Britannica's ENCYCLOPEDIA INFOGRAPHICA

Britannica's ENCYCLOPEDIA INFOGRAPHICA

1,000s OF FACTS & FIGURES

about Earth, space, animals, the body, technology, & more

REVEALED IN PICTURES

Infographics by **Valentina D'Efilippo**

Written by **Andrew Pettie** & **Conrad Quilty-Harper**

BRITANNICA BOOKS

CONTENTS

YOU ARE HERE!

Keep going to find out about humans —though personally I find penguins more interesting!

Welcome!

Did you know that around 70 percent of the way our brain perceives the world is visual? Or that people can identify a picture of a familiar object in just 13 thousandths of a second? That is eight times faster than a blink of the eye!

We humans, you see, are a very visual species. And this is why infographics are so powerful. They are a useful and elegant way to reveal information using pictures.

Most of the 200 infographics that you will find in this book represent collections of facts, which we call data. Translating data into pictures helps us to understand information at a glance and can even make us go "Wow!"

You can find examples of infographics all around you. Common types include maps, charts, graphs, and timelines.

In fact, when space scientists were thinking of the clearest and simplest way to communicate with alien lifeforms, they decided to use an infographic. It was inscribed on a gold-plated plaque and blasted into outer space on board NASA's *Pioneer 10* spacecraft, which was launched in 1972 and completed the first ever mission to the planet Jupiter.

Alongside other important information about Earth, *Pioneer 10*'s infographic included a map of the solar system, so that if aliens ever found the spacecraft, they would hopefully understand where it came from. So far, however, we've yet to hear back...

Before you dive in to explore the world of infographics for yourself, turn the page for a brief guided tour of some of their common features and how they work.

Below: This simple map of the solar system was placed on board NASA's ***Pioneer 10*** spacecraft (illustrated opposite). It shows ***Pioneer 10*** traveling from Earth on a path between Jupiter and Saturn.

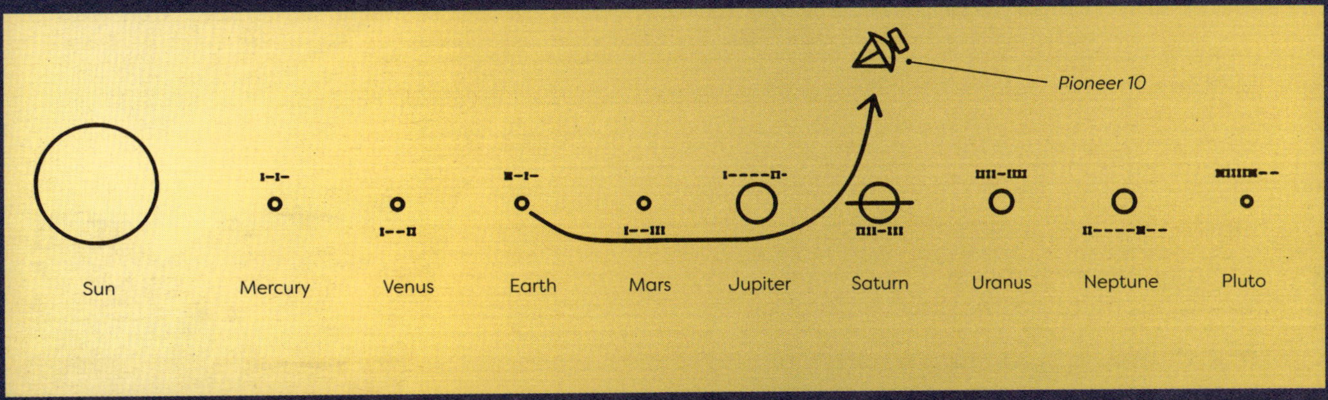

How to Read This Book

Here are some of the main ways in which the infographics in this book organize and present information.

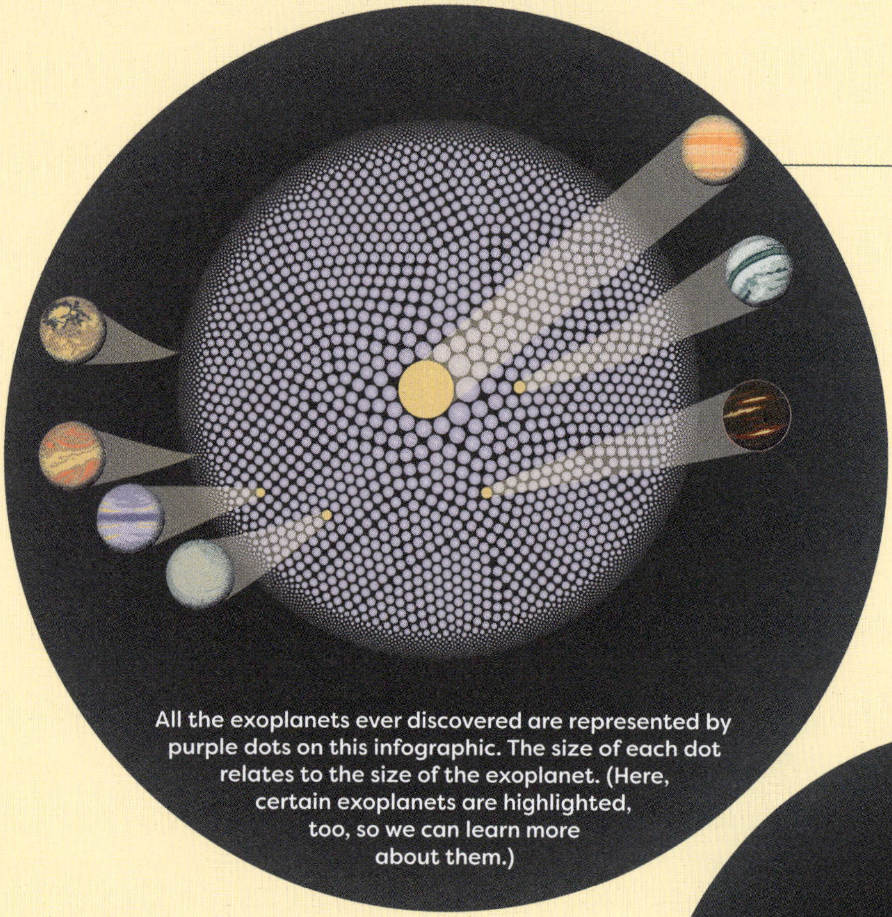

All the exoplanets ever discovered are represented by purple dots on this infographic. The size of each dot relates to the size of the exoplanet. (Here, certain exoplanets are highlighted, too, so we can learn more about them.)

COUNTING AND ORDER

Infographics can be as simple as showing *how many* of a certain thing there are. They might also contain extra information, including, for example, what size they are, or what temperature they are, or what they are made of.

MEASUREMENT AND RULES

Many infographics are about measuring things, such as height, weight, length, and speed. Look out for measurements running along the top, bottom, or up the side of charts, and measuring rules that run across illustrations. All of them will show the unit of measurement being used—for example, feet, years, pounds, or percentages.

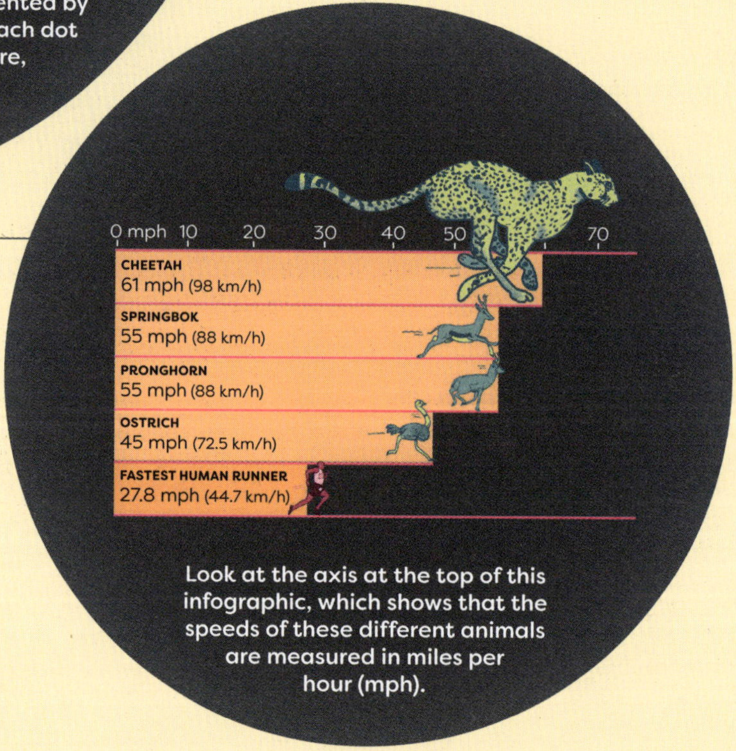

Look at the axis at the top of this infographic, which shows that the speeds of these different animals are measured in miles per hour (mph).

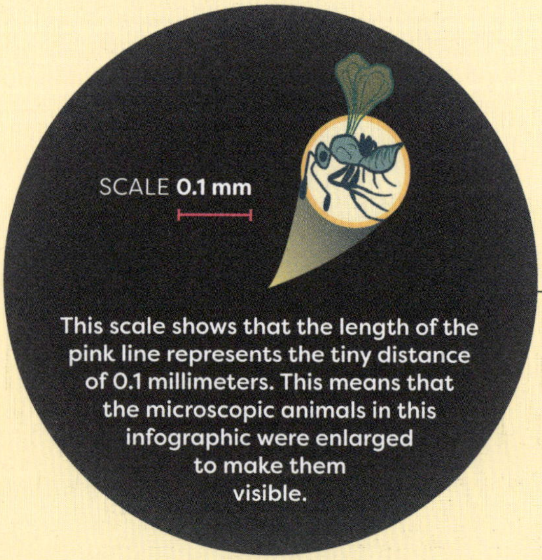

This scale shows that the length of the pink line represents the tiny distance of 0.1 millimeters. This means that the microscopic animals in this infographic were enlarged to make them visible.

SCALE

Some infographics show things "to scale." This means we are not seeing a picture of the *real* distance or size, but a fixed measurement that represents a much bigger or much smaller size in the real world. For example, scales are often used on maps.

COLOR AND PATTERN

The colors and patterns in infographics can be an important part of the story they're telling. Look for the "key" on the infographics, which tells you if the colors or patterns represent measurements, such as temperature.

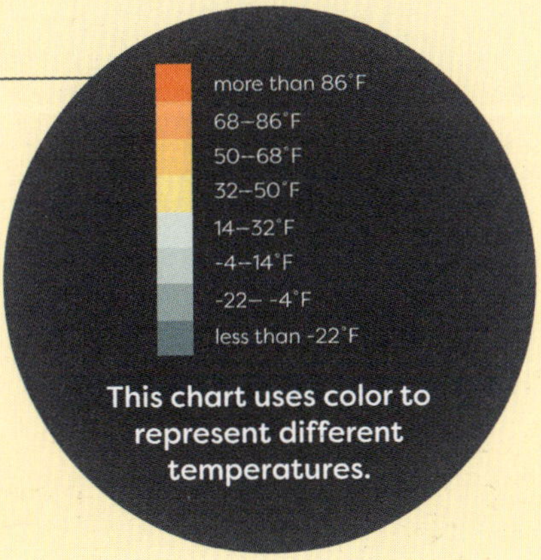

This chart uses color to represent different temperatures.

The key objects in this infographic of the ocean are all in orange, so it is easy to compare their relative depths.

Where two or more things are being directly compared, they might be the *same* color. This can make it easier to look at one thing alongside another in a fair way, or to help you notice important information.

POSITION

The position of items might also be telling you something about their location (such as where things are on a map), timing (such as points along a timeline), or the categories they belong to (such as a family or group).

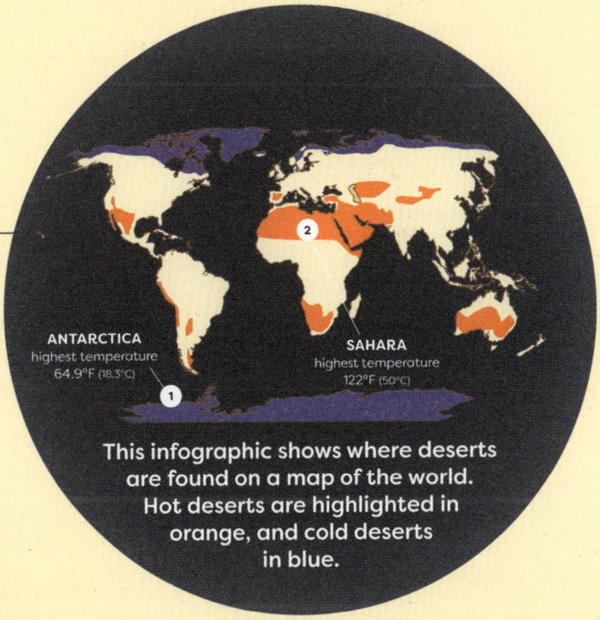

This infographic shows where deserts are found on a map of the world. Hot deserts are highlighted in orange, and cold deserts in blue.

To give a sense of the circumference of a giant tree trunk, this infographic shows how many children holding hands you would need to hug it!

FAMILIAR COMPARISONS

How do you make sense of the size of a gigantic tree? Infographics can help us translate these measurements into things that are more familiar to us.

Some infographics in this book include a note on **How to Read It**. Where you spot these notes, read them first.

Now set off on an adventure through these pages and get ready to see our world in a whole new way...

SPACE

A timeline of everything

Where did the stars come from? Where did you come from? Where did this book come from? The theory is that about 13.8 billion years ago, in a fraction of a second, absolutely everything was created. That includes time, space and all the matter in the universe. We call this mind-boggling event the Big Bang.

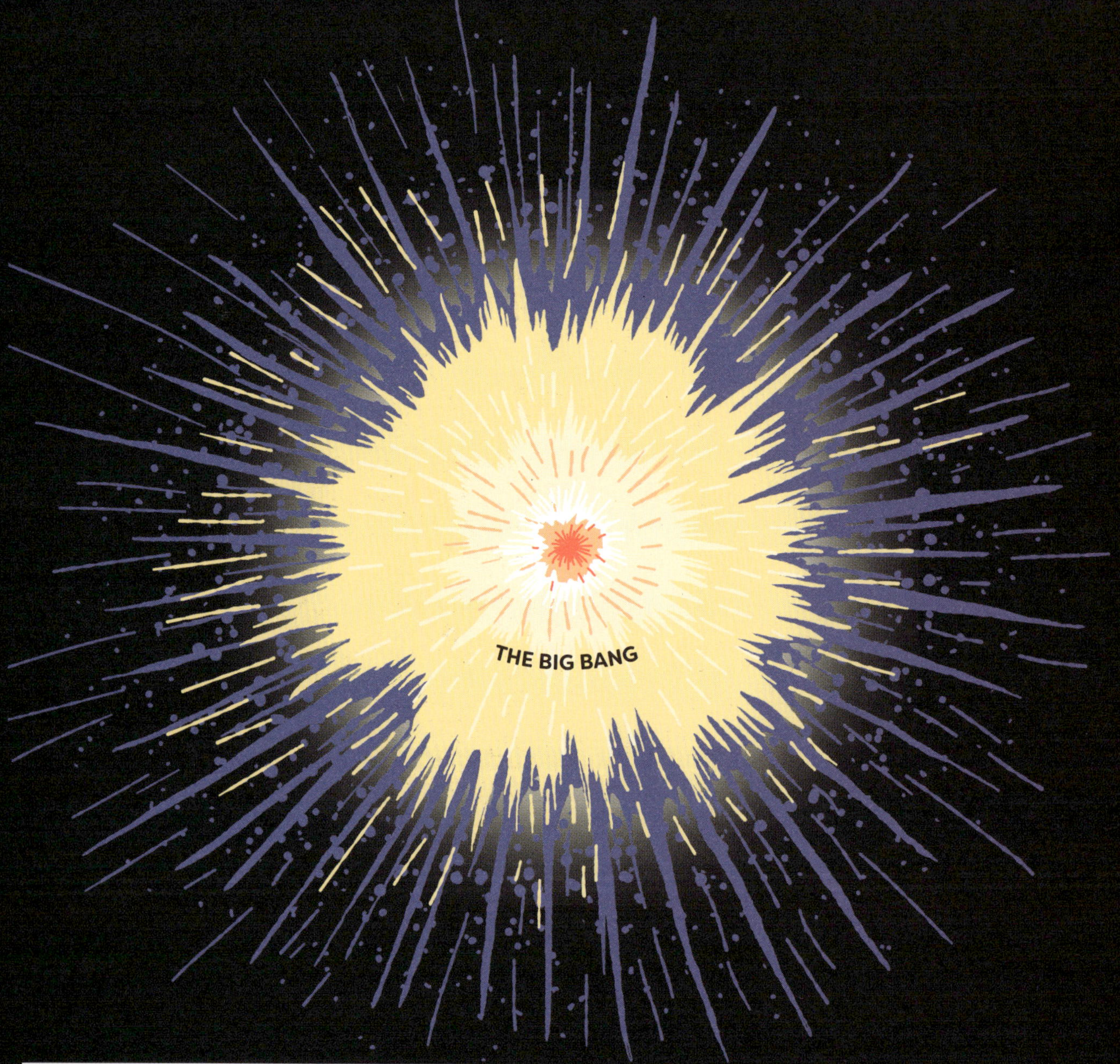

WHAT HAPPENED NEXT?

Scientists think that at the moment of the Big Bang, everything existed in a tiny dot called a singularity. After the Big Bang, the universe began cooling and expanding. Within minutes, particles of matter started to form hydrogen and helium. These elements later formed stars, which led to the creation of planets. According to astronomers, the universe is still cooling and expanding.

If the entire 13.8-billion-year history of the universe was scaled down to fit into a single, 365-day year, this is what the 'cosmic calendar' would look like. The universe begins at 00:01 on 1 January with the Big Bang. Earth forms in September. Dinosaurs go extinct on Christmas Day. Humans appear only after 10pm on 31 December!

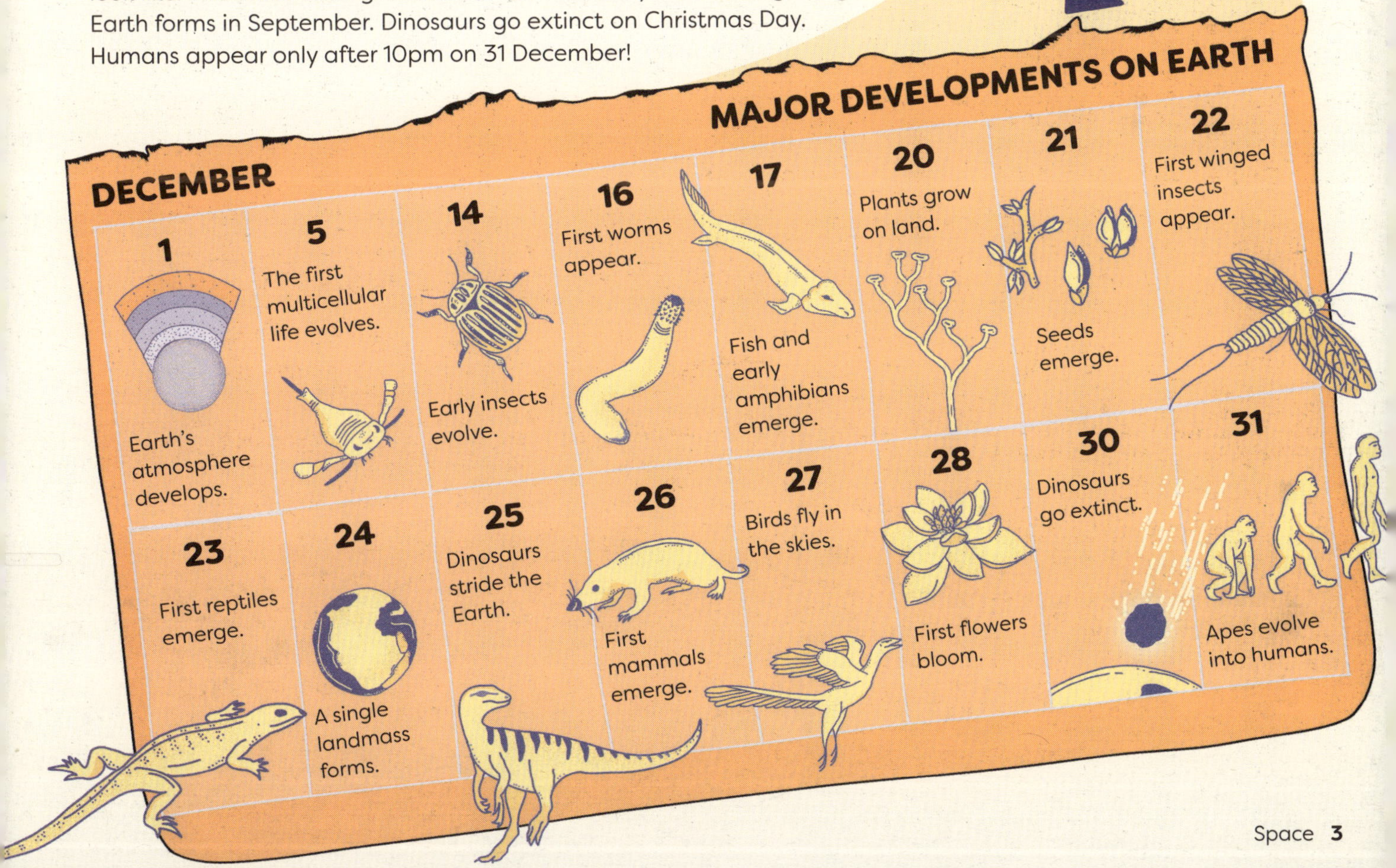

Where are we in the universe?

It's likely that, if you're reading this book, you live on planet Earth. But where exactly *is* Earth? The best way to work it out is to look at a series of space maps. The first map, at the top, shows Earth's position within our solar system. The second map zooms out to show the solar system's position within our galaxy, the Milky Way. And the third map zooms out even further to show the Milky Way's position within the observable universe, which is all the known universe that astronomers have so far been able to see through powerful telescopes.

...IN THE SOLAR SYSTEM

The solar system consists of the Sun and everything that orbits, or travels around, the Sun. This includes the eight planets (including Earth!) and their moons, dwarf planets, and countless asteroids, comets and other small, icy objects. Earth is the third planet in our solar system, about 150 million kilometres away from the Sun.

...IN THE MILKY WAY GALAXY

A galaxy is a collection of stars, clouds of gas and dust particles that move together through the universe. Our galaxy, the Milky Way, has four spiral arms. The solar system is located in one of these spiral arms, and it orbits the centre of the galaxy once every 250 million years.

...IN THE OBSERVABLE UNIVERSE

The Milky Way is part of a neighbourhood of about 30 galaxies called the Local Group. The nearest major galaxy to the Milky Way is called Andromeda.

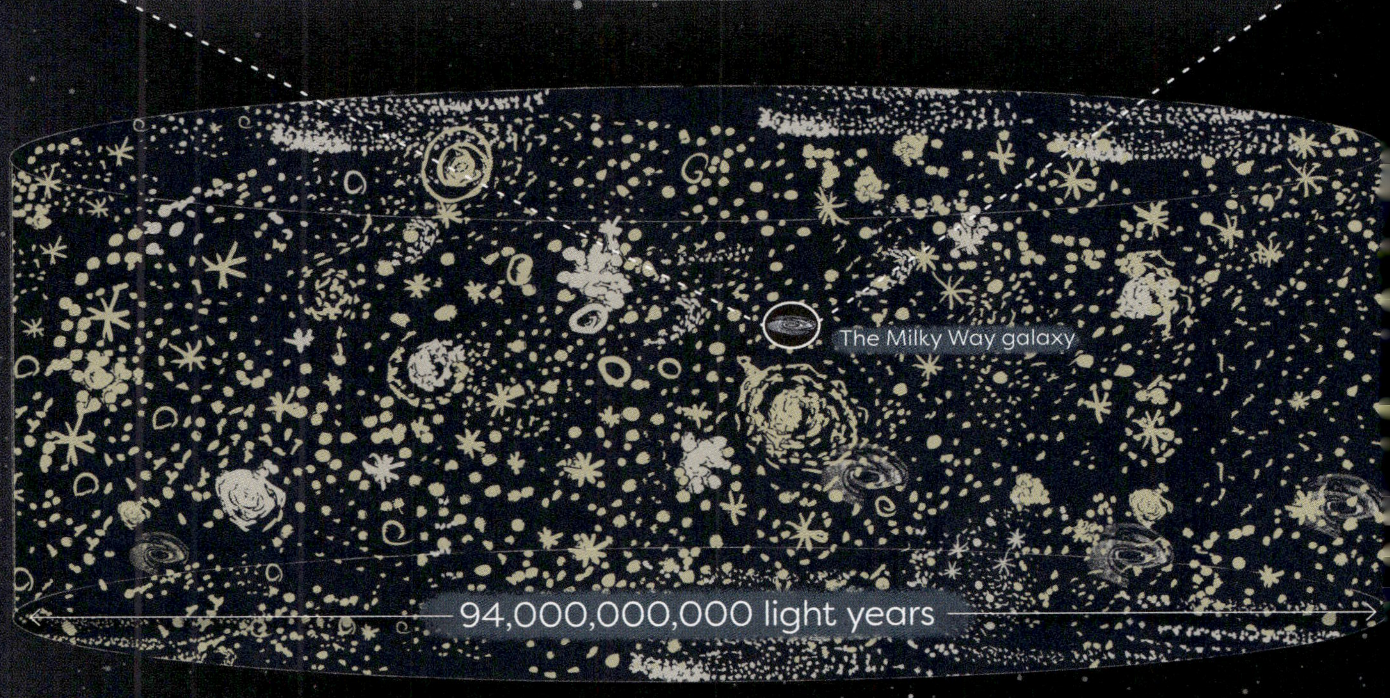

Welcome to our solar system!

Our space neighbourhood is called the solar system because everything in it orbits the Sun (solar means relating to the Sun). Within the solar system there are eight planets, more than 200 moons, five dwarf planets including Pluto, countless comets and asteroids, and huge clouds of dust and gas. The largest objects in the solar system after the Sun are the planets.

All planets rotate on an axis. This is an imaginary line that you can draw through the centre of a planet. The axis of each planet is represented with a grey arrow.

	MERCURY	VENUS	EARTH	MARS
DIRECTION OF ROTATION				
	Rocky, terrestrial worlds			
DIAMETER kilometres, km	4,879 km	12,104 km	12,756 km	6,792 km
ORBIT	88 Earth days to orbit the Sun	225 Earth days	365 Earth days (1 Earth year)	1.9 Earth years

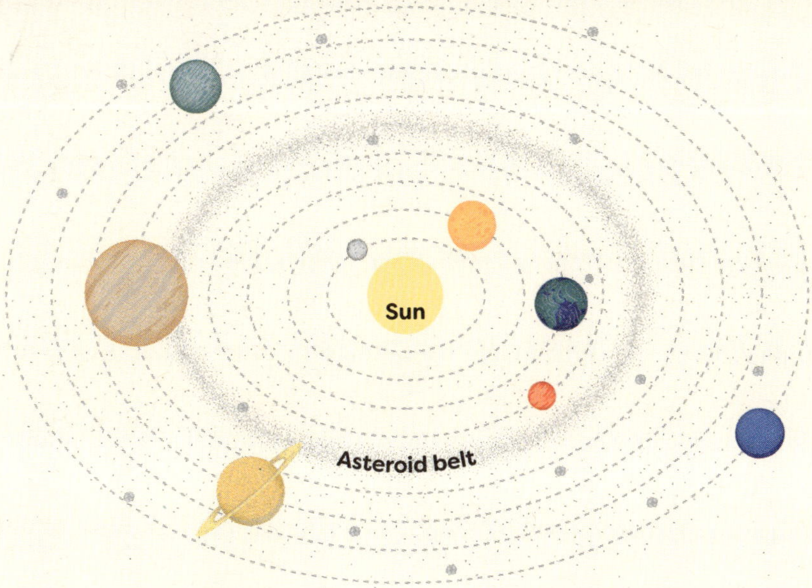

At the centre of our solar system is a star called the Sun. The eight planets orbit the Sun in paths shaped like flattened circles. As they travel on their journeys around the Sun, the planets also spin on their own axes – and they do this at very different speeds. A full rotation of Earth on its axis takes 24 hours, which gives us our day. Jupiter, the fastest, takes about 10 hours to spin once. Venus, the slowest, takes 243 Earth days!

JUPITER **SATURN** **URANUS** **NEPTUNE**

Gas giants

Ice giants

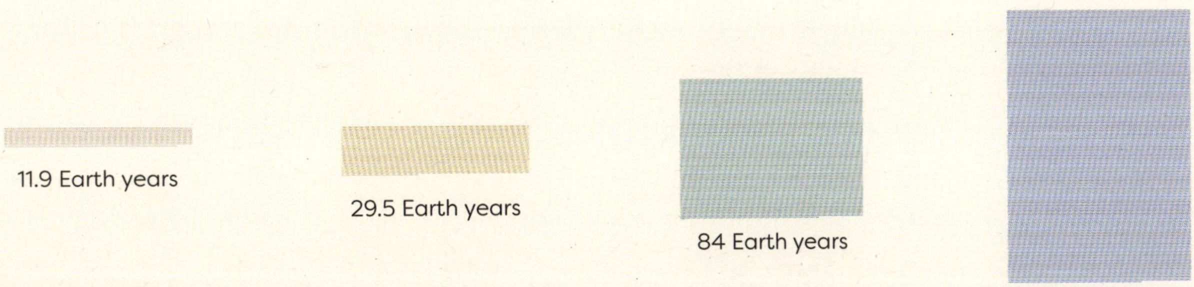

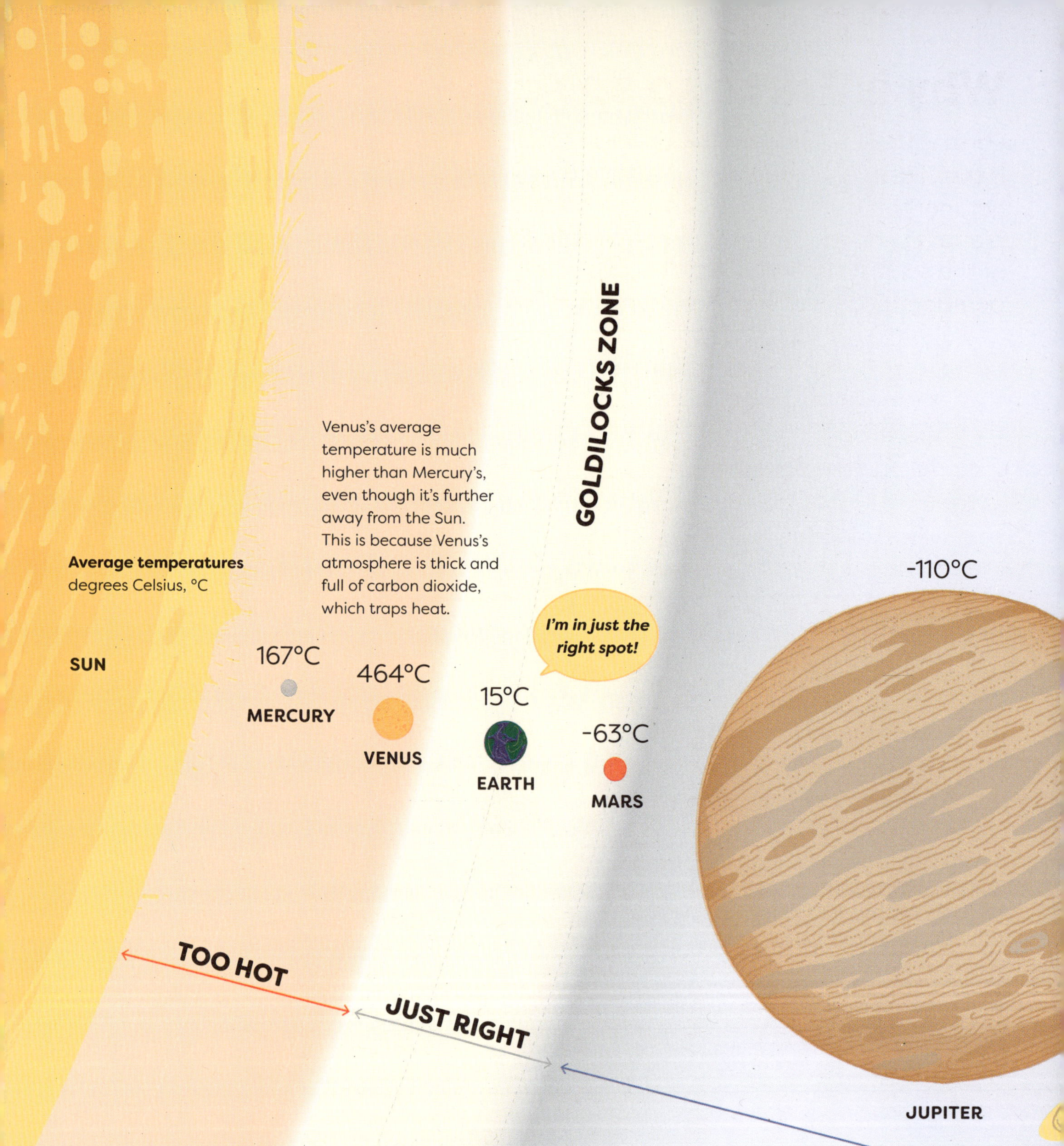

IS THERE LIFE ON OTHER PLANETS?

The sheer number of stars in the universe means that there are probably billions of planets orbiting *other* stars within a Goldilocks zone like Earth's. Scientists have estimated that there could be as many as 300 million potentially habitable planets within our galaxy, the Milky Way. This means that it is mathematically likely that other planets in the universe also host life. So far, however, we have yet to find a single one.

Why is Earth so special?

Earth is the only place in the universe that we know hosts life. One reason for this is that Earth is just the right distance away from its star, the Sun, so it's not too hot, nor too cold. This allows water, which helps make life possible, to lie on the planet's surface without it all evaporating or freezing. Scientists call the region of the solar system that Earth occupies the 'Goldilocks zone' – like the bowl of porridge that Goldilocks eats in the fairy tale, its temperature is just right!

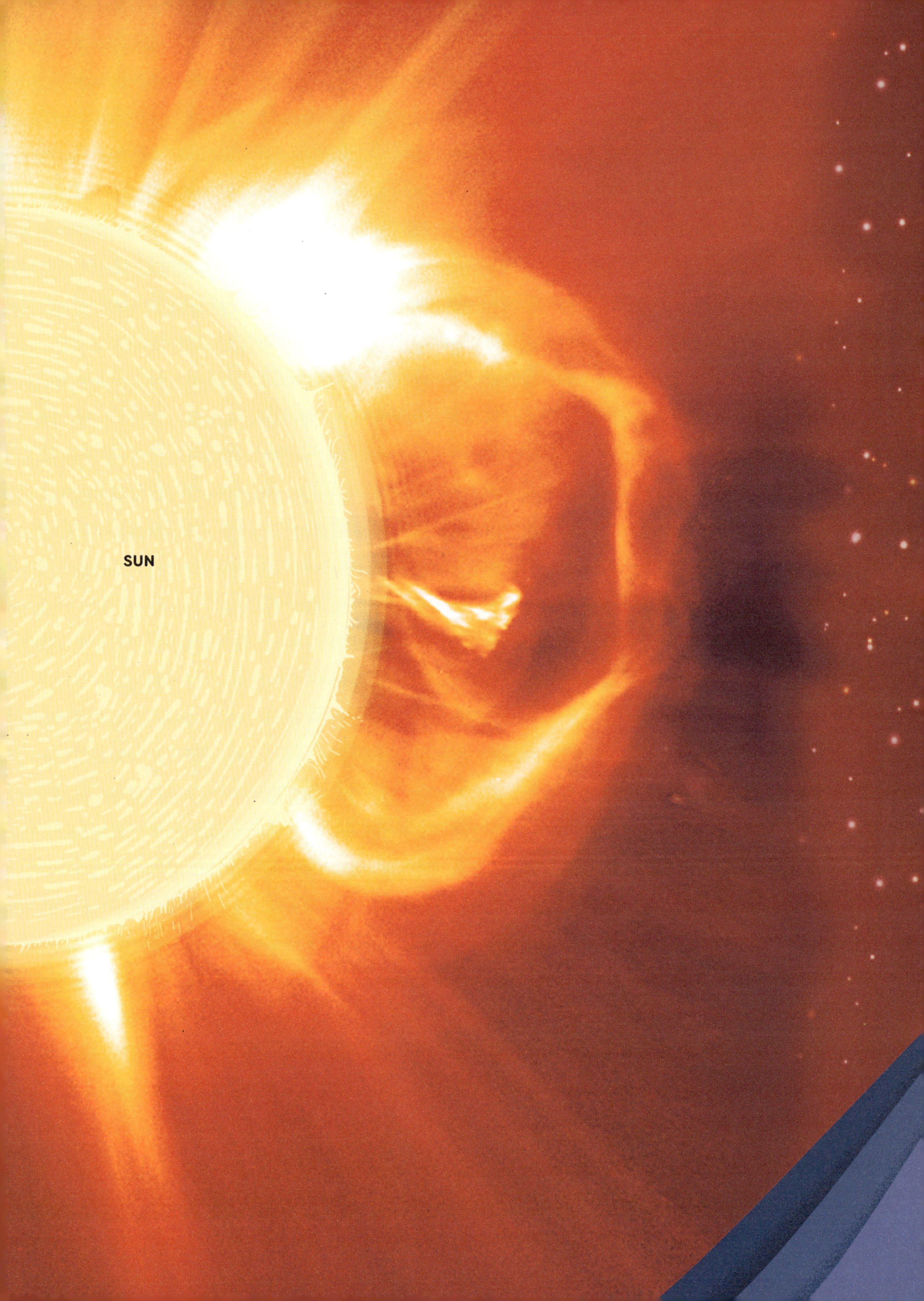
SUN

The magnetosphere creates light displays we can see from Earth – turn to page 74.

What protects Earth from the Sun?

The burning Sun continually throws out heat and light energy, called solar radiation, and a stream of hot, charged particles known as solar wind. Thankfully, Earth has an invisible shield protecting it from these powerful solar emissions. The shield is created by Earth's magnetic field and is called the magnetosphere. It is highlighted with blue lines in the image above. There would be no life on Earth without the magnetosphere for protection.

How many moons do the planets have?

Planets orbit stars. Moons, on the other hand, orbit planets. There are more than 200 moons in our solar system, and they orbit every planet except Mercury and Venus. Pluto, other dwarf planets and many asteroids also have moons. Moons come in all shapes and sizes.

EARTH

1 moon

Our **Moon** is the fifth largest moon in the solar system.

MARS

2 moons

One of Mars's two moons, **Phobos**, is gradually spiralling inwards, getting 1.8 metres closer to the planet every century. Within 50 million years, Phobos will either crash into Mars or break up into smaller pieces, forming a planetary ring.

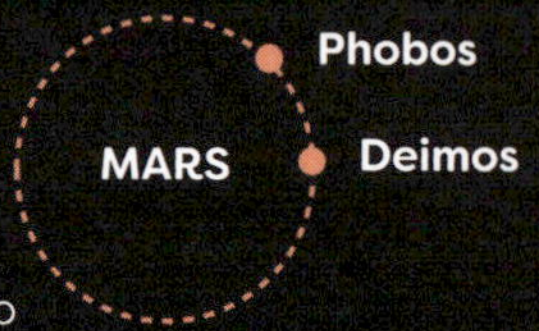

NEPTUNE

14 moons

Triton is one of Neptune's moons. Its icy surface reflects so much of what little light reaches it from the Sun that it is one of the coldest objects in the solar system.

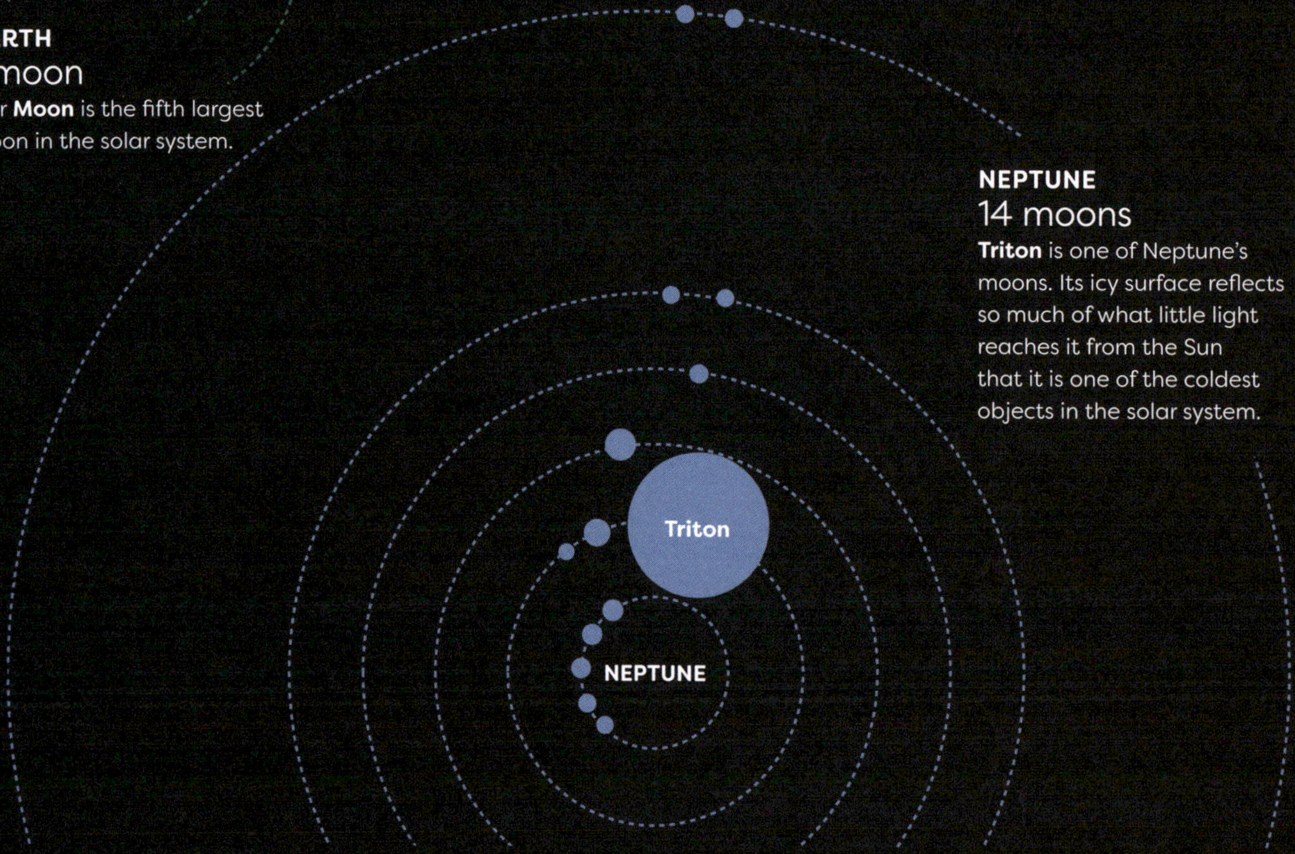

HOW TO READ IT

The dotted lines represent the moons' distance away from the planet. Moons that orbit a planet at roughly the same distance have been placed on the same dotted line.

Average distance of moon from planet

kilometres, km

Radius of moon

kilometres, km

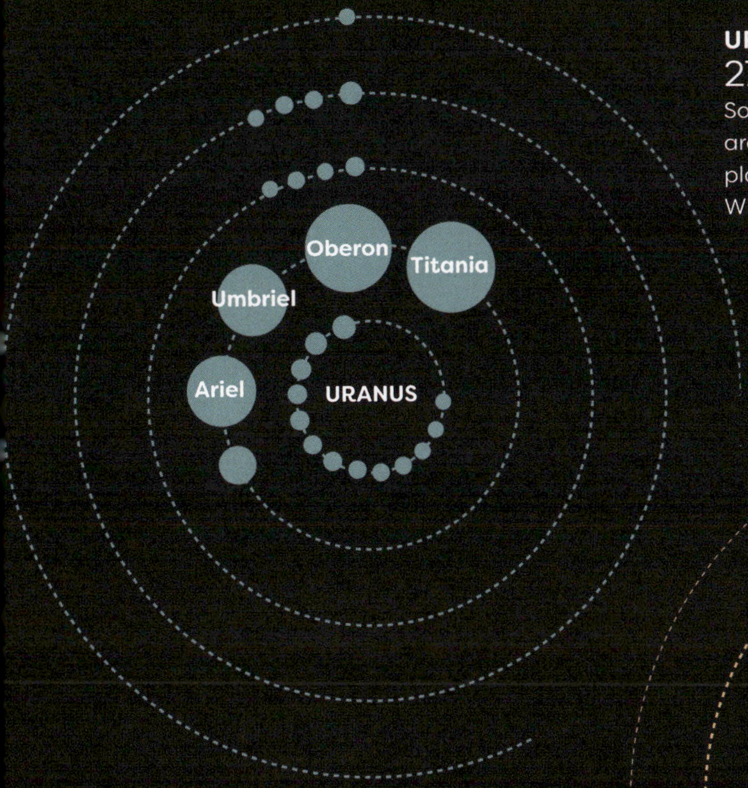

URANUS
27 moons
Some of Uranus's moons are named after characters in plays by the 16th-century writer William Shakespeare.

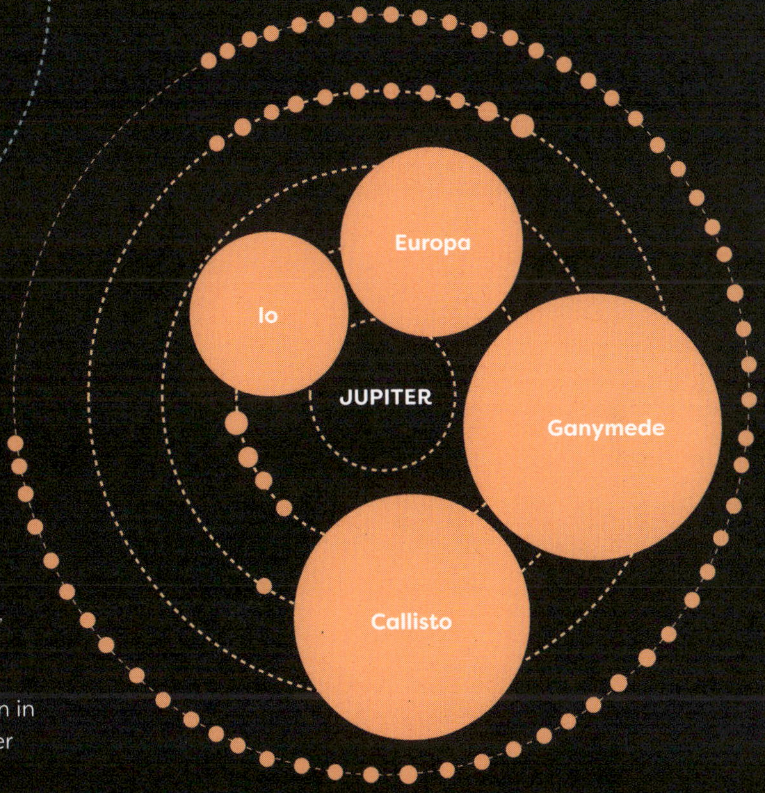

JUPITER
95 moons
Not all moons are pictured, *see note on page 289*
Ganymede, which orbits Jupiter, is the largest moon in the solar system. It is bigger than the planet Mercury.

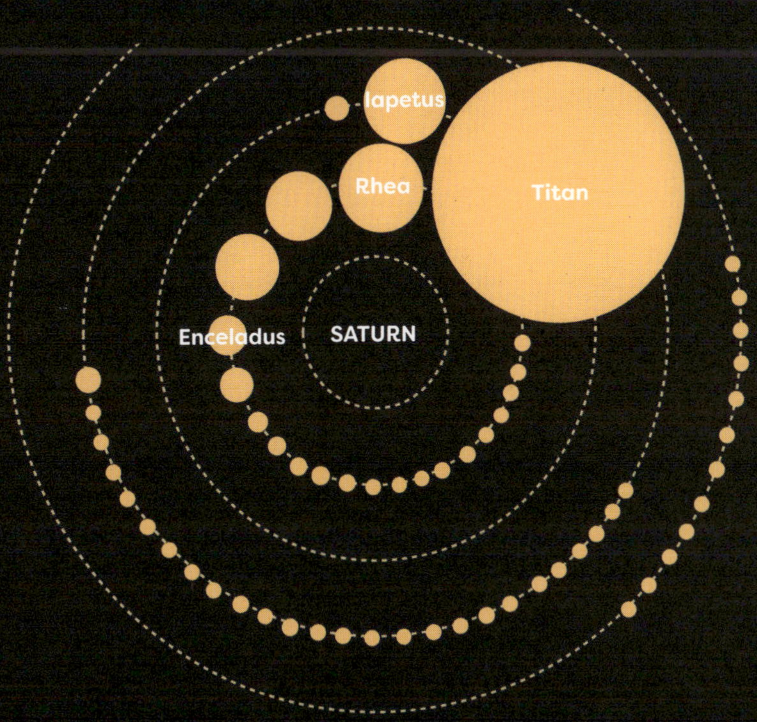

SATURN
145 moons
Not all moons are pictured, *see note on page 289*
The force of gravity is so weak on one of Saturn's moons, **Enceladus**, that a human jumping on its surface would stay off the ground for a whole minute.

How far away is the Moon?

As we stand on Earth, the Moon feels relatively close to us, but it is actually hundreds of thousands of kilometres away. If you lined up the seven other planets in our solar system in a row, they would fit in the space between Earth and the Moon. In fact, in a strange coincidence, they would fit rather neatly!

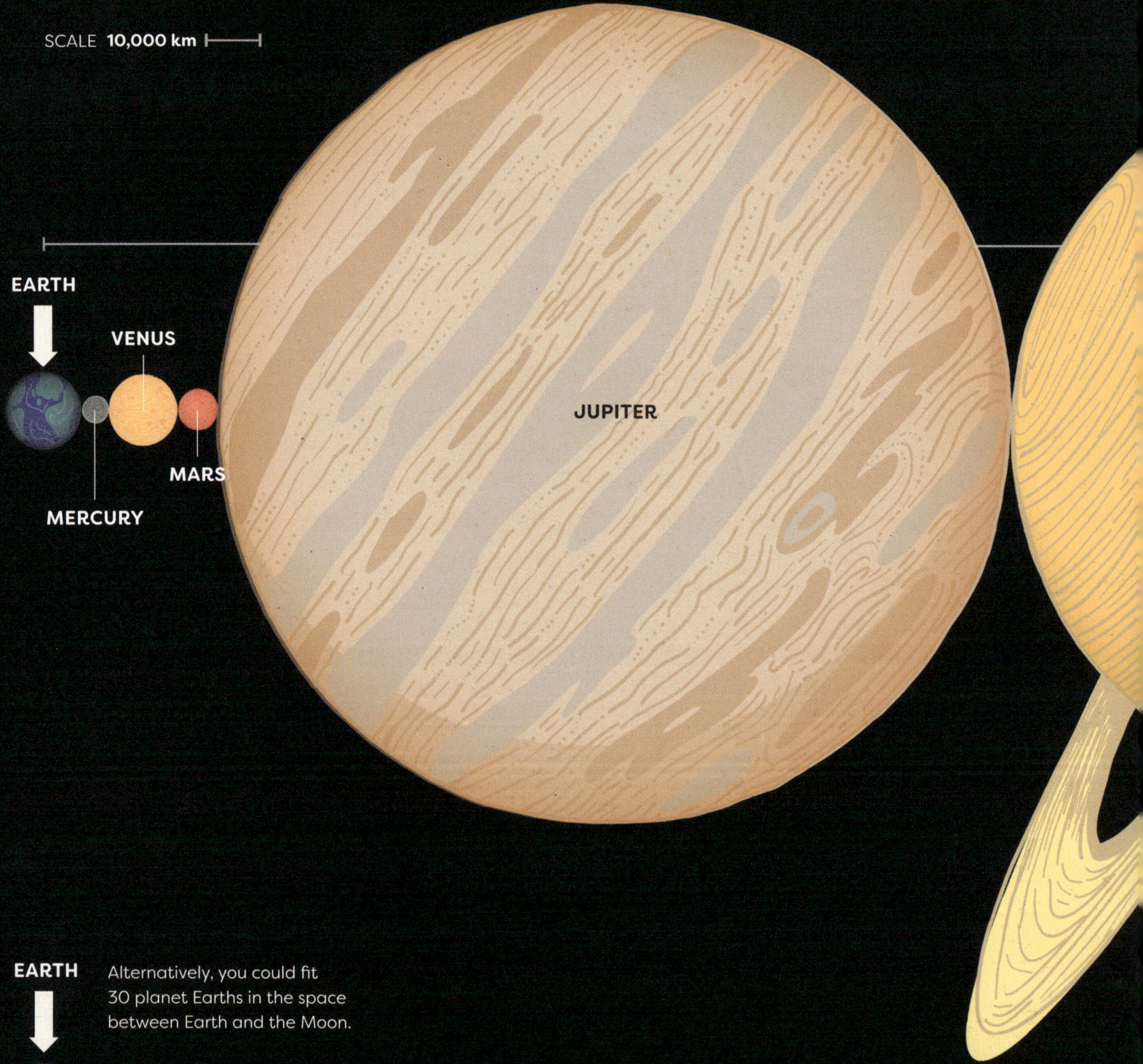

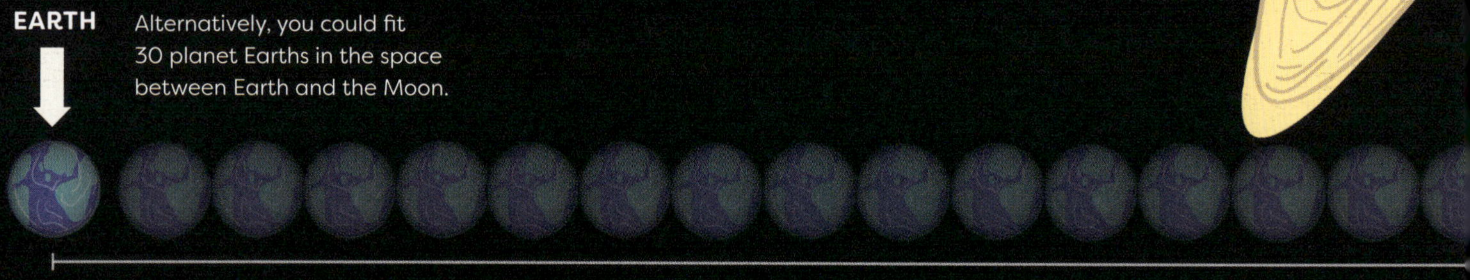

Alternatively, you could fit 30 planet Earths in the space between Earth and the Moon.

THE MOON'S ORBIT

The Moon's orbit around Earth is not a perfect circle. It's more like a slightly flattened circle. At its furthest point from Earth, called the apogee, the Moon is 405,500 kilometres away. At its closest point, the perigee, the Moon is 363,000 kilometres away. On average the gap is about 384,000 kilometres. That's the measurement we've used for this infographic.

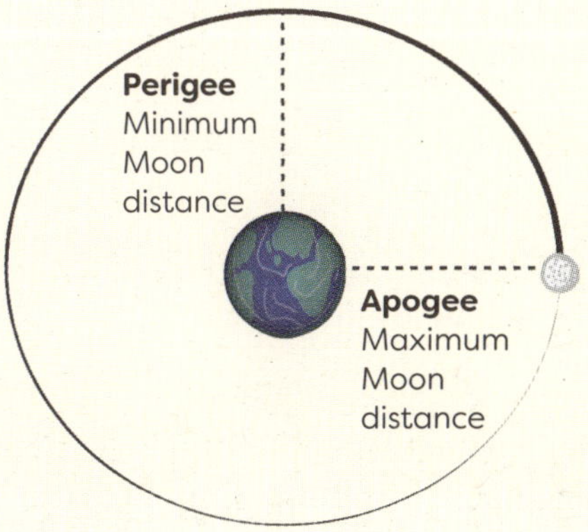

Phases of the Moon

Half of the Moon is always lit up by the Sun (except during a lunar eclipse). But as the Moon orbits Earth, which takes about 27 days, we see different amounts of sunlight reflected by the Moon. These eight recognisable changes in the Moon's appearance are known as phases.

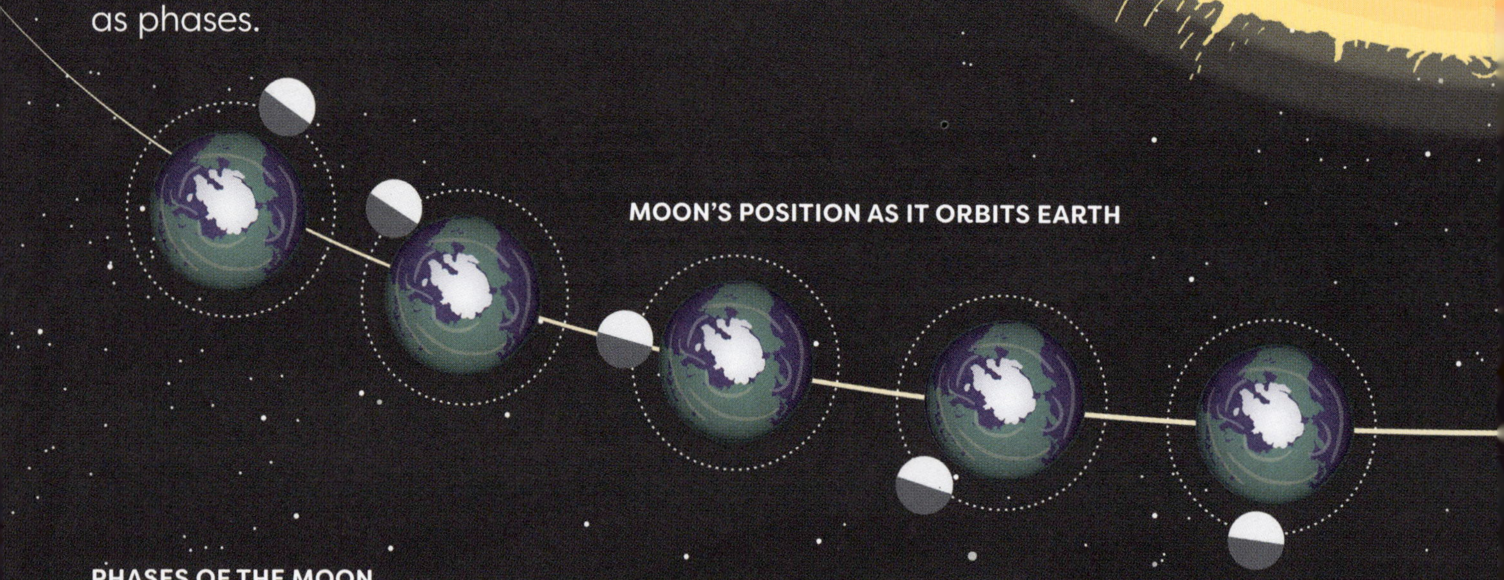

PHASES OF THE MOON

THE FAR SIDE OF THE MOON

If you look carefully at the surface of the Moon, perhaps through a telescope, you will notice an interesting fact: the same side of the Moon, called the 'near side', is always facing Earth. The other side of the Moon, called the 'far side', can never be seen from Earth. This is because the Moon rotates on its axis at the same rate that it orbits Earth. So, as the Moon moves around Earth, its far side is always rotating away from us, keeping it out of sight. However, space rockets and probes have taken photographs of the far side of the Moon, so we now know what it looks like.

THE MOON AND THE TIDES

Tides are the regular rise and fall of water levels in oceans, seas and lakes. The Moon is the major cause of the tides (the Sun plays a role, too). Like a magnet, the Moon pulls all of Earth's water towards it. The Moon's gravity causes a bulge in the oceans on the side of Earth closest to it. We call this bulge a high tide. The fact that Earth is continuously rotating causes a second high tide to occur on the opposite side of Earth to the Moon. These two high tides draw water away from the rest of the oceans, which creates two low tides in between.

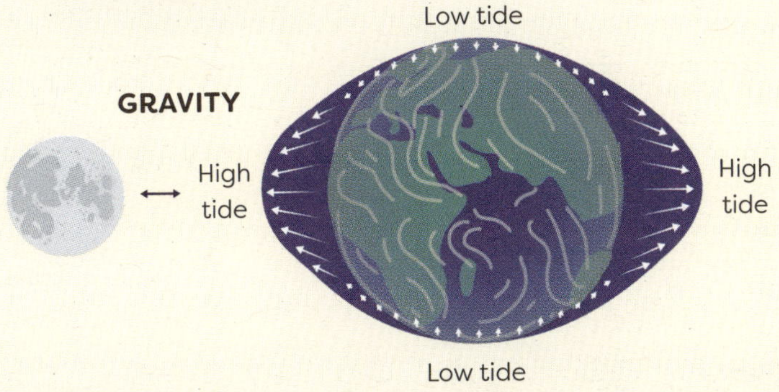

The constellation Pegasus is named after the winged horse in Greek mythology.

NORTHERN HEMISPHERE

Constellations that are easy to spot if you live north of the equator include Cassiopeia, which forms a W shape, Orion (look for three stars that form Orion's belt) and Cygnus, the Swan, in the form of a cross.

Ursa Major is also called the Great Bear. Its seven brightest stars, which form the shape of a saucepan, are known as the Big Dipper.

Find out about all types of telescopes on page 272.

Spica is the brightest star of Virgo, the second largest constellation in the sky.

Hydra, also known as the female watersnake, stretches across the southern sky.

SOUTHERN HEMISPHERE
One of the brightest constellations you can see from the Southern Hemisphere is the Southern Cross (Crux), which looks like a kite.

Mapping the stars

Since ancient times, people have created stories and pictures from the patterns made by the stars. We call these patterns constellations. Constellations can also be useful for mapping the night sky. The oldest known star atlas was created in China around the year 700 CE. Today, there are 88 standard constellations used by astronomers. The graphics above show which of these constellations are easiest to see from the northern half of Earth (the Northern Hemisphere) and the southern half of Earth (the Southern Hemisphere).

What is an eclipse?

When one space object, such as a planet or a moon, moves into the shadow of another space object, it is called an eclipse. There are two types of eclipse commonly seen from Earth: a solar eclipse and a lunar eclipse.

SOLAR ECLIPSE

A solar eclipse occurs when the Moon blocks light from the Sun from reaching Earth, casting a shadow on part of the Earth.

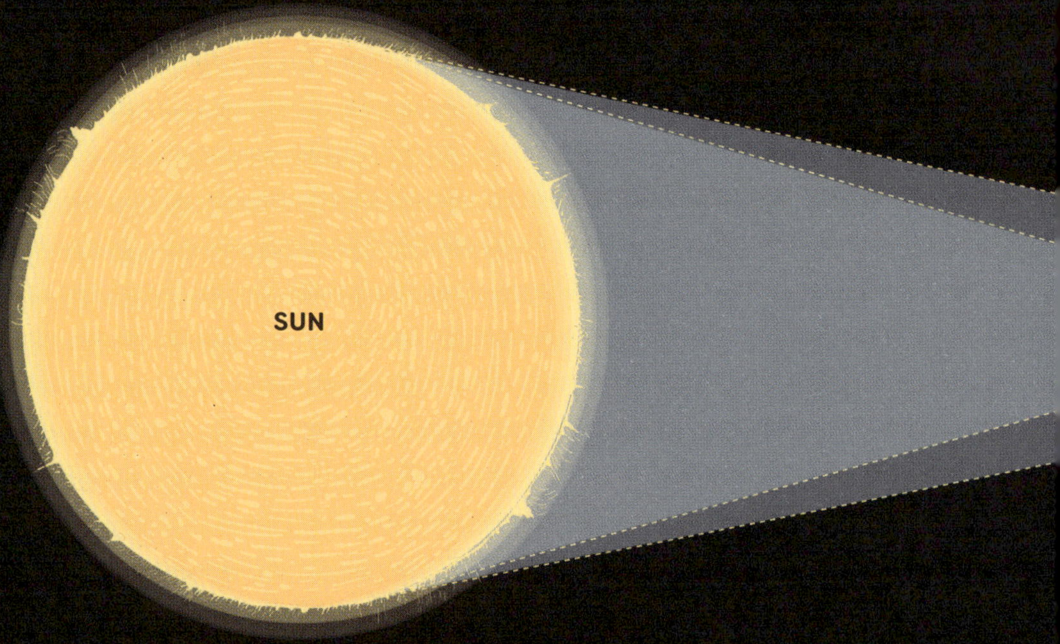

TOTAL SOLAR ECLIPSE, AS SEEN FROM EARTH

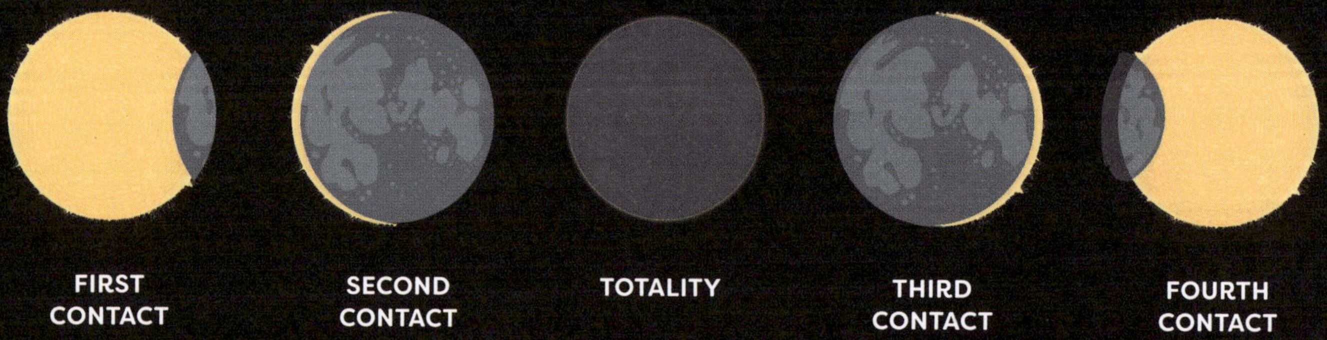

When the Sun, Moon and Earth line up exactly, it causes a total solar eclipse in which the Moon completely covers the Sun, blocking out its light. This perfect alignment of the Sun and Moon in the sky, which astronomers call a totality, is possible only because of an astonishing coincidence, which is that the Sun is both 400 times bigger than the Moon and 400 times further away. This combination means that the Moon covers the Sun perfectly in the sky. Only people in the umbra (see above) can see the totality.

TOTAL ECLIPSE
The complete shadow cast by the Moon, called the umbra, is quite small where it hits Earth. People standing in the umbra will see a total solar eclipse.

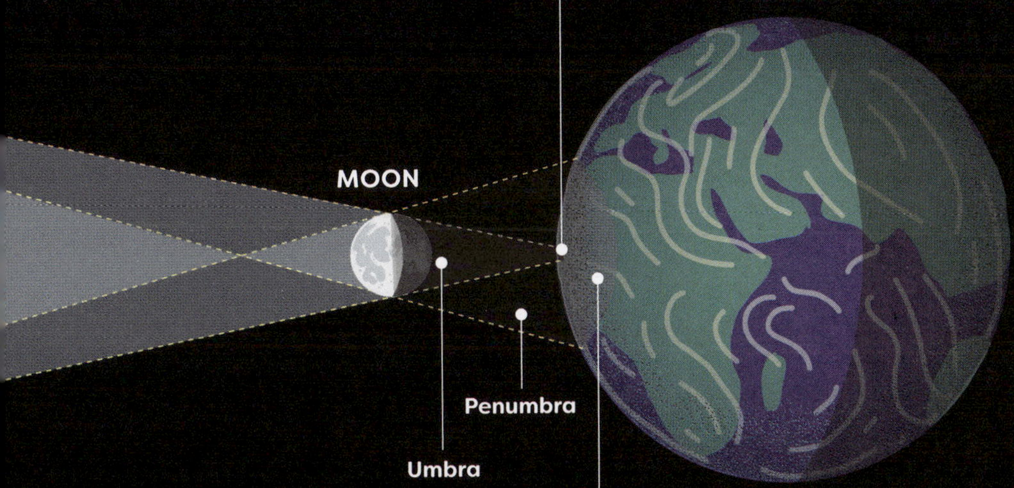

PARTIAL ECLIPSE
The area in partial shadow, called the penumbra, is much bigger than the umbra. People standing in the penumbra will see a partial solar eclipse.

LUNAR ECLIPSE

A lunar eclipse occurs when Earth comes between the Sun and the Moon, blocking out the Sun's light and casting its shadow on the Moon.

LUNAR ECLIPSE		SOLAR ECLIPSE
Two times a year, on average	**OCCURRENCE**	Two to five times a year
1 h 45 min	**LASTS FOR**	7 min 32 sec
Anywhere on Earth (at night!)	**VISIBLE FROM**	Only some places on Earth

Fly me to the Moon!

Only 12 humans have experienced what it feels like to walk on the Moon, starting with the US astronaut Neil Armstrong in 1969. This infographic shows more than 100 Moon missions: successful missions, failed missions and some Moon missions that are planned for the future.

HOW TO READ IT

Each line represents a mission to the Moon, anchored on the timeline on its launch date:

- Successful past mission
- Failed past mission
- Ongoing/future mission

Missions that had human crews are highlighted with circles at each end:

- Crewed missions

NASA's Apollo missions are highlighted in yellow. The six Apollo missions that successfully landed astronauts on the Moon have a yellow circle containing the number of that specific mission:

Landed crewed missions

- Apollo 11 Jul 1969
- Apollo 12 Nov 1969
- Apollo 14 Jan 1971
- Apollo 15 Jul 1971
- Apollo 16 Apr 1972
- Apollo 17 Dec 1972

The marker shows where on the Moon's surface the astronauts touched down.

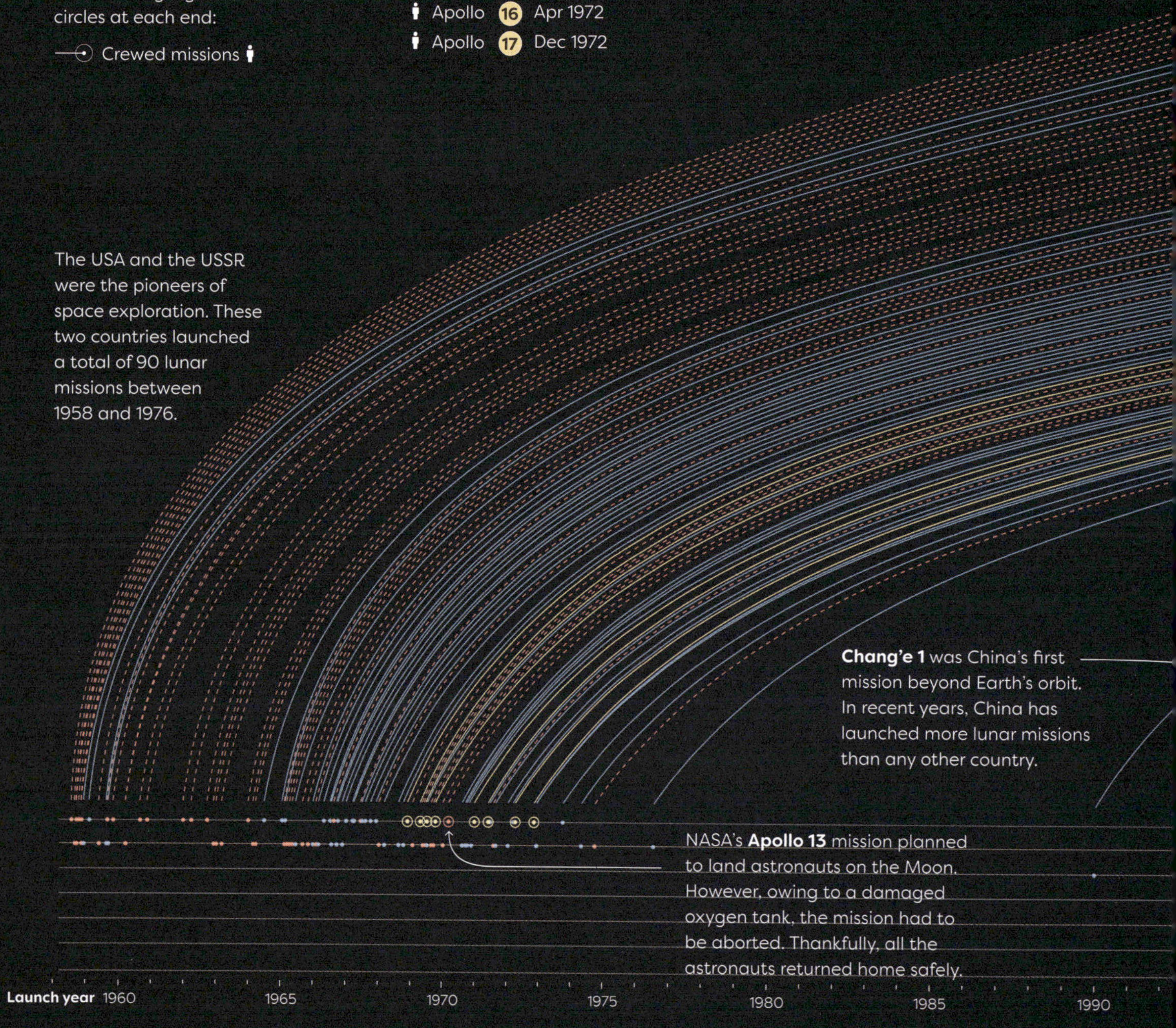

Hi, I'm US astronaut Eugene Cernan. I walked on the Moon in 1972 – and nobody has done it since!
15
17
11
12
14
16
11
12
14
15
16
17
NASA's Artemis missions are planning to land the first woman and the first person of colour on the Moon during the 2020s.
Place of origin
USA
USSR/Russia
Japan
Europe
China
India
Israel
1995
2000
2005
2010
2015
2020
2025

Humans in space

Every dot on this page represents a person's first trip to outer space. The first person to go to space was the Soviet cosmonaut Yuri Gagarin, who orbited Earth in 1961. Since then, more than 600 people from 41 other countries have been to space.

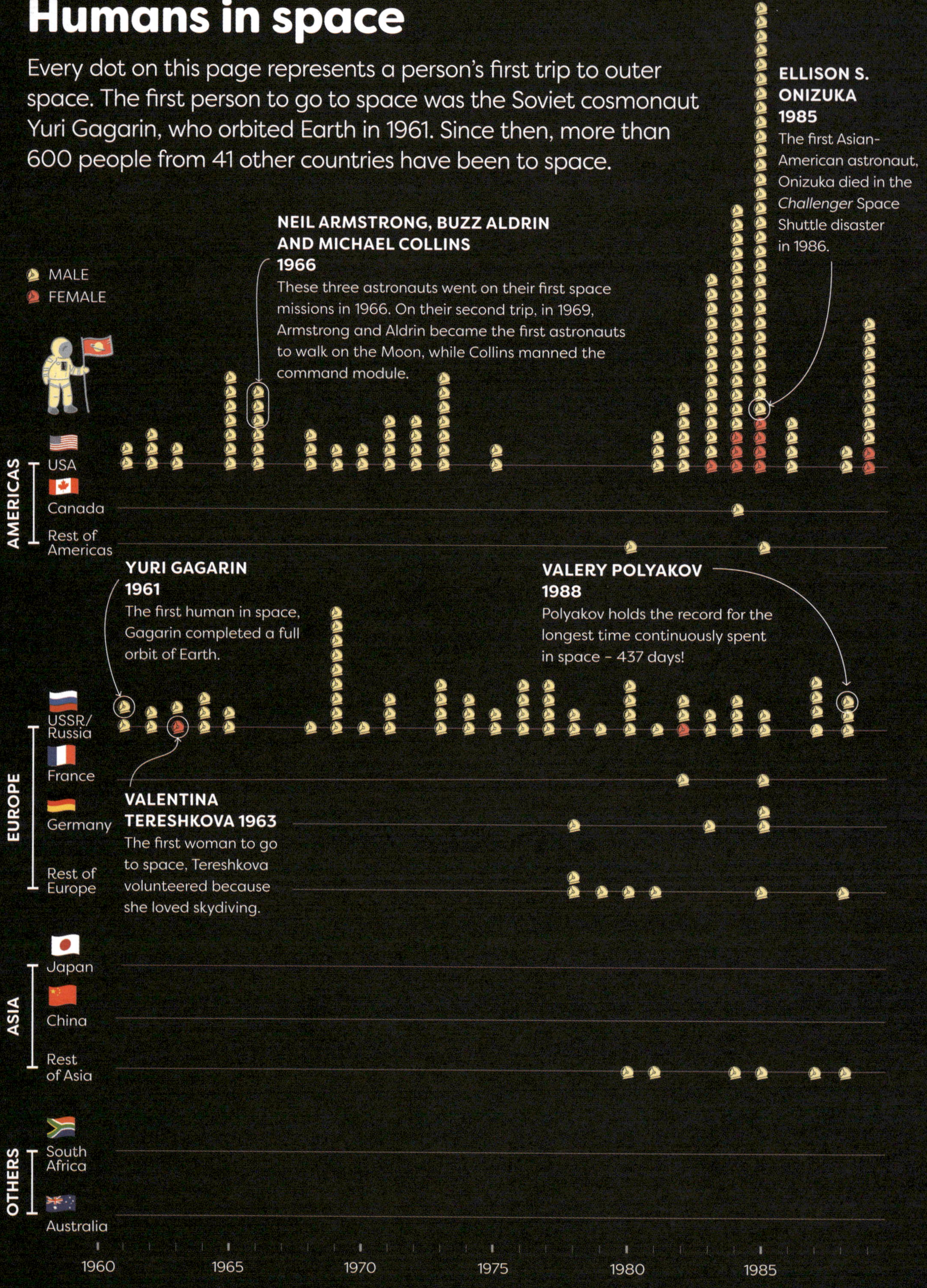

ABOUT 9 OUT OF 10 ASTRONAUTS ARE MEN

Only about 10 per cent of all astronauts who have been into space are women. However, more female astronauts will travel on future missions.

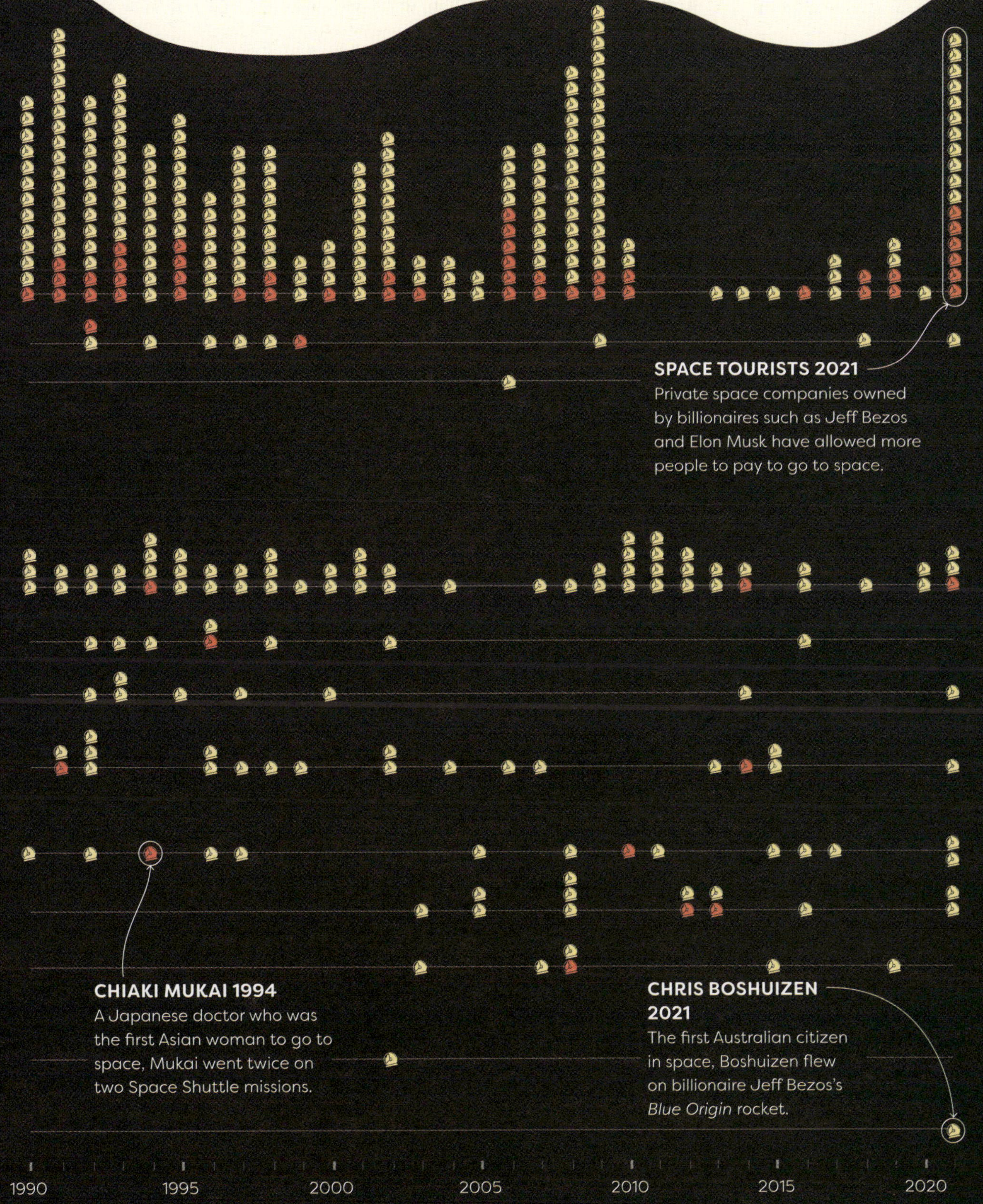

What is the Sun?

Our Sun is a star – a giant ball of burning gas. It's made mostly of hydrogen and helium, with some metals at its core. It would be impossible to visit the Sun's core in person because the temperature there can reach 15,000,000°C. However, by collecting information about the Sun from a distance, using space probes and telescopes, scientists can work out what is happening inside.

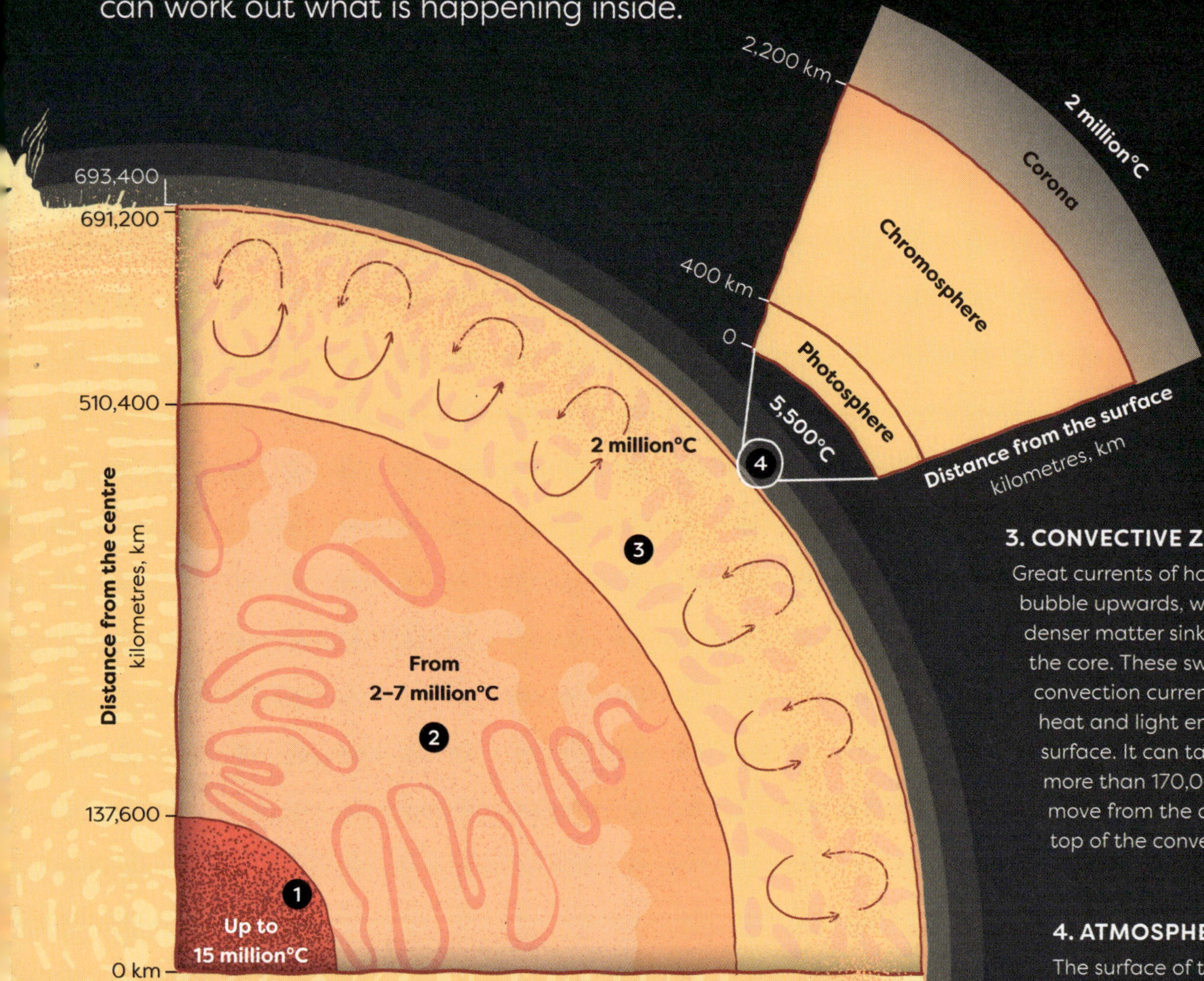

3. CONVECTIVE ZONE

Great currents of hot gases bubble upwards, while cooler, denser matter sinks towards the core. These swirling convection currents transport heat and light energy to the surface. It can take energy more than 170,000 years to move from the core to the top of the convective zone.

4. ATMOSPHERE

The surface of the Sun is called the photosphere. Outside it is a thin middle layer called the chromosphere, followed by a very thin outer atmosphere called the corona.

1. CORE

The core is the hottest part of the Sun. At the core, nuclear reactions, in which hydrogen fuses to form helium, generate the Sun's heat and light.

2. RADIATIVE ZONE

Light and heat energy radiate slowly outwards, taking a long, zigzagging path towards the surface.

LIFE CYCLE OF THE SUN

The Sun formed around 4.6 billion years ago from a giant cloud of dust and gas that was pulled together by gravity over thousands of years. Like all stars, the Sun then started to develop through a series of stages, each of which has its own name and characteristics. Today, the Sun is a main sequence star, which is sometimes called a yellow dwarf. It is about halfway through its 10-billion-year life cycle.

Turn the page to see what a nebula like me looks like!

START HERE!

BIRTH INSIDE A NEBULA
Stars are formed inside clouds of dust and gas called nebulae.

THE SUN AS IT IS TODAY

4 billion years

MAIN SEQUENCE STAR
The Sun will stay the size and shape it is today for billions of years.

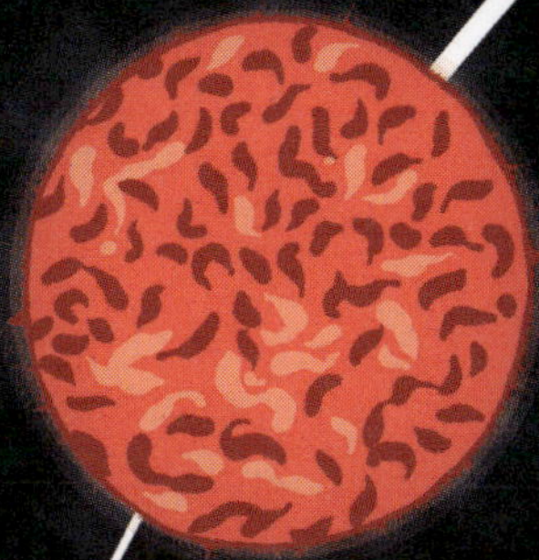

8–10 billion years

RED GIANT
As the Sun approaches the end of its life, its inner core will contract, and the outer layers will expand and cool. At this stage it is called a red giant.

11 billion years

PLANETARY NEBULA
As the Sun runs out of hydrogen, it will cast off its outer layers of gas.

Hundreds of billions of years

WHITE DWARF, BLACK DWARF
The Sun's remaining core will become a white dwarf, shining as a star for billions of years. Scientists believe the white dwarf will cool to become a black dwarf.

END

LIFE CYCLE OF A GIANT STAR

MASSIVE STAR
Stars with a mass more than 1.5 times bigger than the Sun's go through a different life cycle. Big stars use up their hydrogen more quickly and the largest will burn themselves out in just a few million years.

RED SUPERGIANT
Towards the end of its life, a massive star becomes a red supergiant, which can be 1,000 times bigger than our Sun.

SUPERNOVA
Finally, the red supergiant casts off its outer layers in a massive explosion.

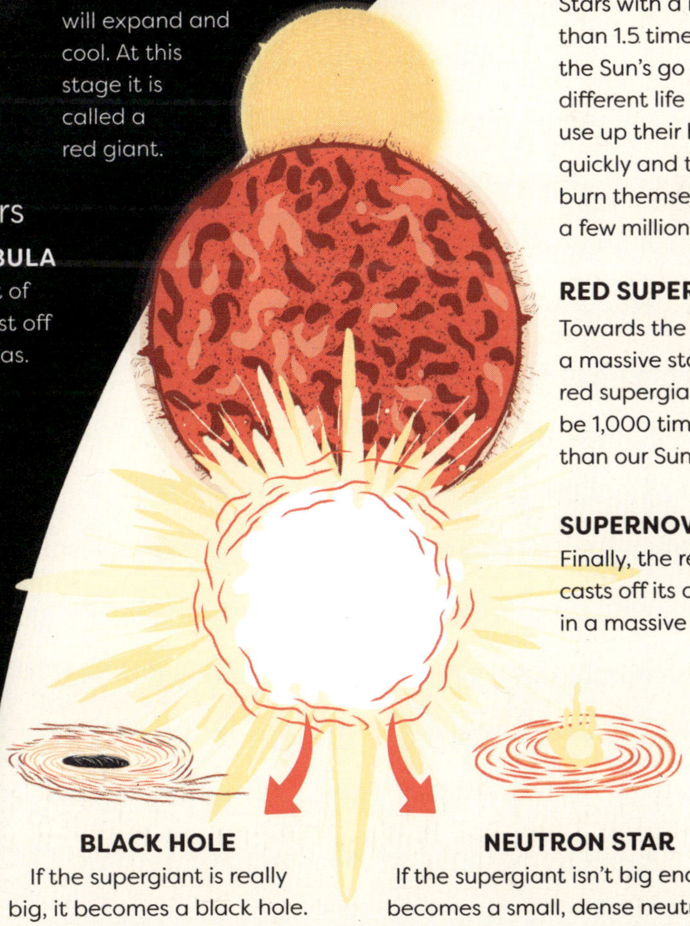

BLACK HOLE
If the supergiant is really big, it becomes a black hole.

NEUTRON STAR
If the supergiant isn't big enough, it becomes a small, dense neutron star.

SCALE
1 light year

1 light year = about 9 trillion kilometres

The place where stars are born

This sparkling image of space shows a nebula, or 'star nursery'. The photo, which was taken by the James Webb Space Telescope, shows how the edge of the nebula, which looks like the peaks and valleys of a mountainous brown landscape, is being eaten away by the radiation created by massive young stars. The scale of the nebula is mind-boggling: the tallest 'peaks' in this image are about seven light years high. (A light year is the distance light travels in a year.)

The fastest thing in the universe

What's the fastest thing you can think of? A car? An aeroplane? A space rocket? In fact, the fastest-moving thing in the universe is light. A car driving on a motorway travels at around 100 kilometres per hour. Light's top speed is ten million times faster than that!

THE SPEED OF LIGHT

The white lines on the chart show how far different things can travel in just one hour. As you can see, light, which has the longest white line, travels by far the furthest, which means it is also the fastest.

FASTEST AIRCRAFT
7,274 km (in 1 hour)

FASTEST SPACE PROBE
692,017 km

OUR SOLAR SYSTEM
720,000 km

SPEED
million km per hour

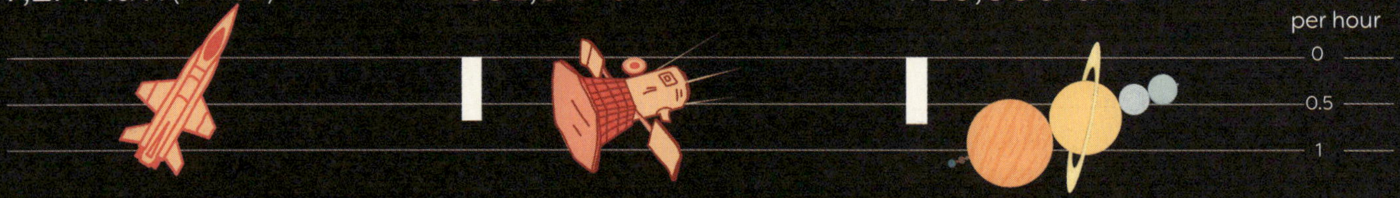

The fastest rocket-powered aircraft can travel more than six times faster than the speed of sound.

Launched in 2018, the fastest-moving space probe is NASA's Parker Solar Probe.

The solar system is moving very quickly through space as it orbits the centre of our galaxy, the Milky Way.

LIGHT IN A VACUUM
1,079,252,849 km (in 1 hour)

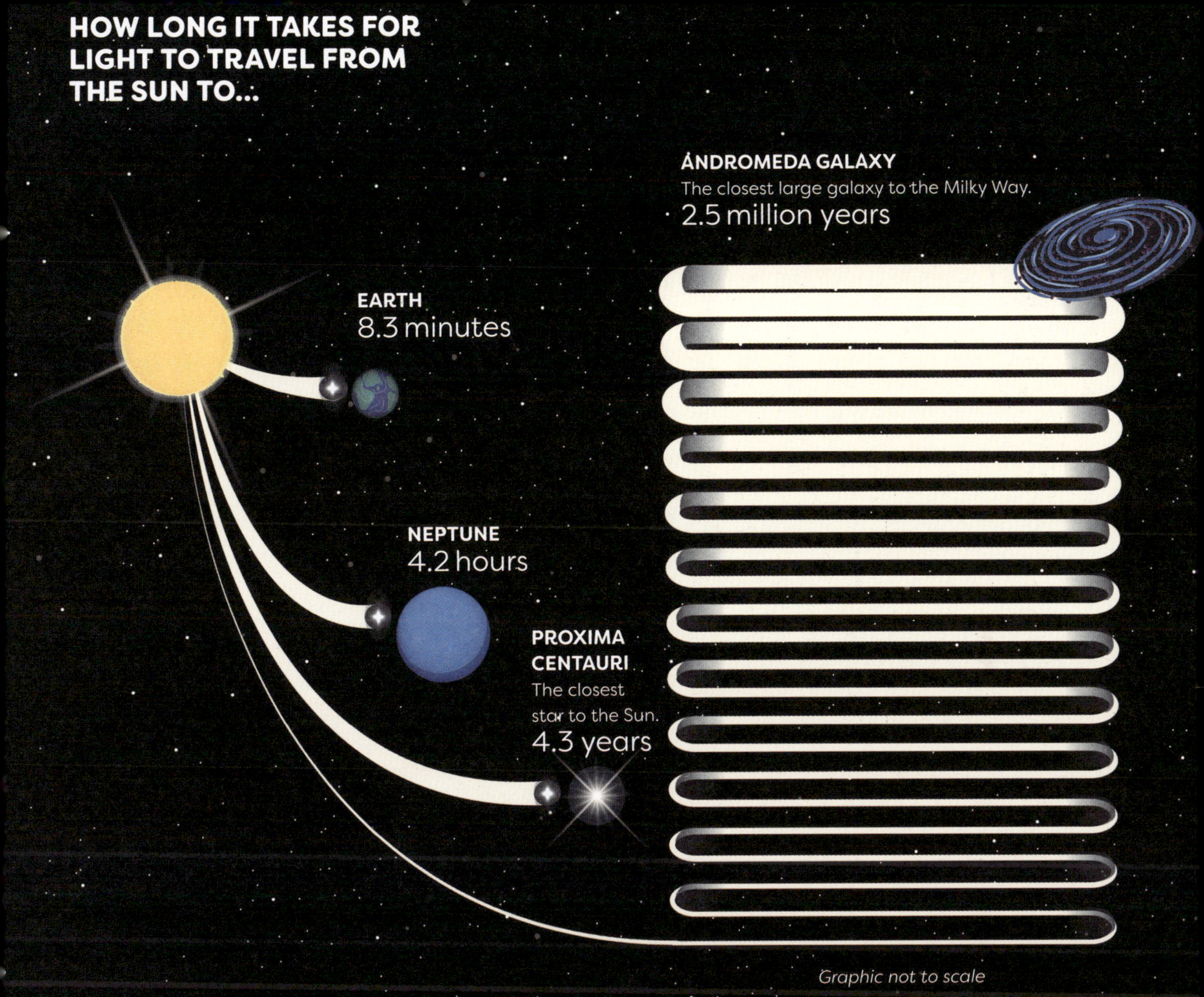

SOUND VS LIGHT

Sound, which travels at about 1,225 kilometres per hour, is much slower than light. This is why you see the light from a bolt of lightning or an exploding firework before you hear it.

If you feel like looking at some really tiny things now, turn to page 148.

The largest known star in the universe!

Our Sun might seem big to us, but it's actually pretty average-sized compared to other stars. Some stars are smaller than the Sun. Some are bigger. And some are MUCH bigger. One of the biggest that astronomers have ever seen is UY Scuti, a hypergiant star near the centre of our galaxy, the Milky Way. Here's what it would look like if we put UY Scuti and our Sun next to each other.

UY SCUTI

2,375,900,000 km across

That's 1,708 times wider than the Sun

Located near the centre of the Milky Way, UY Scuti is a hypergiant star, which is even bigger than a supergiant star. You could fit at least a quadrillion planet Earths inside UY Scuti.

SUN

1,391,016 km across

The Sun looks tiny next to UY Scuti. However, the Sun is much, much bigger than Earth. You could fit 1,300,000 planet Earths inside the Sun.

You are made of stars!

Your body is made of different chemical elements, such as oxygen and carbon. Where did these elements come from in the first place? Well, some of them were created inside exploding stars! Other elements in your body could have been created in the Big Bang itself. So, as you're about to discover, you really are made of stars.

ELEMENTS IN THE HUMAN BODY

Most of your body is made of five elements: oxygen, carbon, hydrogen, nitrogen and calcium. Traces of lots of other elements, such as sodium and iron, make up the remaining 2.5 per cent (and there is even a bit of gold in there, too).

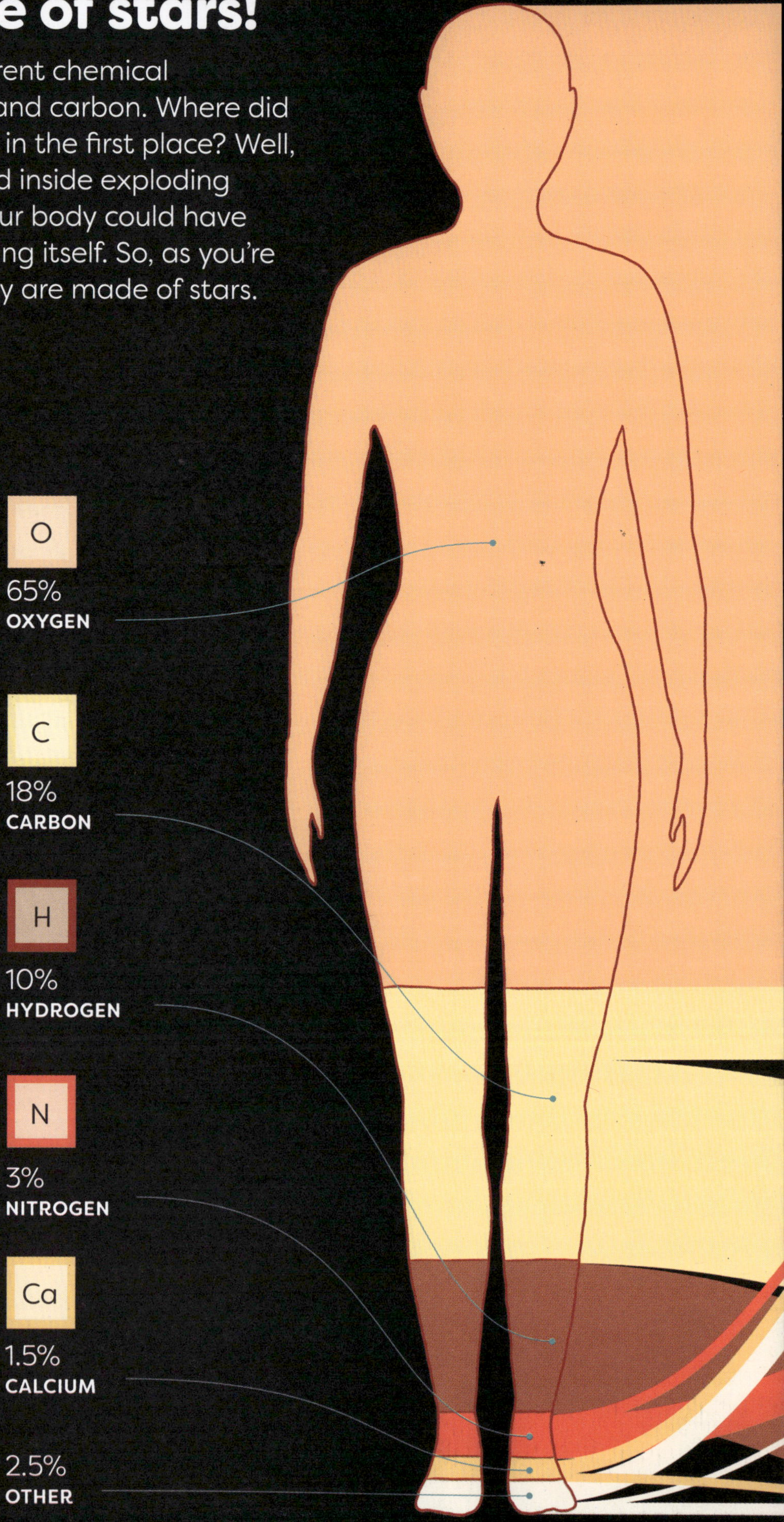

WHERE THESE ELEMENTS WERE CREATED

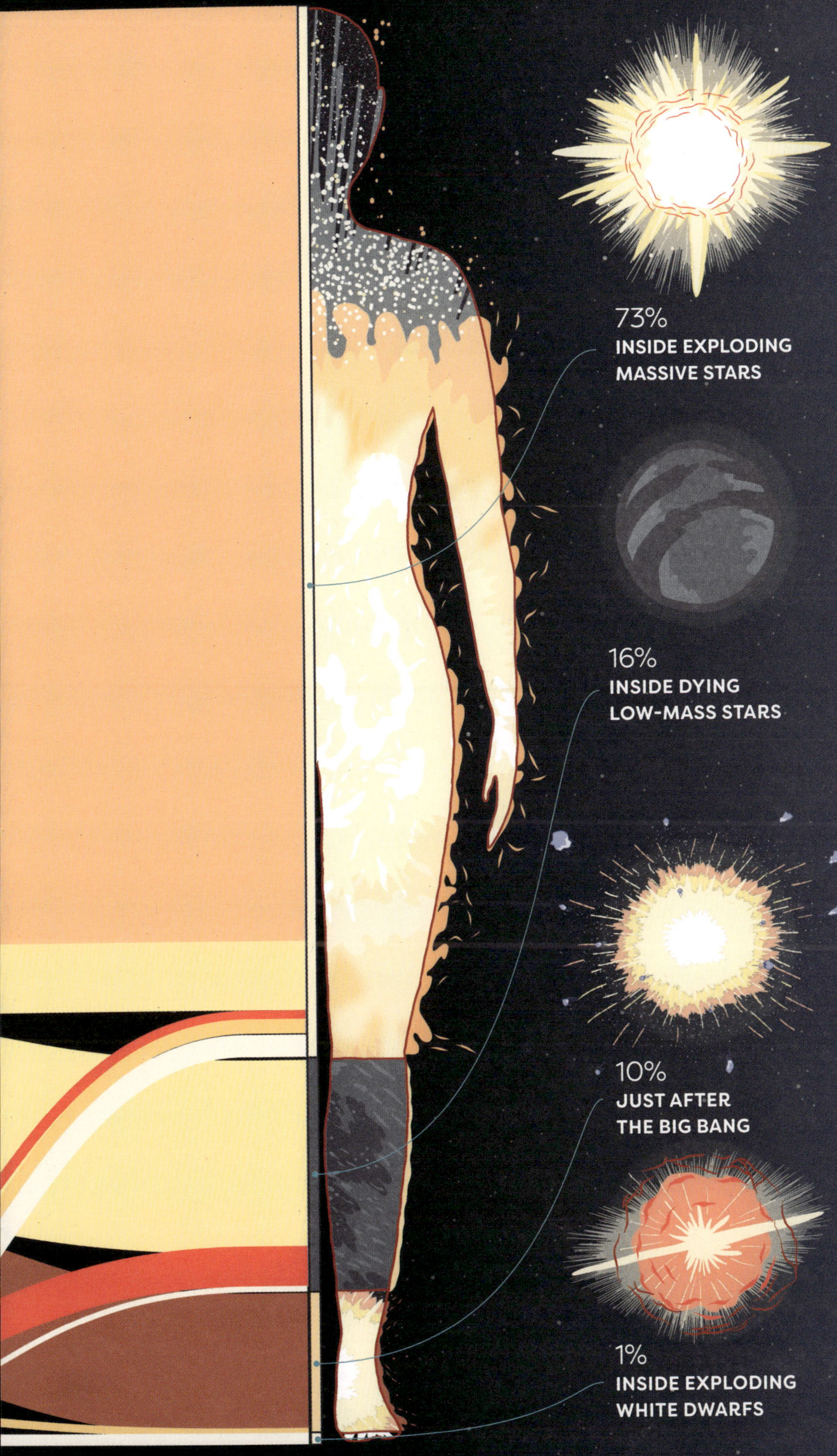

Three-quarters of your body was made in giant star explosions called supernovae. These spectacular explosions fuse lighter elements together to form heavier elements, such as oxygen.

Elements such as nitrogen are also created inside smaller low-mass stars. These stars burn up less dramatically than exploding massive stars.

Some of the most simple elements in your body, such as hydrogen, could have been created shortly after the Big Bang!

Towards the end of their life cycles, some stars turn into white dwarfs. And some white-dwarf stars explode, creating new elements, such as iron.

The awesome power of black holes!

Black holes are areas of space that contain huge amounts of matter packed very tightly together. All this densely packed matter creates an enormously powerful gravitational pull. In fact, nothing that passes close to a black hole can escape its inward pull. Not even light. This is why we call them *black* holes.

WHAT WOULD HAPPEN IF A SPACECRAFT ENTERED A BLACK HOLE?

As the rocket approached the event horizon, gravity would bend and twist the light from the stars, creating a fantastic light show. Total blackness would surround the rocket. What happens next is one of the universe's biggest mysteries. Falling faster and faster, the rocket would probably be stretched and ripped apart from every direction – called 'spaghettification'. Or it might be burned to a crisp in an instant. The remains of the rocket might leak out over millions of years as radiation, or even be burped out from a wormhole (a passageway in space-time).

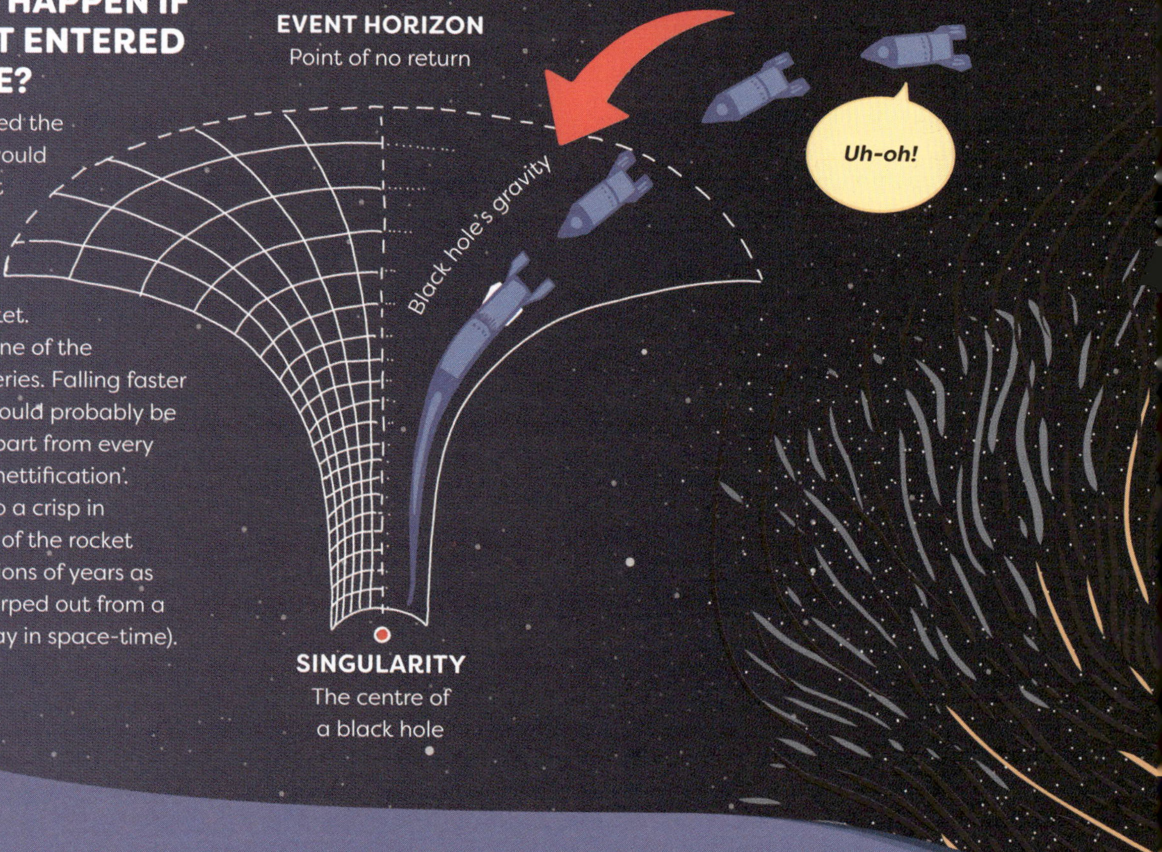

TYPES OF BLACK HOLE

MINI

Tiny black holes might have formed just after the Big Bang. Even if they were as small as a single atom, they would still have the same mass as a mountain.

STELLAR

Stellar black holes are made when massive stars die and collapse inwards. They are the most common type of black hole and are usually bigger than our Sun.

SUPERMASSIVE

Like stellar black holes, except millions of times larger, some supermassive black holes are bigger than our solar system. Most galaxies have one at their centre.

The supermassive black hole at the centre of the Milky Way (our galaxy) is called Sagittarius A*. It has a mass equivalent to the mass of 4 million Suns.

HOW DO WE FIND BLACK HOLES?

With difficulty. Because black holes don't give off light, scientists have to look at the effect their gravitational pull has on other space objects. By studying the movement of stars and galaxies in this way, astronomers can calculate a black hole's location and size. A black hole will also sometimes move close to a star. This heats the black hole up, causing it to give off a strong glow, as in the illustration above. Luckily for us, black holes are a very, very long way from Earth. This makes it harder to detect them, but also means that Earth isn't in danger of being sucked into one.

Rocks from outer space

Most of the solar system is empty space. But as well as the Sun, planets, dwarf planets and moons, you can find asteroids and comets. They are made from dust and rock left over from the formation of the solar system.

HOW TO RECOGNISE SPACE ROCKS

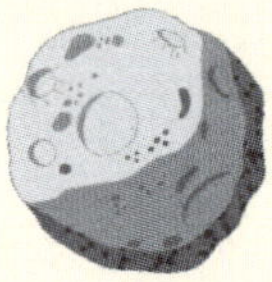

ASTEROIDS
Asteroids are rocky objects that aren't big enough to form a planet.

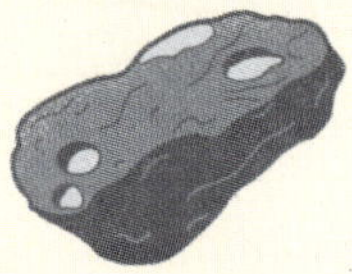

METEOROIDS
Meteoroids are small pieces of rock or metal less than 1 metre across.

METEORS
Often called 'shooting stars', meteors are meteoroids that burn up as they enter Earth's atmosphere, giving off a streak of light.

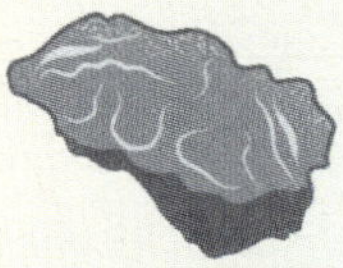

METEORITES
Meteorites are parts of meteors that don't vaporise as they enter Earth's atmosphere and land on the surface of the planet intact.

COMETS
Comets are clusters of rock, dust and ice orbiting the Sun. There could be as many as a trillion comets in the outer reaches of the solar system.

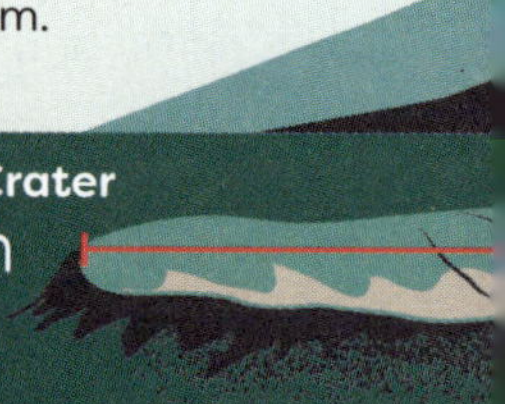

COMETS

Comets are born in two outer regions of the solar system, the Kuiper Belt, a vast icy region beyond the orbit of Neptune, and the Oort Cloud, an even more distant region far beyond dwarf planet Pluto. Sometimes comets pass close to the Sun. When this happens, some of their solid ice turns to gas, producing the comet's spectacular tail.

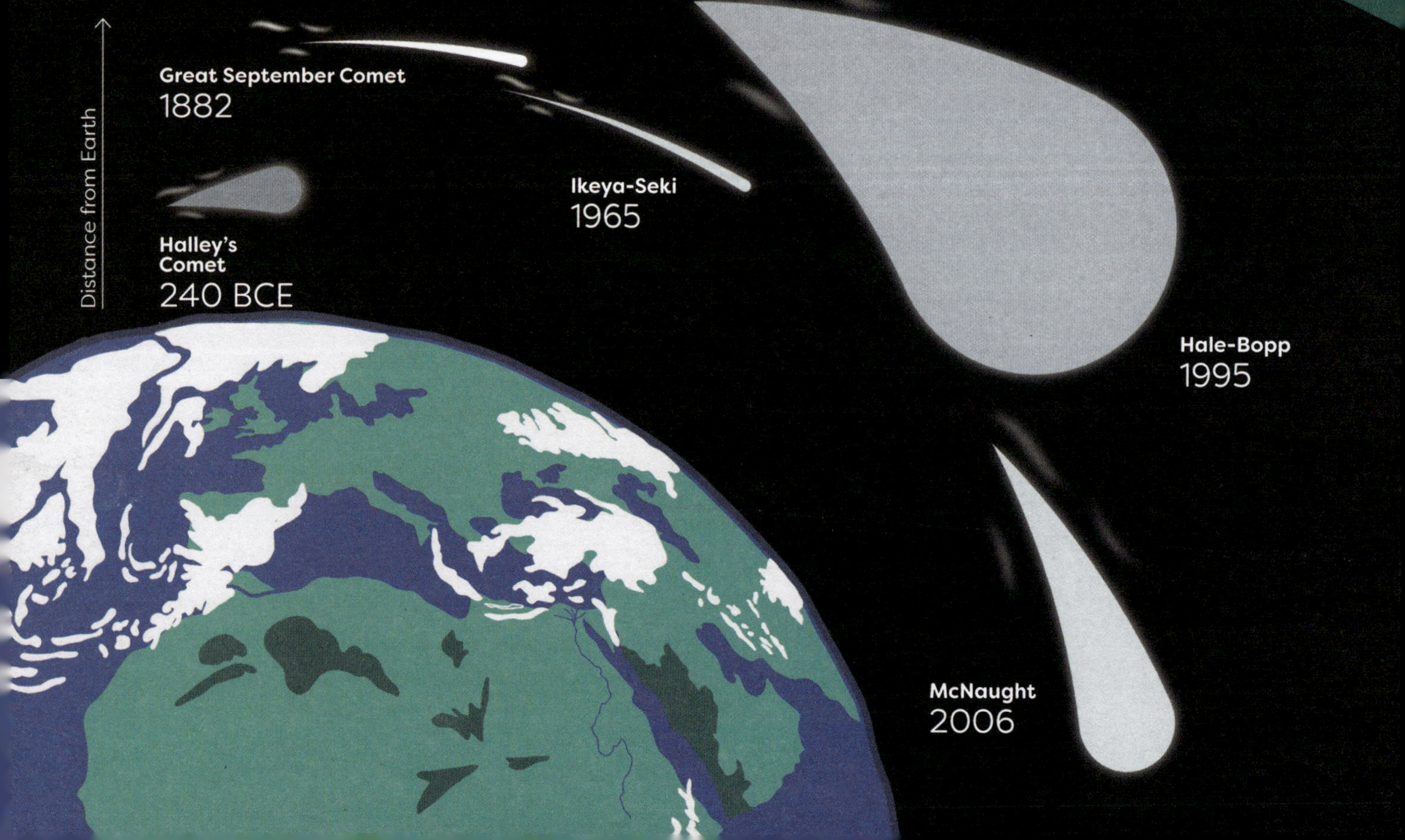

BIGGEST ASTEROID IMPACTS ON EARTH

Most asteroids that hit Earth's atmosphere burn up before they reach Earth's surface. However, once every few million years, an asteroid collides with Earth that is large enough to cause significant damage – and leave behind a giant crater. The faster the asteroid is travelling, the bigger the crater it can make. These are five of the biggest known asteroid impacts on Earth.

The asteroid that caused the extinction of the dinosaurs 66 million years ago is estimated to have been 14 kilometres wide and travelling 150 times faster than a jet aeroplane when it struck Earth.

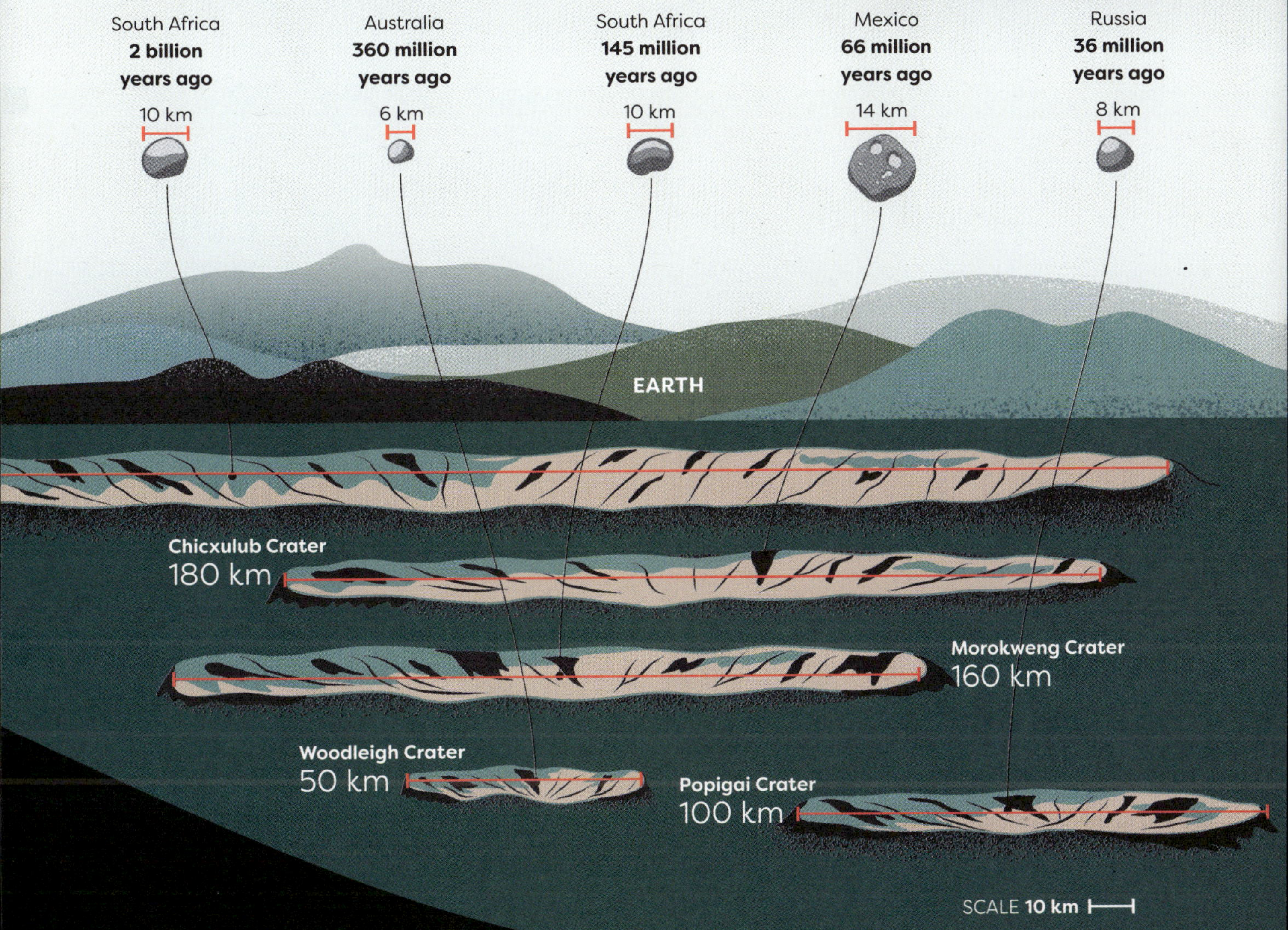

HOW TO READ IT

The diameter of each comet is relative to its dimensions in real life. The length of the tail is measured by how many degrees across the night sky it appeared to stretch (each degree is equivalent to about two full Moons in a row). The colour of the comet indicates how bright it looked from Earth (lighter colour = brighter comet). The year is the year the comet was first recorded.

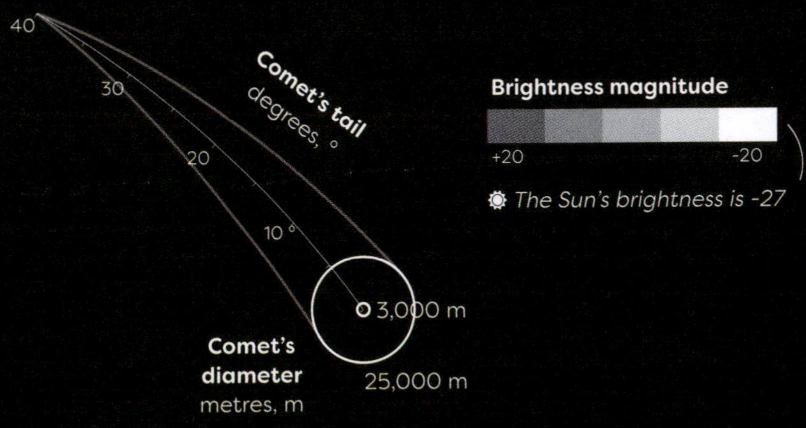

BIGGEST ASTEROIDS

IN THE SOLAR SYSTEM
Diameter in kilometres, km

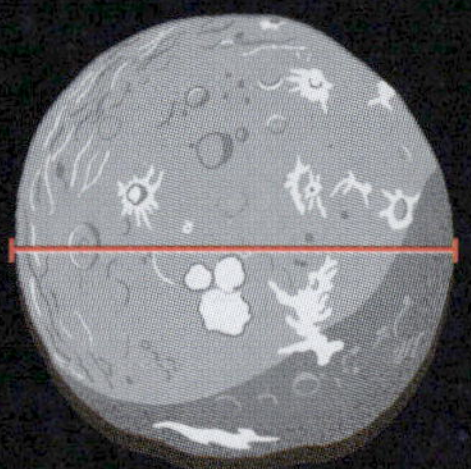

CERES
939 km

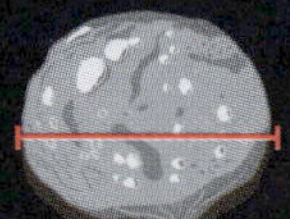

4 VESTA
525 km

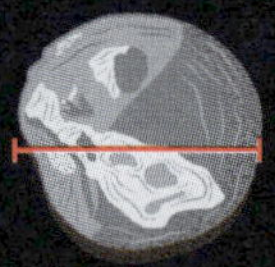

2 PALLAS
513 km

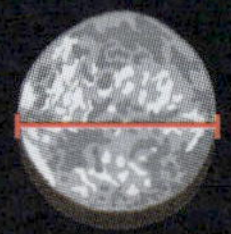

10 HYGIEA
407 km

SCALE
UK (North to South)
965 km

Ceres is the largest object in the asteroid belt. It is also classified as a dwarf planet, like Pluto. The bright spots on its surface are believed to be salty crusts, left behind when salt water evaporated into space.

Mega asteroids!

There are more than 1.1 million large asteroids in the solar system. Most of them are located in the asteroid belt between Mars and Jupiter. Asteroids are usually created from the rock, metals and other stuff left over when planets form. Many asteroids are only the size of large boulders, but the biggest can be hundreds of kilometres across.

Extraordinary exoplanets!

Planets found outside our own solar system are called exoplanets. The first exoplanets were discovered in 1992. Since then, astronomers have found more than 5,000 of them, with the number of discoveries doubling roughly every two years. Exoplanets vary in size. Some are smaller than Earth. Others are several times larger than Jupiter. This infographic shows every exoplanet that we have discovered so far.

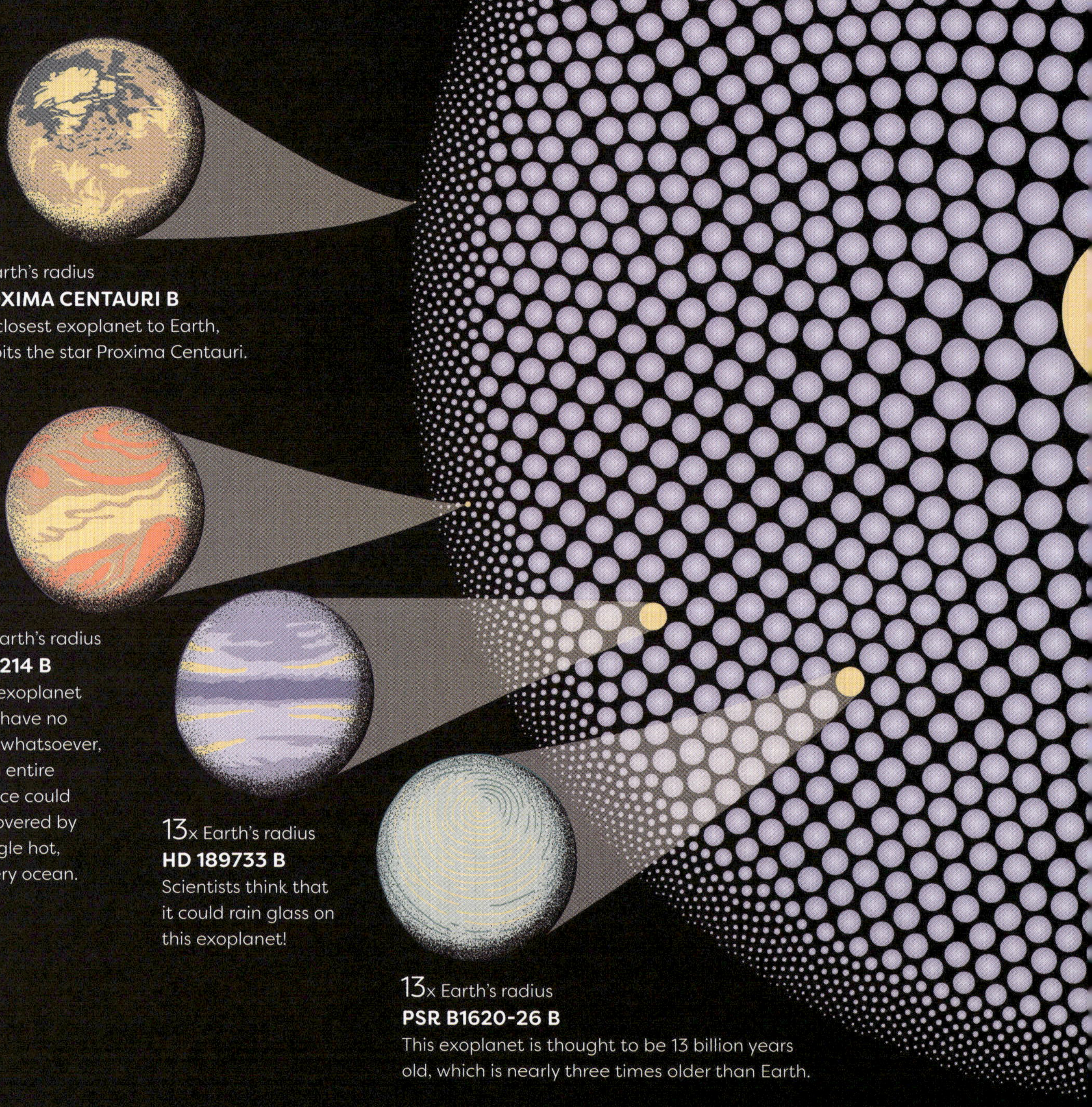

1x Earth's radius
PROXIMA CENTAURI B
The closest exoplanet to Earth, it orbits the star Proxima Centauri.

3x Earth's radius
GJ 1214 B
This exoplanet may have no land whatsoever, as its entire surface could be covered by a single hot, watery ocean.

13x Earth's radius
HD 189733 B
Scientists think that it could rain glass on this exoplanet!

13x Earth's radius
PSR B1620-26 B
This exoplanet is thought to be 13 billion years old, which is nearly three times older than Earth.

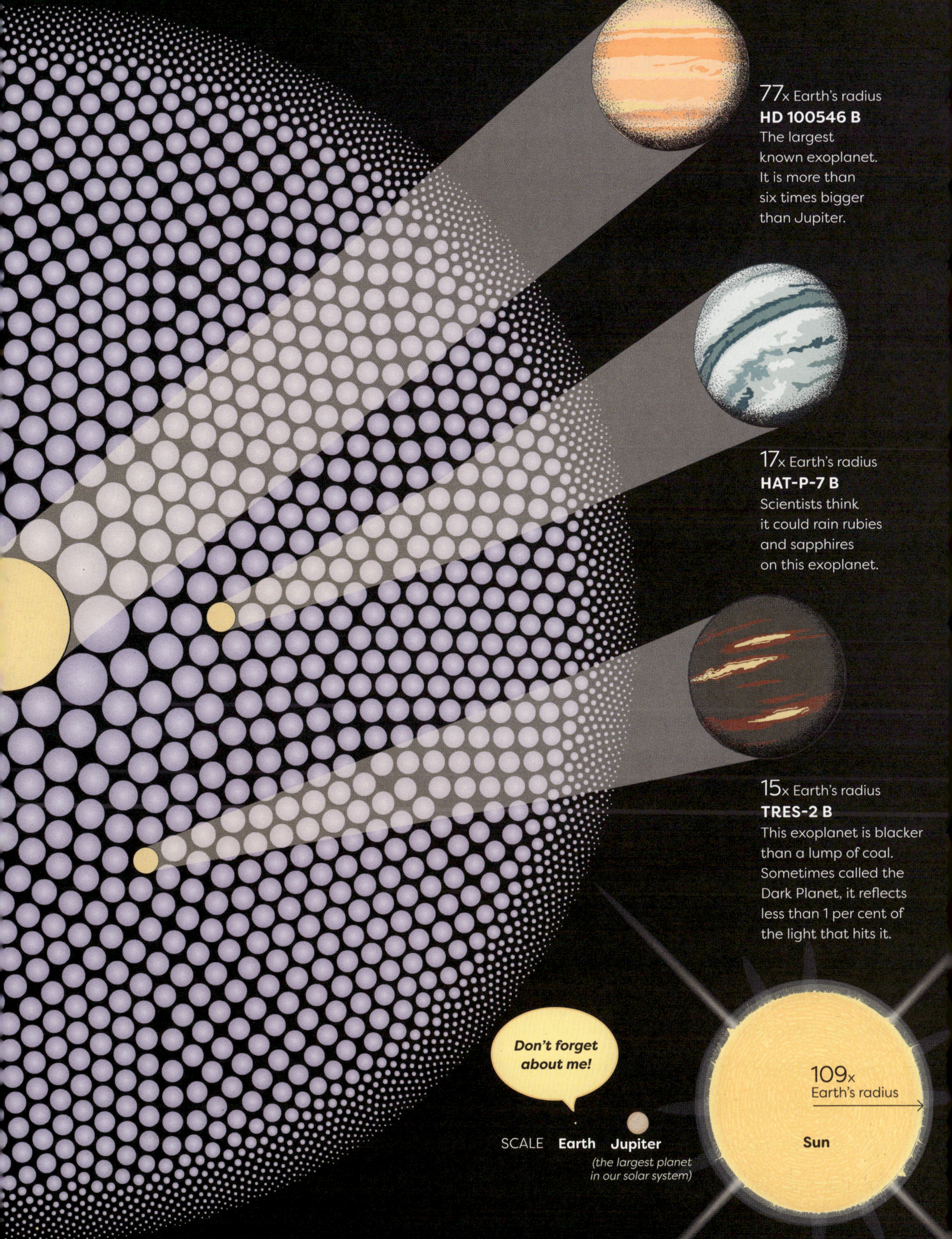

77x Earth's radius
HD 100546 B
The largest known exoplanet. It is more than six times bigger than Jupiter.
17x Earth's radius
HAT-P-7 B
Scientists think it could rain rubies and sapphires on this exoplanet.
15x Earth's radius
TRES-2 B
This exoplanet is blacker than a lump of coal. Sometimes called the Dark Planet, it reflects less than 1 per cent of the light that hits it.
Don't forget about me!
SCALE
Earth
Jupiter
(the largest planet in our solar system)
109x Earth's radius
Sun

The end of the universe

We know that from the Big Bang onwards, the observable universe has been expanding. But we don't know for certain how the story of the universe will end. Most scientists agree that the universe will die at some point in the very, very, very distant future. There are three main theories that predict how this might happen.

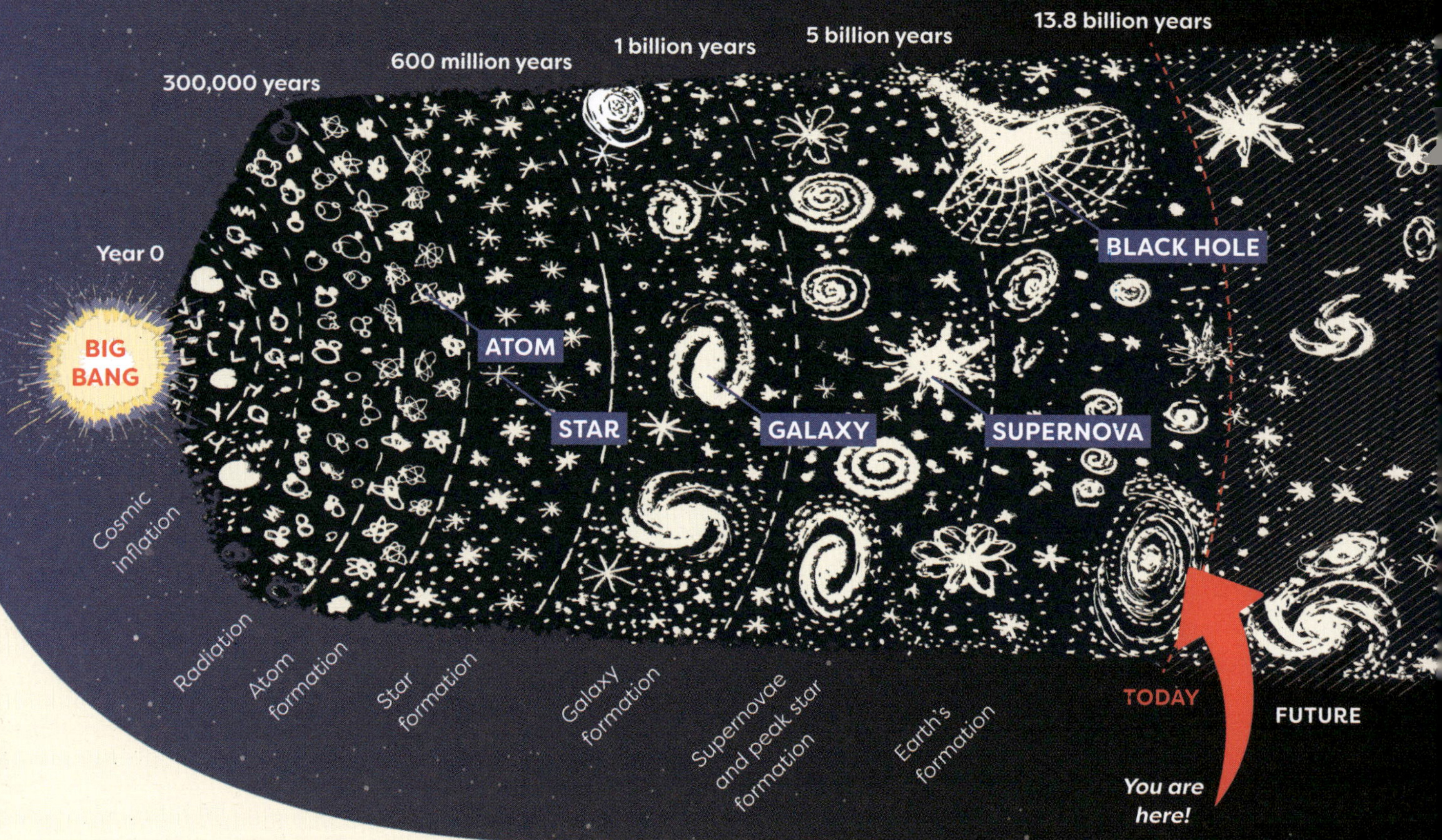

WHAT IS THE UNIVERSE MADE OF?

Everything in the observable universe, including all the stars, planets and comets you can see in the night sky, is made of atoms. This sounds like a lot of stuff, but during the 20th century, scientists were shocked to discover that all the matter and energy we can observe adds up to only about 5 per cent of the universe's *total* matter and energy. So what makes up the remaining 95 per cent? In truth, we don't really know. But scientists have come up with two theoretical ideas to explain the extra matter and energy: dark matter and dark energy.

5%

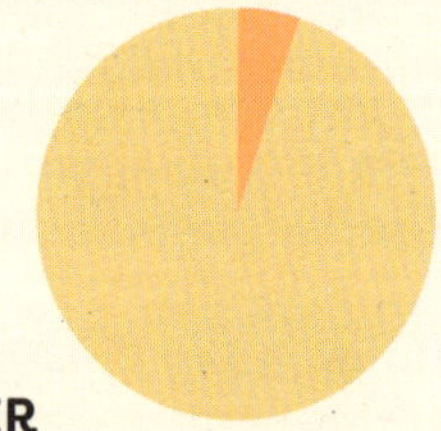

VISIBLE MATTER

Everything that we can see in the universe around us is made of atoms – including you! Scientists call all this stuff 'matter'. According to scientists' calculations, this accounts for just 5 per cent of the universe's total mass.

27%

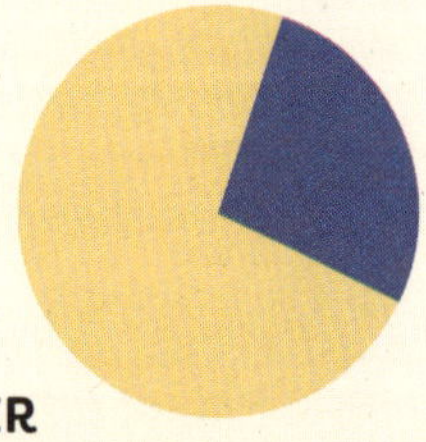

DARK MATTER

Dark matter is made of an invisible substance that doesn't give off, reflect or absorb light, which is why we can't see it. However, scientists think dark matter must exist because they've noticed the gravitational effects it has on objects we can see, such as galaxies and stars.

68%

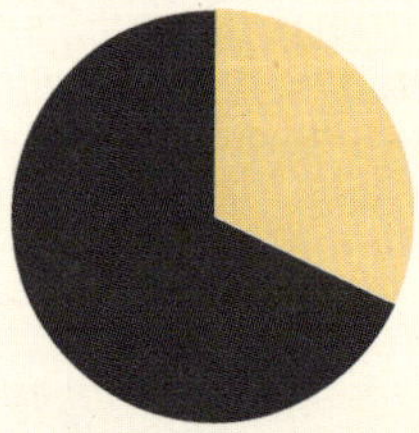

DARK ENERGY

According to the laws of gravity, the rate at which the universe is expanding should be slowing down. However, it's actually speeding up! No one has the faintest idea how or why this is happening. Scientists call the mysterious force causing it dark energy.

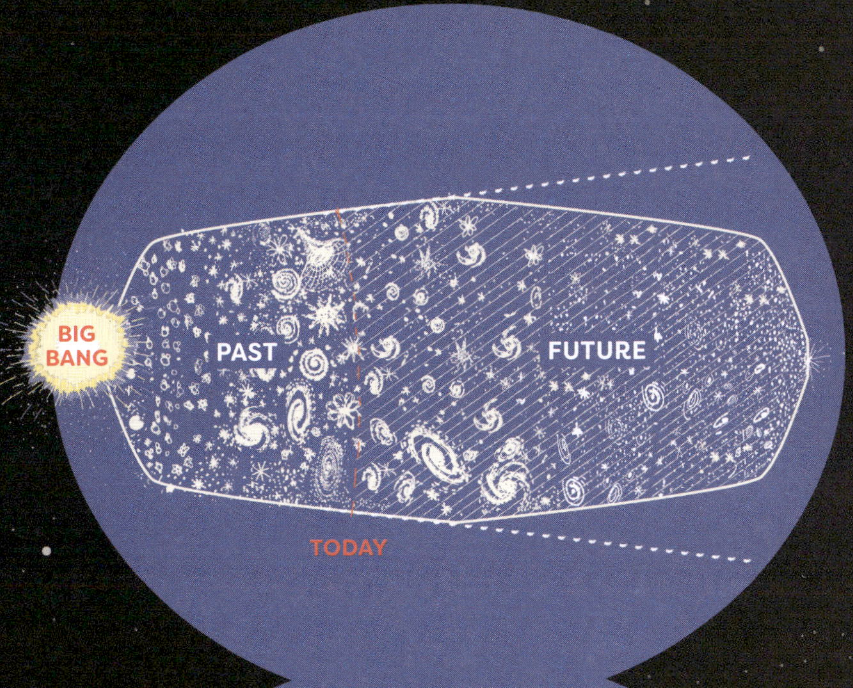

Theory 1

THE BIG CRUNCH

This theory says that the current expansion of the universe will slow down and then reverse, pulling all the matter in the universe together again in a Big Crunch.

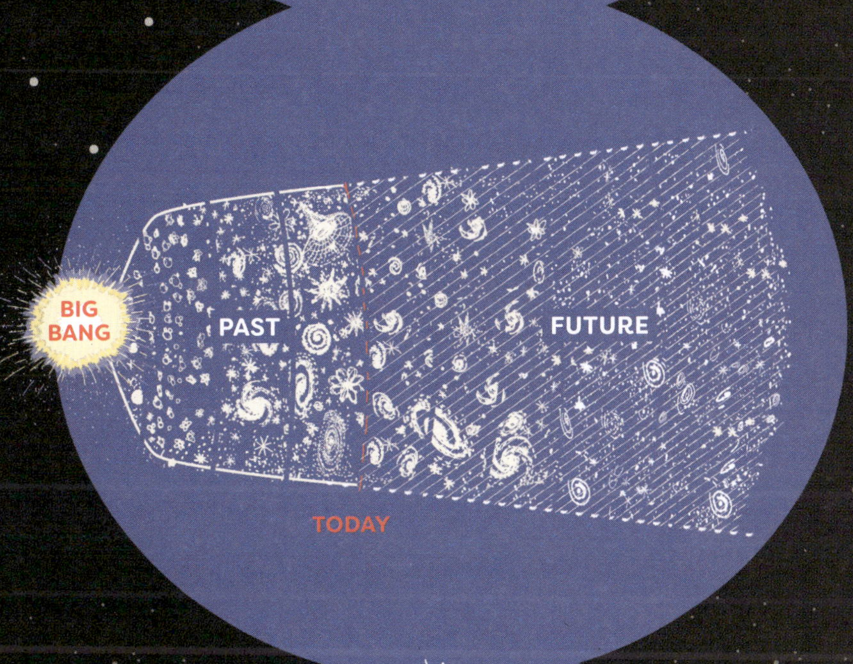

Theory 2

THE BIG FREEZE

An alternative theory says that the universe will continue to expand until it is so spread out that it loses all its energy in a Big Freeze. Most scientists think that the Big Freeze, which is also known as Heat Death, is the most likely scenario.

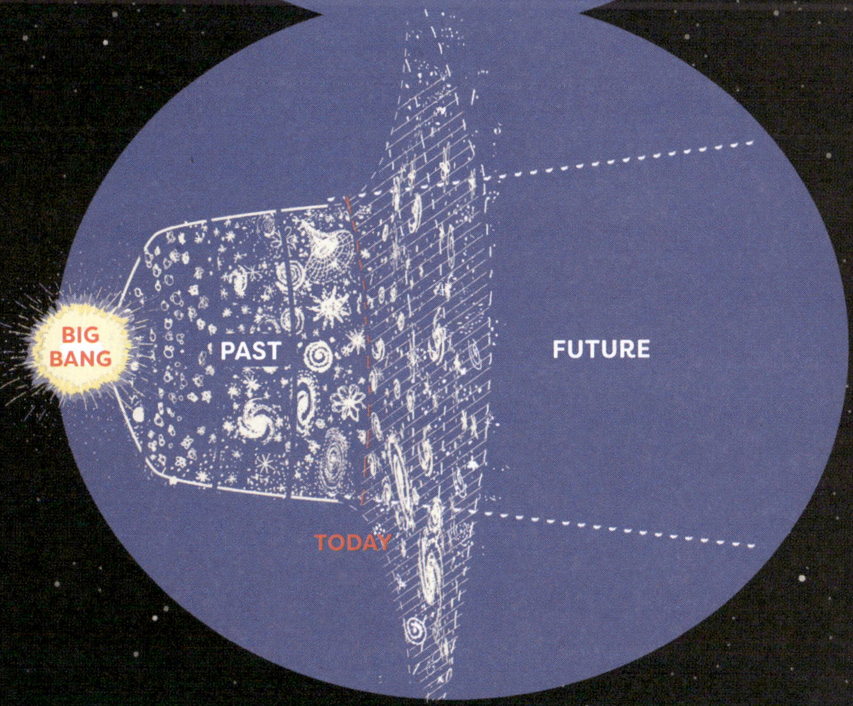

Theory 3

THE BIG RIP

A third theory says that the expansion of the universe will accelerate, becoming so fast that galaxies, stars, planets and even atoms are torn apart in a Big Rip.

MEET THE EXPERT CONSULTANT

Dr James O'Donoghue

Planetary scientist

WHEN DID YOU KNOW THAT YOU WANTED TO STUDY SPACE?

From a young age I loved looking up at the Moon and stars in the night sky and imagining what was happening in space. There was a giant *Encyclopaedia Britannica* on our bookshelf as well, so I used to leaf my way through to pages about space and dinosaurs. It's also really interesting that these two topics are related in Earth's ancient history, as a big asteroid from space wiped out the dinosaurs some 66 million years ago!

TELL US ABOUT YOUR JOB

I am a planetary astronomer, so I use huge telescopes around the world and in space to look at planets in our solar system and planets orbiting other stars. In particular, I measure the temperatures in the atmospheres of the giant planets Jupiter and Saturn. My favourite part is staying up all night at an observatory drinking tea and watching Jupiter's Great Red Spot (a storm larger than Earth!) move around the planet.

WHAT EXCITING DISCOVERY ARE YOU LOOKING FORWARD TO SEEING IN THE FUTURE?

I am excited to see the results from crewed science missions to the Moon in the late 2020s, as people will walk on the lunar surface and collect samples that will reveal the history of the Moon. I'm also looking forward to seeing images beamed back to Earth from Jupiter's moons by the space probes Europa Clipper and Jupiter Icy Moons Explorer ('JUICE') in 2030 and 2031. Even further ahead, hopefully a spacecraft will orbit Uranus by 2045, allowing us to understand the planet as never before – Uranus has never been orbited by a spacecraft!

WHAT IS YOUR FAVOURITE FACT ABOUT SPACE?

Take a deep breath! The observable universe is 94 billion light years wide, meaning it would take 94 billion years for light to travel from one side to another, but that's *just* the universe we can see. The universe is at least 15 million times larger and is expanding so fast that we will never see all of it!

SCAVENGER HUNT!

Can you track down the answers to this quiz in the pages of this book? (Turn to page 305 to see if you are right!)

1. How many Earths could you fit inside the Sun?

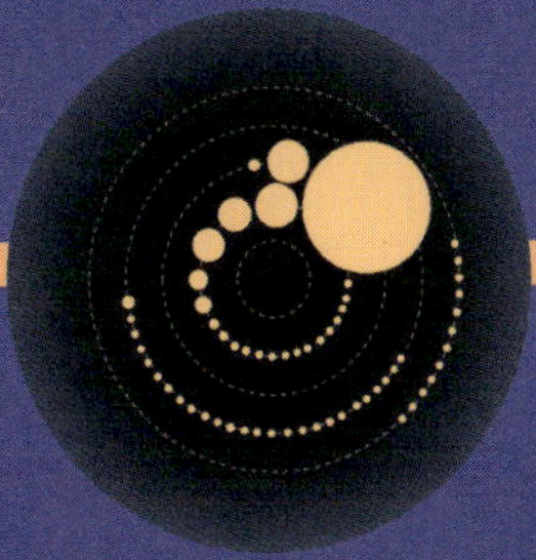

2. Which planet in our solar system is orbited by a moon called Titan?

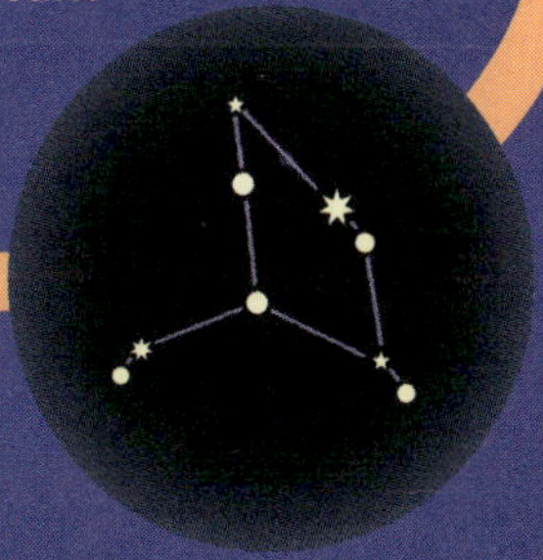

3. Which constellation is this?

4. Which moves faster, sound or light?

5. In what year did astronauts last walk on the Moon?

6. The asteroid that caused the extinction of the dinosaurs was travelling how many times faster than a jet aeroplane: 5 times, 50 times or 150 times?

7. What is the name of the supermassive black hole at the centre of the Milky Way?

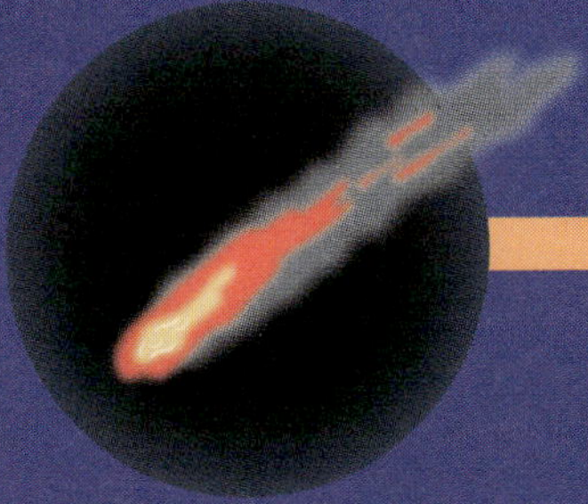

8. What is the scientific name for a shooting star?

LAND, SEA, SKY

Introducing Earth

Earth is a unique planet – as far as we know, it is the only place in the universe that supports life. Life thrives here because of the liquid water on Earth's surface, the abundant oxygen in its atmosphere and a comfortable average temperature.

71%
OF EARTH'S SURFACE IS WATER
Water covers almost three-quarters of Earth's surface, and almost all of this is ocean.

Earth is not quite a perfect sphere! It's actually something called an oblate spheroid, a shape that's wider at the equator than at the poles.

POLAR CIRCUMFERENCE
39,941 km

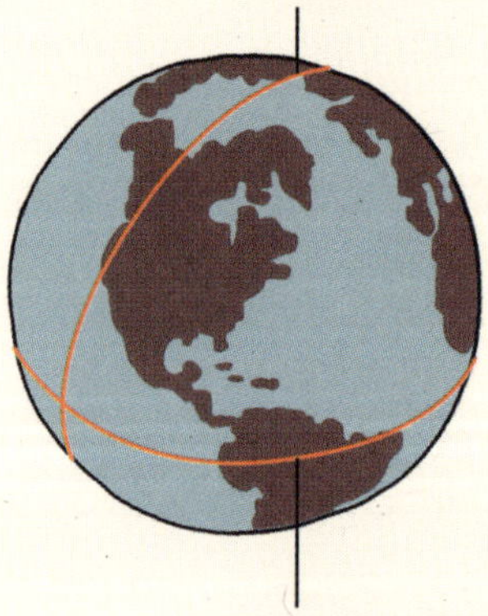

EQUATORIAL CIRCUMFERENCE
40,075 km

AGE
4.4–4.6 billion years

DIAMETER (POLE TO POLE)
12,714 km

Find out how Earth measures up against other planets in the solar system on page 6.

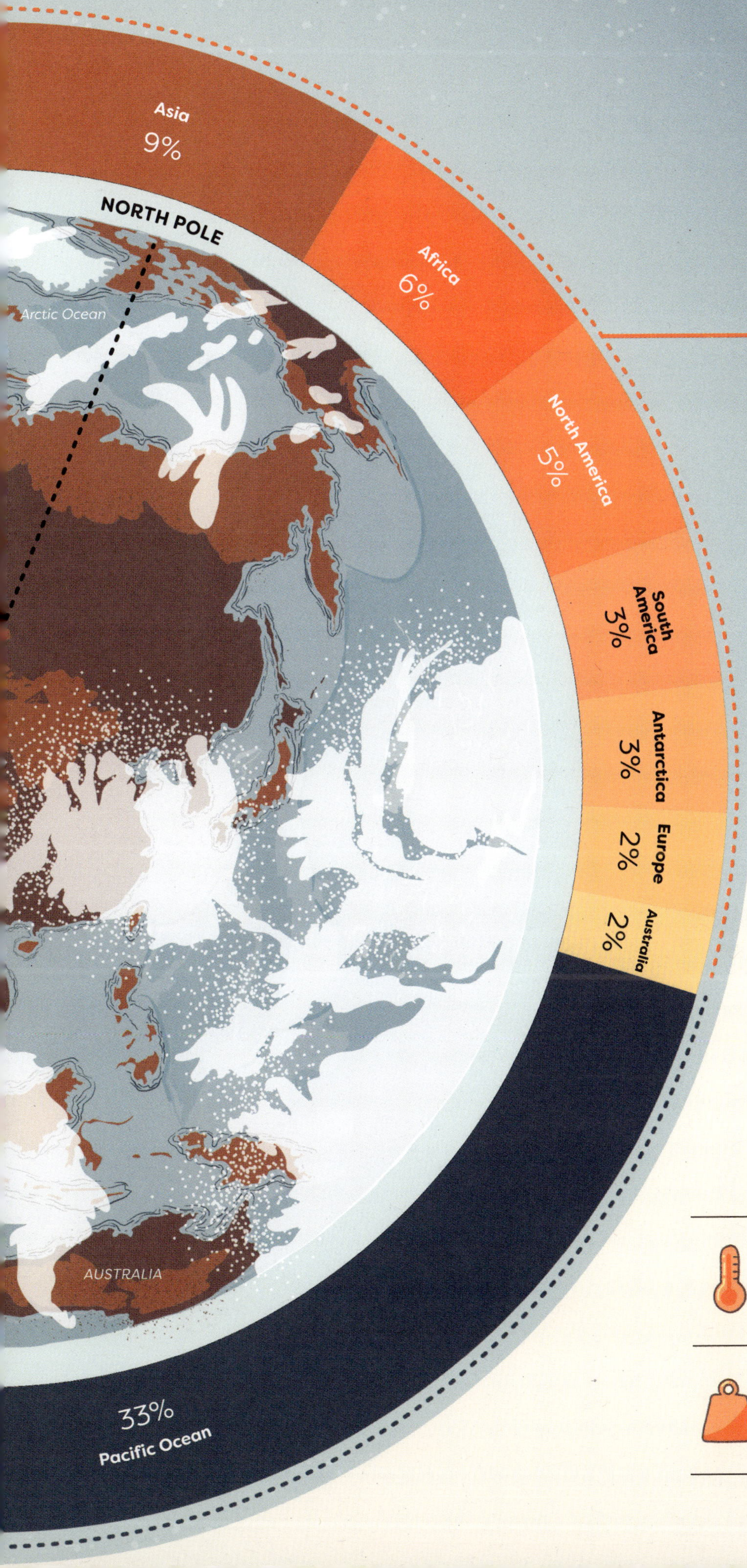

29%

OF EARTH'S SURFACE IS LAND

Just over a quarter of Earth's surface is land, made up of continents and islands. *(Percentages for each continent have been rounded up to the nearest whole number.)*

SPEED OF ROTATION AT THE EQUATOR
1,670 km/h

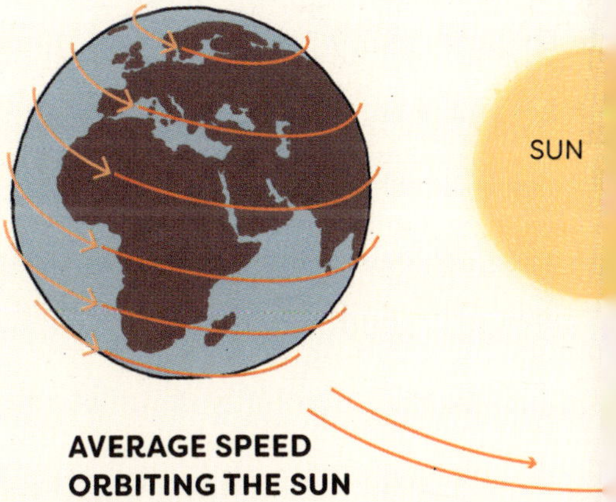

AVERAGE SPEED ORBITING THE SUN
29.8 km/s

AVERAGE TEMPERATURE
15°C

MASS
5,970,000,000,000,
000,000,000,000 kg
(that's 5.97 septillion kilograms)

What's inside Earth?

When Earth first formed it was a ball of very, very hot liquid rock. Over time, it cooled and heavier elements such as iron and nickel sank into the centre of the planet, which we call the core. Surrounding the core is the mantle, a layer of hot, semi-solid rock that contains crystals. Earth's outermost layer is the crust, which is mostly made of solid basalt and granite rock.

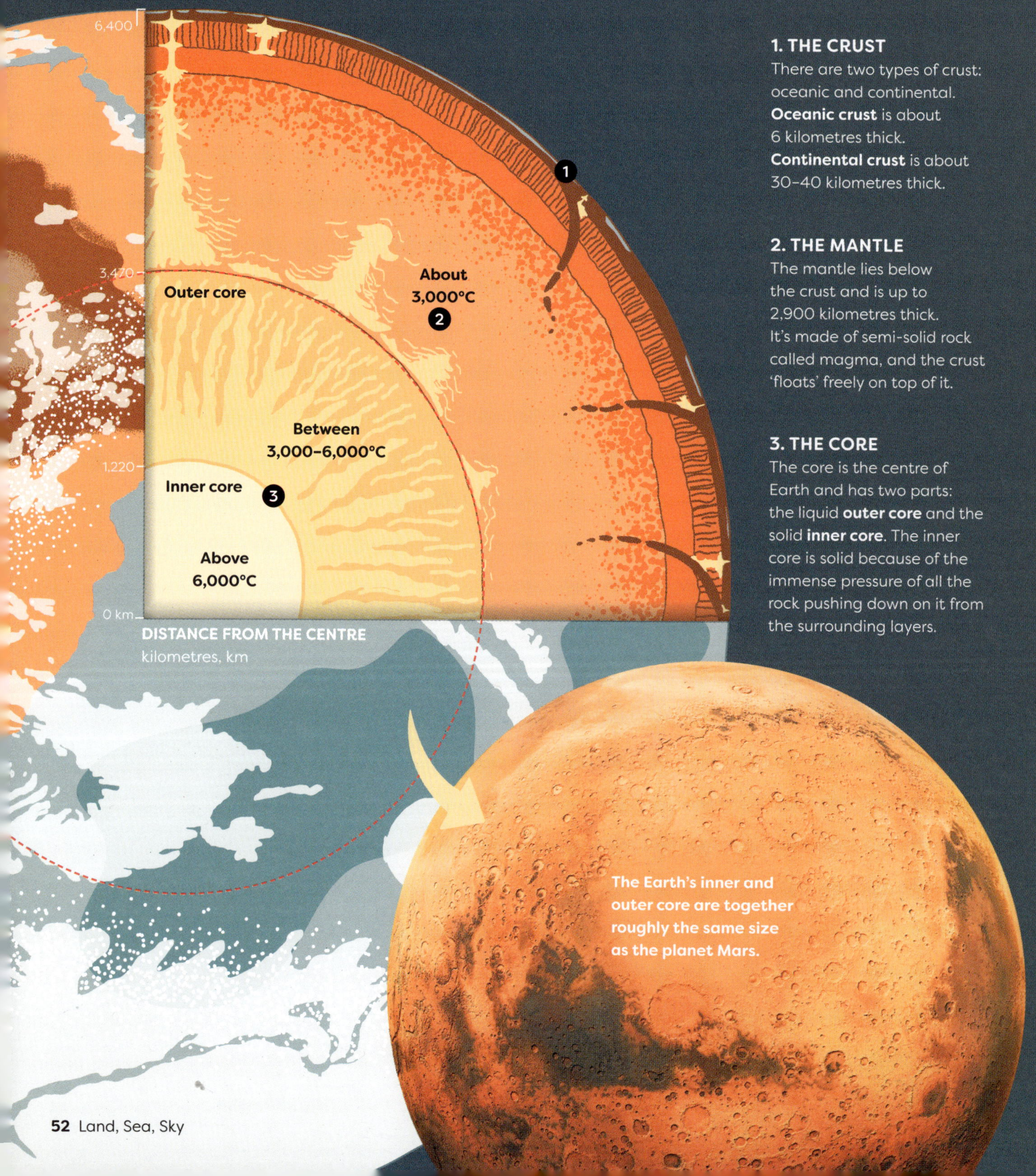

1. THE CRUST

There are two types of crust: oceanic and continental. **Oceanic crust** is about 6 kilometres thick. **Continental crust** is about 30–40 kilometres thick.

2. THE MANTLE

The mantle lies below the crust and is up to 2,900 kilometres thick. It's made of semi-solid rock called magma, and the crust 'floats' freely on top of it.

3. THE CORE

The core is the centre of Earth and has two parts: the liquid **outer core** and the solid **inner core**. The inner core is solid because of the immense pressure of all the rock pushing down on it from the surrounding layers.

Want to know more about cyanobacteria? Turn to page 107.

HOW DID EARTH FORM?

Earth formed about 4.6 billion years ago from clouds of gas and dust left over from the formation of the Sun. Pulled together by gravity, these clouds created a ball of hot compacted rock, which eventually became our planet.

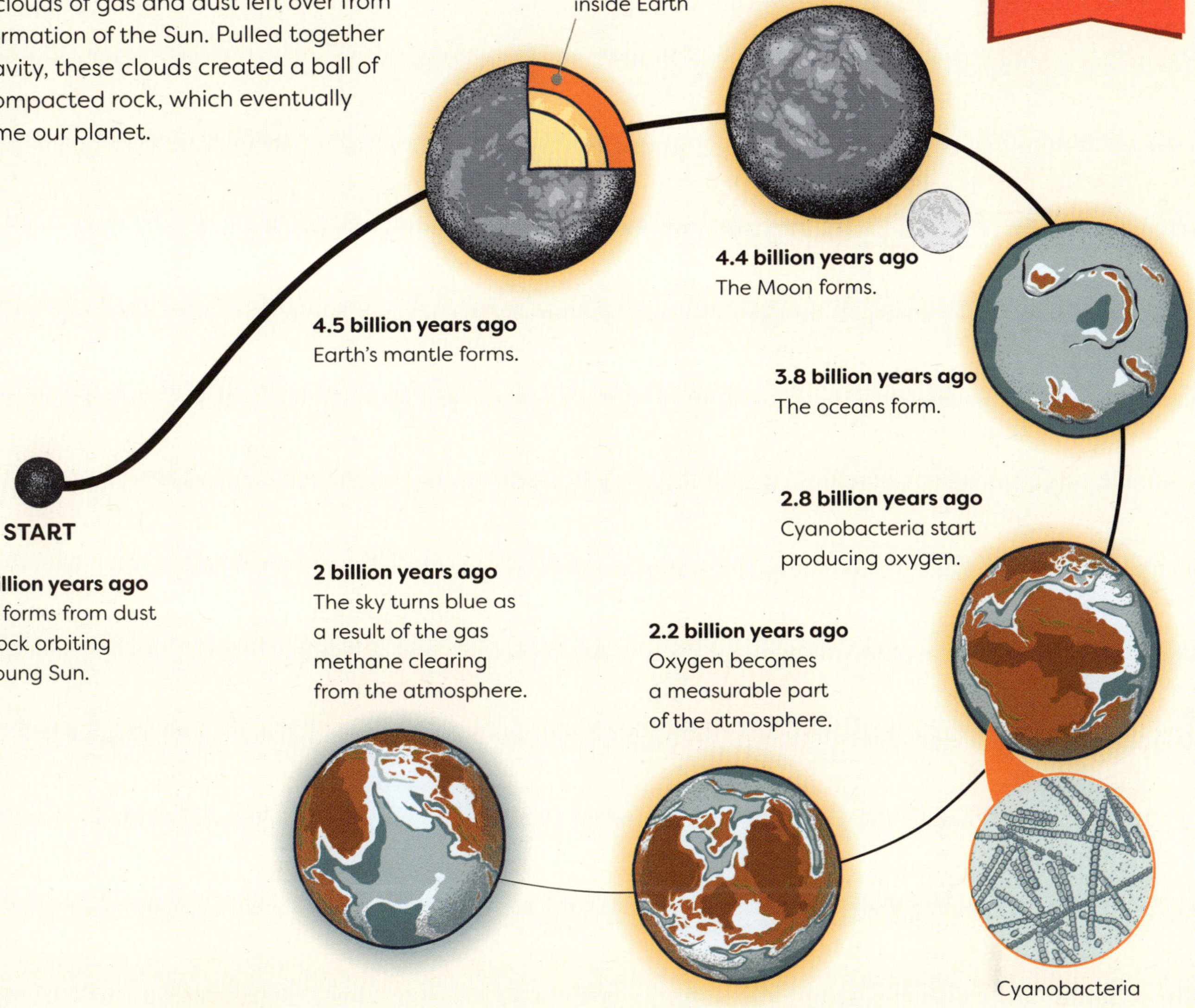

THE EARTH IS A BIT LIKE A BOILED EGG!

The proportions of a boiled egg are a good way to imagine the relative sizes of Earth's crust, mantle and core. Just like a boiled egg, Earth has a thin, hard outer shell. And the size of Earth's core relative to the rest of the planet is roughly the same as the size of an egg yolk relative to the rest of the egg.

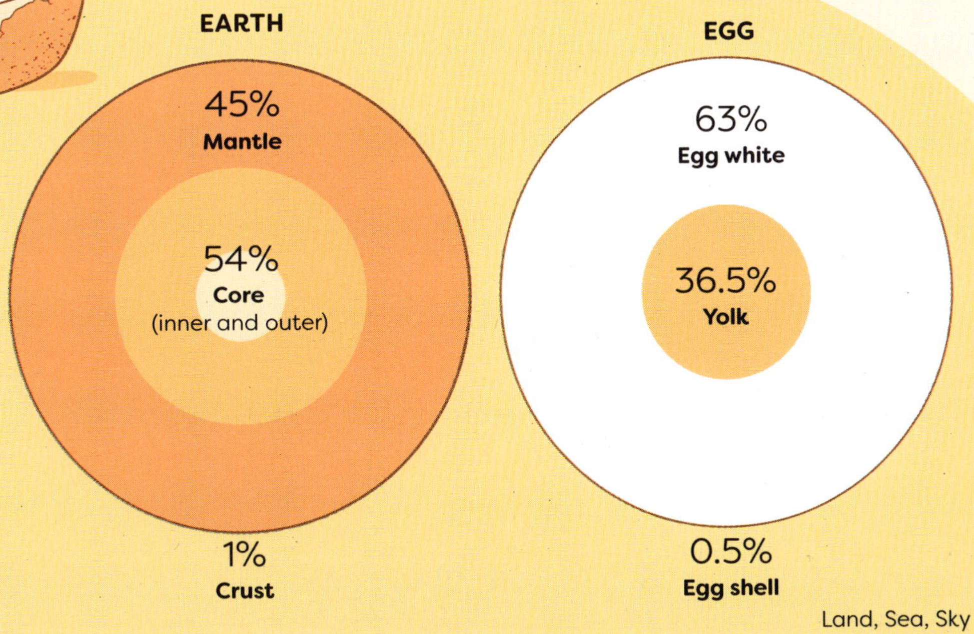

Volcanic explosion!

During a volcanic eruption, magma escapes from an opening in Earth's crust. Magma released by a volcano is called lava. In some eruptions, lava flows slowly out of a crack in the ground. In others, lava, rock, ash and other materials are thrown high into the air. The type of eruption depends on several things, including the stickiness of the magma, the size and upwards thrust of the bubbles of hot gases it contains, and the rock formation through which the magma escapes.

We use the volcanic explosivity index (VEI) to compare volcanic explosions. The index ranges from 0 to 8, with each number representing an eruption ten times more powerful than the last.

Volcanic Explosivity Index (VEI)	0 EFFUSIVE	1 SEVERE	2 EXPLOSIVE	3 CATASTROPHIC	4 CATACLYSMIC
Volume of ash cubic kilometres	<0.0001	0.0001–0.001	0.001–0.01	0.01–0.1	0.1–1
Eruption column height kilometres (<1, 1, 5)	<0.1	0.1–1	1–5	3–15	10–25
Example	**Mauna Loa** Hawaii 1984	**Kīlauea** Hawaii 1961	**Fourpeaked** Alaska 2006	**Nevado del Ruiz** Colombia 1985	**Lakagigar** Iceland 1783

Eruption type

HAWAIIAN ERUPTION (VEI OF 0 AND 1)

Though small and gentle compared to stronger eruptions, these can still send fountains of hot rock reaching 50 metres into the air!

VULCANIAN ERUPTION (VEI OF 2, 3 AND 4)

These types of eruption are named after Vulcano Island near Stromboli, Italy. They have dense clouds of billowing ash that explode into the sky.

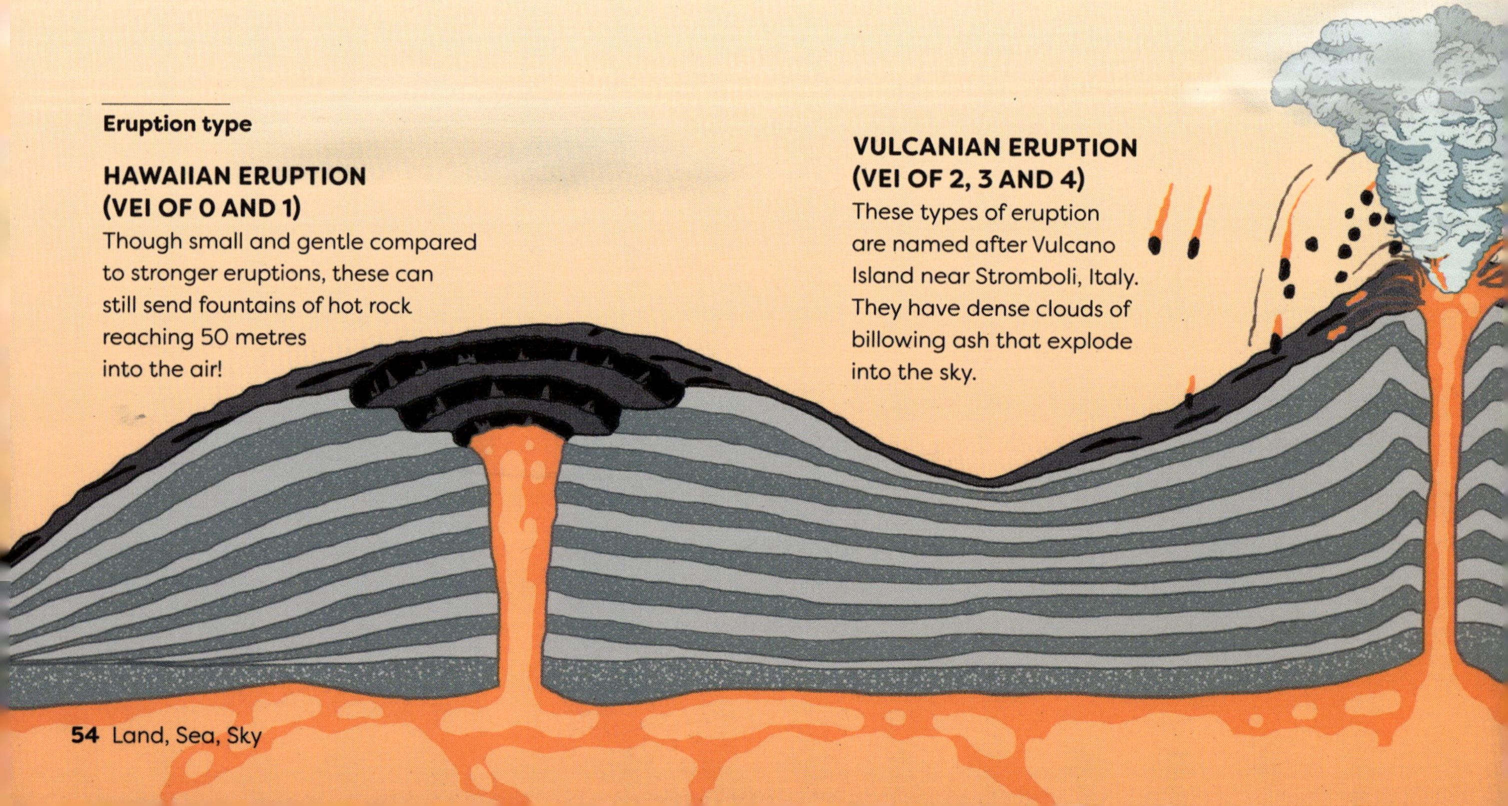

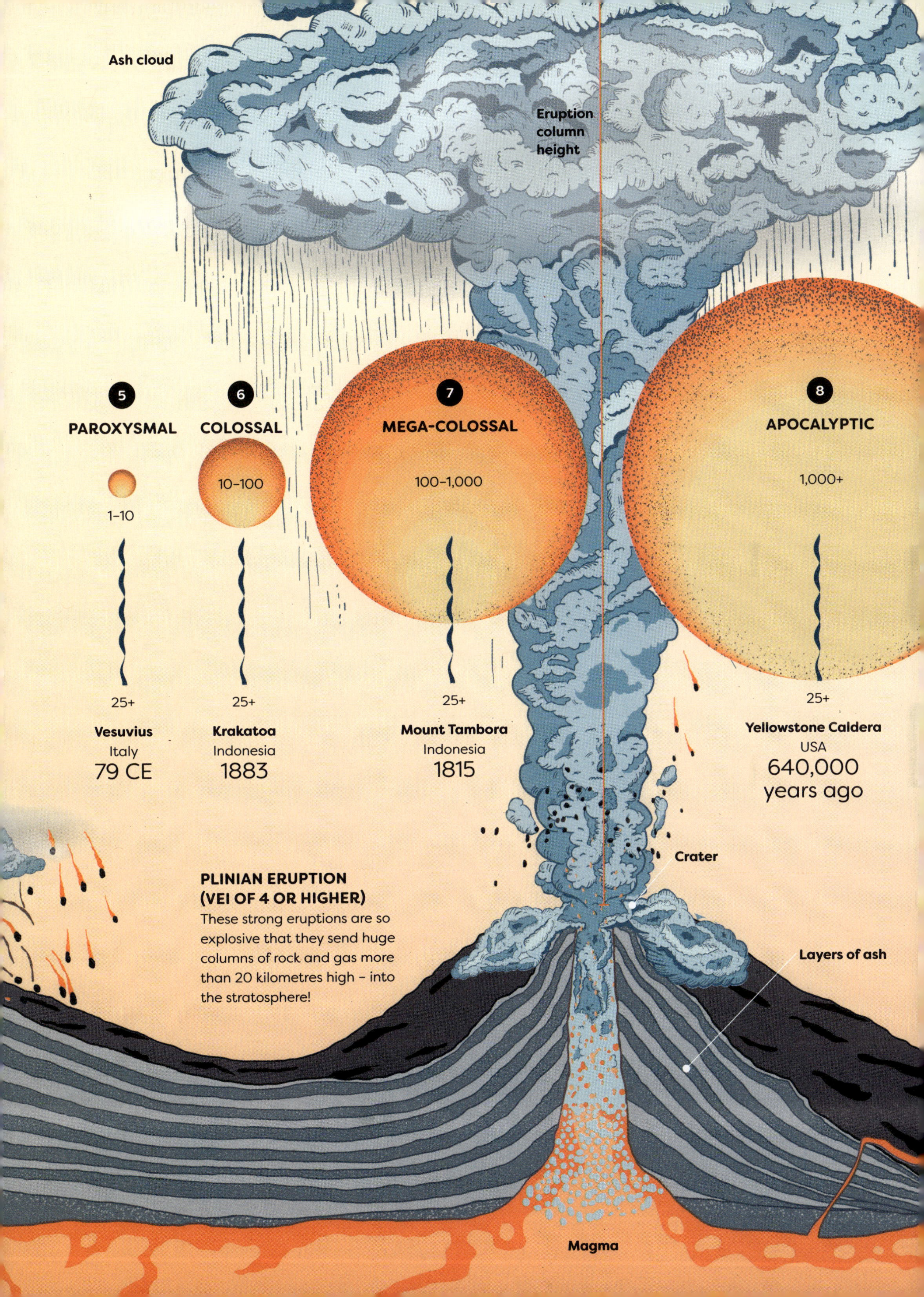

PLINIAN ERUPTION (VEI OF 4 OR HIGHER)

These strong eruptions are so explosive that they send huge columns of rock and gas more than 20 kilometres high – into the stratosphere!

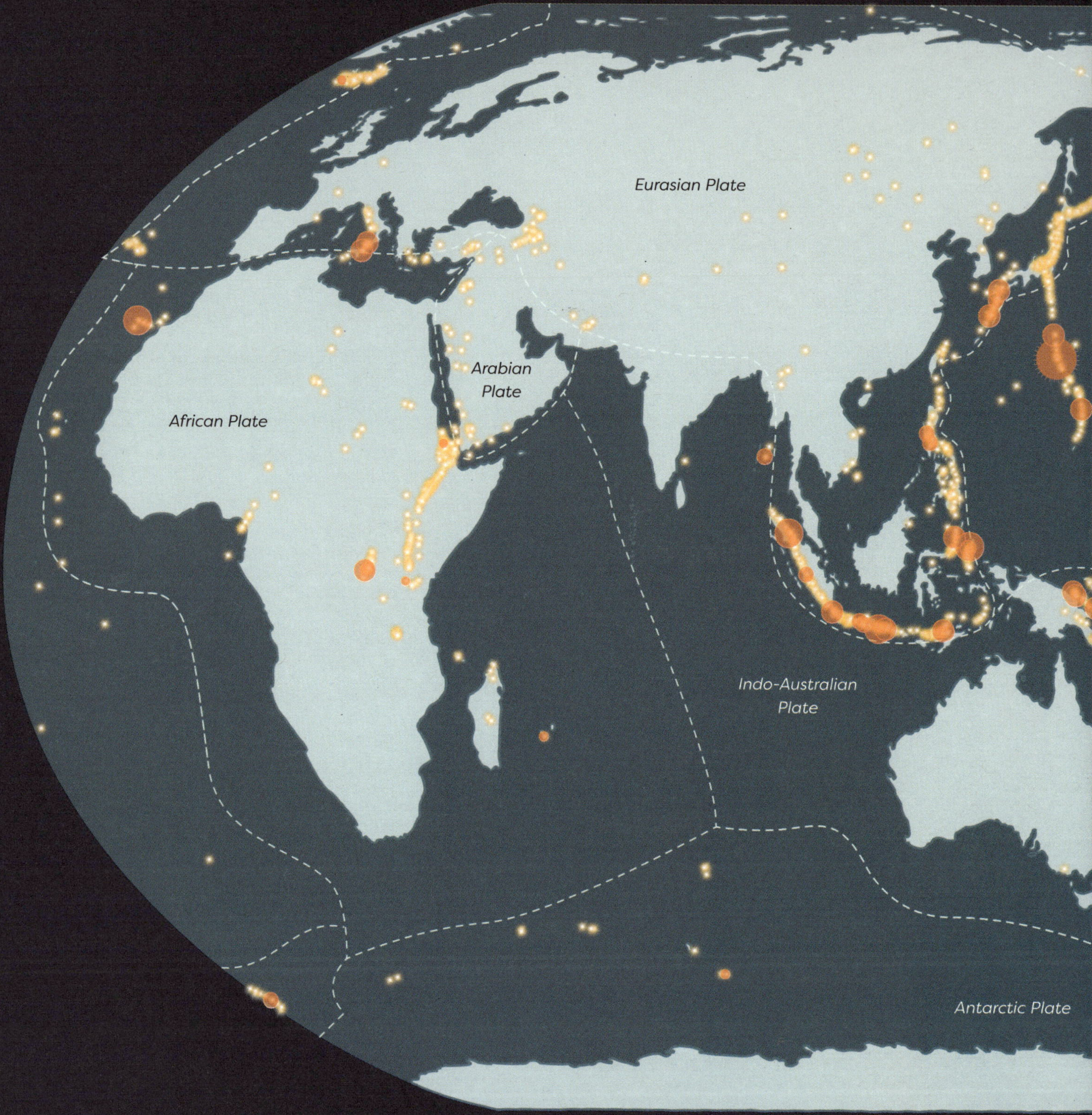

The Ring of Fire

Where do volcanoes happen on Earth? Earth's crust is divided into giant slabs of rock called tectonic plates. These are slowly moving around on the liquid rock beneath. Most volcanoes and earthquakes occur at the plate edges (margins), where different tectonic plates meet and grind against each other. About 75 per cent of all volcanoes erupt at the margins of the Pacific Plate, around what is known as the Ring of Fire.

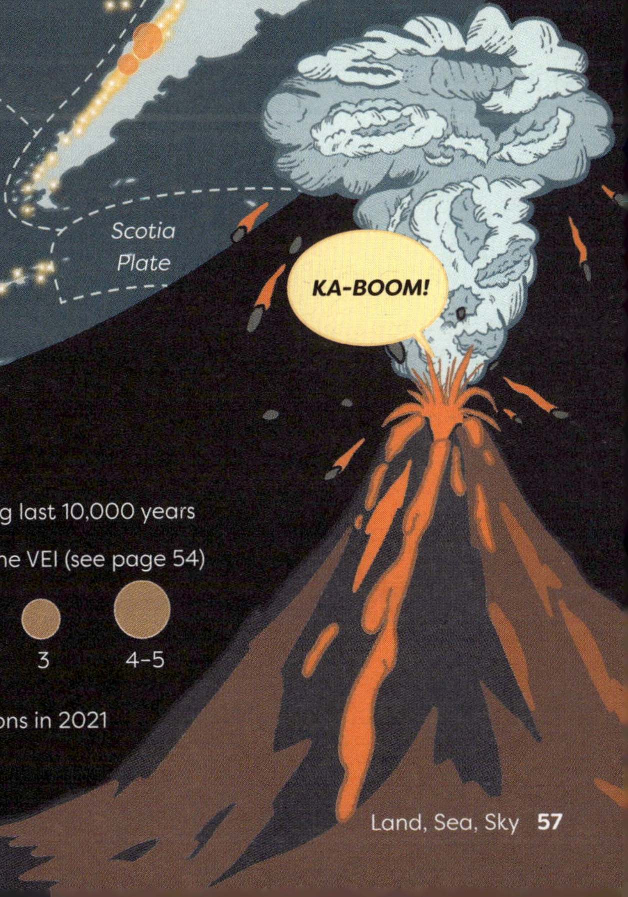

HOW TO READ IT

The dotted lines show the margins of the major tectonic plates. The bright yellow dots show volcanoes that have been active during the last 10,000 years. Major volcanic eruptions in 2021 are highlighted with a red circle. The bigger the red circle, the bigger the eruption.

Volcanoes active during last 10,000 years

Size of 2021 eruptions on the VEI (see page 54)

0 1 2 3 4–5

Major volcanic eruptions in 2021

--- Tectonic plates

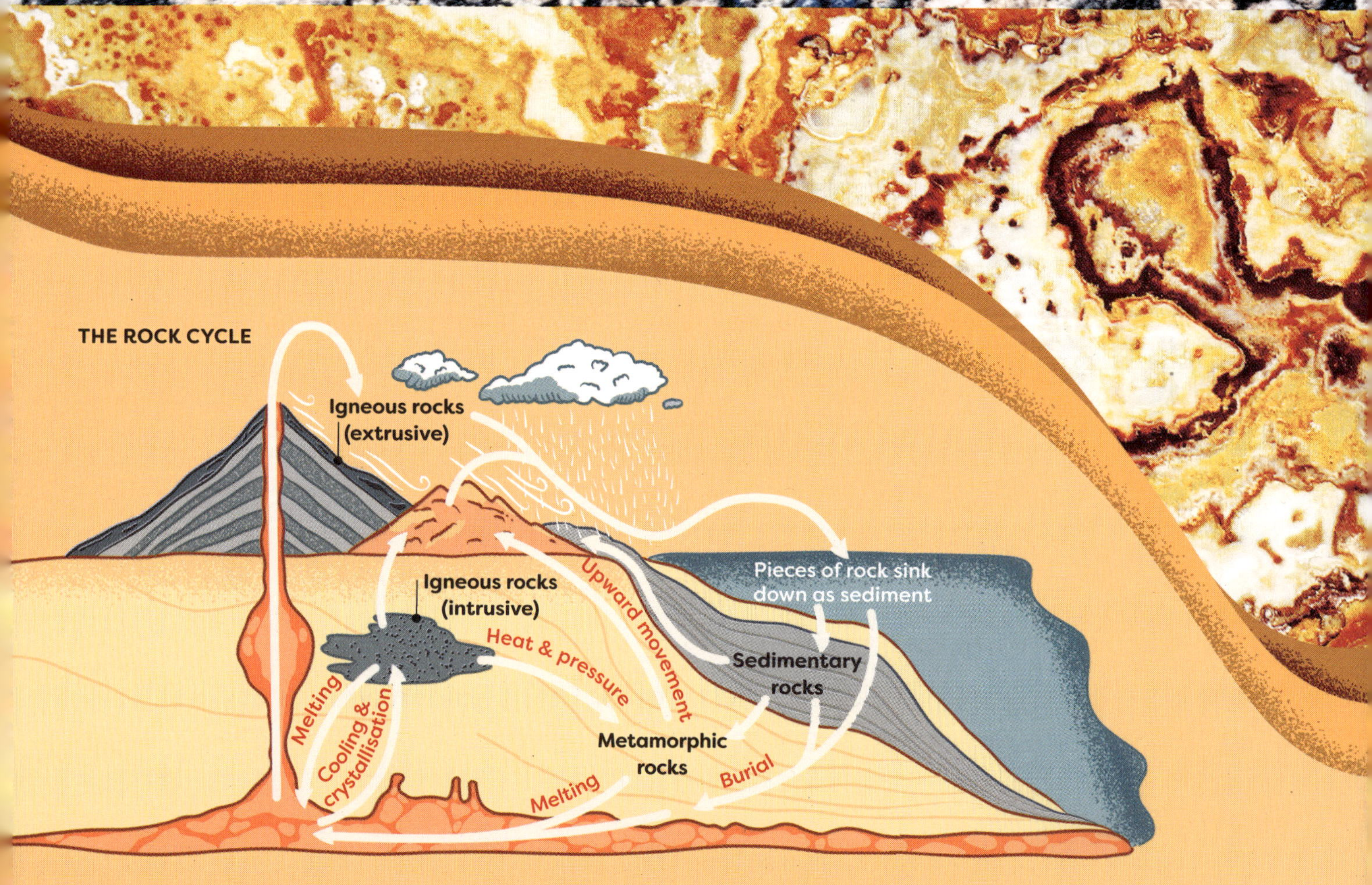
THE ROCK CYCLE
Igneous rocks (extrusive)
Igneous rocks (intrusive)
Upward movement
Heat & pressure
Pieces of rock sink down as sediment
Sedimentary rocks
Metamorphic rocks
Melting
Cooling & crystallisation
Burial
Melting

SEDIMENTARY ROCK

Sedimentary rock is made of soft, loose sediment that gets squashed together in visible layers. Fossils can be found in sedimentary rock.

IGNEOUS ROCK

Igneous rock is hardened magma. Intrusive igneous rocks are made when magma cools and hardens underneath Earth's surface. Extrusive igneous rocks form when magma breaks through the surface of Earth and cools and hardens above ground. Igneous rocks made from rapidly cooled magma contain small crystals, and those made from slowly cooled magma contain large crystals (like the ones shown here).

METAMORPHIC ROCK

Metamorphic rock is formed when existing igneous or sedimentary rock is squeezed under great heat and pressure inside Earth's crust. It often has a folded texture.

Reading the rocks

Rock is always being formed, worn down into smaller pieces, and then formed again in what is called the rock cycle. There are three different types of rock that form as part of this cycle: sedimentary, igneous and metamorphic. They all have different appearances, which you can see in the images above.

How to measure a mineral

Earth's surface is made of rocks, most of which are combinations of one or more minerals. There are thousands of minerals and they can look and feel very different – from diamond, which is one of the hardest naturally occurring substances on Earth, to talc, which is crumbly and soft. This infographic shows the Mohs Scale, which geologists use to compare the relative hardness of different minerals and gemstones.

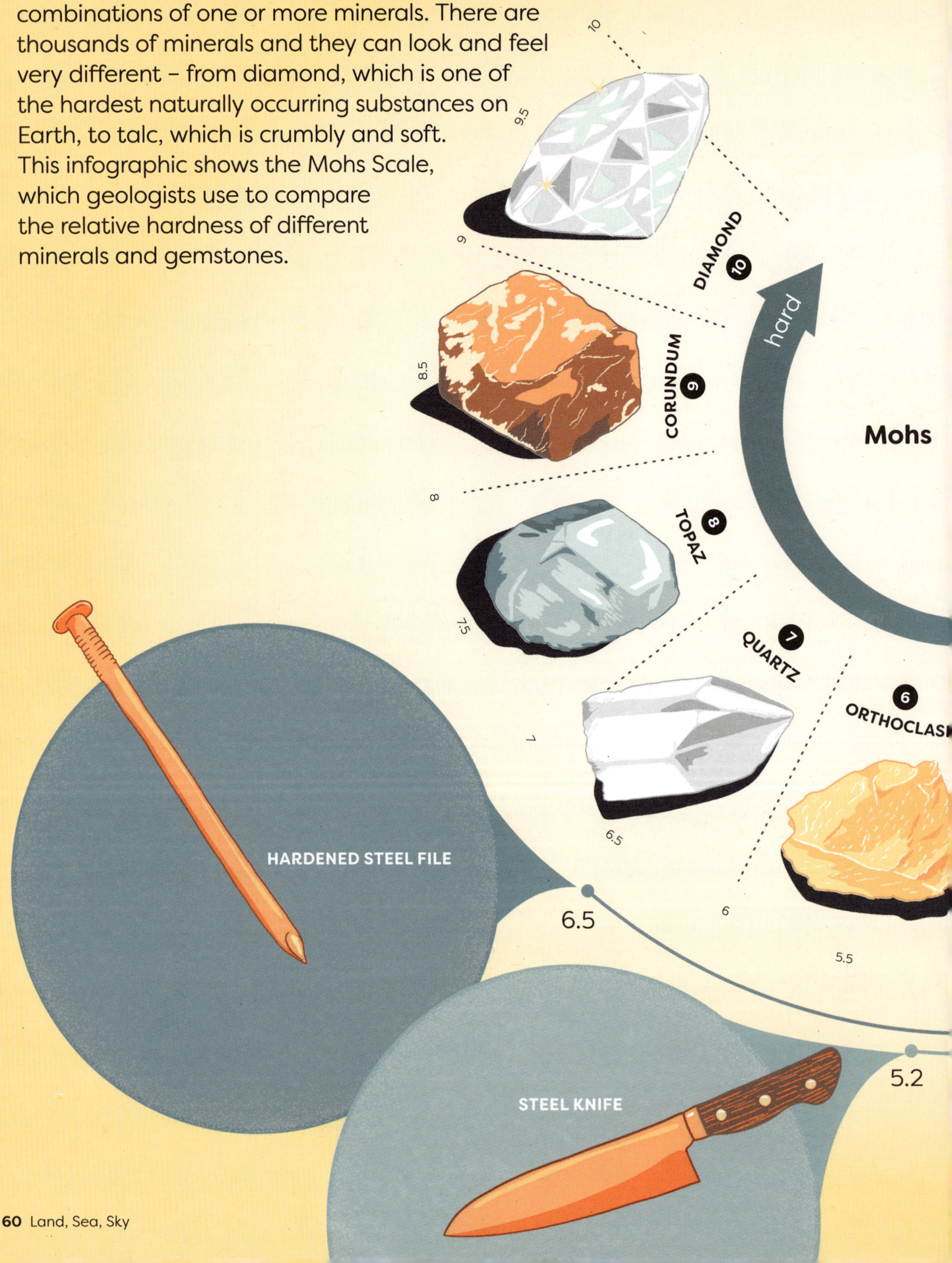

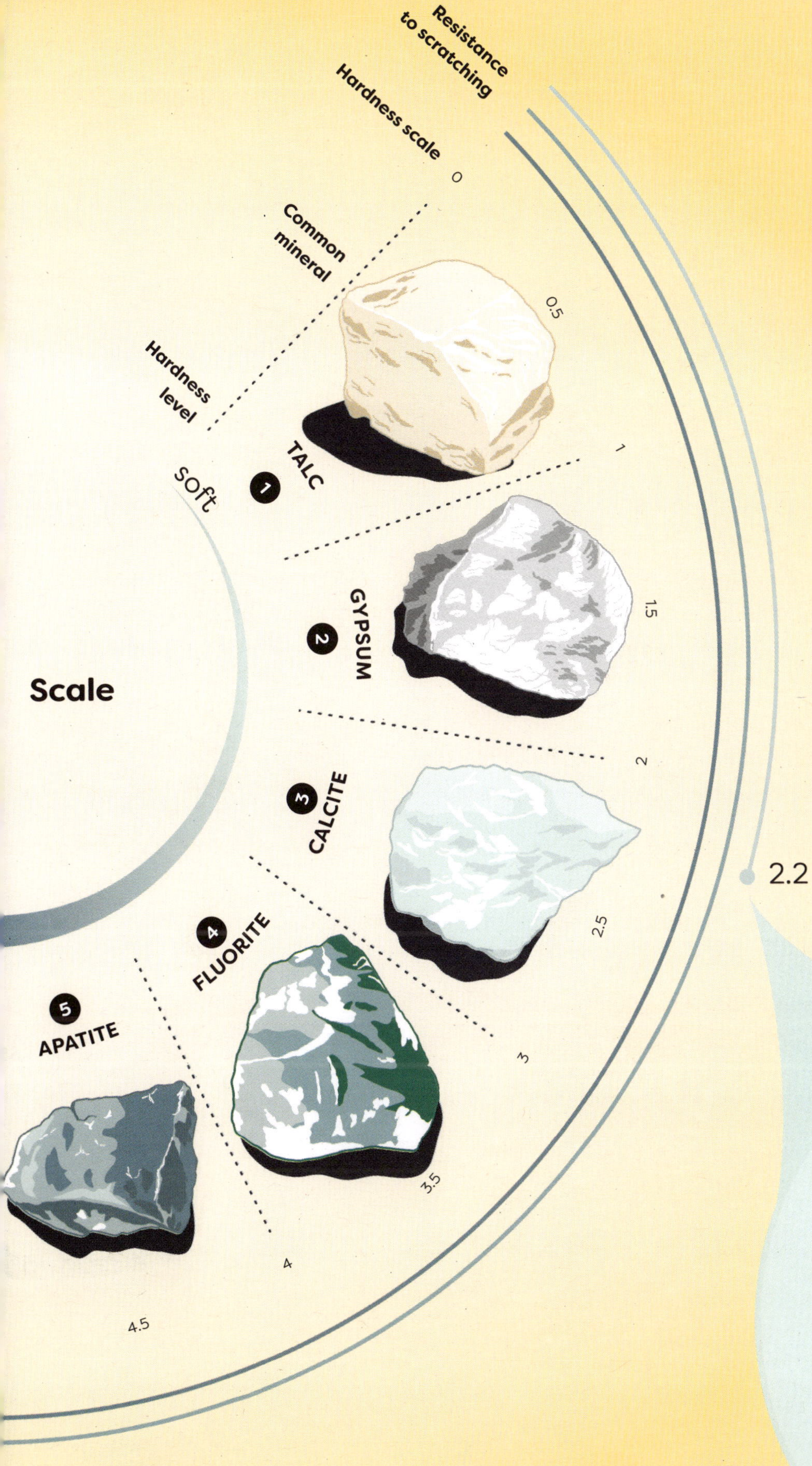

THE MOHS SCALE OF HARDNESS

German geologist Friedrich Mohs invented the Mohs Scale to measure how easily we can scratch a substance. The scale ranks ten common minerals from one to ten, with each mineral being able to scratch all those below it. So the higher the number on the scale, the harder the mineral. We can also use the Mohs Scale to measure the hardness of other materials. For example, you would be able to scratch gypsum with your fingernail, but not calcite. This gives your fingernail a score of 2.2 on the Mohs Scale – it is harder than gypsum but softer than calcite.

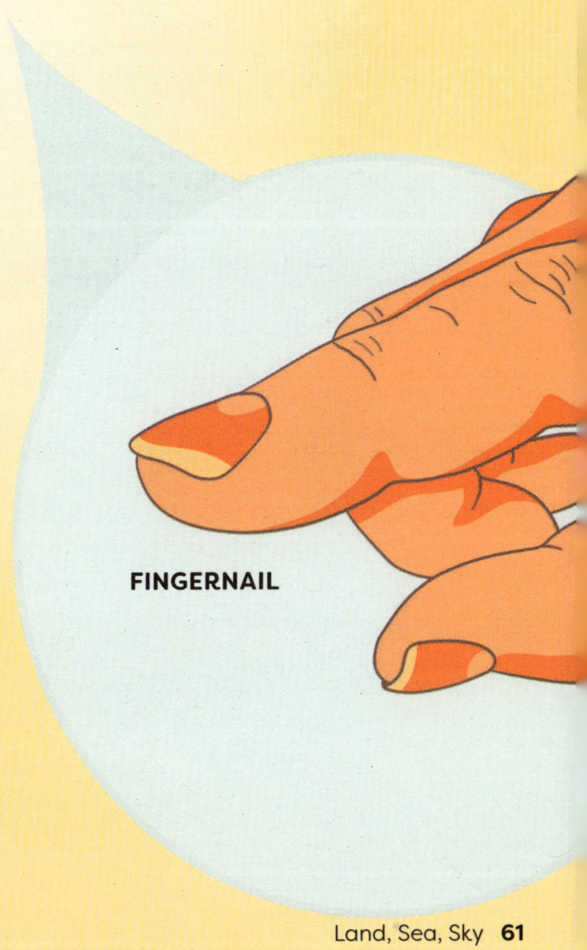

Where's all the water?

Viewed from space, Earth appears to be a blue planet. That's because the oceans cover such a high percentage of the surface (see page 50). This infographic shows what it would look like if all the water on Earth was stripped from the surface. The blue water droplets, which represent all the water on Earth, are drawn to scale.

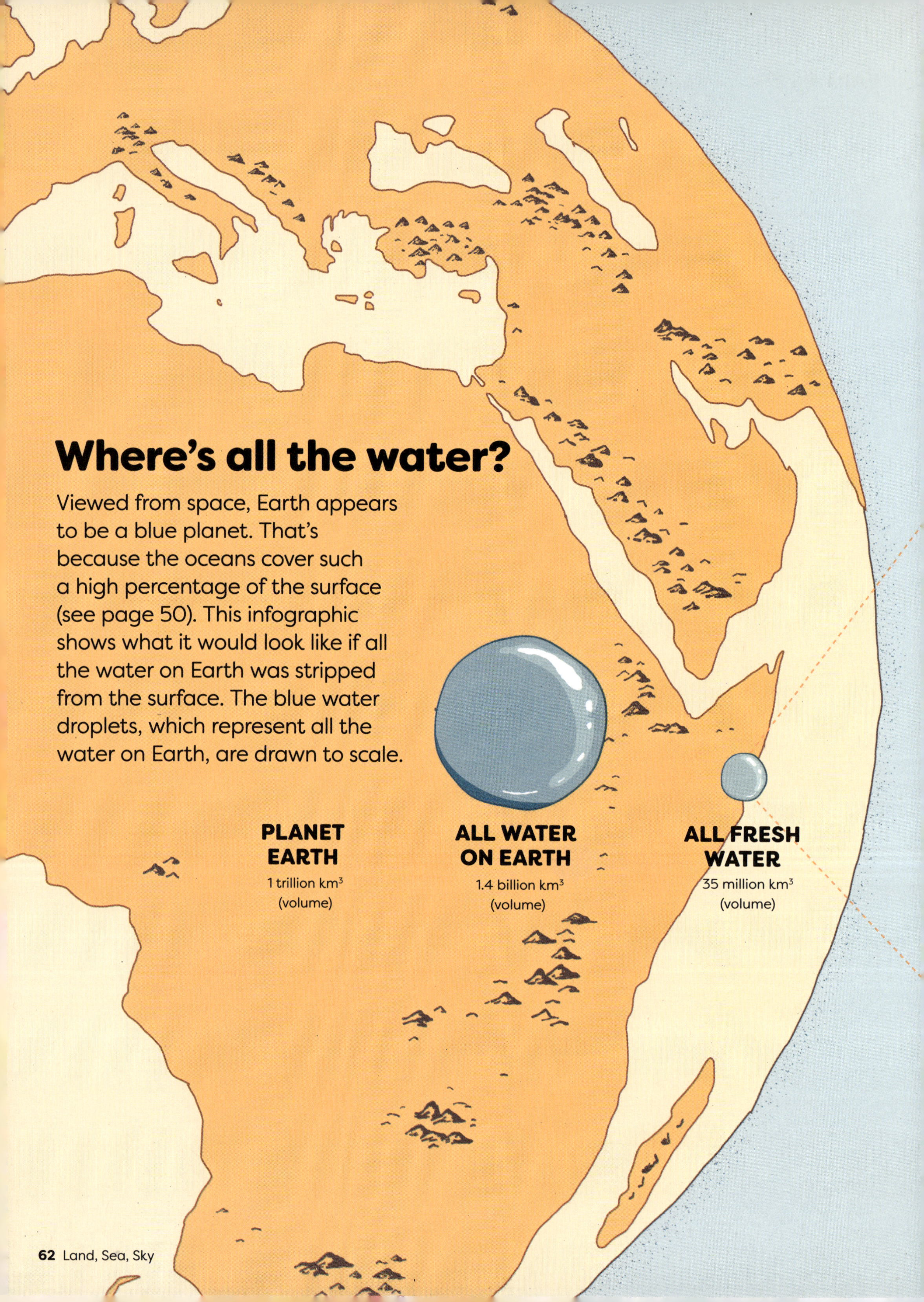

EARTH'S FRESH WATER IN ONE GLASS

Almost all of the water on Earth is salt water in the oceans – only a small proportion is fresh water, and an even smaller part of that is *liquid* fresh water. The infographic below shows what it would look like if we put all Earth's fresh water into a giant glass. Most of the water would be ice from glaciers and the ice caps. The next biggest source of fresh water is groundwater underneath Earth's surface. What's left over is fresh liquid water on the surface, which makes up a tiny proportion of all the water in the world.

How many people in the world have access to safe drinking water? Find out on page 243.

0.3%

SURFACE WATER

This tiny sliver of water in the glass represents all the water in every lake, swamp and river and inside every animal and plant on Earth – plus all the water in the atmosphere.

30.1%

GROUNDWATER

There are huge amounts of water underneath our feet. This unseen, giant store of moving water is very important for life, because it continually refills lakes and rivers, keeping them topped up.

69.6%

GLACIERS, GROUND ICE AND PERMAFROST

Most of Earth's fresh water is locked up in frozen glaciers and in the ice caps, mainly in Greenland and at the North and South poles.

Iceberg ahead!

Icebergs are chunks of ice that break off from glaciers or ice shelves and float in the ocean. They're found in oceans around Antarctica, in the Arctic and near lakes fed by glaciers. Icebergs are made of solid freshwater ice, and they are mostly hidden underwater, making them dangerous to ships. They can drift on the ocean for thousands of kilometres, but when they reach warm waters they melt away.

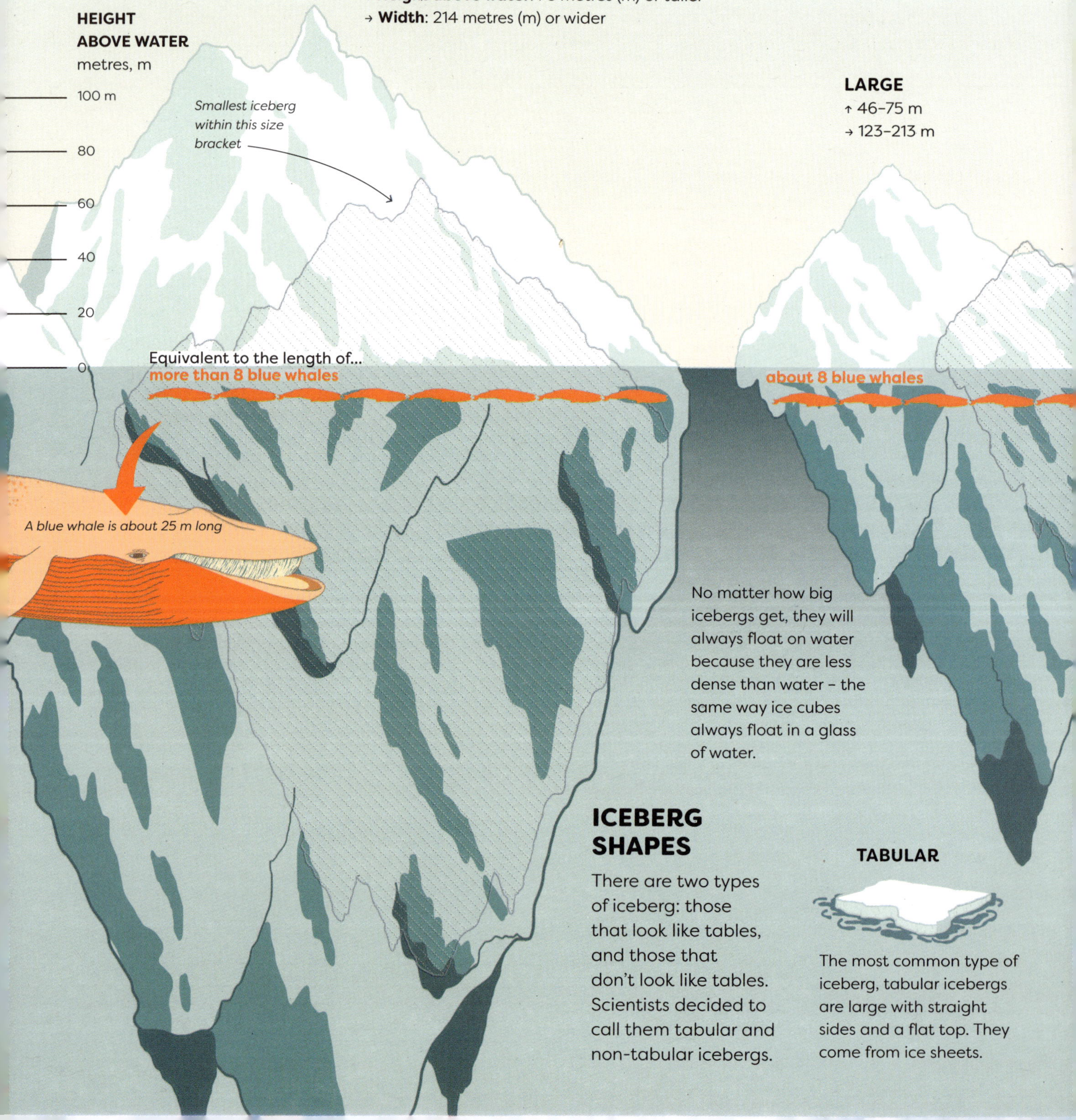

No matter how big icebergs get, they will always float on water because they are less dense than water – the same way ice cubes always float in a glass of water.

ICEBERG SHAPES

There are two types of iceberg: those that look like tables, and those that don't look like tables. Scientists decided to call them tabular and non-tabular icebergs.

TABULAR

The most common type of iceberg, tabular icebergs are large with straight sides and a flat top. They come from ice sheets.

CALVING GLACIERS

Some icebergs come from glaciers, or large masses of slowly moving ice. Glaciers are made of snow that has been pressed together over hundreds of years. In a process called calving, pieces of a glacier break off into the ocean. On the maps to the right, you can see that there is much more ice in the Antarctic than in the Arctic. This is because the ice in the Antarctic sits on top of land, and the ice in the Arctic sits on top of ocean. Ocean holds more heat than land, and so the Arctic is warmer than the Antarctic.

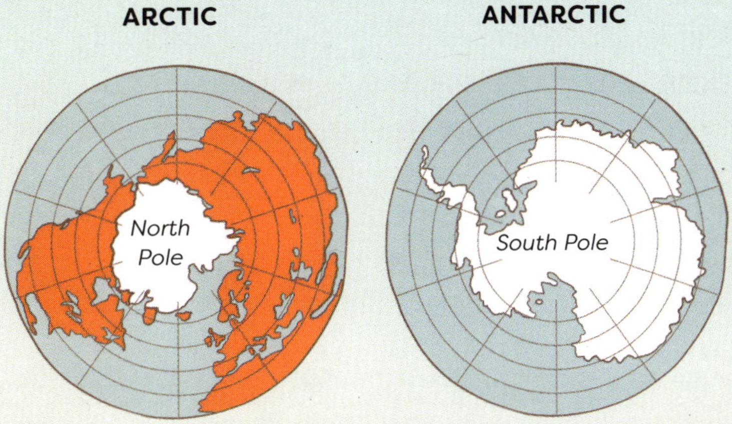

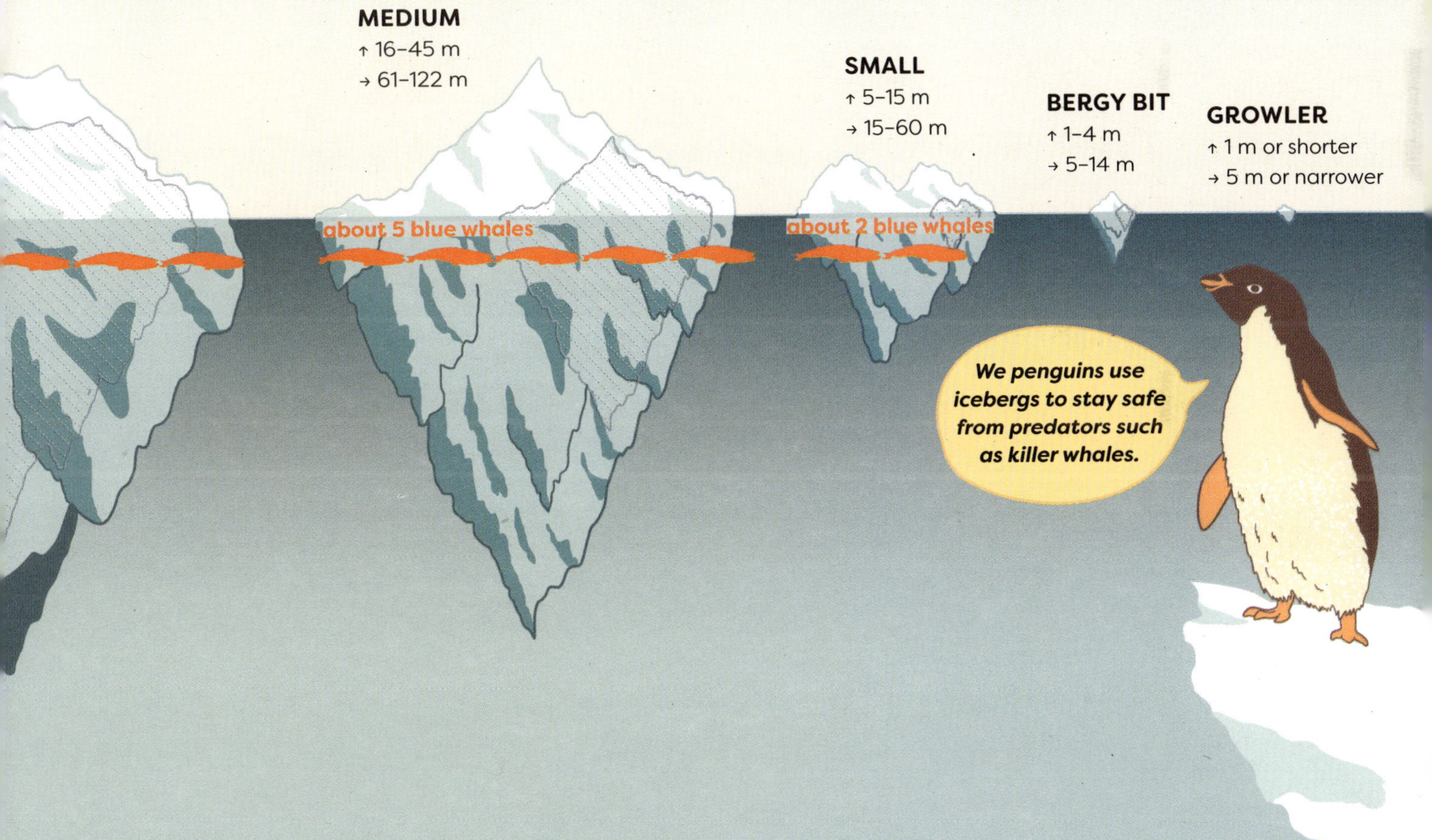

NON-TABULAR

Dome
These have rounded tops, usually with a smooth surface.

Pinnacle
Spires of ice that stick out from the submerged part of the iceberg.

Wedge
These are like a wedge of cheese with a steep face on one side and a smooth slope.

Drydock
Two or more tall columns of ice that make a U-shape.

Blocky
Steep, vertical sides and a flat top that look like huge ice cubes.

Longest rivers

Although rivers hold only a tiny fraction (0.0001%) of all the water on Earth, they are important because they carry freshwater to plants, animals and people. Rivers also carve out valleys and canyons in the land to shape the planet's surface.

HOW TO READ IT

Here are the world's ten longest rivers and the average volume of water each one carries to the sea (known as the river's discharge). Use the numbers on the map to find where each of these ten rivers is located around the world. The numbers are shown at the river mouths, and the rivers are represented by the blue lines.

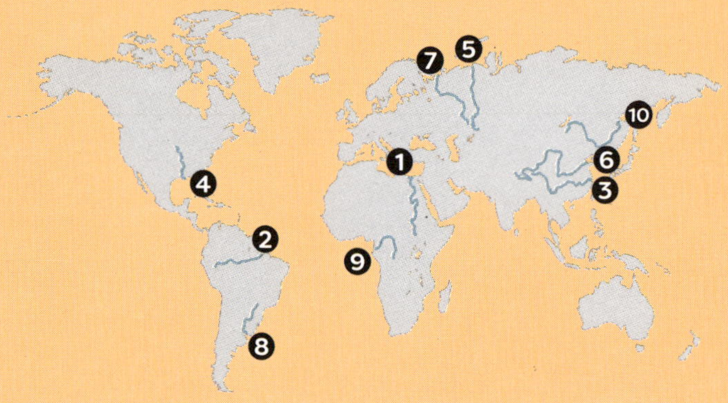

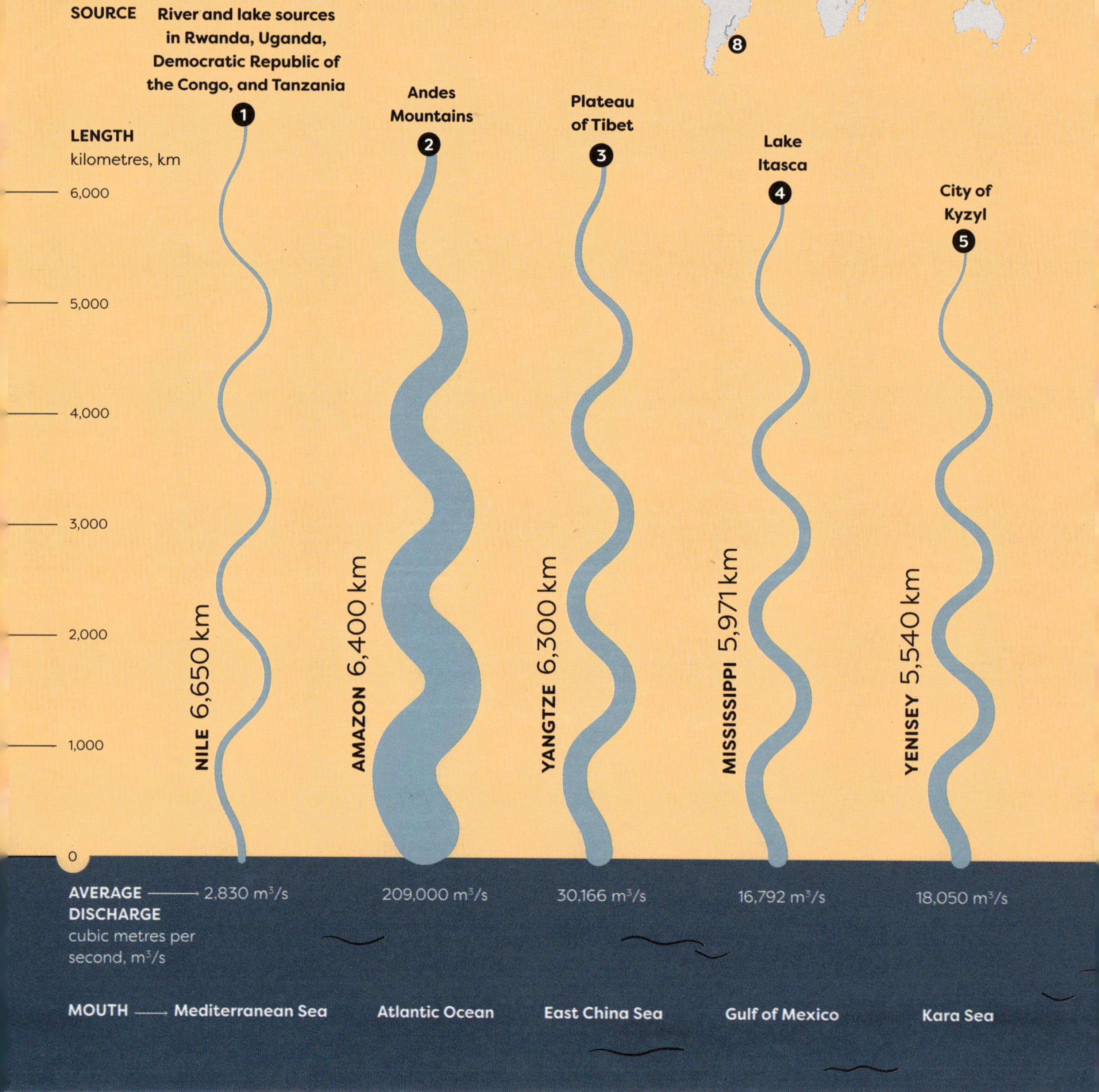

TALL WATERFALLS

Angel Falls, the world's biggest waterfall, is so tall that in warmer weather, all the water flowing over the top turns into a fine mist before it hits the bottom.

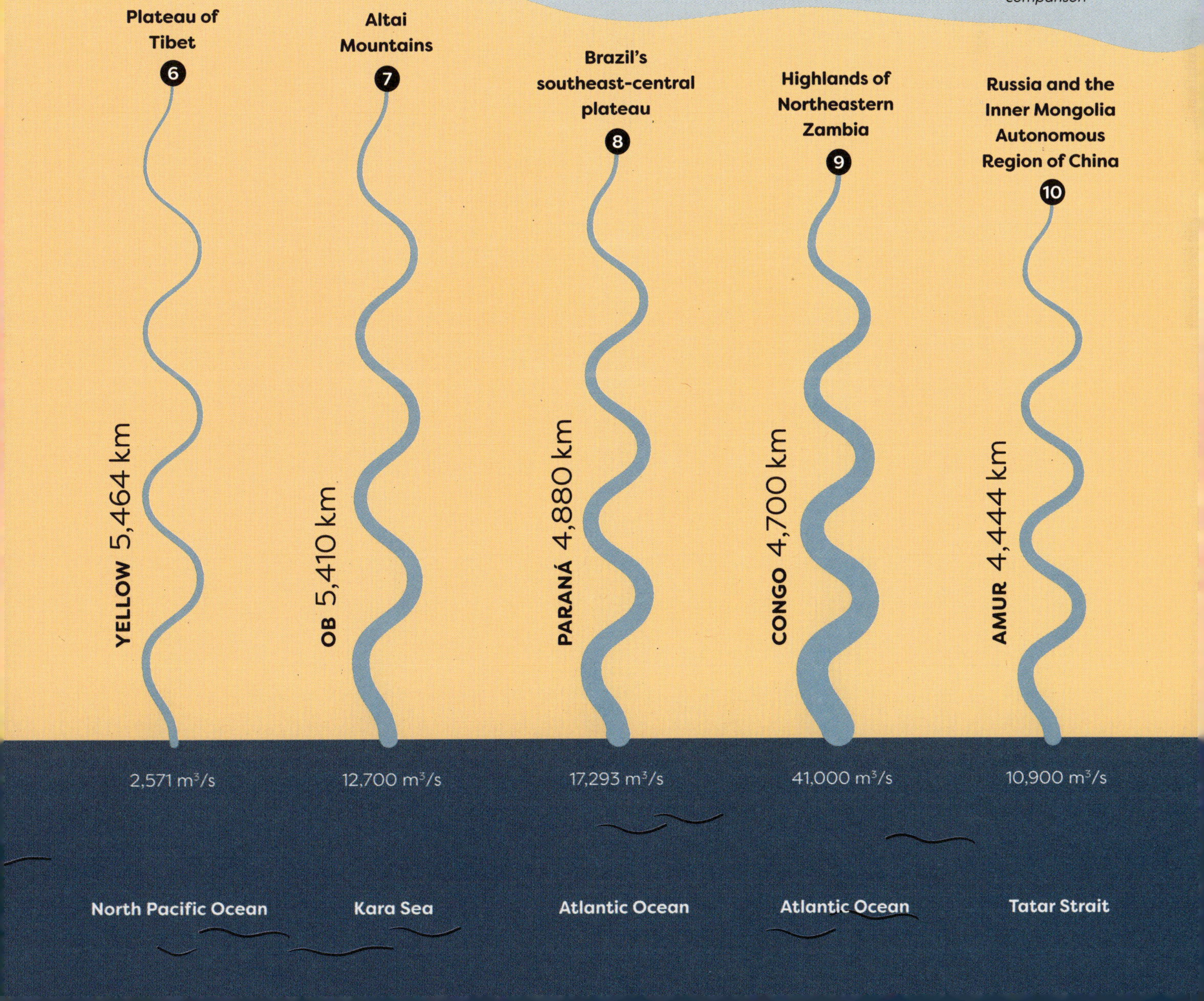

Deep caves

Caves can form in different ways, including when rocks are dissolved by water, by the flow of molten lava from volcanoes or when earthquakes cause large rocks to crack. The world's longest cave systems extend for hundreds of kilometres under the ground.

LONGEST CAVES

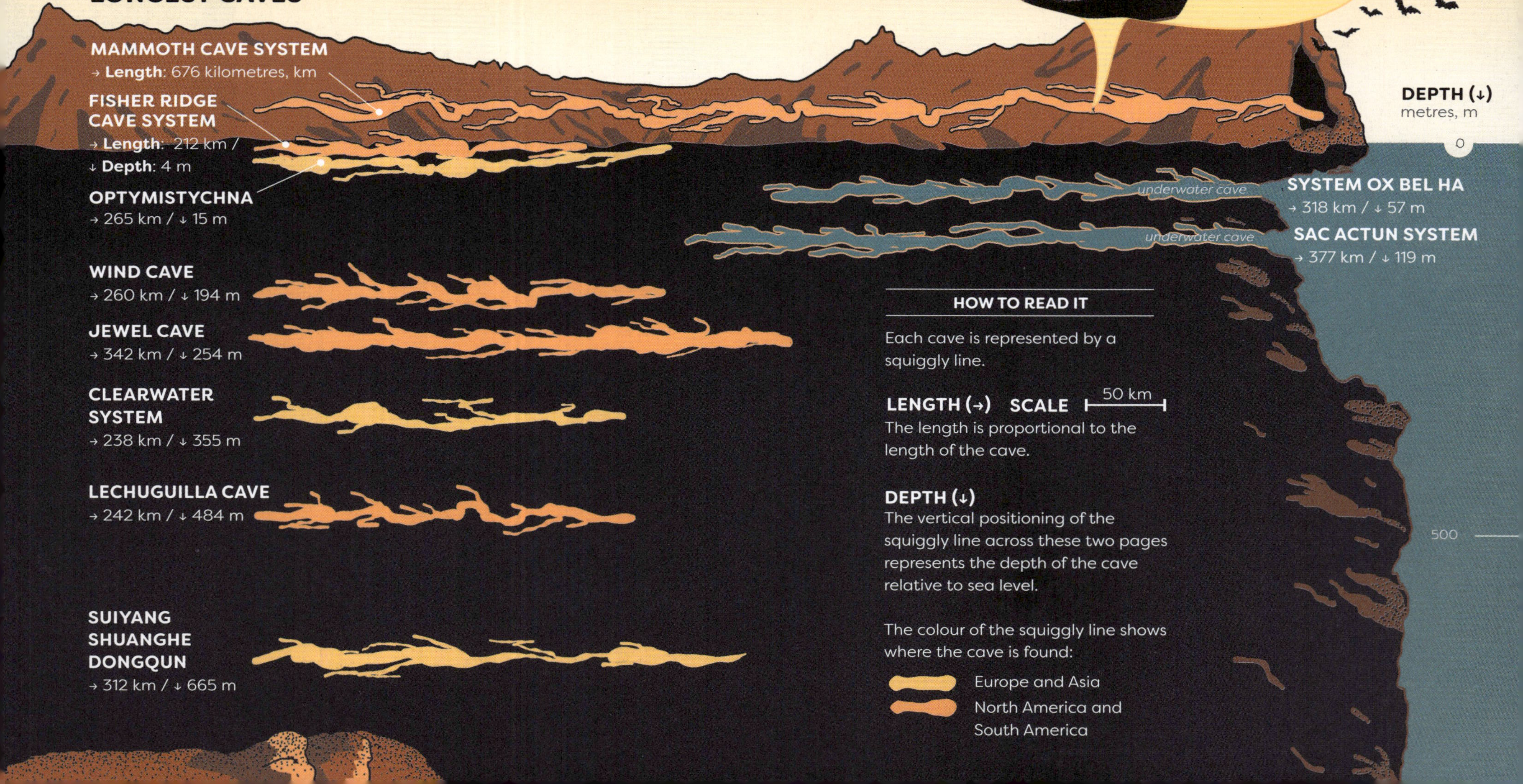

DEEPEST CAVES

Here you can see the eight deepest known caves in the world. The four deepest of these are found in Georgia in Europe and Asia. Veryovkina Cave was discovered in 1968. It takes specialist cave scientists called speleologists around a week to complete the risky journey deep into the cave and back up to the surface again.

1,000

1,500

TORCA DEL CERRO DEL CUEVÓN
→ 7 km / ↓ 1,589 m

RESEAU JEAN BERNARD
→ 26 km / ↓ 1,625 m

GOUFFRE MIROLDA – LUCIEN BOUCLIER
→ 13 km / ↓ 1,733 m

LAMPRECHTSOFEN VOGELSCHACHT
→ 60 km / ↓ 1,727 m

ILLYUZIA-MEZHONNOGO-SNEZHNAYA
→ 24 km / ↓ 1,760 m

SARMA
→ 6 km / ↓ 1,830 m

2,000

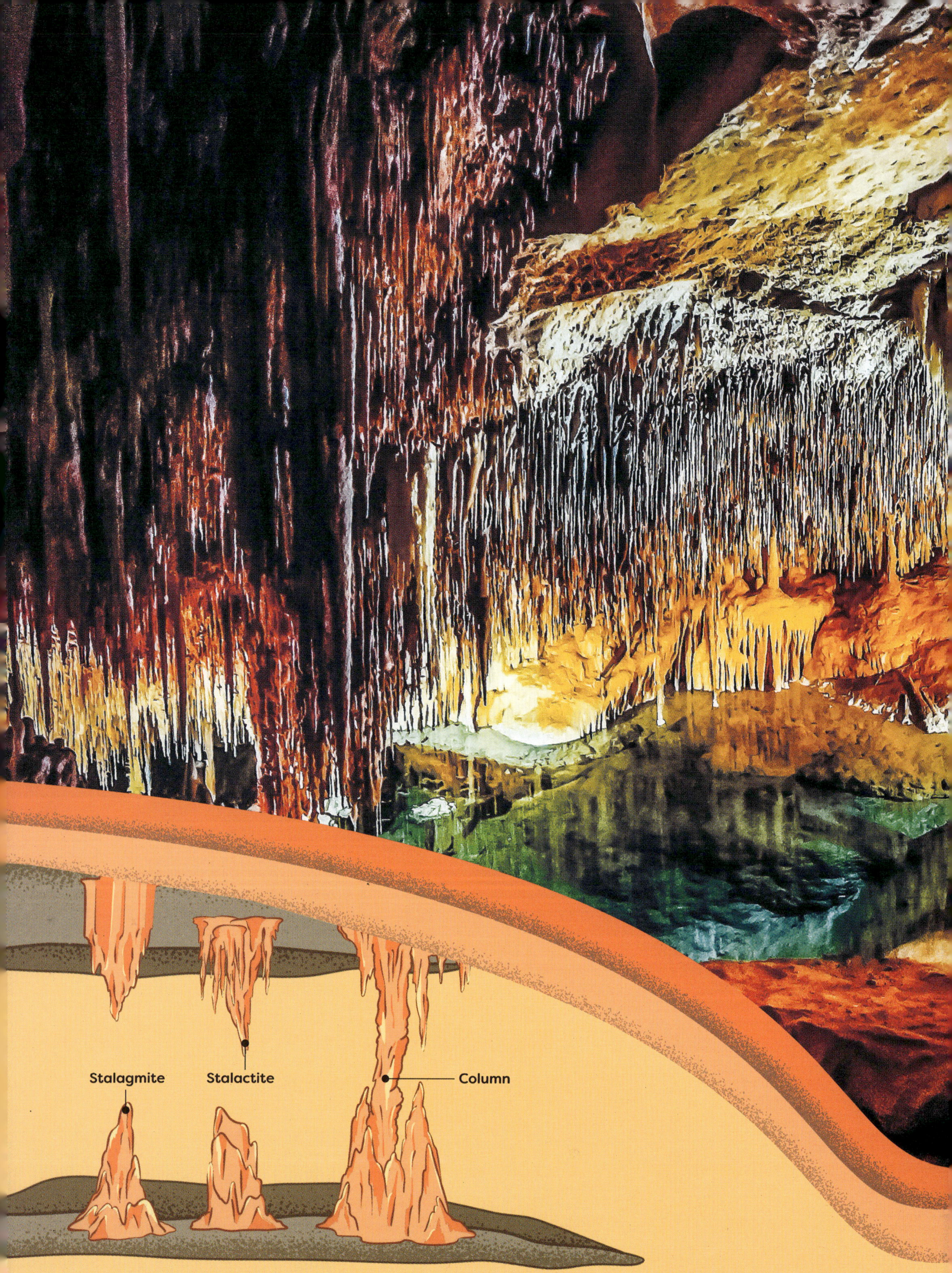
Stalagmite
Stalactite
Column

Stalactites and stalagmites

As water drips from the roof of a cave, it leaves behind small amounts of minerals on the cave roof and on the cave floor below. Over time, these small mineral deposits create cone-shaped rock formations that rise up from the cave floor and are called stalagmites. Cones of rock that hang down from the cave roof are called stalactites. Eventually, stalagmites and stalactites can join together to form columns.

The sky and beyond

Although you can't see them with the naked eye, there are five major layers in Earth's atmosphere. We spend nearly all our lives in the troposphere, where clouds and weather form. Higher up, air particles spread further and further apart and the atmosphere gets lighter (sometimes called 'thinner'). Eventually, Earth's atmosphere ends as you reach the vacuum of outer space.

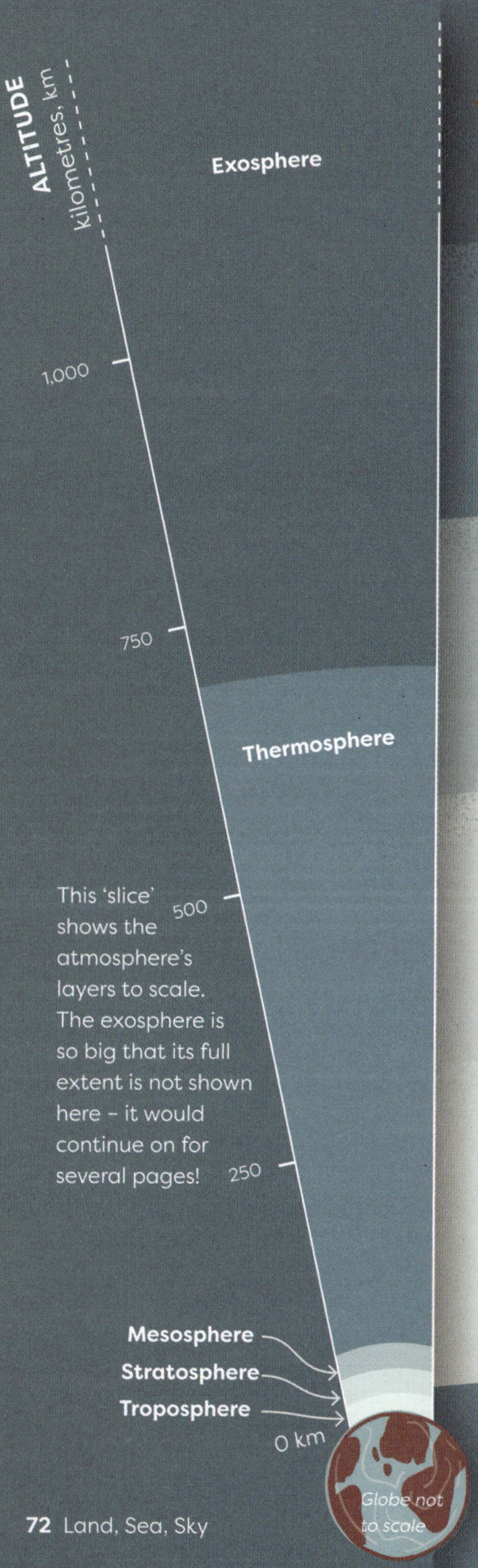

This 'slice' shows the atmosphere's layers to scale. The exosphere is so big that its full extent is not shown here – it would continue on for several pages!

EXOSPHERE
700–10,000 km

The exosphere is the outermost layer of Earth's atmosphere. Light and fast-moving gas particles sometimes even escape to space. Many satellites orbit here.

THERMOSPHERE
80–700 km

This layer is called the thermosphere because the Sun's energy can heat the air in the daytime to a temperature 200°C hotter than it is at night.

MESOSPHERE
50–80 km

The air in the mesosphere is similar to that in lower layers, but it's much lighter and there is very little water vapour. Shooting stars (meteors that are burning up) are found in this layer of the atmosphere.

STRATOSPHERE
20–50 km

The stratosphere is home to the ozone layer, a protective layer of oxygen that absorbs most of the Sun's ultraviolet radiation. Without the ozone layer, humans would be at much greater risk of skin cancer. There's not enough oxygen to breathe here.

TROPOSPHERE
0–20 km

Most of the clouds and weather systems are here. It's the heaviest (or 'thickest') layer of the atmosphere and the closest to Earth's surface. Above 8 kilometres, the air is too thin for humans to breathe.

WHAT IS THE AIR WE BREATHE MADE OF?

Earth's atmosphere in the troposphere is largely made up of nitrogen, a gas that has no colour or taste, and doesn't react with other gases at room temperature. The rest is mostly oxygen. The remaining 1 per cent is a gas called argon, plus small amounts of carbon dioxide, methane, hydrogen, and other elements.

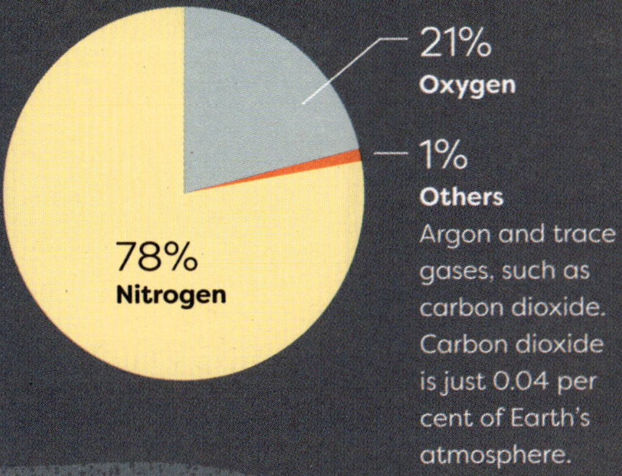

ATMOSPHERIC PRESSURE

The weight of air is known as atmospheric pressure. Air becomes lighter farther away from Earth's surface. As the weight of the air decreases, so does the air pressure. Most aeroplanes fly at about 11,000 metres and use a cabin pressure control system so that the air pressure inside the plane remains similar to the air pressure on the ground.

Auroras occur around Earth's poles, shown in the green banding on this map.

Dazzling auroras

An aurora is a display of shimmering, coloured light that sometimes appears in the night sky. Auroras mostly happen in Earth's far northern and far southern regions. In the Northern Hemisphere, these beautiful displays are known as *aurora borealis*, or the northern lights (shown here). In the Southern Hemisphere, they are called *aurora australis*, or the southern lights. Auroras are caused when electrically charged particles from the Sun collide with atoms of gases in the thermosphere, one of the upper layers of Earth's atmosphere.

Cloudy skies

Clouds are formed when water vapour, which is invisible, turns into tiny droplets of water or ice crystals. The droplets of water or crystals, or a mixture of both, float in the air as clouds until they become large and heavy enough to fall to the ground as rain, snow or hail. Here are ten common types of cloud, each of which typically appears at a certain altitude in the sky.

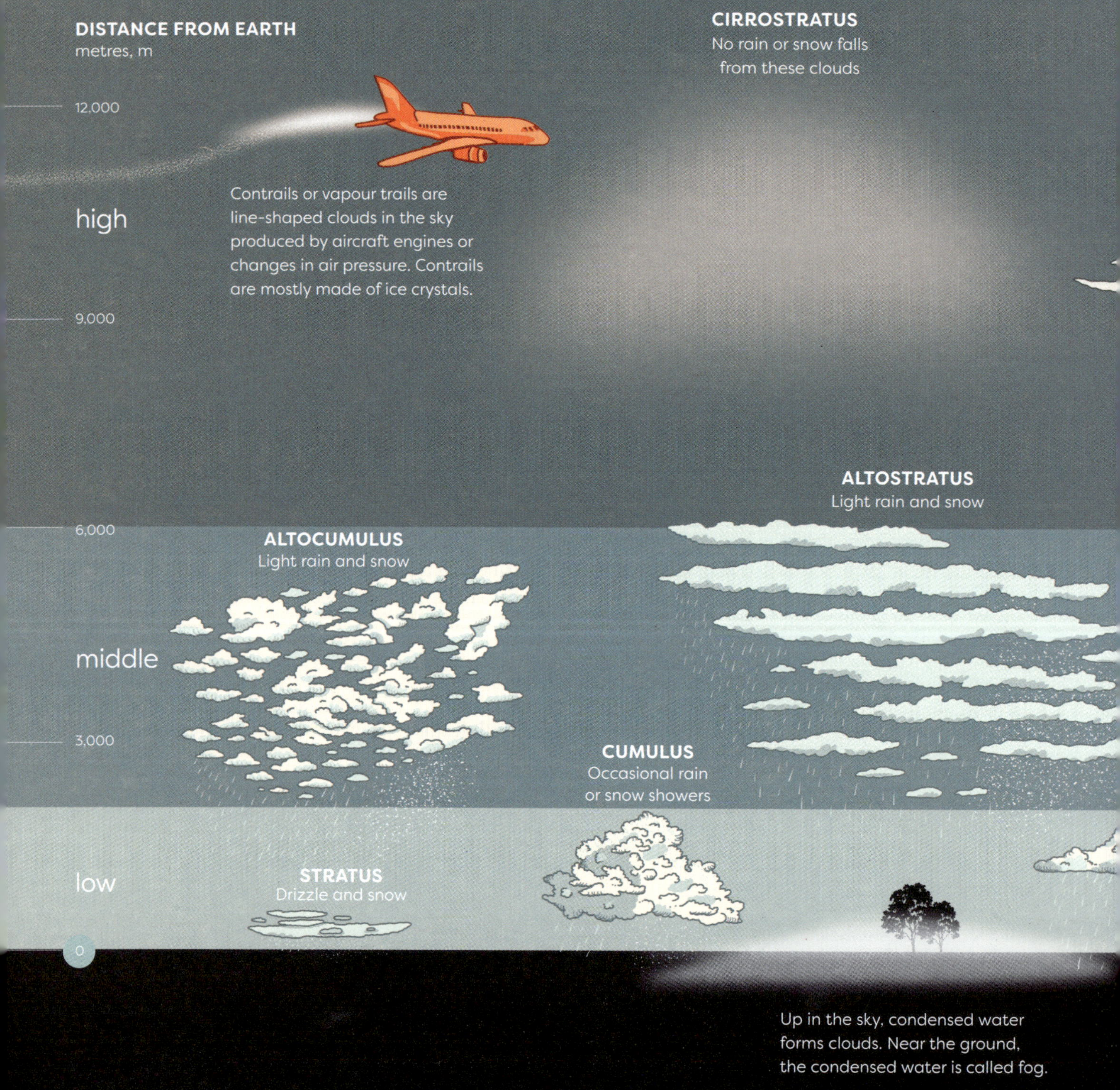

THE WATER CYCLE

Water is constantly moving around the planet in a process called the water cycle. The Sun heats water on Earth's surface, causing the water to evaporate as water vapour. When the vapour cools and condenses, it forms clouds, before falling back down on to Earth's surface as rain, snow or hail. Thanks to gravity, water then flows downhill in rivers and under the ground until it rejoins the ocean, ready for the cycle to begin again. Human action impacts the water cycle, for example through our creation of dams, and water usage to supply homes and communities.

Extreme planet

From scorching deserts to frozen glaciers, and towering mountains to deep waters, Earth is a planet of extremes. This map is colour-coded with average temperature levels measured over several years. Extreme features and weather events on each continent are pointed out, too.

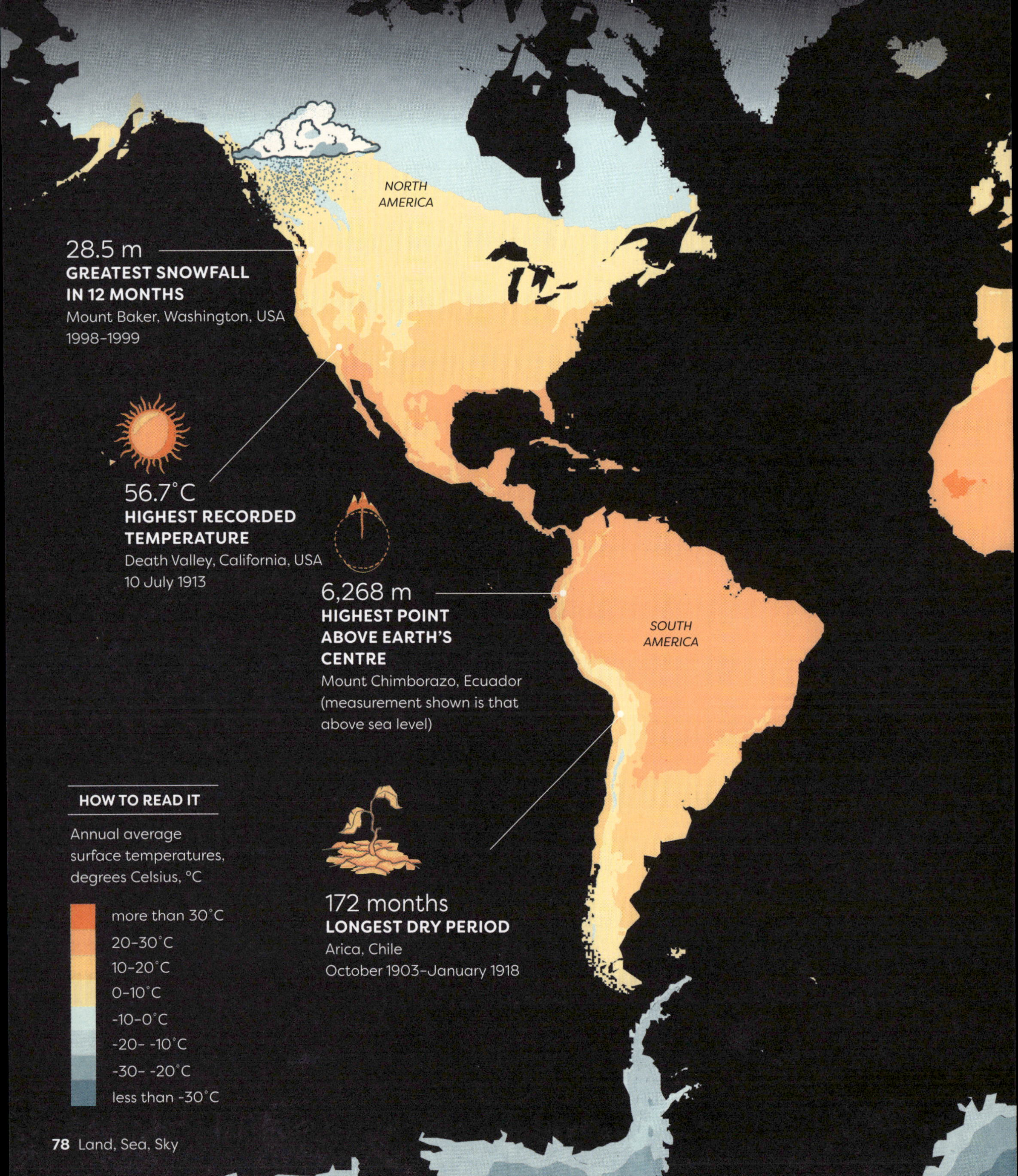

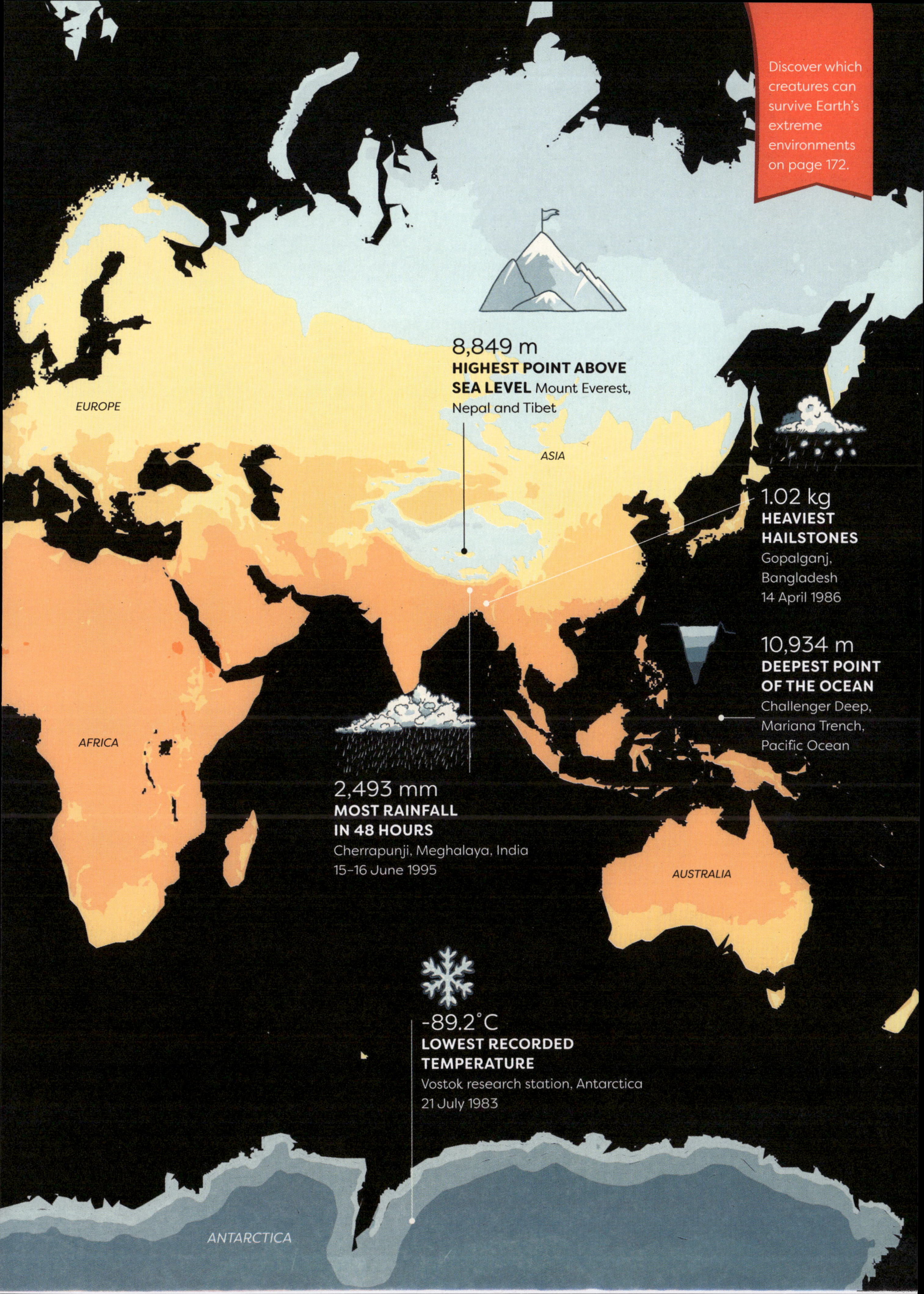

Discover which creatures can survive Earth's extreme environments on page 172.

1 Antarctica is a cold, icy desert, where the average precipitation (mostly snow) is equivalent to 150 mm of water per year.

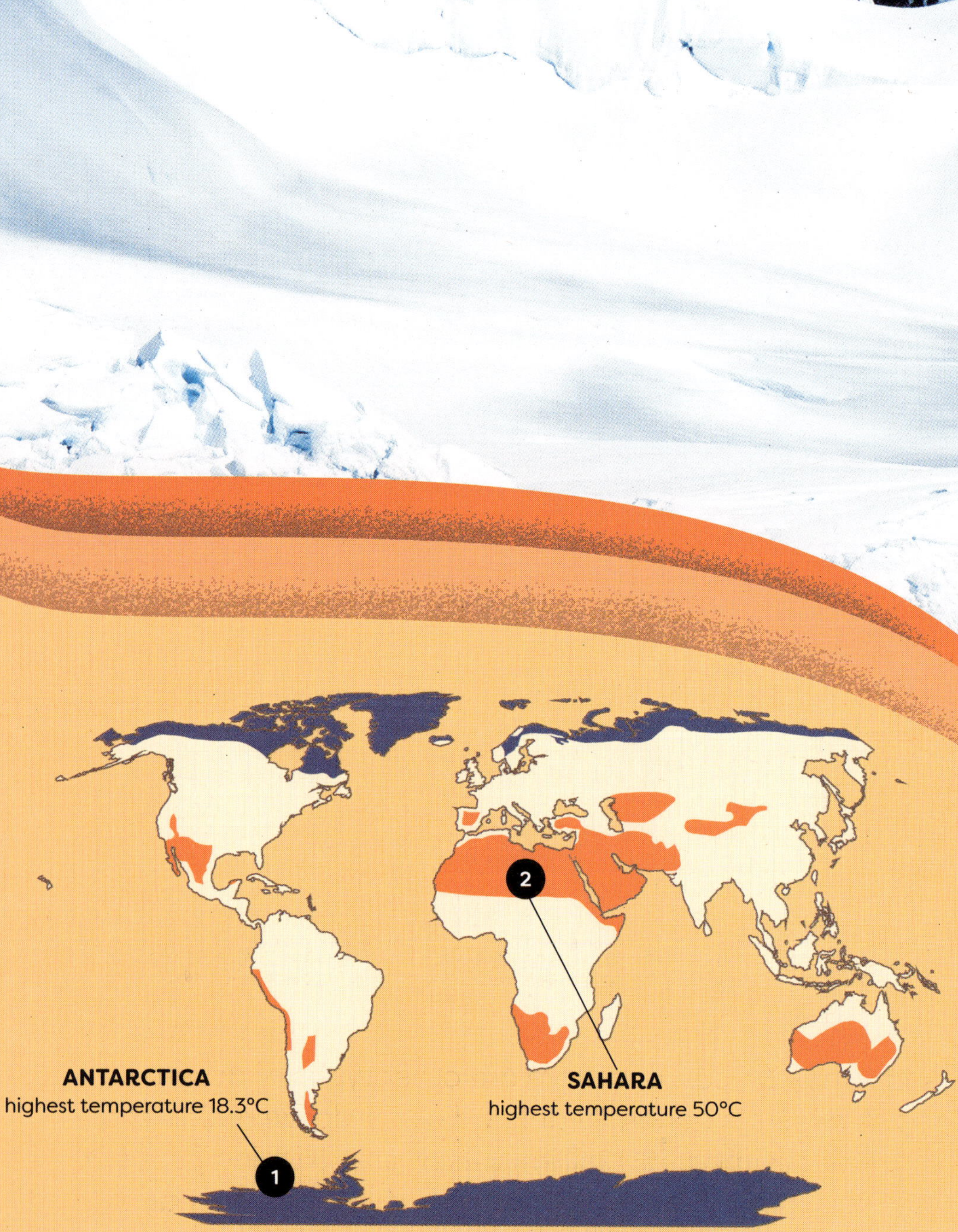

EARTH'S LAND SURFACE COVERED BY DESERTS

- Hot deserts
- Cold deserts

2 The Sahara is a hot, sandy desert, where the average precipitation is 76 mm per year.

The driest places on Earth

When people think of deserts, they usually think of hot and sandy places. But there are other types of desert, too. A desert is generally defined as any large region that receives less than 250 millimetres of precipitation per year. This means that Antarctica is also a desert. More than 20 per cent of Earth's land surface is covered by deserts.

Lightning and thunder

Lightning is a bolt of electricity that is usually produced by a thunder storm. Thunder is the sound caused by lightning. Because light travels faster than sound, you see lightning before you hear it.

EXTREME LIGHTNING BOLTS

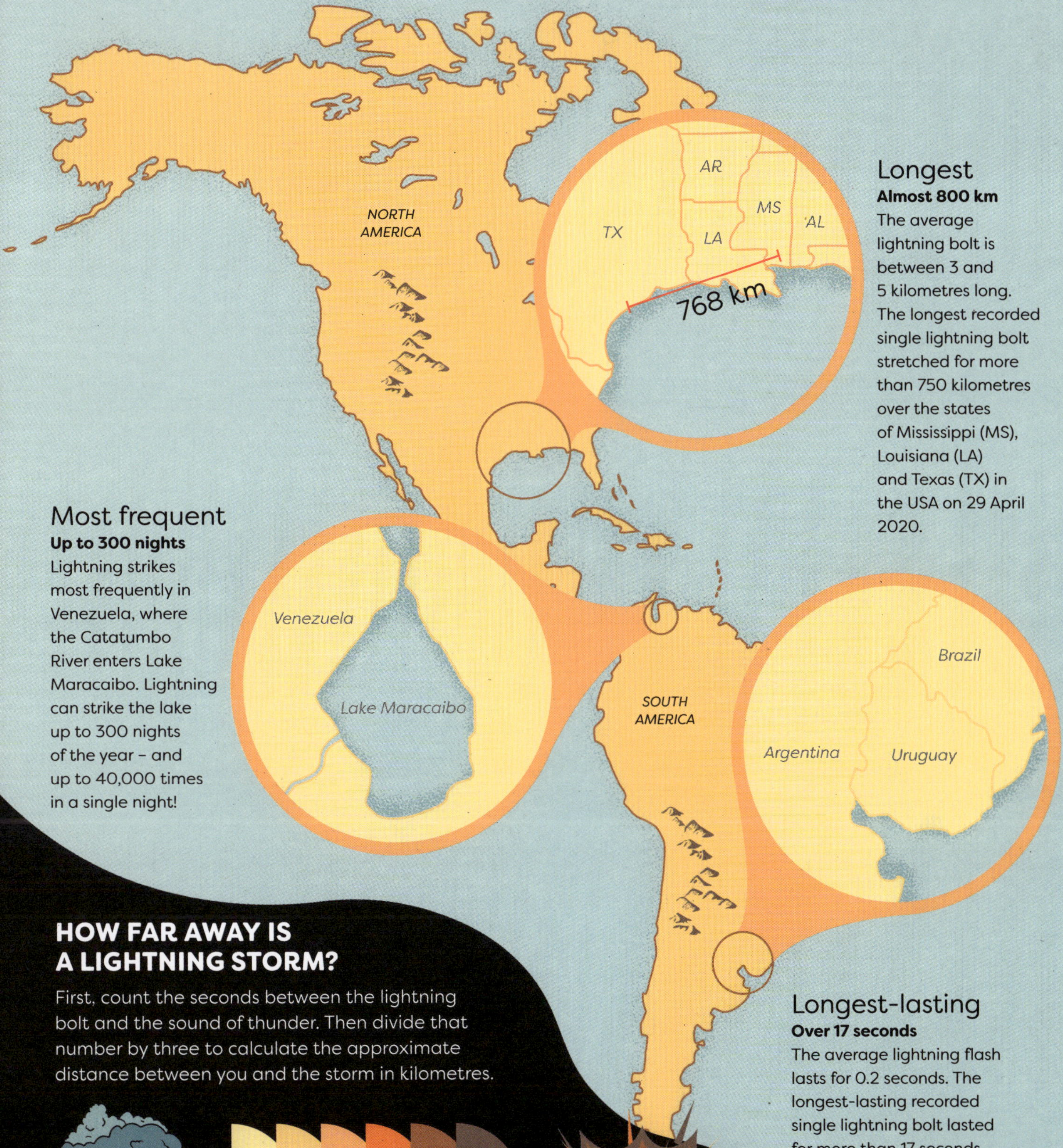

Longest

Almost 800 km

The average lightning bolt is between 3 and 5 kilometres long. The longest recorded single lightning bolt stretched for more than 750 kilometres over the states of Mississippi (MS), Louisiana (LA) and Texas (TX) in the USA on 29 April 2020.

Most frequent

Up to 300 nights

Lightning strikes most frequently in Venezuela, where the Catatumbo River enters Lake Maracaibo. Lightning can strike the lake up to 300 nights of the year – and up to 40,000 times in a single night!

Longest-lasting

Over 17 seconds

The average lightning flash lasts for 0.2 seconds. The longest-lasting recorded single lightning bolt lasted for more than 17 seconds, over parts of Uruguay and Argentina in June 2020.

HOW FAR AWAY IS A LIGHTNING STORM?

First, count the seconds between the lightning bolt and the sound of thunder. Then divide that number by three to calculate the approximate distance between you and the storm in kilometres.

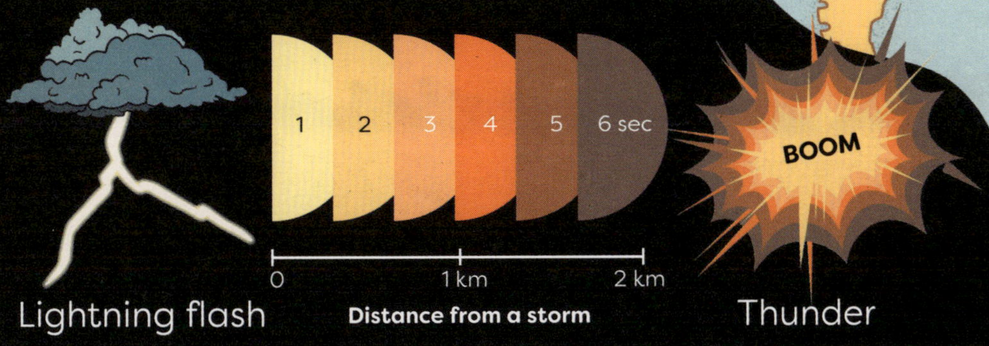

Wind made visible!

Wind is a swirling mass of air that is created by differences in air pressure. In areas of high pressure, air is heavier, and in areas of low pressure, air is lighter (see page 73). Wind is the flow of air from high to low pressure areas. These movements of the wind create the waves and ripples you can see on this map. It shows a snapshot of a very windy day in September 2017, with several hurricanes. As you can see from the map, hurricanes get stronger over oceans and weaker over land.

Map created by Cameron Beccario

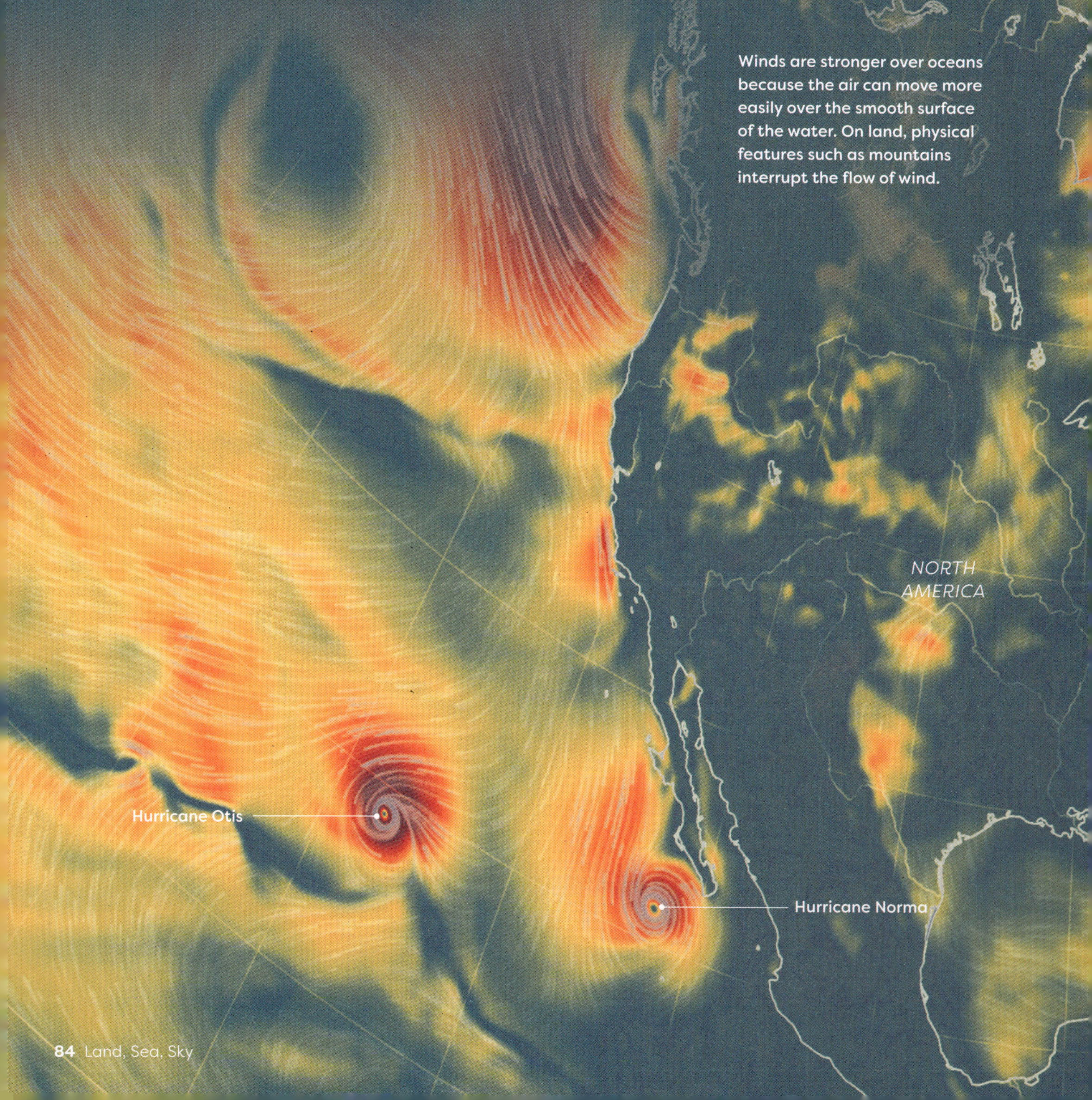

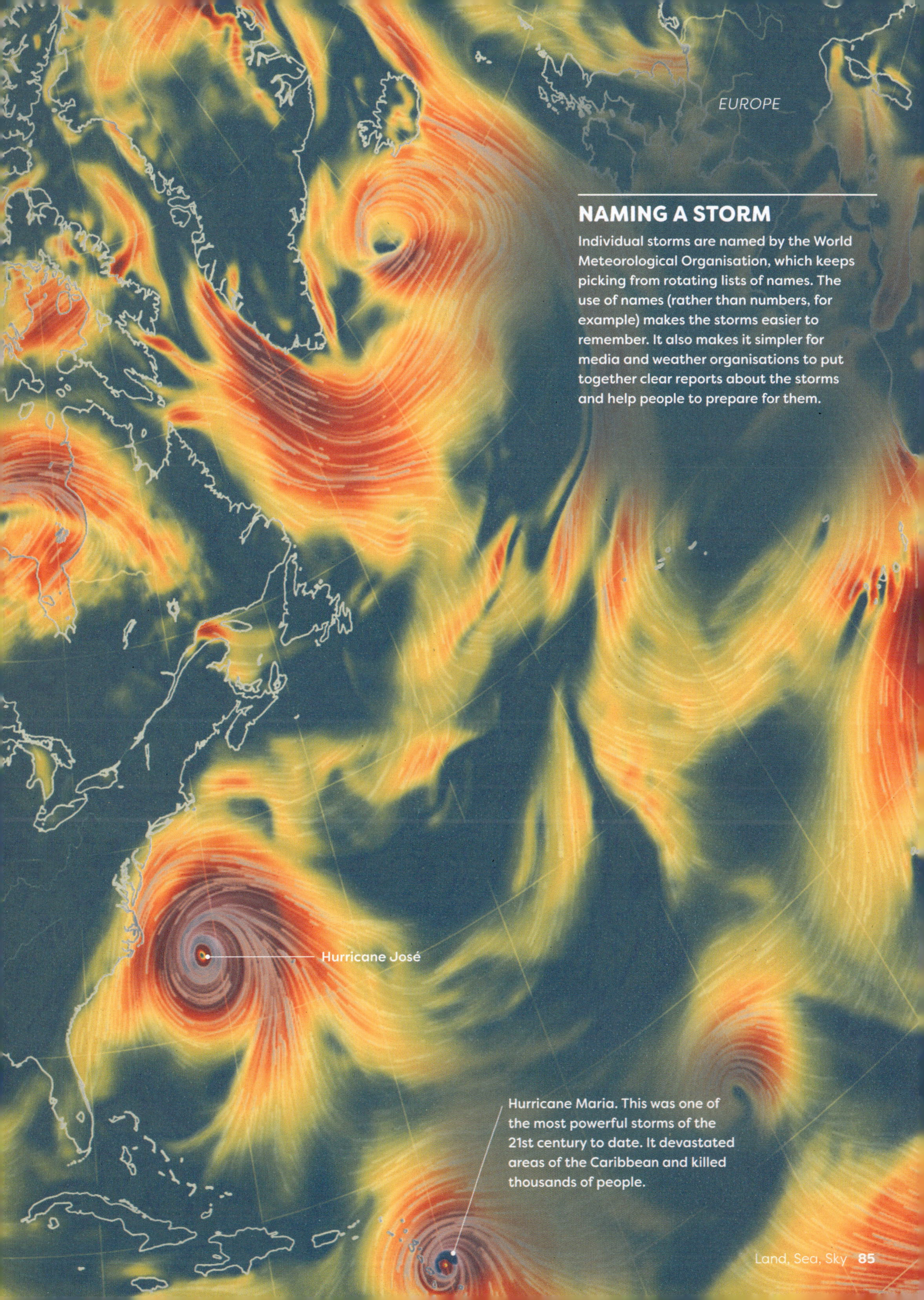

NAMING A STORM

Individual storms are named by the World Meteorological Organisation, which keeps picking from rotating lists of names. The use of names (rather than numbers, for example) makes the storms easier to remember. It also makes it simpler for media and weather organisations to put together clear reports about the storms and help people to prepare for them.

Pronounced soo-NAH-mee, the word tsunami comes from the Japanese *tsu*, meaning port or harbour, and *nami*, meaning wave.

Tsunamis

A tsunami is a series of large sea waves caused by an underwater earthquake, landslide or volcanic eruption or, more rarely, a giant meteor impact. Tsunami waves can be up to 1,000 kilometres long and travel across the ocean for thousands of kilometres. When they reach the coast, these giant waves can cause enormous devastation and loss of life.

HOW DO TSUNAMIS FORM?

A sudden movement under the ocean, such as an earthquake, causes waves to spread out. As the waves approach a coast, they hit land under the water. This makes the waves rise higher above the surface of the sea.

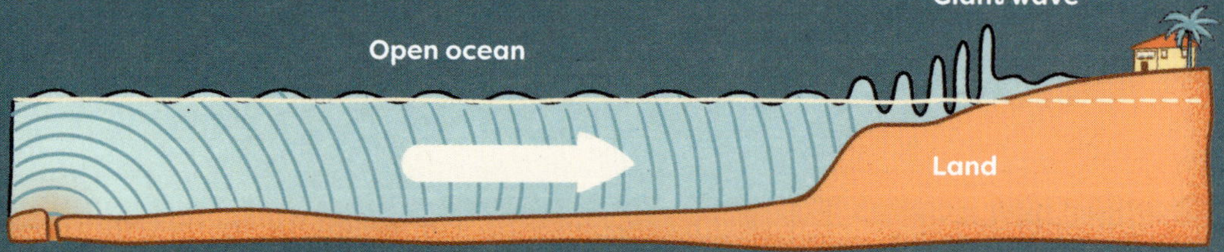

THE TSUNAMI THAT KILLED DINOSAURS

When the asteroid that caused the extinction of the dinosaurs landed on Earth 66 million years ago, it created a giant tsunami. Scientists estimate that this gigantic wave was 1,500 metres tall, which is almost twice the height of the Burj Khalifa, the world's tallest building. This wave is not drawn to the same scale as the waves illustrated on the right because it would be taller than this page.

Burj Khalifa,
for scale comparison

BIGGEST TSUNAMIS IN THE PAST 200 YEARS

The amount of damage a tsunami does depends more on the area it hits than on the size of the waves. The five waves below, drawn to scale, highlight this fact.

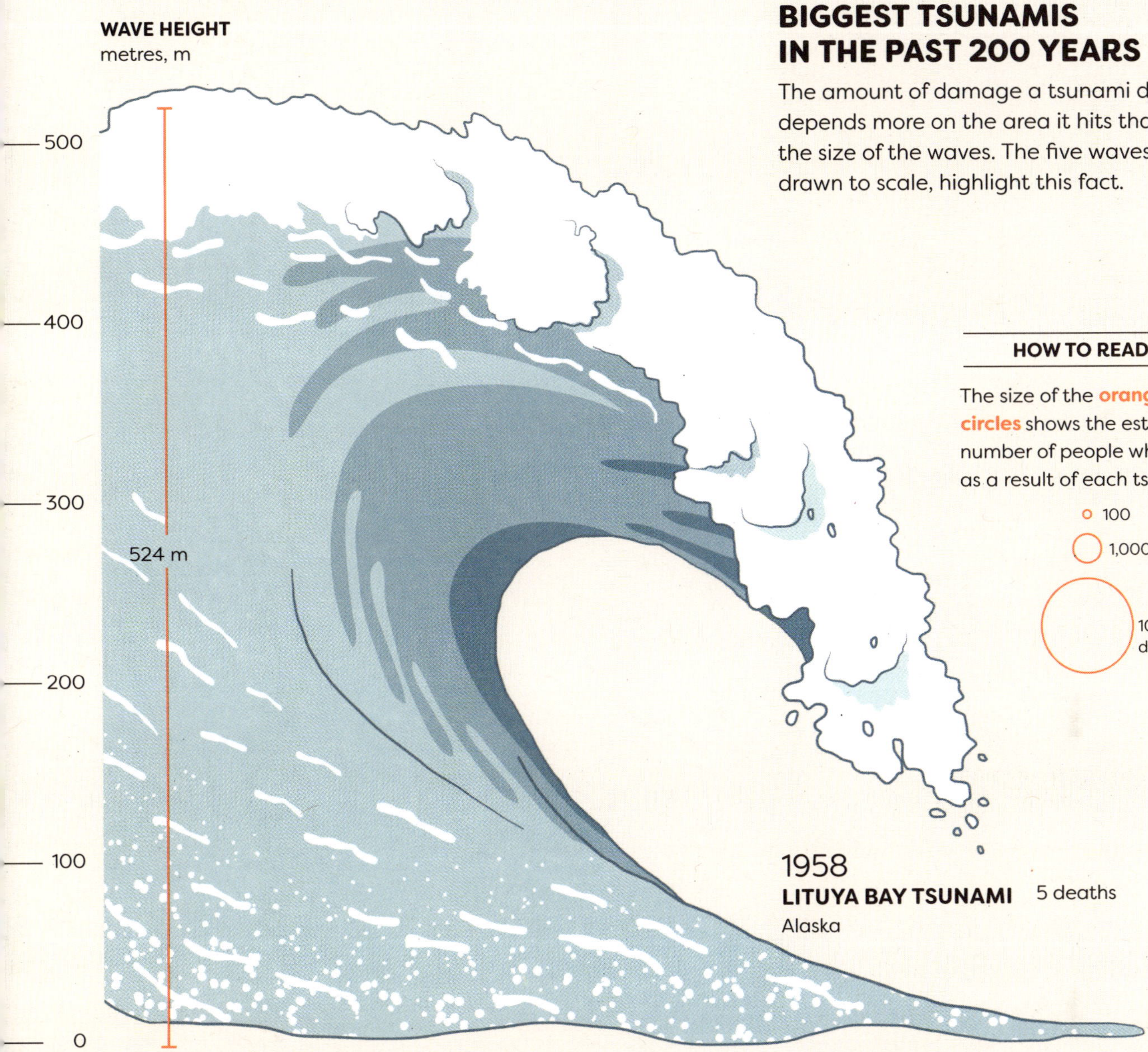

HOW TO READ IT

The size of the **orange circles** shows the estimated number of people who died as a result of each tsunami.

100

1,000

10,000 deaths

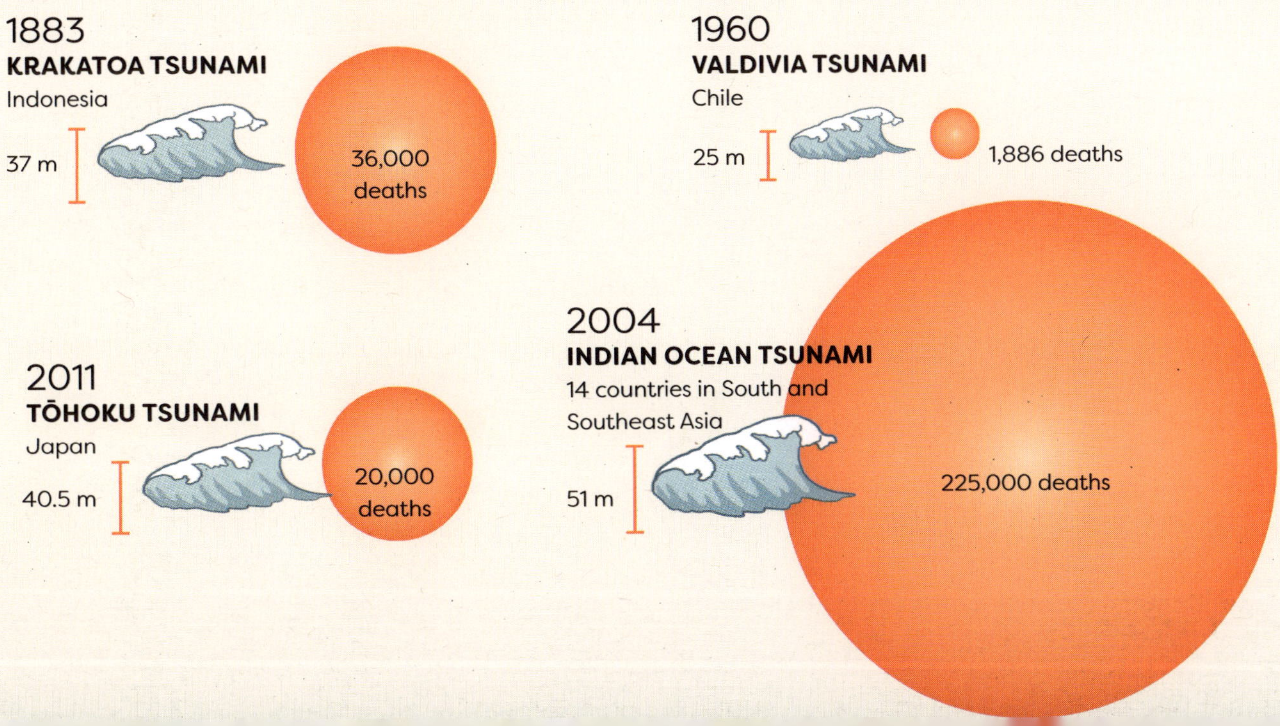

Highest points on Earth

The highest point on Earth is the summit of Mount Everest in the Himalayan mountain range in Nepal and Tibet. Nearly 9,000 metres up, it's almost as high as some jet aeroplanes fly. In this infographic you can compare some of the tallest natural features, human-made structures and living things on Earth.

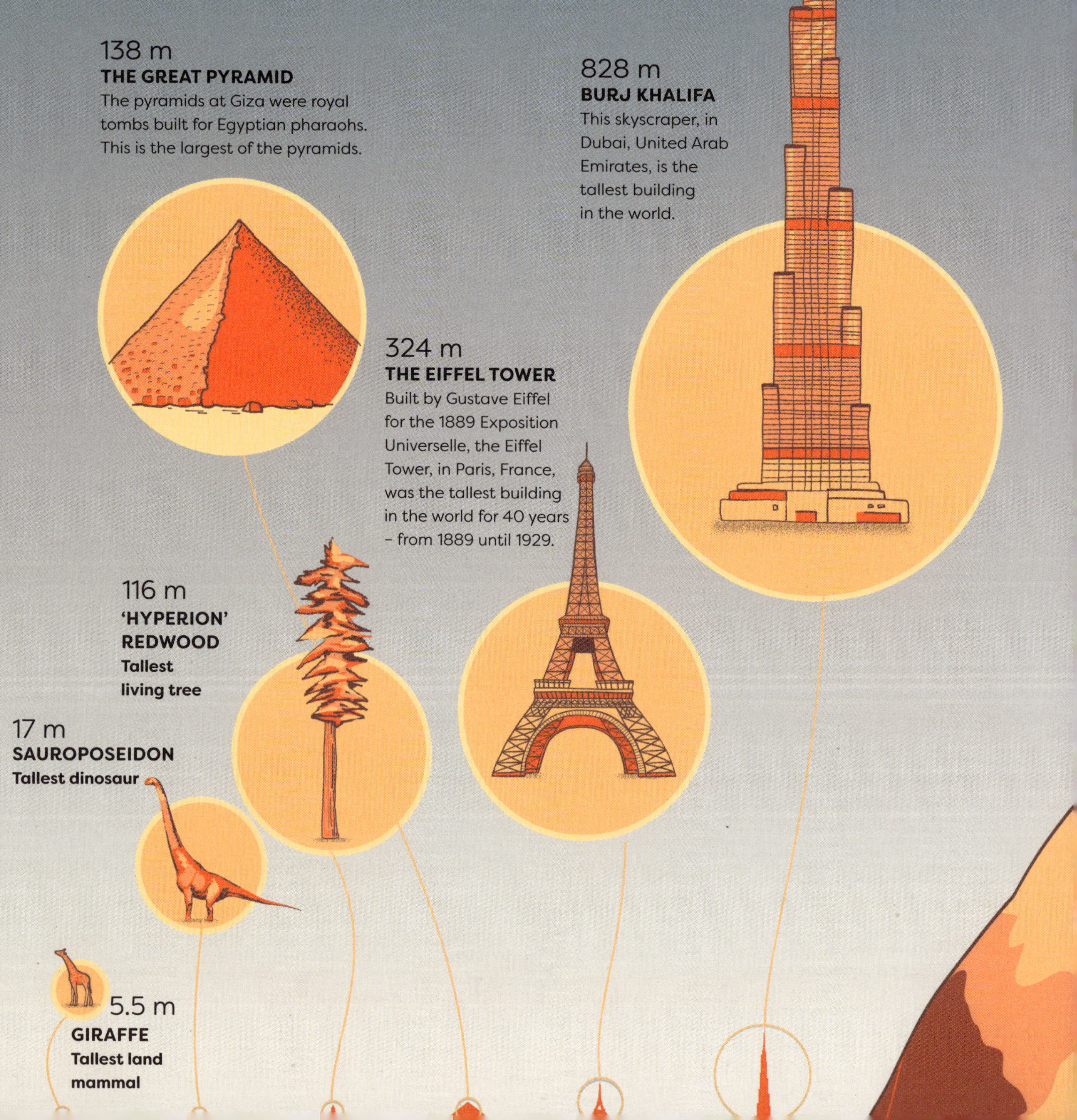

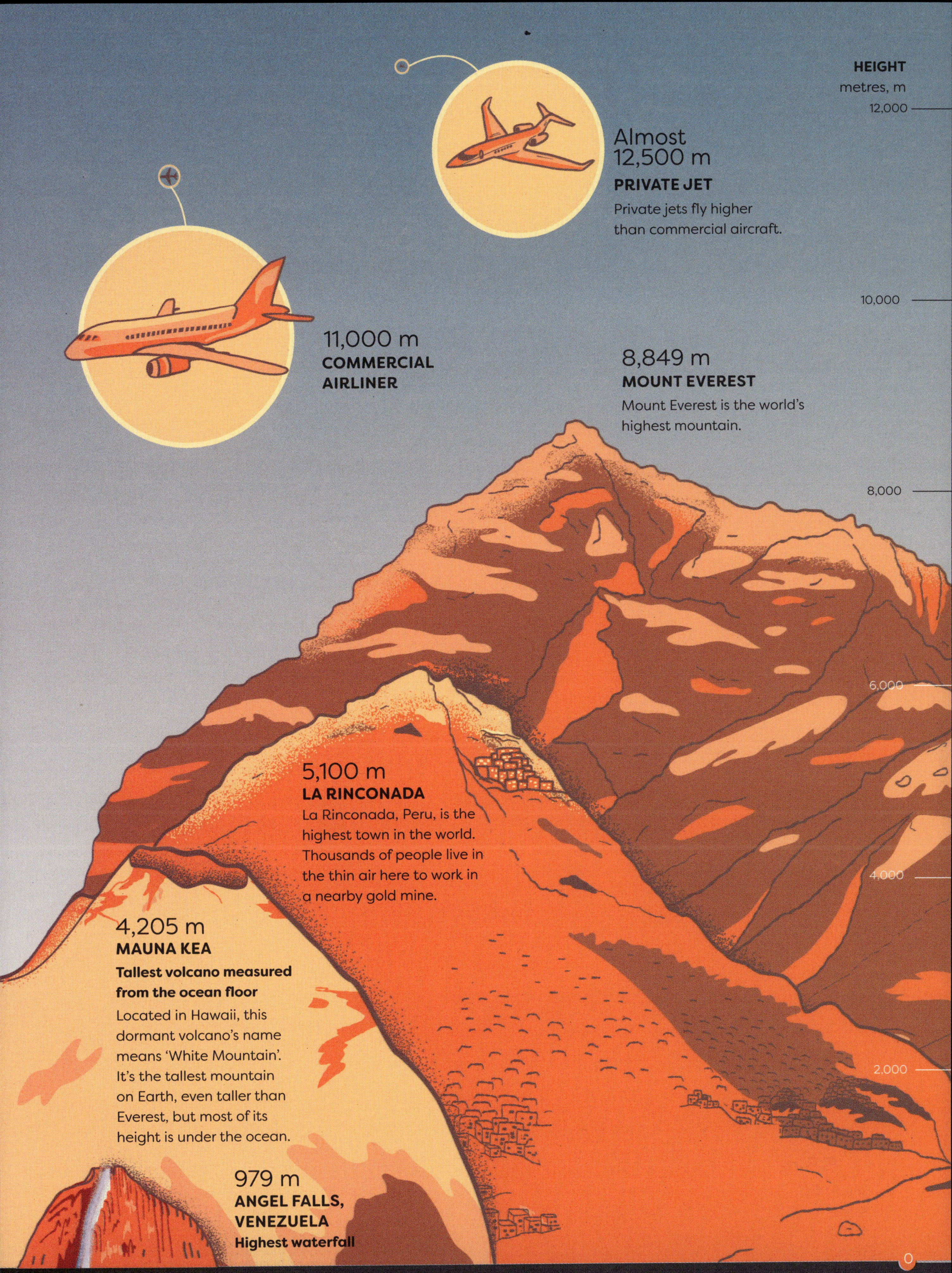
HEIGHT
metres, m
12,000
10,000
8,000
6,000
4,000
2,000
0
Almost
12,500 m
PRIVATE JET
Private jets fly higher
than commercial aircraft.
11,000 m
COMMERCIAL
AIRLINER
8,849 m
MOUNT EVEREST
Mount Everest is the world's
highest mountain.
5,100 m
LA RINCONADA
La Rinconada, Peru, is the
highest town in the world.
Thousands of people live in
the thin air here to work in
a nearby gold mine.
4,205 m
MAUNA KEA
Tallest volcano measured
from the ocean floor
Located in Hawaii, this
dormant volcano's name
means 'White Mountain'.
It's the tallest mountain
on Earth, even taller than
Everest, but most of its
height is under the ocean.
979 m
ANGEL FALLS,
VENEZUELA
Highest waterfall

NUMBER OF PEOPLE WHO HAVE SUCCESSFULLY CLIMBED MOUNT EVEREST, YEAR BY YEAR

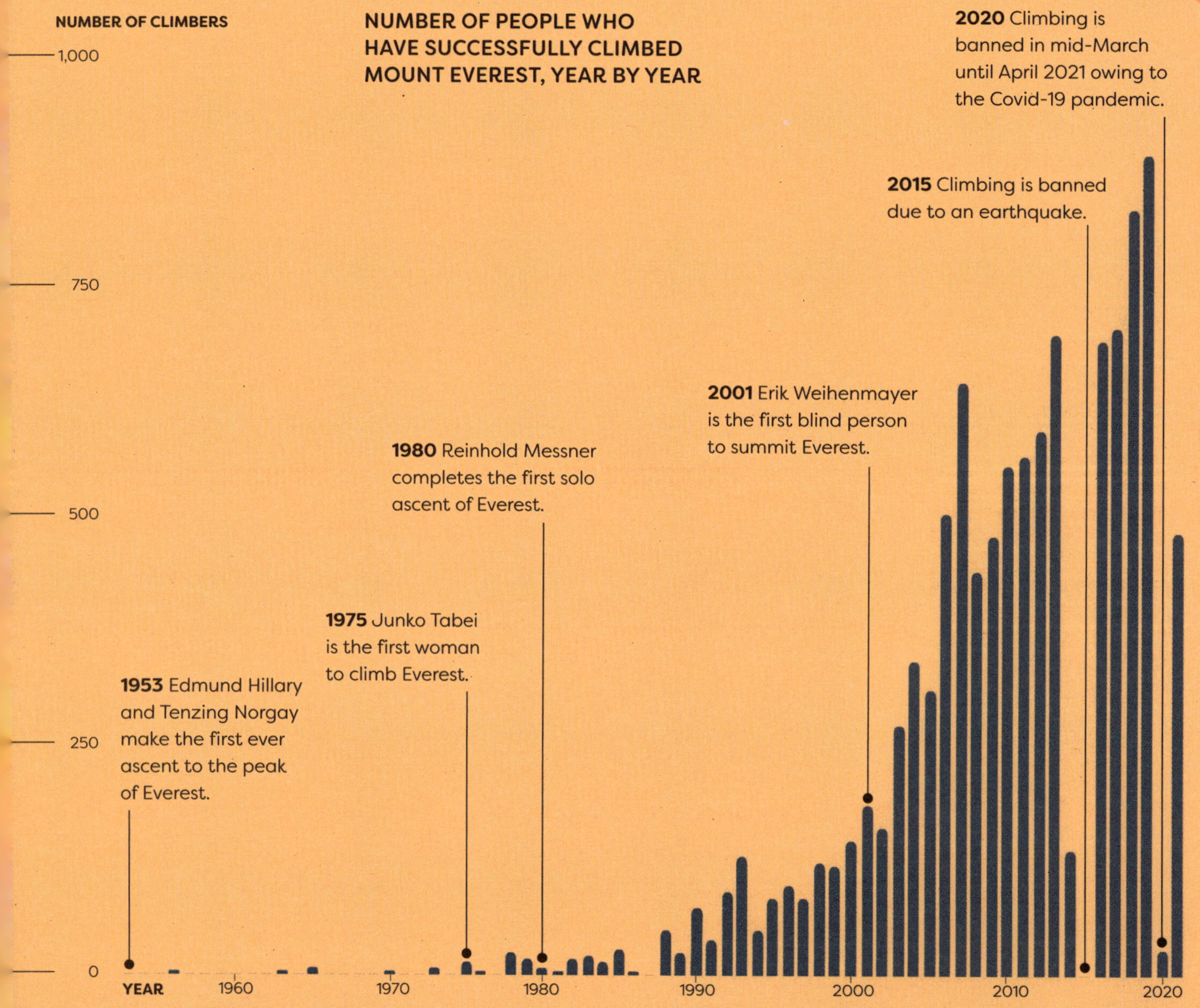

Mount Everest

Mount Everest is the tallest peak in the Himalayas, a mountain system of southern Asia. They started to form between 40 and 50 million years ago, when two of Earth's tectonic plates, the Indo-Australian Plate and the Eurasian Plate (see page 56), collided. The pressure of this collision led to the formation of the mountain range. Himalaya means 'house of snow' in the ancient language of Sanskrit.

UNDERWATER DEPTH
metres, m

0

-900 m
GIANT SQUID
Deepest recorded depth.

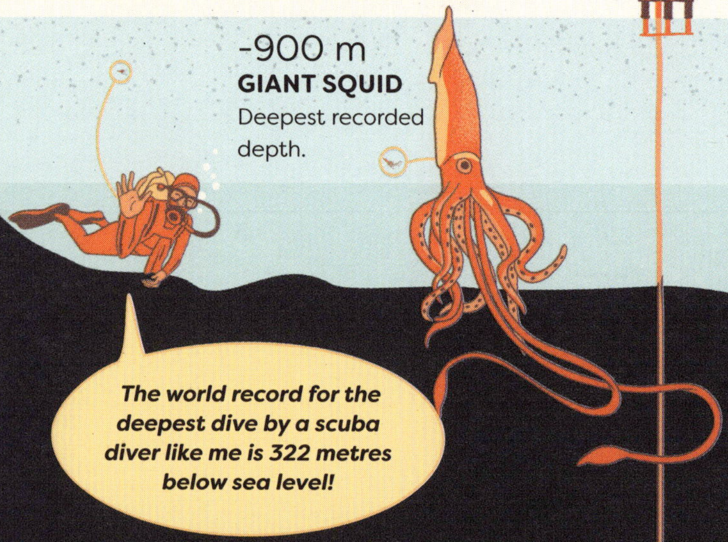

-2,000

DRILLING FOR OIL

Oil is trapped beneath the surface of Earth, and humans drill down into the ground or seabed to extract it for fuel and other products. The world's deepest oil well drilled from a floating rig is located in the Gulf of Mexico.

-1,800 m
WHALE SHARK
Deepest recorded depth.

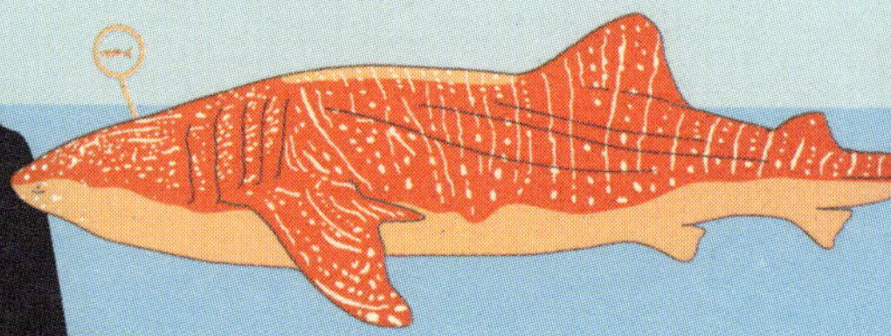

-4,000

-3,840 m
TITANIC SHIPWRECK

The RMS *Titanic*, a luxury passenger liner, sank 740 kilometres off the coast of Newfoundland, Canada, in the North Atlantic Ocean on 15 April 1912, after colliding with an iceberg. The shipwreck was discovered in 1985.

-6,000

In deep water

Scientists have divided the ocean into different layers, or zones, depending on how far away they are from the surface. The deepest point on Earth's surface is found in the Mariana Trench in the Pacific Ocean. The bottom of the Mariana Trench is a greater distance below sea level than the summit of Mount Everest is above sea level. Here are some other extraordinary things to be found in the watery depths.

-8,000

-10,000

-10,685 m
OIL

HMS *CHALLENGER*

HMS *CHALLENGER II*

The HMS *Challenger*'s three-and-a-half year voyage around the world between 1872 and 1876 led to the scientific naming of thousands of new marine species. Scientists on board the ship took readings and measured the depth of the ocean floor by lowering lead weights and scientific instruments attached to long lengths of rope.

Scientists on board HMS *Challenger II* discovered the Mariana Trench, the deepest known point of the ocean, in 1951. They measured the trench's depth using a sonic depth finder, which emits sound waves that bounce off the seabed before returning to the ship. The shape and frequency of the returning sound waves can tell scientists how far away the sea bed is from the surface.

THE SUNLIGHT ZONE

-1,000 m
The depth to which sunlight can reach.

THE MIDNIGHT ZONE

sound waves

-2,992 m
BEAKED WHALE
The deepest recorded diving mammal.

THE ABYSS

-8,178 m
MARIANA SNAILFISH
The deepest-swimming fish.

THE TRENCHES

lead weight

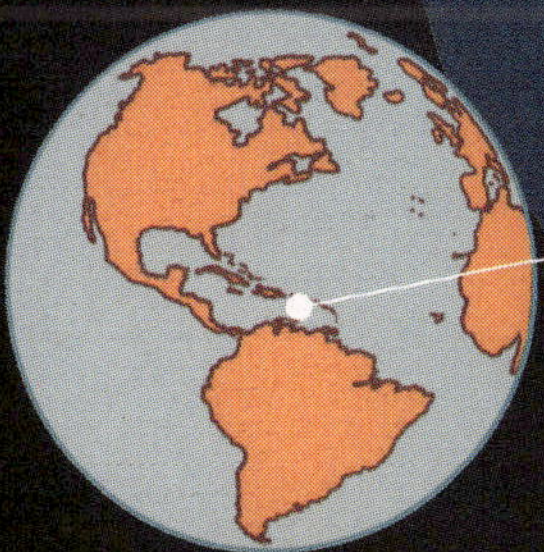

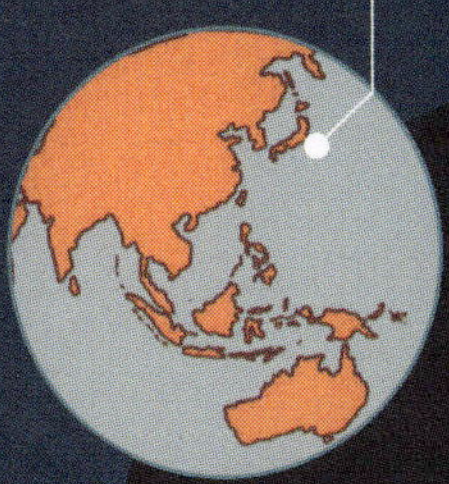

-8,376 m
PUERTO RICO TRENCH
Located off the coast of the island of Puerto Rico in the Caribbean, the Puerto Rico Trench is the deepest point in the Atlantic Ocean.

-10,925 m
DEEPEST DIVE BY A CREWED VESSEL
On 28 April 2019, Victor Vescovo descended almost 11,000 metres into the Mariana Trench in his submersible *Limiting Factor*.

-10,934 m
MARIANA TRENCH
Located in the western Pacific Ocean, the Mariana Trench is a deep crescent-shaped scar in Earth's crust. It is more than 2,550 kilometres long and 69 kilometres wide. Its deepest point is called the Challenger Deep.

MEET THE EXPERT CONSULTANT

Professor Christopher Jackson

Geoscientist

WHEN DID YOU REALISE THAT YOU WANTED TO STUDY EARTH SCIENCE?

I had a creeping realisation, over many, many years, that Earth science was not only fascinating, but also really important. Earth's rocks hold the clues about our planet's past and its changes in climate over geological time. Studying the rocks will help us better understand climate change today.

WHAT IS YOUR FAVOURITE FACT ABOUT EARTH?

It's that Earth isn't a perfect sphere! It's slightly flattened at the poles.

WHAT EXCITING DISCOVERY ARE YOU LOOKING FORWARD TO SEEING IN THE FUTURE?

I really hope that we can combine our geological knowledge, engineering skills, and belief in social justice to tackle the climate crisis, and provide safe, cheap and reliable energy for all.

WHAT IS THE BEST THING ABOUT YOUR JOB?

I use Earth science knowledge to research how to permanently store hazardous materials, such as nuclear waste and carbon dioxide, deep within Earth, and to store and recover useful resources, such as geothermal heat and hydrogen.

SCAVENGER HUNT!

Can you track down the answers to this quiz in the pages of this book? (Turn to page 305 to see if you are right!)

1. What percentage of Earth's surface is covered by water?

2. On which page of this book can you find a boiled egg?

3. In which layer of Earth's atmosphere can you find one of these?

4. On which continent is the coldest recorded place on Earth?

5. What type of cloud is this?

6. What number does diamond score on the Mohs Scale of hardness?

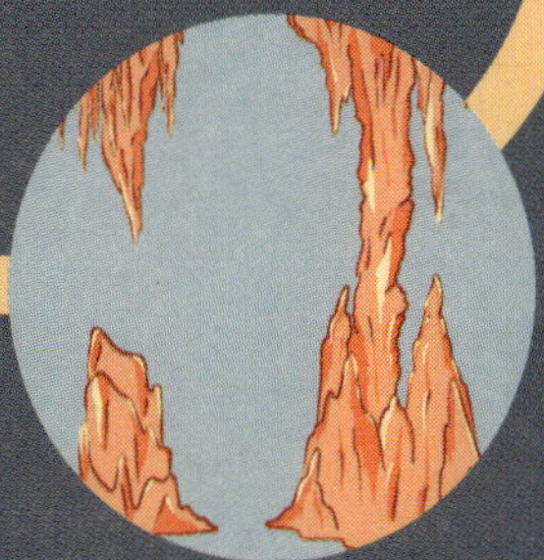

7. Do stalactites point upwards or downwards?

8. What is the name of this deep-swimming fish?

LIVING PLANET

Survival and extinction

Life on Earth began between 3.5 and 3.7 billion years ago, with simple, single-celled organisms called microbes. It took another 2 billion years for complex, multicellular life to evolve and another billion years after that for the first plants and animals to evolve. The infographic running along the bottom of these pages shows what happened next, as some species thrived, others became extinct and new species developed. (If you can't wait to see when dinosaurs and humans arrived on the scene, then turn the page.)

WHERE THE CONTINENTS WERE
The shape and position of the continents have been changing throughout Earth's history.

MASS EXTINCTION
A mass extinction is a period of history during which 75% or more of the species on Earth became extinct in just a few million years.

PERCENTAGE OF SPECIES THAT BECAME EXTINCT
percent, %

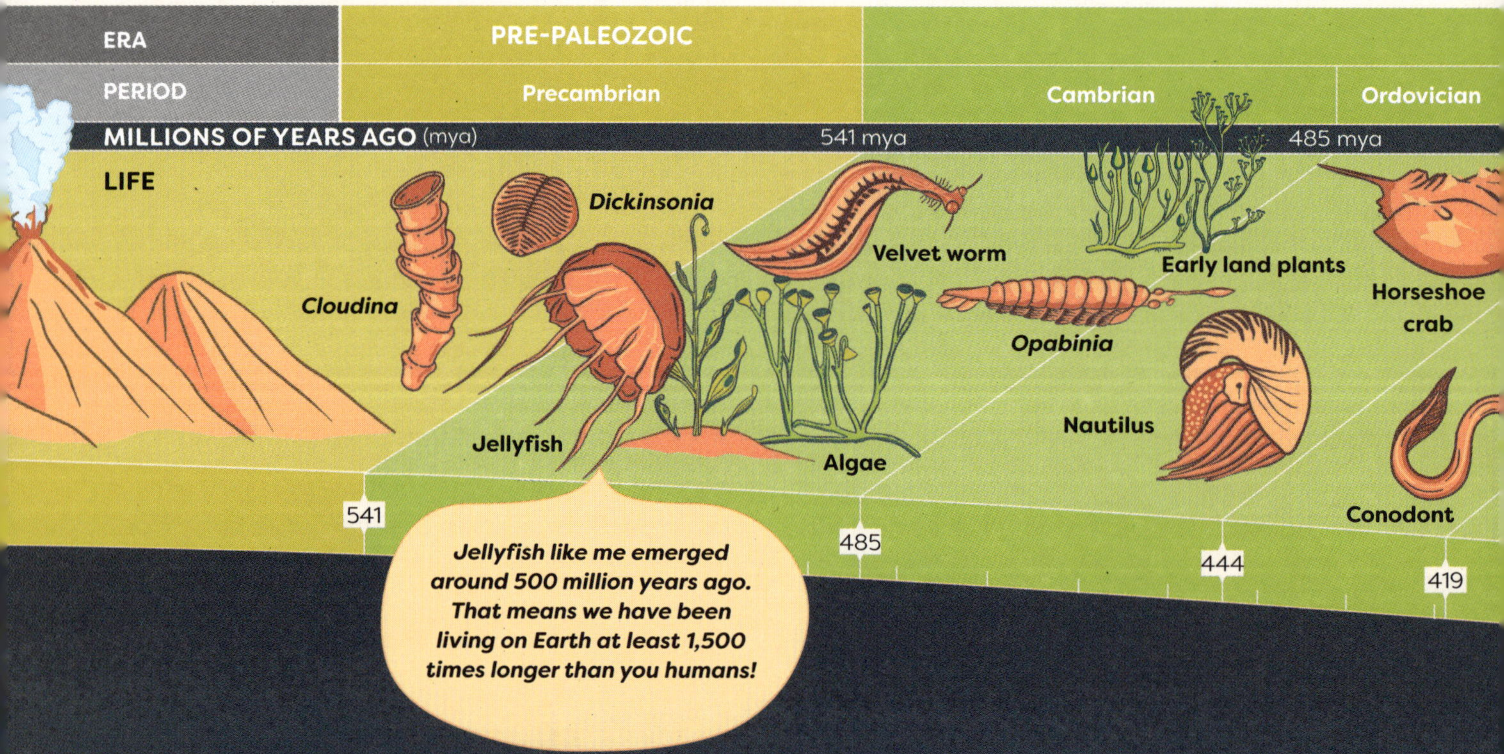

Turn the page!

444 million years ago

1ST MASS EXTINCTION

The Ordovician-Silurian extinction was caused by Earth getting much colder. Huge glaciers formed, which lowered sea levels. This was followed by a period of rapid warming.

85% of all species died out

359 million years ago

2ND MASS EXTINCTION

The Devonian extinction may have had several environmental causes, including periods of global warming and cooling, which changed sea levels and the amount of oxygen seas contained.

75% of all species died out

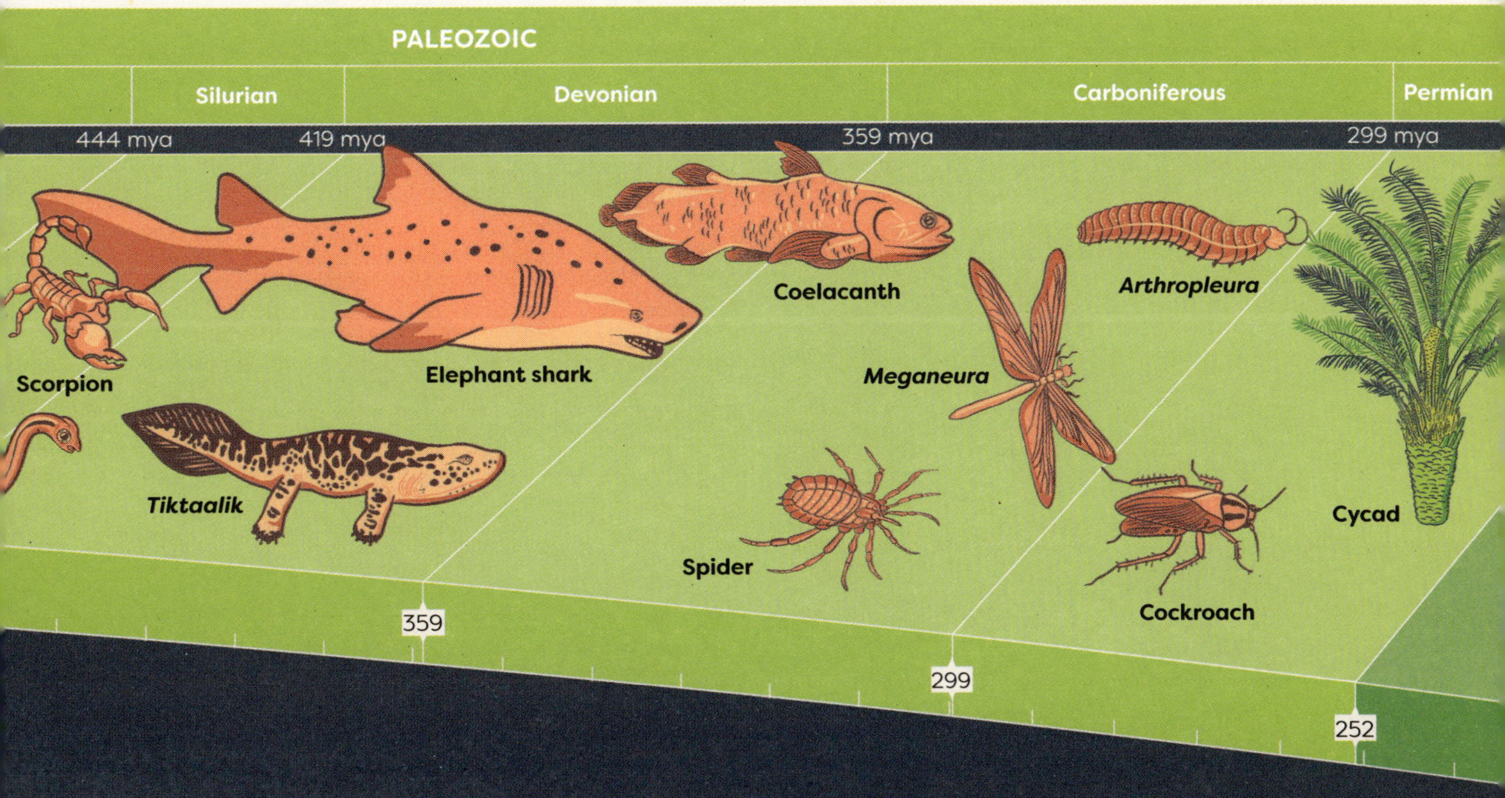

252 million years ago

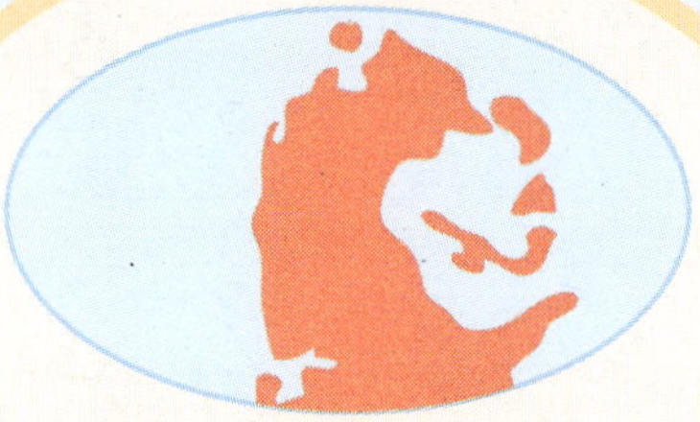

3RD MASS EXTINCTION

The Permian-Triassic extinction was perhaps the biggest threat to life on Earth. It may have been caused by massive volcanic eruptions. 96% of marine species and 70% land species went extinct.

90% of all species died out

201 million years ago

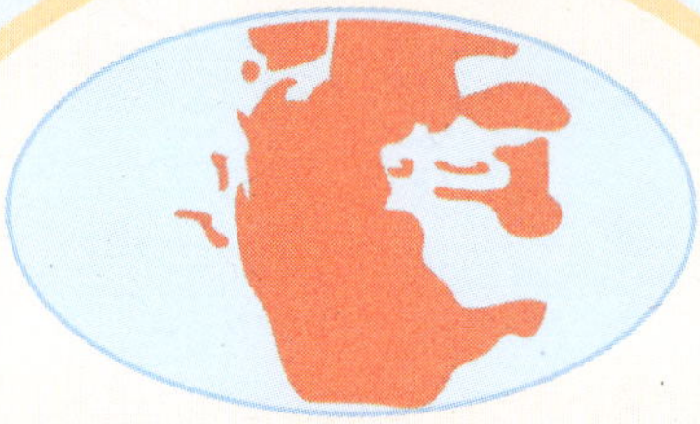

4TH MASS EXTINCTION

The Triassic-Jurassic extinction is thought to have lasted 18 million years. It was caused by climate change resulting from a rise of CO_2 in the atmosphere.

80% of all species died out

66 million years ago

5TH MASS EXTINCTION

The Cretaceous-Paleogene extinction was primarily caused by an asteroid hitting Earth. The extinction killed three-quarters of all species, including all dinosaurs (except birds).

76% of all species died out

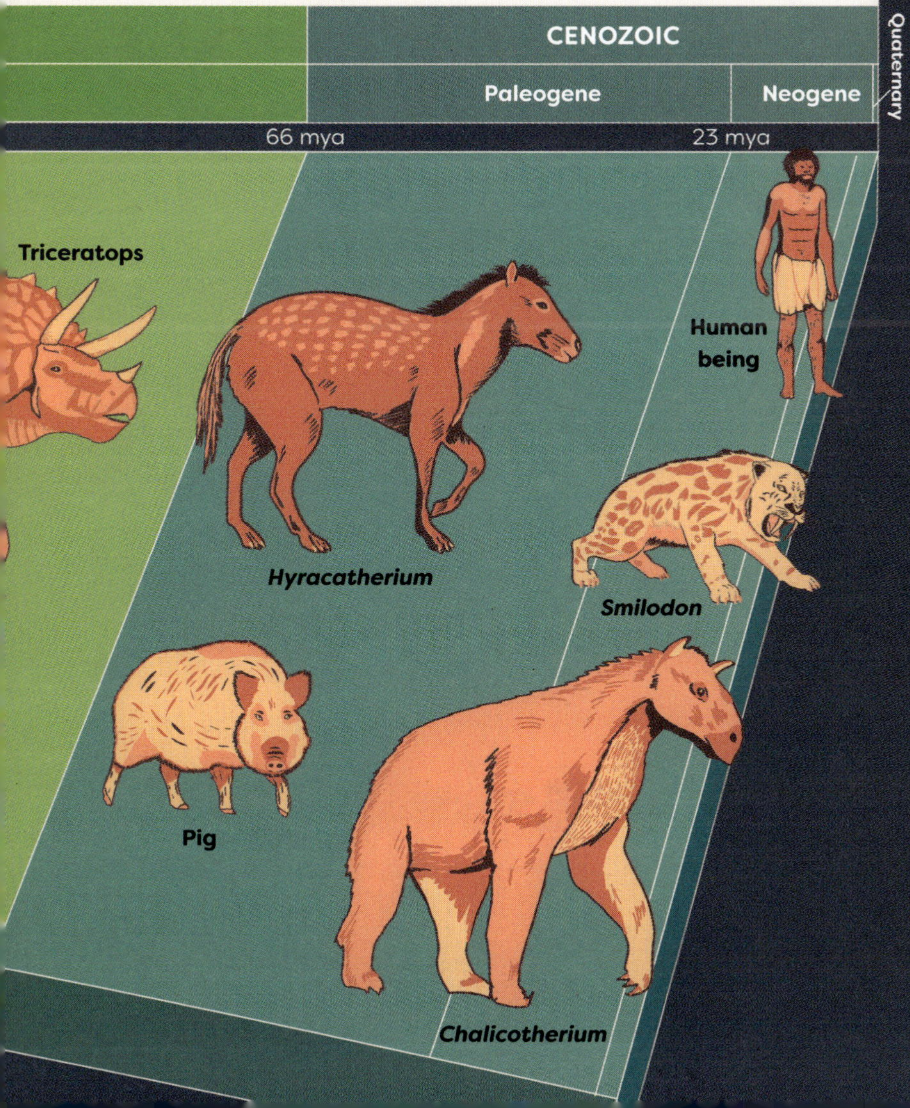

IS EARTH IN THE MIDDLE OF A 6TH MASS EXTINCTION?

Species on Earth will always experience extinction—in fact, more than 99 percent of all creatures that have ever lived have become extinct. But the current *rate* of extinction is far more rapid than is natural thanks to human activities, such as burning fossil fuels and deforestation. We need to act now to slow the rate of extinctions.

Examples of species that have become extinct in the last 500 years	Extinction rate compared to the 5th mass extinction
Chiriqui harlequin frog 	AMPHIBIANS 165x faster
Dodo 	BIRDS 103x faster
Longjaw cisco 	BONY FISH 65x faster
Tasmanian tiger (thylacine) 	MAMMALS 48x faster
Pinta giant tortoise 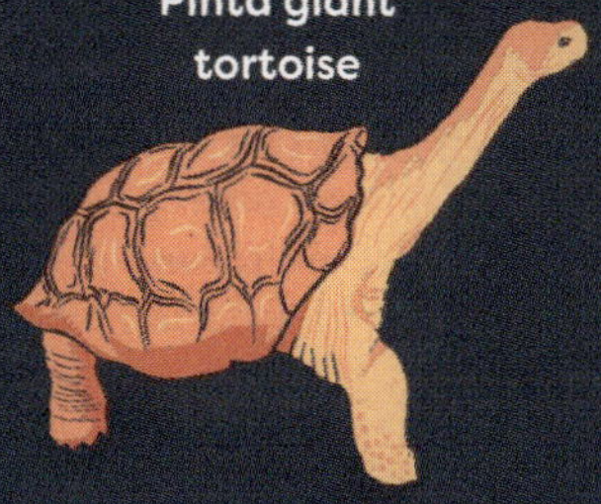	REPTILES 16x faster

Archaeopteryx fossil

EXAMPLES OF DINOSAUR FOSSILS FOUND AROUND THE WORLD

Clues about the past

Fossils are the remains or traces of plants and animals that lived long ago—and they can give scientists clues about extinct animals such as the dinosaurs, including where, when, and how they lived. Dinosaur fossils have been discovered on all seven of Earth's continents, including Antarctica.

Life on Earth now

This infographic shows the different categories of organisms on our planet. Each leaf represents how much the carbon in all the organisms in that category would weigh if you collected it all together.*

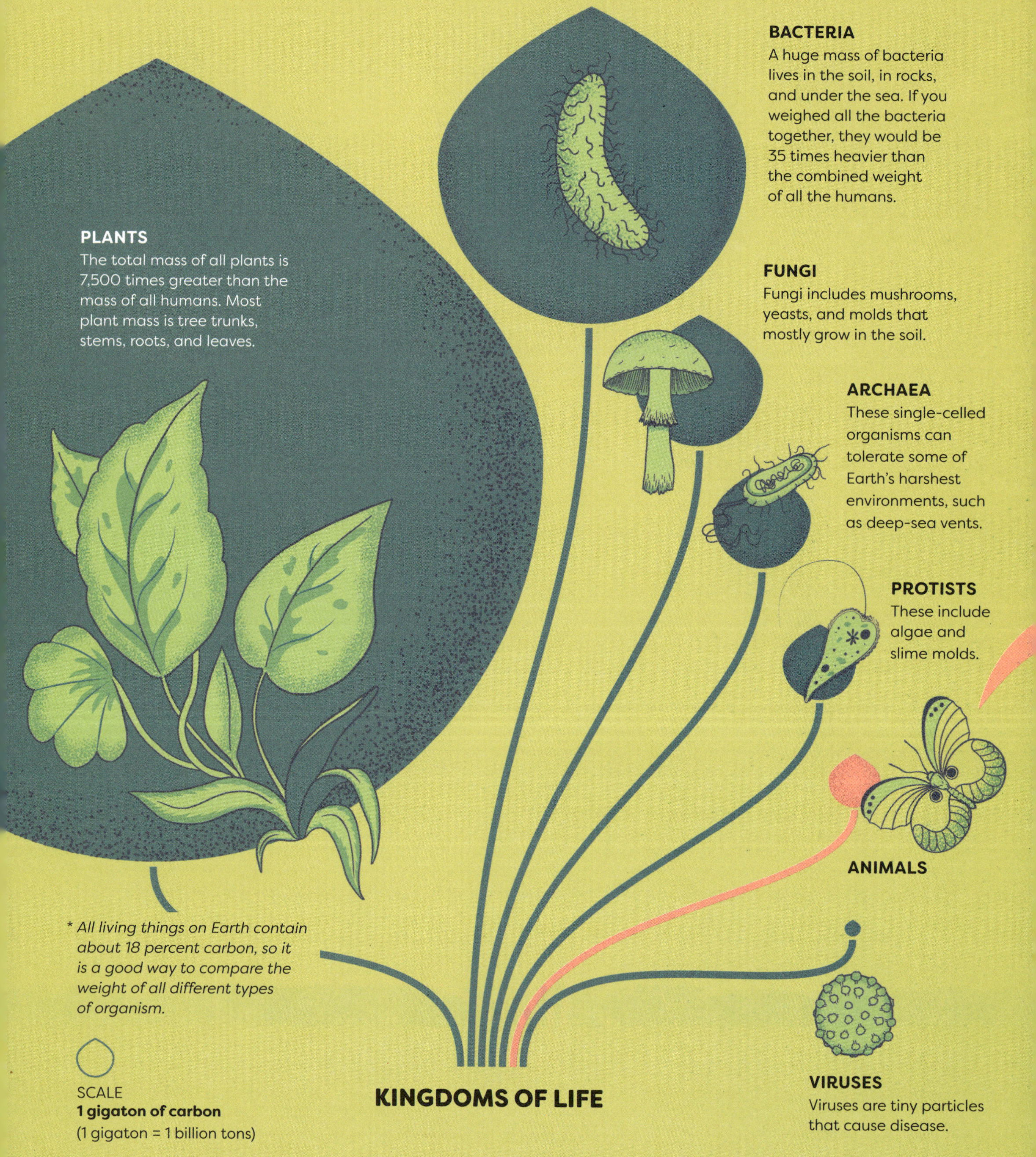

** All living things on Earth contain about 18 percent carbon, so it is a good way to compare the weight of all different types of organism.*

Find out how many species of beetle there are on Earth on page 146.

Zooming in to see animal life in more detail shows humans in relation to the rest of the animal kingdom. The combined carbon weight of reptiles and amphibians is so tiny that they don't even appear here.

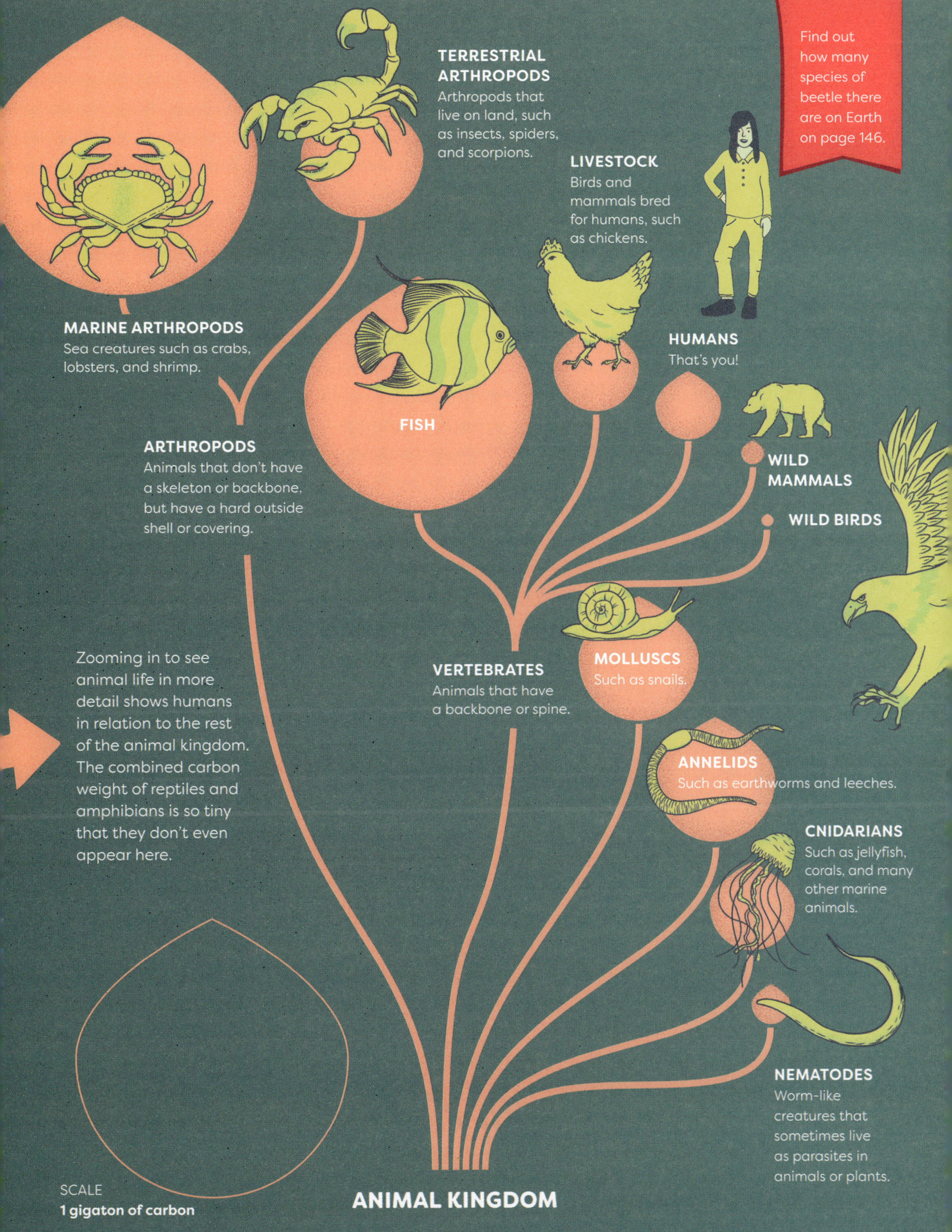

Where does oxygen come from?

Almost all animals need oxygen to survive. But where does all the oxygen in the atmosphere come from? Most comes from tiny plants called phytoplankton that live in the ocean and produce oxygen during photosynthesis (see opposite). There are so many phytoplankton that satellites can see their colorful blooms from space.

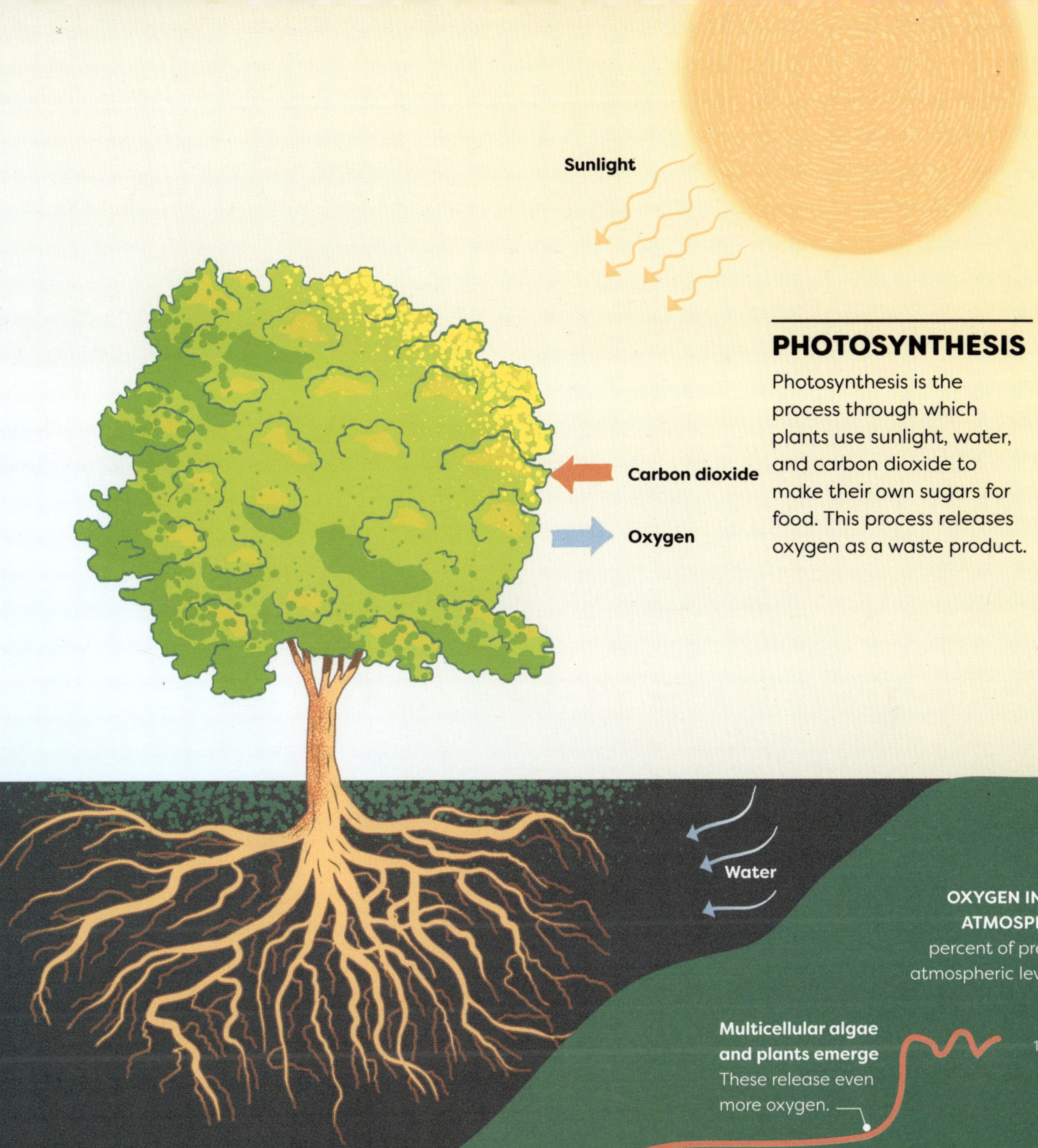

PHOTOSYNTHESIS

Photosynthesis is the process through which plants use sunlight, water, and carbon dioxide to make their own sugars for food. This process releases oxygen as a waste product.

HOW OXYGEN FILLED EARTH'S ATMOSPHERE

At the beginnings of life on Earth, there was almost no oxygen in the atmosphere. The only organisms that could survive were microbes that could live without it. But around 2.8 billion years ago, oxygen gas accumulated in the atmosphere for the first time, which scientists think was as a result of a type of bacteria that was able to photosynthesize.

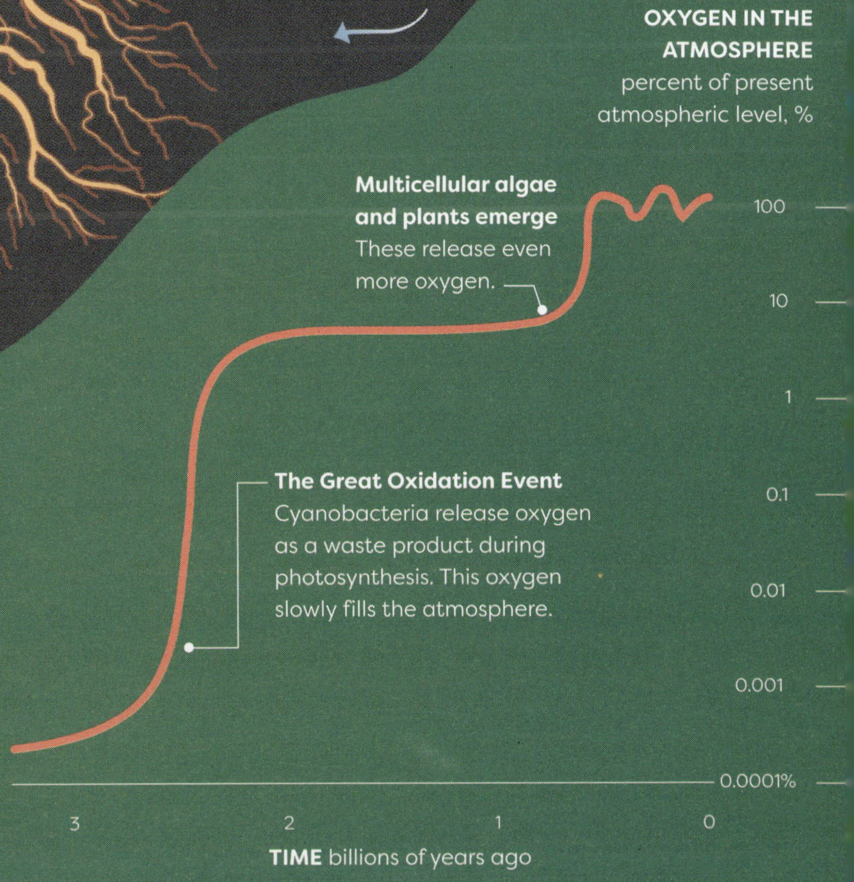

Tremendous trees

Scientists estimate that there are more than 3 trillion trees on Earth. This means that there are more individual trees on our planet than there are stars in the Milky Way. Here are some of the widest and the tallest trees.

WORLD'S WIDEST TREES

SCALE **3 feet** (1 m)

The width (or thickness) of a tree is measured using its diameter, which is the length of a straight line that passes through the tree's center from one side of the tree's trunk to the other. The tree trunks here are illustrated to scale. To show each trunk's circumference (the length all around the edge), you can see how many children, holding hands, would be needed to hug it.

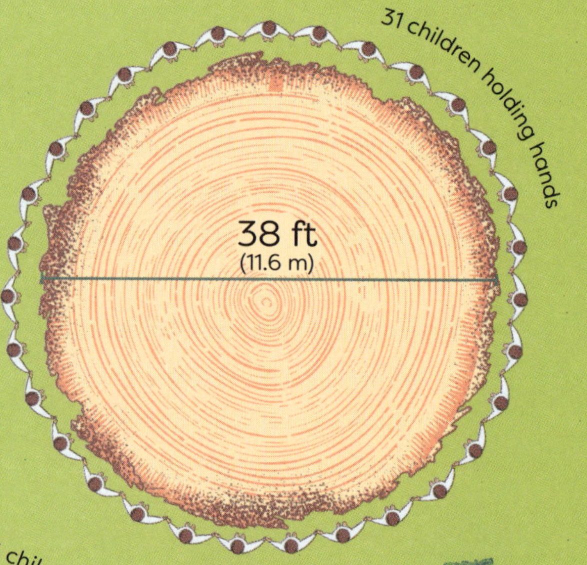

ÁRBOL DEL TULE
Montezuma Cypress
Mexico

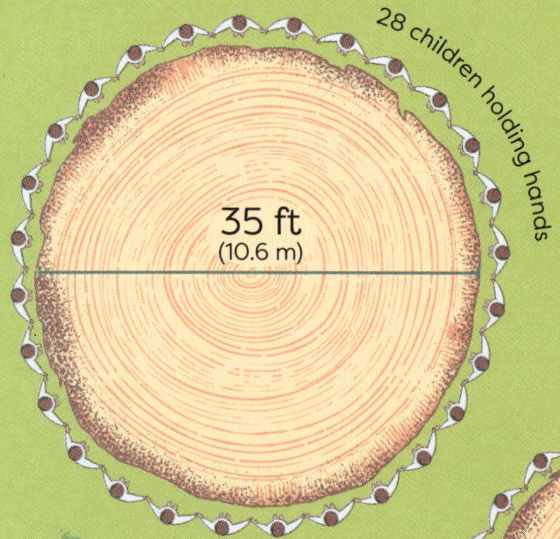

SUNLAND BAOBAB
Baobab
South Africa

THE TEMPLE FIG
White or Strangler Fig
Australia

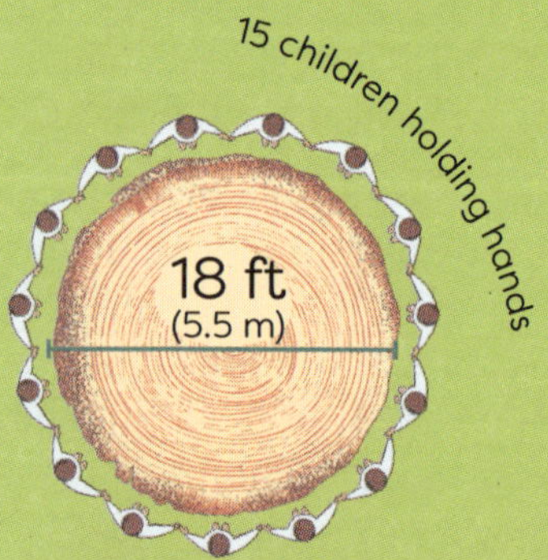

THE BELLINGEN FIG
Moreton Bay Fig
Australia

JUPITER
Coast Redwood
USA

WORLD'S TALLEST TREES

The world's tallest known tree is a Coast Redwood. It was discovered in northern California in 2006 and is now famous enough to have its own nickname: Hyperion. Hyperion's precise location is kept secret to protect it from being damaged.

Leaf spotting

Just like a snowflake, the closer you look at a leaf, the more there is to notice. Here is a guide to common leaf features and how to spot them.

SHAPE

The first thing to identify about a leaf is its overall shape. Here are some of the most common.

ACICULAR
Needle-shaped

ACUMINATE
Ending in a long, thin point

ARISTATE
With a spine-like tip

CORDATE
Heart-shaped with a stem in the cleft

CUNEATE
Wedge-shaped, with narrow base

DELTOID
Triangular

DIGITATE
With lobes like fingers

ELLIPTIC
Oval-shaped, with a small or no point

FALCATE
Shaped like a hook or sickle

FLABELLATE
Shaped like a fan

HASTATE
Triangular with lobes at the base

LANCEOLATE
Pointed at both ends

LINEAR
Long, with parallel margins

LOBED
Deeply indented margins

OBCORDATE
Heart-shaped, stem at the point

OBOVATE
Egg-shaped, narrower at the base

OBTUSE
With a blunt tip at the end

ORBICULAR
Round

OVATE
Egg-shaped, wider at the base

PALMATE
Like a hand with fingers

PEDATE
Palmate, but with indented lobes

PINNATISECT
Deep lobing on opposite sides

RENIFORM
Shaped like a kidney

RHOMBOID
Shaped like a diamond

SPATULATE
Shaped like a spoon

SPEAR-SHAPED
With a shape and point like a spear

SUBULATE
Narrowing to a long, thin point

TRUNCATE
Flattened off at the tip or base

MARGIN

The edge of a leaf is called the margin. A leaf's margin can be smooth or wavy or have jagged "teeth."

Find a leaf in a nearby yard or park. What type of margin does it have?

CILIATE
With fine hairs

CRENATE
With rounded teeth

DENTATE
With symmetrical teeth

DENTICULATE
With tiny teeth

DOUBLY SERRATE
With different sizes of teeth

ENTIRE
Smooth and even

LOBATE
With large round indents

SERRATE
With large teeth

SERRULATE
With small teeth.

SINUATE
With indentions like waves

SPINY
With sharp, stiff points

UNDULATE
With curving waves

VEIN PATTERNS

Veins inside a plant carry water to and from its leaves in a similar way to how blood vessels carry blood around your body. Plants' veins also provide the structure and support that give leaves their shape. The arrangement of veins inside a leaf is called venation.

ARCUATE

CROSS-VENULATE

DICHOTOMOUS

LONGITUDINAL

PALMATE

PARALLEL

PINNATE

RETICULATE

ROTATE

ARRANGEMENT

In some plants and trees, leaves are formed from an arrangement of smaller leaves called leaflets.

ALTERNATE
Leaflets arranged alternately

BIPINNATE
Leaflets in pairs of rows

OPPOSITE
Leaflets in adjacent pairs

PELTATE
With the stem attached to the middle of the leaf

PERFOLIATE
With the stem seeming to pierce the leaf

ODD PINNATE
Leaflets in rows, with one at the tip

EVEN PINNATE
Leaflets in rows, with two at the tip

TRIFOLIATE
Leaflets in threes

TRIPINNATE
Groups of leaflets in threes

UNIFOLIATE
A single leaf

WHORLED
Three or more leaflets arranged in rings

Flower power!

The vast majority of flowering plants rely on animals to help them reproduce. Honeybees, wasps, flies, moths, butterflies—and even some lizards, bats, and lemurs—are pollinators. They visit flowers to drink their sugary nectar and, in the process, carry dust-like grains of pollen from flower to flower, which is essential for the plant to make new seeds. This process is called pollination.

HOW POLLINATION BEGINS

Flowers have a male part (stamen) and a female part (stigma). Pollinators such as honeybees carry the pollen from the stamen of one flower to the stigma of the next. This causes fertilization, and a seed grows.

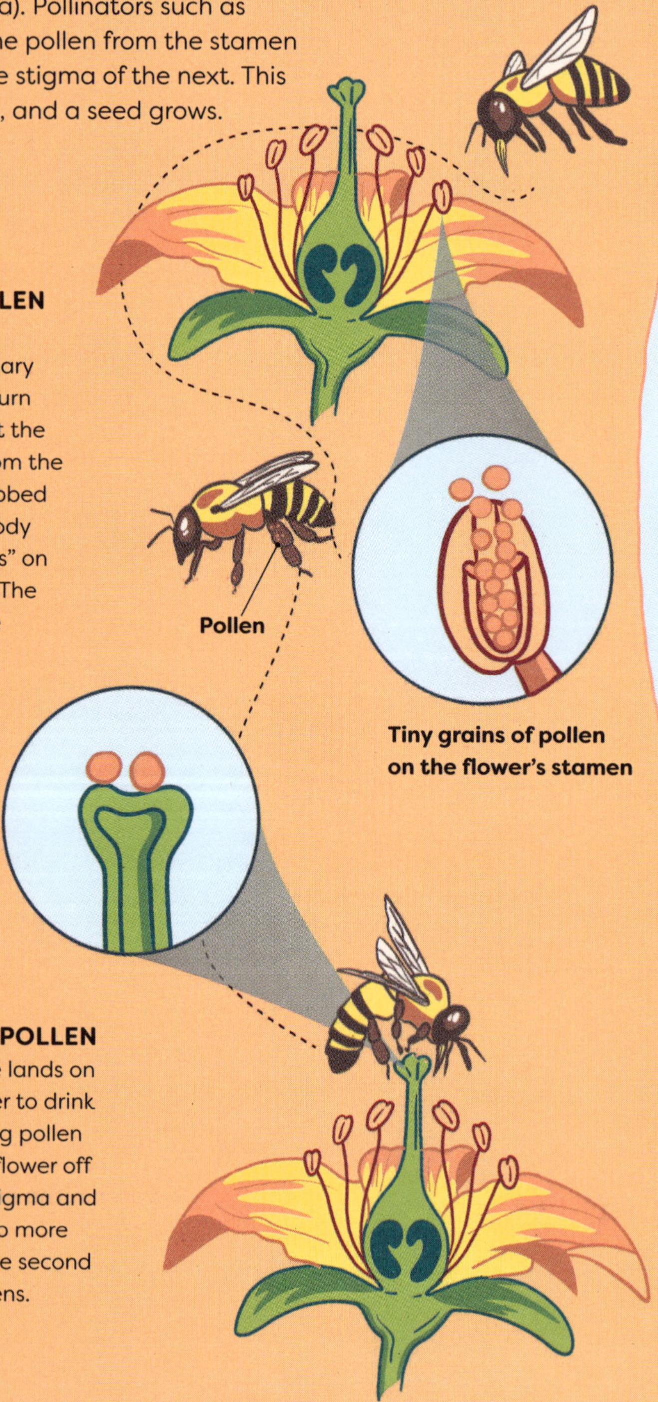

1 COLLECTING POLLEN
The honeybee visits flowers to collect sugary nectar. (Honeybees turn nectar into honey.) At the same time, pollen from the flower's stamen is rubbed on the honeybee's body and sticks to "baskets" on the honeybee's legs. The honeybee flies to the next flower.

2 RELEASING POLLEN
The honeybee lands on the next flower to drink nectar, rubbing pollen from the first flower off against the stigma and also picking up more pollen from the second flower's stamens.

Bees need to visit 660 flowers to make 1 drop of honey.

1 drop = 150 milligrams

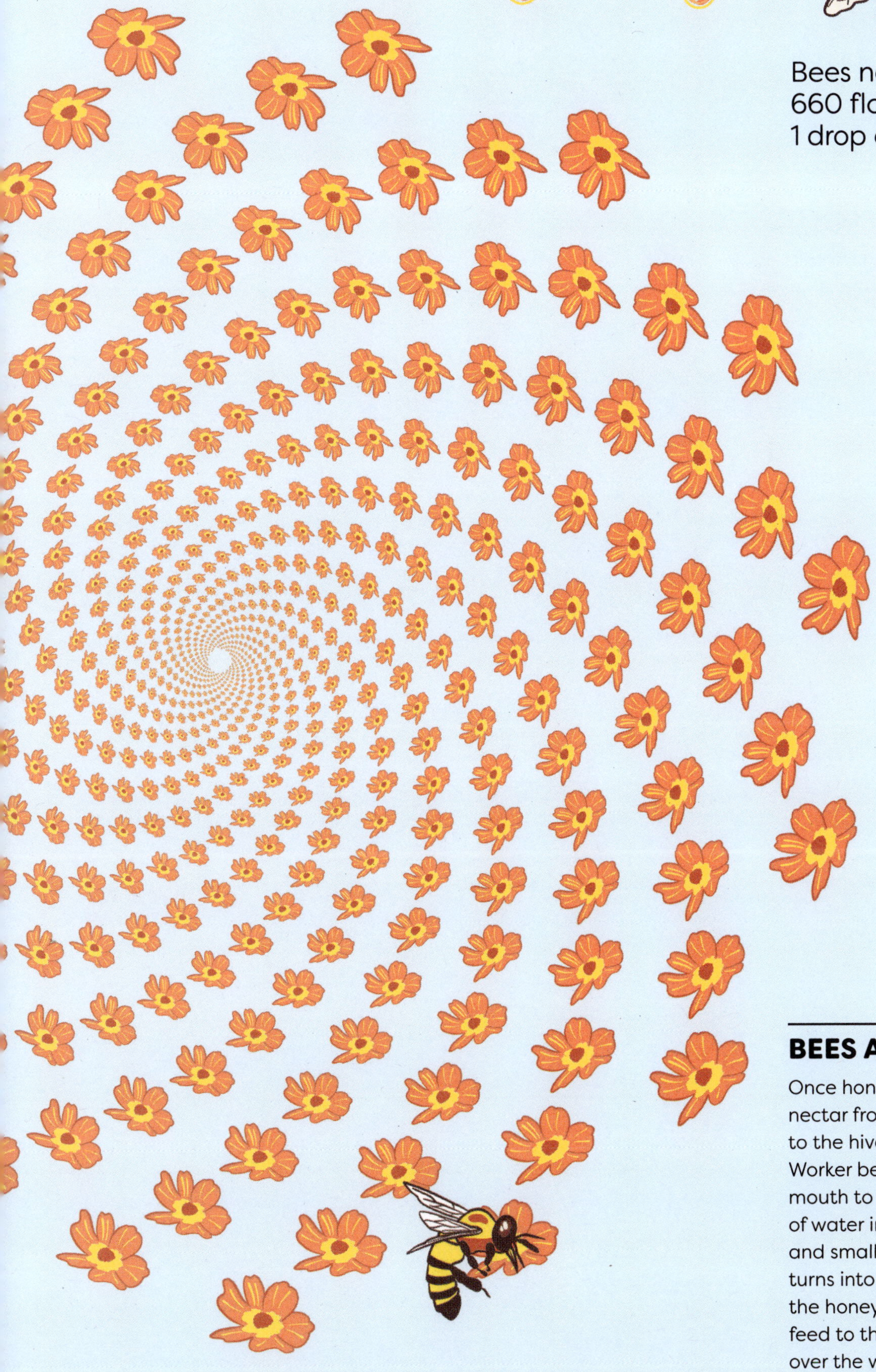

BEES AND HONEY

Once honeybees have drunk the nectar from flowers, they return to the hive and regurgitate it. Worker bees pass it to each other, mouth to mouth, and the amount of water in the nectar gets smaller and smaller. Eventually the nectar turns into honey. The bees store the honey in wax chambers to feed to their larvae and to eat over the winter.

The world's biggest flower

The orange-brown and white plant *Rafflesia arnoldii* holds the world record for having the largest flowers. Even the smallest *Rafflesia* flowers are the size of dinner plates, and the biggest ever recorded measured more than 3 feet (1 m) across! *Rafflesia arnoldii* flowers are also very smelly, giving off a foul odor similar to rotten meat in order to attract insects, such as flies and beetles, which then pollinate the plant.

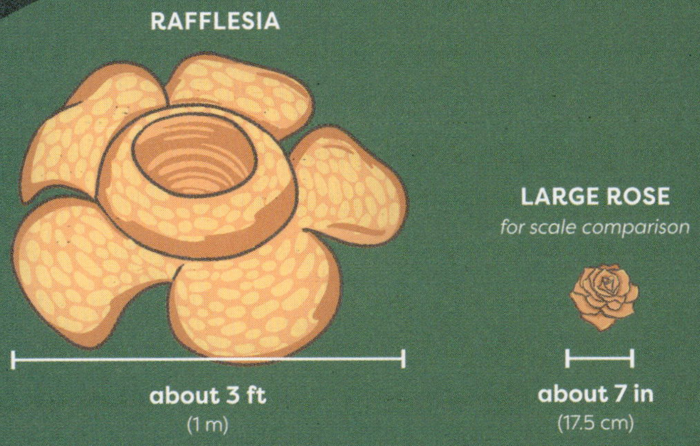
RAFFLESIA
about 3 ft
(1 m)
LARGE ROSE
for scale comparison
about 7 in
(17.5 cm)

Seeds great and small

Most plants start their lives as seeds. Each seed contains a young plant, called an embryo, which can develop into a fully grown plant. Seeds come in all shapes and sizes, adapted to travel away from their parent plant—or, in the case of the coco de mer, not to go anywhere at all!

DANDELION

There are around 150 to 200 seeds on a single dandelion stem. They have feathery bristles that act a little like a parachute, helping the seeds float through the air. The wind can carry them over distances of about 60 miles (100 km)!

HOW DO SEEDS SPREAD?

It is important for most seeds to travel away from their parent plant. If a seed landed and grew near its parent plant, the new plant would compete with its parent for light and water, meaning that both plants would be less likely to survive. Seeds can spread in many different ways. Here are five of the most common.

ANIMALS

Animals swallow seeds, or seeds can get stuck to an animal's feathers or fur. The seeds are then deposited elsewhere in the animal's poop or simply drop off as the animal moves around.

FARMING AND GARDENING

Farmers and gardeners collect and plant many different types of seeds to grow new flowers, fruit, and other crops.

WIND

The wind blows seeds such as dandelion seeds (see above) through the air.

BURSTING SEED PODS

Some plants fling their seeds away from them with explosive force.

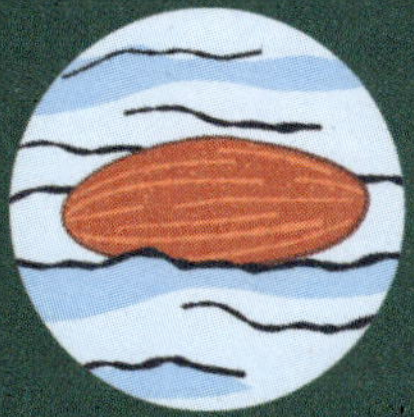

WATER

Some seeds, such as coconuts, are carried on rivers and across oceans.

WHAT THIS GIANT SEED GROWS INTO

The coco de mer is a rare palm tree found on the Seychelles in the Indian Ocean. It can take up to 50 years to grow from a seed to a fully mature tree and can produce flowers and fruit for as long as 800 years. The tree's enormous fruit, which takes years to ripen, is among the biggest of any plant.

COCO DE MER (IT REALLY IS THIS BIG!)

The coco de mer palm tree produces the largest and heaviest seeds in the world. A single seed can weigh as much as 55 pounds (25 kg). This seed doesn't travel far at all—it can't float in water or through the air. It appears to be one of the few seeds in nature that benefits from growing in the shadow of its parent plant.

SCALE **1 inch** (2.5 cm)
Dandelion and coco de mer shown at actual size

THE WORLD'S BIGGEST FUNGUS

A mycelium network in Oregon spreads across nearly 4 square miles (10 sq km), making it the largest fungus ever discovered. It is about three times bigger than Central Park in Manhattan, New York. Its nickname is the "humongous fungus!"

Trees that are sick or dying are digested by fungi. Living trees can then access the nutrients through the underground network.

The Wood Wide Web

Did you know that plants and trees share hidden connections with each other? And that it's all thanks to fungi? Underneath the soil, fungi grow on the roots of trees, forming a system of interconnected threads called mycelium. Mycelia transport water, nutrients, and chemical signals from one plant to another through their complex underground network.

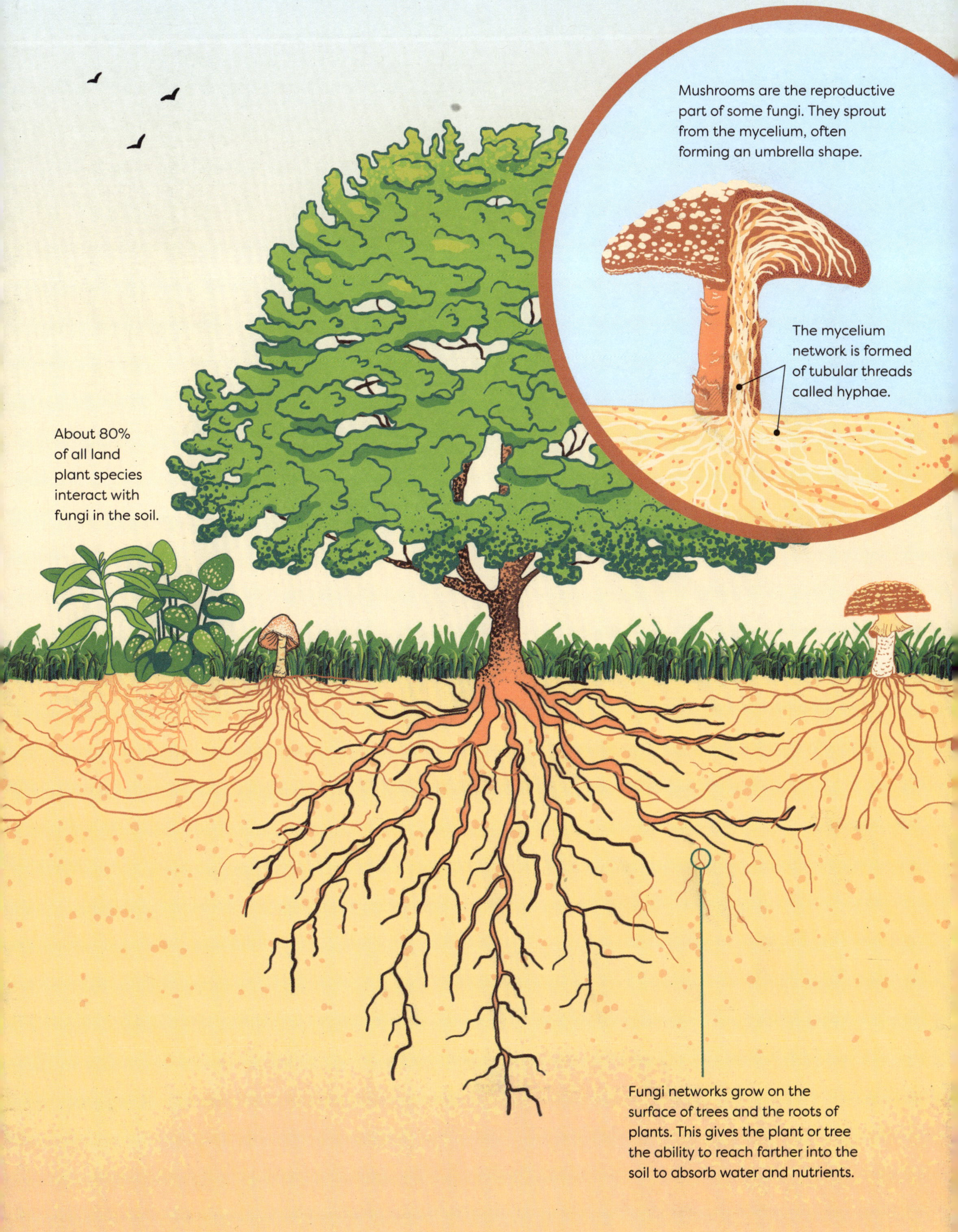

Mushrooms are the reproductive part of some fungi. They sprout from the mycelium, often forming an umbrella shape.
The mycelium network is formed of tubular threads called hyphae.
About 80% of all land plant species interact with fungi in the soil.
Fungi networks grow on the surface of trees and the roots of plants. This gives the plant or tree the ability to reach farther into the soil to absorb water and nutrients.

Heroes of the underground

The most important animal on Earth might just be the humble earthworm. Beneath the ground, worms are quietly keeping the soil healthy so that plants can grow, creating food for lots of animals, including humans. In fact, there are so many earthworms that if you rolled them all into a giant ball, it would weigh eight times more than all the humans!

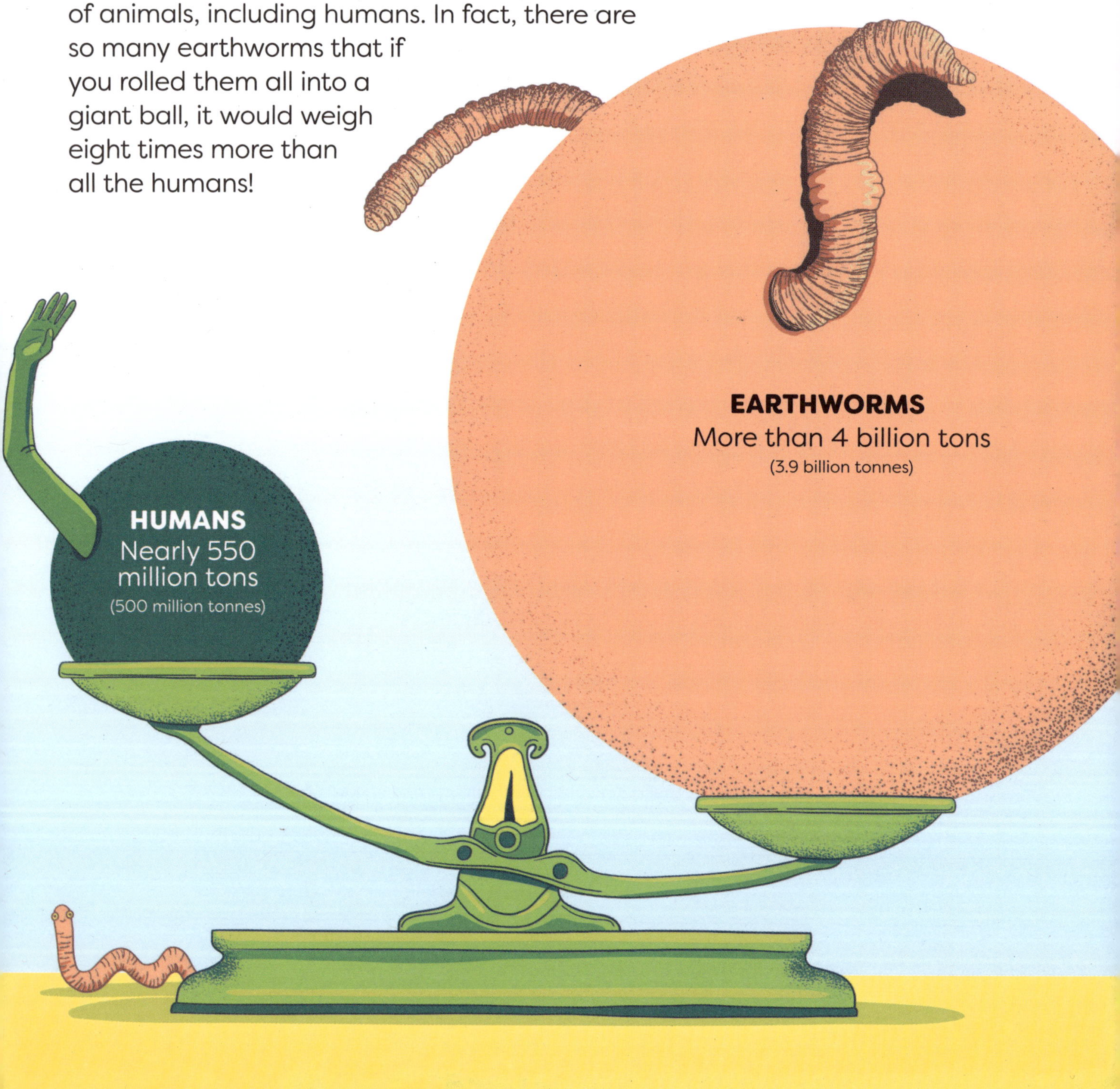

WHY ARE EARTHWORMS SO IMPORTANT?

Earthworms keep the soil healthy for plants. They do this in several ways: by breaking down dead organic matter such as fallen leaves, by burrowing and making holes so the soil can hold more water and plants can reach deeper underground, and by mixing up the soil so that the nutrients it contains are spread around evenly. They also provide a great source of food for many living things.

THE WORLD OF WORMS

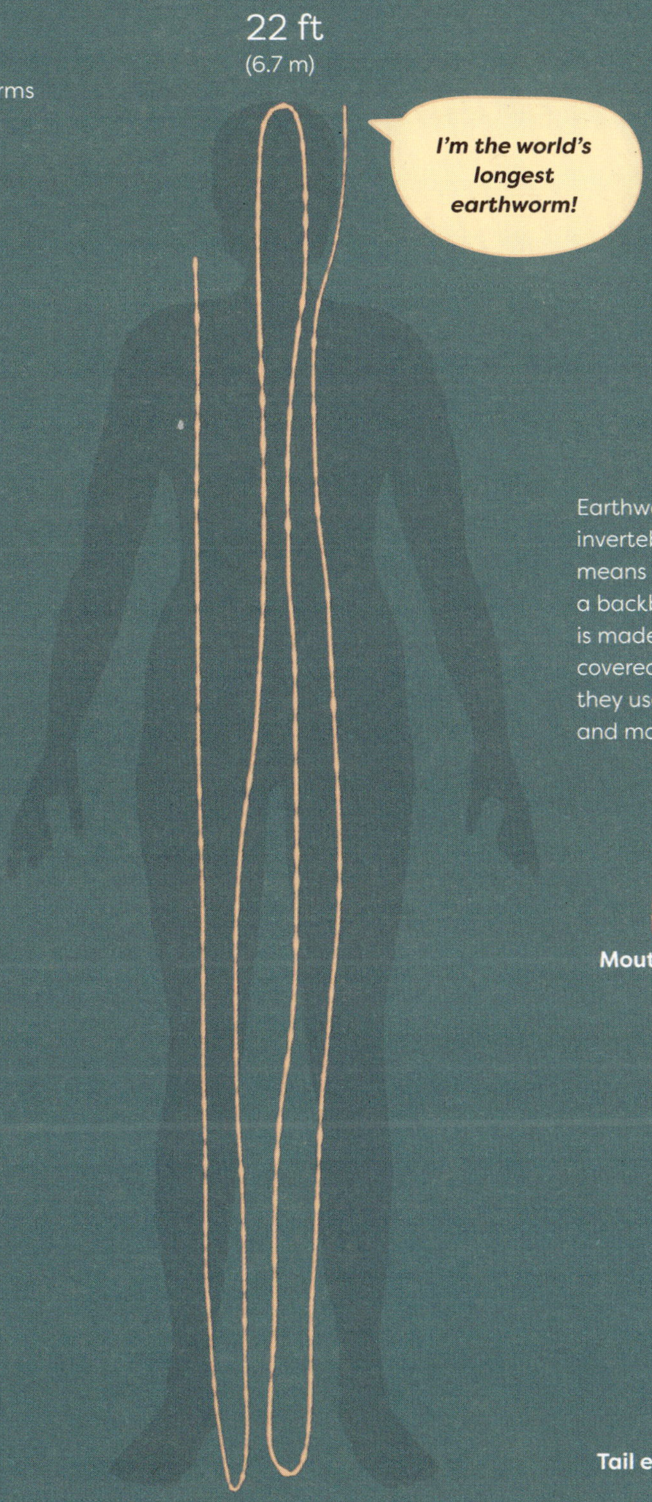

Earthworms are invertebrates, which means they don't have a backbone. Their skin is made up of ridges covered in tiny hairs that they use to grip the soil and move around.

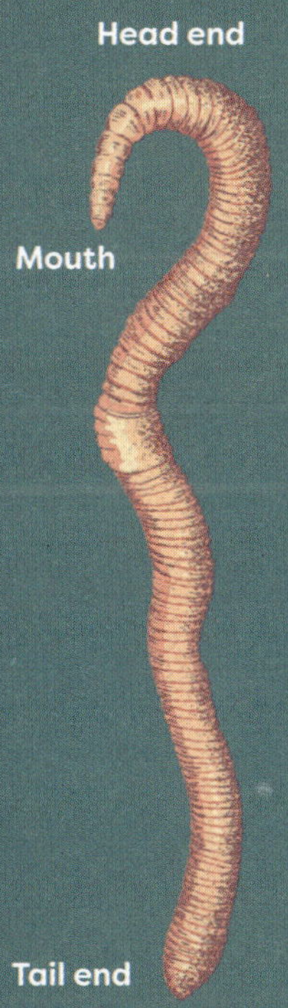

POPULATION
There are about 1,300,000,000,000,000 earthworms on Earth. An average field has about nine earthworms in every spadeful of soil.

SIZE
The world's longest earthworm is the African giant earthworm. It can grow to be 22 feet (6.7 m) long, which is about four times longer than an average-size human.

ANATOMY
An earthworm's digestive system runs the entire length of its body. Earthworms can eat and poop their own body weight in a single day.

Humans and our planet

While there are nowhere near as many people as there are other types of animals, over thousands of years, humans have changed the balance of our living planet. But how did we spread all over the globe in the first place? Many scientists think that the first humans lived in Africa around 300,000 years ago. This is the story of how early humans then migrated, or spread out, to live and settle in other parts of the world—and how our population rapidly expanded.

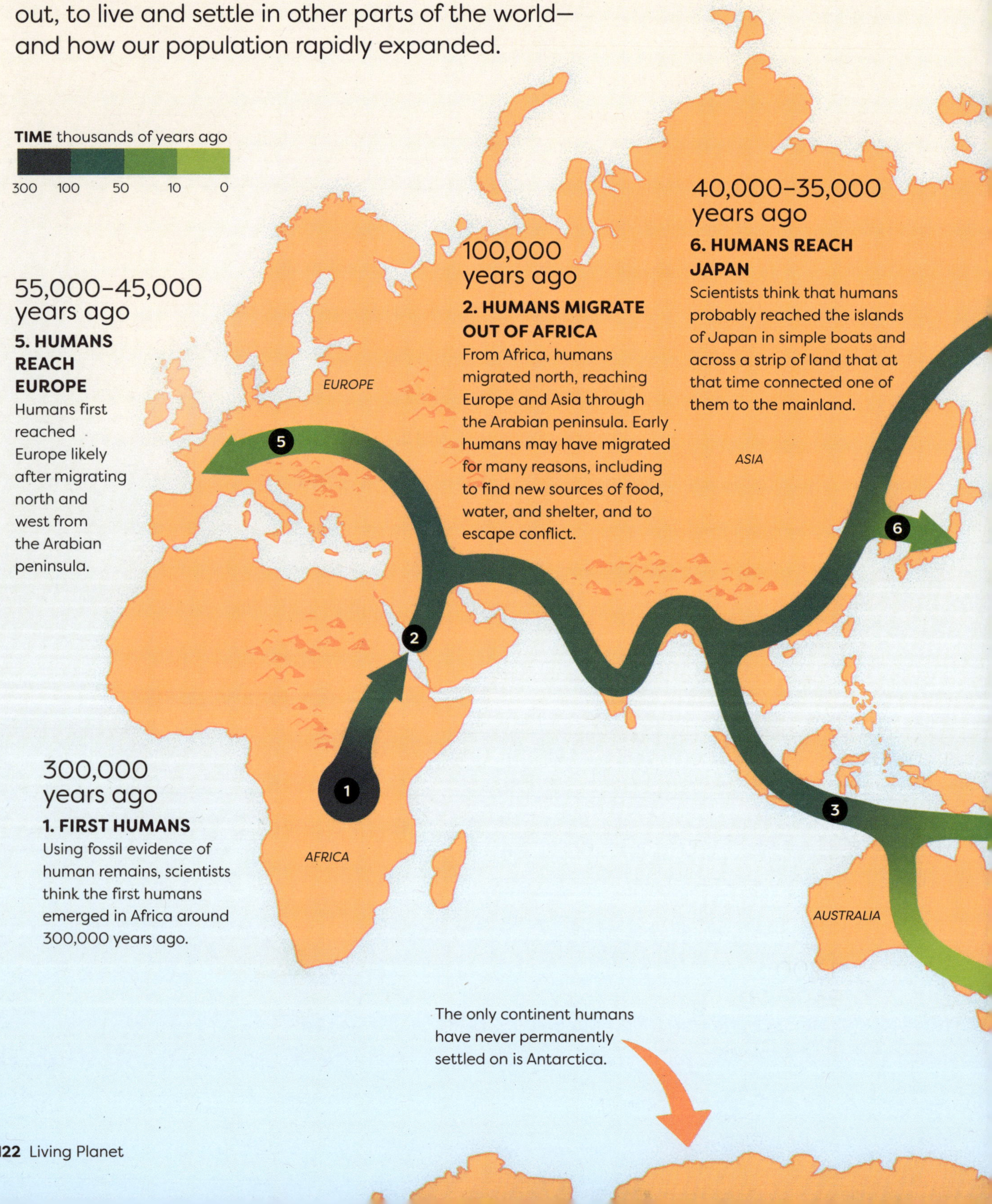

300,000
years ago

1. FIRST HUMANS

Using fossil evidence of human remains, scientists think the first humans emerged in Africa around 300,000 years ago.

100,000
years ago

2. HUMANS MIGRATE OUT OF AFRICA

From Africa, humans migrated north, reaching Europe and Asia through the Arabian peninsula. Early humans may have migrated for many reasons, including to find new sources of food, water, and shelter, and to escape conflict.

55,000–45,000
years ago

5. HUMANS REACH EUROPE

Humans first reached Europe likely after migrating north and west from the Arabian peninsula.

40,000–35,000
years ago

6. HUMANS REACH JAPAN

Scientists think that humans probably reached the islands of Japan in simple boats and across a strip of land that at that time connected one of them to the mainland.

The only continent humans have never permanently settled on is Antarctica.

HOW MANY PEOPLE ARE THERE NOW?

It took hundreds of thousands of years for the total number of human beings on Earth to reach 1 billion. This is estimated to have happened in 1804. It then took just 123 years for the total number of human beings to reach 2 billion, in 1927. During the 20th century, this rapid growth of the global population continued to accelerate. Today, there are about 8 billion people living on our planet.

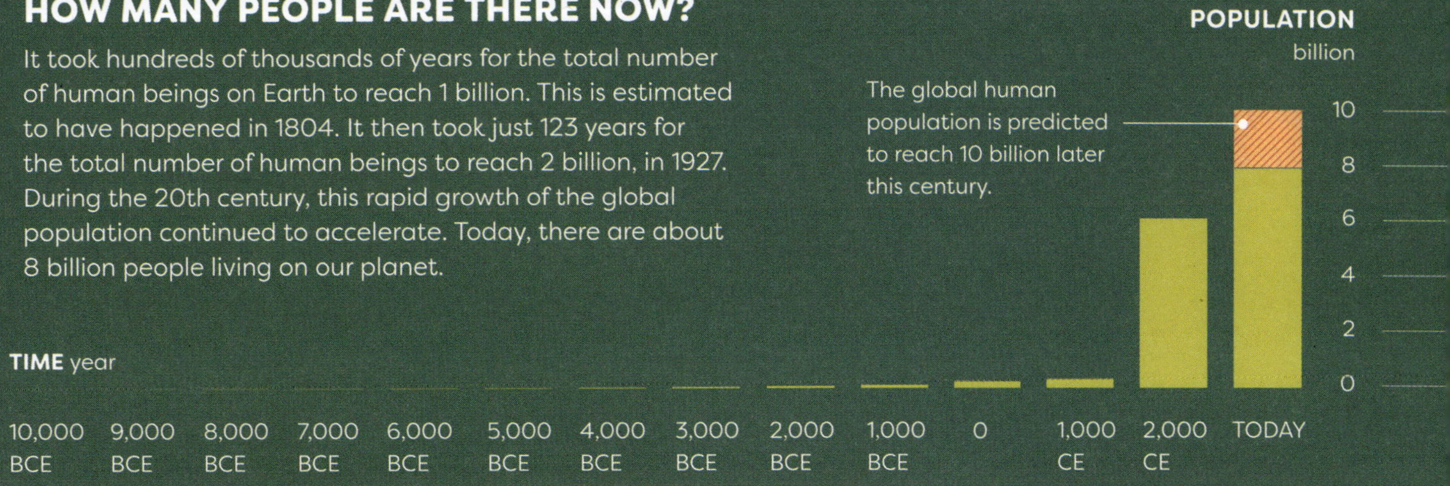

60,000–20,000 years ago

4. HUMANS TRAVEL INTO NORTH AMERICA

From Asia, groups of humans migrated to North America in several waves. Some may have crossed the icy seas in boats. And from 38,000 years ago, there was a strip of land between Asia and North America, which may have allowed humans to walk from one continent to the other. This strip of land is now covered by the Bering Sea.

16,000–8,000 years ago

7. HUMANS MIGRATE TO SOUTH AMERICA

Humans gradually migrated south through Central and then South America.

70,000–50,000 years ago

3. HUMANS REACH SOUTHEAST ASIA AND AUSTRALIA

Some prehistoric peoples set out from Asia in boats, reaching Australia about 50,000 years ago and, eventually, all the large islands of the Pacific Ocean.

1,200 years ago

8. HUMANS REACH NEW ZEALAND

The islands of New Zealand were among the last major places to be settled by humans, around 1,200 years ago.

Where do humans live now?

About 8 billion people live on planet Earth—the spikes on this map show where you can find them. The taller the spike, the more people live in that location. You might be surprised to see how empty parts of North America, Africa, and Russia are compared to India and China. You can also see that lots of people live near the coast, which is why you can still spot the familiar outlines of many countries and continents on the map.

This map, created by Alasdair Rae, shows the global human population in 2020.

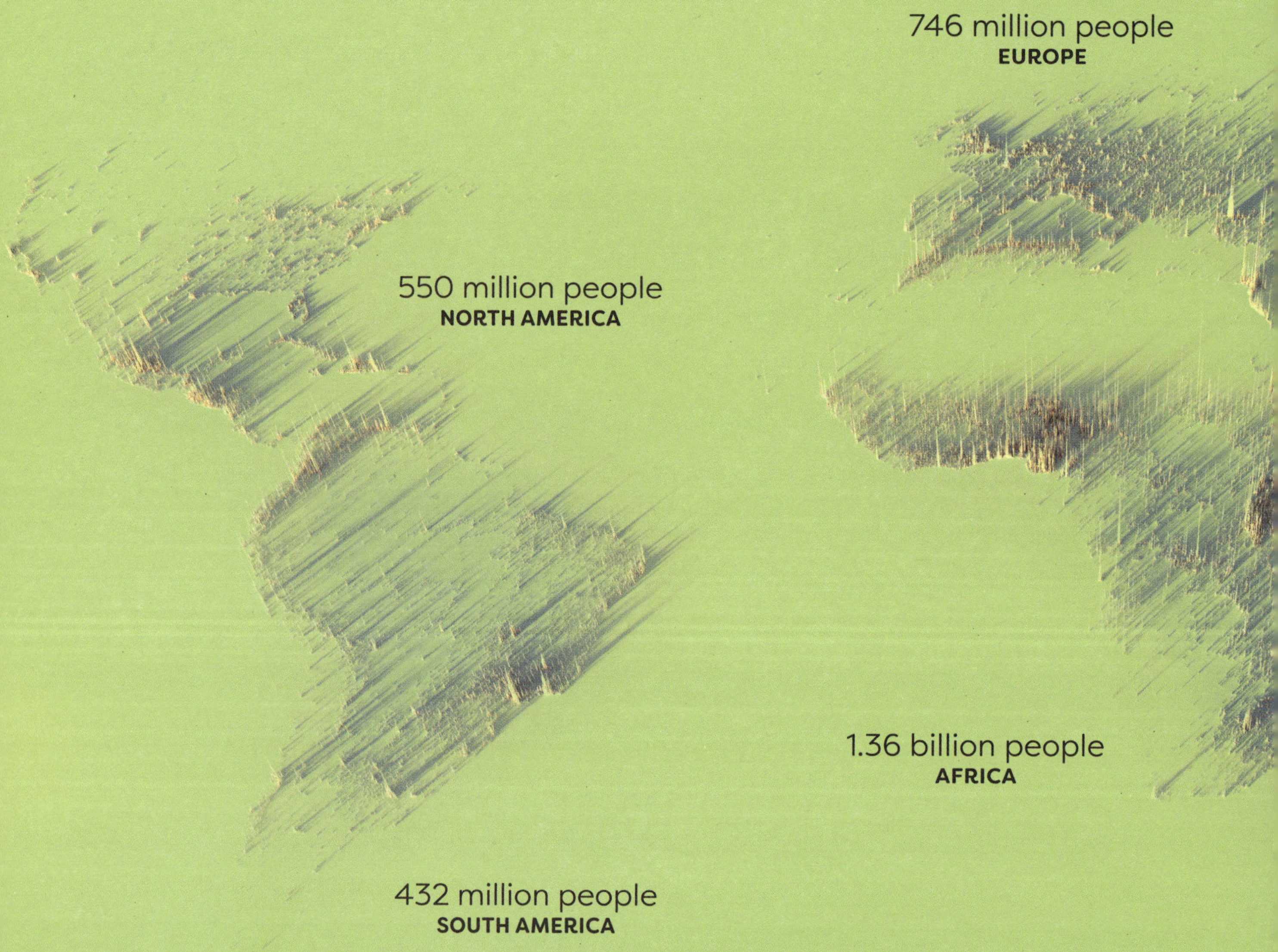

IF THE WORLD WERE EIGHT PEOPLE

Another way to think about such large numbers is to reduce them to a few units. Imagine if the world's population was only eight people, rather than eight *billion* people. The Americas would be inhabited by one person and so would Africa and Europe. The remaining five inhabit Asia and Oceania.

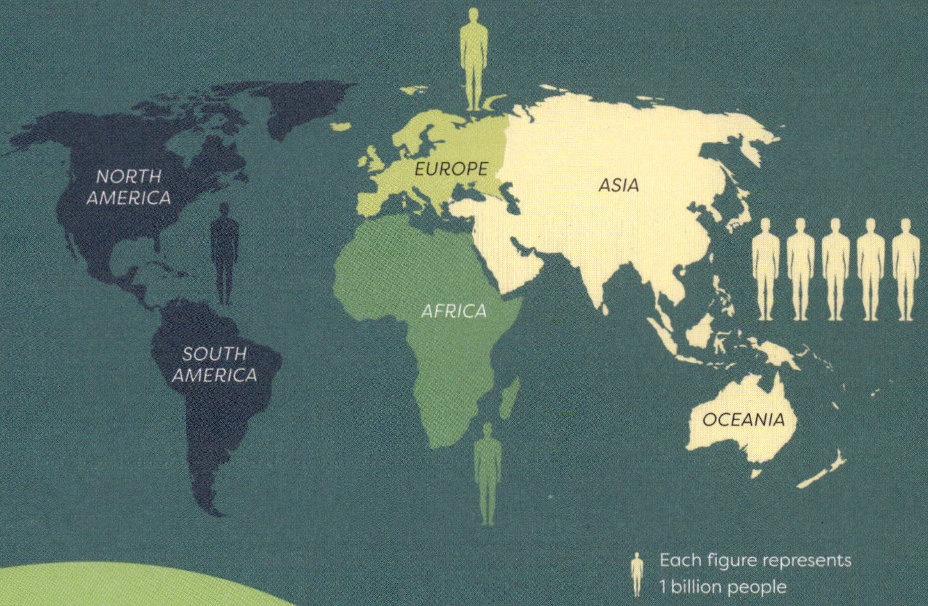

Use the map above to help you detect the outlines of the continents on the population infographic below.

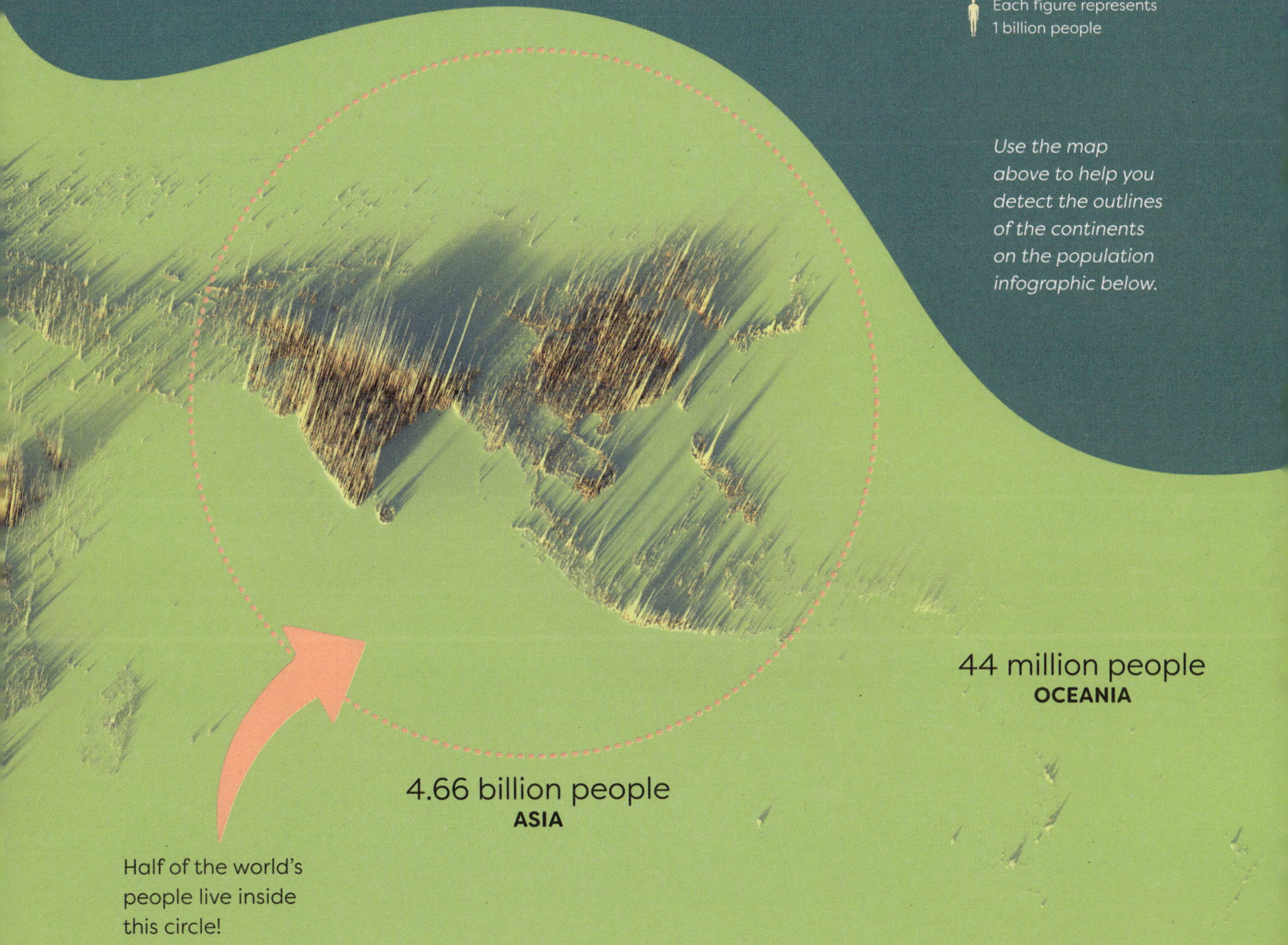

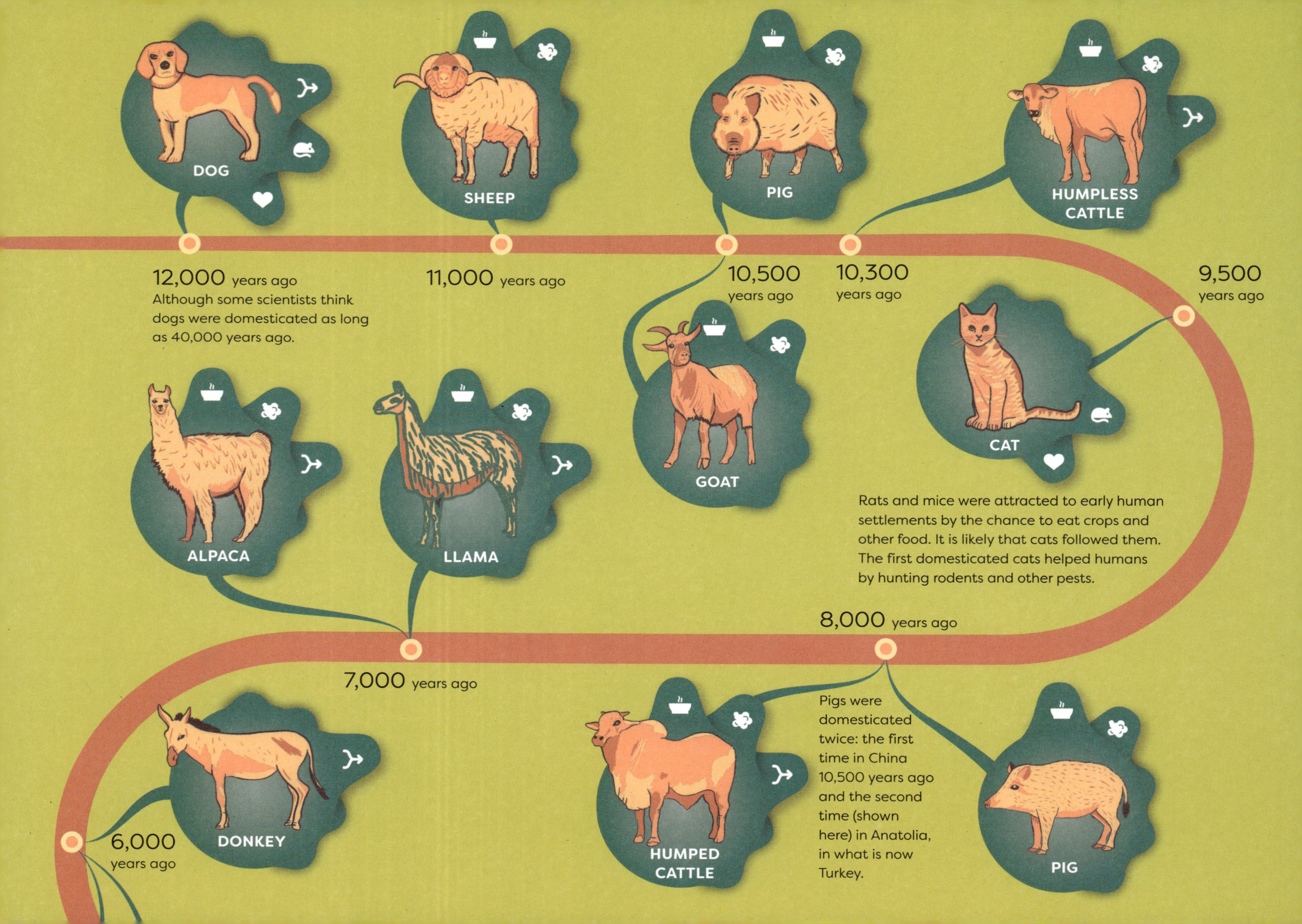
DOG
SHEEP
PIG
HUMPLESS CATTLE
12,000 years ago
Although some scientists think dogs were domesticated as long as 40,000 years ago.
11,000 years ago
10,500 years ago
10,300 years ago
9,500 years ago
CAT
GOAT
ALPACA
LLAMA
Rats and mice were attracted to early human settlements by the chance to eat crops and other food. It is likely that cats followed them. The first domesticated cats helped humans by hunting rodents and other pests.
8,000 years ago
7,000 years ago
Pigs were domesticated twice: the first time in China 10,500 years ago and the second time (shown here) in Anatolia, in what is now Turkey.
DONKEY
HUMPED CATTLE
PIG
6,000 years ago

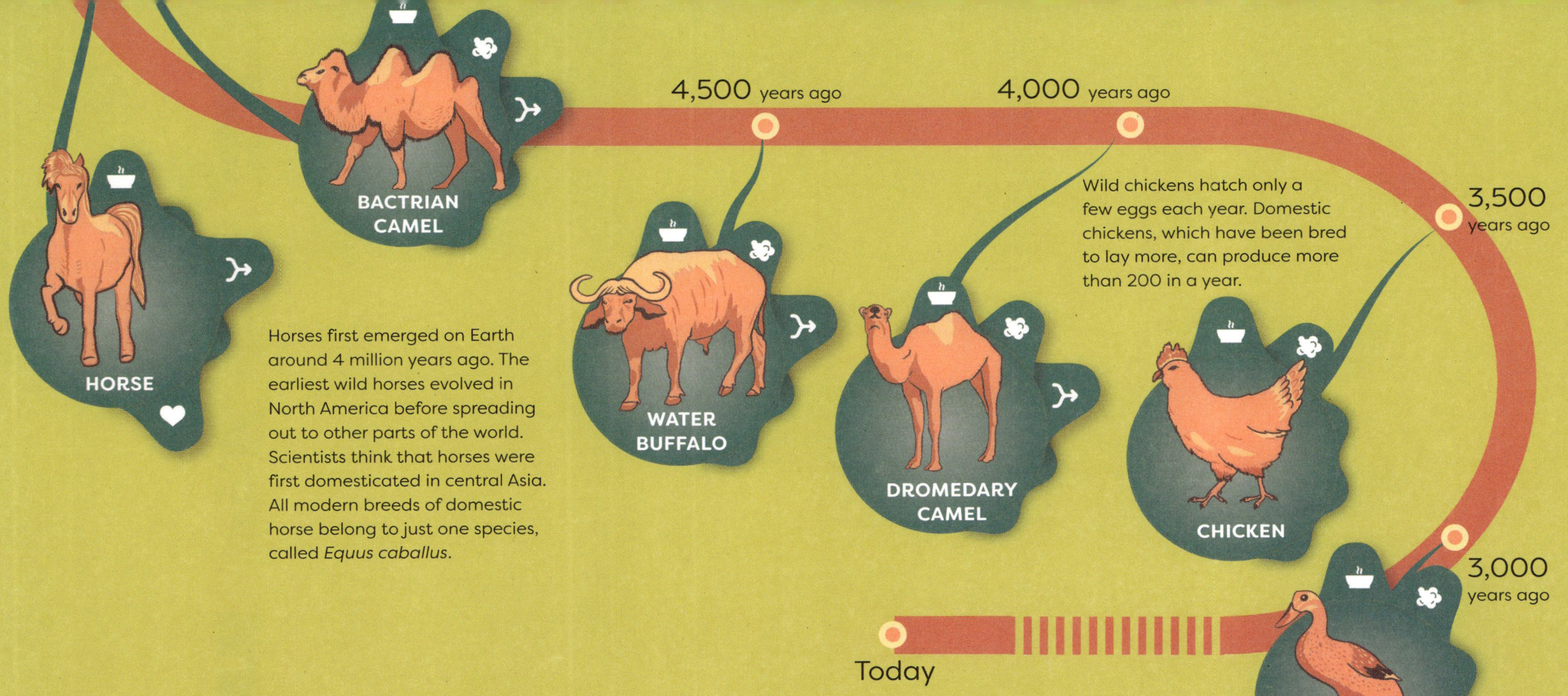

Friends with animals?

The human race's progress on Earth is owed in part to the animals that we have used to help us throughout history. These domesticated animals carry us, pull machinery, and help to cultivate fields. They provide food and clothing. As pets they offer companionship. As you can see in the timeline above, this human harnessing of nature goes back at least 12,000 years.

HOW TO READ IT

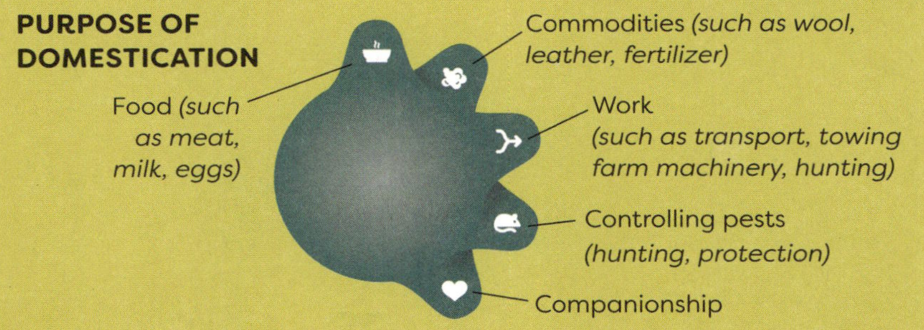

The rise of the chicken

As the human population has grown to about 8 billion people, the number of farm animals has risen, too. There are around 40 billion farm animals living on our planet today—about five for every human. Domesticated mammals such as cows and sheep now vastly outnumber wild mammals, demonstrating the profound impact of human activity on the balance of life on the planet.

COUNTING CHICKENS

The average American eats 23 chickens each year (as well as a third of a pig and a tenth of a cow). Many chickens are bred to grow larger and more quickly than they naturally would, so that they produce more meat for humans to eat.

HOW TO READ IT

The chart shows the increased global number of farm animals over the last six decades. Among all groups, **poultry** (made up of chickens, ducks, and turkeys) had the most growth—with a population eight times bigger now than in the 1960s.

2020 population:

- Horses, **60 million animals**
- Pigs, **1 billion**
- Cattle and buffalo, **1.7 billion**
- Sheep and goats, **2.4 billion**
- Poultry, **34.7 billion**

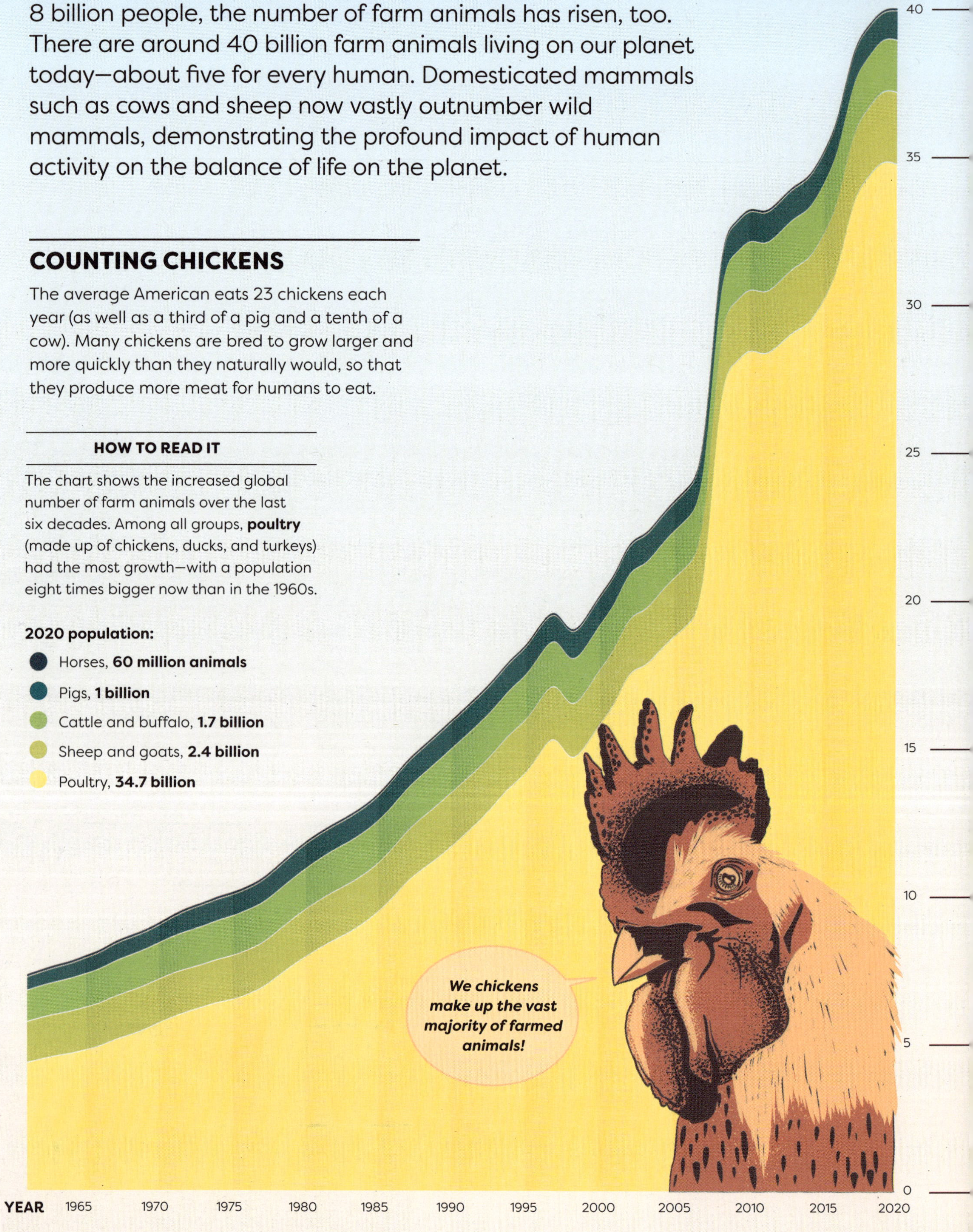

EATING MEAT

As the human population grows, so does the demand for meat, especially in richer and more developed countries. This infographic shows approximately how much meat is produced on farms around the world in a single year. Larger farm animals, such as cows, produce more meat per animal than smaller animals, such as chickens.

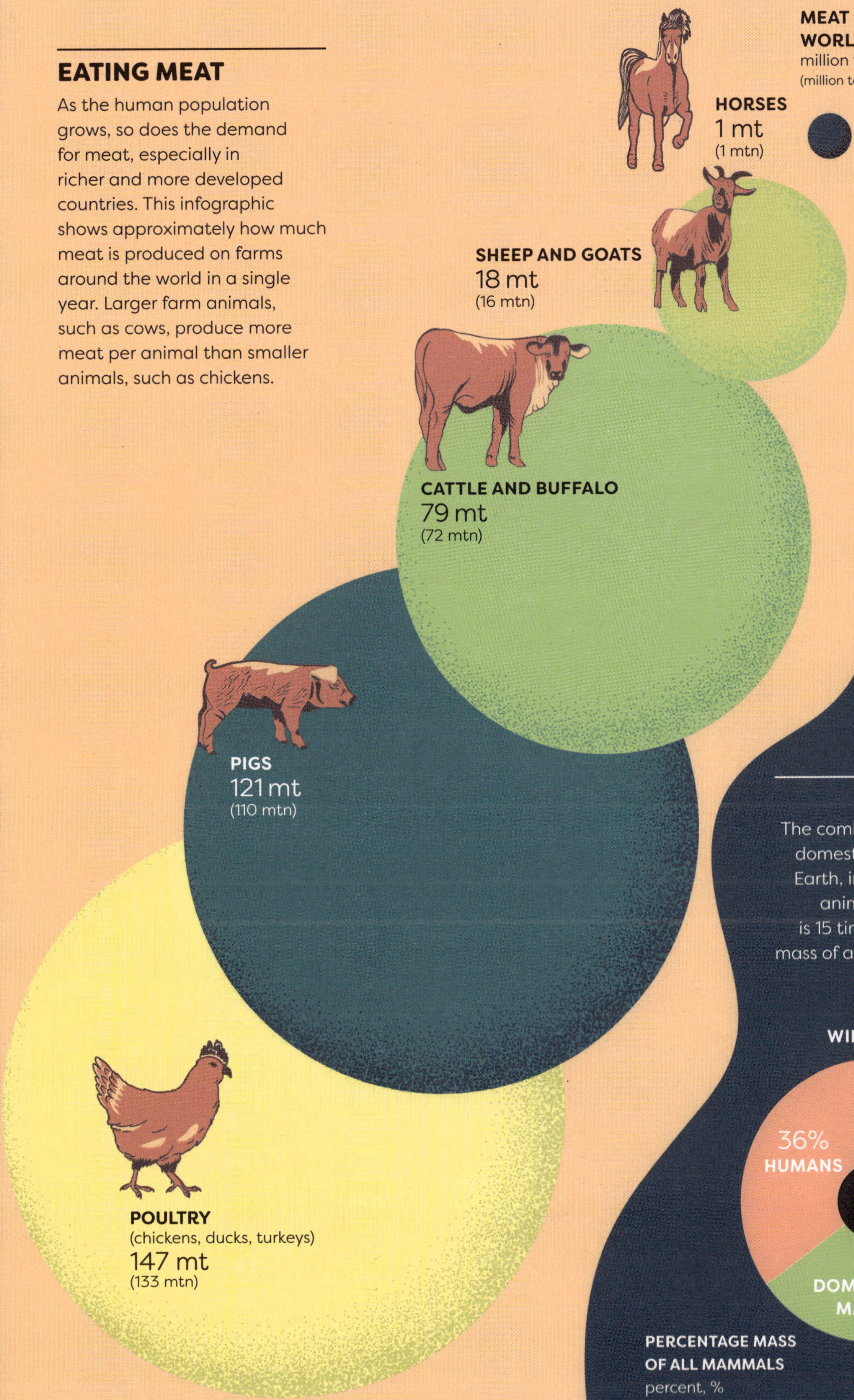

WEIGHING IN

The combined mass of all the domesticated mammals on Earth, including all the farm animals and all the pets, is 15 times greater than the mass of all the wild mammals.

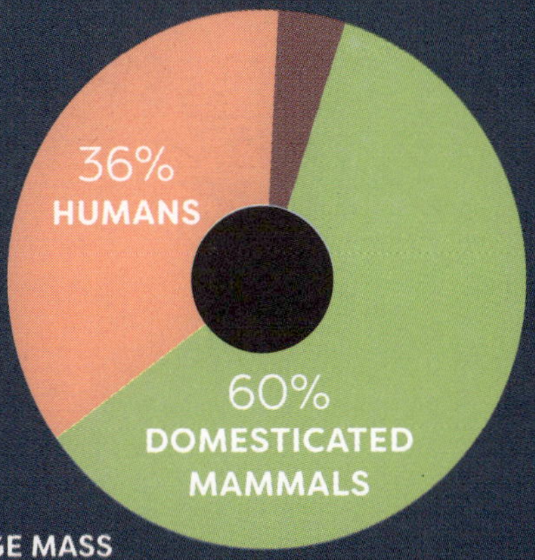

Scientists often divide rainforests into four layers: the emergent layer, the canopy, the understory, and the forest floor. Each layer is different because of the differing amounts of light and water found there. Here are some of the animals you might find living in a rainforest.

Life in the rainforests

Home to an incredible diversity of life, rainforests are among Earth's most extraordinary and important habitats. In fact, more than half of all plant and animal species live in rainforests, even though rainforests cover just 6 percent of the planet's land surface.

Did you know that the Amazon rainforest contains around 10% of all known species—including me, the boa constrictor?

RAINFOREST LOSS

The maps below show two of the world's largest rainforests. The light green area on Map 1 shows the rainforest on the island of Borneo in Asia. The light green area on Map 2 shows the Brazilian Amazon rainforest in South America. The patterned dark green areas on both maps show areas of deforestation, where the rainforest has already been cut down and cleared by humans.

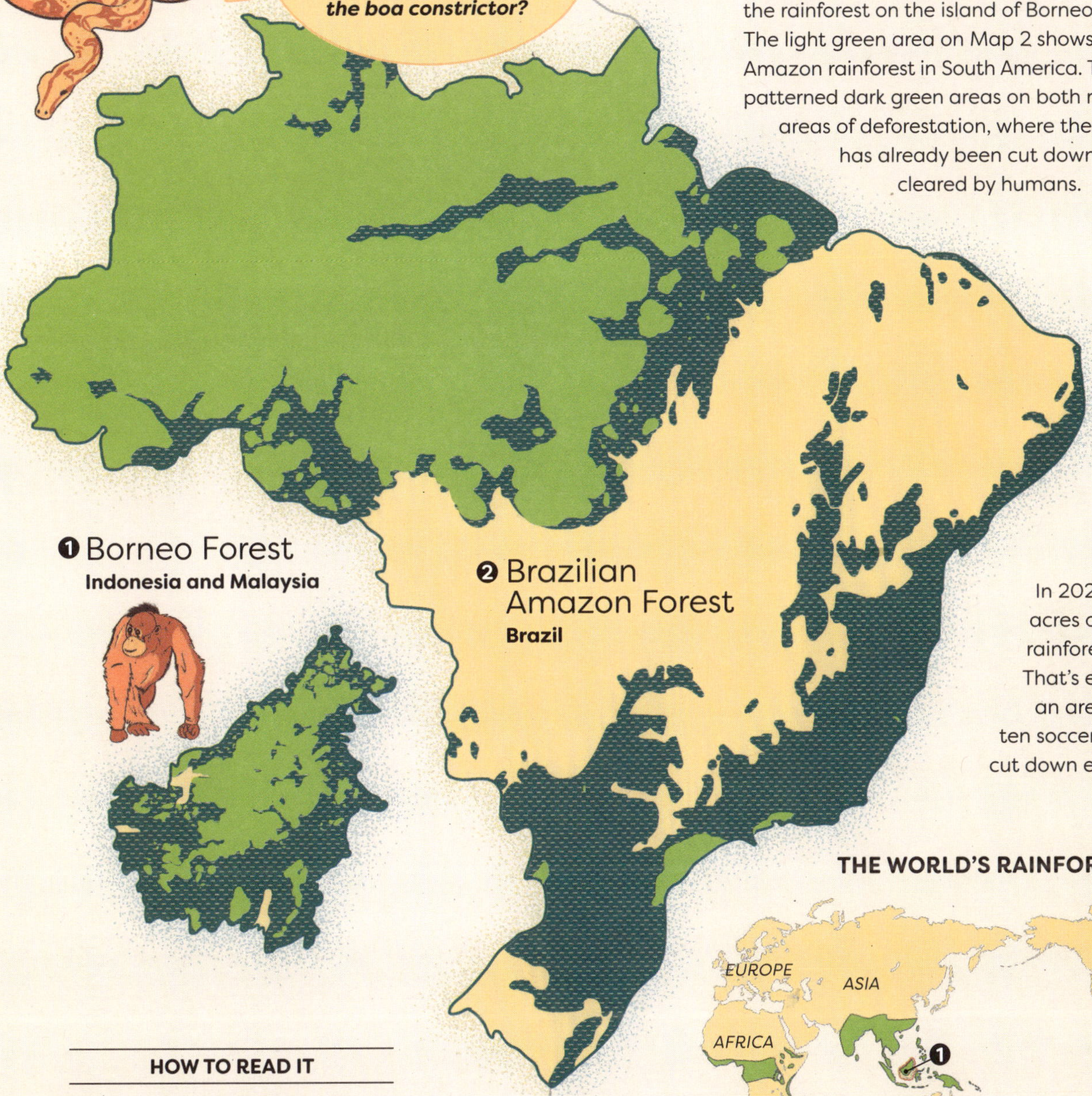

In 2021, 9.4 million acres of the world's rainforest were lost. That's equivalent to an area the size of ten soccer fields being cut down every minute.

THE WORLD'S RAINFORESTS

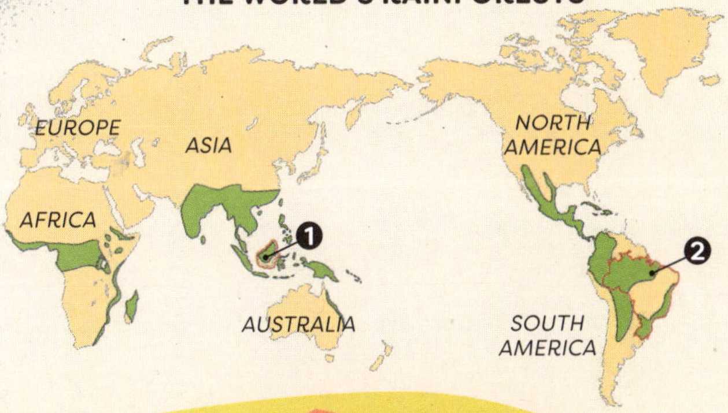

HOW TO READ IT

- Rainforest cut down by humans
- Rainforest that still exists today

SCALE **100 miles** (160 km)

WHY ARE ALL FORESTS UNDER THREAT?

Deforestation, the clearing or cutting down of forests by humans, is causing terrible damage around the world. The chart on the right shows the three main reasons for deforestation and the proportion (as a percentage) of forest lost for each reason. The cutting down of forests is especially damaging to our planet because of the diversity of life they contain and because plants help to combat climate change by absorbing harmful carbon dioxide from the atmosphere through photosynthesis.

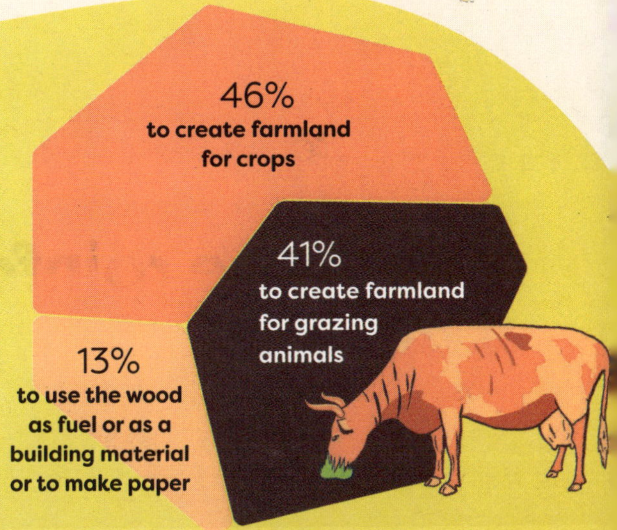

Energy sources

For hundreds of years, humans have been burning fossil fuels, such as petroleum, coal, and natural gas, to generate heat and electricity. However, we need to stop relying on these fuels—not only because one day they will run out, but also because burning fossil fuels pollutes the atmosphere with harmful emissions and heats up the planet, causing climate change. The good news is that solar panels, wind farms, and other renewable energy sources can make electricity without harming the atmosphere.

COAL
44,473 TWh
A crumbly black rock that we can burn to make electricity.

PETROLEUM
51,170 TWh
Petroleum is a liquid that is found deep underground. It is used for heating and is refined into gasoline, which powers cars, planes, and other vehicles.

Non-renewable energy sources

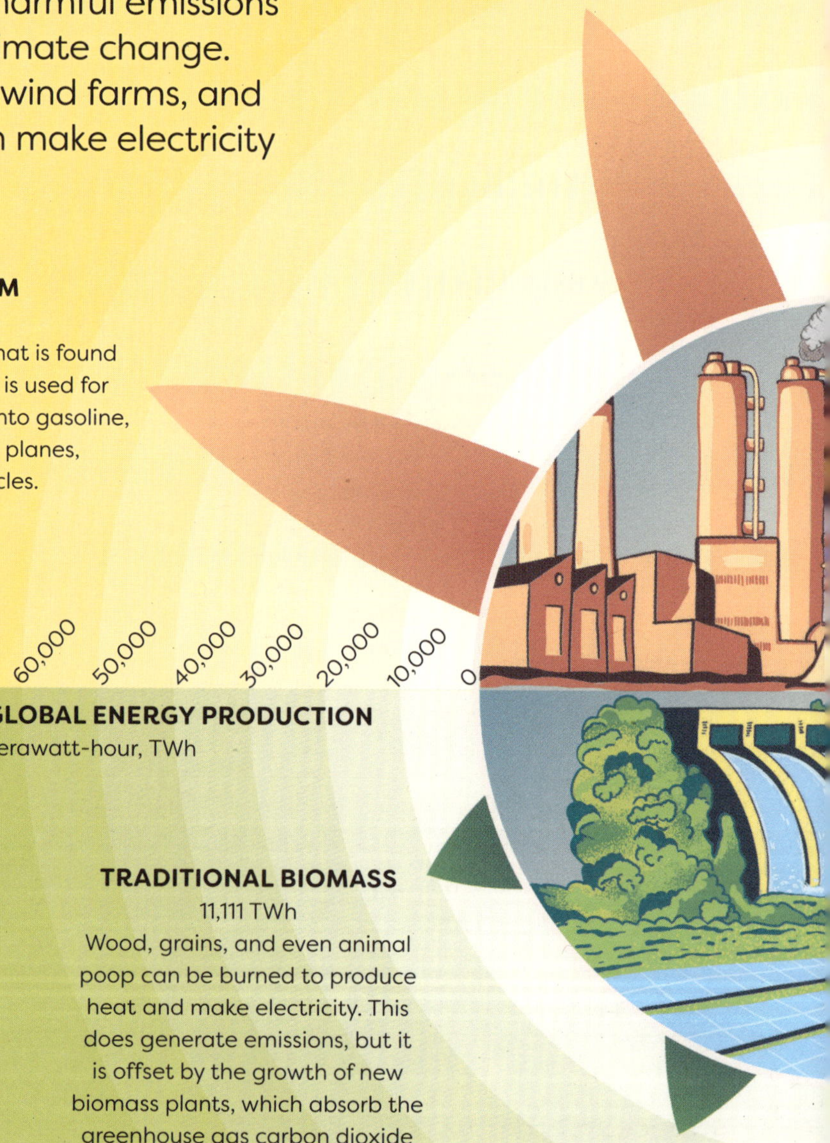

Renewable energy sources

GLOBAL ENERGY PRODUCTION
Terawatt-hour, TWh

TRADITIONAL BIOMASS
11,111 TWh
Wood, grains, and even animal poop can be burned to produce heat and make electricity. This does generate emissions, but it is offset by the growth of new biomass plants, which absorb the greenhouse gas carbon dioxide from the atmosphere.

HYDROPOWER
11,183 TWh
By damming rivers and capturing energy from ocean waves and tides, we can generate electricity from the natural movement of water.

NET-ZERO EMISSIONS

A growing number of countries are promising to achieve net-zero emissions in order to preserve our living planet from the worst effects of climate change. The phrase "net-zero emissions" means that action that reduces the amount of harmful emissions in the atmosphere exactly balances out the harmful emissions created by human activity.

NATURAL GAS
40,375 TWh
A fuel that we get from under the ground and that we can burn for heat and to make electricity.

NUCLEAR
7,031 TWh
Radioactive elements in fuel (such as uranium) release energy in the form of heat, which we can use to make electricity. (Nuclear energy does not give off harmful emissions, but it is powered by non-renewable fuel, which is why it is counted as non-renewable. Nuclear waste is also given off as a hazardous by-product of the process.)

WIND
4,872 TWh
By putting up big windmills, we can capture energy from the wind.

SOLAR POWER
2,702 TWh
Solar panels can capture energy directly from sunlight.

FUTURE FUELS

In order to reach "net-zero" emissions, we will need to generate a decreasing proportion of our energy from fossil fuels—and to generate an increasing proportion of our energy using solar, wind, and water power instead.

SHARE OF ELECTRICITY GENERATION
percent, %

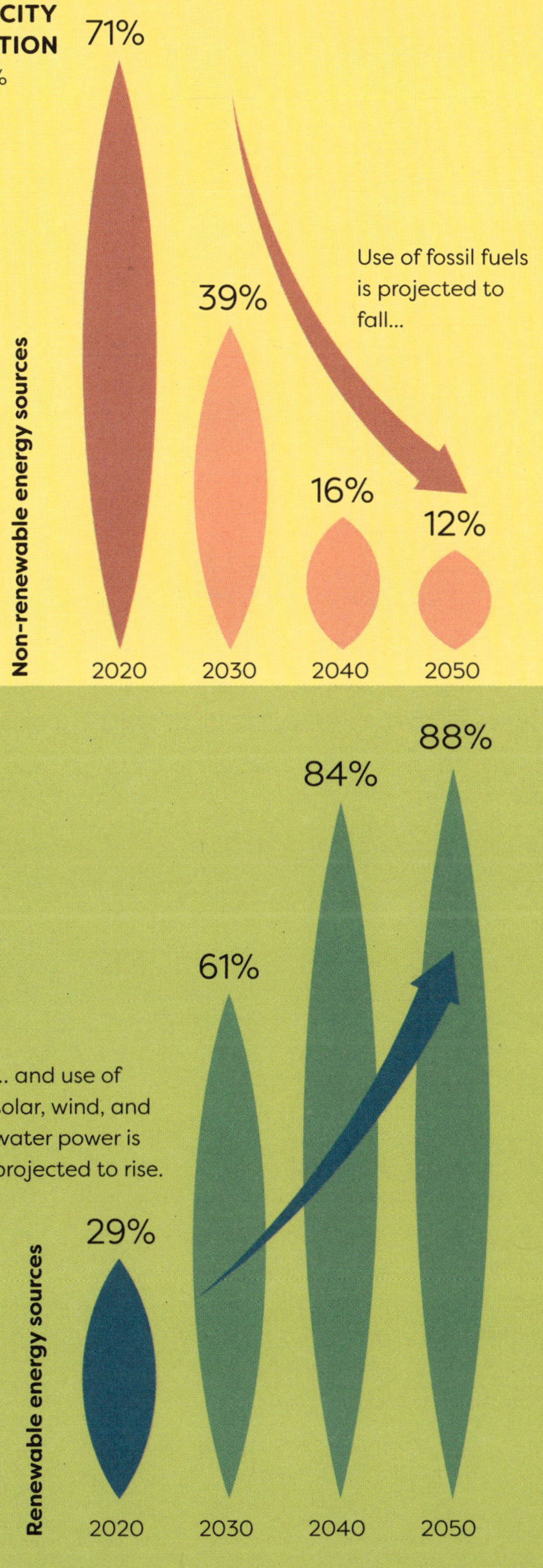

1860
1890
1920

Changing temperatures on Earth

This famous infographic by Professor Ed Hawkins shows the change in Earth's temperature beginning in 1850. Each stripe represents the temperature for an individual year, relative to Earth's average temperature between 1971 and 2000. Shades of blue represent cooler-than-average years, and shades of red represent warmer-than-average years. The noticeable shift to red stripes in the last two decades highlights the recent and worrying increase in Earth's average temperatures.

Shrinking ice

The Arctic is the fastest-warming region of our planet. Temperatures are rising nearly four times as fast there as they are in the rest of the world. Each summer, the Arctic ice cap melts to what scientists call its "minimum" size before colder weather freezes the ocean, making the ice cap bigger again. This map shows how much smaller the Arctic ice cap's minimum size is today than it was 40 years ago (shown by the red outline on the map).

It might not be long until there is no ice at the North Pole during the summer. Scientists think this might happen as soon as 2030.

SHRINKING ARCTIC ICE

The globes along the top show the minimum size of the Arctic ice cap since 1979. The white graph beneath charts the total area covered by the Arctic ice cap over the same period of time.

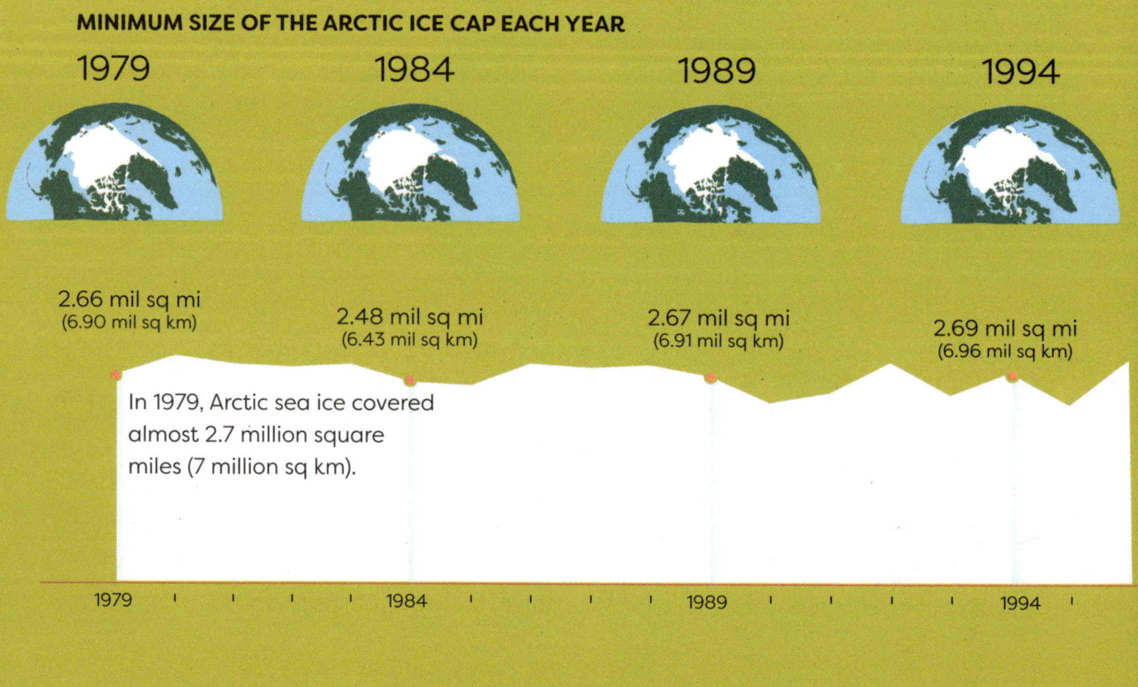

Earth has two ice caps: one at the North Pole called the Arctic ice cap, and one at the South Pole called the Antarctic ice sheet.

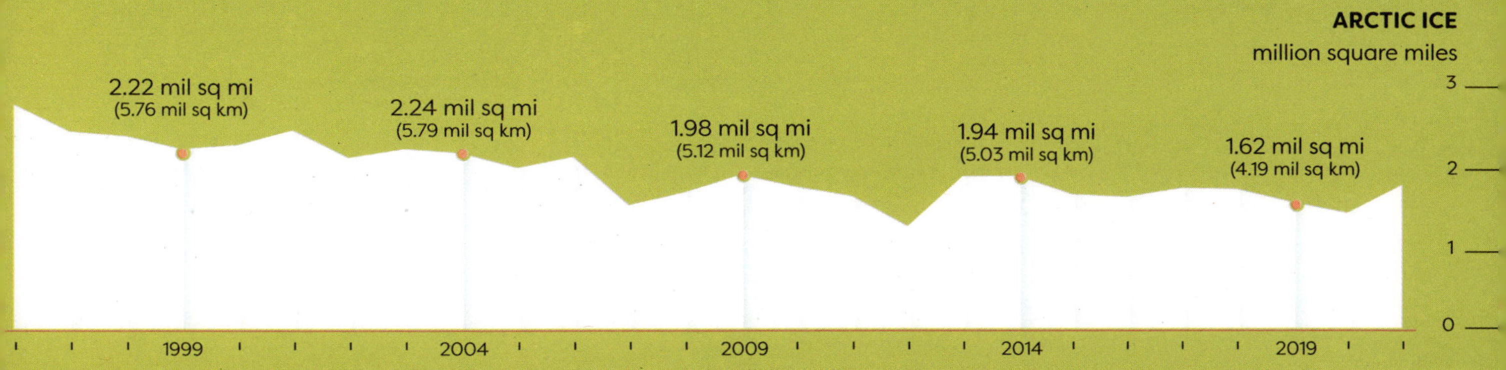

Animals in danger

Because of climate change and human activities, more than 25,000 species are now at risk of extinction. We call these species endangered. Thankfully, conservation programs are helping the populations of some endangered species to recover.

ENDANGERED SPECIES

This infographic shows estimated populations of a variety of wild animals, and whether their numbers are decreasing or increasing. The smaller the animal in the picture, the fewer are left. Scientists consider several factors when assigning the risk status of a species, including the number of animals, population loss over generations, and habitat loss.

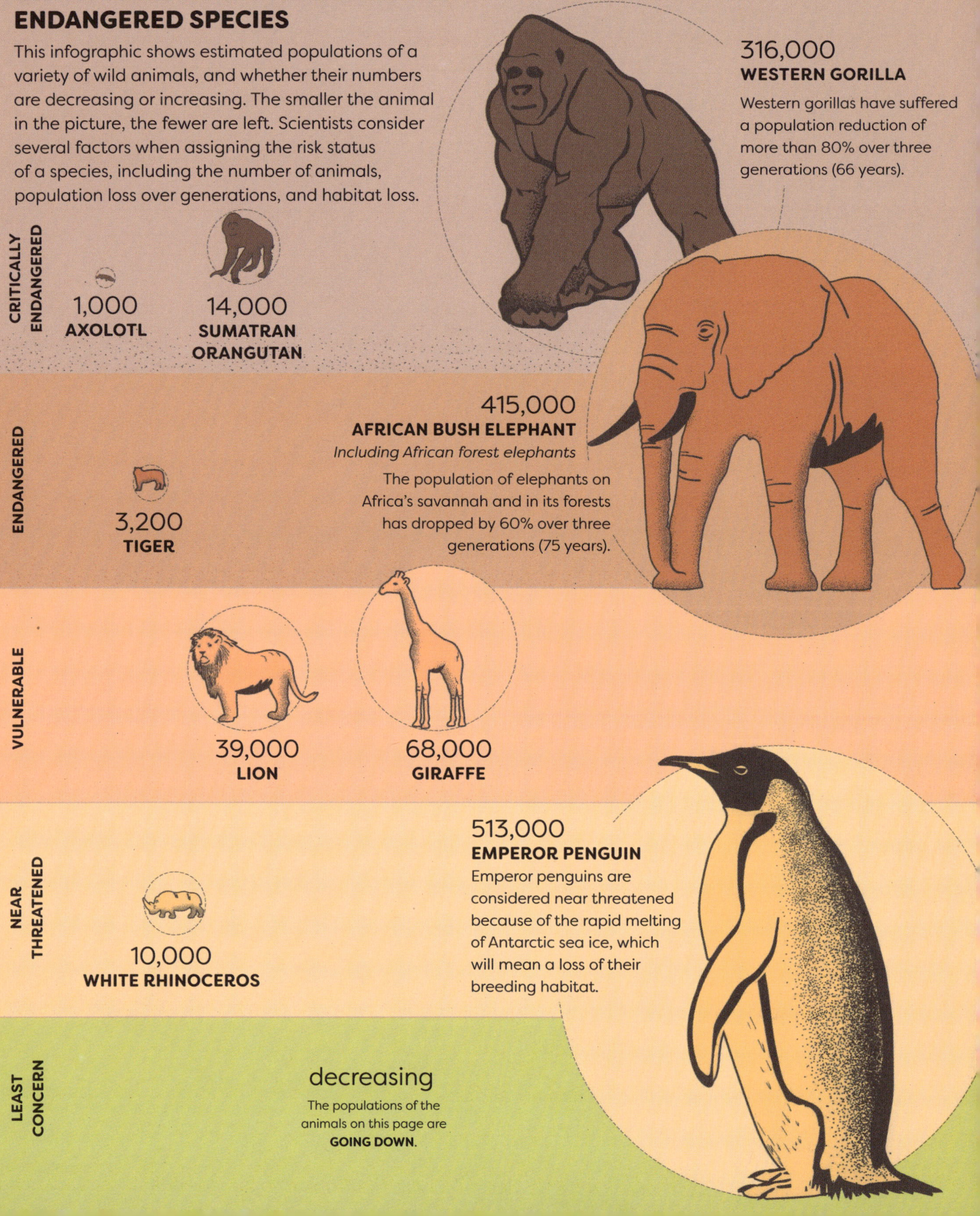

CREATURES AT RISK

This infographic shows the percentage of different categories of animals that are currently threatened by extinction. For example, 41 percent of all amphibians, such as frogs and toads, are now at risk of dying out. This is especially worrying because amphibians are indicator species. Indicator species are very sensitive to shifts in their environment, such as pollution, and so a drop in their numbers gives an early signal that ecosystems are being damaged.

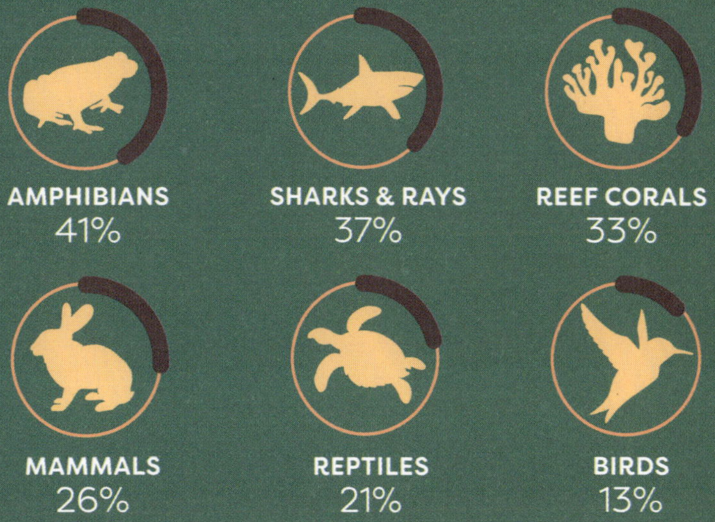

HOW TO READ IT

How endangered the animal is

- Critically endangered
- Endangered
- Vulnerable
- Near threatened
- Least concern

Is the population going up or down?

Decreasing | Increasing | Stable

Estimated animal population

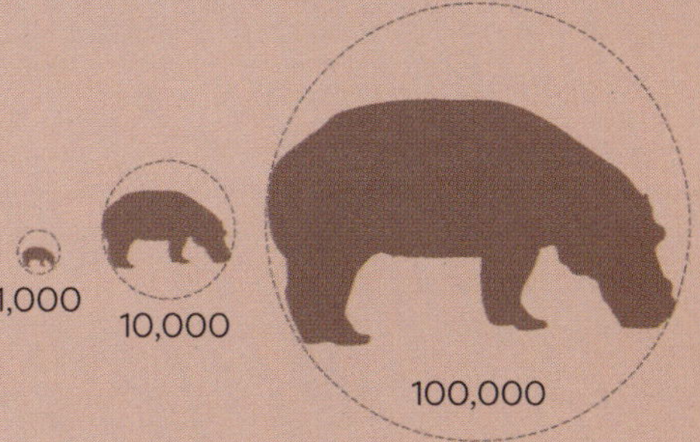

Figures have been rounded

You can see a picture of me on the next page.

443
GRAND CAYMAN BLUE IGUANA

1,000
GIANT PANDA

1,000
YELLOW-EARED PARROT

130,000
HIPPOPOTAMUS

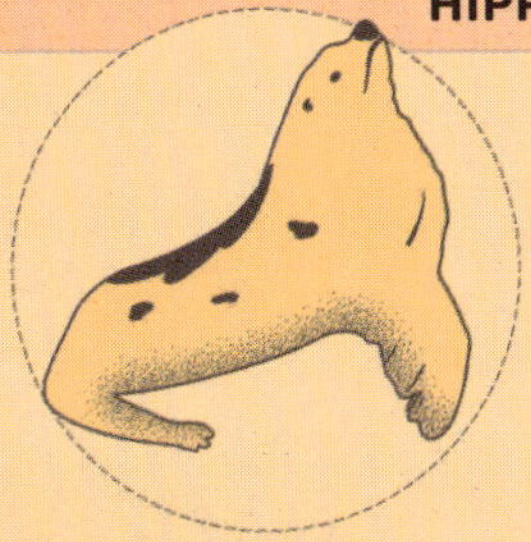

81,000
STELLER SEA LION

1,200,000
EURASIAN BEAVER

At the start of the 20th century, there were only about 1,200 beavers left. Thanks to conservation efforts, there are now around 1.2 million.

increasing

The populations of the animals on this page are stable or **GOING UP**.

Conservation in action

The Grand Cayman blue iguana is an example of the positive power of conservation. Although this magnificent species of iguana is still endangered, its population has recovered from just 10 to 25 animals in the early 2000s to 443 individuals today—all thanks to vital conservation work.

MEET THE EXPERT CONSULTANT

Dr. Christopher Fernandez

Ecologist

WHEN DID YOU KNOW THAT YOU WANTED TO STUDY ECOLOGY?

I have always loved the outdoors, and California, where I grew up, has an incredible diversity of climate and plants. When I learned about the important relationship between plants and fungi and how they help each other access nutrients, I became hooked and decided to specialize in the science of mycorrhizal fungi.

WHAT IS YOUR FAVORITE FACT?

Plants use carbon from the atmosphere to make their own food. The thing that blows my mind is that plants give up to 20 percent of this carbon to the fungi that they are connected to, rather than using it all themselves. This is a great example of how all living things on Earth form part of a complex but connected system.

WHAT EXCITING DISCOVERY ARE YOU LOOKING FORWARD TO SEEING IN THE FUTURE?

I am excited to see developments in our ability to study tiny microbes, such as those in the soil, especially with techniques using DNA sequencing. When we know what these mysterious microbes are doing, it will really help us in our conservation efforts.

WHAT IS THE BEST THING ABOUT YOUR JOB?

The best thing is the fact that my research contributes to human knowledge of the natural world and I get to share this knowledge and my passion with the younger generation of scientists every day.

SCAVENGER HUNT!

Can you track down the answers to this quiz in the pages of this book? (Turn to page 305 to see if you are right!)

1. In which country is the world's tallest tree?

2. How far can seeds from this flower travel in the wind: 6 mi, 60 mi, or 600 mi?

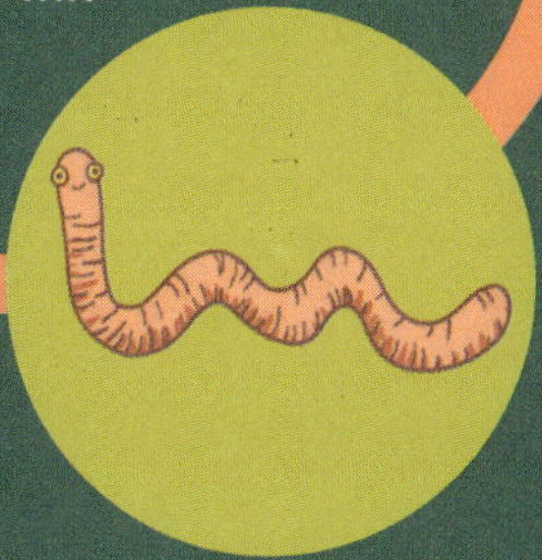

3. Which weighs more, all the humans on Earth or all the earthworms on Earth?

4. What is this animal?

5. At which of Earth's poles could you meet a polar bear?

6. What does the world's biggest flower smell like?

7. Is the number of beavers in the world going up or down?

8. On which page of this book can you find a boa constrictor?

ANIMALS

There are somewhere between 350,000 and 400,000 species of beetle. This means that one in four known animal species on Earth is a beetle!

How many species do we know about?

So far, scientists have identified and described more than one and a half million animal species. However, some scientists also estimate that there are about 8 million animal species in all. This means that there are millions of unidentified creatures living somewhere on Earth – just waiting for scientists to discover them!

8 million
ESTIMATED TOTAL ANIMAL SPECIES

Exactly how many animal species there are on Earth remains one of the mysteries of science. Eight million is one estimate, but other estimates are much bigger. One reason for the uncertainty may be that species are becoming extinct before scientists have even named them.

Fewer than 20% of all 8 million species have been named and described by scientists.

1.6 million
KNOWN ANIMAL SPECIES

almost 1.5 million
INVERTEBRATES

An invertebrate is any species of animal that does not have a backbone. Most animals on Earth are invertebrates and most invertebrate species (almost 70 per cent!) are insects.

almost 74,000
VERTEBRATES

A vertebrate is any animal that has a backbone. Mammals, including we humans, are vertebrates.

Tiny creatures

What is the smallest animal you've ever seen? However tiny, it was probably still a relative giant compared to the animals on these pages, which are among the smallest animals on Earth.

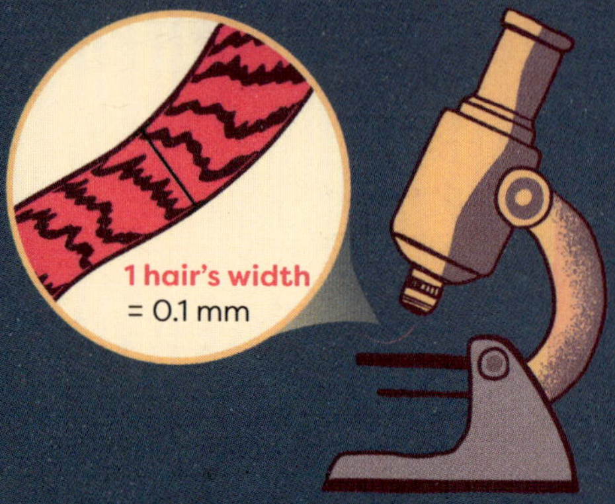

MICROSCOPIC ANIMALS

If these animals were drawn at actual size, you'd need a microscope to see them. So, instead, we have enlarged them 100 times.

SCALE **0.1 mm**
Animals shown enlarged 100 times

PARASITIC WASP

Dicopomorpha echmepterygis

0.14 mm
body length

This is the smallest known adult insect. The larvae feed inside the eggs of other insects.

just over 1 hair's width

SEA SNAIL

Ammonicera minortalis

0.3 mm
diameter

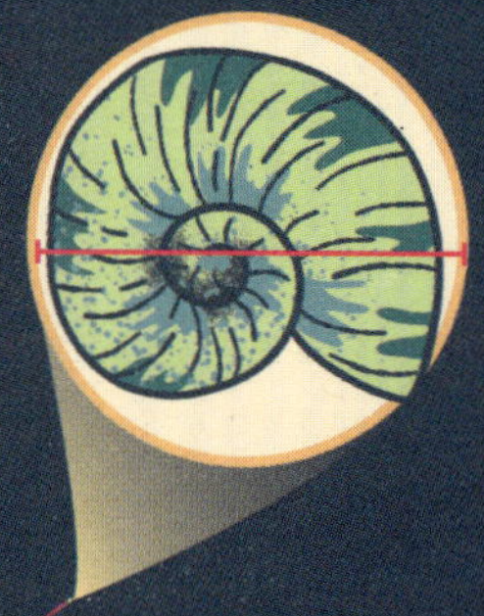

3 hairs' width

FRADE CAVE SPIDER

Anapistula ataecina

0.43 mm
body length

These tiny spiders have been found living in only a few caves in Portugal, and are the smallest spiders in Europe.

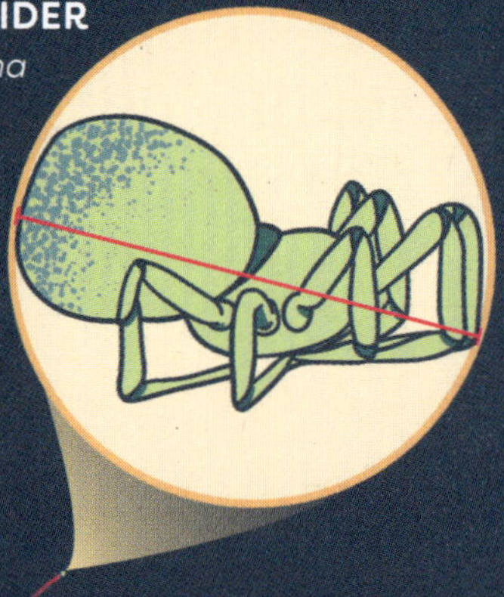

over 4 hairs' width

VIETNAMESE CAVE SNAIL

Angustopila psammion

0.6 mm
diameter

6 hairs' width

This is the smallest land snail in the world, found living in a single cave in Vietnam.

TARDIGRADE

Tardigrada

1 mm
body length

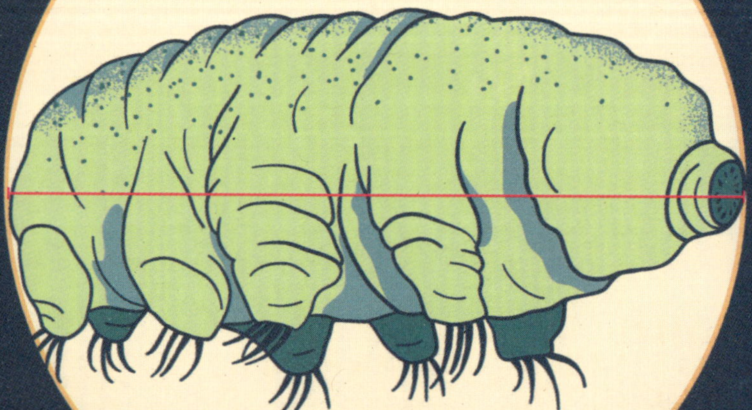

These microanimals can survive in many extreme environments, from deserts to deep-sea vents.

10 hairs' width

SMALLEST KNOWN...

Here is a selection of surprisingly small creatures that we don't need a microscope to see. They are shown here at their actual size.

SCALE **1 cm**
Animals shown at actual size

SMALLEST AMPHIBIAN
Frog
Paedophryne amauensis

0.8 cm
body length

This frog is so small that, to find it, scientists had to scoop up a bag of leaves and soil from the rainforest floor and then carefully inspect the contents to spot the tiny frog hopping inside!

SMALLEST FISH
Dwarf minnow
Paedocypris progenetica

0.8 cm
body length

SMALLEST BIRD
Bee hummingbird
Mellisuga helenae

5.5 cm
body length

SMALLEST REPTILE
Nano-chameleon
Brookesia nana

1.4 cm
body length
(not including tail)

SMALLEST LAND MAMMAL
Etruscan shrew
Suncus etruscus

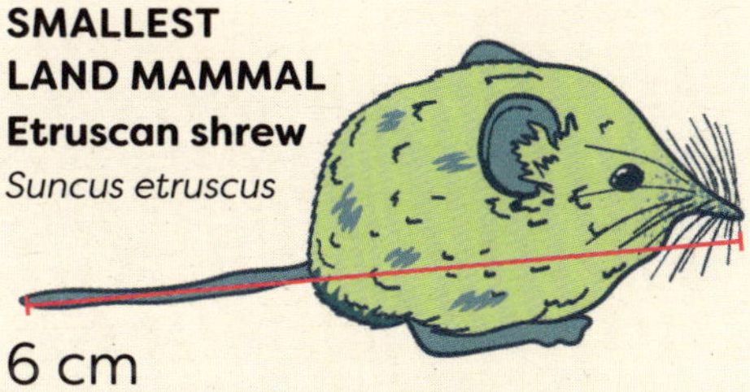

6 cm
body length (including tail)

SMALLEST SNAKE
Barbados threadsnake
Tetracheilostoma carlae

10 cm
length when extended

SMALLEST FLYING MAMMAL
Bumblebee bat
Craseonycteris thonglongyai

This miniature bat is found in only a few limestone caves in Thailand and Myanmar, and it weighs less than 2 grams.

Compare these animals to the size of a banana!

Biggest beasts of the land and sky

The heaviest land animal on Earth today is the elephant, and the tallest is the giraffe. But in prehistoric times even larger animals roamed the planet and soared in the sky. Over the next four pages, you can see how the giants of the animal kingdom – both those alive today and those long extinct – measure up.

HOW TO READ IT

The pink lines show the length, height or wingspan of the animal.

SCALE **1 m**

The pink circles show the weight of the animal.

WEIGHT
kilograms, kg 100 1,000 10,000

Animals that are alive today are coloured in greens, whites and blues. Animals that are extinct are in purples and browns, and highlighted with this symbol ⊗

Living species
Extinct species

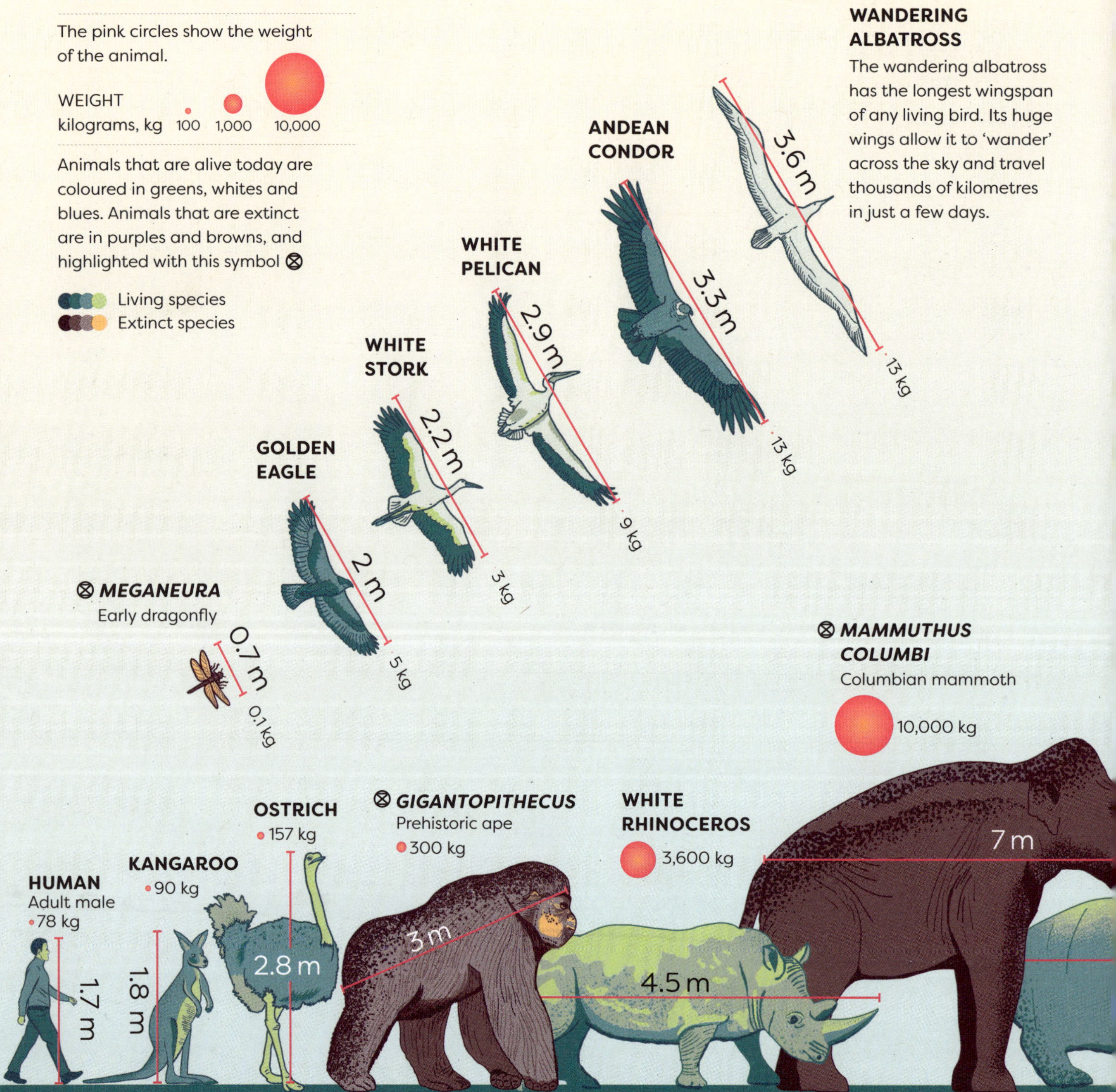

Turn the page

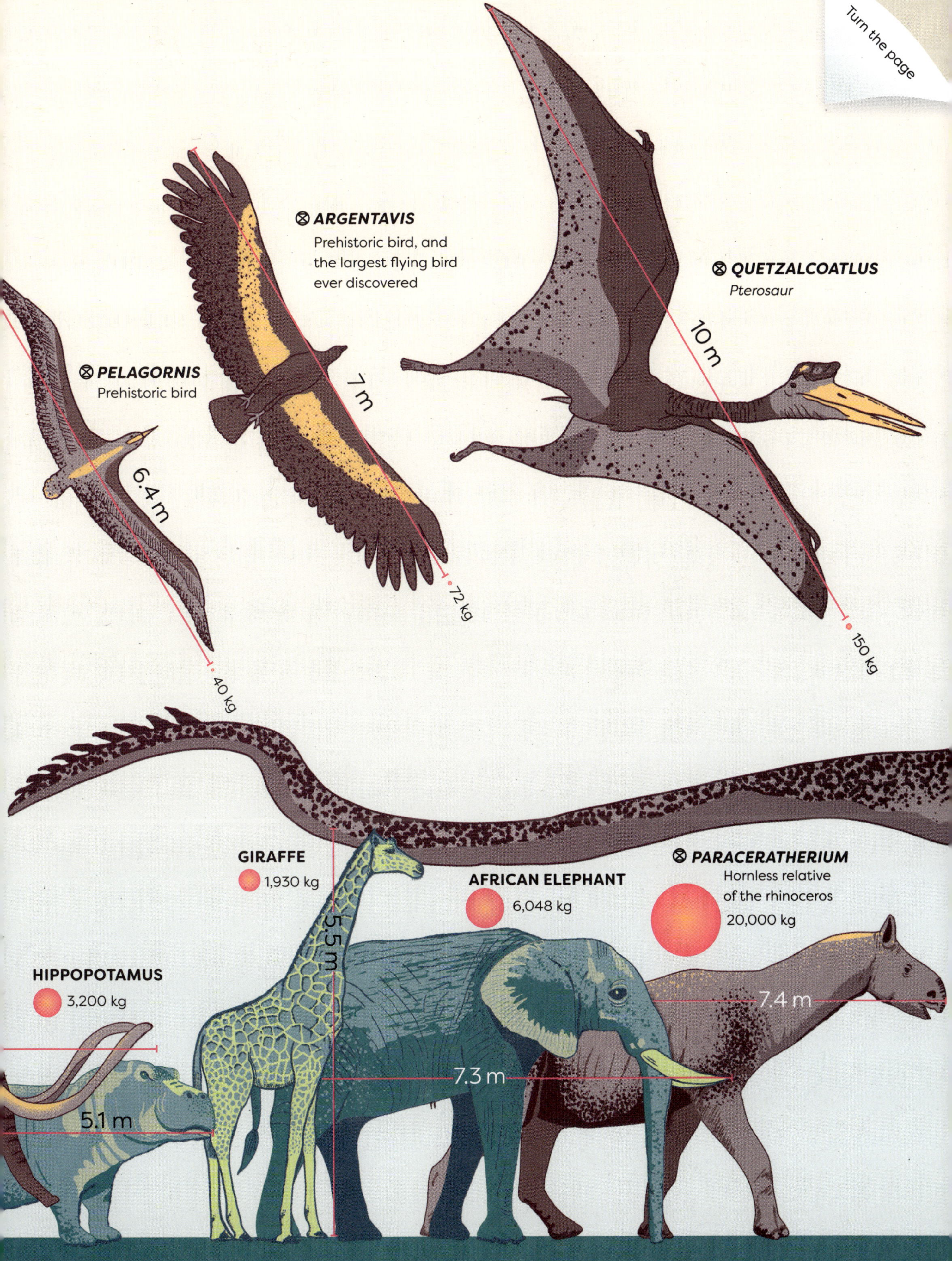

HATZEGOPTERYX
Pterosaur
250 kg
12 m
39.7 m
TYRANNOSAURUS REX
Theropod dinosaur
8,800 kg
13 m
TRICERATOPS
Ceratopsid dinosaur
7,100 kg
8.5 m
12 m
GREEN ANACONDA
227 kg

Where have we found fossils of dinosaurs? Turn to page 102 to find out.

WHEN DID THESE EXTINCT ANIMALS LIVE ON EARTH?

This chart shows the approximate timespan during which the extinct animals featured in this infographic were alive. The **pink lines** represent the number of millions of years each animal species lived on Earth.

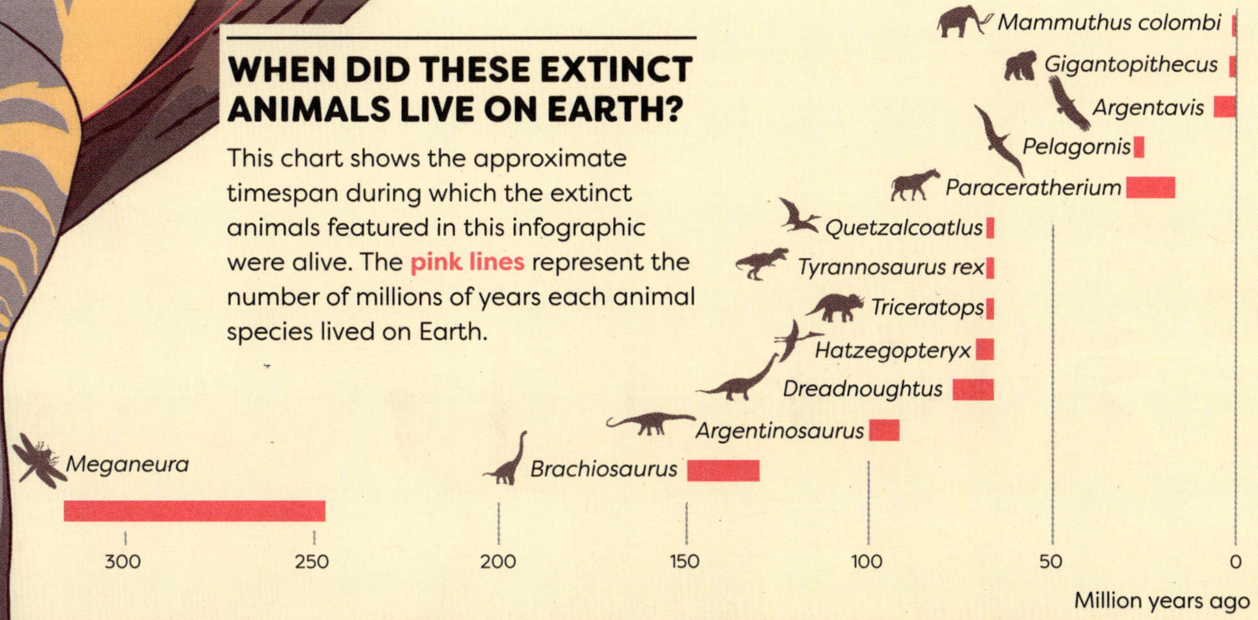

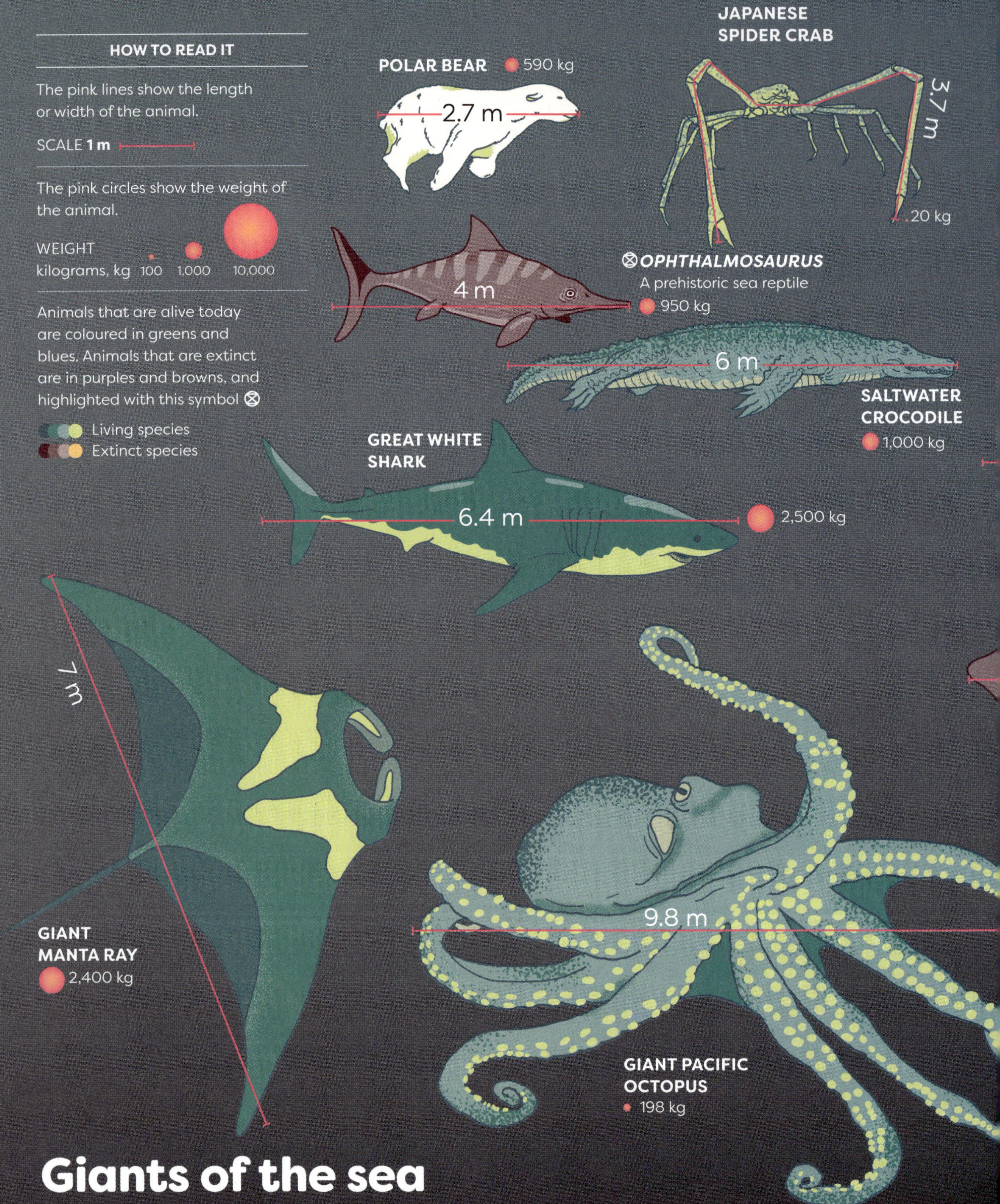

Giants of the sea

The sea is home to billions of organisms – some of them enormous! Here are some of the biggest underwater creatures, from the giant spider crab that lives off Japan's Pacific coast, to the biggest animal of them all, the blue whale (on the next page), whose heart alone is the size of a small car.

Turn the page

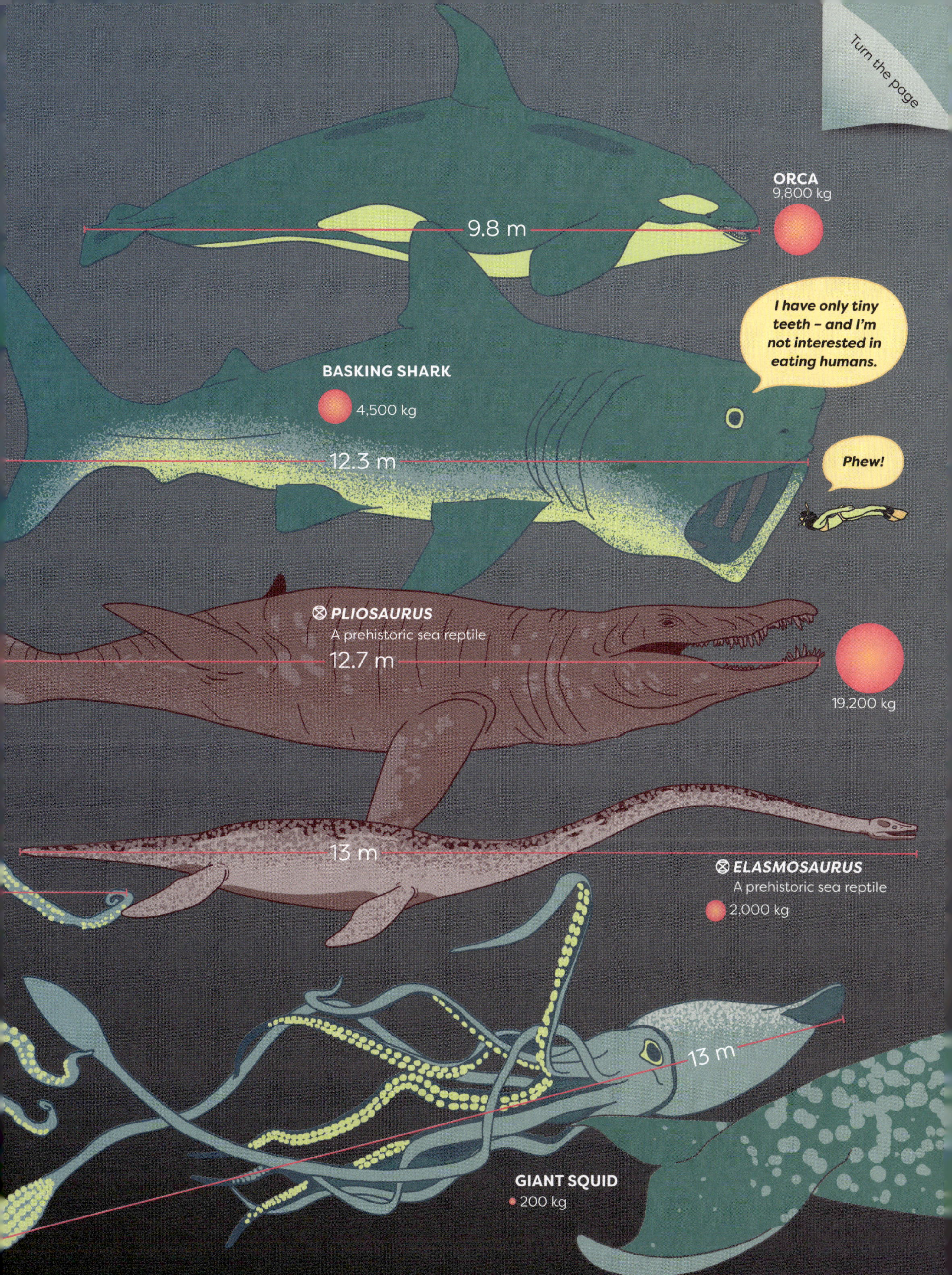

18.8 m
21 m
24 m
25 m
33 m

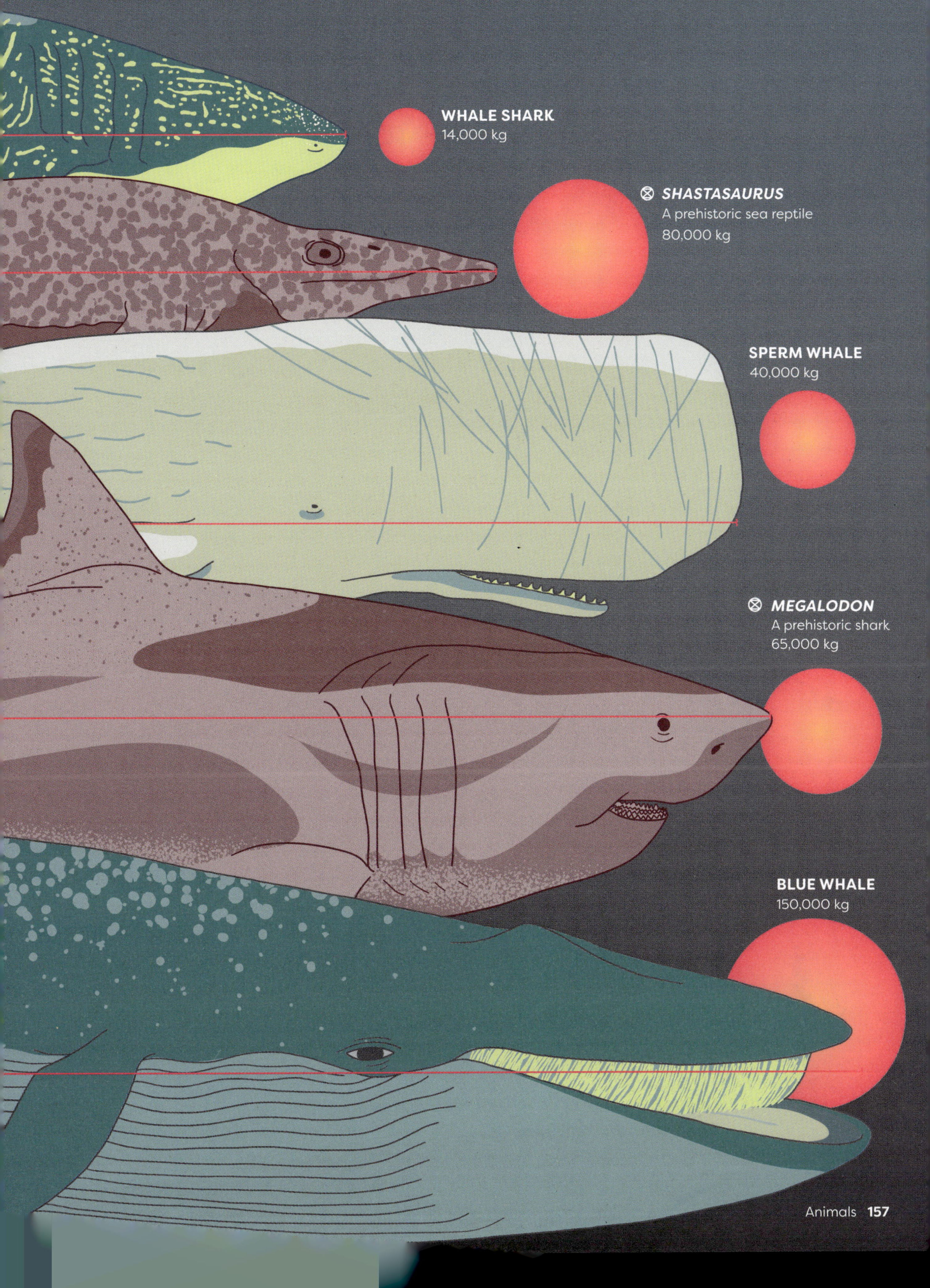
WHALE SHARK
14,000 kg
SHASTASAURUS
A prehistoric sea reptile
80,000 kg
SPERM WHALE
40,000 kg
MEGALODON
A prehistoric shark
65,000 kg
BLUE WHALE
150,000 kg

Most carnivores have carnassial, or shearing, teeth that are good for slicing and tearing meat, and cutting tough sinews.

What's for dinner?

Animals can be divided into three categories depending on what they eat. Animals that eat only meat (from other animals) are called carnivores. They include tigers, sharks and birds of prey. Animals that eat only plants and algae are called herbivores. They include elephants, tortoises and butterflies. And animals that eat a combination of both meat and plants are called omnivores. Omnivorous animals include bears, monkeys, squirrels, pigs and humans.

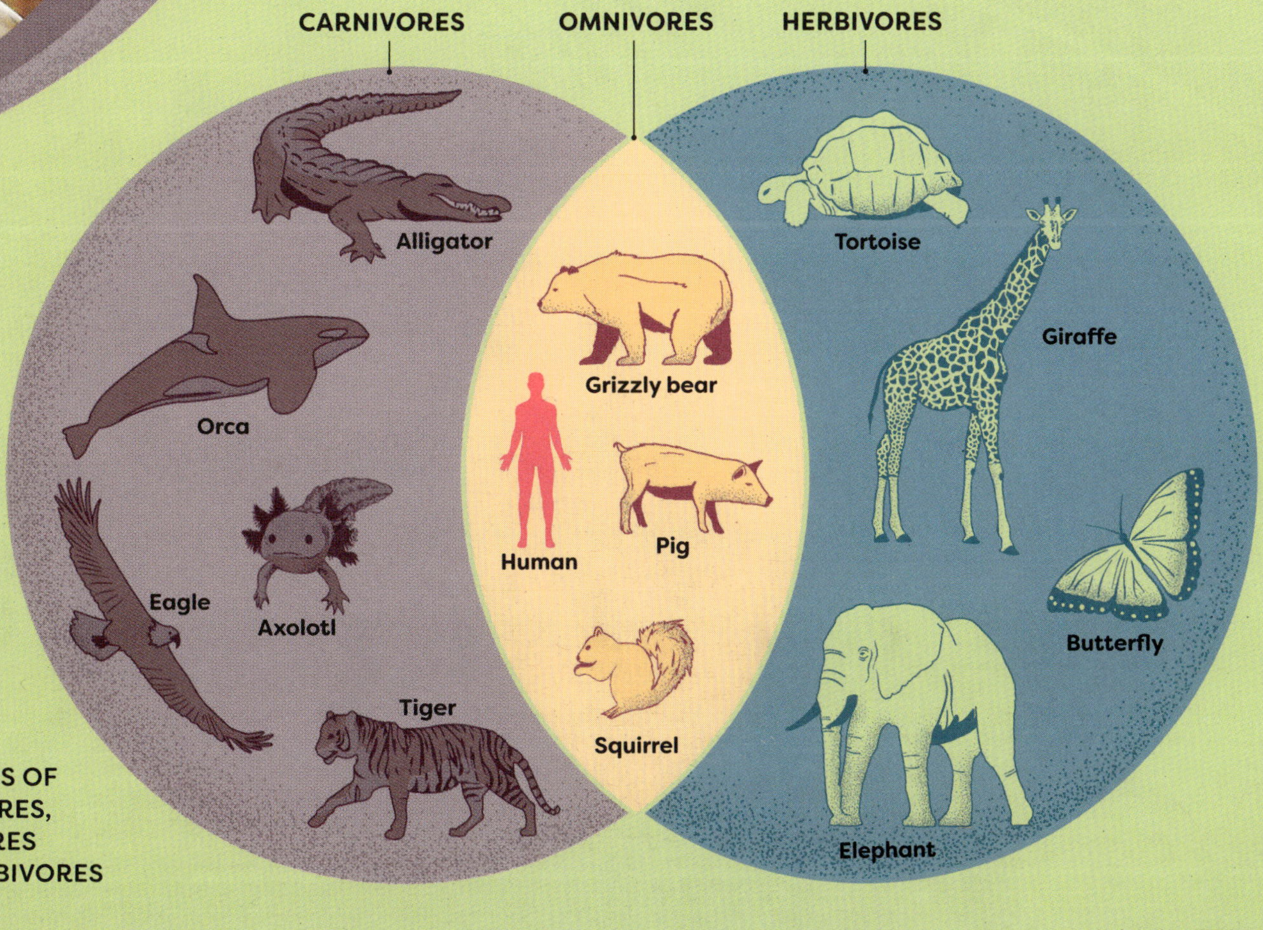

EXAMPLES OF CARNIVORES, OMNIVORES AND HERBIVORES

What goes in... must come out!

All animals eat to absorb the proteins, carbohydrates, fats and vitamins in food. But not everything in food is useful, which is why we poo – to get rid of waste. Bigger animals need to eat more food than smaller animals because they usually need more energy and nutrients to survive. As a result, they also do bigger poos!

THE LAW OF POO

Most mammals, from cats to elephants, take an average of 12 seconds to do a poo, despite excreting very different sizes, shapes and amounts.

HOW TO READ IT

The yellow pile on the left represents how much each animal **eats** in an average day, and the pink pile on the right represents how much it **poos**.

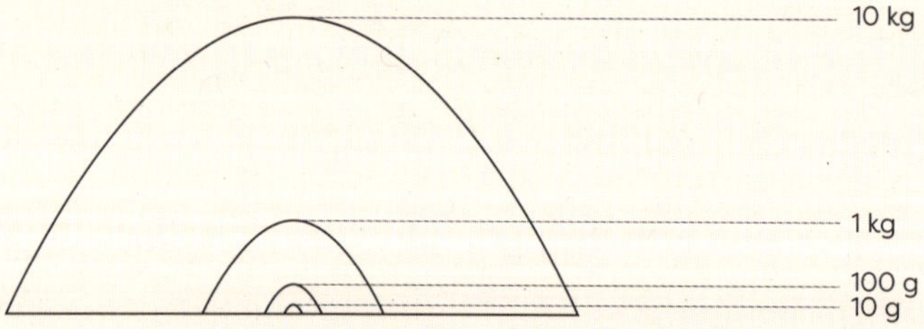

THE WORLD'S LARGEST POO!

The blue whale is the world's largest animal, and its poo is the biggest, too. Scientists who have had the pleasure of seeing blue whale poo say it smells a bit like dog poo, and has the consistency of breadcrumbs.

A blue whale eats more than **3,600 kg** of krill per day.

Animals with a very high-fibre diet, such as rabbits, pandas and elephants, cannot easily digest a lot of their food, and much of it comes out with other waste in their poo!

The blue whale can excrete **200 litres** of poo in one go. Its poos are so big they can be seen from an aeroplane.

Tongues and tails

Would you like to have a curly tail like a monkey? Or a giant tongue like an anteater? Lots of animals rely on their tongues and tails to do important jobs, such as catching prey or for keeping balance. Here are some of the largest and longest tongues and tails in the animal kingdom.

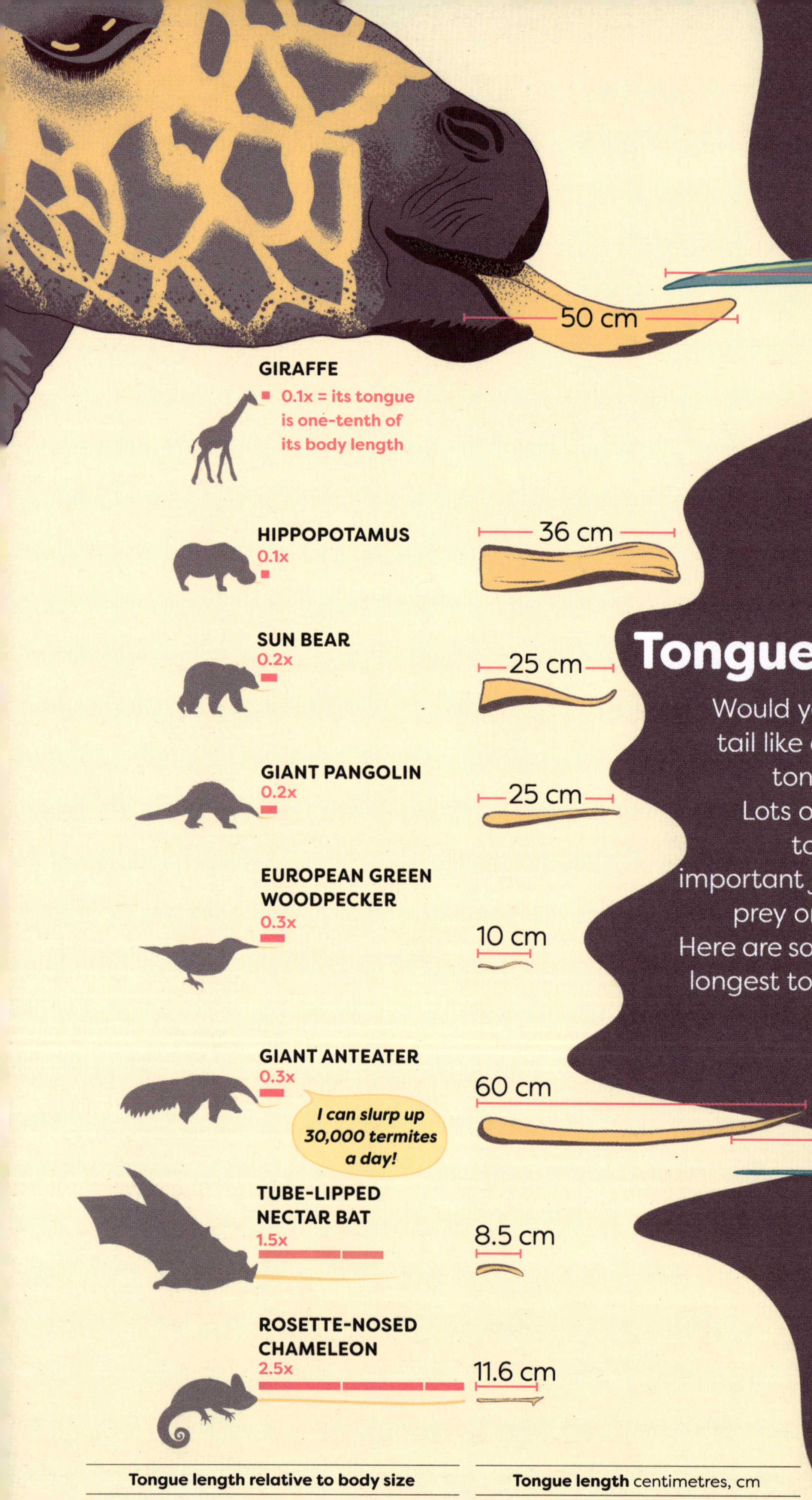

HOW TO READ IT

Tongue or tail length relative to body size:

1x = one times its body length (excluding the tail)

SCALE **10 cm**

Animal	Tail length centimetres, cm	Tail length relative to body size	What's the tail for?
GIRAFFE	100 cm	0.2x (0.2x = its tail is one-fifth of its body length)	Swatting insects
PELAGIC THRESHER SHARK	182.5 cm	1x	Propulsion; Hunting
ANGOLA COLOBUS	75 cm	1.3x	Balance; Swinging between branches
RING-TAILED LEMUR	62 cm	1.4x	Balance; Communication
GEOFFROY'S SPIDER MONKEY	84 cm	1.8x	Balance; Swinging between branches
EUROPEAN LEGLESS LIZARD	78 cm	1.9x	Distracting predators
LONG-EARED JERBOA	16.2 cm	2x	Balance
ROUGHTAIL STINGRAY	170 cm	2.1x	Propulsion; Defence
COMMON BASILISK	39 cm	3x	Balance
AFRICAN LONG-TAILED WIDOWBIRD	50 cm	4.3x	Balance; (Males also use their tails to attract mates.)

LINES OF SYMMETRY IN A BUTTERFLY AND A STARFISH

Bilateral symmetry

Radial symmetry

Symmetry

Nearly all animals display some elements of symmetry, in which two or more parts of their bodies look the same. For example, the butterfly displays bilateral, or two-sided, symmetry: the left and right sides of its body are mirror images of each other. The starfish displays radial symmetry. This means that its body contains multiple lines of symmetry arranged around a central axis, like a wheel. The only group of animals that is classified as asymmetrical are sponges. Their bodies display no symmetry at all.

The strongest animals on Earth

Which animal is stronger: an elephant or an ant? The elephant can carry the heavier weight, of course. But perhaps a fairer way to decide is to measure how much weight each animal can carry relative to the weight of its own body. Looking at it this way, small but powerful animals, such as ants and beetles, are even stronger – relative to the size of their bodies – than gorillas, bears and elephants!

HARPY EAGLE
This eagle can carry 7.5 kg, the same as (**1 time**) its own weight.

GRIZZLY BEAR
A grizzly can carry 250 kg, the same as (**1 time**) its own weight.

AFRICAN ELEPHANT
An African elephant can carry 9,000 kg, **1.5 times** its own weight (6,000 kg).

TIGER
A tiger can carry 400 kg, twice (**2 times**) its own weight (200 kg).

MUSK OX
A musk ox can carry 570 kg, twice (**2 times**) its own weight (285 kg).

GORILLA
A gorilla can carry 640 kg, **4 times** its own weight (160 kg).

HOW STRONG ARE HUMANS?

The world-record-holding weightlifter **Tamara Walcott** can lift 291 kg, about twice (**2 times**) her own weight (134 kg).

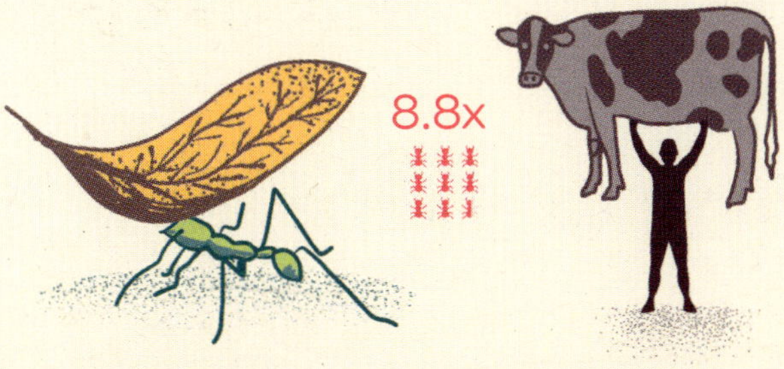

LEAFCUTTER ANT
This remarkable ant can carry **nearly 9 times** its own weight (0.02 g). This is equivalent to a **human carrying a cow**!

RHINOCEROS BEETLE
A rhinoceros beetle can carry **100 times** its own weight (2.4 g). This is equivalent to a **human carrying an elephant**!

ORIBATID MITE
This mite can pull **530 times** its own weight (0.0001 g), which is equivalent to a **human pulling the weight of a *Brachiosaurus* dinosaur**!

DUNG BEETLE
A dung beetle can pull **more than 1,100 times** its own weight (0.09 g). This is equivalent to a **human pulling a tank**!

The fastest animals on Earth

Jamaican athlete Usain Bolt is the world's fastest human, and can run a 100-metre race in just over 9 seconds. He might be a world-record-holder among humans, but he is slow compared to other running, swimming and flying animals. These are the fastest creatures in the animal kingdom.

TOP FLYING SPEED

kilometres per hour, km/h

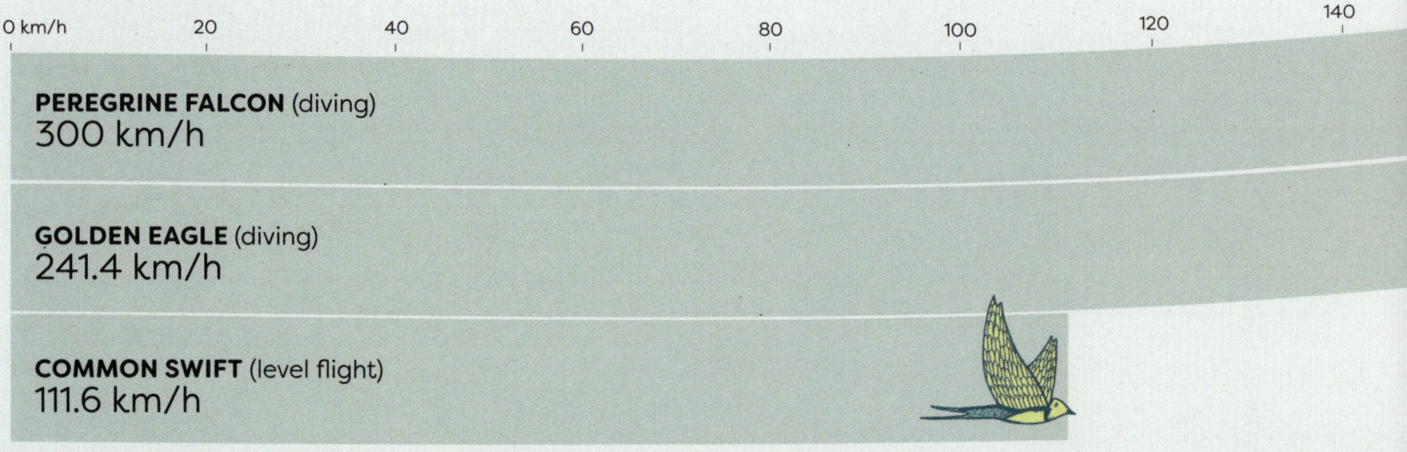

TOP SWIMMING SPEED

The black marlin and other billfish are among the fastest swimmers in the world.

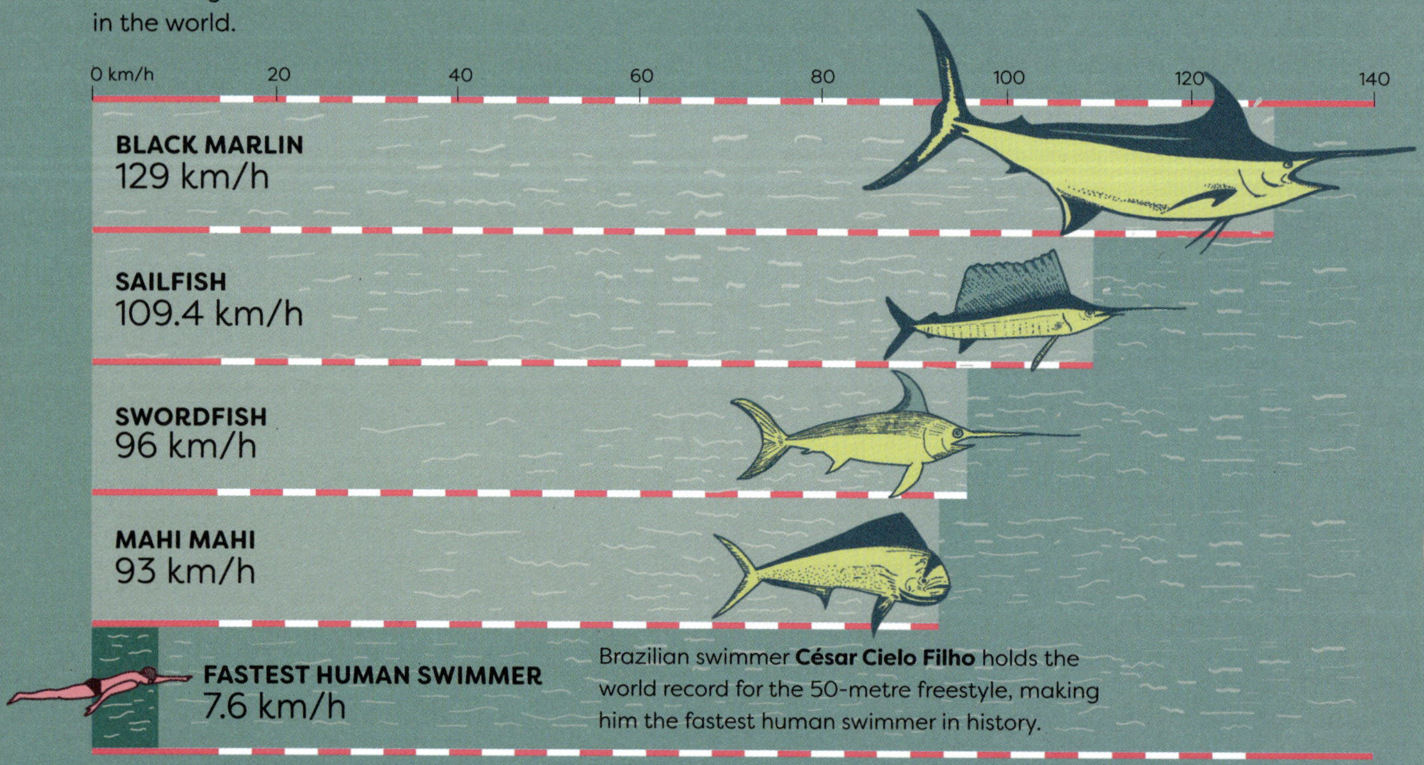

To find out about speedy human-made objects, turn to page 264.

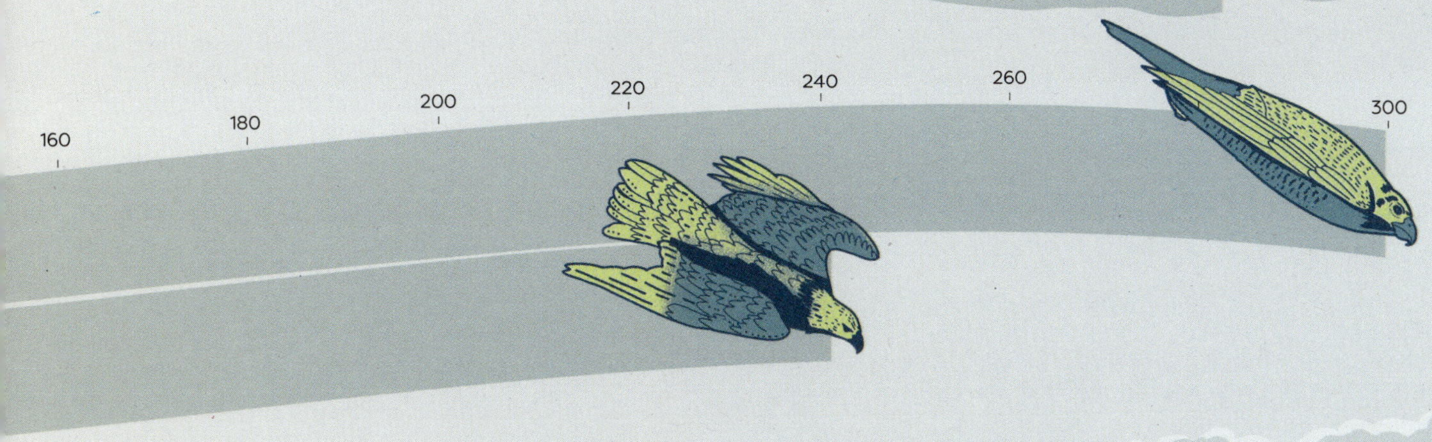

TOP RUNNING SPEED

In 2012, an 11-year-old cheetah called Sarah ran 100 metres in 5.95 seconds, reaching a top speed of 98 kilometres per hour (km/h).

Usain Bolt's top running speed was measured during a 100-metre race in 2009, which he completed in 9.58 seconds.

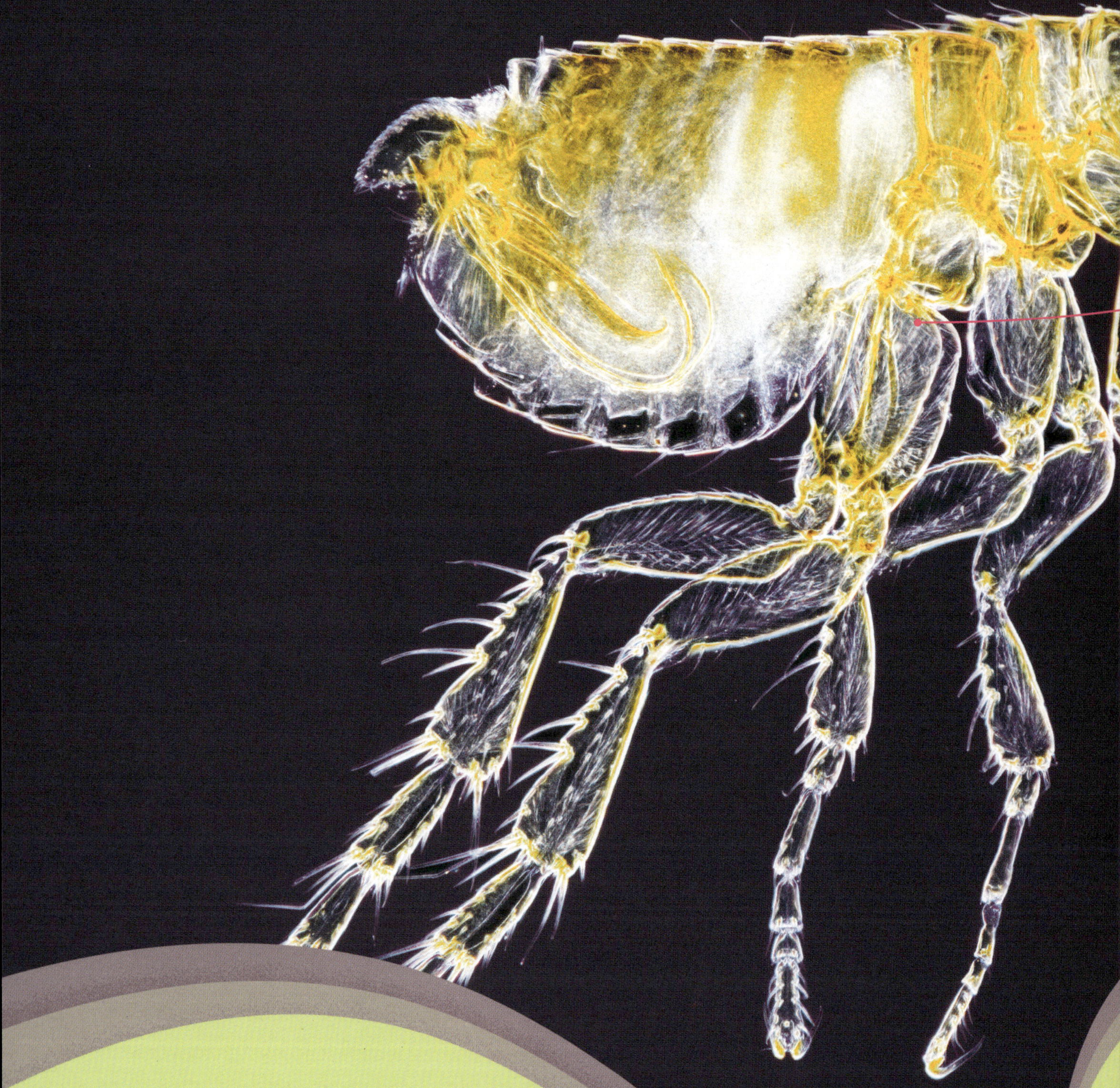

Jumping champions!

When it comes to jumping, fleas are the champions. Kangaroos can jump 9 metres in a single leap, which is five times their body length. Fleas can jump 50 cm, which might not sound like much, but is actually 200 times their body length!

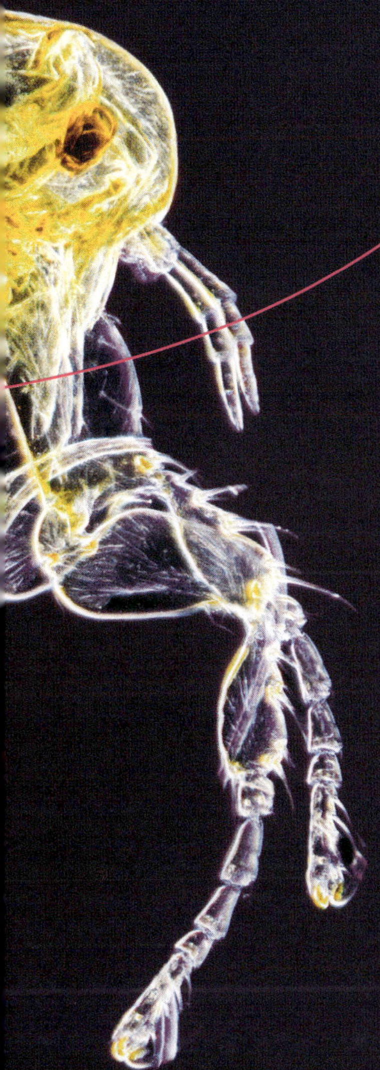

The flea's ability to jump so far isn't only thanks to the muscles in its legs. Inside its thorax, a flea has some rubbery stuff called resilin. When the flea folds its back legs, ready to leap, the muscles in its thorax contract, and this action squishes the resilin. When the flea pushes off with its legs, the resilin bounces back, a bit like a coiled spring, enabling the flea to launch itself up to 50 centimetres away.

A KANGAROO CAN JUMP UP TO...

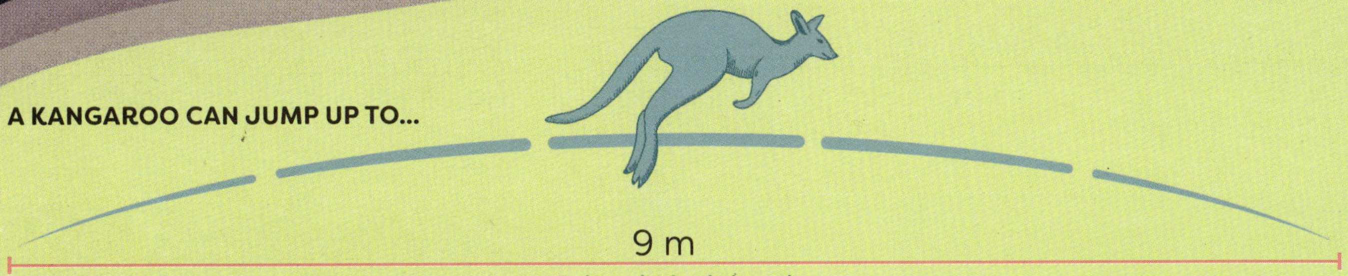

9 m

or 5 times its body length

A FLEA CAN JUMP UP TO...

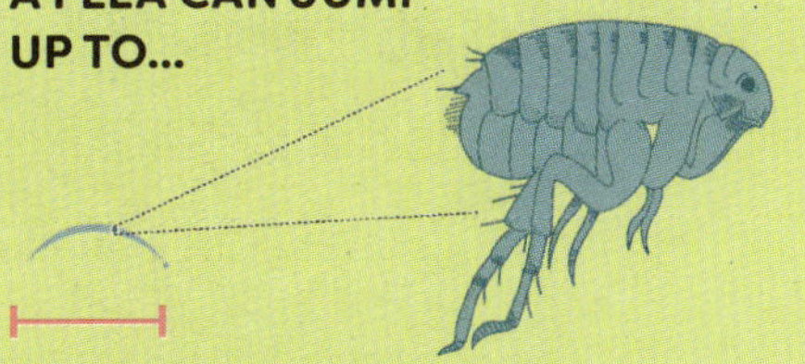

50 cm

or 200 times its body length

...which is equal to a human adult leaping over 340 m or 3.4 football pitches in a single jump.

Nature's survivors

Some animal species are able to live and thrive in very extreme environments, from the scorching Sahara desert to Antarctica's freezing ice sheets. On these pages you can meet a selection of animals that can survive in the hottest, coldest, highest and lowest places on Earth.

HOT AND COLD

The animals in the top half of this chart can survive in extremely hot temperatures. The animals in the bottom half feel more at home in the freezing cold. The tardigrade can cope in both!

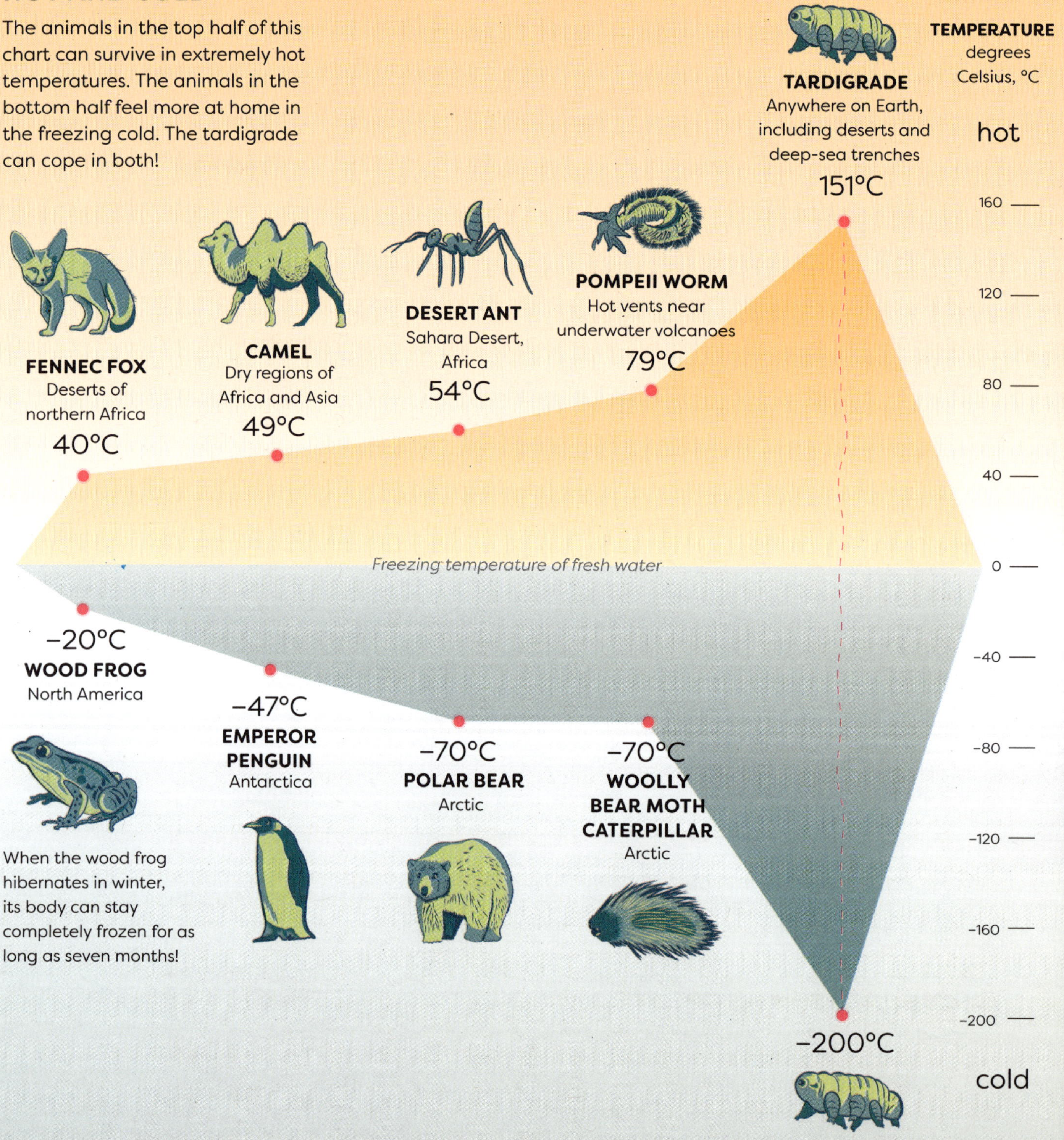

When the wood frog hibernates in winter, its body can stay completely frozen for as long as seven months!

HIGH AND LOW

The animals in the top half of this chart are used to living at high altitudes. The animals in the bottom half live deep underground, or at the bottom of the ocean.

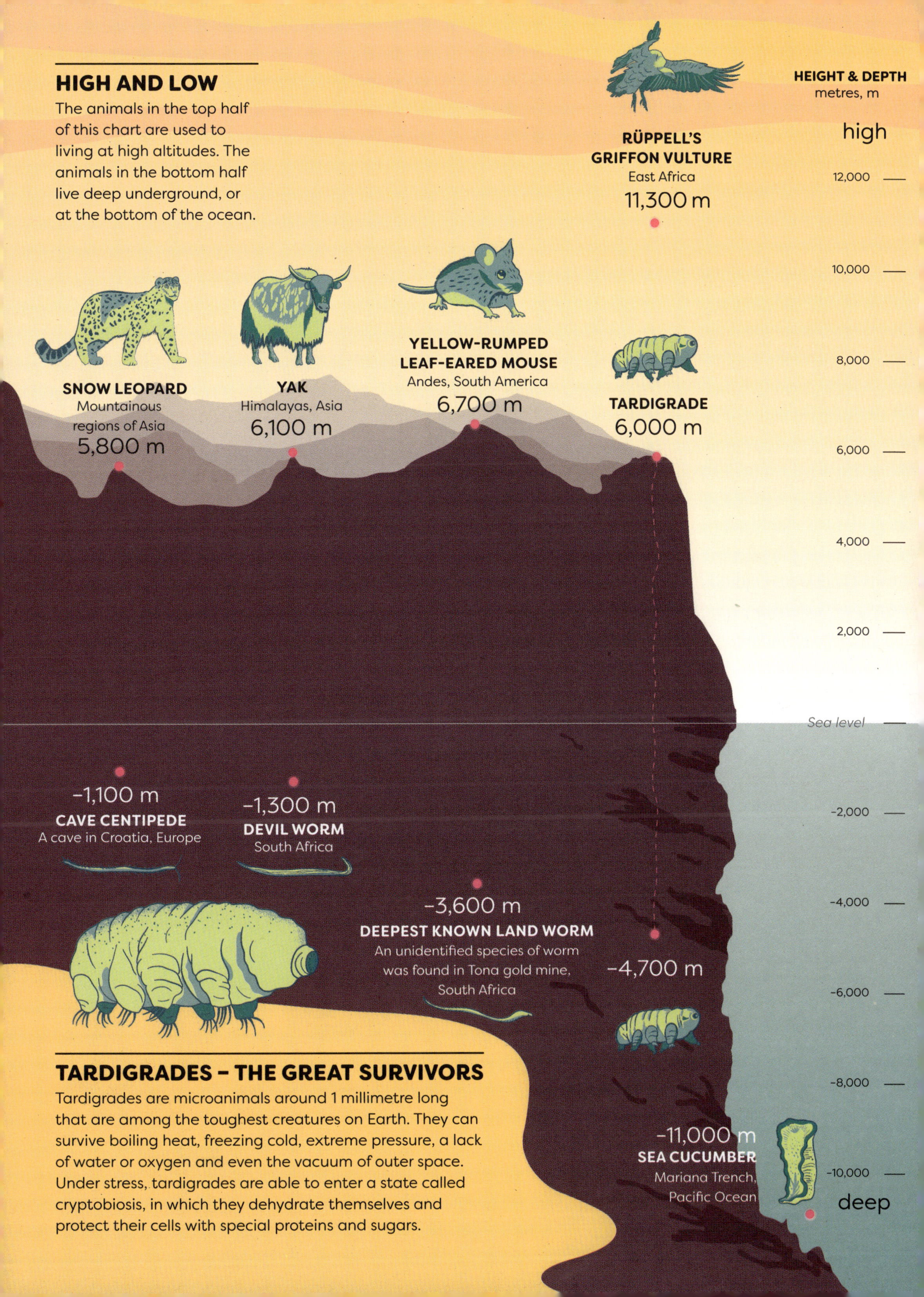

TARDIGRADES – THE GREAT SURVIVORS

Tardigrades are microanimals around 1 millimetre long that are among the toughest creatures on Earth. They can survive boiling heat, freezing cold, extreme pressure, a lack of water or oxygen and even the vacuum of outer space. Under stress, tardigrades are able to enter a state called cryptobiosis, in which they dehydrate themselves and protect their cells with special proteins and sugars.

How big is a penguin?

The largest species of penguin alive today is the emperor penguin. Emperor penguins can be up to 1.3 metres tall. However, around 40 million years ago, an even bigger species of penguin lived on the frozen plains of Antarctica. Scientists estimate that *Palaeeudyptes klekowskii*, which is now extinct, would have been around 1.6 metres tall and weighed 115 kilograms – which is almost twice the weight of the average adult human being!

Gentoo penguins are the third largest species of penguin alive today. This photograph captures them leaping on to an ice sheet in Antarctica.

PENGUIN HEIGHT metres, m

Epic migrations

A migration is a seasonal movement of animals from one part of the world to another. Mammals, reptiles, birds, insects and fish all include species that migrate for a variety of reasons. These reasons include finding food, mating and giving birth to offspring. As you can see from this map, some animals migrate for tens of thousands of kilometres each year.

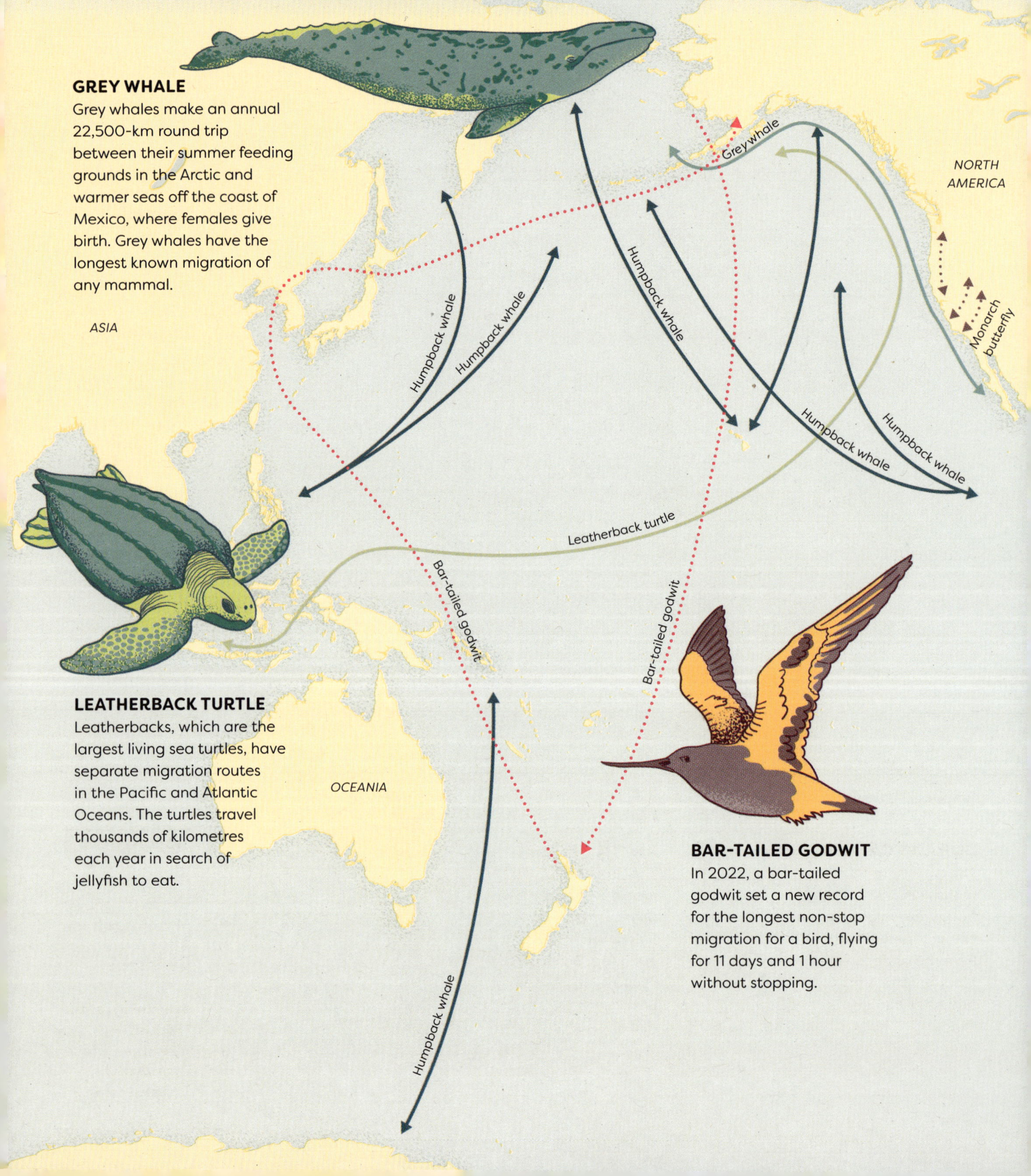

GREY WHALE

Grey whales make an annual 22,500-km round trip between their summer feeding grounds in the Arctic and warmer seas off the coast of Mexico, where females give birth. Grey whales have the longest known migration of any mammal.

LEATHERBACK TURTLE

Leatherbacks, which are the largest living sea turtles, have separate migration routes in the Pacific and Atlantic Oceans. The turtles travel thousands of kilometres each year in search of jellyfish to eat.

BAR-TAILED GODWIT

In 2022, a bar-tailed godwit set a new record for the longest non-stop migration for a bird, flying for 11 days and 1 hour without stopping.

MONARCH BUTTERFLY

Monarch butterflies in North America are divided into two main groups. One group migrates each year between the Rocky Mountains and southern California. The other migrates between Canada and central Mexico. The butterflies use the Sun to navigate and have an internal magnetic compass that helps them to stay on course on cloudy days.

HUMPBACK WHALE

Humpback whales live in every ocean on the planet. In the summer they feed in the polar regions (both north and south), and then migrate closer to the equator in the winter.

GREAT SNIPE

Scientists think that the great snipe is the fastest bird flying over very long distances. They recorded one great snipe flying 6,800 km from Northern Europe to sub-Saharan Africa in just three and a half days.

DORADO CATFISH

The two-metre-long dorado catfish has the longest freshwater migration of any fish, swimming from the Andes to the mouth of the Amazon and back again.

ARCTIC TERN

The arctic tern holds the record for the longest animal migration as it flies around the world each year on its 96,000-km journey between the Arctic Circle and Antarctica.

Super senses!

Animals respond to the world around them through their senses, to help them find food and water, to navigate, and to escape predators. But they don't only have the familiar senses that humans possess – some have extraordinary senses that allow them to experience the world in ways we can only imagine.

ECHOLOCATION
By monitoring how their high-frequency squeaks are reflected back, some animals – including bats, dolphins and whales – can detect objects in the dark.

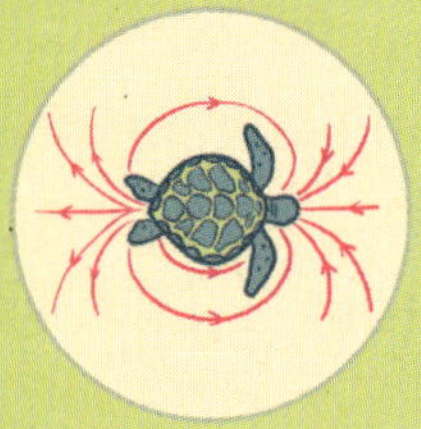

MAGNETORECEPTION
Migrating animals, such as salmon, eels and sea turtles, can use Earth's magnetic field to navigate long distances without getting lost.

ELECTRORECEPTION
Predators, including sharks, rays and duck-billed platypuses, can detect electrical signals emitted by the muscles of prey animals and hunt them in the dark.

UV VISION
Many birds, bees and spiders can see ultraviolet light, which is mostly invisible to human eyes. This allows them to see the world in richer detail.

STORM FORECASTING
Weather loaches are fish with an uncanny ability to detect changes in pressure, such as before a storm, thanks to special bones in their heads.

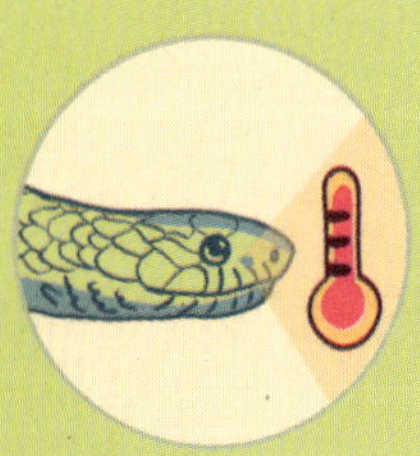

THERMAL VISION
Some snakes can hunt in the dark, using holes under their eyes called pit organs, which can detect the heat of warm-blooded animals from up to a metre away.

The hammerhead shark in this illustration is using its sense of electroreception to detect the electromagnetic energy being given off by the fish hiding on the seabed below. The hammerhead shark's distinctive head allows it to search for prey over a large area of the ocean floor as it swims.

Transformers!

Some creatures can dramatically change their appearance in order to help them escape danger, become stealthier hunters, regulate their temperature, impress a male or female partner, or just communicate! The mimic octopus is one of the most impressive shape-shifters, and can change its appearance in an instant to look like a whole host of other animals.

REASON Why does it change?	TRANSFORMATION What changes?	TIME How long does the change take?
MIMIC OCTOPUS This octopus can change its colour to conceal itself or impersonate other sea creatures – including lionfish, jellyfish and sea snakes – to fool potential predators.	Colour Skin texture Shape	Instant
CHAMELEON A chameleon can change the colour of its skin to regulate its body temperature (darker colours absorb more light and heat) and to communicate with other chameleons.	Colour Pattern	Instant
CUTTLEFISH A cuttlefish can change the colour, pattern and texture of its skin to blend in with its surroundings. Male cuttlefish also change colour to impress females and to compete with rival males.	Colour Pattern Skin texture	Instant

PUFFERFISH

Pufferfish can fill their stomachs with water and expand like a beach ball, more than doubling in size. The pufferfish suddenly puffs up in this way to deter predators from eating it.

GOLDEN TORTOISE BEETLE

This beetle normally looks gold because of the way light reflects off fluid in its outer shell. When it is threatened, the beetle can dry up the fluid, revealing a bright colour beneath that makes it look like a poisonous insect to predators.

MUTABLE RAIN FROG

This rare frog, roughly the size of a fingernail, can change the texture of its skin from smooth to spiny in just a few minutes. Scientists think this change of appearance helps the frog to blend in with its surroundings on the mossy rainforest floor.

ARCTIC FOX

The colour of the Arctic fox's fur changes from a thin brown/grey coat in summer to a heavy white coat in the winter, so that it can blend in with its snowy winter habitat. This makes it a stealthy hunter, and harder for predators to spot.

Which animals kill the most humans?

Which animal do you think poses the greatest danger to humans? If you said a hungry shark or a poisonous spider you would be... completely wrong! Because the deadliest animal for humans is actually the tiny mosquito.

WHY ARE MOSQUITOES SO DEADLY?

Mosquitoes do not kill humans directly. But they do transmit dangerous diseases between animals and humans when they bite them and drink their blood. The deadliest of these diseases is malaria, which is found only in certain parts of the world but has killed millions of people throughout human history.

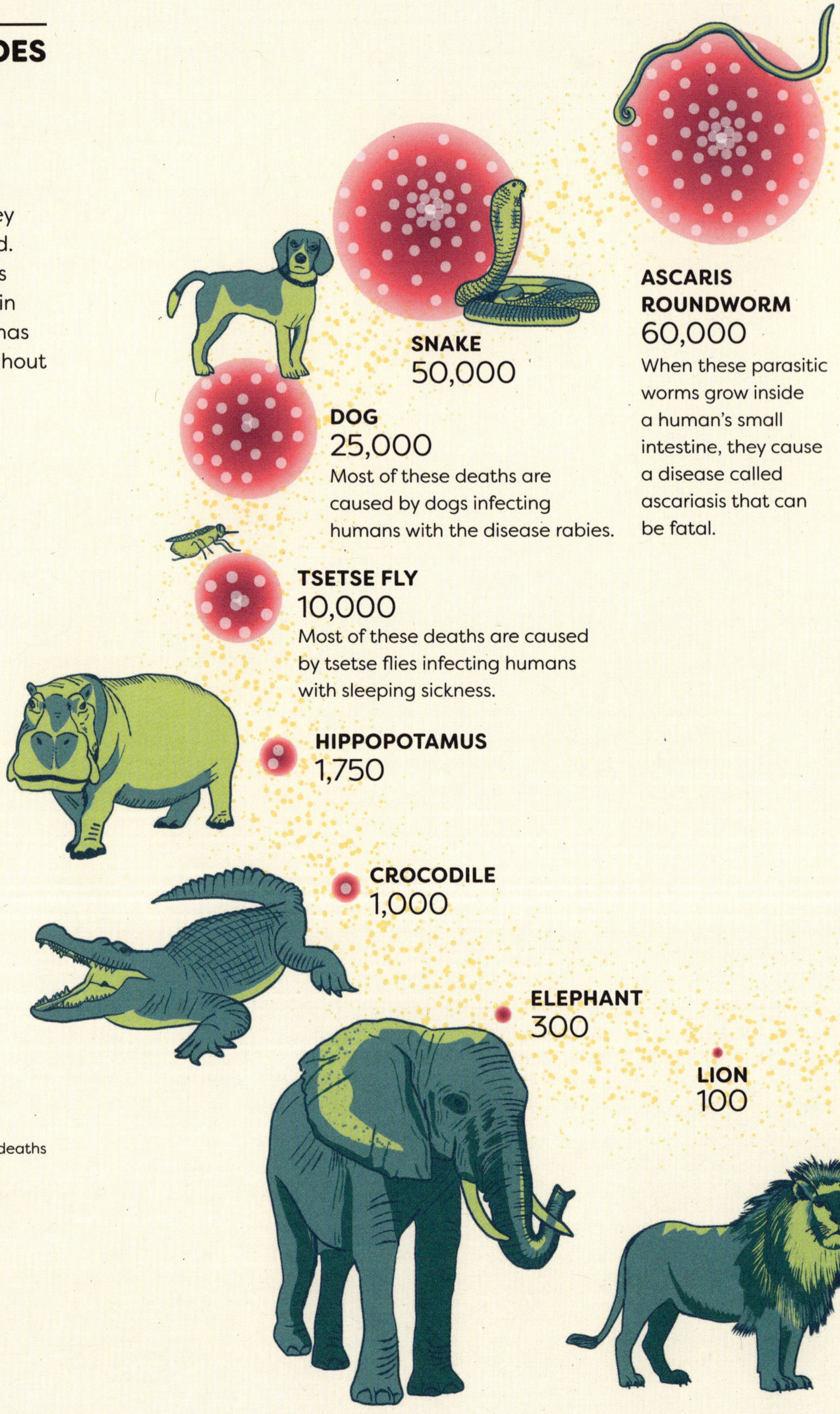

HOW TO READ IT

The size of the **pink circles** shows the estimated number of humans that each animal species kills per year.

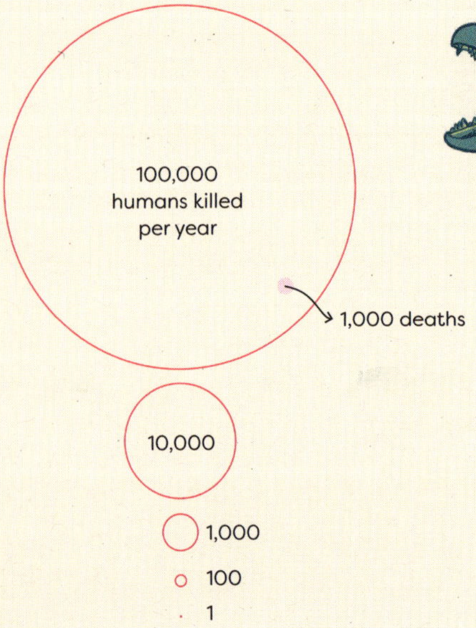

FRESHWATER SNAIL
200,000
Freshwater snails carry parasitic worms that can infect humans with a potentially fatal disease called schistosomiasis, which is also known as 'snail fever'. Schistosomiasis infects nearly 250 million people around the world each year.

HUMAN
500,000
Thanks to wars and other forms of violence, humans kill hundreds of thousands of other humans every year. This makes us by far the deadliest mammal on Earth.

Mosquitoes like me can transmit as many as 15 diseases, including malaria, yellow fever and zika.

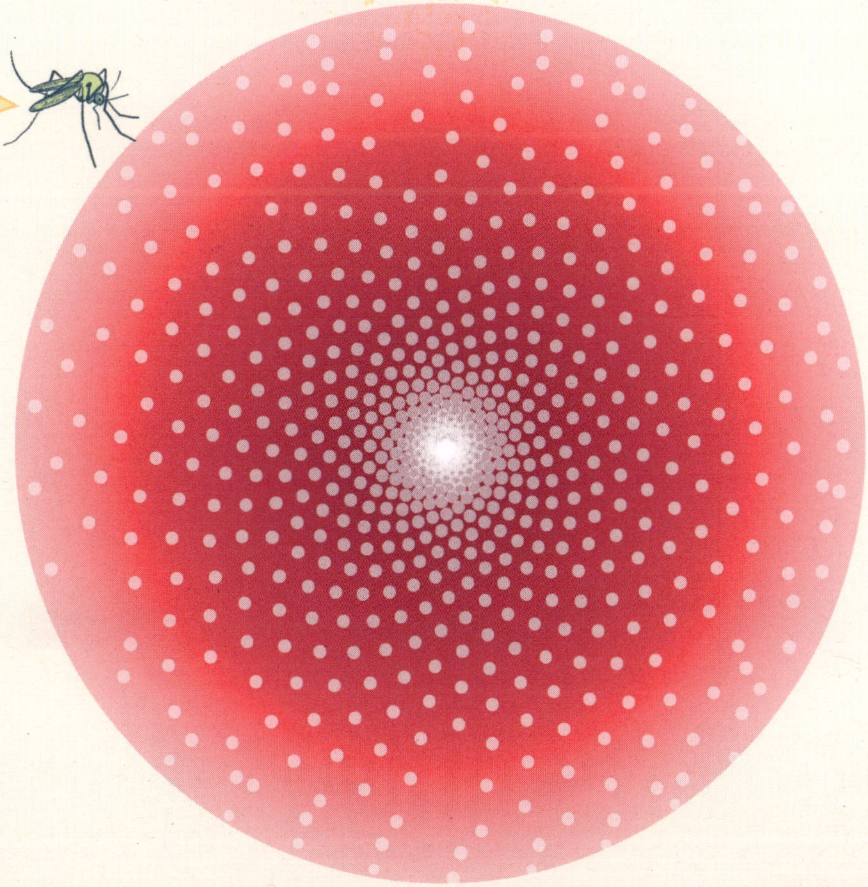

MOSQUITO
725,000
These deaths are mostly caused by mosquitoes infecting humans with the disease malaria.

SHARK
5

On average, sharks kill just five humans per year. Humans, however, kill more than 100 million sharks each year for their fins or teeth, or for sport.

Eggs great and small

With all the ingredients for life inside its shell, the bird's egg has been described as 'the most perfect thing in the universe'. But it's not only birds that lay eggs: reptiles, amphibians, fish, insects and even some mammals do too!

COMMON BIRD EGGS, BY SIZE

Birds grow in fragile but hard shells that get their colours from just two pigments: a red-brown pigment and a green pigment.

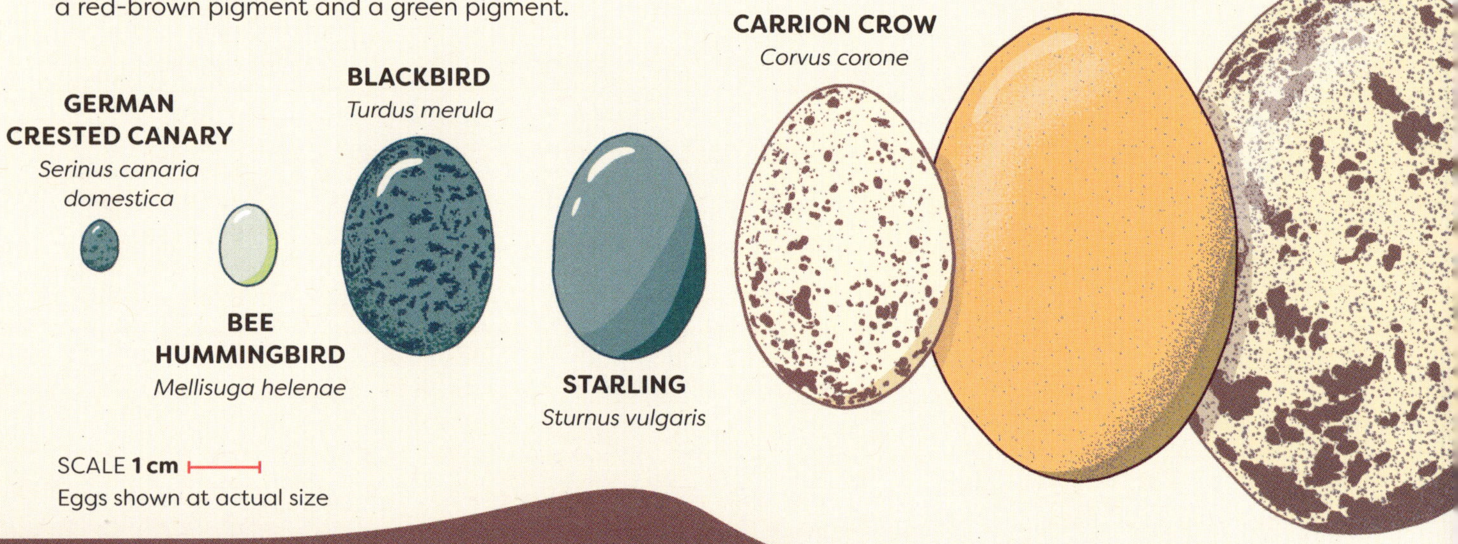

SCALE **1 cm**
Eggs shown at actual size

NOT ONLY BIRDS LAY EGGS

Reptile eggs are tough and elastic, and fish and frog eggs often float in a protective jelly in the water.

OCELLARIS CLOWNFISH
Amphiprion ocellaris
A popular fish to keep in saltwater aquariums, female clownfish lay up to 1,500 eggs at once.

COMMON OCTOPUS
Octopus vulgaris
The female octopus lays up to 500,000 eggs about the size of a grain of rice, and stays with them for up to 5 months until they hatch. She normally dies shortly after the final egg has hatched.

GOLIATH FROG
Conraua goliath
The largest living frog, the Goliath frog lays eggs that are about the same size as other frogs' eggs – around 4 mm across. It lays a few thousand eggs at a time.

SCALE **1 cm**
Eggs shown at actual size

STICK INSECT
Haaniella echinata
The stick insect's eggs are so large they are eaten by some people in Malaysia, where it lives.

CARPENTER BEE
Xylocopa auripennis
This is one of the largest eggs laid by an insect.

PLATYPUS
Ornithorhynchus anatinus
The duck-billed platypus is one of only two egg-laying mammals on Earth. The other is the echidna, or spiny anteater.

LEATHERBACK SEA TURTLE
Dermochelys coriacea
Female sea turtles migrate long distances to lay their eggs at night on particular beaches, which they return to repeatedly throughout their lives.

LITTLE SPOTTED KIWI
Apteryx owenii

TRUMPETER SWAN
Cygnus buccinator

OSTRICH
Struthio camelus

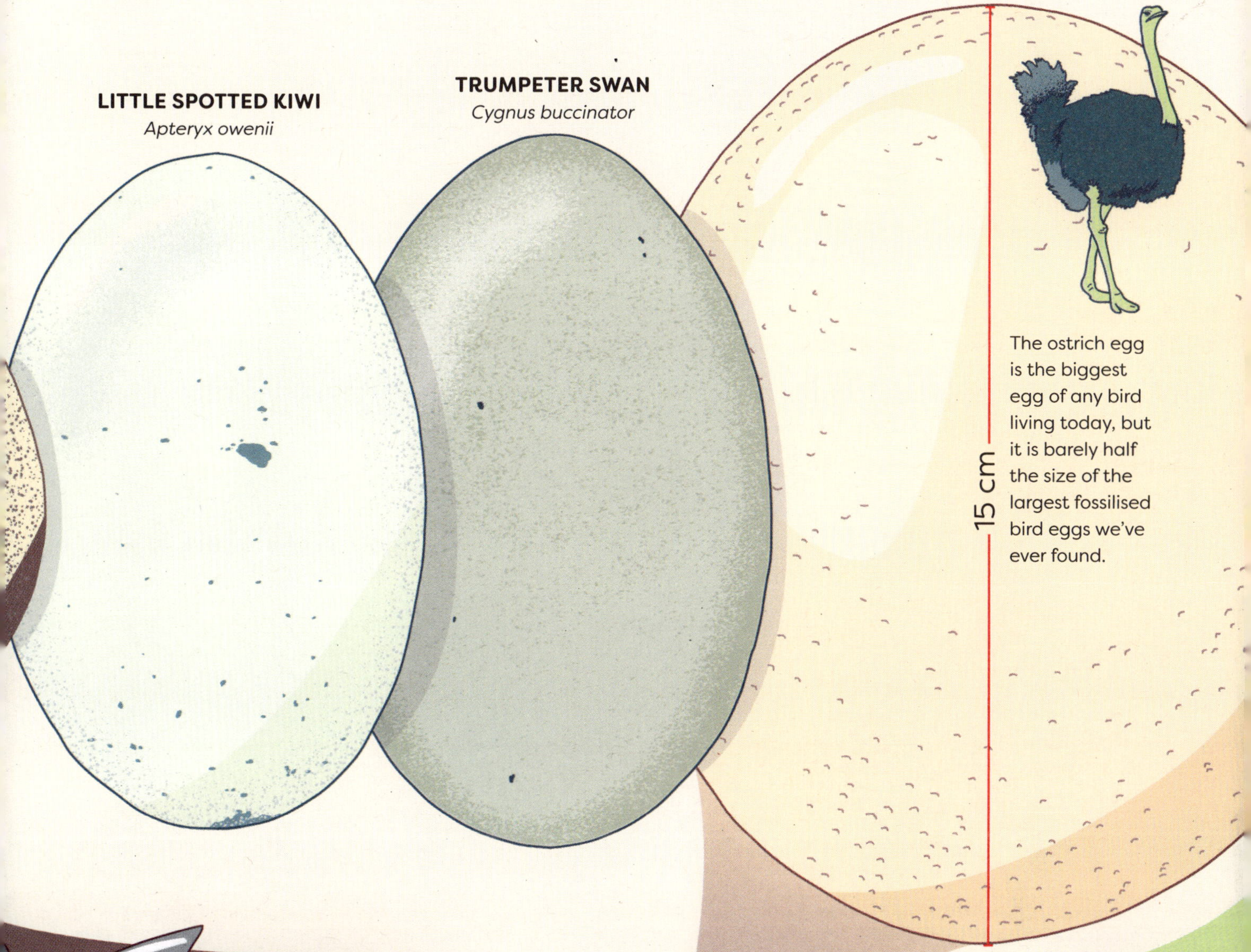

The ostrich egg is the biggest egg of any bird living today, but it is barely half the size of the largest fossilised bird eggs we've ever found.

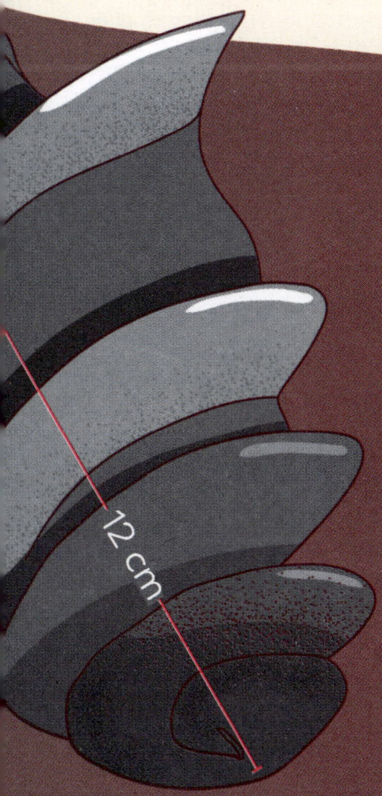

HORN SHARK
Heterodontus francisci
The horn shark has one of the most unusual eggs in the animal kingdom. The eggs are corkscrew-shaped, which helps hold them in place in rocks and crevices, so they don't wash away.

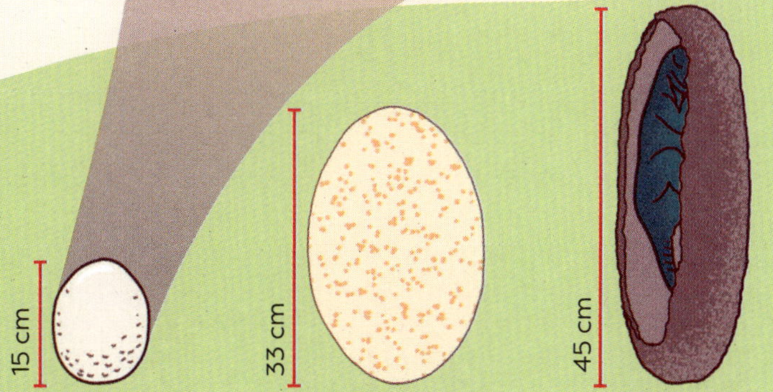

OSTRICH
Largest egg of living bird

MADAGASCAN ELEPHANT BIRD (EXTINCT)
Aepyornithidae
Largest known bird egg

BEIBEILONG (EXTINCT)
Beibeilong sinensis
Largest known dinosaur egg

SCALE **10 cm**
Eggs shown at one-tenth of actual size

How long do animals sleep?

All humans need to sleep – and it's an important part of the lives of many other animals, too. However, as you can see here, some animals sleep very little, and others are champion snoozers!

HOW TO READ IT

Each clock shows two circles that each represent 12 hours, and so add up to a 24-hour day. The **pink portion** shows the average time each animal sleeps per day.

Giraffes sleep standing up for several ten-minute stints with their eyes barely closed. They sometimes lean against a tree or another giraffe for support.

GIRAFFE
40 minutes

AFRICAN ELEPHANT
2 hours

HORSE
3 hours

COW
4 hours

GOAT
5 hours

Dolphins, like whales and other aquatic mammals, sleep differently from humans. Instead of its whole brain going to sleep as ours does, one side of a dolphin's brain gets some rest, while the other side keeps the dolphin semi-alert and breathing. Dolphins even sleep with one eye open!

BOTTLE-NOSED DOLPHIN
8 hours

CHIMPANZEE
9 hours, 30 minutes

Koalas eat more than a kilogram of leaves every day. All that eating and digesting requires a lot of energy, so they spend a long time sleeping to recover.

HUMAN SLEEP

Humans need different amounts of sleep at different stages of their lives. A new baby may sleep for as many as 16 hours a day, whereas an adult needs to sleep for only about 8 hours a day.

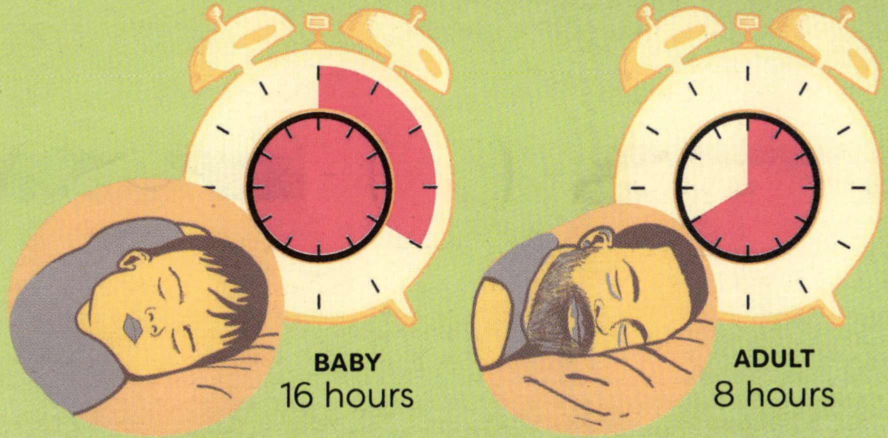

Staying alive

The average lifespan for different types of animal varies enormously and depends on many factors, including the animal's size. Small animals, such as insects and rodents, often live for just a few days, weeks, months or years. Larger mammals, reptiles and fish can live for decades – or centuries!

HOW LONG DO ANIMALS LIVE?

Below you can see the average lifespan of different animals.

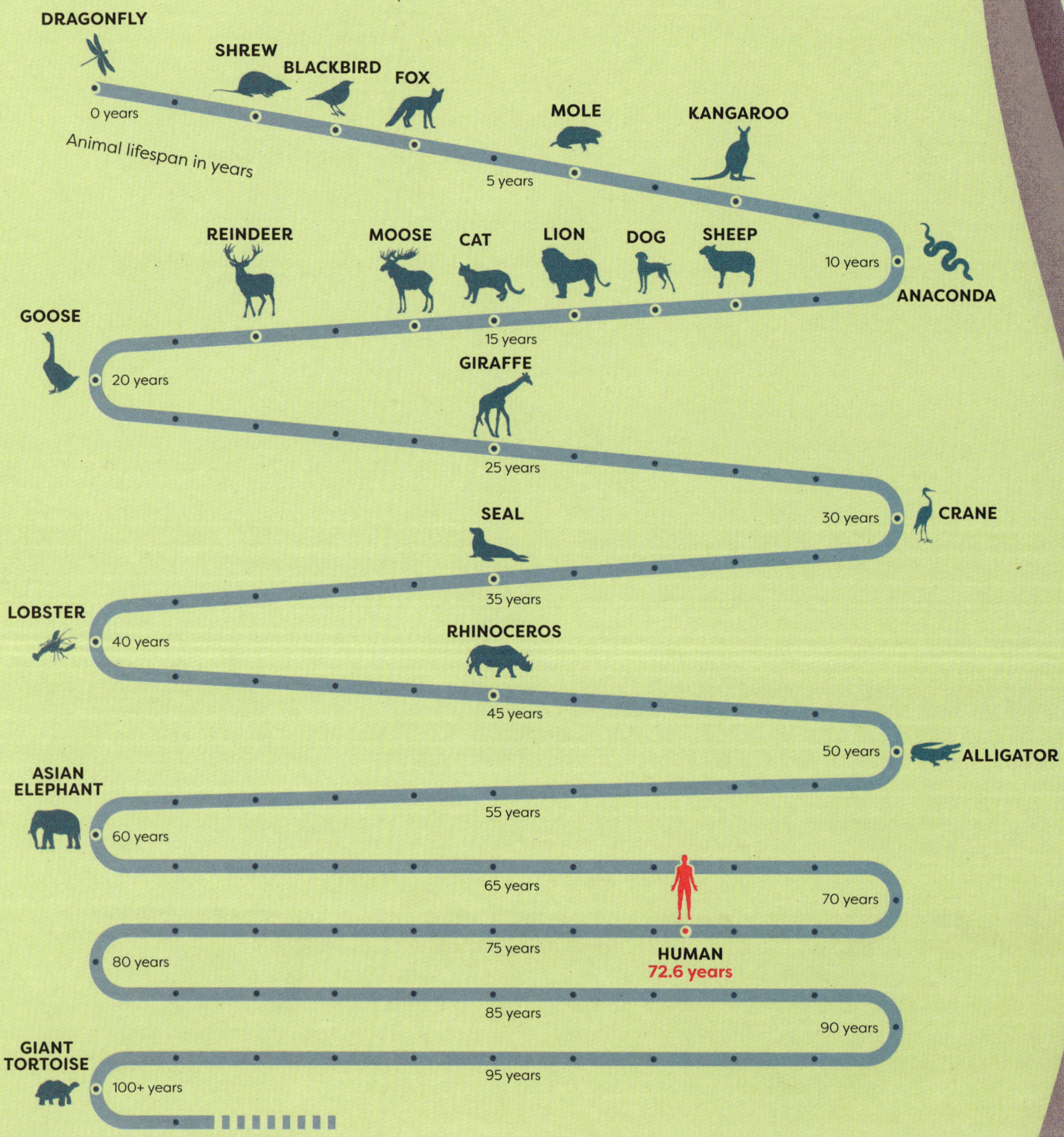

Discover which animal species are endangered on page 138.

Tortoises are the longest-living land animals on Earth. The oldest recorded individual tortoise was a giant Aldabra tortoise that died in 2006 in Calcutta, India, at the age of 225. Its name was Adwaita, which means 'The one and only'.

MEET THE EXPERT CONSULTANT

Miranda Lowe CBE

Curator and scientist

WHAT SPARKED YOUR INTEREST IN ANIMALS?

As a child I loved wildlife, animals, nature and photography, so family trips to museums and green spaces spurred my interest to pursue a career in science. I took my camera on visits to the New Forest in Hampshire and Kew Gardens in London to take lots of images of flowers, birds and horses. Looking down the lens of a camera allowed me to observe nature close up.

TELL US ABOUT YOUR JOB

I'm responsible for the Natural History Museum's historical collections of marine invertebrates – such as crabs, shrimps and lobsters – to keep them accessible for the next 100 years or more of scientific research. I use my microscope to see the detailed structures of very tiny animals from the ocean. Then, I produce scientific work and articles on everything from corals to crustacea to help people all over the world understand environmental science. With my colleagues, other scientists and artists, I help to design exhibitions that enable the public to engage positively with the natural world.

WHAT DISCOVERY ARE YOU LOOKING FORWARD TO SEEING IN THE FUTURE?

Since the 1950s, Earth has lost half of its coral reefs because of the stress of climate change. So, I'm really excited about some current research that's looking into how transplanting healthy corals on to dying reefs may help them to recover. This would help to save the reefs that are home to such a diverse variety of animals.

WHAT IS YOUR FAVOURITE ANIMAL FACT?

Jellyfish have no brain, lungs or heart and have been floating in our world's oceans for about 500 million years! That means they have outlived the dinosaurs.

SCAVENGER HUNT!

Can you track down the answers to this quiz in the pages of this book? (Turn to page 305 to see if you are right!)

1. How much poo can a blue whale excrete in one go: 100 litres, 200 litres or 300 litres?

2. On average, how many humans are killed by sharks each year?

3. Is an axolotl a herbivore, an omnivore or a carnivore?

4. For how many days did a bar-tailed godwit fly non-stop to set a new migration record in 2022?

5. Which animal lays corkscrew-shaped eggs: the horn shark or the leatherback sea turtle?

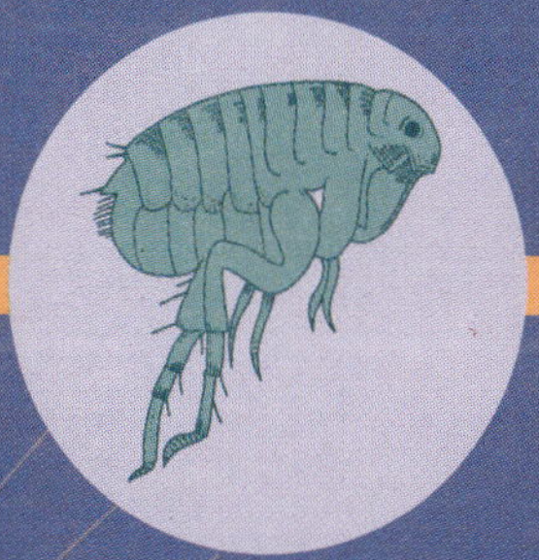

6. How many times its body length can a flea jump?

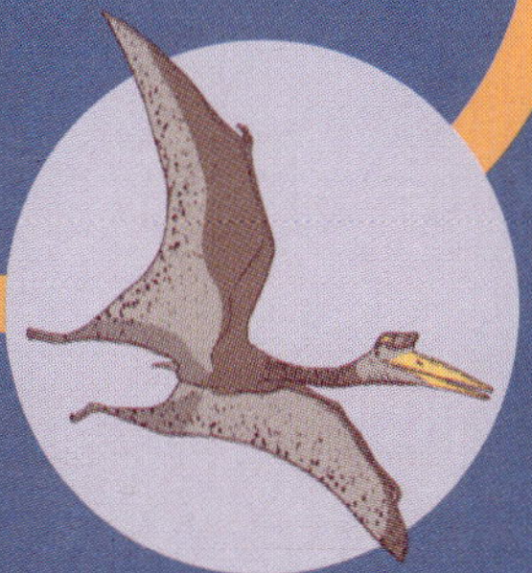

7. What is the wingspan of a *Quetzalcoatlus* in metres?

8. On average, how many hours do koalas sleep each day?

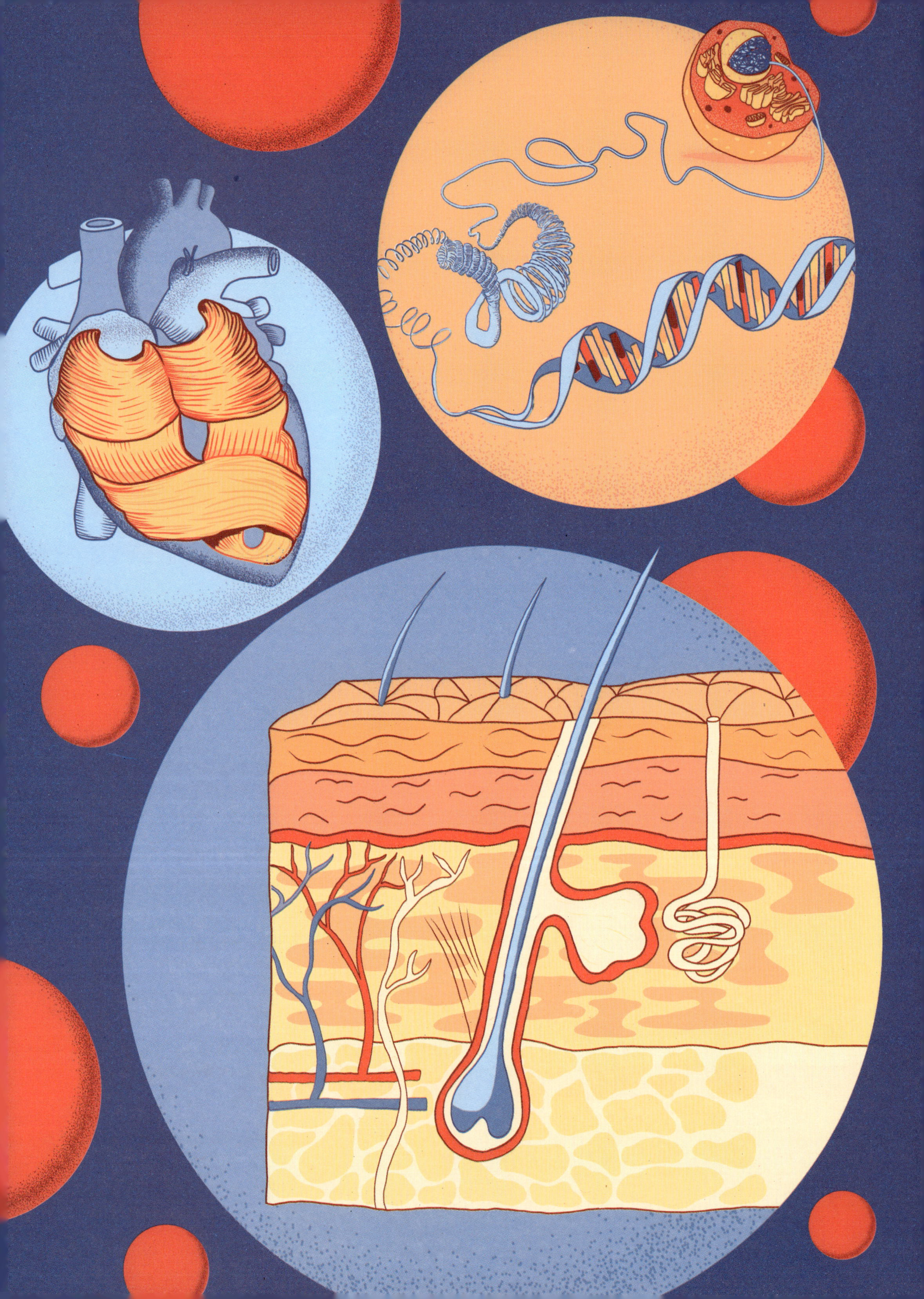

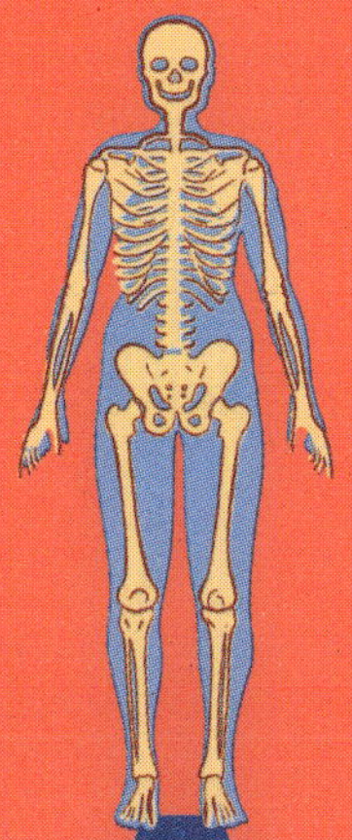

HUMAN BODY

The building blocks of the body

The human body is an astonishingly sophisticated living thing that is made of more than 30 trillion tiny cells. Cells are your body's building blocks. They join together to form tissues and organs, which in turn are part of larger systems that allow your body to move, eat, sleep... and read this book! Here's how all those different parts of the body work together to create the living, breathing human being that is YOU.

CELLS

Every living thing is made up of **cells**. Most cells are extremely small—you could fit about 10,000 human cells on the head of a pin. There are more than 200 different types of cells in your body. They perform a huge variety of jobs, from providing structure and support to making and storing energy. The cell shown here is a neuron, which is found in the brain and spinal cord.

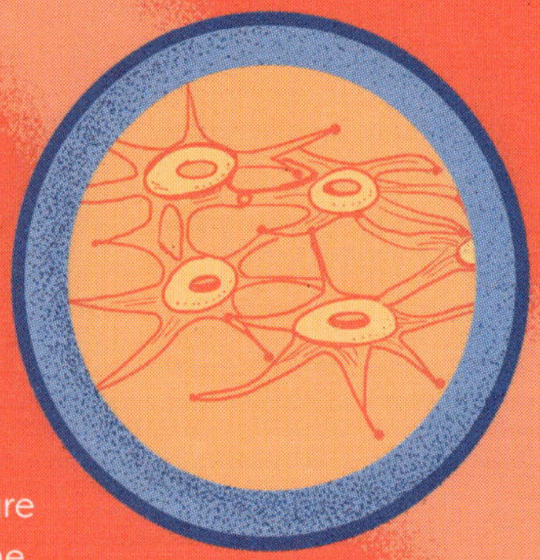

TISSUES

Some cells work alone. Others are grouped together as **tissues**. The body has four main types of tissues. Connective tissue supports other tissues, binding them together. Nerve tissue (shown here) carries messages between different parts of the body. Muscle tissue creates movement. Epithelial tissue, such as the outer layer of your skin, provides a covering or lining.

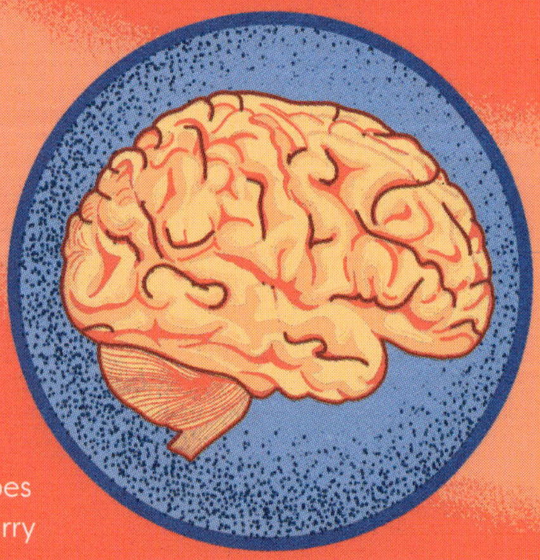

ORGANS

Organs are groups of different types of tissues that work together to carry out a specific job. The brain (shown here), lungs, and heart are three of the body's most important organs. The main job of the heart, for example, is to pump blood around the body (see page 209).

Even though all humans are made of the same building blocks, I am unique, and so are you! For example, some people have extra muscles or bones, and the exact sizes and patterns of our blood vessels are different. Every human body is distinctive.

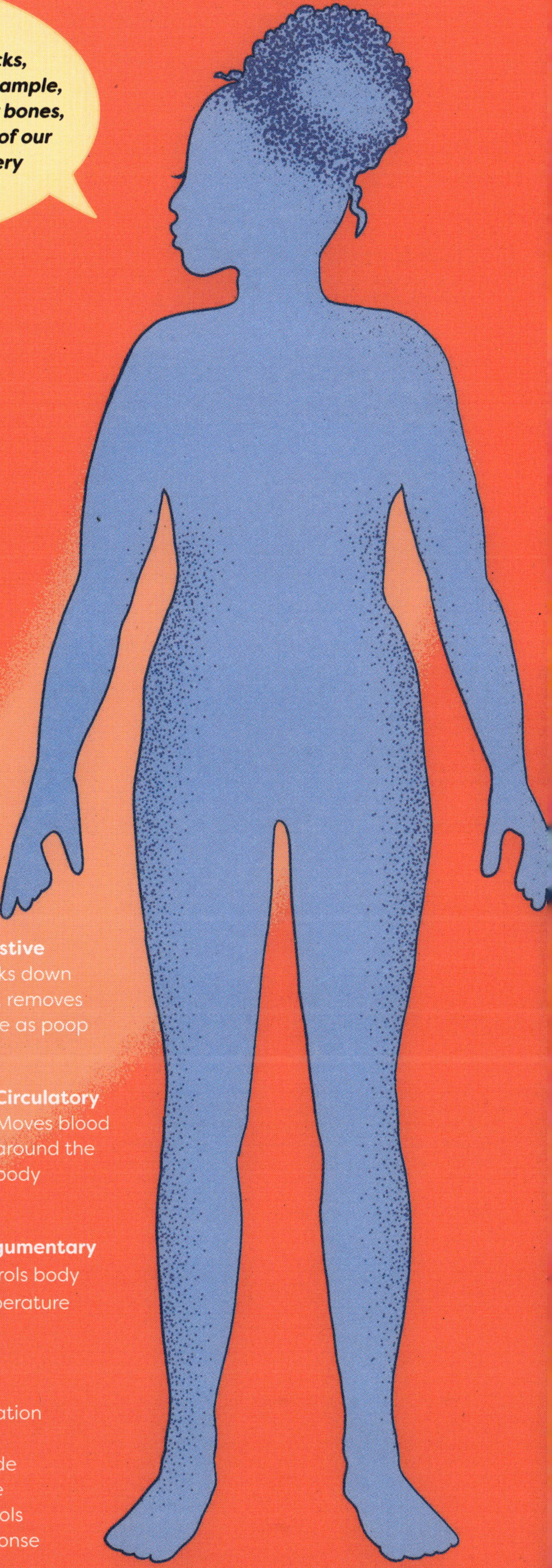

SYSTEMS

Each of the body's 11 main **systems** contains one or more organs and tissues that team up to perform a specific function. Here is a list of the systems and what each one does.

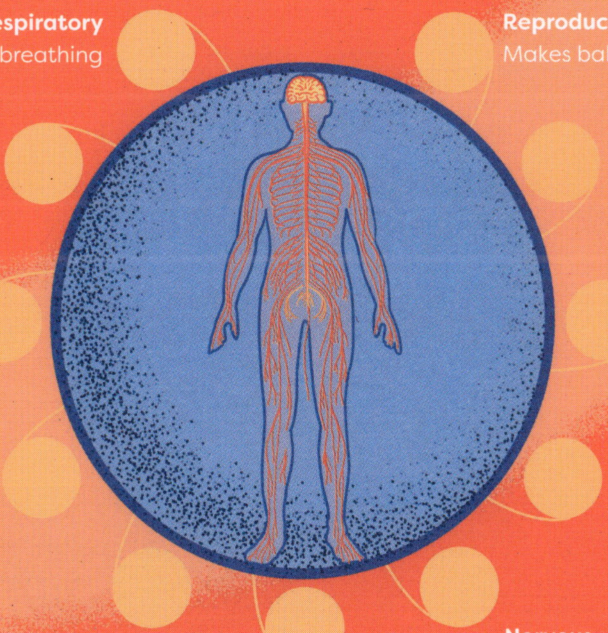

Respiratory
Controls breathing

Skeletal
Supports and protects the body

Urinary
Removes waste as pee

Muscular
Helps the body move

Lymphatic and immune
Fight disease and infection

Endocrine
Controls and coordinates body functions with hormones

Nervous
Collects information about what is happening inside and outside the body and controls the body's response

Integumentary
Controls body temperature

Circulatory
Moves blood around the body

Digestive
Breaks down food, removes waste as poop

Reproductive
Makes babies

How bony are you?

The skeleton does several vital jobs: it supports the body, protects the squishy internal organs, and, in partnership with the muscles, allows you to move. Here, we count *all* the bones in a skeleton—and pick out a few of the most remarkable.

HOW MANY BONES IN A SKELETON?

An adult human skeleton typically has between 206 and 213 bones.

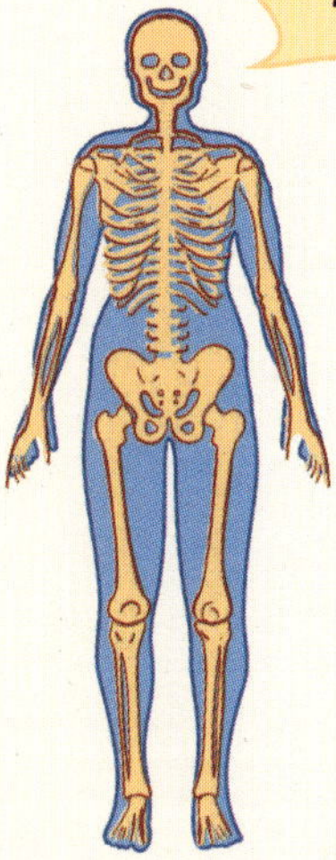

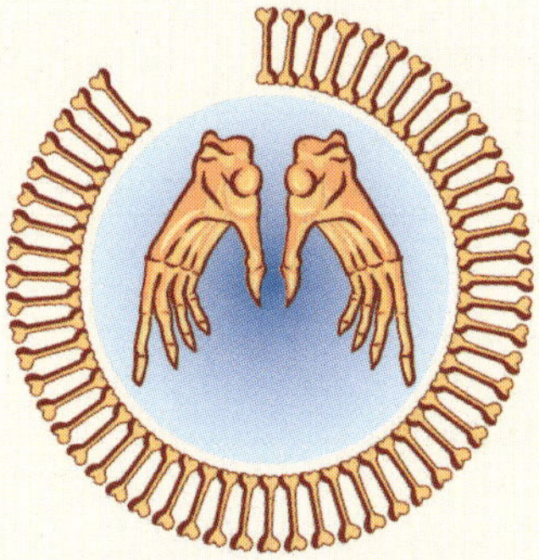

54 bones
HANDS

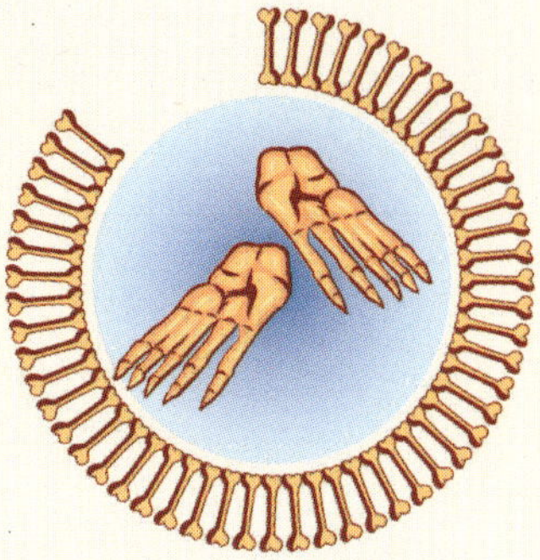

52 bones
FEET

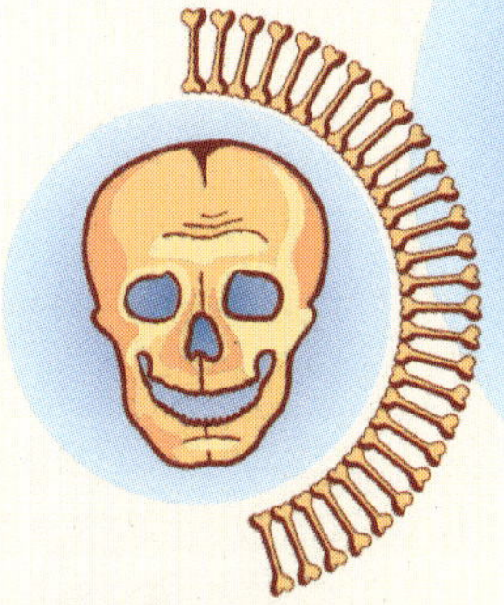

28 bones
SKULL and JAW

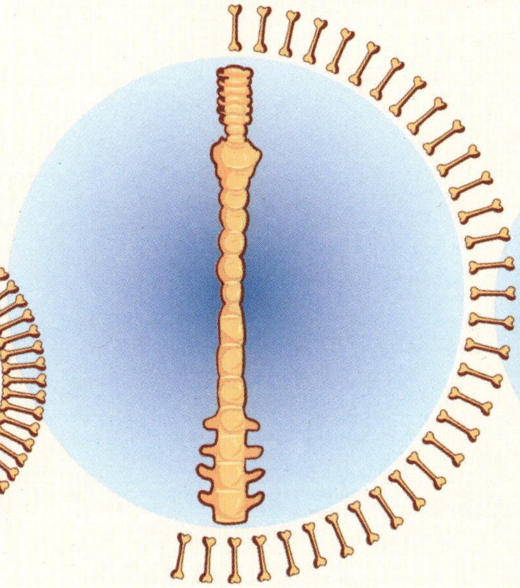

33 bones
NECK and SPINE

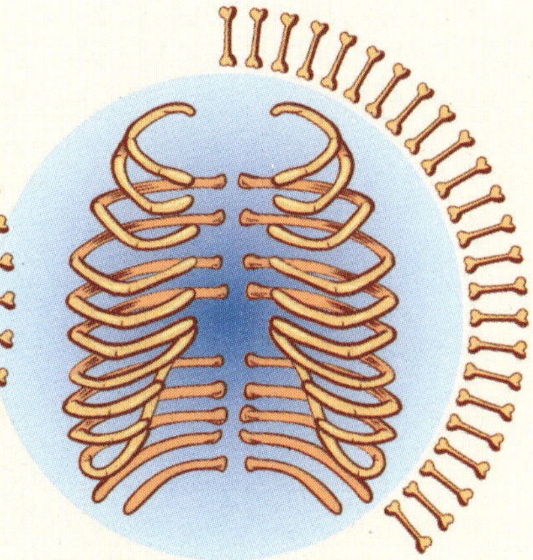

24 bones
RIBS

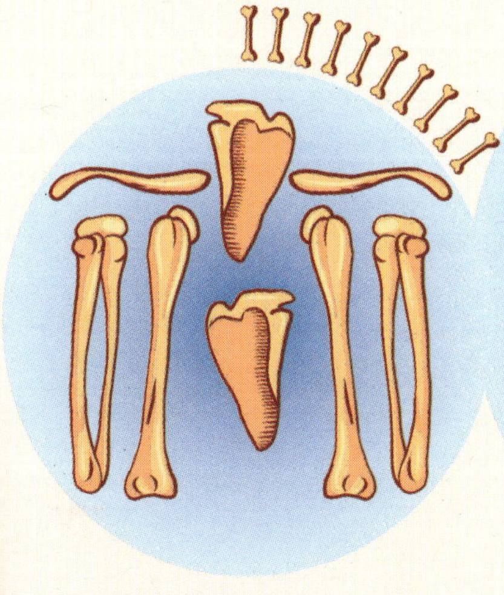

10 bones
ARMS and SHOULDERS

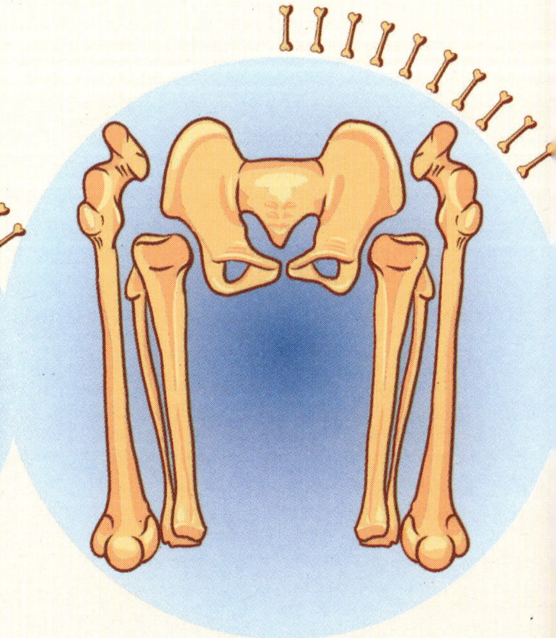

10 bones
LEGS and HIPS

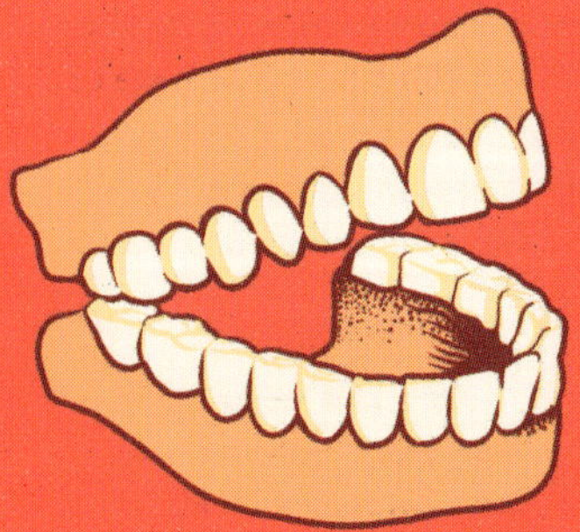

WHAT ABOUT TEETH?

Although teeth are part of the skeleton, they are not bones. You have two sets of teeth: 20 baby teeth that fall out during childhood and 32 adult teeth that replace them (see next page). Enamel, which covers and protects teeth, is the hardest substance in the human body.

EXTRAORDINARY BONES

Bones perform different roles and so come in different shapes and sizes. Here are four extraordinary examples.

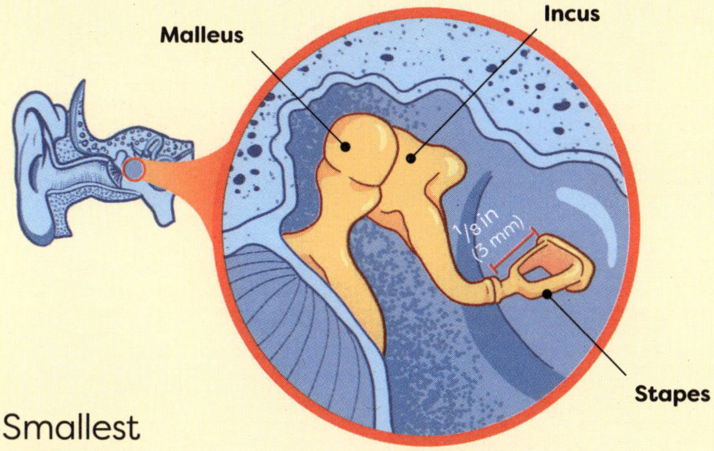

Smallest

OSSICLES

The malleus, incus, and stapes, which together are called the ossicles, are the body's smallest bones. Found in the ear, they transmit sound vibrations. The stapes is the smallest bone of all. It would easily fit on the tip of your finger.

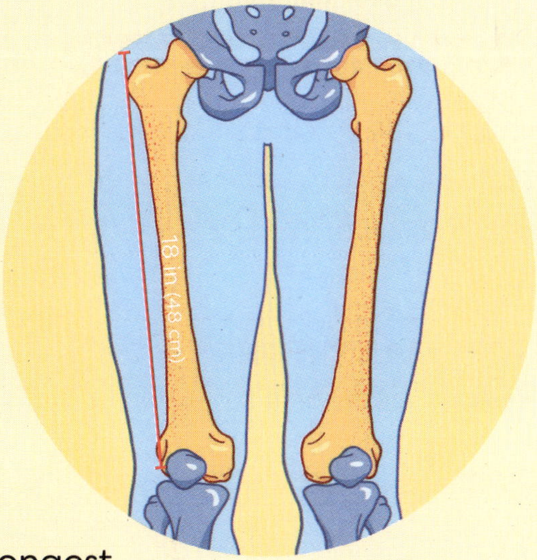

Longest

FEMUR

The femur, or thigh bone, connects the hip to the knee. It is both the longest and the strongest bone in the body.

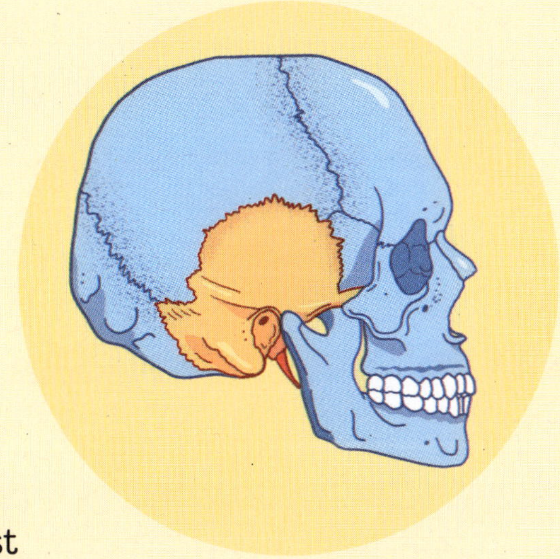

Hardest

PETROUS

The petrous forms part of the temporal bones on either side of the skull. Its main job is to protect the inner ear. It is the hardest bone in the body.

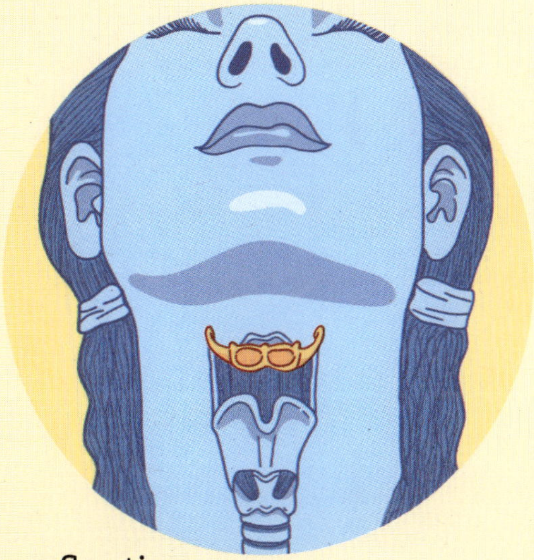

Free floating

HYOID

The hyoid is a small U-shaped bone below the tongue that helps you talk, breathe, and swallow. It is held in place by muscles and by tough bands of tissue called ligaments. The hyoid is unusual as it is not directly connected to any other bones in the body.

X-RAYS

An X-ray machine directs X-rays, which are rays of light that are invisible to humans, through the body. X-rays pass easily through the body's softer parts, such as skin and muscle, but are blocked by the harder parts, such as bone. This creates a black-and-white photograph of the inside of the body, with the lighter, whiter areas of the photo representing bones.

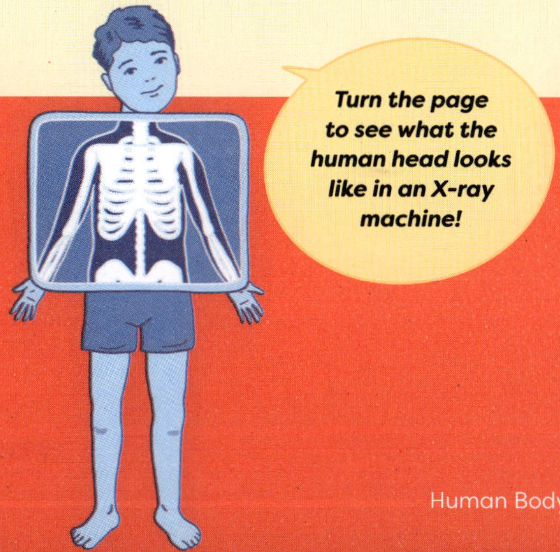

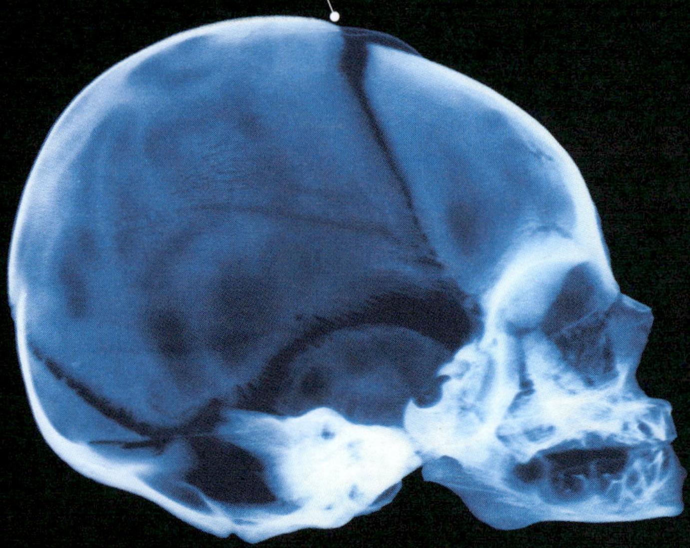

SKULL OF A NEWBORN

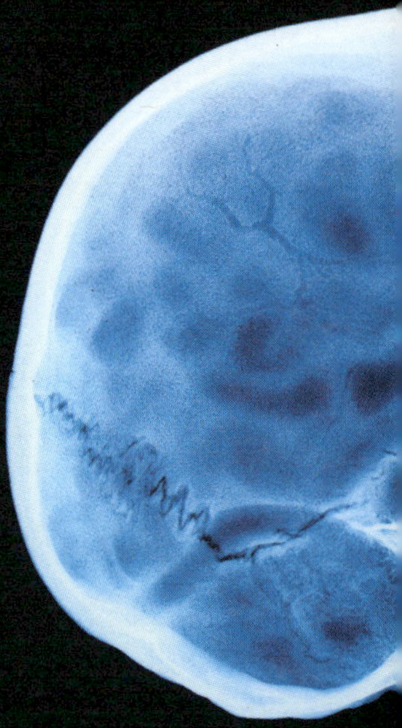

SKULL OF AN ELEMENTARY-SCHOOL-AGE CHILD

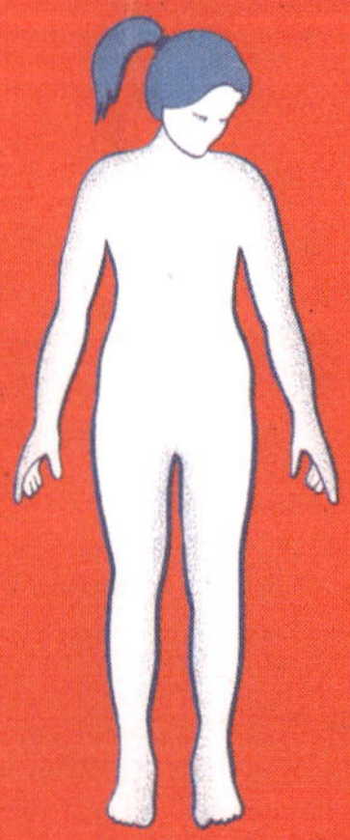

Adult
206–213 bones
in whole body

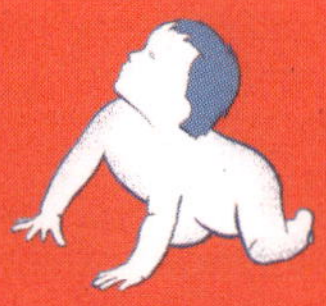

Baby
about 300 bones
in whole body

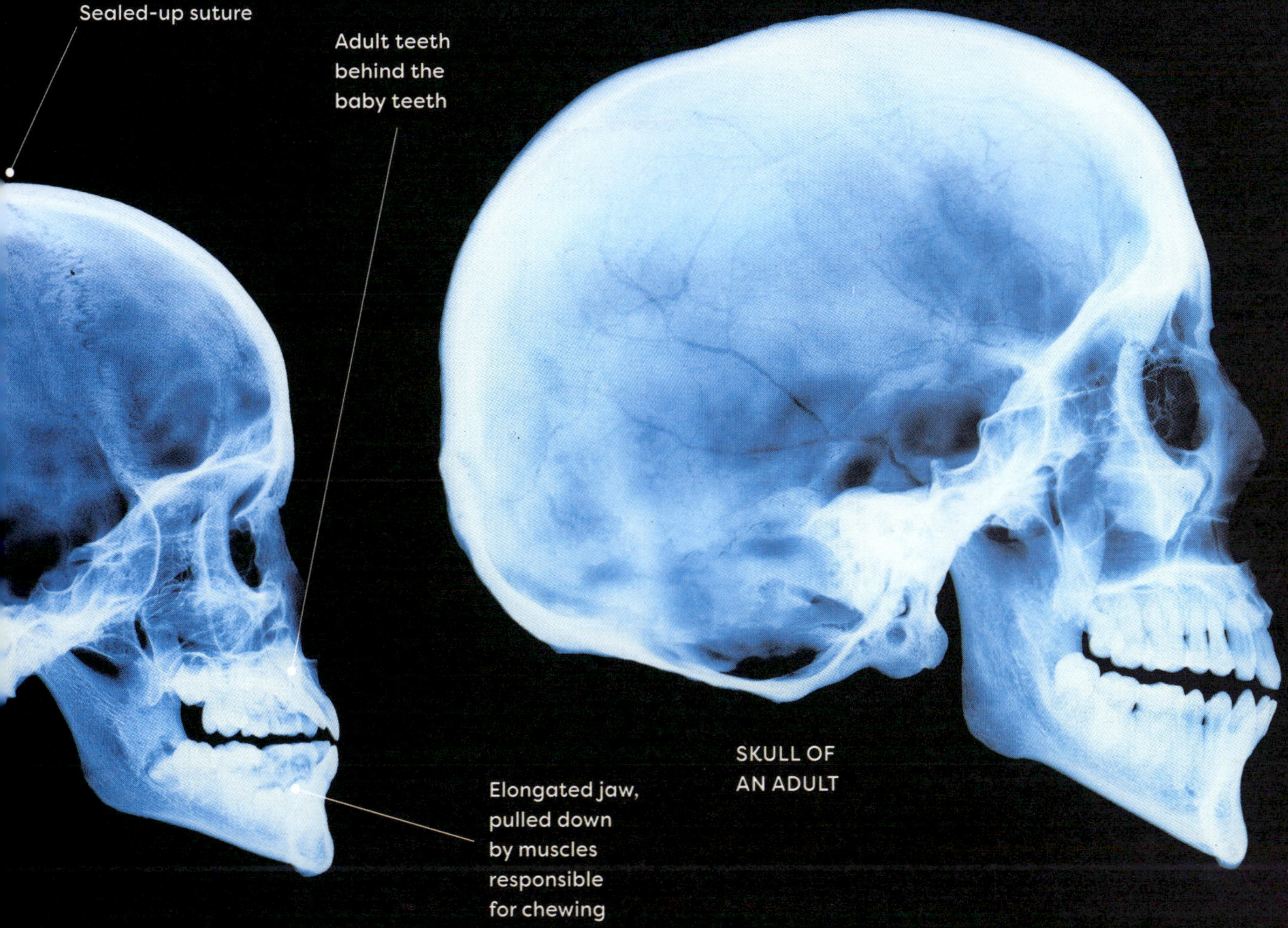

The growing skull

These X-rays show the growth and development of the human skull from birth to adulthood. The newborn baby's skull has gaps in it called sutures, which allow the skull to enlarge as the brain grows. By the time a child reaches about two years of age, these gaps seal up. Many bones through the body do this. That's why adults have fewer bones than children do.

Your biggest muscle is... behind you!

Muscles help you do all kinds of important things, from running and jumping to breathing and digesting food. The human body has more than 600 muscles in total, and their size, shape, and strength varies depending on the job that they are designed to do. Here is a selection of your body's most extraordinary muscles.

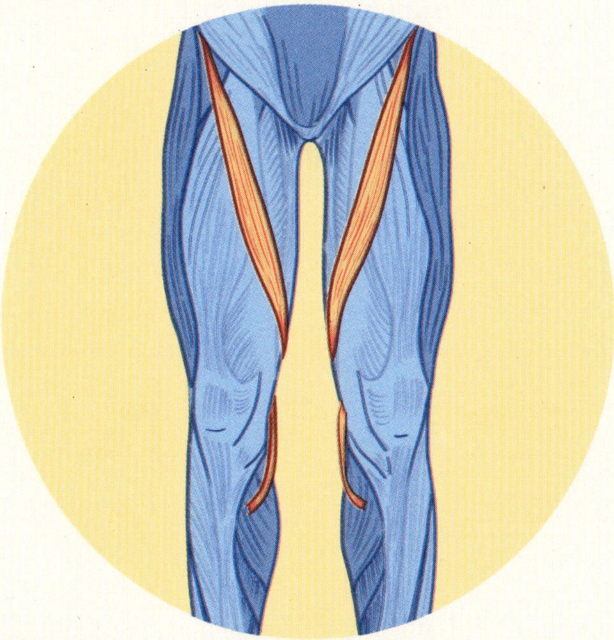

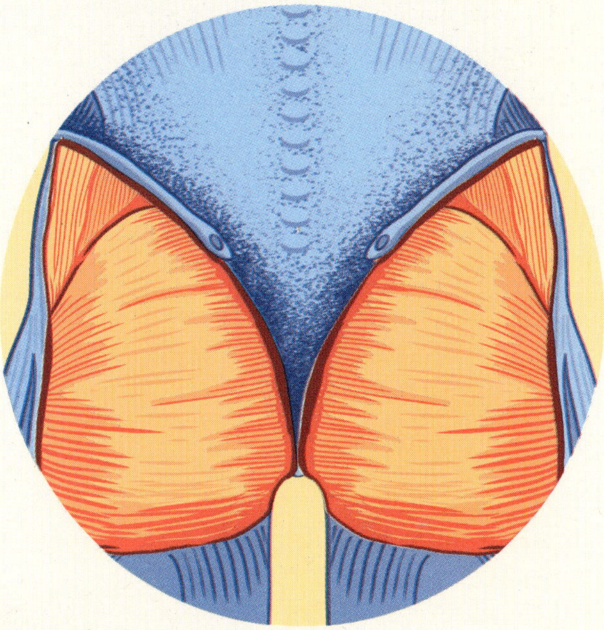

Largest
GLUTEUS MAXIMUS

The scientific name for the largest muscle in the body is the gluteus maximus—it's the muscle on your bottom. The gluteus maximus helps the body stand upright. You can feel it working when you walk up a flight of stairs.

Longest
SARTORIUS

The sartorius muscle runs down the length of your thigh and can be up to about 23 inches (60 cm) long. It helps to control the movement of the hip and knee joints.

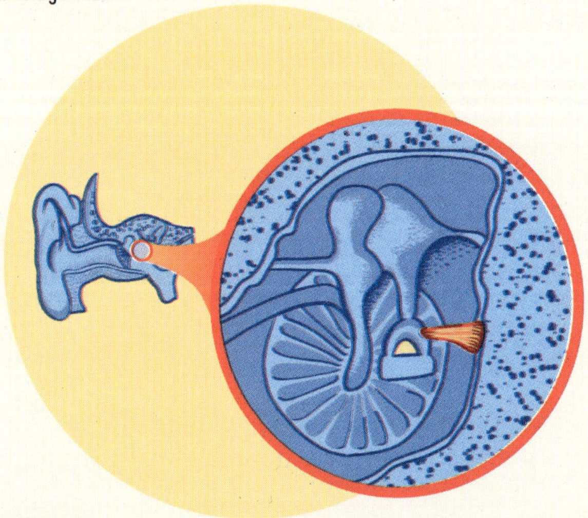

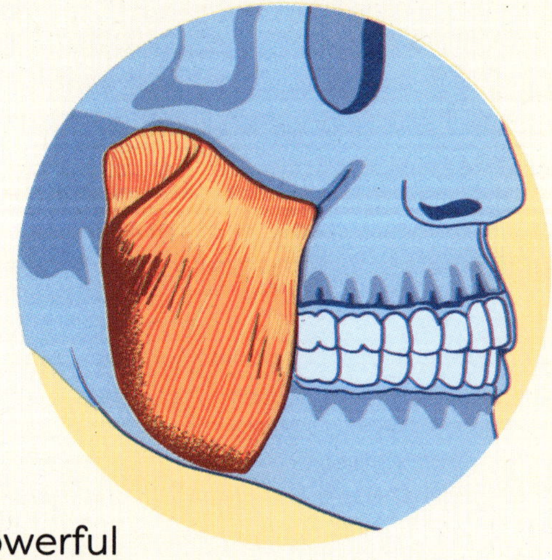

Powerful
MASSETER

The masseter's main job is to pull your jaw shut as you chew on food. It is among the most powerful muscles in the body for its size, allowing you to bite with tremendous force.

Smallest
STAPEDIUS

Located inside the middle ear, and ranging from $\frac{1}{25}$–$\frac{1}{3}$ inch (1–9 mm) long, the stapedius is the smallest muscle in the body. It controls the vibration of the stapes, which is the body's smallest bone (see page 197).

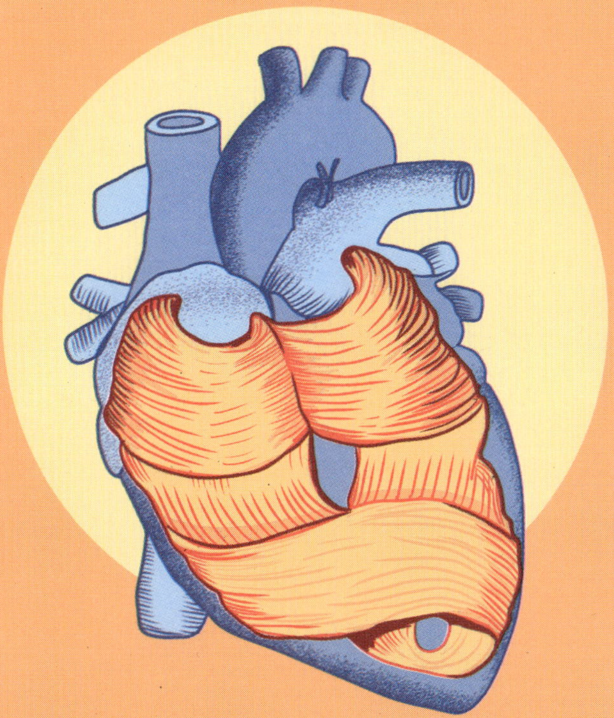

Resilient
HEART

The heart is one of the most hard-working muscles in your body. It can pump up to 2,000 gallons (about 7,000 liters) of blood around the circulatory system each day and will beat as many as 3 billion times during an average human lifetime.

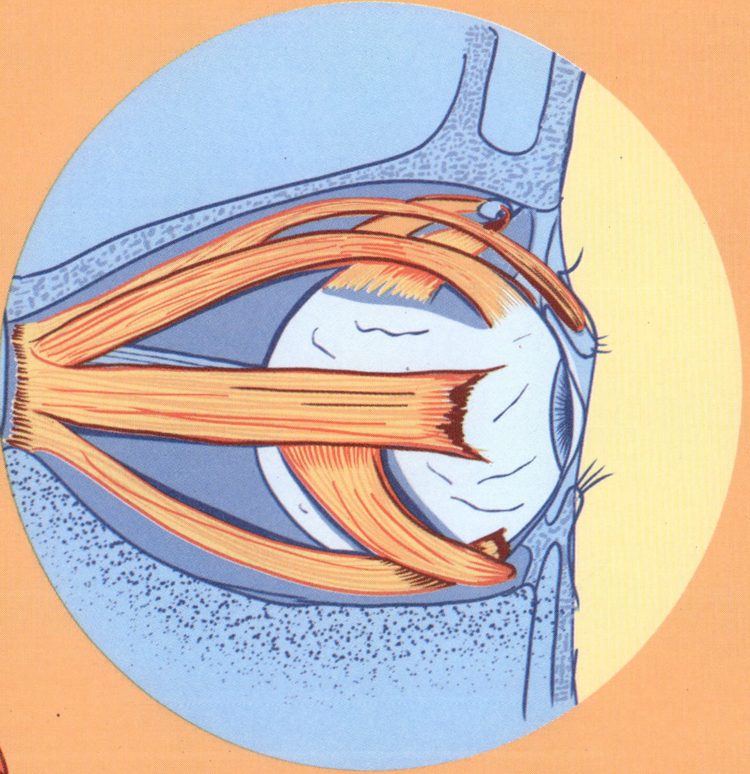

Fast-moving
EXTRAOCULAR MUSCLES

This group of six muscles controls the movement of each eye. If you read this book for an hour, during that time these muscles will make about 10,000 coordinated movements.

Highly flexible
TONGUE

The tongue is actually a set of eight interwoven muscles, which gives it a unique ability to move in almost any direction. Your tongue has a similar structure to an elephant's trunk and the arms of an octopus.

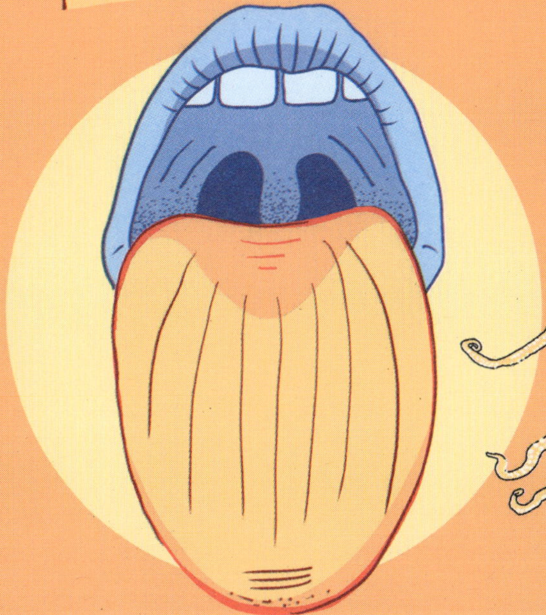

Take a deep breath!

Your body needs oxygen to do everything, from moving muscles and digesting food to growing and even thinking. You get oxygen from the air, and it's the job of the lungs to absorb the oxygen into your bloodstream, which then takes it wherever it needs to go. We call this process the respiratory system—and this is how it works.

BREATHE IN...

There are four main steps that happen so that air can enter your body—they are labeled 1 to 4 on this infographic. When you breathe in (inhale), your body takes in oxygen from the air.

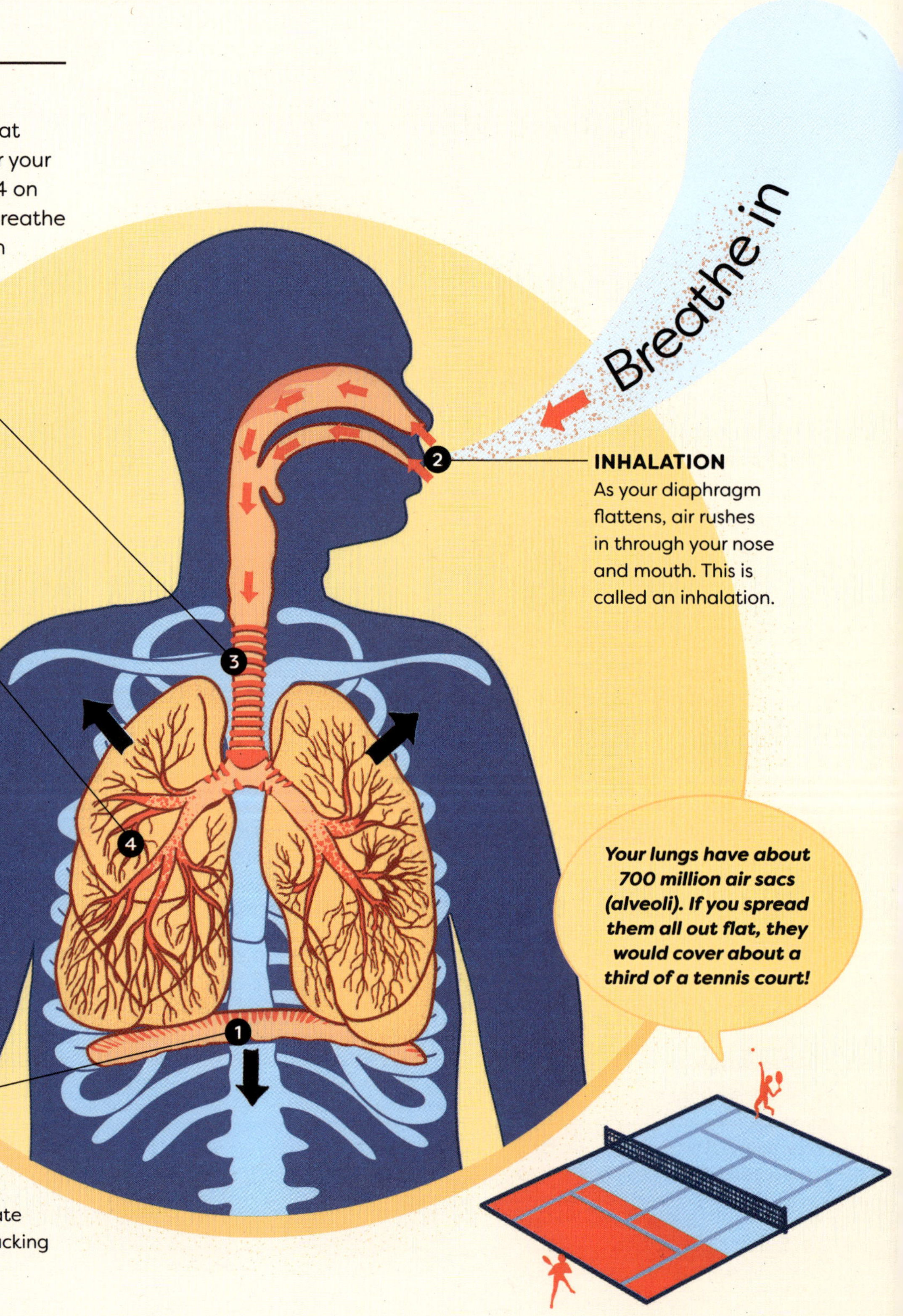

TRACHEA
Air travels through this tube, the trachea, to get to your lungs.

LUNGS
Inside the lungs are air sacs called alveoli. Oxygen passes through the alveoli and into your blood vessels, which then carry the oxygen around your body. At the same time, the waste gas carbon dioxide moves from the blood into the alveoli, ready to be breathed out (see opposite).

DIAPHRAGM
The diaphragm is a long muscle that pushes down when it contracts. As you take a breath, it flattens to create more space inside your lungs, sucking air into the body in the process.

INHALATION
As your diaphragm flattens, air rushes in through your nose and mouth. This is called an inhalation.

Your lungs have about 700 million air sacs (alveoli). If you spread them all out flat, they would cover about a third of a tennis court!

HOW LONG CAN WE SURVIVE ON A LUNGFUL OF AIR?

● = 1 minute of holding your breath

Average human
1 or 2 mins

World record for holding a breath of air
24 mins 37 secs

Longest recorded dive for a sperm whale
2 hours

Whales like me are mammals, so we can't breathe under water and need to hold our breath. We can do this for an impressively long time!

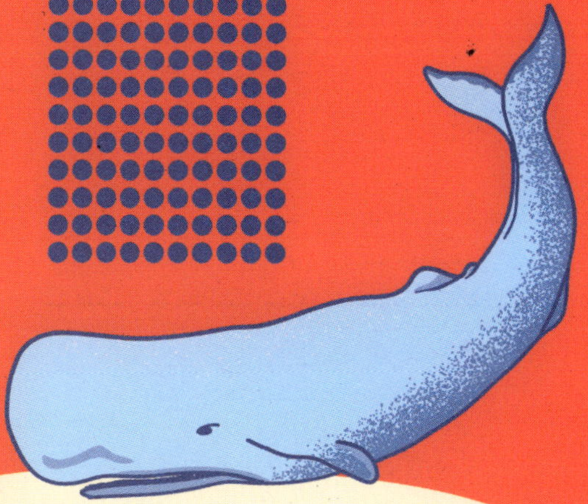

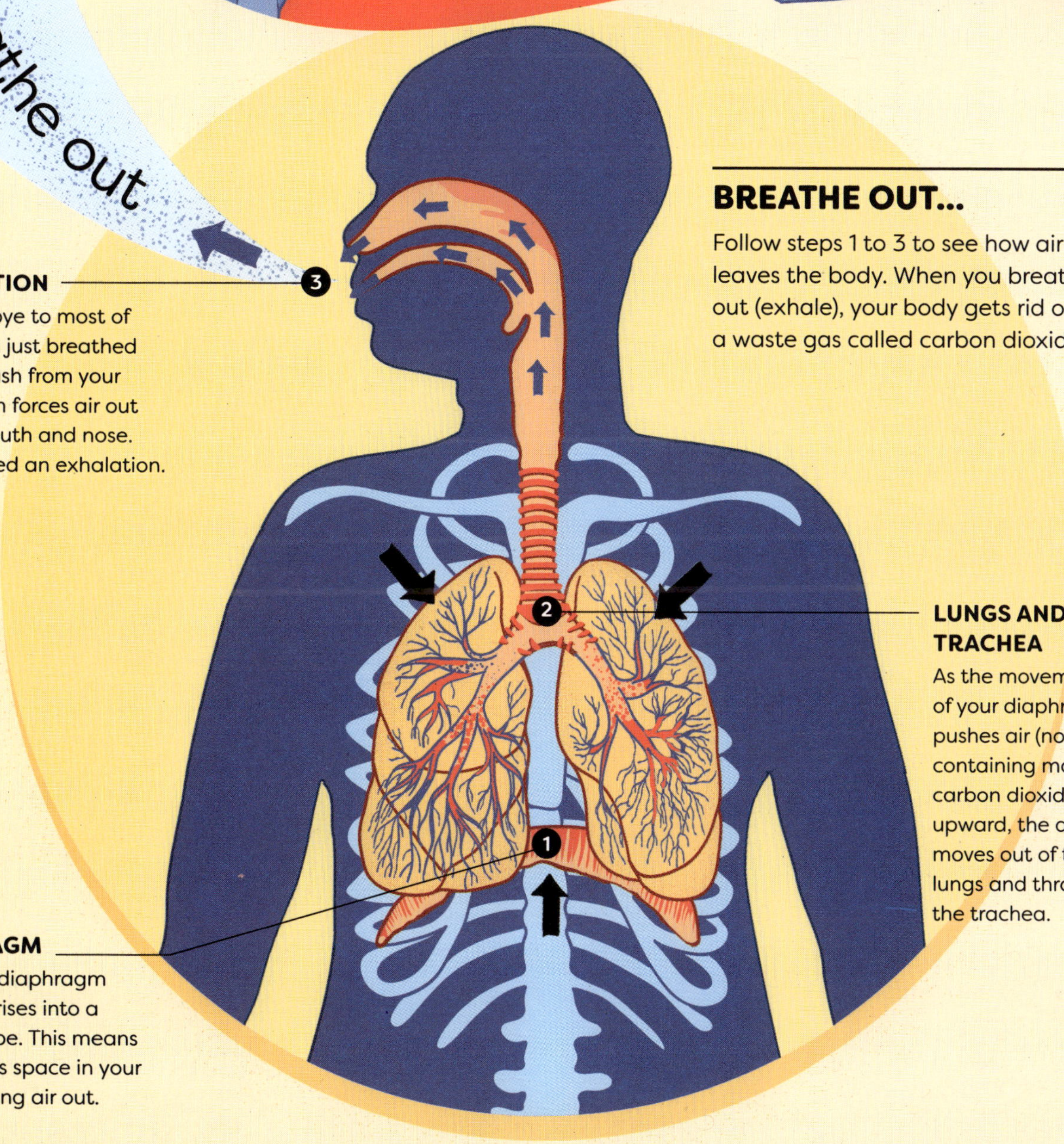

BREATHE OUT...

Follow steps 1 to 3 to see how air leaves the body. When you breathe out (exhale), your body gets rid of a waste gas called carbon dioxide.

EXHALATION
Say goodbye to most of the air you just breathed in! That push from your diaphragm forces air out of your mouth and nose. This is called an exhalation.

LUNGS AND TRACHEA
As the movement of your diaphragm pushes air (now containing more carbon dioxide) upward, the air moves out of the lungs and through the trachea.

DIAPHRAGM
When the diaphragm relaxes, it rises into a dome shape. This means there is less space in your lungs, forcing air out.

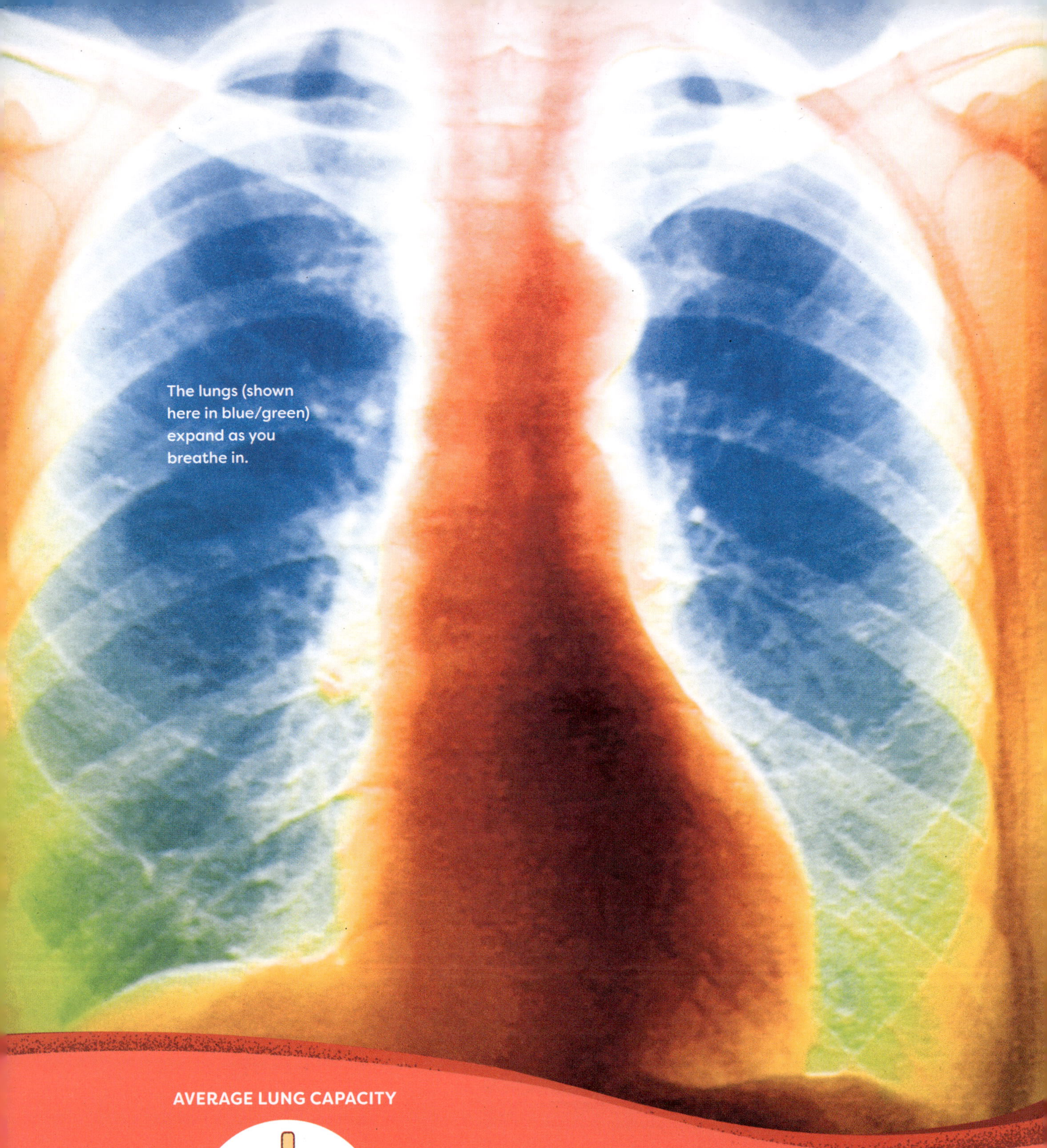

The lungs (shown here in blue/green) expand as you breathe in.

AVERAGE LUNG CAPACITY

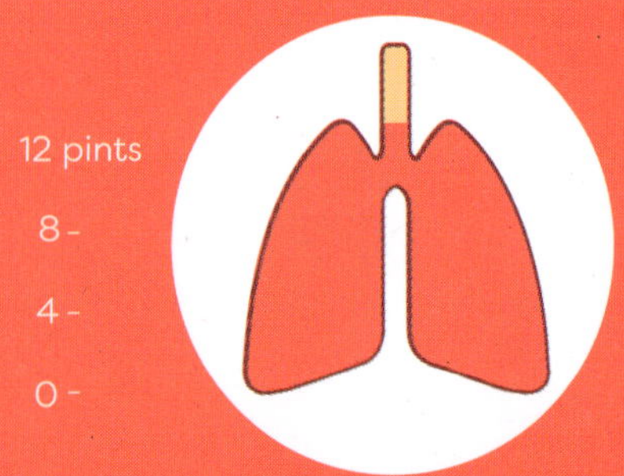

An adult's lungs can hold just over 12½ pints (6 liters) of air.

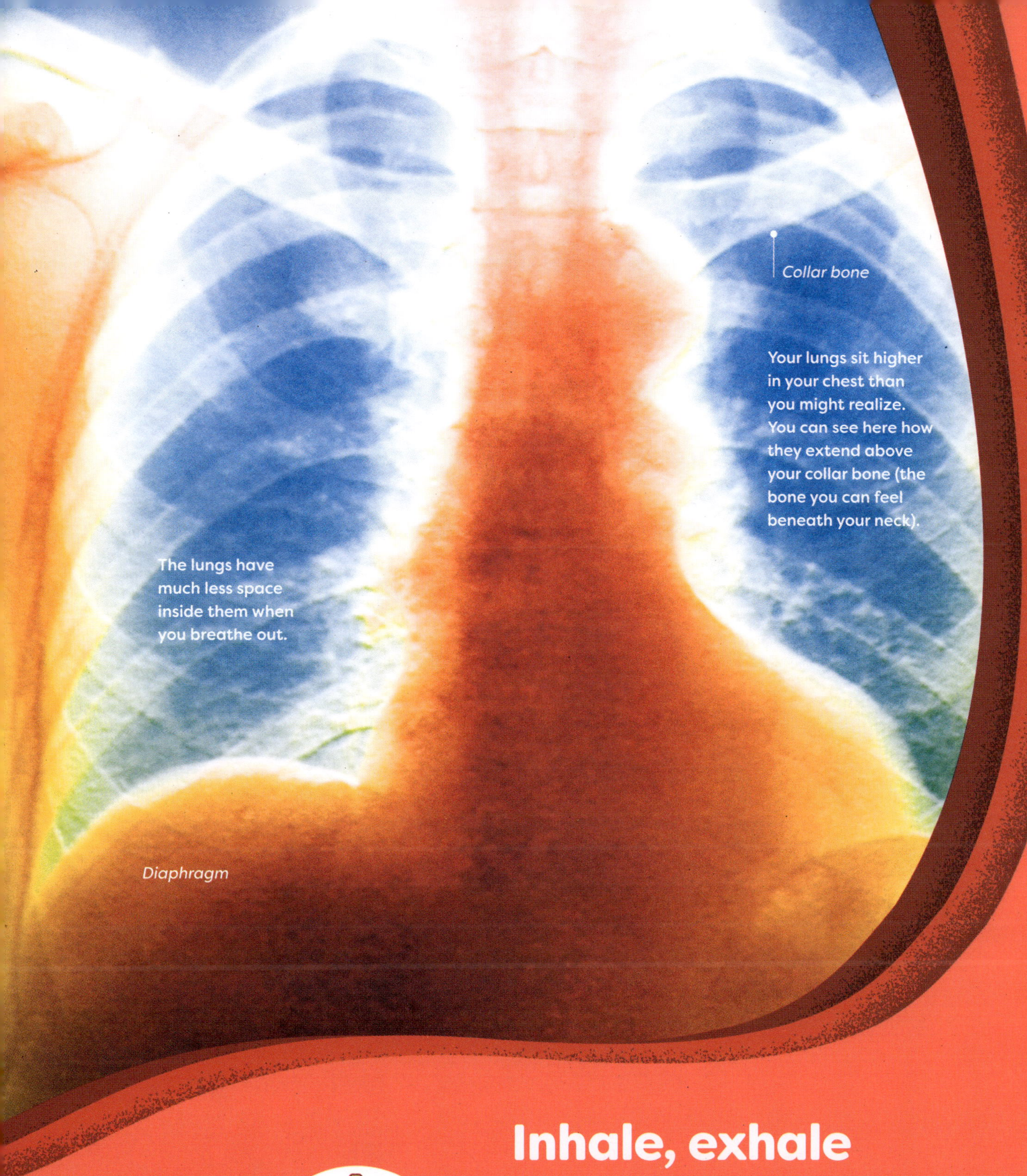

Inhale, exhale

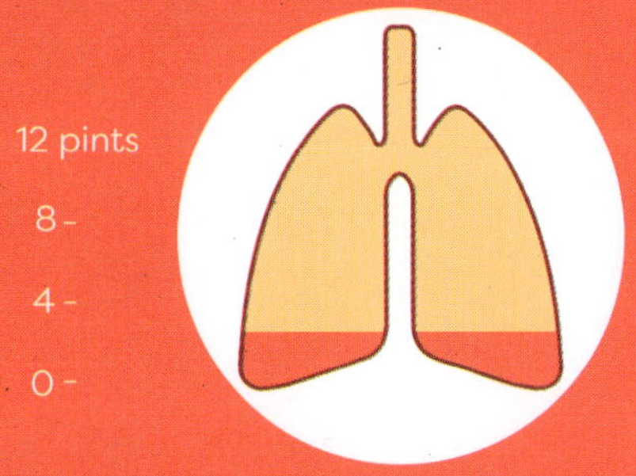

Around 2½ pints (1.2 liters) of air stay inside the lungs even after fully breathing out.

These colored X-rays show what happens inside your body as you breathe in and out. In the X-ray on the left, the diaphragm has flattened, allowing space for air to rush in to the lungs (as you inhale). In the X-ray on the right, the domed-up diaphragm forces air out of the lungs (as you exhale).

How does blood get around the body?

Your heart and all the blood vessels inside your body are known as the circulatory system. Like a complex network of roads, their job is to transport blood to all the different parts of your body, delivering oxygen and nutrients and removing waste.

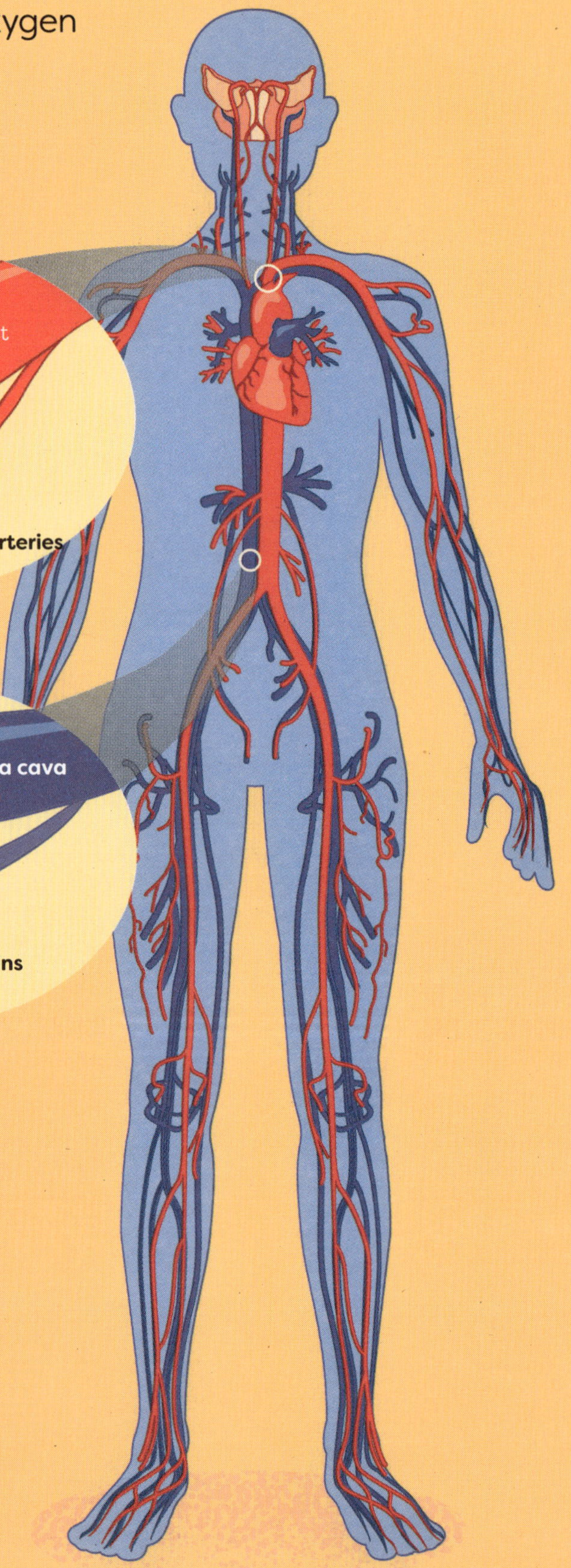

ARTERIES

Arteries, which are your body's biggest blood vessels, carry blood away from the heart and so have to be thick and strong to cope with the pressure of your heartbeat. The blood in arteries is bright red because it has just picked up lots of oxygen from the lungs.

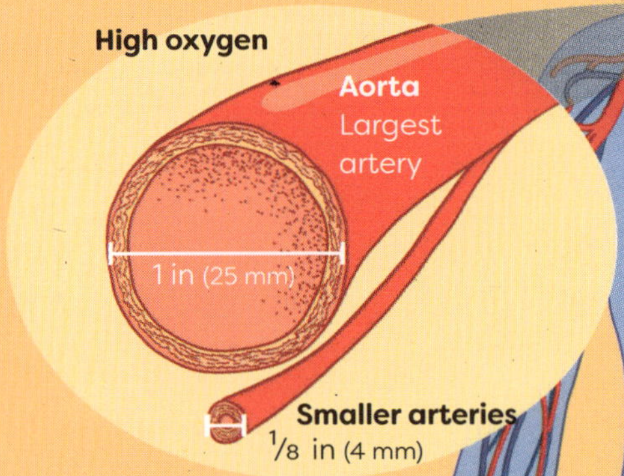

VEINS

Veins, which carry blood back to the heart after it has delivered oxygen to your organs and muscles, are mostly thinner and more fragile than arteries because the blood pressure inside them is lower. The blood in your veins isn't actually blue—that's just a trick of the light. It is dark red.

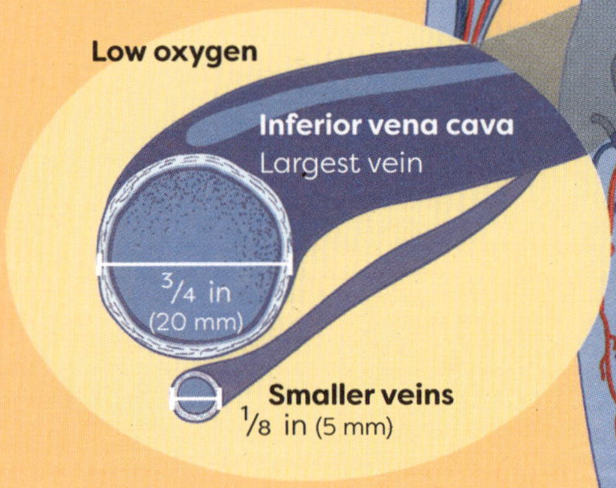

CAPILLARIES

The thinnest and most delicate of your blood vessels are capillaries. They are tiny tubes that connect the arteries and veins, and deliver blood, oxygen, and nutrients to the cells in the body.

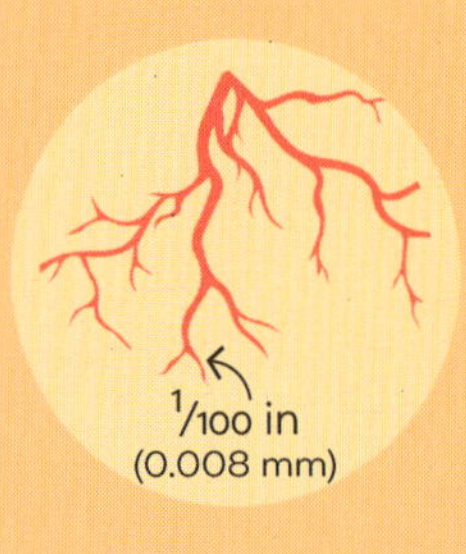

WHAT IS BLOOD MADE OF?

On average, blood makes up around 10 percent of a human's total body weight. The exact volume of blood in your circulatory system depends on how big you are. An adult has just over 1.3 gallons (5 liters) of blood. This is what it's made of.

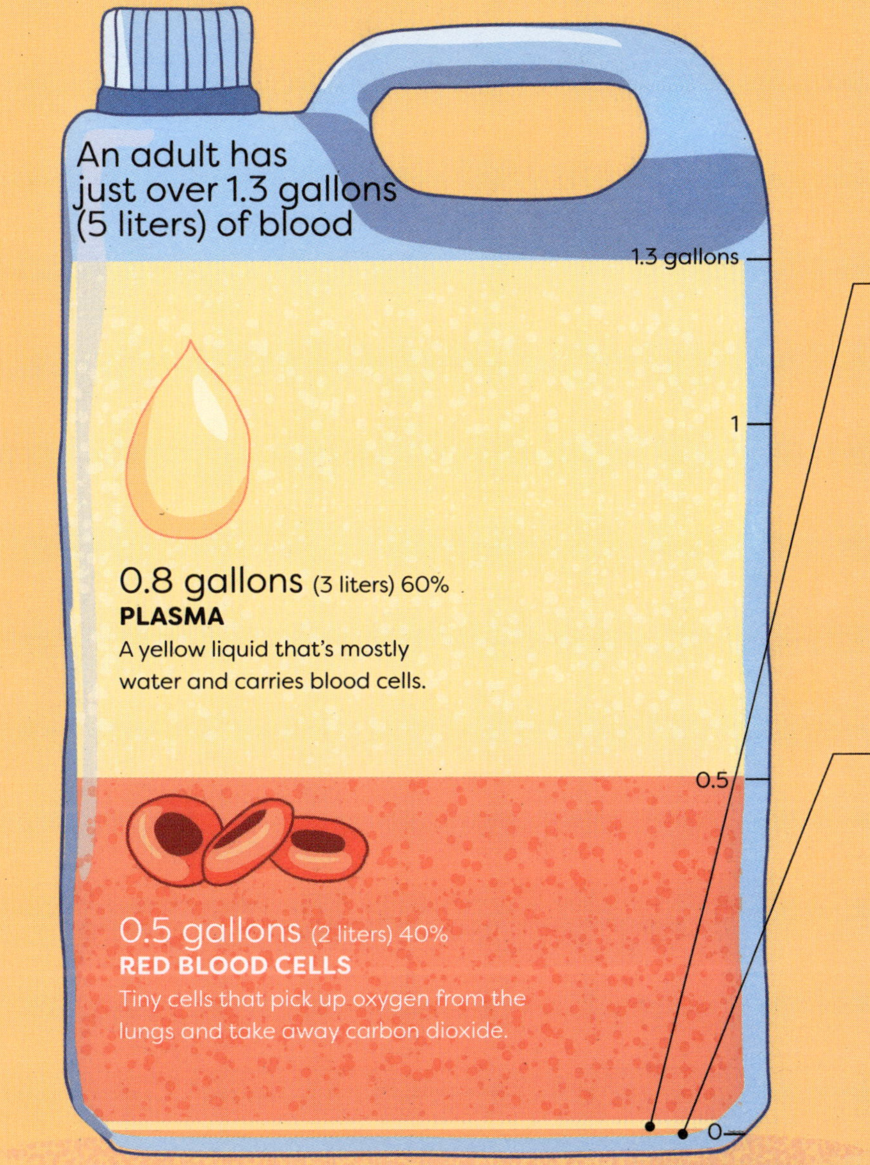

<1 ounce (0.02 liters) less than 0.5%
WHITE BLOOD CELLS
Protective cells that fight harmful bacteria and viruses to help prevent you from getting sick.

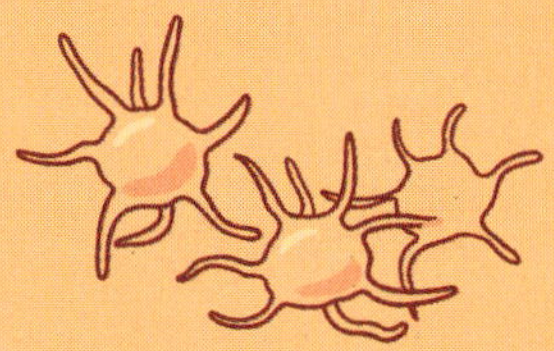

<1 ounce (0.02 liters) less than 0.5%
PLATELETS
Platelets help to make your blood sticky so that it clots when, for example, you cut yourself and you need to stop bleeding.

If you stretched out all the blood vessels in your body end to end, they would be more than 60,000 miles (100,000 km) long—that's long enough to wrap around Earth two and a half times!

60,000–90,000 miles long
(100,000–150,000 km)

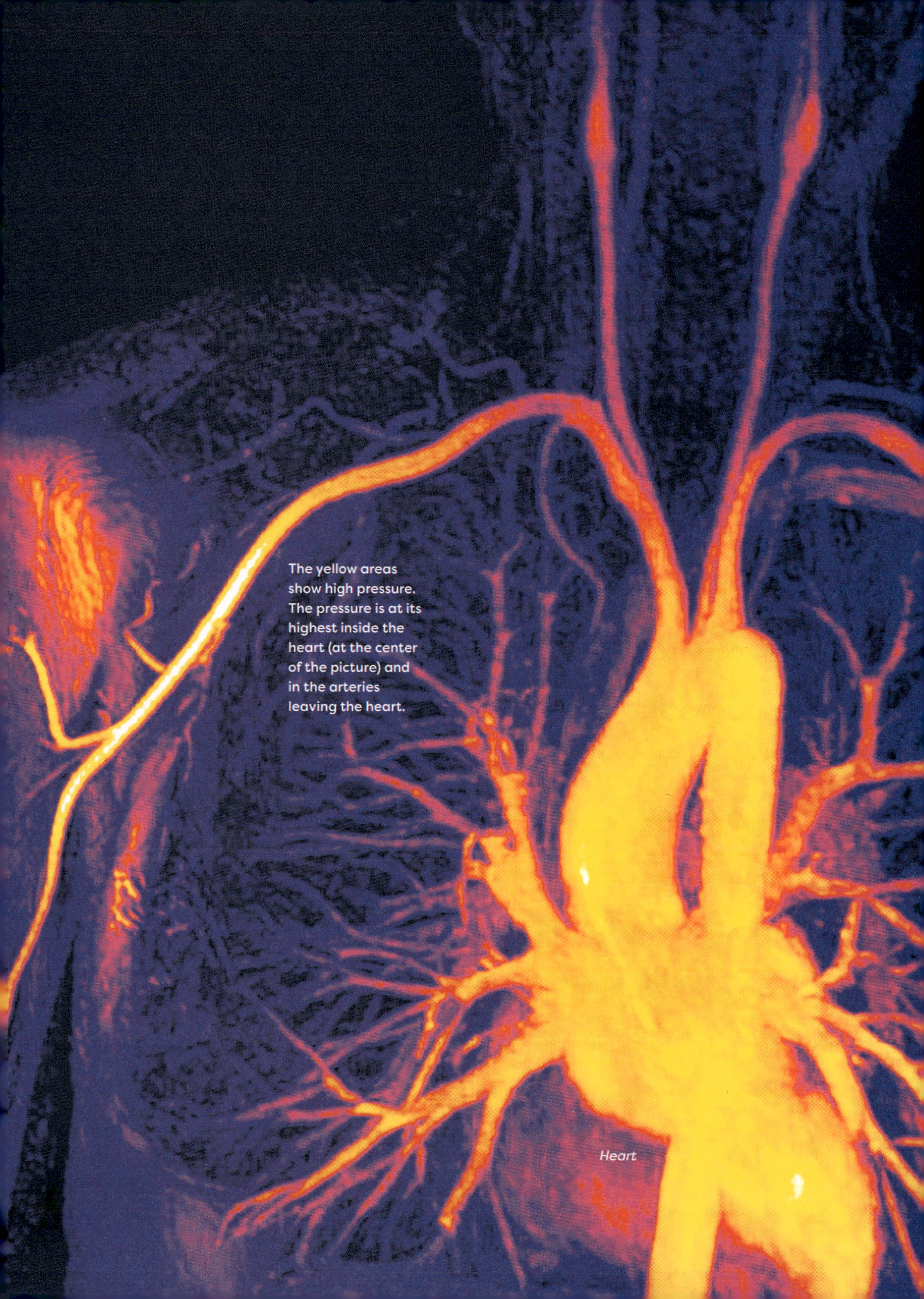

The yellow areas show high pressure. The pressure is at its highest inside the heart (at the center of the picture) and in the arteries leaving the heart.

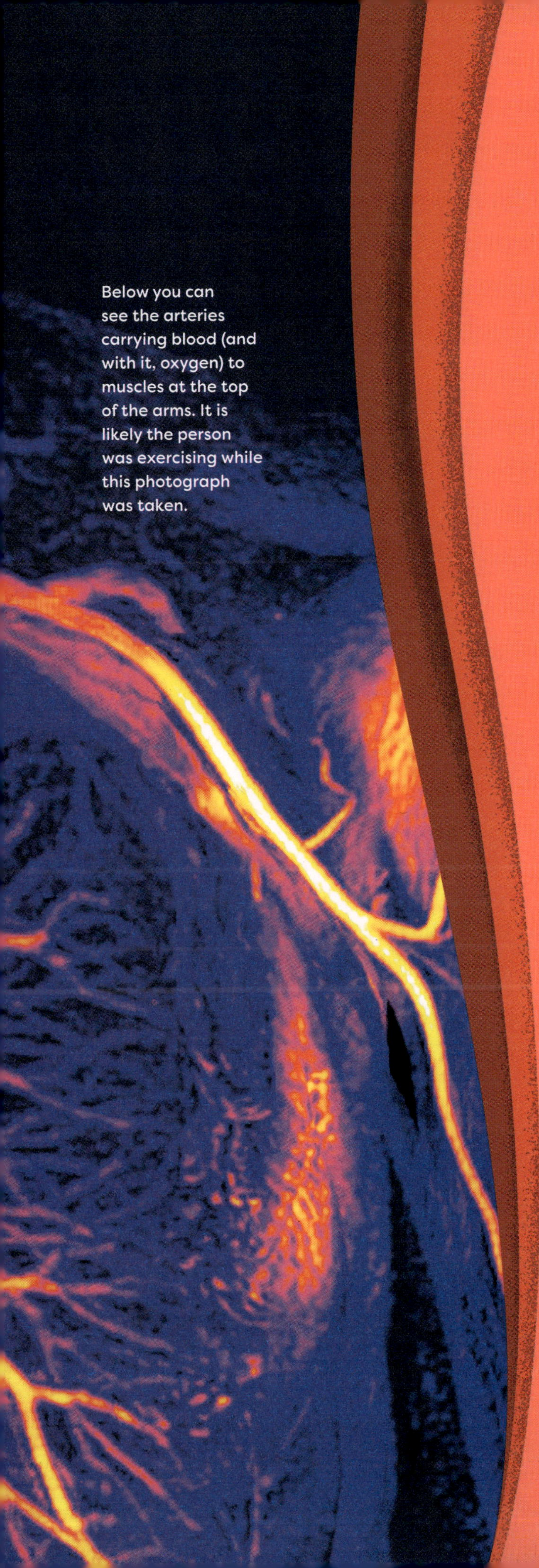

Below you can see the arteries carrying blood (and with it, oxygen) to muscles at the top of the arms. It is likely the person was exercising while this photograph was taken.

Pump, pump, pump

This image shows the blood vessels branching out from the heart. When you are moving, the heart squeezes harder and faster because your muscles need more oxygen from your blood. This is why your heart rate—the speed at which your heat is beating—increases when you're exercising.

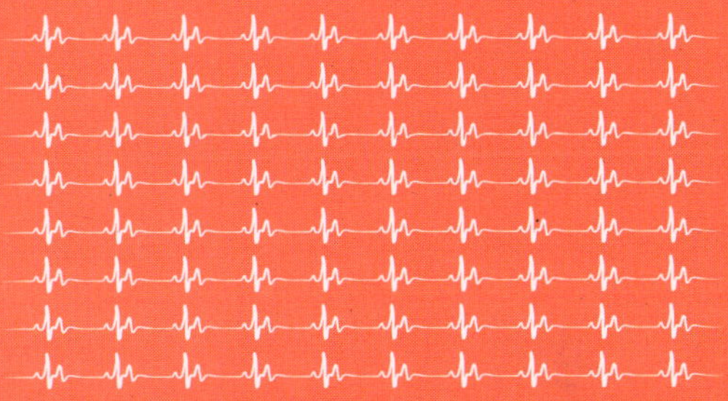

An adult's resting heart rate is usually between 60 and 100 beats per minute.

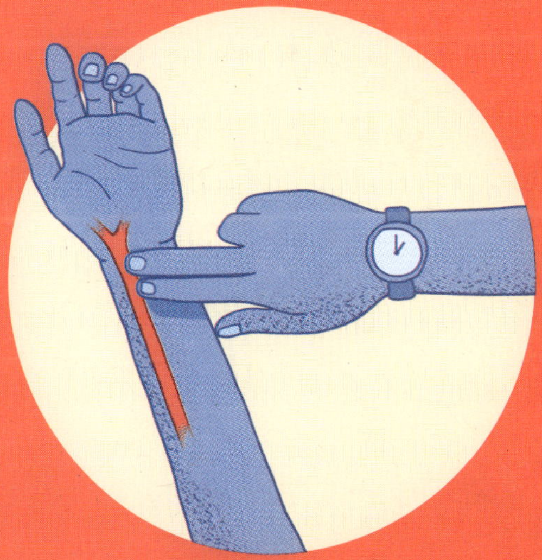

You can calculate your heart rate by placing two fingers on your wrist and counting the beats for 1 minute.

Eat, then excrete!

When you eat a meal, it takes about 24 hours for the food to pass all the way through the digestive tract, which is a long twisting tube that starts at the mouth and ends at the anus. Here, we follow the food on its epic journey through the body. (And if you want to find out what happens next, turn to page 214.)

HOW THE BODY DIGESTS FOOD

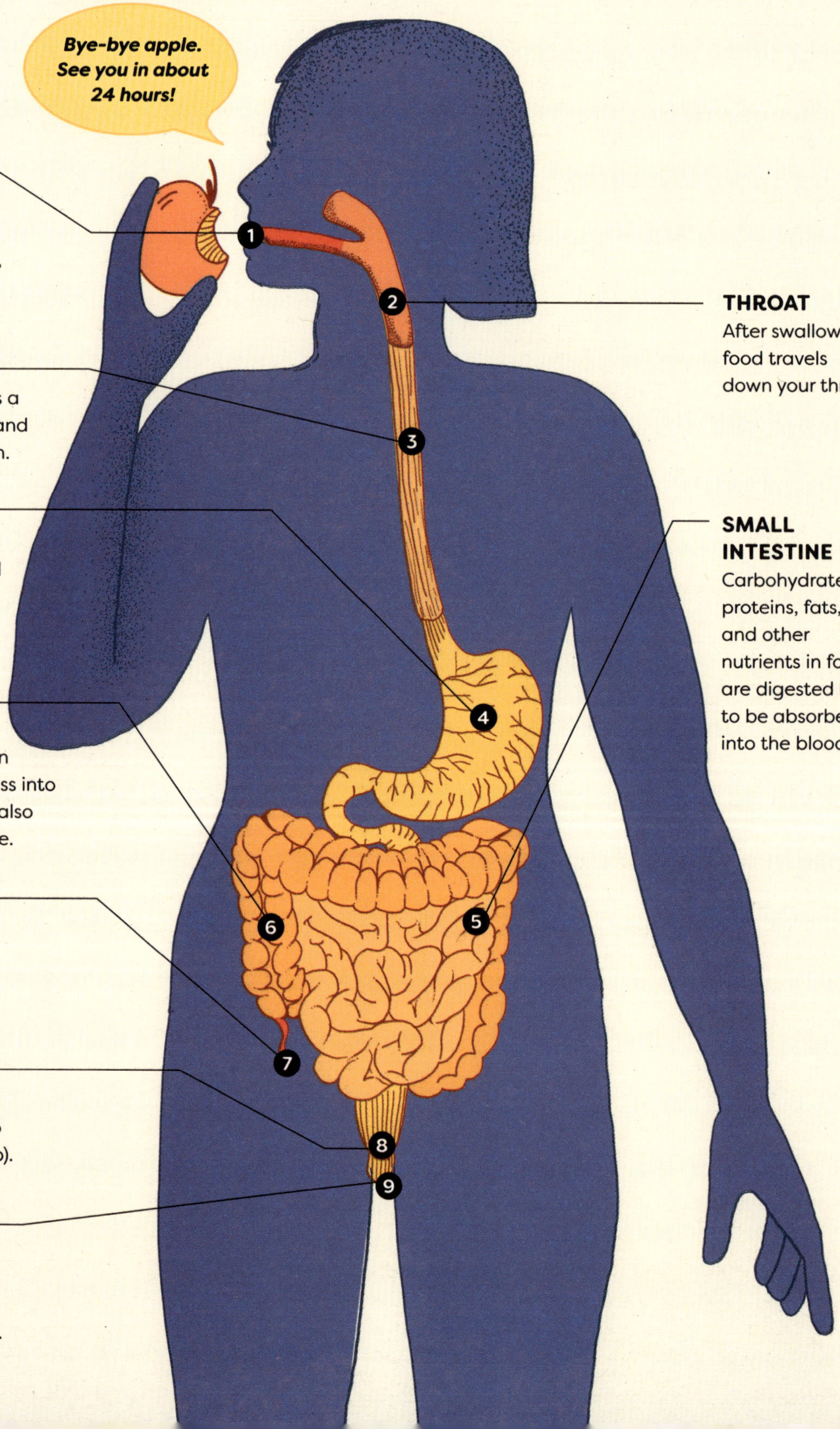

MOUTH
The digestive process starts in the mouth. Your teeth break food into smaller bits while your saliva moistens it, making it easier to swallow.

THROAT
After swallowing, food travels down your throat.

ESOPHAGUS
From the throat, food enters a thin tube—the esophagus—and travels down to the stomach.

STOMACH
Inside the stomach, acid and enzymes kill off harmful bacteria and break down food so it is easier to digest.

SMALL INTESTINE
Carbohydrates, proteins, fats, and other nutrients in food are digested here to be absorbed into the blood.

LARGE INTESTINE
Food materials that your body can't easily break down (mainly fiber from plants) pass into the large intestine. Water is also absorbed into the blood here.

APPENDIX
The appendix is a tube attached to the large intestine. It is not clear if it serves any purpose.

RECTUM
Undigested bits of your food then pass into the rectum to be stored as feces (aka poop).

ANUS
The anus is the opening at the very end of the digestive tract through which poop leaves the body.

HOW LONG IS THE DIGESTIVE TRACT?

So that the digestive tract takes up less space inside your body, most of it is curled up on itself like a big ball of spaghetti. However, if you stretched the digestive tract of an adult all the way out to its full height, it would be about 30 feet (9.3 m) tall. That's roughly the height of a three-story building!

How much snot do you make?

Snot may be pretty disgusting, but it's actually really important and useful stuff. It is a type of mucus produced in glands in your nose. Snot traps dust and harmful bacteria and also helps you smell things. Mucus is also made in your mouth, where it forms part of your saliva. Saliva moistens your food so that it's easier to eat and swallow. Your stomach produces mucus, too—here, it stops acid from leaking. This is what it would look like if you poured *all* that gloop together in one place.

A DAY OF MUCUS

Your body produces about five cups of mucus every 24 hours.

A LIFETIME OF MUCUS

Your body produces about 209 bathtubs of mucus in your lifetime.

Your body makes mucus all the time, even while you're asleep!

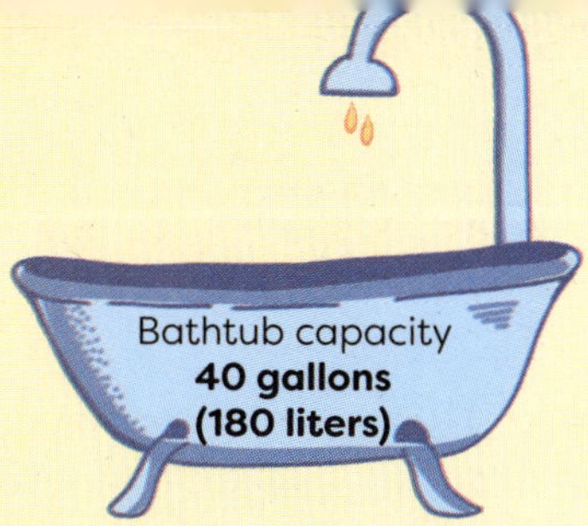

Poop and farts

At the end of food's digestive journey, a lump of smelly brown waste material is left over, which is then pushed out of the body. The scientific name for this unwanted waste material is feces, but you probably know it as... poop!

WHAT'S IN POOP?

On average, an adult human excretes between 3½ and 9 ounces (100–250 g) of poop each day. Most of it is made of water, which is what helps to give poop its mud-like texture. The solid matter in your poop is made up of dead bacteria, dead cells, stuff your body can't digest (such as cellulose, which is found, for example, in the husks of corn kernels), as well as some proteins, fats, and various other waste materials.

The main elements in poop are oxygen, carbon, and hydrogen. We also flush tiny amounts of valuable minerals in our poop down the toilet, including gold!

WHY DO WE PASS GAS?

Gas gradually builds up inside the human digestive tract. Some of this gas is swallowed as air. Other gases are produced when helpful bacteria inside our digestive system ferment our food. When this gas finally leaves the body through the anus, it makes a ring-shaped muscle called the sphincter vibrate. This causes a funny farting sound.

VOLUME OF PASSED GAS PER DAY
pints

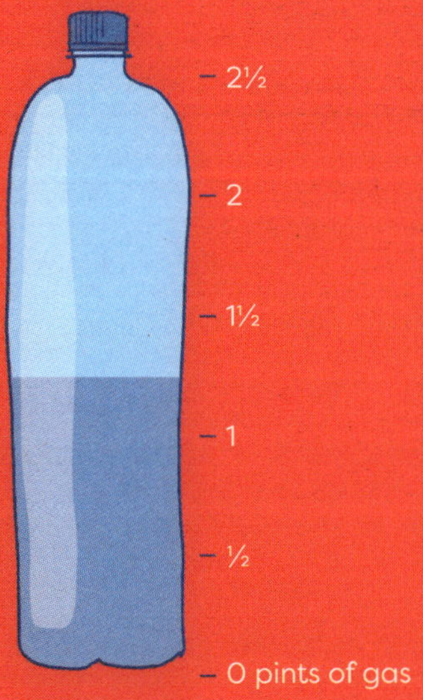

On average, humans produce just over a pint of gas a day.

THE SEVEN TYPES OF POOP

Scientists at the University of Bristol in the UK have created a scale that divides human poop into seven different categories depending on what the poop looks and feels like. It is called the Bristol Stool Scale. (Stool, like feces, is a medical name for poop.)

Want to find out about an animal that eats its own poop? Turn to page 160.

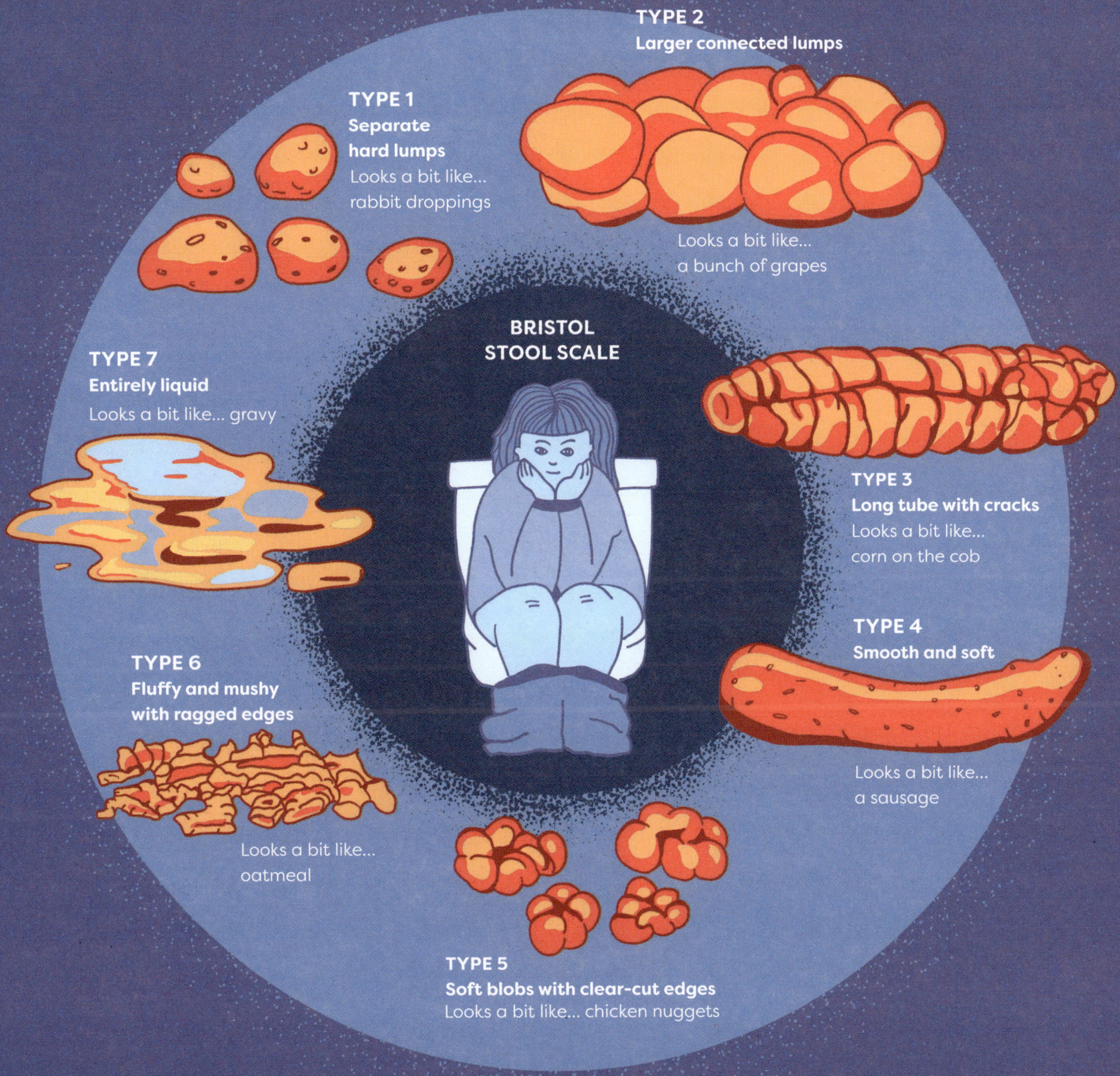

The power of pee

Peeing is your body's way of getting rid of extra water and unwanted toxins. Also known as urine, pee comes from your blood, not your digestive system. This is the journey pee takes from your kidneys to your bladder on its way to the toilet...

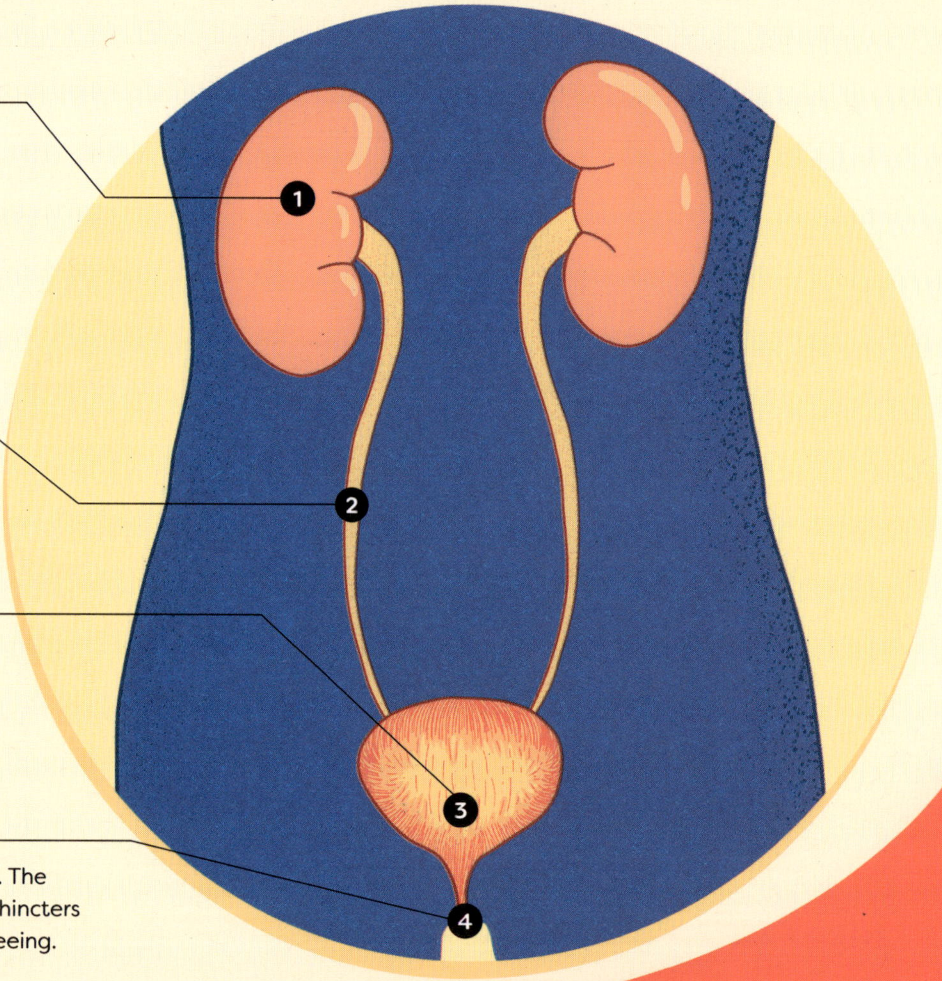

KIDNEYS
When you drink a glass of water, it's absorbed into the blood in your digestive system. The kidneys, which keep blood clean, filter out the harmful stuff in the blood plus any extra water your body doesn't need and turns them into pee.

URETERS
The ureters are tubes that carry urine from the kidneys to the bladder. There is one ureter for each kidney.

BLADDER
This is a bag inside your body where pee is stored. When your bladder is full, it tells your brain you need to go to the bathroom.

URETHRA
Pee leaves your body through this tube. The urethra has muscles around it called sphincters that control when you start and stop peeing.

HOW MUCH PEE?

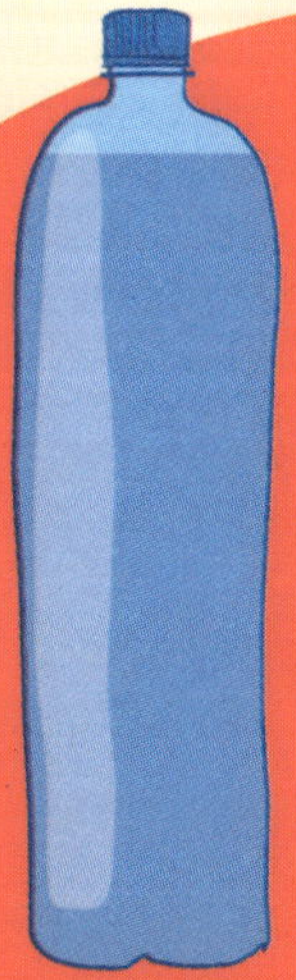

DAILY PEE
An average day's worth of pee could fill a large water bottle, about 3 pints (1.5 quarts).

LIFETIME OF PEE
The amount of pee you produce over a lifetime could fill a large tanker truck—about 10,000 gallons (40,000 liters)!

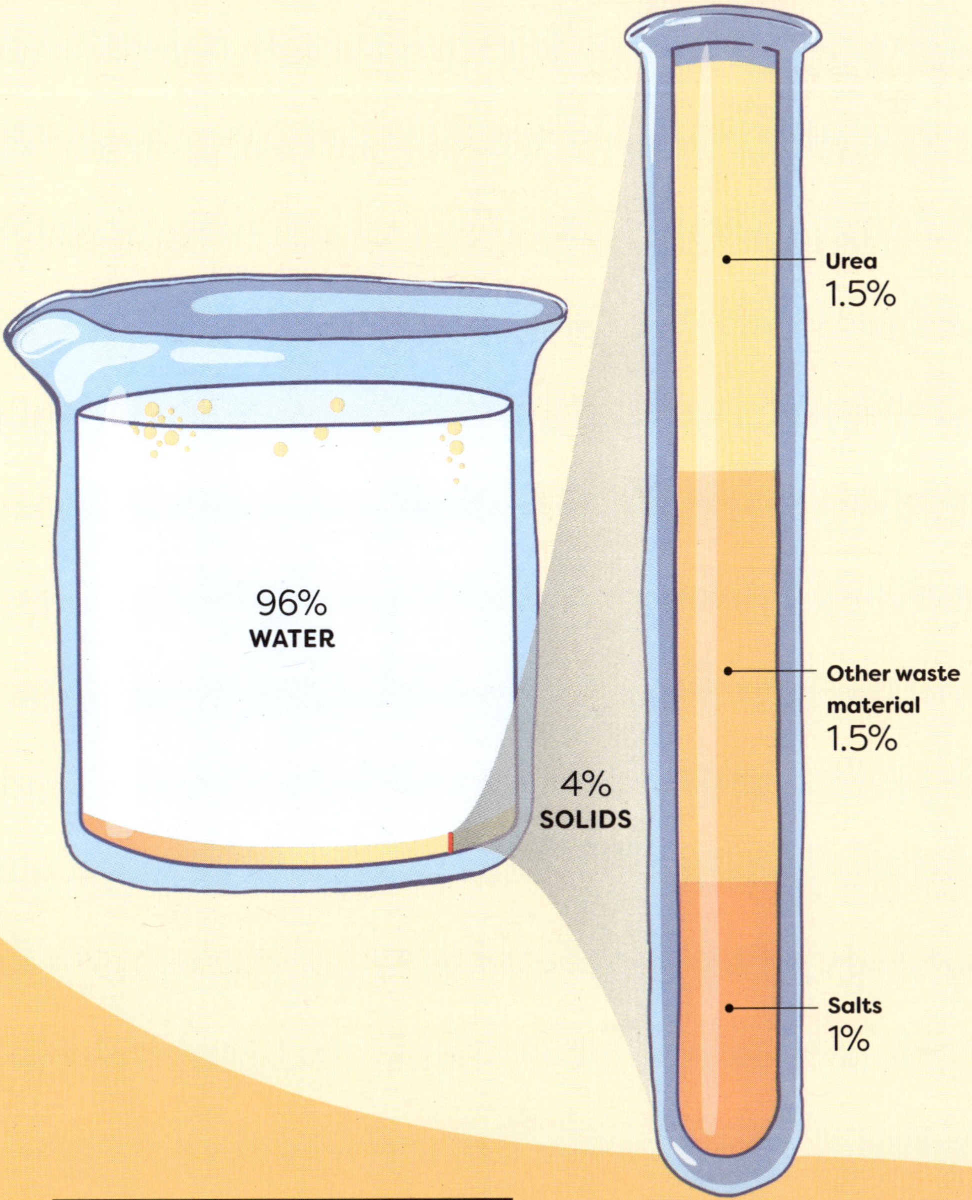

WHAT'S INSIDE PEE?

Most of your pee—about 96 percent—is water. The remaining 4 percent, shown in the test tube illustration, is made of urea (a waste product from your digestive system), salts, and other waste material. This other waste material includes a yellow pigment called urochrome—which comes from your blood and gives pee its yellowish color—and also ammonia, which gives pee its distinctive smell.

THE "LAW OF URINATION"

The time it takes for a human to pee is usually between 20 and 30 seconds. It takes elephants and lots of other mammals roughly the same time to pee as humans—even though elephants have a bladder that is 100 times bigger than ours!

	CAT	HUMAN	GORILLA	HORSE	ELEPHANT
BODY MASS pounds, lbs (kilograms, kg)	11 lbs (5 kg)	137 lbs (62 kg)	220 lbs (100 kg)	1,318 lbs (598 kg)	13,334 lbs (6,048 kg)
PEE DURATION	about 20–30 seconds				

What does skin do?

The skin connects your body to its surroundings, through the sense of touch, while also shielding it from outside threats. If we zoom in to see what skin looks like beneath the surface, we can see the many ingenious ways it helps your body.

UNDERNEATH THE SKIN

The diagram below shows a cross section of human skin from the surface to the skin's deepest layers. The cross section has been magnified so you can see the different features of each layer in detail.

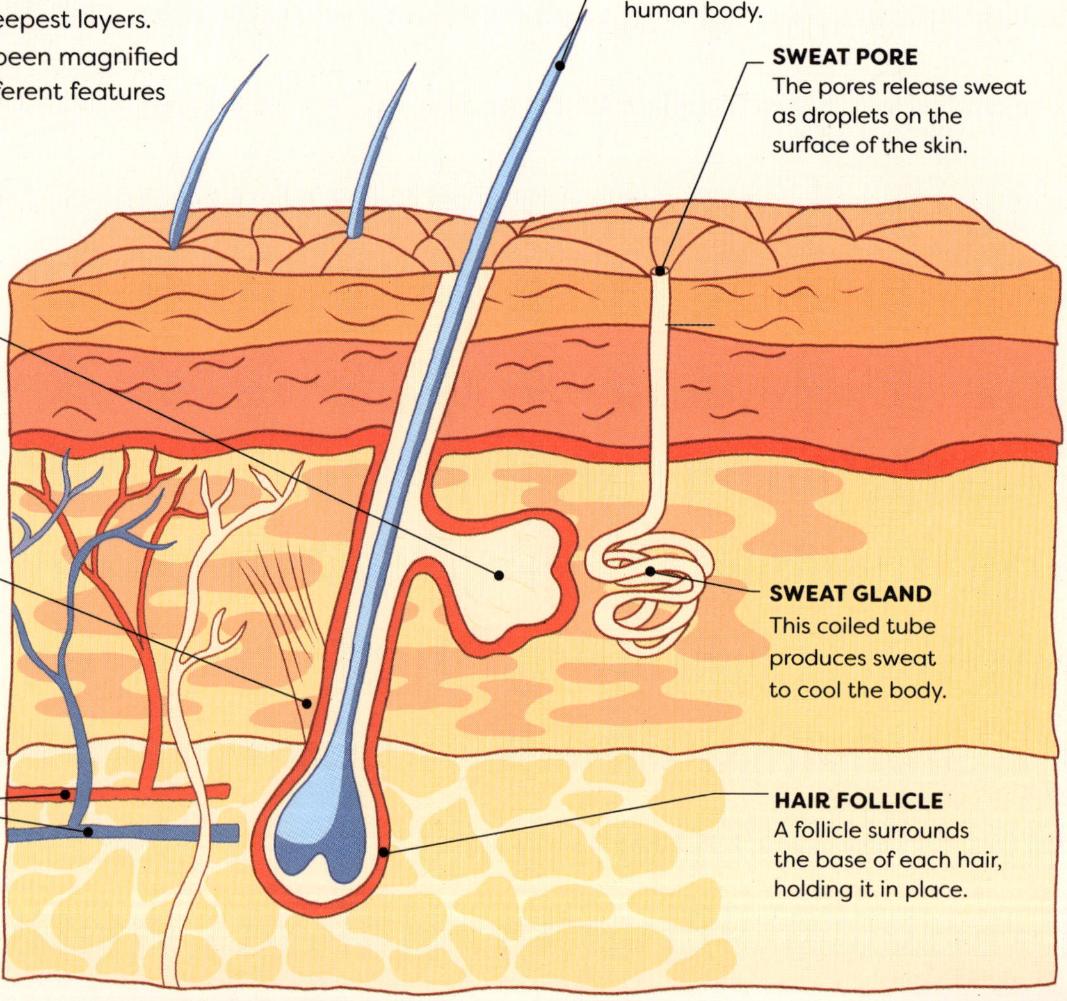

HAIR
Hairs cover most areas of the human body.

SWEAT PORE
The pores release sweat as droplets on the surface of the skin.

OIL GLAND
This releases a greasy oil that helps keep skin waterproof and flexible.

ARRECTOR PILI MUSCLE
This pulls your hair up when you are cold or experience strong emotion, which gives you "goosebumps."

SWEAT GLAND
This coiled tube produces sweat to cool the body.

BLOOD VESSELS
These carry blood between the heart and the skin.

HAIR FOLLICLE
A follicle surrounds the base of each hair, holding it in place.

HOW SKIN HELPS YOUR BODY

Your skin does an impressive variety of jobs. Here are six of the most important, from protecting the body against harmful bacteria to helping you communicate with other people.

PROTECTION
Skin helps protect you against germs and injury and keeps you waterproof.

TEMPERATURE REGULATION
Sweat helps cool the body; hair keeps it warm and dry.

HOW BIG IS YOUR SKIN?

The skin is your body's biggest organ. It is both the heaviest by weight and the largest by total surface area. This illustration shows what surface area an adult's skin and child's skin would cover if each were stretched out flat.

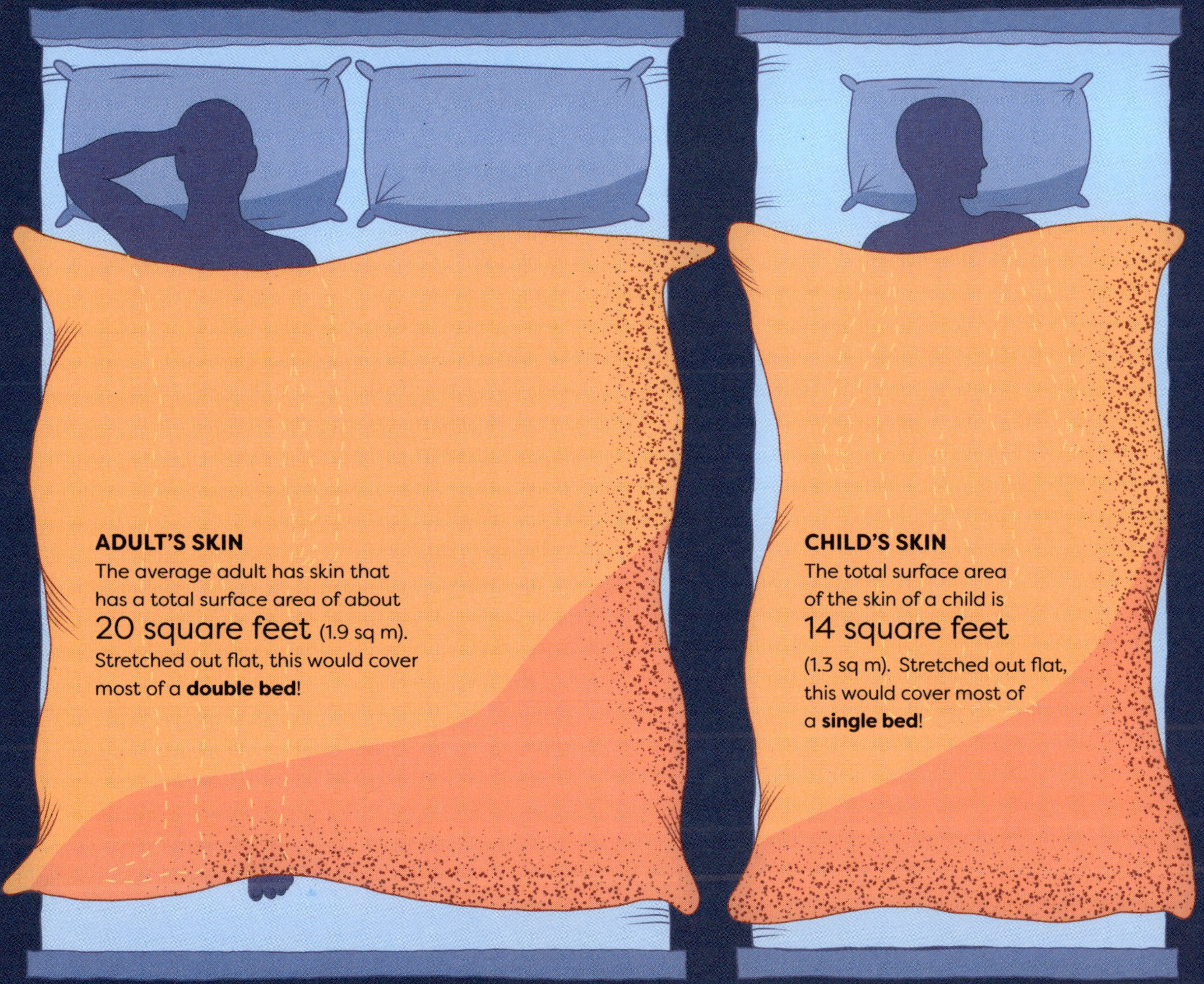

COMMUNICATION
Skin can reveal emotions, as it does when you blush.

GRIP
By regulating moisture, ridges on your fingers help you to grip.

VITAMIN-D PRODUCTION
Skin produces vitamin D when exposed to sunlight.

SENSITIVITY
Through touch, skin tells the brain about your environment.

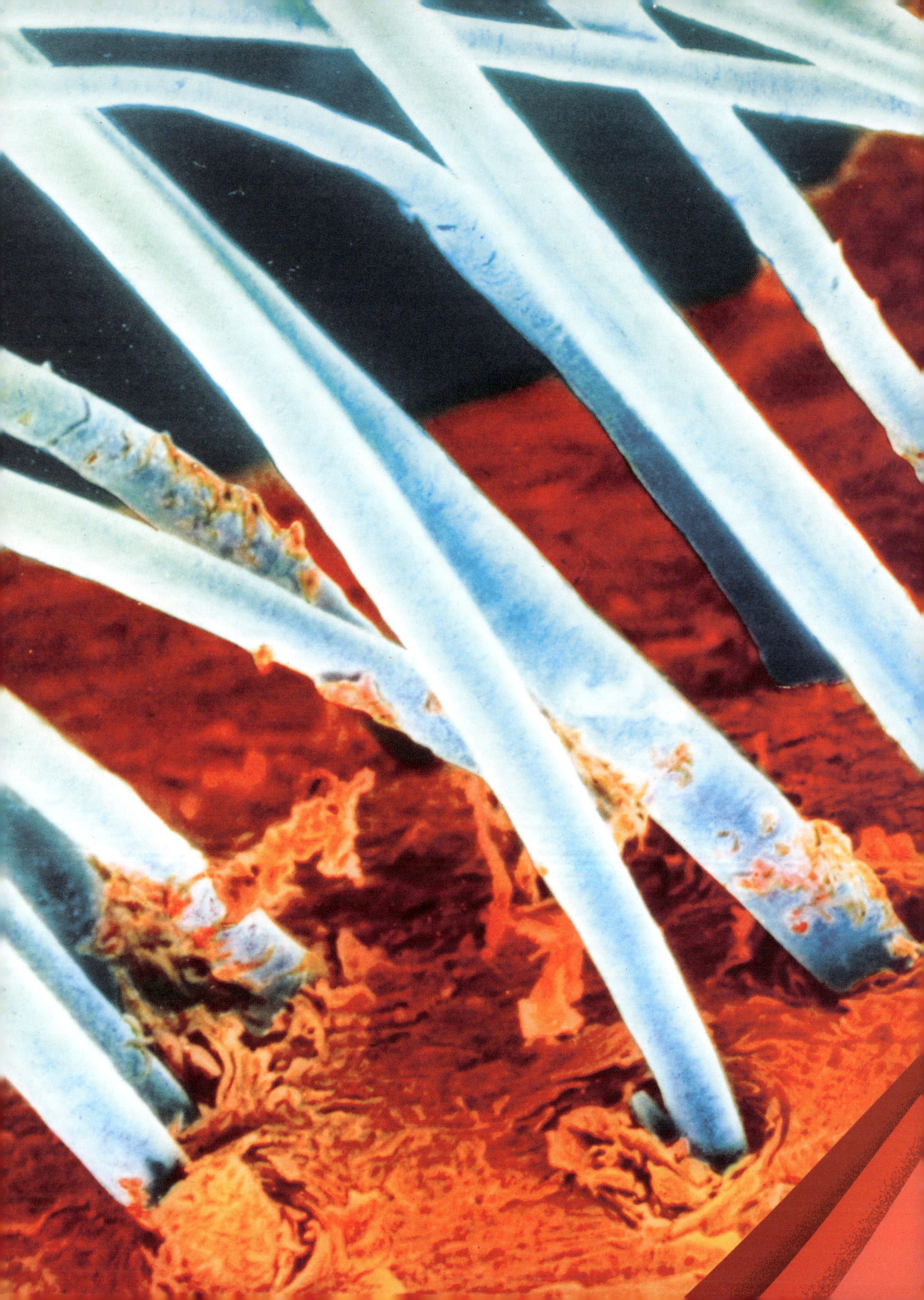

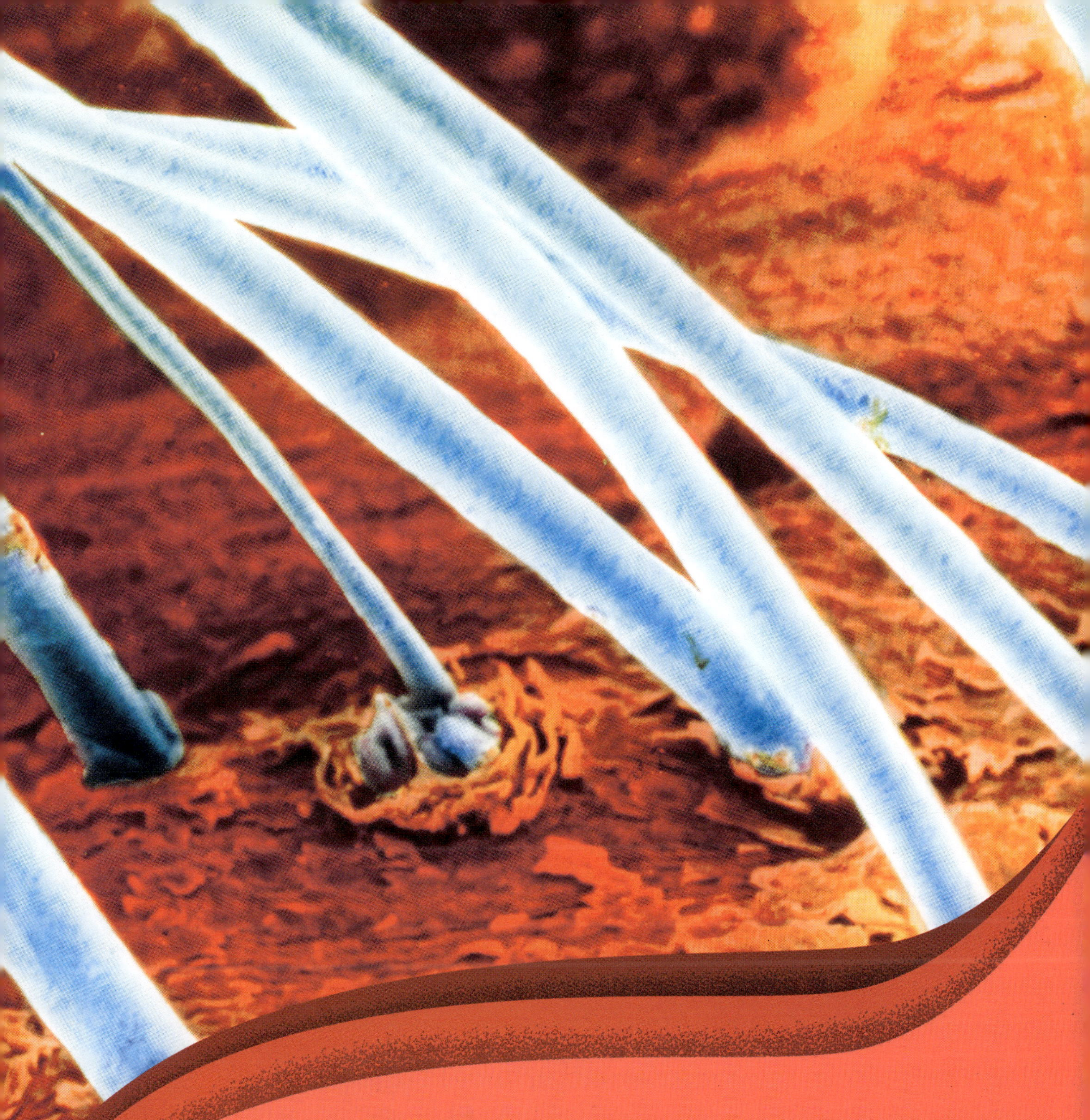

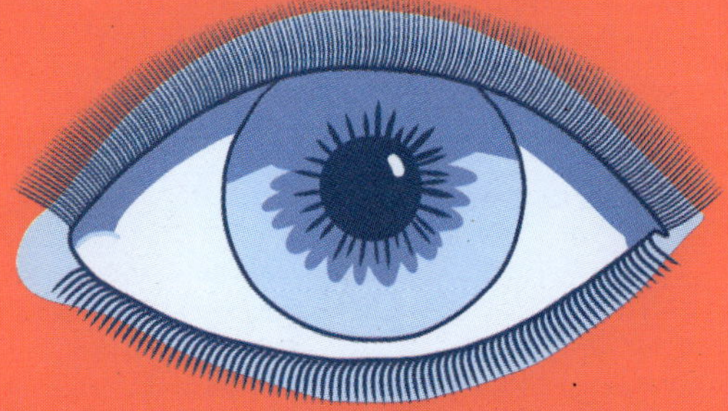

Long lashes

This microscope image shows human eyelashes (in blue) growing out of the skin of the eyelid, magnified 42 times. Humans can have up to double the number of lashes on their top lid as on their bottom lid. We lose around four lashes per day.

Can you hear me?

Ears are vibration detectors—they hear vibrations in the air, which can range in speed, or "frequency." High-pitched sounds, such as a whistle, are fast vibrations, and low-pitched sounds, such as the rumble of a train, are slow vibrations.

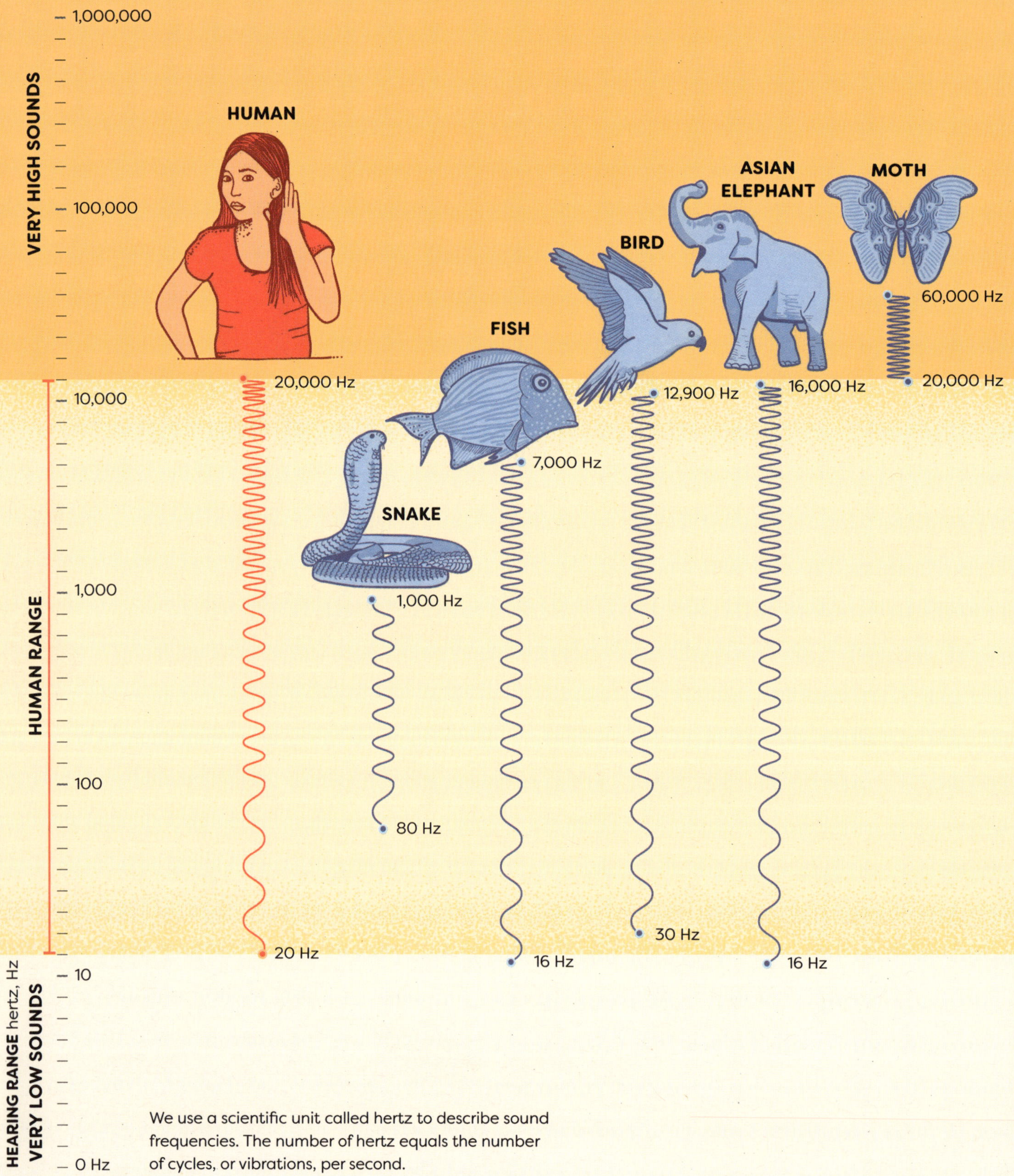

We use a scientific unit called hertz to describe sound frequencies. The number of hertz equals the number of cycles, or vibrations, per second.

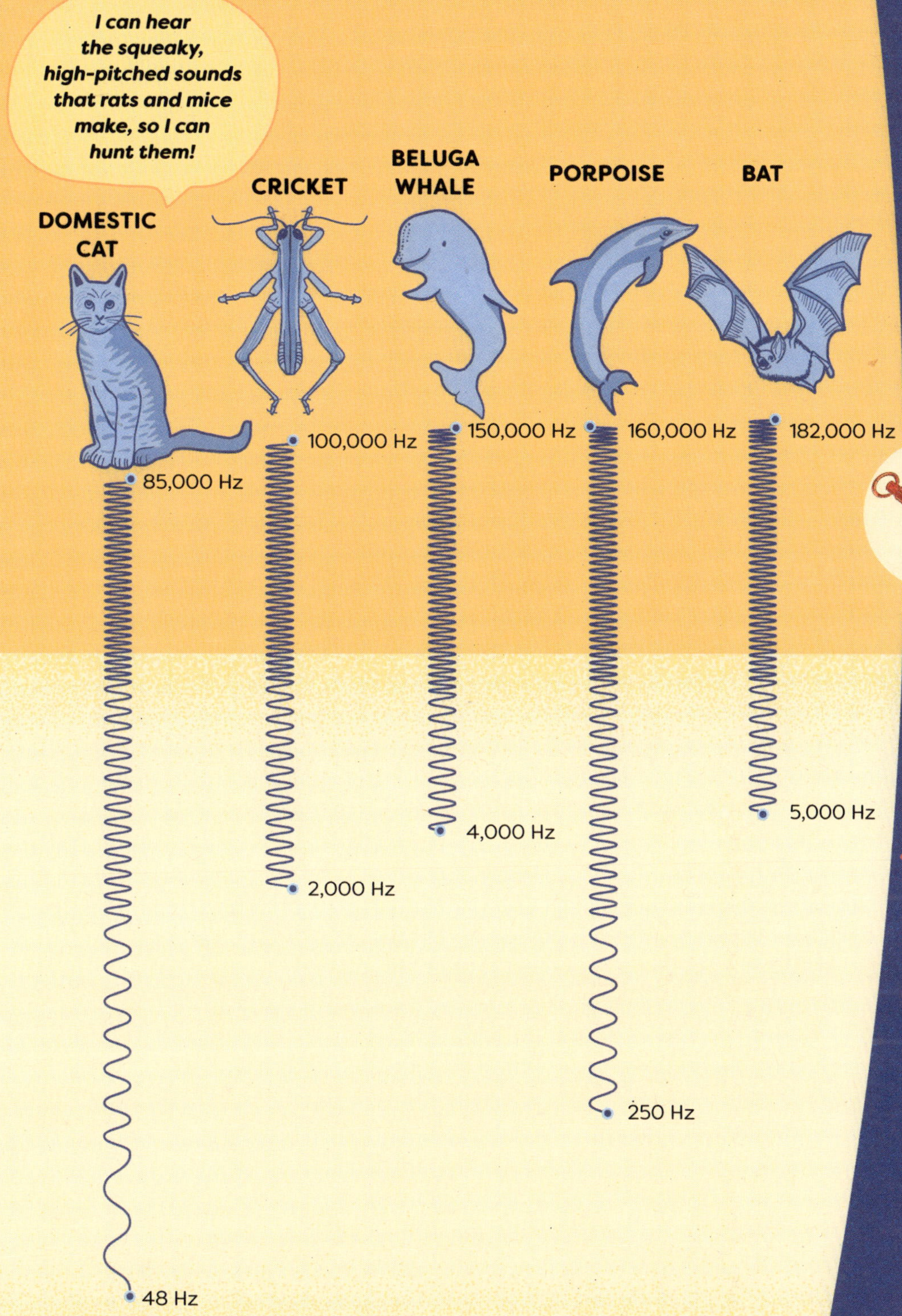

EXAMPLES OF SOUNDS

Dog whistle

The dog whistle is so high-pitched that humans and sheep can't hear it, but dogs can. It is used for training dogs to perform tasks such as herding sheep without disturbing the flock.

Ambulance siren

There's a reason sirens on ambulances and police cars are in the middle of our hearing range: so we can hear them clearly and get out of the way!

Earthquake

We don't need ears to hear the sound of an earthquake approaching. We can feel its vibrations in our bones and body.

The eye cells

Inside your eye is a layer of highly specialized cells called rods (with the narrow tips) and cones (with the flower-like tips). Rod cells help the body to see in dim light, and cone cells are sensitive to color. These cells work together to pass visual information through to the brain, as part of your nervous system. The human eye contains about 130 million rods and about 7 million cones.

HUMANS

have **more cone cells** than cats and dogs, making humans better than cats and dogs at seeing in color.

CATS AND DOGS

have **more rod cells** than humans, making cats and dogs better than humans at seeing things in the dark.

Your body's control center

The brain takes all the information from your different senses and processes it, allowing you to act and decide what to do about... well, everything. For centuries, how the brain worked was largely a mystery to humans. But scientists now know that different areas of the brain are responsible for different things. This illustration shows some of the jobs performed by different parts of your brain.

STRUCTURE OF THE BRAIN

The brain has three main sections: The **forebrain**, at the front; the **midbrain**, in the middle; and the **hindbrain**, at the back. These are shown in the diagram below. The sections of the brain are divided into smaller regions called lobes. The illustration on the right shows the lobes of the forebrain and hindbrain, with each lobe highlighted in a different color. The pictures show some of the brain functions that each lobe specializes in.

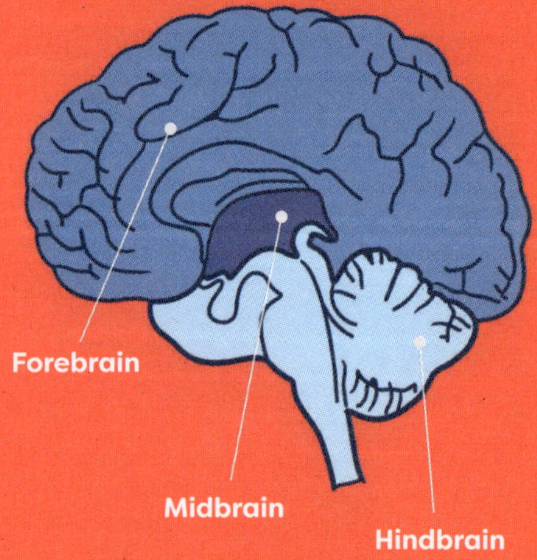

MOVEMENT
TOUCH AND PRESSURE
AWARENESS OF THE BODY'S ENVIRONMENT
PARIETAL LOBE
TASTE
LANGUAGE
YES
SI
OUI
PROCESSING IMAGES
HEARING
READING
OCCIPITAL LOBE
TEMPORAL LOBE
RECOGNIZING FACES
BALANCE AND COORDINATION
CEREBELLUM

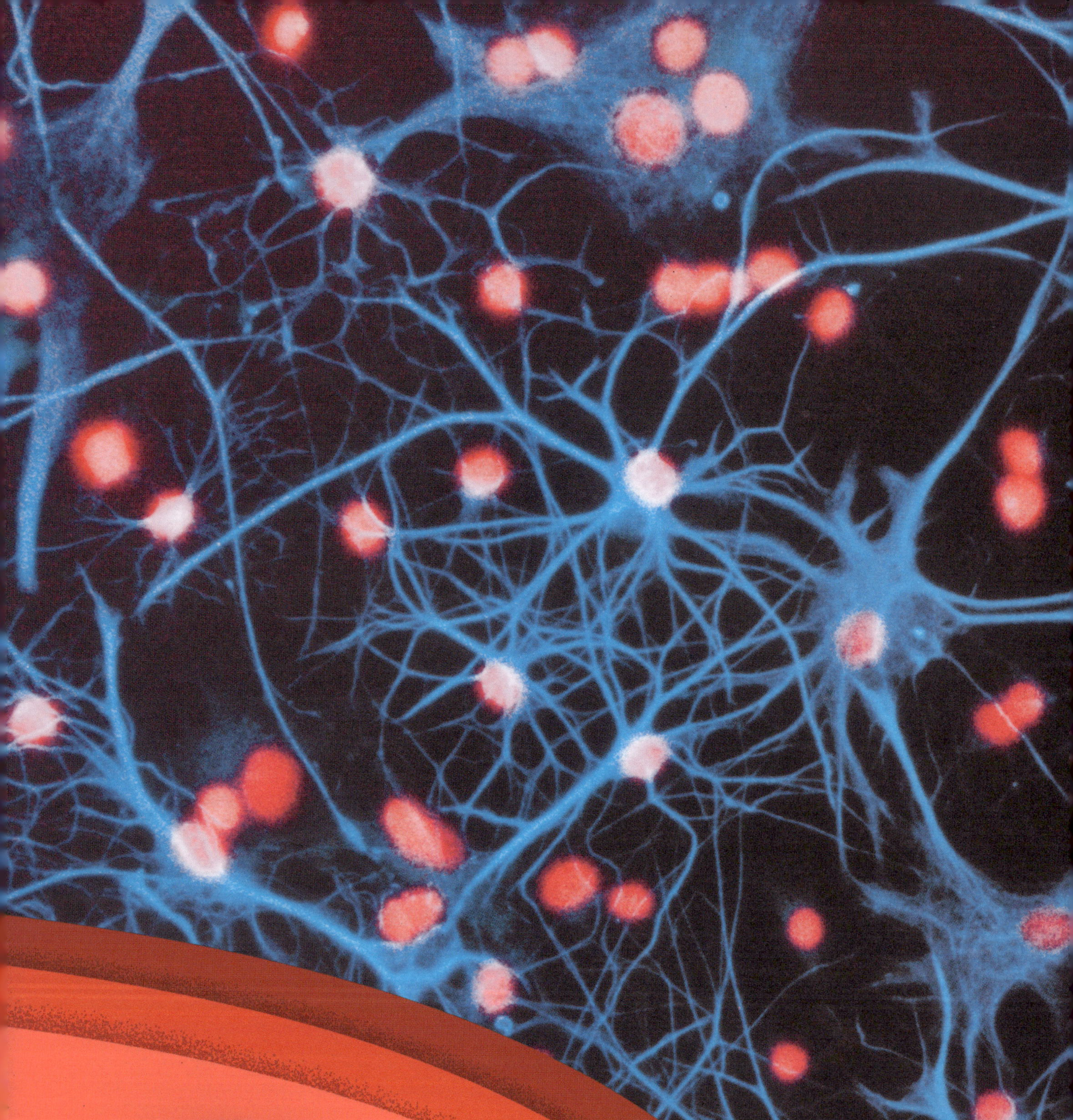

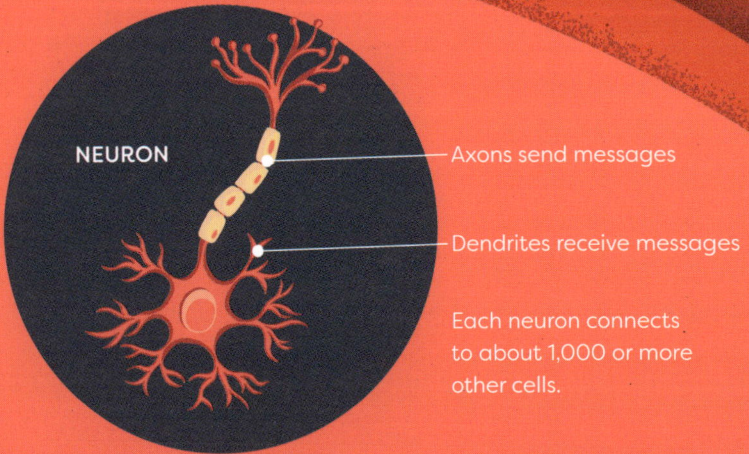

Each neuron connects to about 1,000 or more other cells.

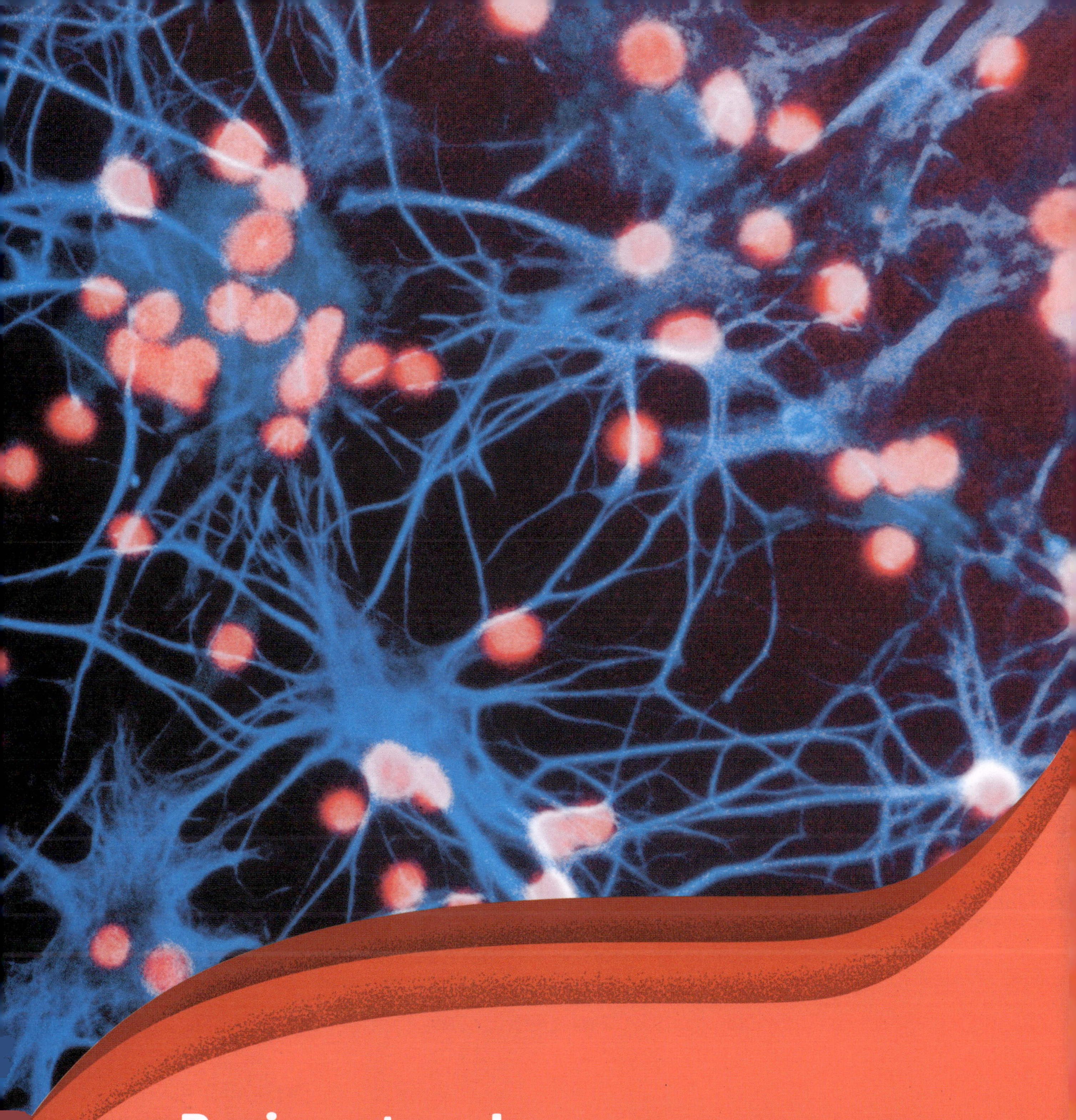

Brain networks

This image might look like it's from a sci-fi movie, but it's actually a picture of the inside of the brain! Neurons, shown in this magnified image, are the information carriers inside your brain. Each neuron consists of a cell body with branching structures that extend from the cell body like the branches of a tree. The average neuron is connected to 1,000 or more other cells through a complex network of axons and dendrites, which send and receive messages. The networks and pathways in your brain are constantly changing as you grow and learn.

How brainy are humans?

Human brains are really big for the size of our bodies, especially when they're compared to the brains of other mammals of our size. Scientists think it might explain why humans can do things like read books and play chess, and other animals can't. But the size of the brain is likely to be just one of several reasons why some animals are smarter than others.

To work out each mammal's EQ (Encephalization Quotient) number, scientists use a special calculation that compares how much of each mammal's body its brain takes up. Humans' EQ number is seven, which is the highest score of any mammal. This means that, relative to body size, a human's brain is seven times larger than the average mammal's brain.

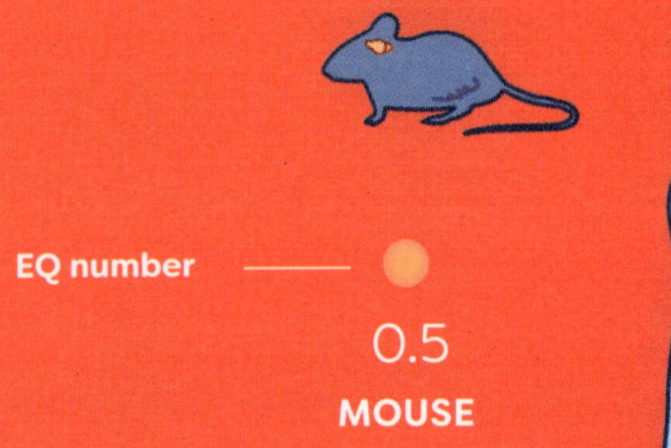

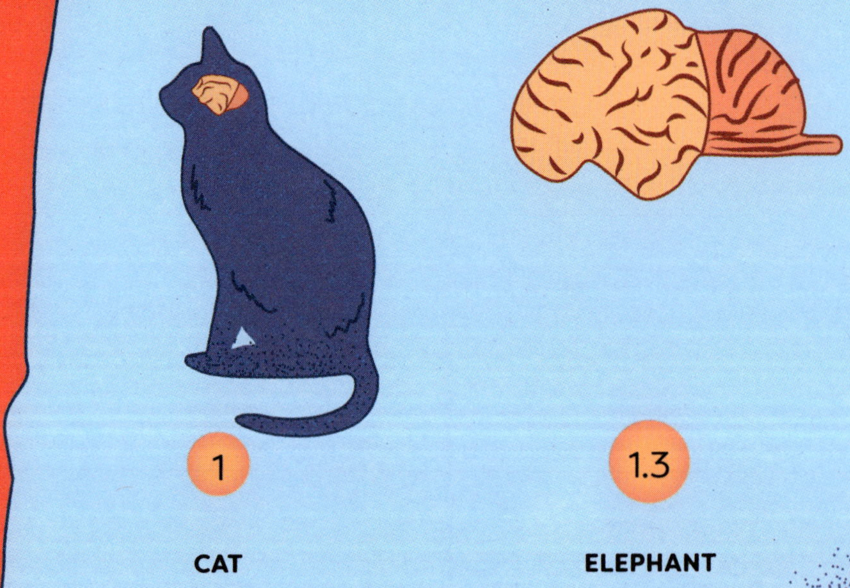

SCALE **2 inches** (5 cm)

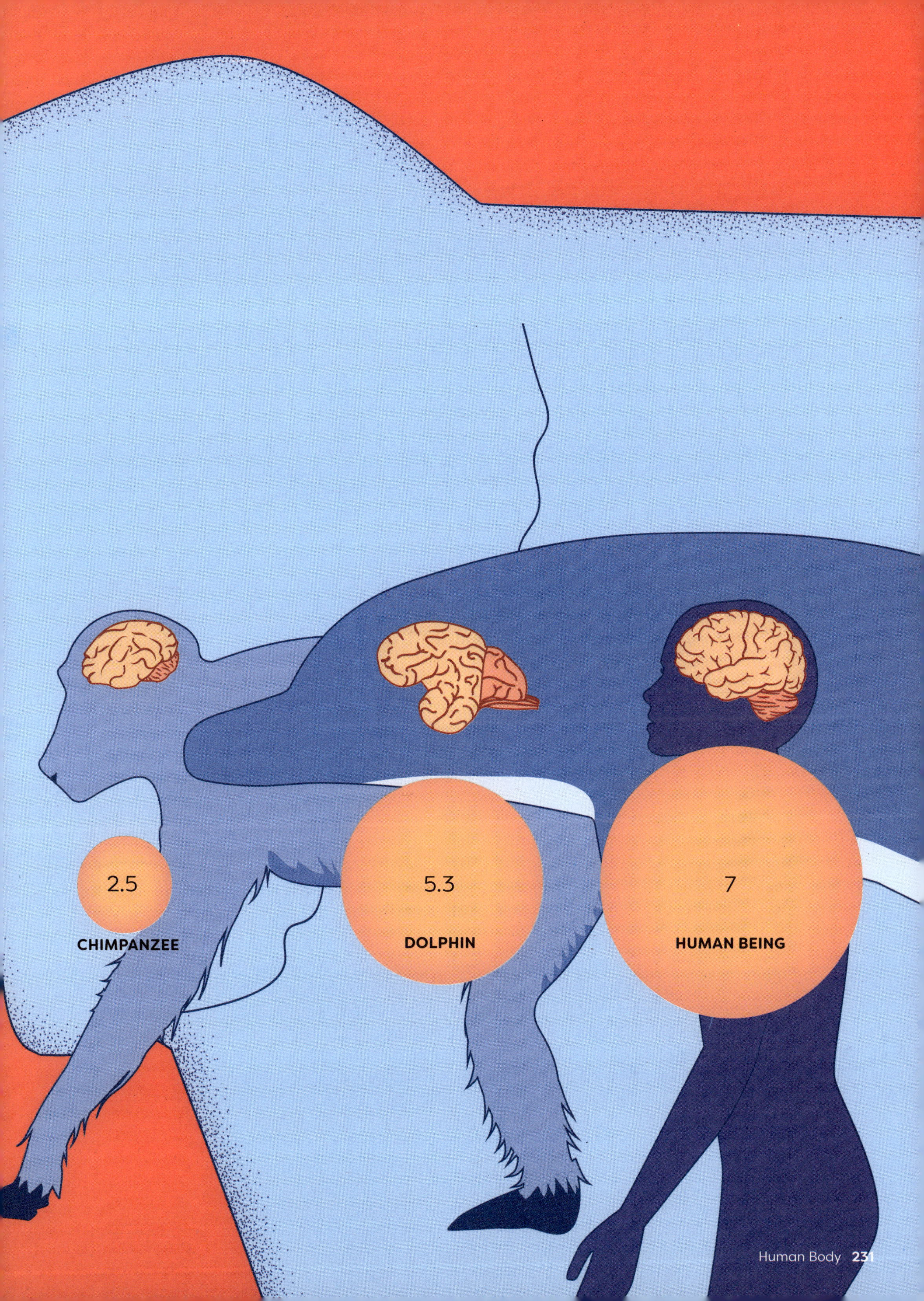
2.5
CHIMPANZEE
5.3
DOLPHIN
7
HUMAN BEING

What is DNA?

DNA is found inside the cells of all living things. It is a set of genetic codes that tells an organism how to develop and grow and controls how it will look and function. DNA in humans controls everything from our eye color to how our lungs work.

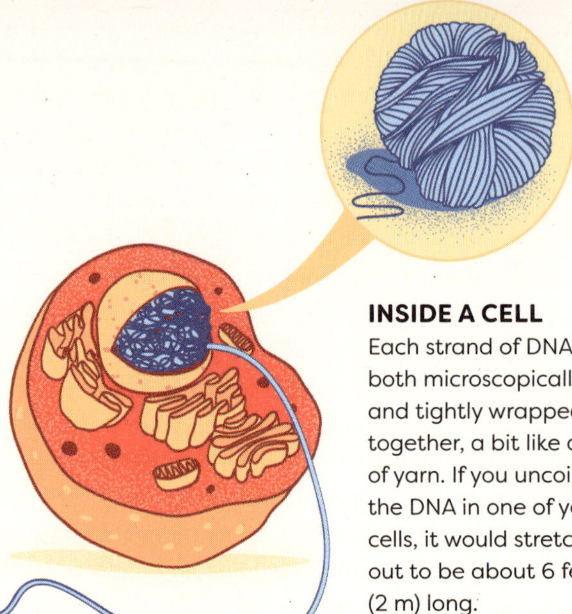

INSIDE A CELL

Each strand of DNA is both microscopically small and tightly wrapped together, a bit like a ball of yarn. If you uncoiled the DNA in one of your cells, it would stretch out to be about 6 feet (2 m) long.

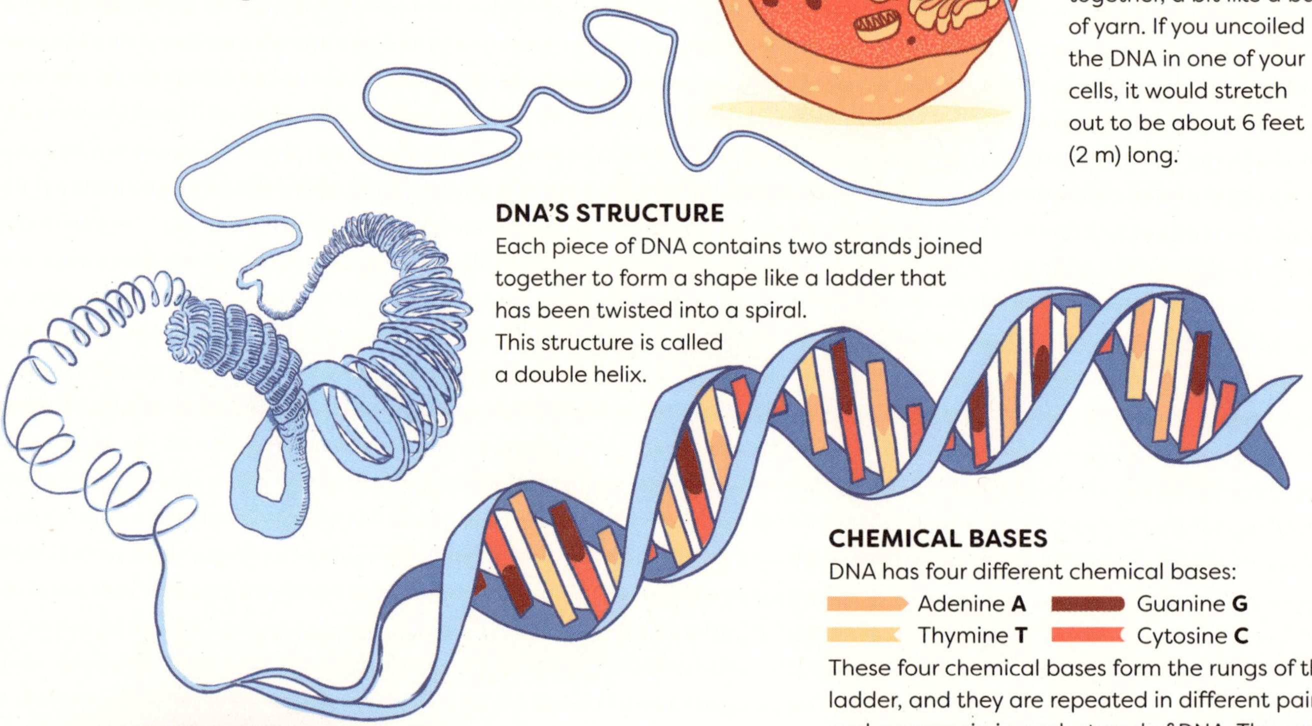

DNA'S STRUCTURE

Each piece of DNA contains two strands joined together to form a shape like a ladder that has been twisted into a spiral. This structure is called a double helix.

CHEMICAL BASES

DNA has four different chemical bases:

- Adenine **A**
- Guanine **G**
- Thymine **T**
- Cytosine **C**

These four chemical bases form the rungs of the ladder, and they are repeated in different pairs over and over again in each strand of DNA. The order of the bases is important because it creates a code that tells cells what types of protein to make. It is the differences between these proteins that create the differences between all living things and between all the parts of the body.

HOW LONG IS YOUR DNA?

If the uncoiled DNA from one of your cells is 6 feet (2 m) long, how far would *all* the DNA in your body stretch if it was uncoiled and connected end to end, like a giant piece of string? The answer is **67 billion miles (108 billion km), which is about 171 times the distance between Earth and the planet Jupiter**.

DISTANT RELATIVES

Members of the same species have most of their DNA in common. For example, 99.9 percent of your DNA's genetic code is also found in every other human being. Here's how much of our DNA we share with other living things.

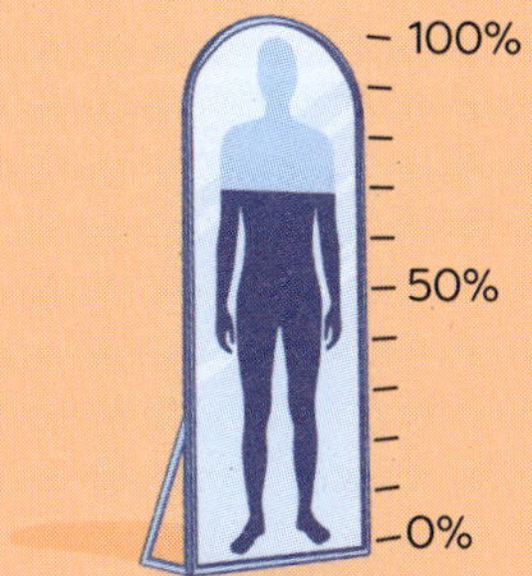

PERCENTAGE SHARED DNA

HOW TO READ IT

Look at the human silhouettes in the mirrors below. The size of the lower, **dark blue** section of each silhouette shows what percentage of our human DNA we share with the animal, plant, or fruit facing that mirror.

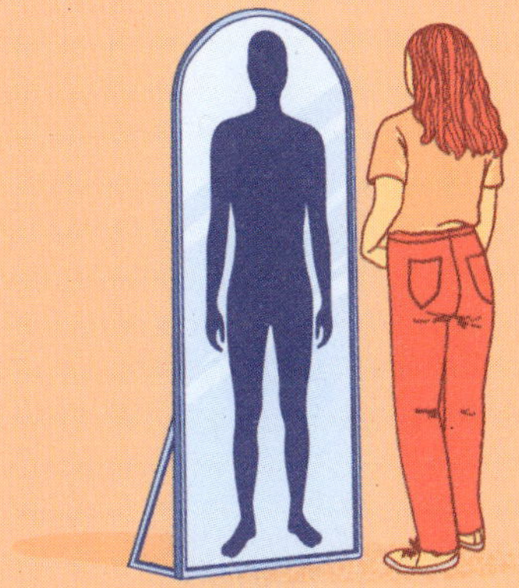
ANOTHER HUMAN
99.9%

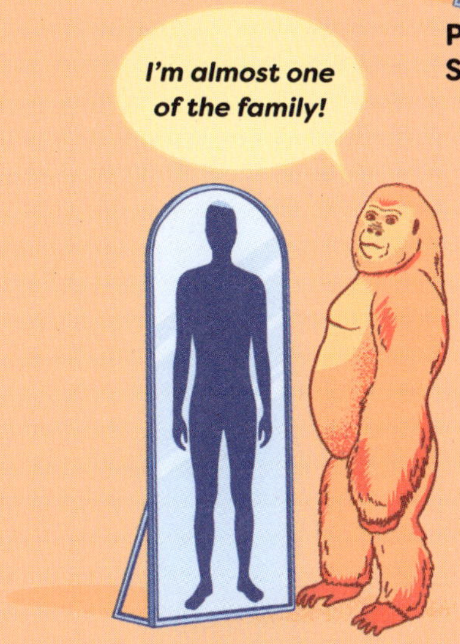

GORILLA
98%

MOUSE
85%

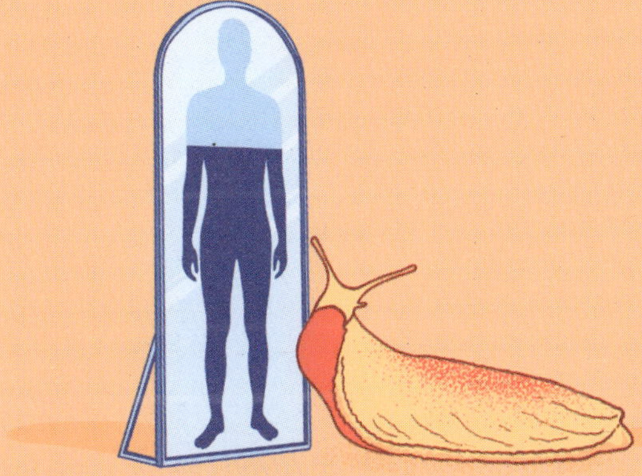
SLUG
70%

CHICKEN
60%

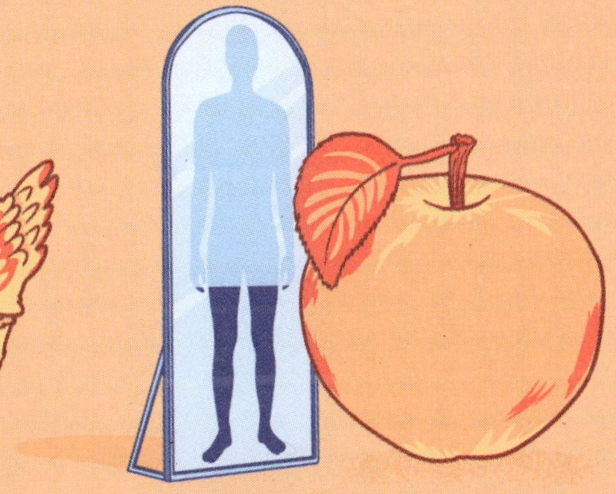
APPLE
40%

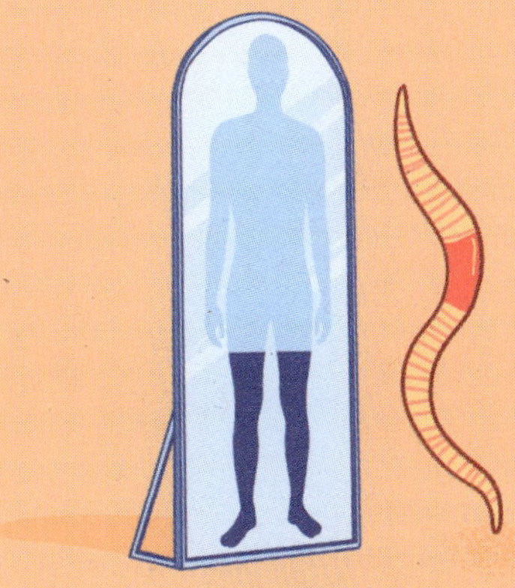
ROUNDWORM
38%

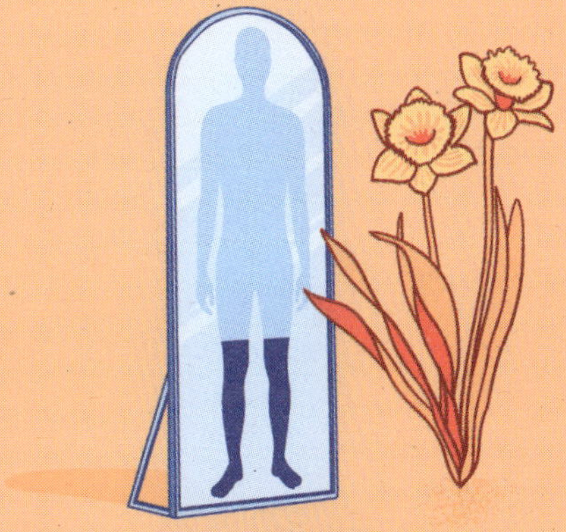
DAFFODIL
35%

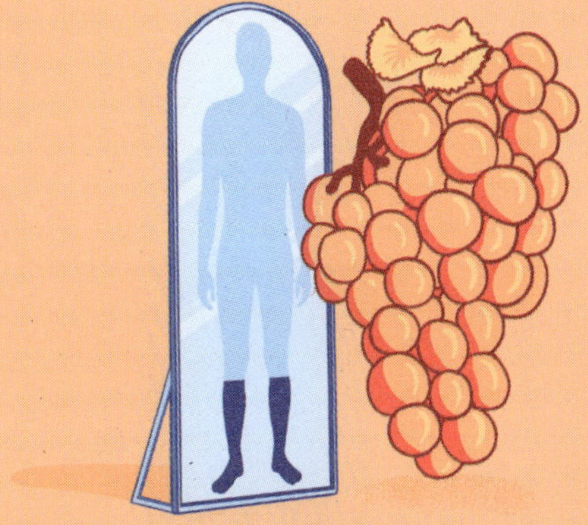
GRAPE
24%

How old is your body? (Younger than you think!)

You might not notice it, but your body is constantly changing. Some body features, such as your hair and nails, never stop growing. And the cells in most parts of your body need to be replaced by new cells as they age and become damaged over time. Depending on where the cells are in your body, this process of regeneration can happen every few days—or it can take years and years.

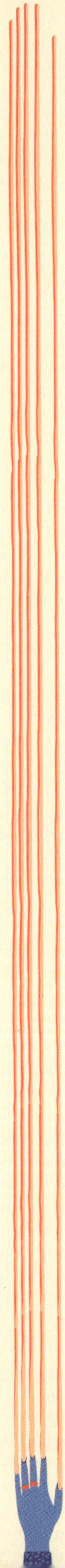

HAIR AND NAILS

What would happen if you never had a haircut or cut your fingernails again? They would just keep growing! And growing. And growing. Your hair would grow as long as a bus, and your nails would grow so long that they would start curling in on themselves, eventually forming spirals. If you stretched out the spirals, though, your nails would be long enough to touch the ceiling!

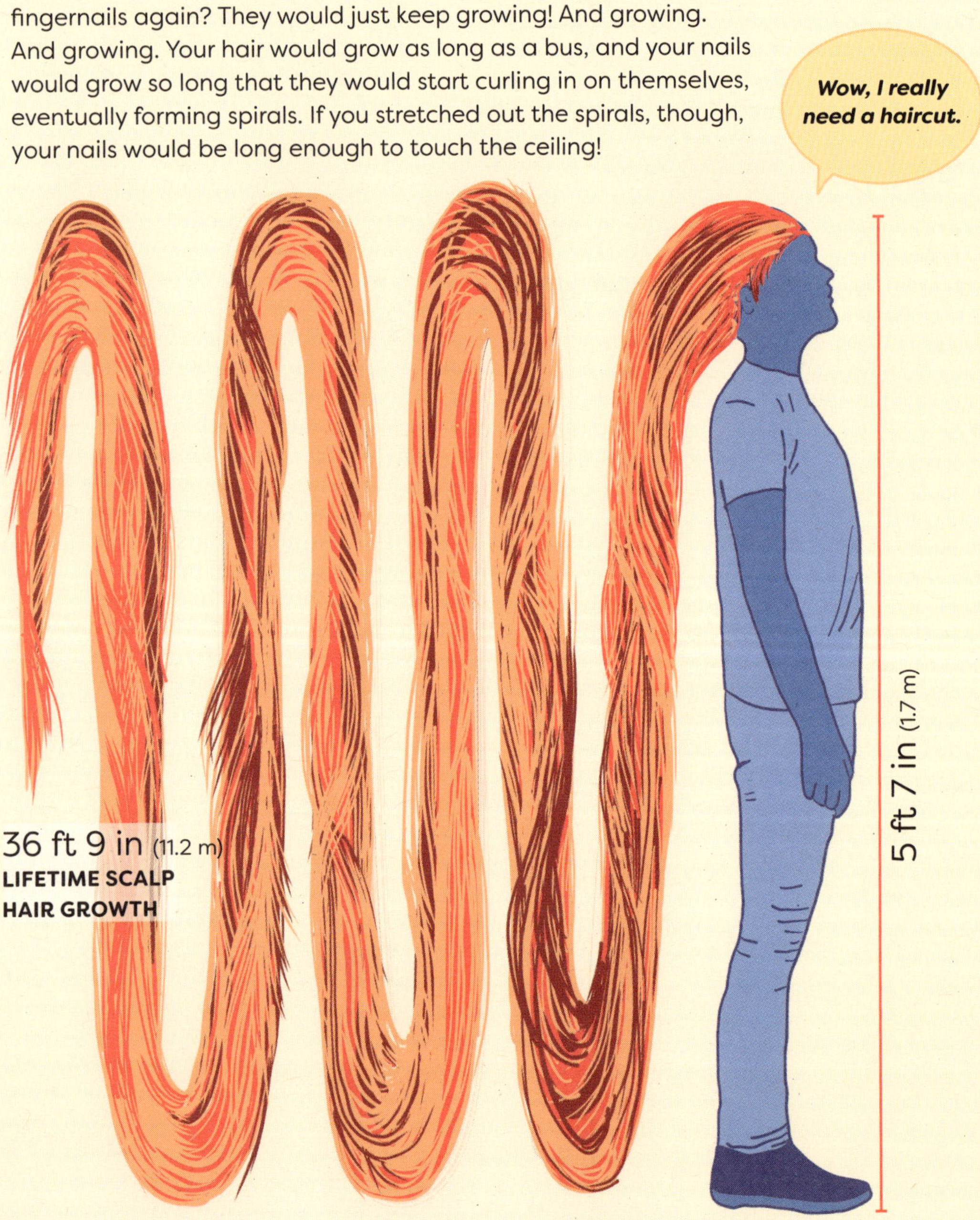

NEW BODY, OLD BRAIN

How many of the cells inside your body stay with you throughout your life? The answer is surprisingly few. In fact, the only part of your body that is truly with you from birth until death is your brain.

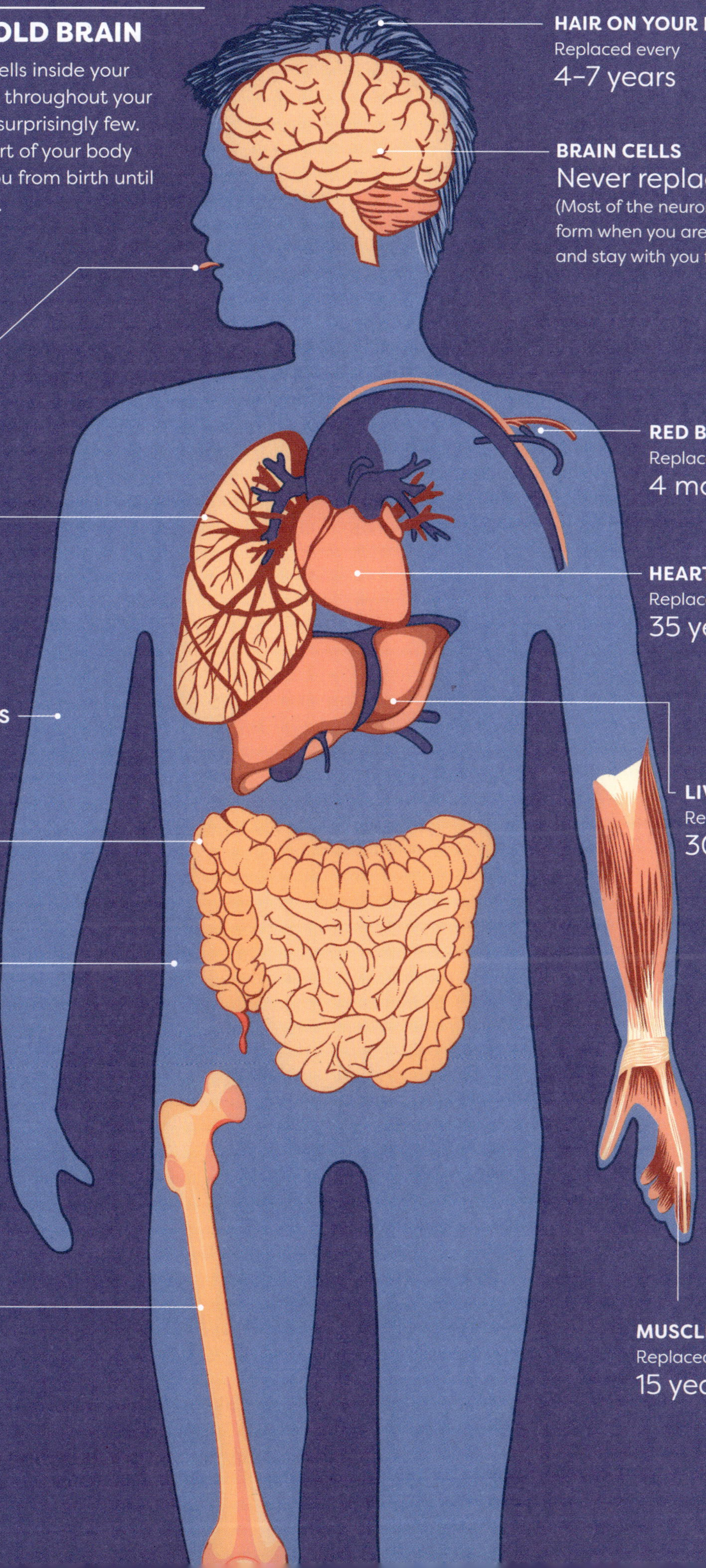

How long does it take to grow a baby?

A lot of changes happen to your body even before you are born, as you develop and grow inside your mother's womb. This process is called gestation. Here you can see how a baby grows inside its mother—and how the nine-month period of the average human pregnancy compares with other mammals.

Month	1				2				3				4				
Week	1	2	3	4	5	6	7	8	9	10	11	12	13	14	15	16	17	18

BABY'S APPEARANCE

SIZE COMPARISON

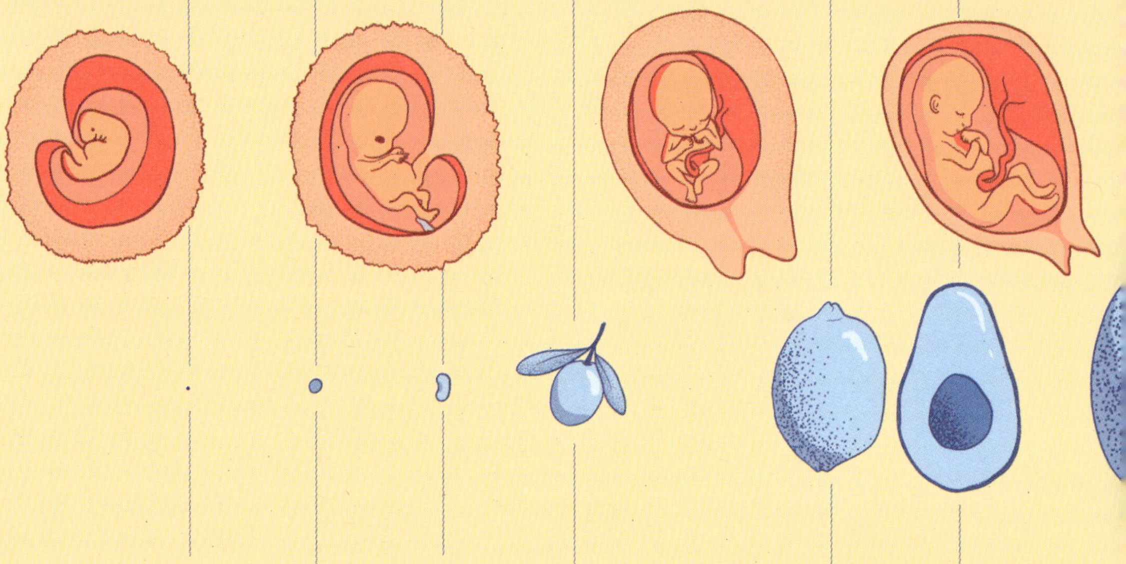

SIZE COMPARISON	**Poppy seed**	**Lentil**	**Kidney bean**	**Olive**	**Lemon**	**Avocado**
KEY DEVELOPMENTS	**4 weeks** Big enough for us to see without a microscope.	**6 weeks** Heart starts beating.	**8 weeks** Starts to pee.	**10 weeks** Can kick and move its limbs.	**14 weeks** Can stretch and suck its thumb.	**16 weeks** Can hear sounds.

WHAT ABOUT OTHER MAMMALS?

Larger mammals tend to have longer gestation periods than smaller mammals. For example, an Indian elephant's pregnancy lasts for almost two years!

■ = 1 week of gestation

HUMAN
40 weeks

VIRGINIAN OPOSSUM
almost 2 weeks

RAT
just over 3 weeks

GUINEA PIG
almost 10 weeks

How many babies are born every second? Turn to page 246.

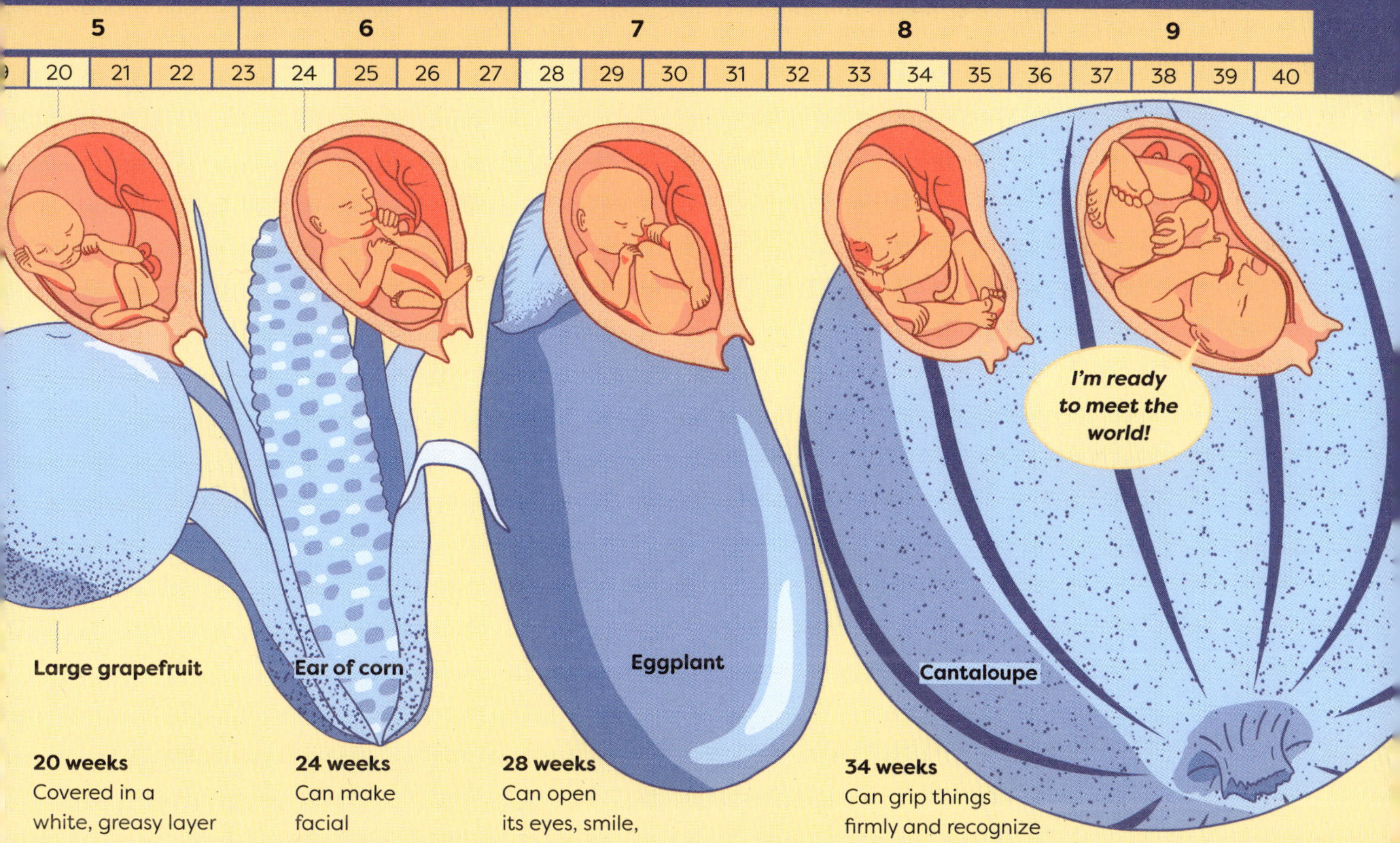

20 weeks
Covered in a white, greasy layer that protects its skin.

24 weeks
Can make facial expressions.

28 weeks
Can open its eyes, smile, and cry.

34 weeks
Can grip things firmly and recognize its mother's voice.

CHINCHILLA
almost 16 weeks

SHEEP
21 weeks

HORSE
47 weeks

INDIAN ELEPHANT
almost 96 weeks

MEET THE EXPERT CONSULTANT

Professor Claire Smith

Anatomist

WHAT WAS THE MOMENT YOU KNEW THAT YOU WANTED TO STUDY THE HUMAN BODY?

As a kid I did loads of dancing and wanted to understand more about the human body and how it moved. What were the sore and aching muscles in my legs?

WHAT IS YOUR FAVORITE FACT ABOUT THE BODY?

That when you are an embryo your eyes are where your ears are now, on the side of your head. As the face develops, your eyes move round to the front of the face.

WHAT EXCITING DISCOVERY ARE YOU LOOKING FORWARD TO SEEING IN THE FUTURE?

I'm looking forward to us understanding more about what causes cancer and how it can be prevented.

WHAT IS THE BEST THING ABOUT YOUR JOB?

My favorite part is working with medical students, and seeing that light-bulb moment when they dissect a human body as part of their training and start to see and understand the body from a new perspective.

SCAVENGER HUNT!

Can you track down the answers to this quiz in the pages of this book? (Turn to page 305 to see if you are right!)

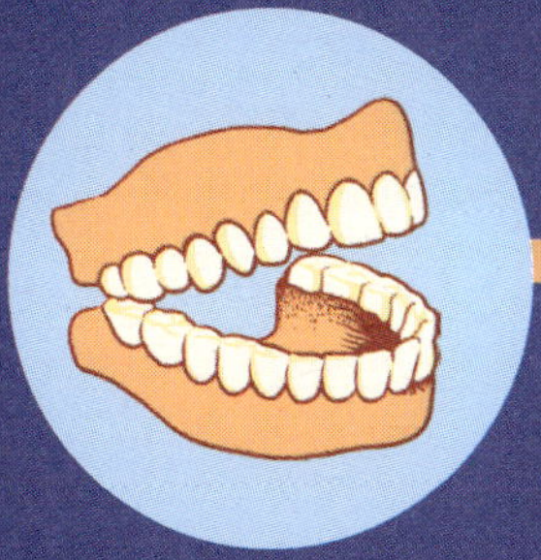

1. What is the hardest substance in the body?

2. Which of your organs has muscles that resemble those in an octopus's arm?

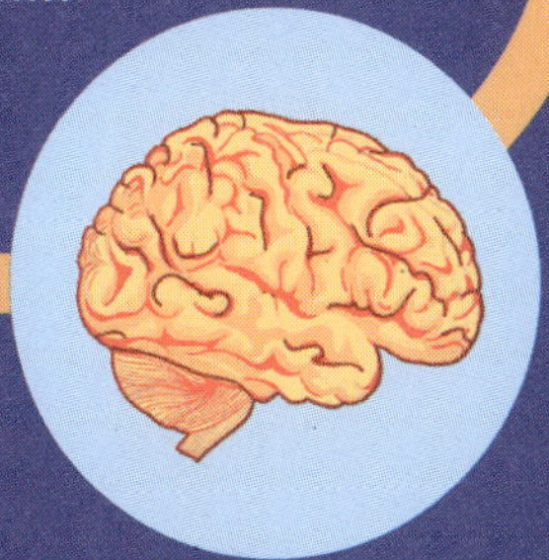

3. Which has a bigger brain, a cat or a human?

4. Roughly how many cups of mucus does your body produce each day?

5. What percentage of DNA do humans share with chickens?

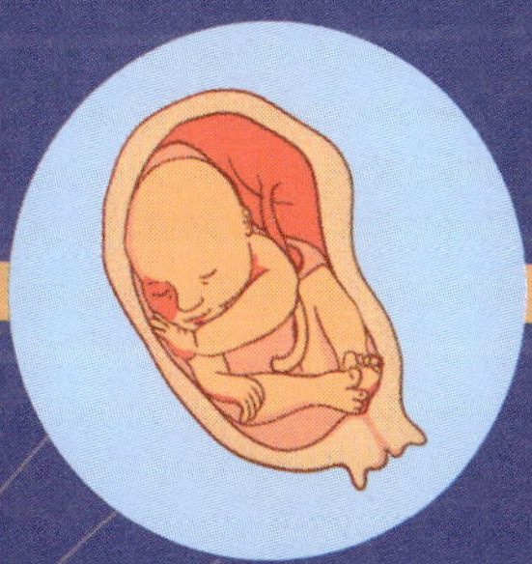

6. Is a 34-week-old fetus the size of an avocado or a cantaloupe?

7. Traces of which highly precious metal can be found in your poop?

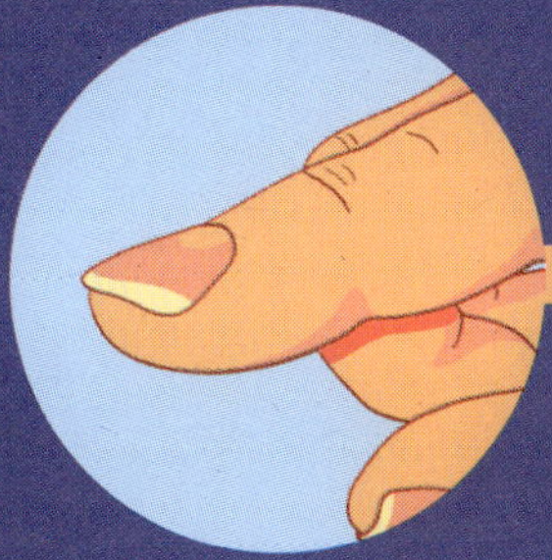

8. Roughly how long do human fingernails grow in a lifetime?

HUMAN WORLD

The world as 100 people

Imagine that the total global population of 8 billion people was scaled down and represented by just 100 people. For example, as 89 percent of humans are right-handed, 89 of these 100 representative people would also be right-handed. Now that we've imagined the world as 100 people, what else can we say about them?

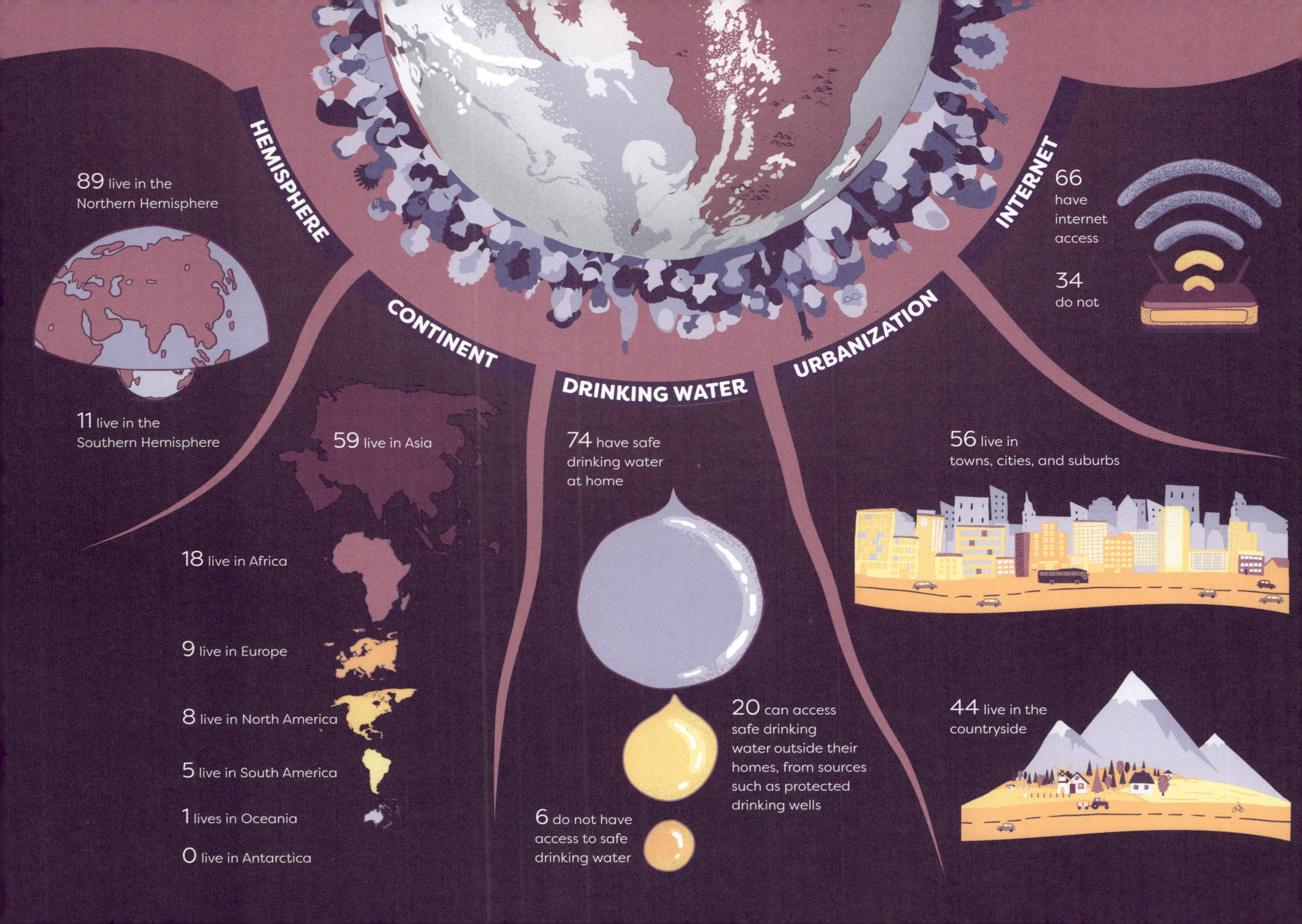
HEMISPHERE
89 live in the Northern Hemisphere
11 live in the Southern Hemisphere
CONTINENT
59 live in Asia
18 live in Africa
9 live in Europe
8 live in North America
5 live in South America
1 lives in Oceania
0 live in Antarctica
DRINKING WATER
74 have safe drinking water at home
20 can access safe drinking water outside their homes, from sources such as protected drinking wells
6 do not have access to safe drinking water
URBANIZATION
56 live in towns, cities, and suburbs
44 live in the countryside
INTERNET
66 have internet access
34 do not

Life and death

Scientists estimate that, across almost 200,000 years of human history, approximately 117 billion people have been born. Of those 117 billion, around 8 billion people, or 7 percent of the total, are alive today—including you!

ALL PEOPLE WHO HAVE EVER LIVED Each human figure = 1 billion people

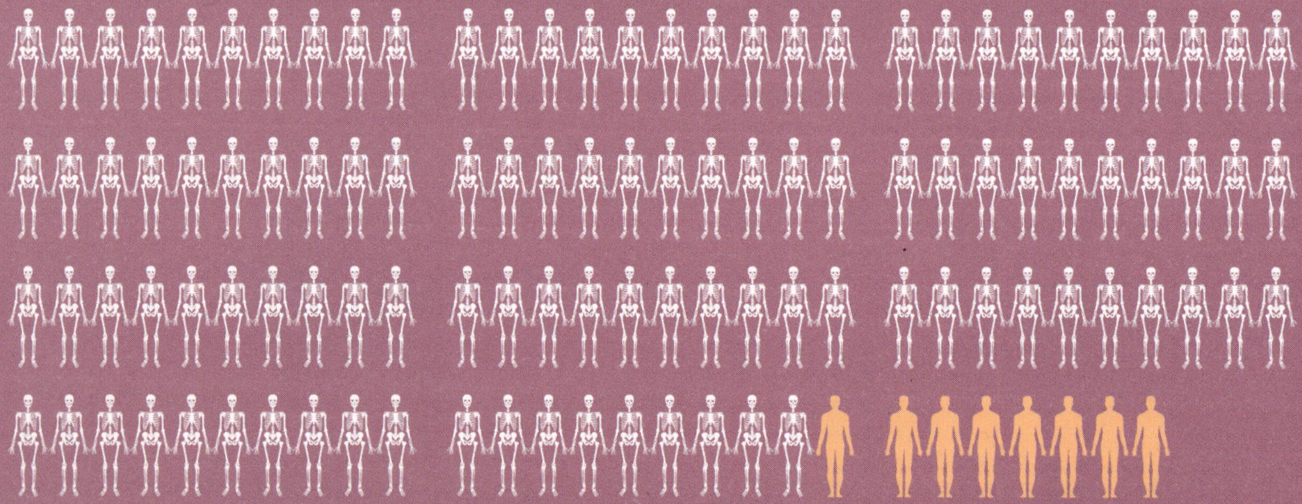

109 billion deceased people

8 billion people alive today

The Day of the Dead, or *Día de los Muertos*, as it is known in Spanish, is celebrated in Mexico and other parts of Latin America on November 1st and 2nd each year. The festival is a time to remember loved ones who have died. This photograph shows an altar that has been specially decorated for the celebrations.

Every second...

Have you ever wondered what all the people on Earth are up to? At any one moment, lots of them are laughing, cycling, or reading a book (just like you). Here's an estimate of how many times various things are happening, on average, every single second.

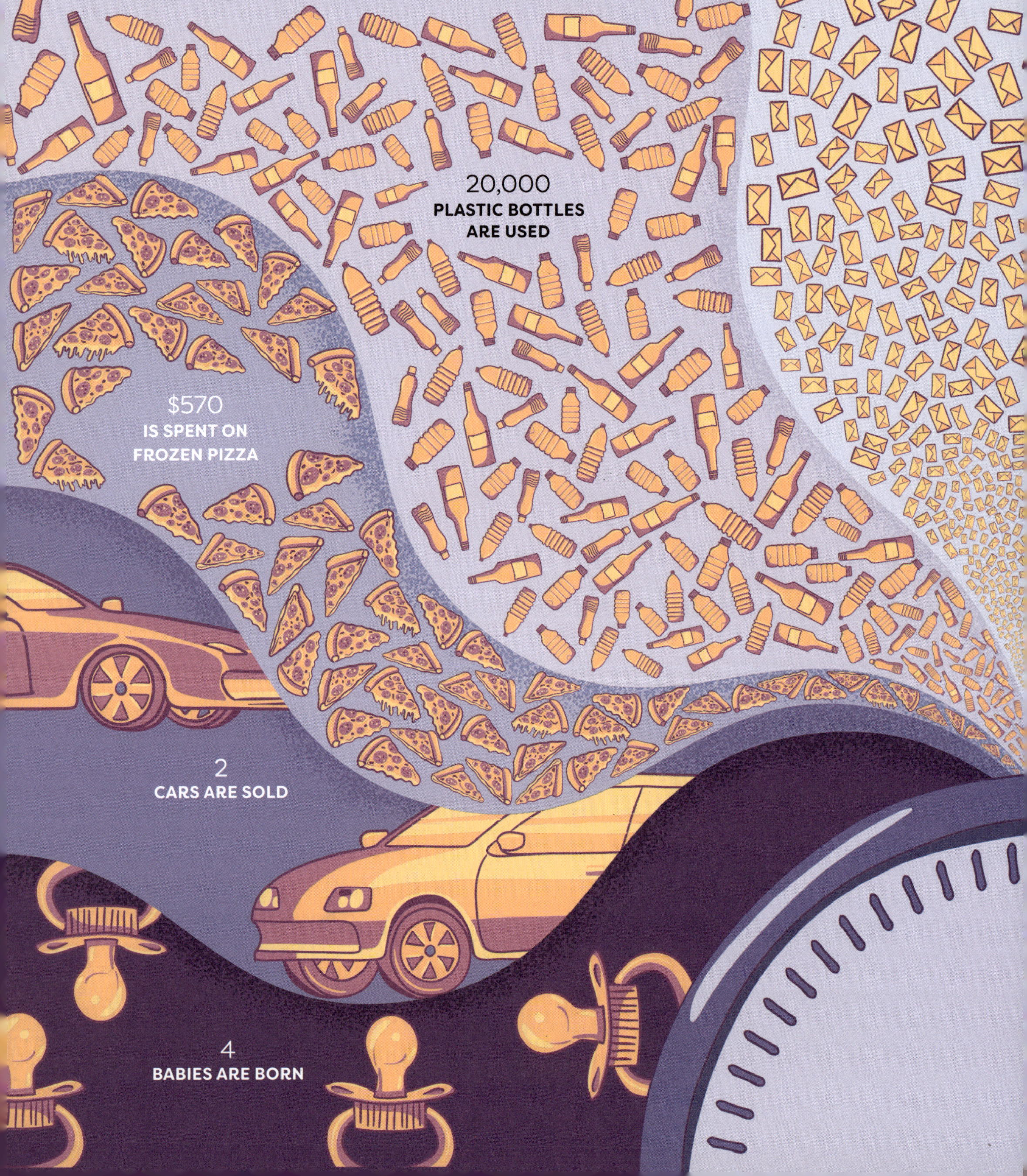

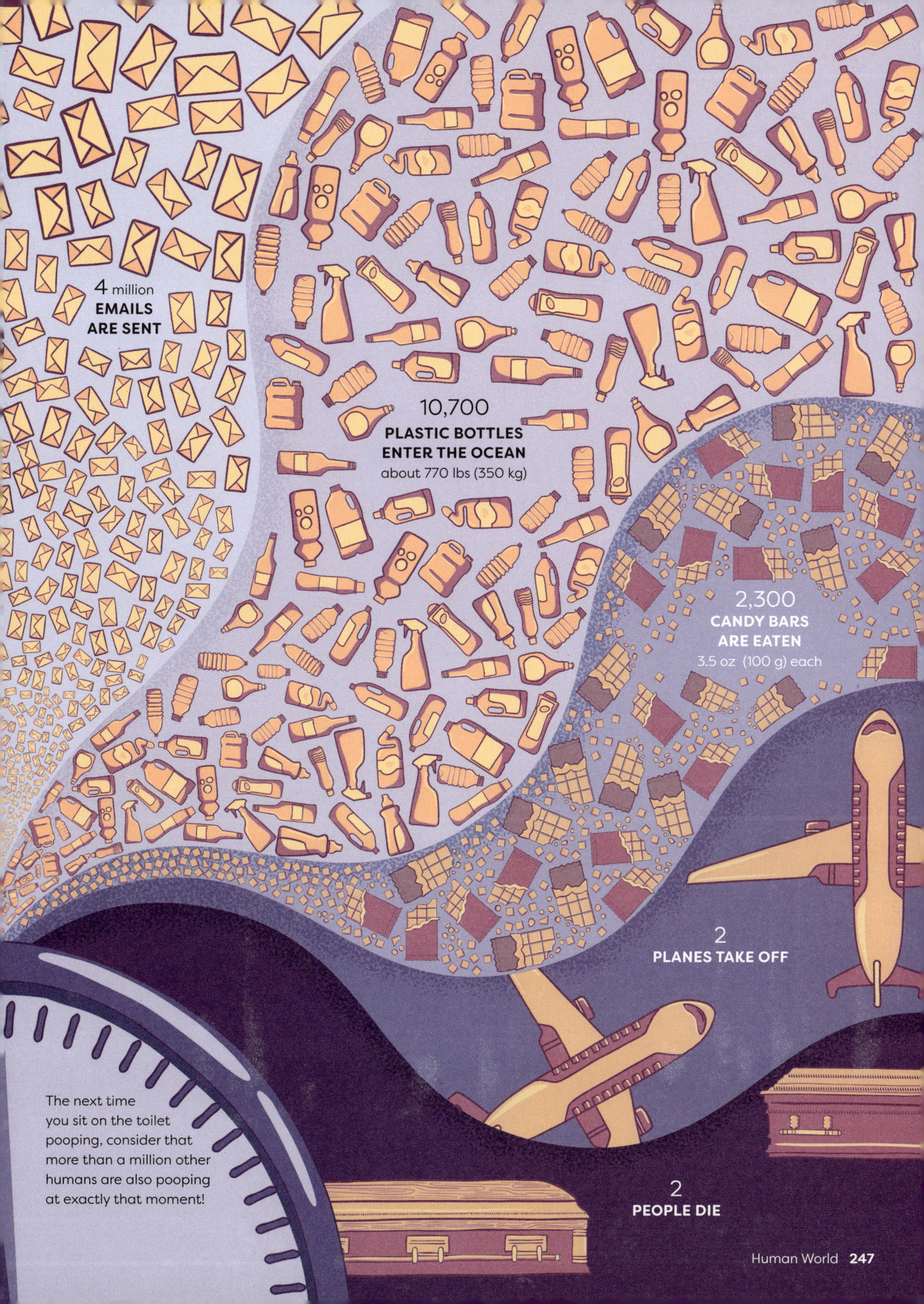
4 million
EMAILS ARE SENT
10,700
PLASTIC BOTTLES ENTER THE OCEAN
about 770 lbs (350 kg)
2,300
CANDY BARS ARE EATEN
3.5 oz (100 g) each
2
PLANES TAKE OFF
2
PEOPLE DIE
The next time you sit on the toilet pooping, consider that more than a million other humans are also pooping at exactly that moment!

How much money do people have?

If you added up the value of all the cash in every bank, every house, and every apartment, as well as every piece of gold, every diamond, every Bitcoin, and everything else, and put it into an imaginary pie, it would be worth about 464 trillion US dollars. Here's how that pie is divided. As you can see, almost half the world's wealth is owned by just 1 percent of the global population.

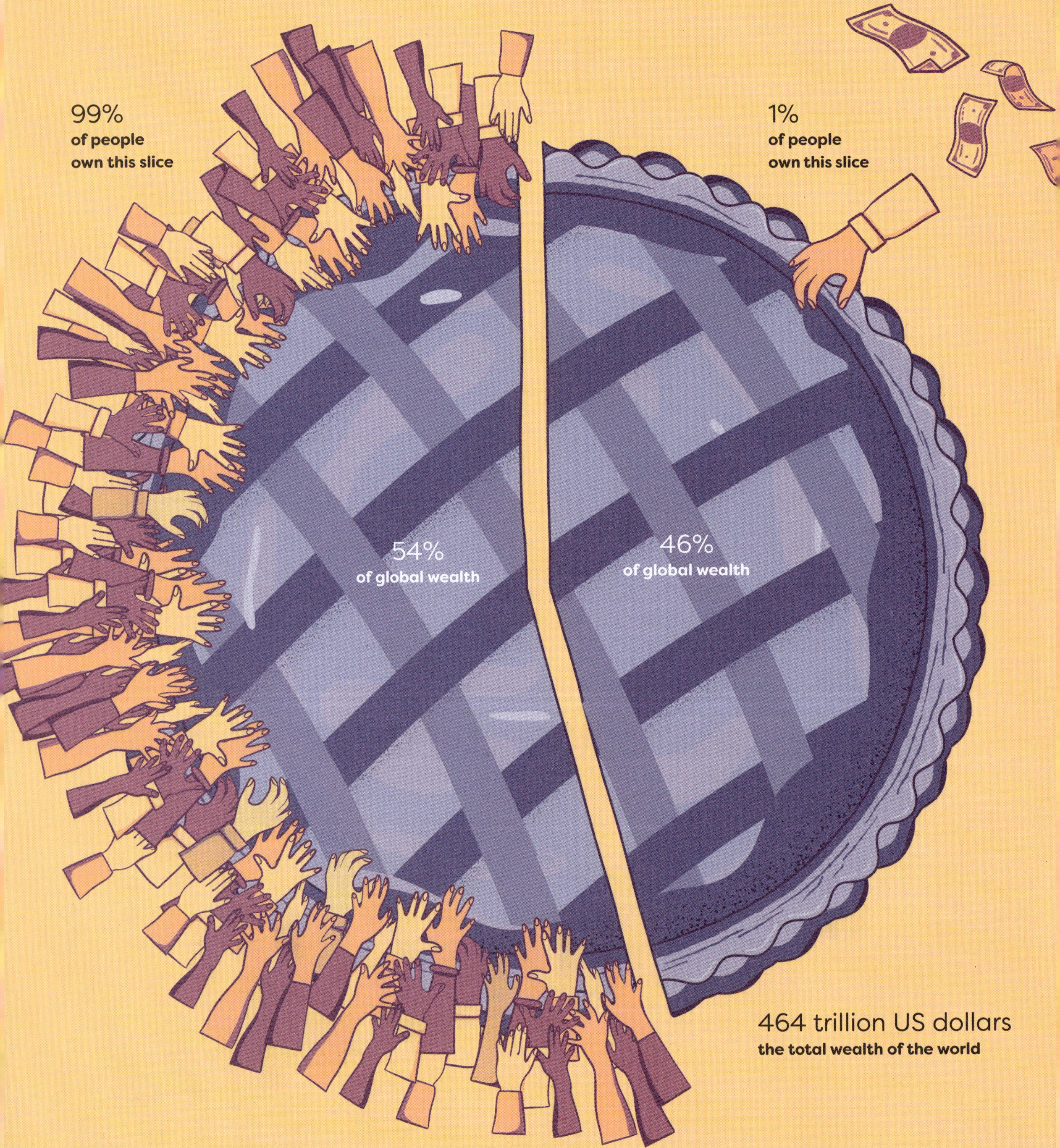

HOW MUCH MONEY?

A million dollars sounds like a lot of money, but it's nothing compared to a billion dollars. Here's a simple way to get your head around what those huge sums of money look like.

The wealthiest person in history was probably **Mansa Musa**, the emperor of Mali, West Africa, in the 14th century. In 1324, he went on a pilgrimage to Mecca, taking with him more than eighty camels each carrying over 200 pounds (100 kg) of gold.

1 million US dollars
standard briefcase

A million US dollars in $100 bills can fit inside a briefcase. That's 10,000 bills.

1 billion US dollars
10 standard pallets

You'd need a large truck to carry a billion dollars. That's the equivalent of 1,000 briefcases each filled with 10,000 $100 bills!

Coming together

Kumbh Mela is a Hindu religious festival in India. It is held four times every 12 years at different religious sites around the country and lasts for several weeks. When Kumbh Mela was held in 2019, more than 200 million people attended, including 50 million people on a single day. This meant that, on that day, more people came together to celebrate Kumbh Mela than currently live in Tokyo, the world's most populated city.

Hindu pilgrims gather on the banks of the sacred River Ganges during the Kumbh Mela festival.

The number of people attending the Kumbh Mela on a single day (2019), in comparison to the number of people who live in the world's most populated cities.

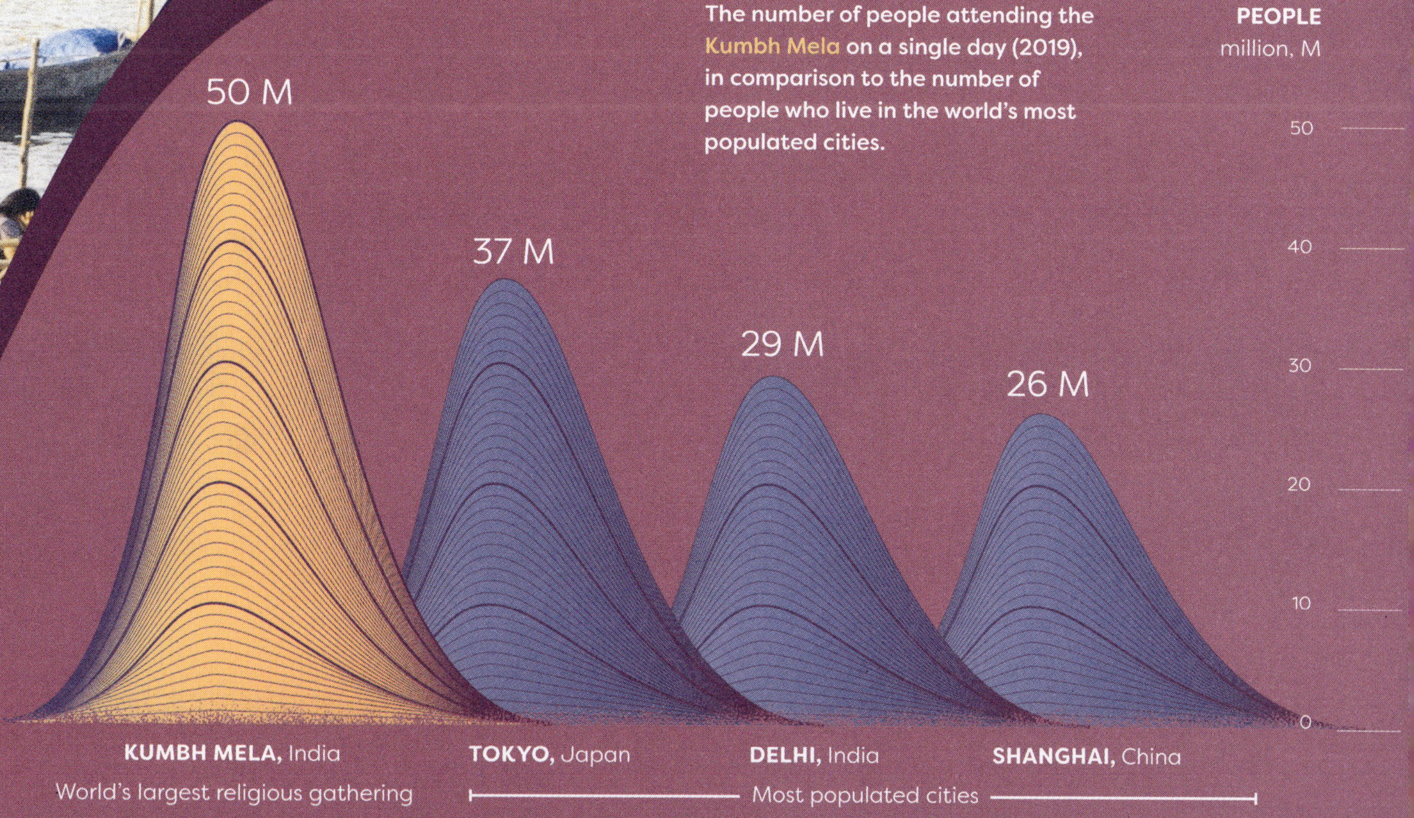

Human conflict

Throughout history, groups of people have attempted to settle their differences through fighting. Wars have always been destructive, but after the invention of modern weapons, such as tanks and machine guns, they have become even more devastating. Here, you can see the enormous human and economic costs of the two World Wars.

THE FIRST WORLD WAR

Fought over four years between July 1914 and November 1918, the First World War was the largest war that the world had seen up to that time. More than 30 countries were involved, and most of the major battles took place in Europe and the Middle East.

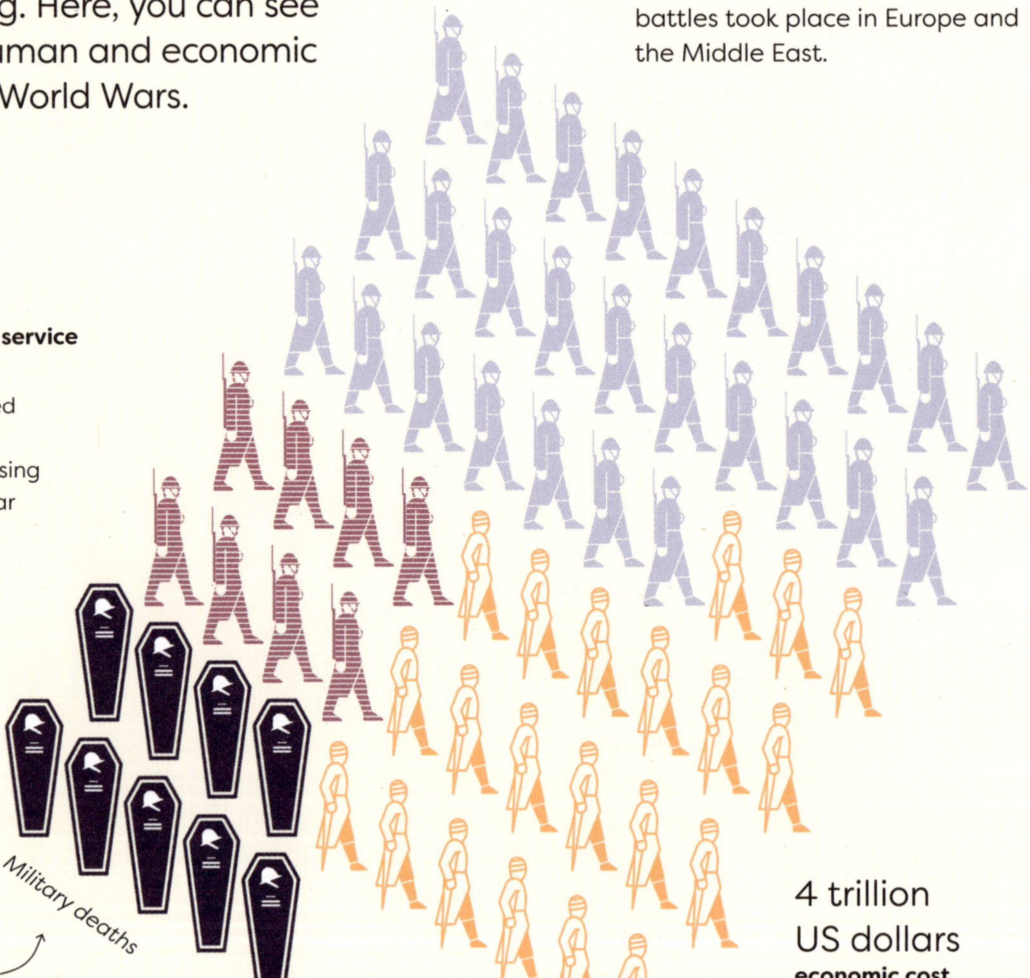

65 million
people in active military service

Of these:

- 9 million people were killed
- 21 million were wounded
- Almost 8 million went missing or became prisoners of war

22 million
people killed

Almost 9 million military personnel and 13 million civilians died

Civilian deaths

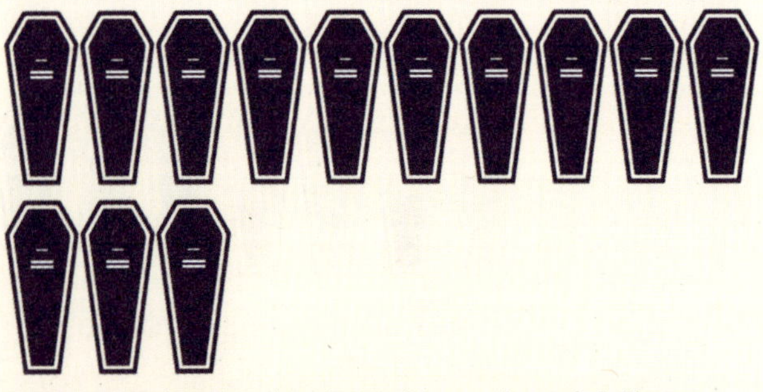

It is hard to be certain about the number of civilian deaths caused by the war, as no one kept any official records. The most destructive outbreak of influenza in the 20th century occurred in 1918, which also led to the deaths of many people, both military and civilian.

4 trillion
US dollars
economic cost
(equivalent in today's money)

HOW TO READ IT

Each soldier = 1 million people

- Soldiers who returned home
- Military wounded
- Military prisoners/missing
- Military or civilian deaths

Each stack of money = 1 trillion US dollars

THE SECOND WORLD WAR

Fought over six years between September 1939 and September 1945, the Second World War is the largest and bloodiest war in history. More than 50 countries were involved in the fighting, with battles taking place in almost every part of the world. Estimates of the number of people killed vary. The highest figures suggest that as many as 60 million people were killed.

70 million

people in active military service

Of these:

- 20 million people were killed
- 14 million were wounded
- More than 6 million went missing or became prisoners of war

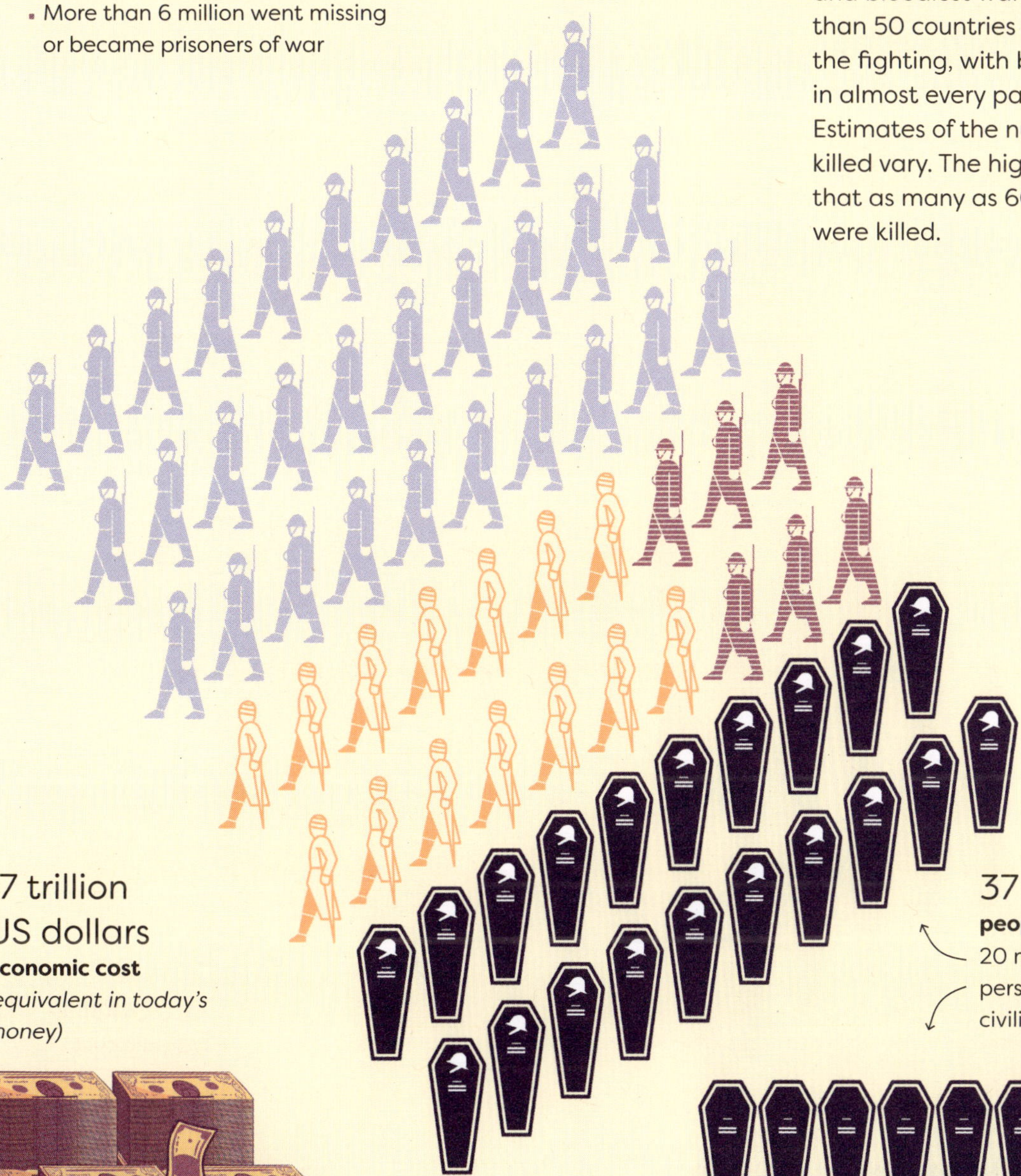

17 trillion US dollars

economic cost

(equivalent in today's money)

37 million

people killed

20 million military personnel and 17 million civilians died

Civilian deaths include 5,700,000 Jews, which was more than a third of all Jews in the world at this time, who died in Nazi concentration and death camps.

Eureka! A timeline of inventions

Throughout history, human beings have used their creativity and ingenuity to invent things to make our lives easier and better (or, in the case of weaponry, to cause more destruction). Across the next four pages, we chart the history of invention over hundreds of thousands of years, from prehistoric arrowheads to the latest digital technology.

HOW TO READ IT

Origin

- Africa
- Americas
- Asia
- Europe
- Middle East
- Europe & Asia

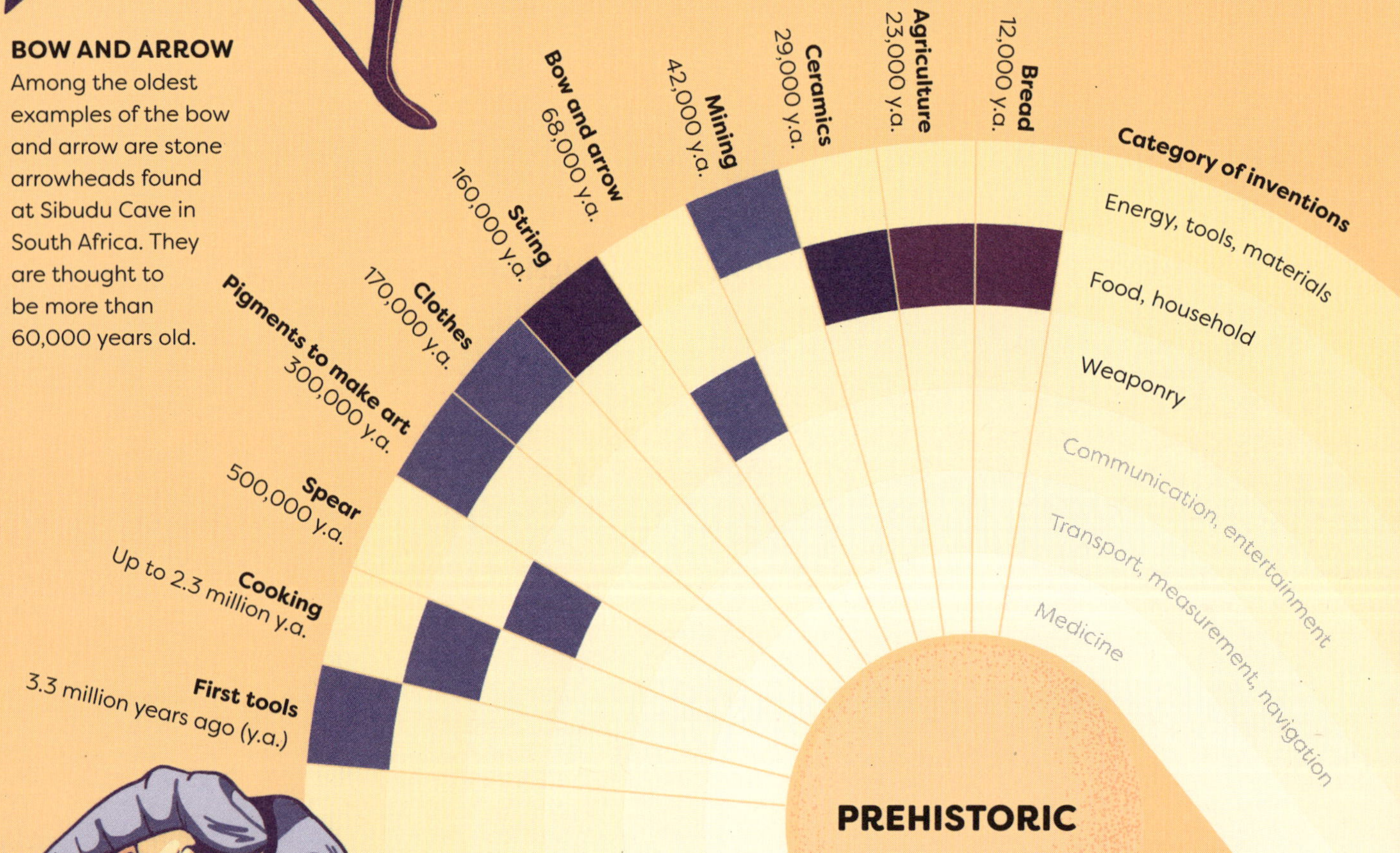

BOW AND ARROW

Among the oldest examples of the bow and arrow are stone arrowheads found at Sibudu Cave in South Africa. They are thought to be more than 60,000 years old.

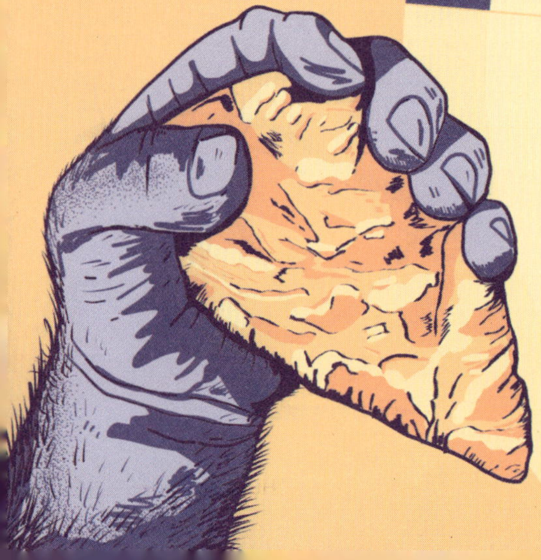

FIRST TOOLS

The earliest tools that we have discovered so far are around 3.3 million years old. Scientists think that they were made by an ape-like species that might have been an evolutionary ancestor of modern humans.

Turn the page

CHESS

The game of chess was probably invented in India. From there, it spread to the Middle East and Europe.

THE WHEEL

No one knows exactly when the wheel was invented or who invented it. There is evidence that wheels were used to make pottery around 5,500 years ago, in the region of the Middle East that is now in Iraq.

LIGHT BULB

The US inventor Thomas Edison was among several people who developed the first electric light bulb. He also invented the first string of electric lights for a Christmas tree!

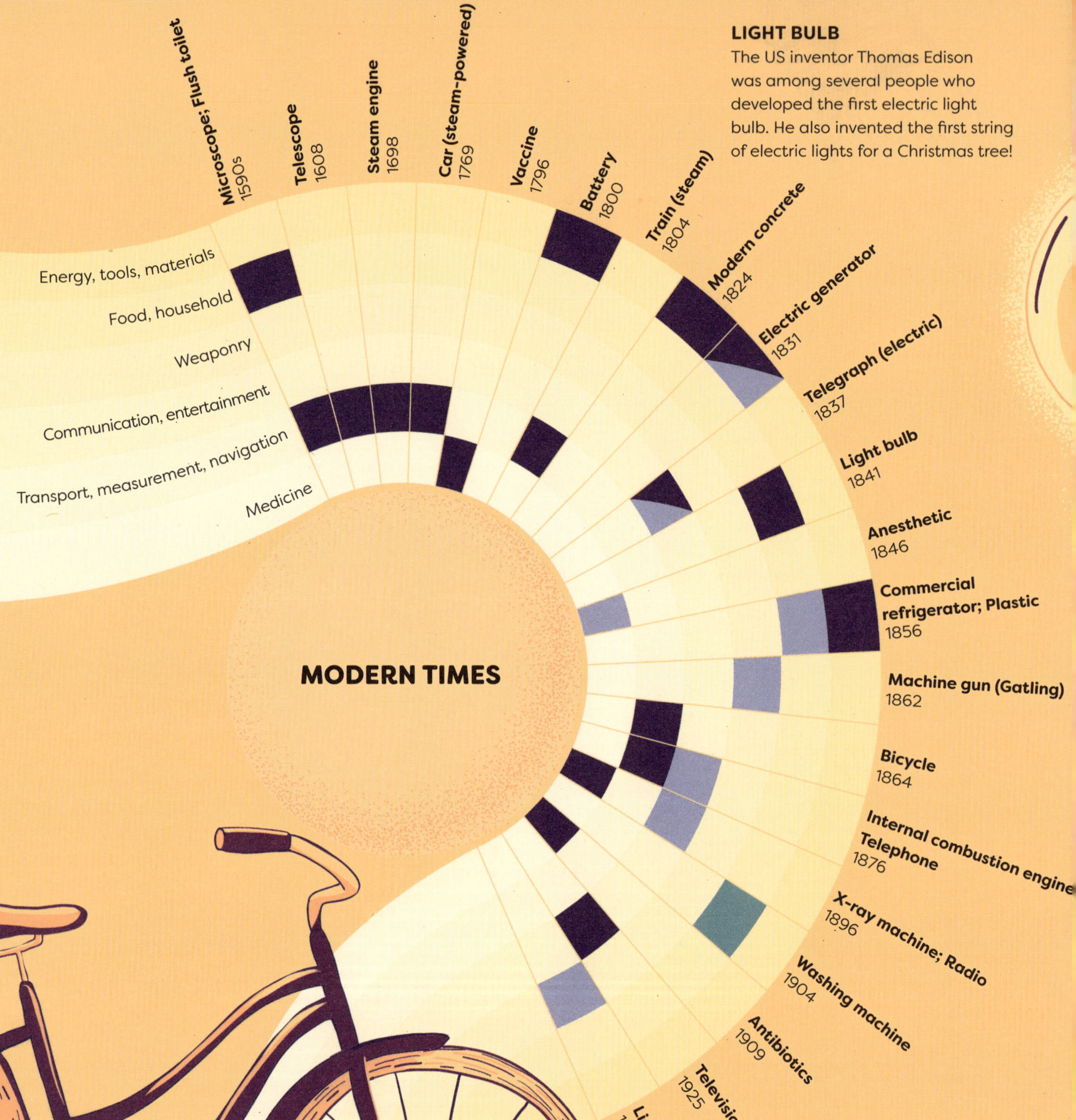

BICYCLE

French blacksmith Pierre Michaux and his son Ernest built an early “pedal-driven velocipede.” Evidence suggests they built it in 1864. The word bicycle came into use a few years later.

HOW TO READ IT

Origin

- Africa
- Americas
- Asia
- Europe
- Europe & Asia
- Europe & Americas
- Unknown

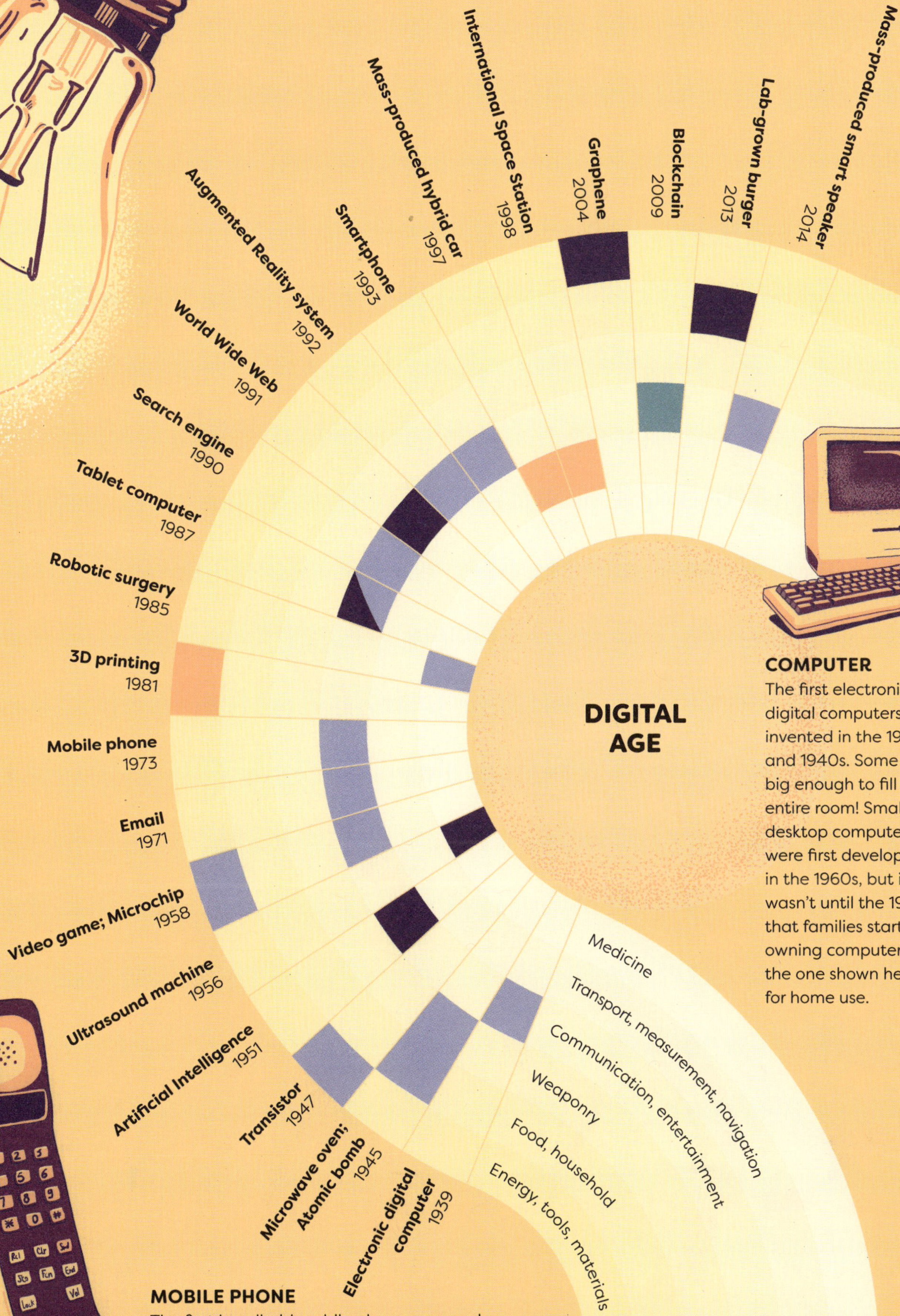

COMPUTER

The first electronic digital computers were invented in the 1930s and 1940s. Some were big enough to fill an entire room! Smaller desktop computers were first developed in the 1960s, but it wasn't until the 1980s that families started owning computers, like the one shown here, for home use.

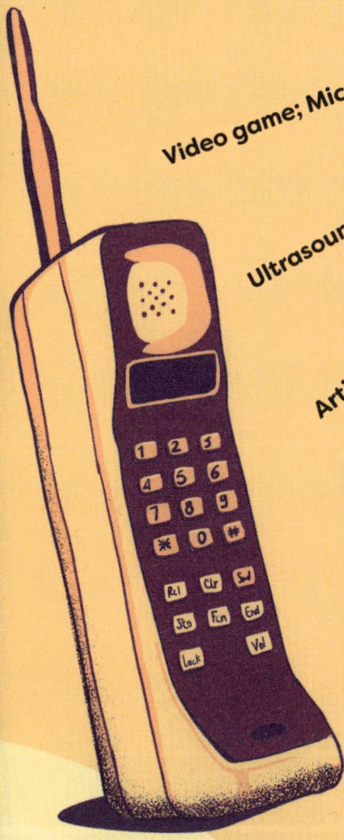

MOBILE PHONE

The first handheld mobile phone was made in New York in 1973. It was the size of a shoebox and could make calls for 35 minutes before needing 10 hours to recharge.

How smart is AI?

Artificial intelligence, or AI, is an area of computer science that deals with teaching machines how to learn and adapt to real-life situations in ways that a human being might. For example, AI programs are taught to recognize things by being shown lots of examples of that thing, so they can then spot and remember its key characteristics as a repeating pattern. The AI program applies this stored information to new situations and objects that it encounters, gathering more information all the time. Although this technological advance is impressive, AI programs are still far less sophisticated than a human brain. If the images looked similar enough, AI programs could easily confuse a picture of a dog with a picture of a blueberry muffin!

Which pictures are of dogs, and which are of blueberry muffins? It might seem like an easy question for you, but it could be bamboozling for an AI program!

An AI computer program learns how to recognize a dog by being given an "input." In this case, the input is a set of pictures of dogs. It will then remember and identify the characteristics that the dogs have in common. This process is called "feature extraction and classification." The computer program then stores the information and uses it to decide whether other pictures are of dogs, too.

LONGEST RAILWAY
Trans-Siberian Railway
Russia, Mongolia, China
5,771 mi (9,288 km)
1916

LONGEST ROAD
Pan-American Highway
North America to South America
19,000 mi (30,600 km)
1923

The Pan-American Highway is the world's longest road. It stretches from Alaska in the USA down to the southern tip of Argentina. The fastest anyone has ever completed the journey on a bicycle was 84 days, 11 hours and 50 minutes!

TALLEST BUILDING
Burj Khalifa
United Arab Emirates
2,717 ft (828 m)
2010

LONGEST CANAL
Jing-Hang Canal
China
1,100 mi (1,800 km)
1327

LONGEST TUNNEL
Delaware Aqueduct
USA
105 mi (170 km)
1965

LONGEST BRIDGE
Danyang-Kunshan Grand Bridge
China
102 mi (165 km)
2011

LENGTH miles, mi (kilometers, km)

HEIGHT feet, ft (meters, m)

YEAR COMPLETED
MEASUREMENT

Engineering masterpieces

Humans have collaborated to create awe-inspiring structures. Here are some of the most impressive, from the world's tallest building to the longest bridge and the deepest mine.

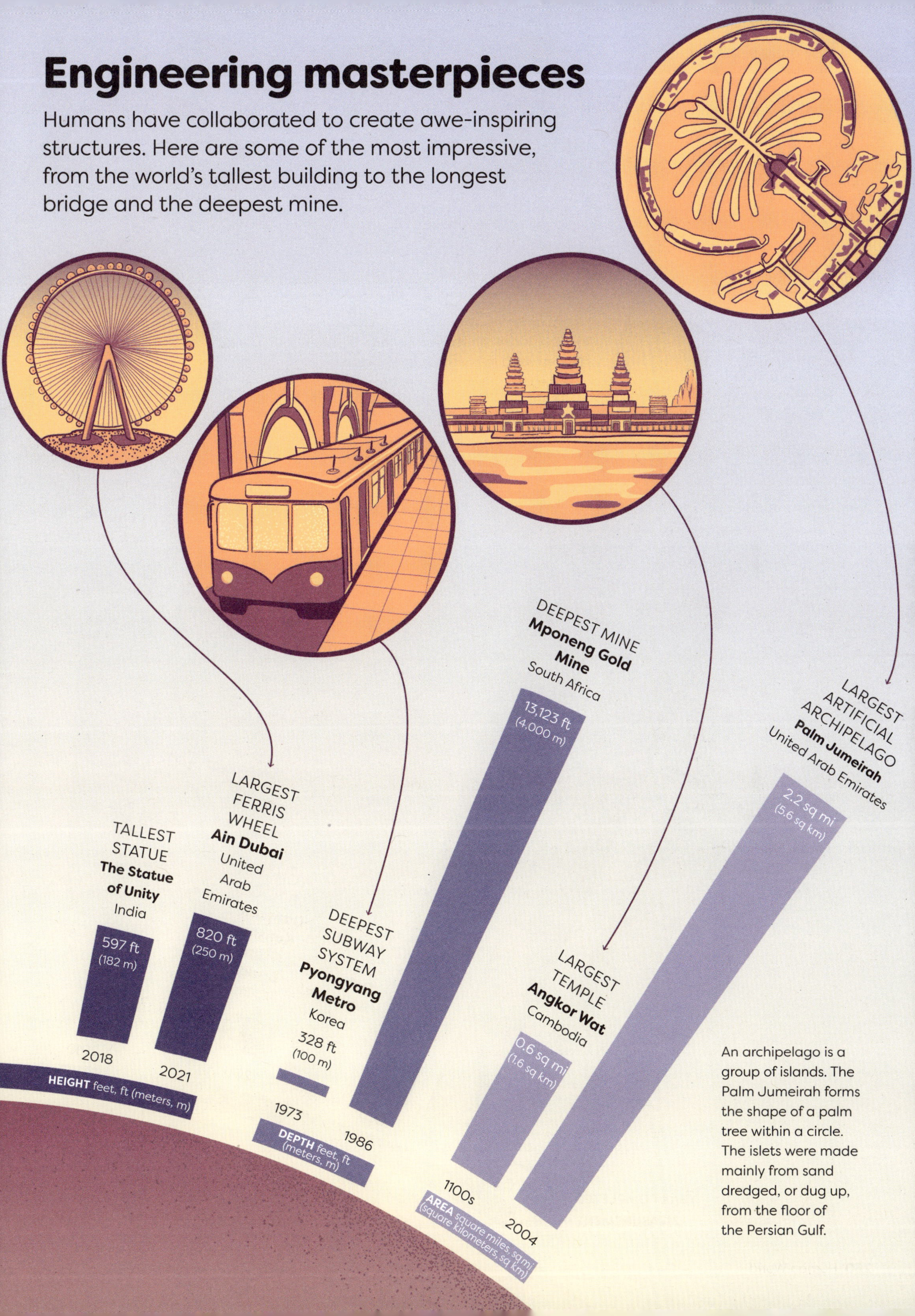

An archipelago is a group of islands. The Palm Jumeirah forms the shape of a palm tree within a circle. The islets were made mainly from sand dredged, or dug up, from the floor of the Persian Gulf.

LEGO MINIFIGURE AND HUMAN POPULATIONS, 2010–2030

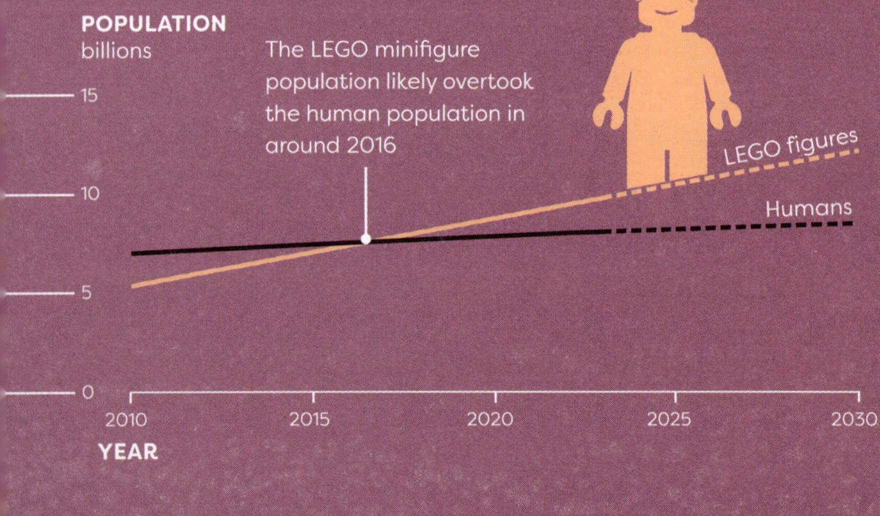

The **black line** shows the growth in the global human population between 2010 and 2030. The **orange line** shows the growth in the number of LEGO minifigures over the same period. The dotted sections of both lines show how the numbers of humans and LEGO people are projected to rise across the rest of this decade.

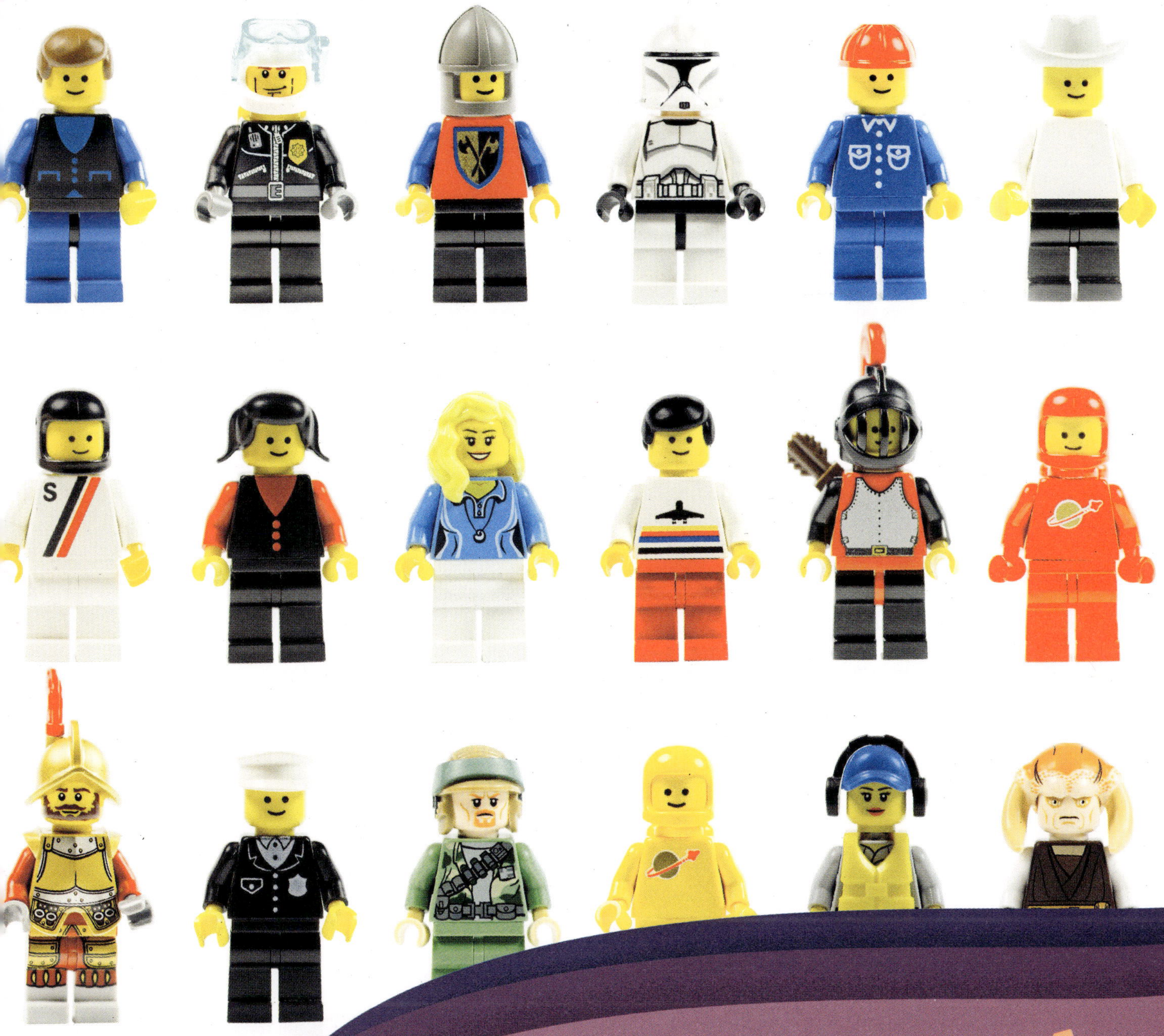

Rise of the toys

Do you like playing with LEGOs? Well, so do millions of other children around the world. In fact, there are an estimated 9 billion individual LEGO minifigures on Earth! This means that there are more than a billion more LEGO people on our planet than there are human beings. Look at the graph opposite to find out when the LEGO population overtook the human population for the first time—and see how both populations are projected to grow in the future.

Moving at speed!

Since they were invented more than 200 years ago, trains and cars have gotten faster and faster—and faster! On these pages, you can see some record-breaking vehicles that have helped humans to zoom around the world at ever-increasing speeds.

The first steam locomotive, which was invented in Wales, UK, in 1804, traveled only slightly faster than the average human's walking speed.

FIVE HIGH-SPEED TRAINS

Maximum speed

STEPHENSON'S ROCKET

1829, UK

This train won the Rainhill trials, a race to see which of five early steam locomotive designs was the fastest.

13 ft **(4 m)**

Train length feet, ft (meters, m)

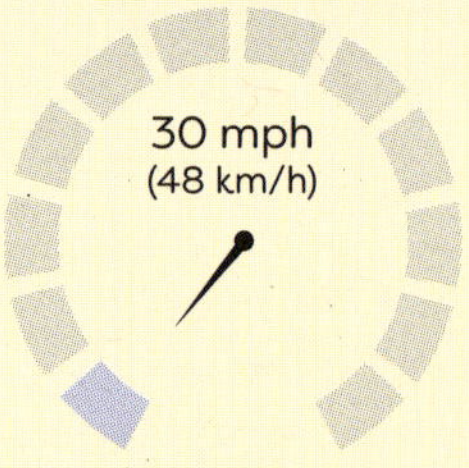

MALLARD

1938, UK

In 1938, this train set the record for fastest steam locomotive—a record it still holds today.

72 ft **(22 m)**

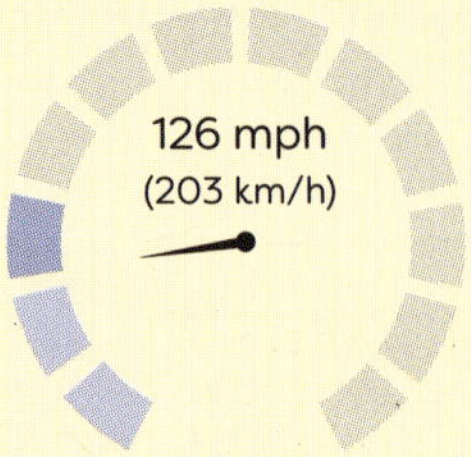

TGV

1981, France

This train held the record for world's fastest train between 1981 and 1988.

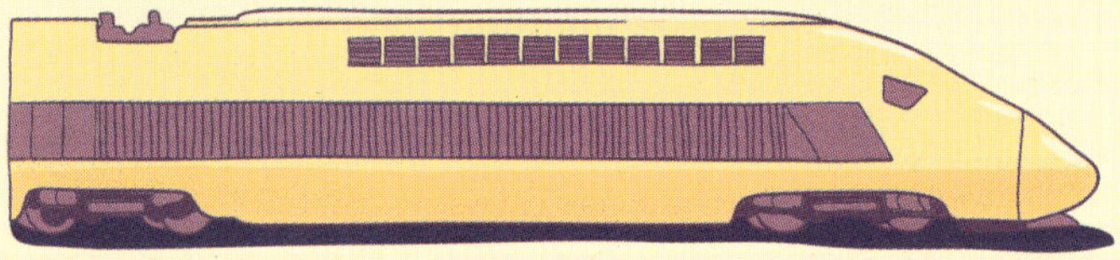

656 ft **(200 m)**

CRH380BL

2010, China

This train set a new world record travelling between Beijing and Shanghai.

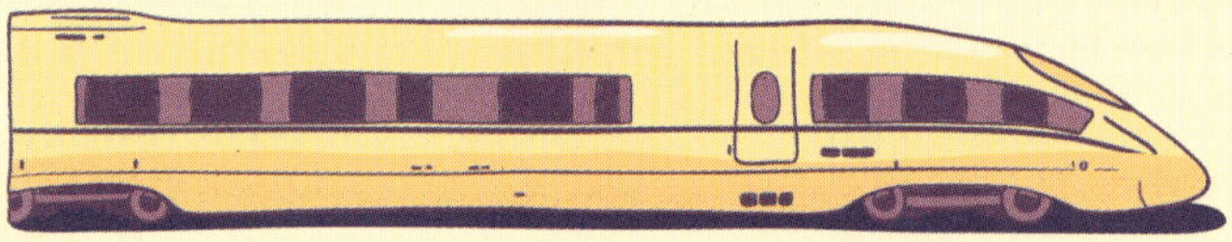

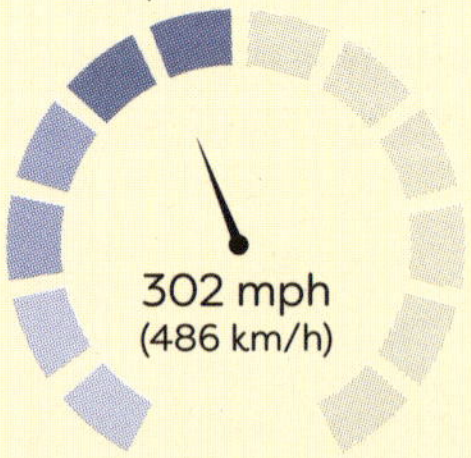

1,322 ft **(403 m)**

SERIES LO MAGLEV

2015, Japan

The world's fastest train, it uses powerful magnets to float above the tracks.

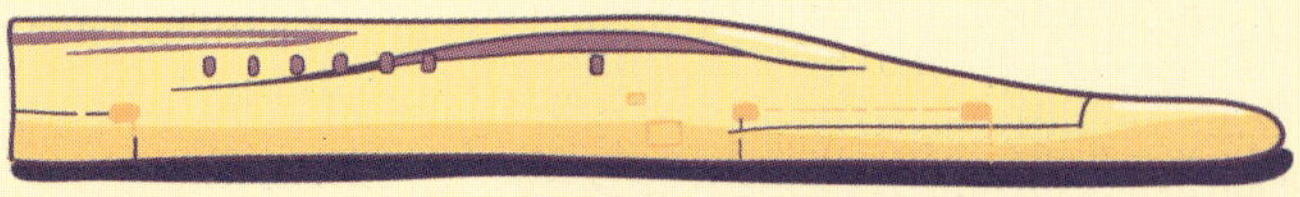

581 ft **(177 m)**

FIVE HIGH-SPEED CARS

LA JAMAIS CONTENTE
1899, France
La Jamais Contente was the first car ever to travel faster than 60 mph (100 km/h).

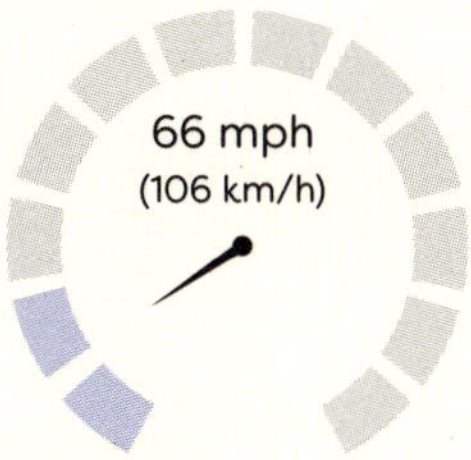

HONDA RA106
2006, UK
This car achieved the fastest recorded speed by a Formula-1 racing car.

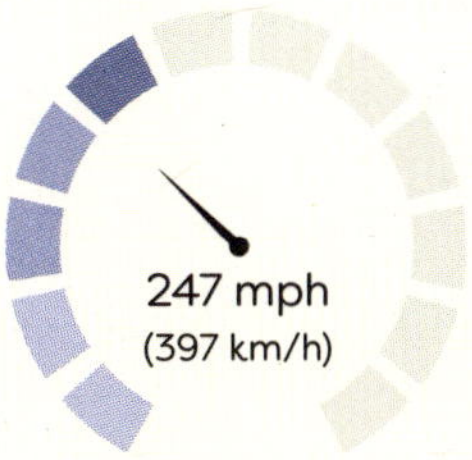

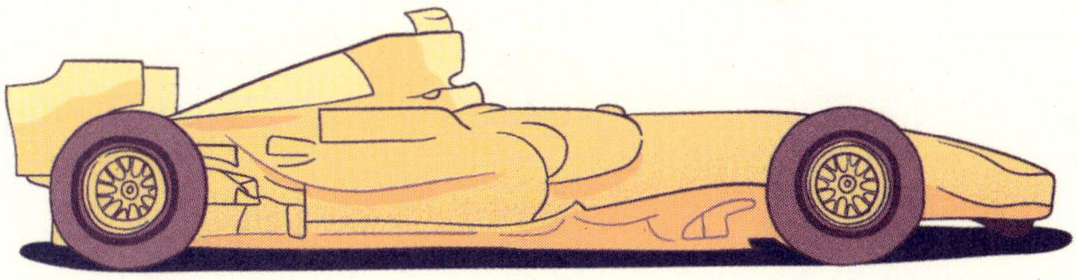

BUGATTI CHIRON
2022, France
This is the world's fastest car that is designed to drive on normal roads.

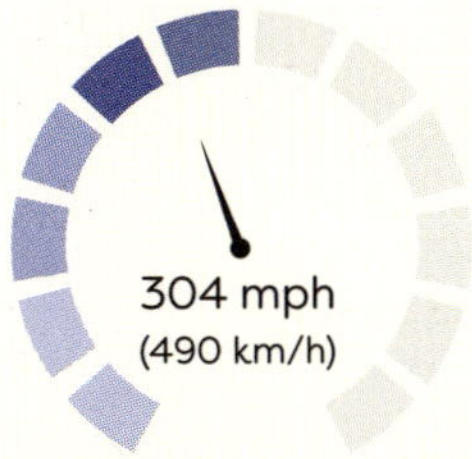

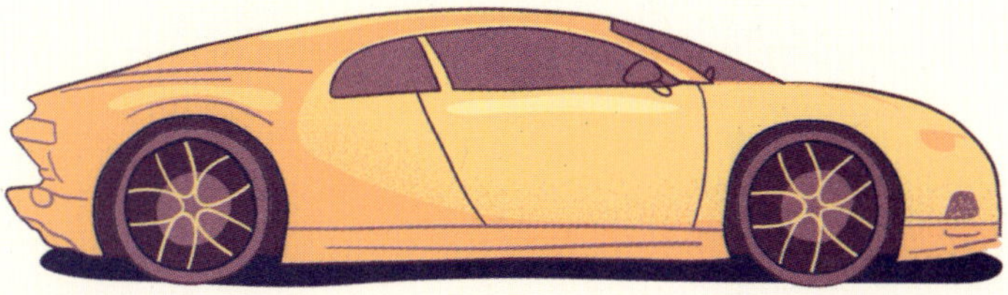

BLUEBIRD CN7
1964, UK
This car holds the record for the fastest car not powered by a jet engine.

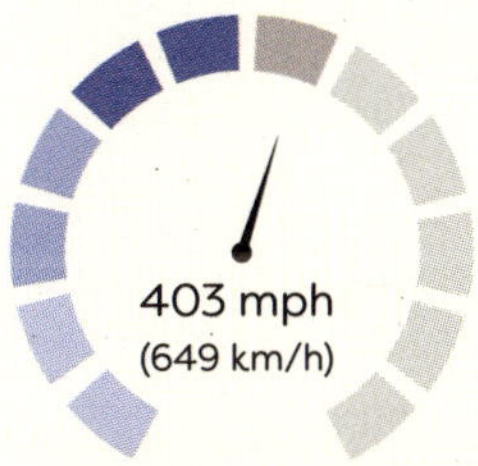

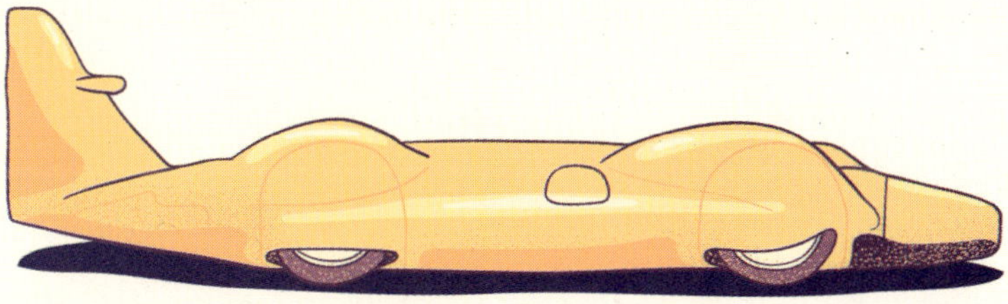

THRUST SSC
1997, UK
Powered by two jet engines, this was the first car to travel faster than the speed of sound (see page 31).

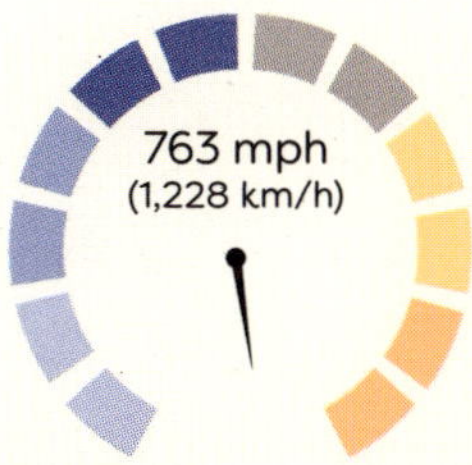

The very first car, which was invented in Germany in 1886, had a top speed of 10 mph (16 km/h).

HOW TO READ IT

Maximum speed
miles per hour, mph
(kilometers per hour, km/h)

The black arrow points to the fastest speed that the train or car achieved.

How many planes are in the sky?

Humans are constantly on the move across the globe, but how many of us are traveling in the air at any one moment?

This map gives you a good idea of how many planes are flying in the air at once, because each yellow airplane on it represents a real plane that was flying at 3 p.m. on July 13th, 2022, one of the busiest days for flights on record. In total, there were 17,916 planes in the sky at that time. This means that if there were, on average, 100 passengers traveling in each plane, more than 1.5 million people were in the sky at the same time!

✈ = one plane flying in the sky

Map created by Flightradar24

Want to find out about how high up planes fly? Turn to page 73.

THE FIRST PLANE TO FLY NONSTOP AROUND THE WORLD

On March 2nd, 1949, an American Boeing B-50A military airplane named *Lucky Lady II* landed at Carswell Air Force Base in Texas to become the first ever plane to fly all the way around the world without stopping. This record-breaking flight, piloted by James G. Gallagher, took 94 hours and 1 minute, as *Lucky Lady II* covered a distance of 23,452 miles (37,742 km) at an average speed of 249 miles per hour (401 km/h). In order to keep flying nonstop for almost four days, *Lucky Lady II* had to be refueled four times in midair, using a long hose to take on additional fuel from a tanker plane that flew close by.

Mega space rockets

If you were to travel 62 miles (100 km) straight up into the sky, you would reach the Kármán Line, an imaginary boundary separating Earth's atmosphere from space. It takes a lot of energy to escape the pull of Earth's gravity and fly this high, a feat that humans first achieved in 1944. Since then, we have launched thousands more rockets into space. Here are some of the biggest.

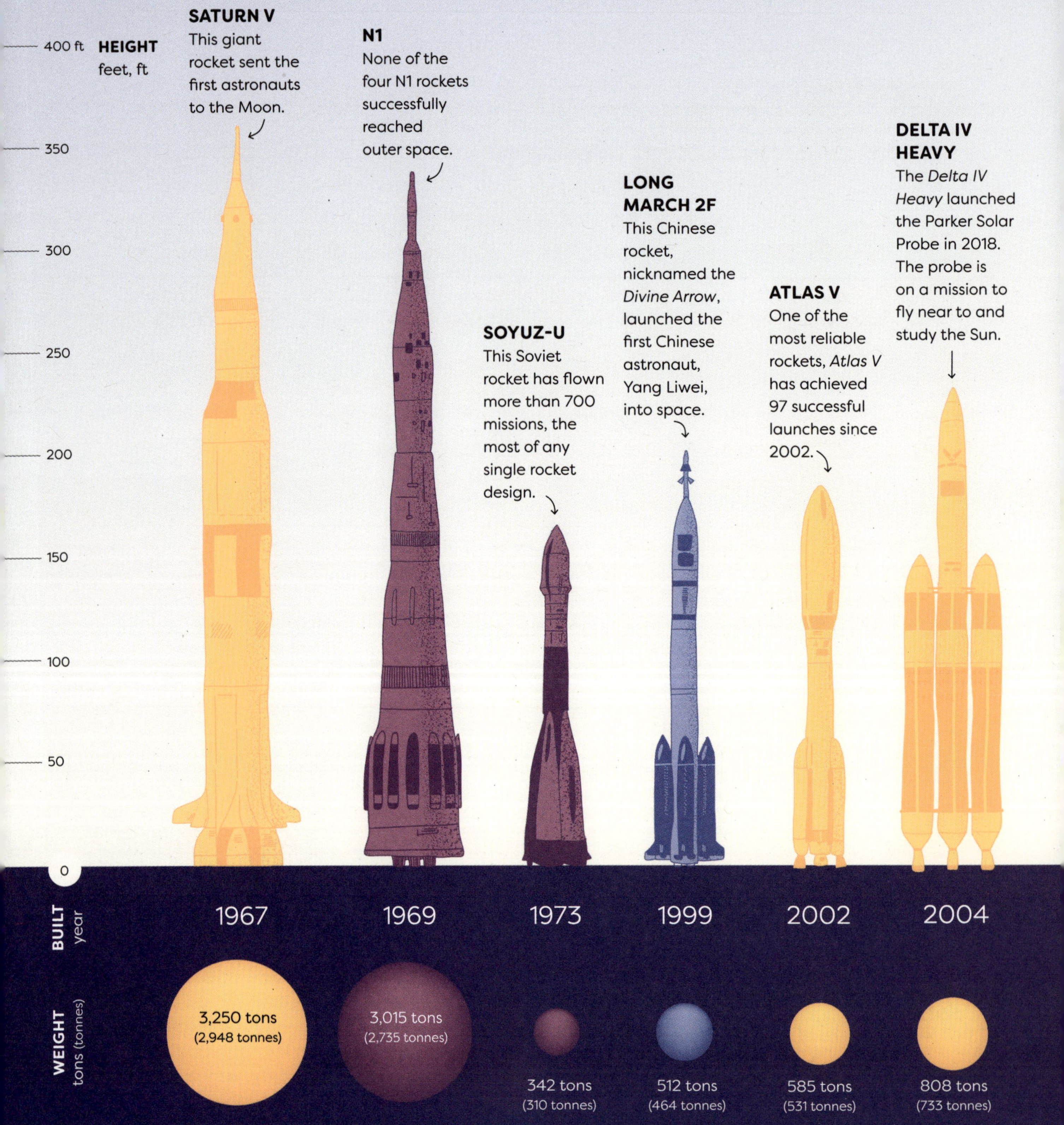

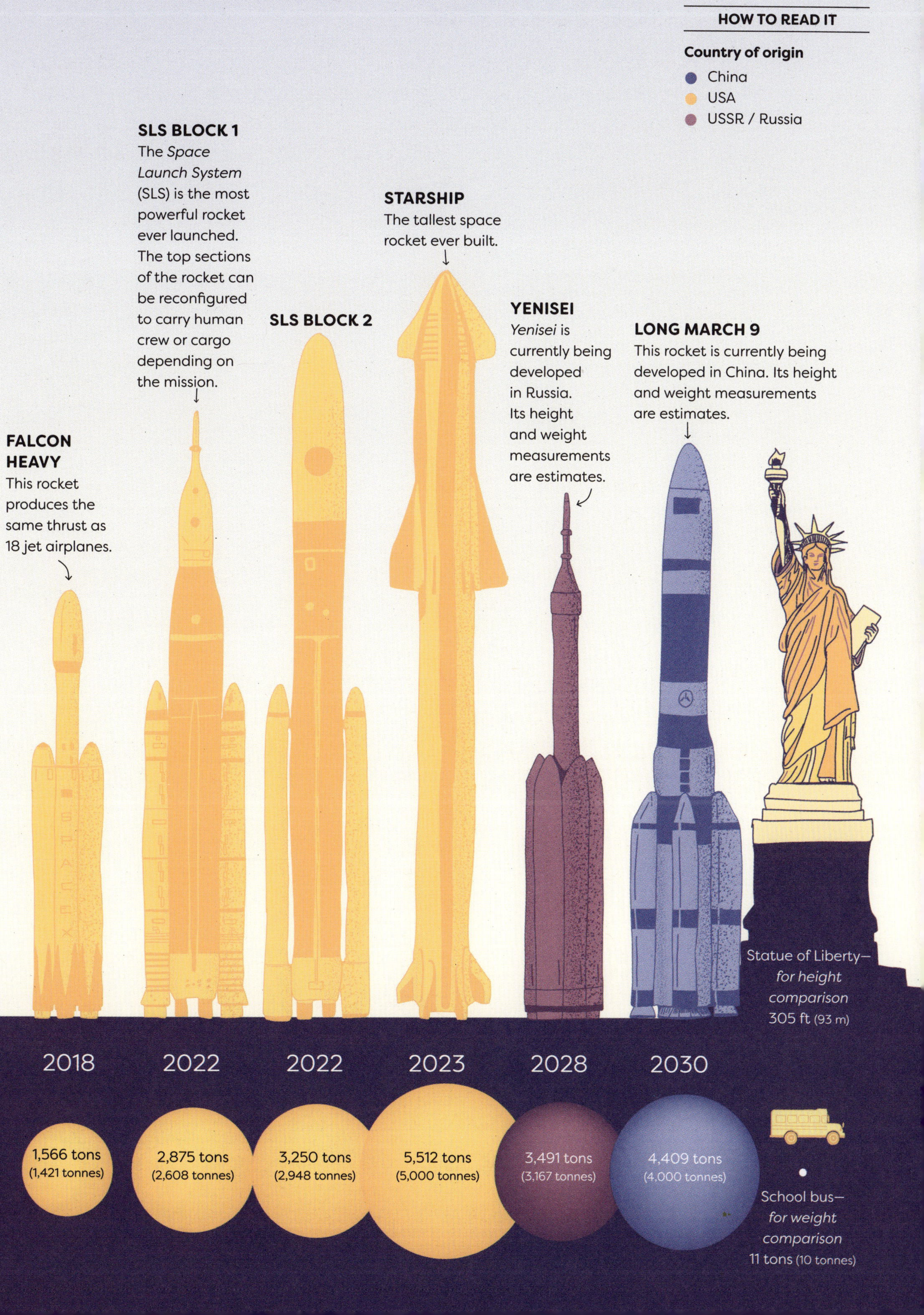

HOW TO READ IT
Country of origin
China
USA
USSR / Russia
SLS BLOCK 1
The *Space Launch System* (SLS) is the most powerful rocket ever launched. The top sections of the rocket can be reconfigured to carry human crew or cargo depending on the mission.
STARSHIP
The tallest space rocket ever built.
SLS BLOCK 2
YENISEI
Yenisei is currently being developed in Russia. Its height and weight measurements are estimates.
LONG MARCH 9
This rocket is currently being developed in China. Its height and weight measurements are estimates.
FALCON HEAVY
This rocket produces the same thrust as 18 jet airplanes.
Statue of Liberty—
for height comparison
305 ft (93 m)
2018
2022
2022
2023
2028
2030
1,566 tons
(1,421 tonnes)
2,875 tons
(2,608 tonnes)
3,250 tons
(2,948 tonnes)
5,512 tons
(5,000 tonnes)
3,491 tons
(3,167 tonnes)
4,409 tons
(4,000 tonnes)
School bus—
for weight comparison
11 tons (10 tonnes)

Space junk

Since the 1950s, humans have launched thousands of rockets into space and an even larger number of satellites into orbit around Earth. When these machines stop working or break up into smaller bits, they become space junk. Some space junk burns up as it re-enters Earth's atmophere. However, satellites and debris at higher altitudes can continue orbiting Earth for hundreds or even thousands of years. Scientists are now working on ways to clean up all this unwanted junk, including picking it up with magnets and catching it in a giant net.

SPACE JUNK IN NUMBERS

more than
30,000 pieces
of space junk are larger than 4 inches (10 cm) across. They include dead satellites that have failed or been left in orbit at the end of their mission.

around
1,000,000 pieces
are between 1/3 inch and 4 inches (1–10 cm) across. They include dropped tools, screws, cables, and space cameras.

more than
100 million fragments
are smaller than 1/3 inch (1 cm) across. They include fragments that fall off satellites due to wear and tear.

Space junk in orbit around Earth.

Looking into space

Telescopes allow us to see distant objects in space and reveal the universe's secrets. Early telescopes used glass lenses to see faraway objects. Today's telescopes use curved mirrors instead of lenses because they're better at collecting the dim light from deep space.

HOOKER
1917 (first recorded images)
Mount Wilson, California
This telescope was used to prove the Milky Way is not the only galaxy.

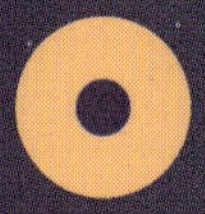

HALE
1948
Mount Palomar, California
This telescope collects visible light, magnified by a giant curved mirror.

MULTI-MIRROR TELESCOPE
1979 (updated in 2000)
Mount Hopkins, Arizona
Originally a six-mirror telescope design, it was replaced with a single lens in 2000 to create sharper images.

HUBBLE
1990
Low-Earth orbit
The first telescope located in space, Hubble revolutionized astronomy and produced many famous space images.

KECK
1993 and 1996
Mauna Kea, Hawaii
Keck's twin telescopes each contain 36 reflective hexagons that combine to form two giant mirrors.

HOBBY-EBERLY
1996
Davis Mountains, Texas
This telescope is designed to capture visible and infrared light from super distant and faint stars and galaxies.

VERY LARGE TELESCOPE
1998–2000
Cerro Paranal, Chile
The Very Large Telescope produced the first direct image of an exoplanet.

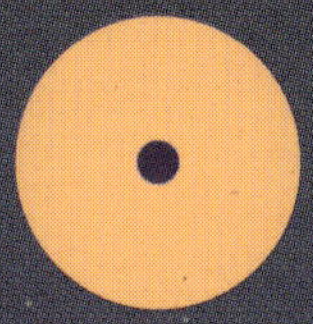

SUBARU TELESCOPE
1999
Mauna Kea, Hawaii
The Subaru Telescope can observe 2,400 galaxies at once.

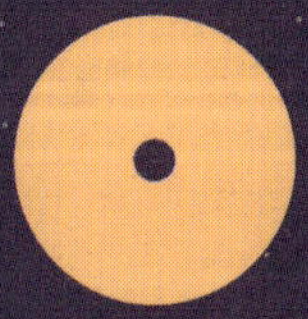

GEMINI NORTH
1999
Mauna Kea, Hawaii

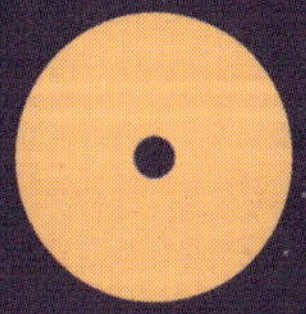

GEMINI SOUTH
2000
Cerro Pachón, Chile

The two Gemini telescopes can view the entire sky. Astronomers have used both these telescopes, along with other telescopes, to uncover a massive explosion of colliding neutron stars.

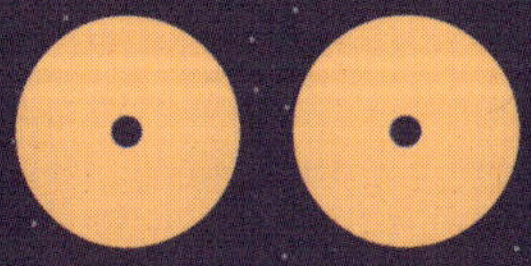

MAGELLAN TELESCOPES
2000 and 2002
Las Campanas, Chile
Their location high up in the dry Atacama desert gives the Magellan telescopes good visibility of the sky for 300 nights of the year.

LARGE ZENITH TELESCOPE
2004
British Columbia, Canada
With a liquid mirror made of mercury, the Large Zenith Telescope (now no longer in use) could be pointed only in one direction—but it cost a fraction of what a solid-mirror telescope does.

HOW TO READ IT

- ● Located on Earth
- ● Located in space
- ○ Under construction

Single mirror telescopes are called monolithic mirrors because they use a single rigid piece of glass, which collects and reflects light into the sensor. The largest single mirror is about 26 feet (8 m) across.

Segmented mirror telescopes are made up of lots of smaller, hexagonal mirrors that are positioned by computers to form a single mirror. In theory, there's no limit to how big a mirror can be with this design.

Check out the photograph of a nebula taken by the JWST on page 28.

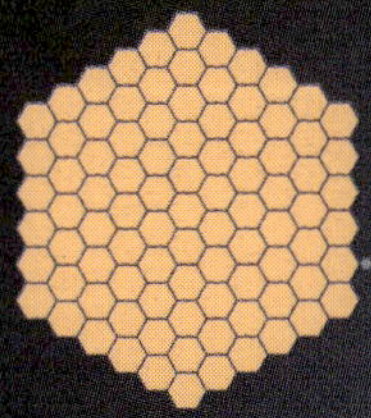

SOUTHERN AFRICAN LARGE TELESCOPE

2005

Sutherland, South Africa

This telescope has been used to detect black holes.

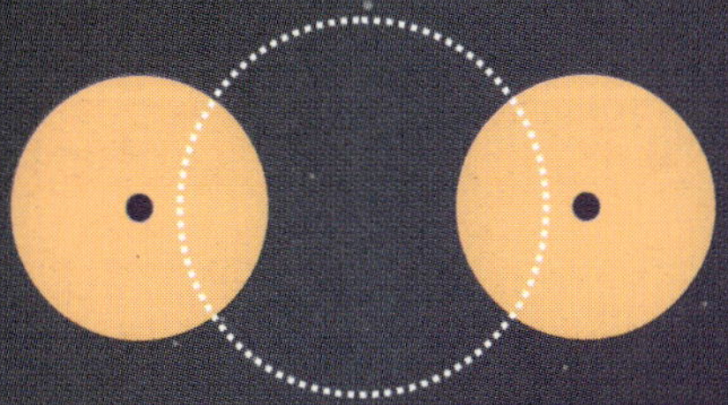

LARGE BINOCULAR TELESCOPE

2005 and 2008

Mount Graham, Arizona

This telescope has twin mirrors to collect more light and create a sharper picture. It looks like a giant pair of binoculars.

GRAN TELESCOPIO CANARIAS

2007

La Palma, Canary Islands, Spain

The giant mirror of this telescope is 34 feet (10.4 m) across. It is the largest optical, or light-gathering, telescope in the world.

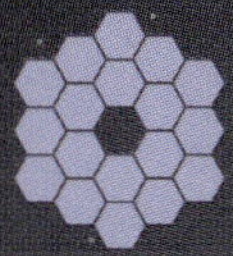

JAMES WEBB SPACE TELESCOPE (JWST)

2021

Earth-Sun L2 point

JWST is the largest and most powerful space telescope ever built, with a sunshield the size of a tennis court to protect its massive mirror. Aside from creating stunning images of stars, galaxies, and nebulae, it is capable of finding galaxies that formed very early in the history of the universe, only 200 million years after the Big Bang.

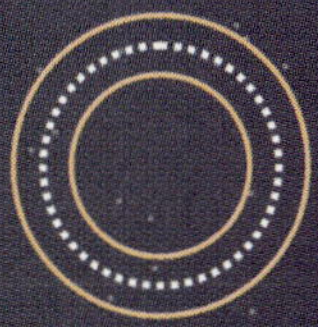

VERA C. RUBIN OBSERVATORY

2024

Cerro Pachón, Chile

Unlike other telescopes, which look very closely at small numbers of space objects, this telescope is designed to create a ten-year "movie" that maps the night sky.

EXTREMELY LARGE TELESCOPE

2025

Cerro Armazones, Chile

This telescope will be nearly four times bigger than any built before.

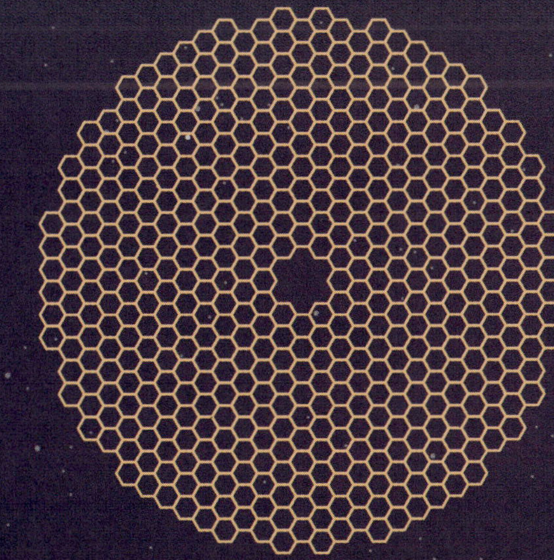

THIRTY METER TELESCOPE

2027

Mauna Kea, Hawaii

Locals oppose the plans for this telescope, which will be three times bigger than any built before.

GIANT MAGELLAN TELESCOPE

2029

Las Campanas, Chile

This telescope will use seven of the largest mirrors ever built to explore the distant universe and look for signs of alien life.

Human at the same scale as the telescope mirrors

SCALE **30 feet** (10 m)

Going for gold

Every four years, athletes from more than 200 countries around the world gather to compete in the Olympic Games. The Games were held in ancient Greece until 393 CE, before being revived centuries later, in 1896. Here are some of the countries and athletes to have won the most Olympic medals in modern times.

MICHAEL PHELPS / *Swimming*
Phelps competed in four Olympic Games between 2004 and 2016 and won a total of 28 medals, making him the most successful modern Olympian. Phelps also holds the record for winning the most Olympic gold medals (23).

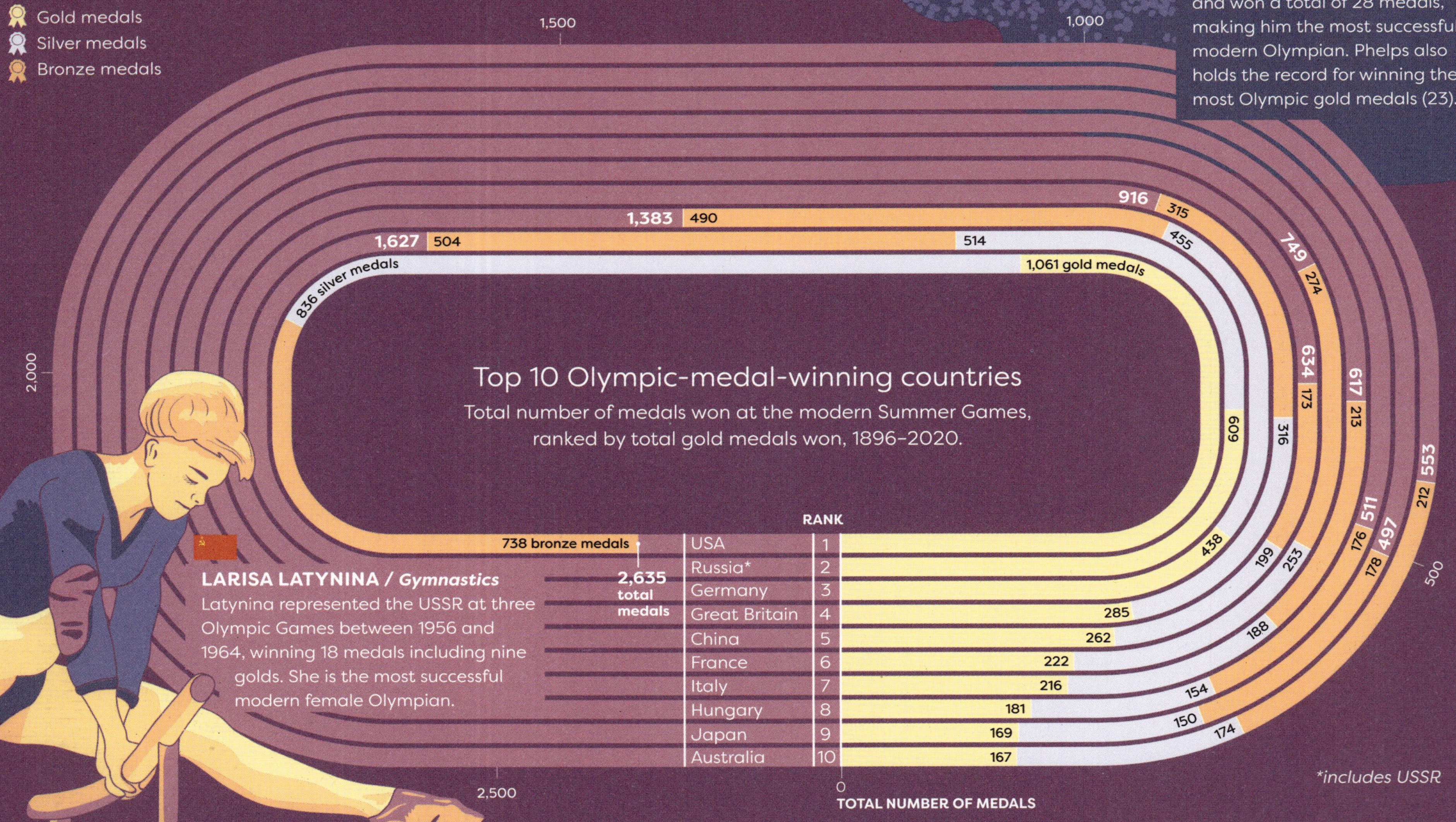

LARISA LATYNINA / *Gymnastics*
Latynina represented the USSR at three Olympic Games between 1956 and 1964, winning 18 medals including nine golds. She is the most successful modern female Olympian.

OLYMPIC MEDALS VS POPULATION SIZE

As you might expect, countries with larger populations, such as the USA and Russia, tend to win more Olympic medals because they have more potential Olympic athletes to choose from. The chart below shows what the top-ten Olympic medals table looks like when calculated by the average number of medals for each million people in the country's population.

ALADÁR GEREVICH / *Fencing*
Hungary's Aladár Gerevich won ten medals across six different Olympic Games, including seven golds. He won his first gold in 1932 and his last 28 years later, in 1960.

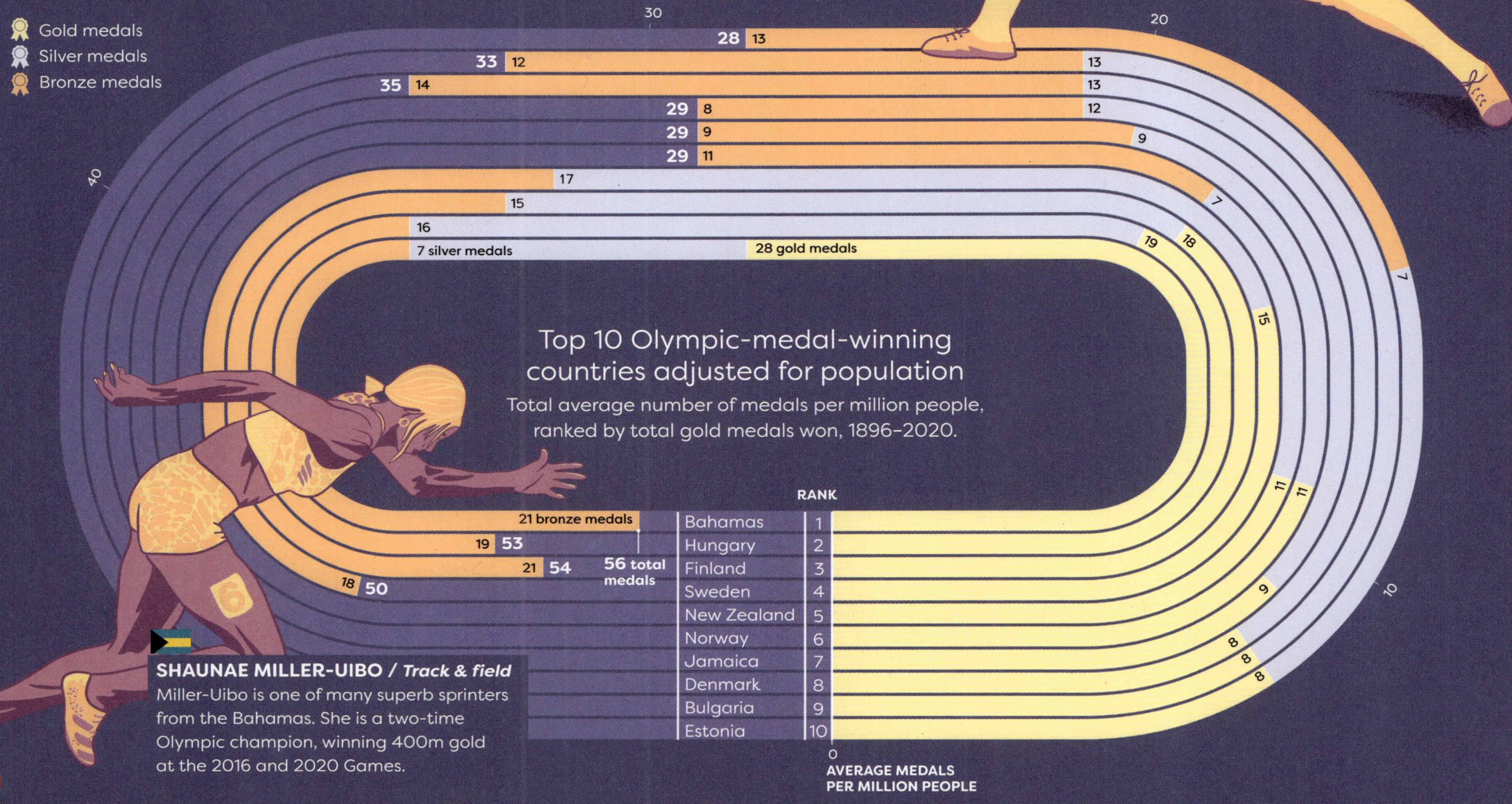

SHAUNAE MILLER-UIBO / *Track & field*
Miller-Uibo is one of many superb sprinters from the Bahamas. She is a two-time Olympic champion, winning 400m gold at the 2016 and 2020 Games.

Sporting success

Some of the world's greatest athletes compete in the Paralympic Games, an international sports competition for elite athletes with disabilities. The Paralympic Games are held in the same host city as the Olympic Games (*para* means alongside). The first ever Paralympics were held in 1960 in Rome, Italy. Since then, the Paralympics have grown in size and popularity, with thousands of athletes from more than 150 countries now competing. An estimated global TV audience of 4.25 billion people watched the 2020 Paralympic Games when they were held in Tokyo, Japan.

NUMBER OF PARALYMPIC ATHLETES

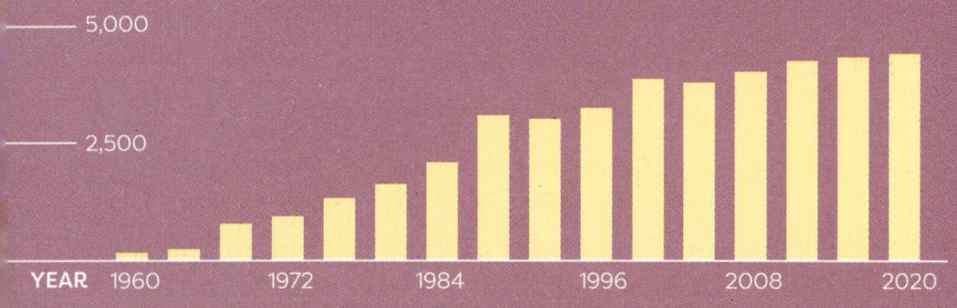

NUMBER OF PARALYMPIC SPORTS

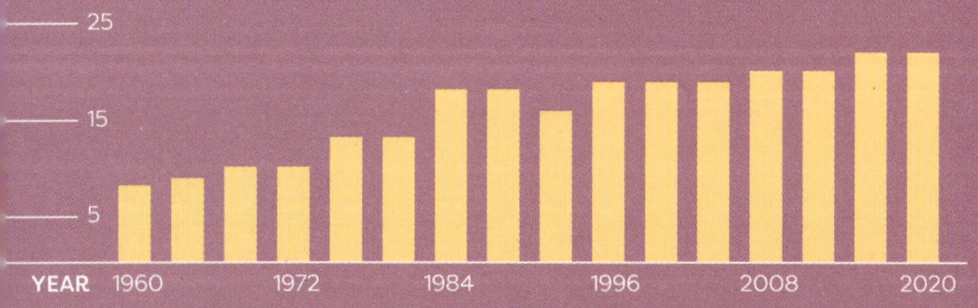

NUMBER OF COUNTRIES COMPETING

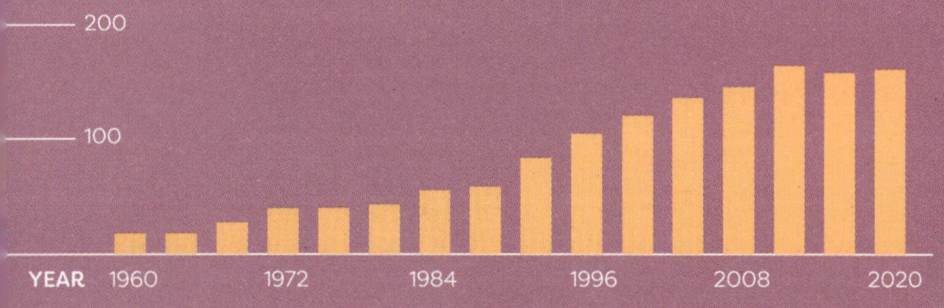

This photograph shows Zheng Tao of China competing in a men's 100-meter freestyle swimming race at the 2020 Paralympic Games in Tokyo, Japan.

Read all about it

Humans have been making books for more than 3,000 years, but we only invented the technology to create more than one identical copy of the same book 1,000 years ago. We have only been able to print lots of copies *really fast* much more recently. Here's how it happened.

HOW PRINTING CHANGED THE WORLD

This timeline shows how different methods of printing have evolved over the past 1,300 years. As printing became more efficient, the number of books printed each year went up and the average cost of printing them went down. The growing availability of cheaper books helped millions of people around the world to learn how to read and write. It also meant that people gained better and broader access to other people's ideas and direct access to sacred texts.

WOODBLOCK PRINTING
8th century, China
This is the earliest known form of printing, in which carved wooden blocks covered in dye or ink are used to press words or symbols onto paper or textiles.

MOVEABLE TYPE
1041–1048, China
In this printing technique, individual letters or characters (known as "type") made of porcelain are arranged in a rack before being used for printing. The same type can then be rearranged to form different words. By the 12th century, metal moveable type had been invented in China.

ROTARY PRESS
1847, USA
Instead of printing on individual sheets of paper, as Gutenberg's press did, rotary presses use rotating rolls of paper to print multiple pages in a continuous stream. They are widely used in newspaper printing.

OFFSET PRESS
1904, USA
An offset press transfers the ink from a metal printing plate onto a rubber sheet, which then prints onto sheets of paper. This helps protect the metal plate from wear and tear. The book you are holding in your hands is printed on a modern offset press.

E-BOOK
1971, USA
The first electronic book, or e-book, is a copy of the US Declaration of Independence. It is made in 1971, although e-books only start to be used widely in the 1990s.

MECHANICAL PRINTING PRESS
1455, Germany
The first mechanical printing press, invented by Johannes Gutenberg, makes it possible to print books much faster and more cheaply. It works by pressing metal pieces of type onto individual sheets of paper.

STANHOPE PRESS
1800, England
This is the first printing press made entirely from metal, allowing it to print more quickly and efficiently.

Today, it is estimated that 86% of people over the age of 15 can read and write, which is more than double the percentage of people who could read and write in 1940.

BESTSELLING BOOKS

Here are five of the bestselling books of all time. Each of these books has sold at least 150 million copies around the world. *Harry Potter and the Sorcerer's Stone* by J.K. Rowling is not far behind, with 120 million copies sold.

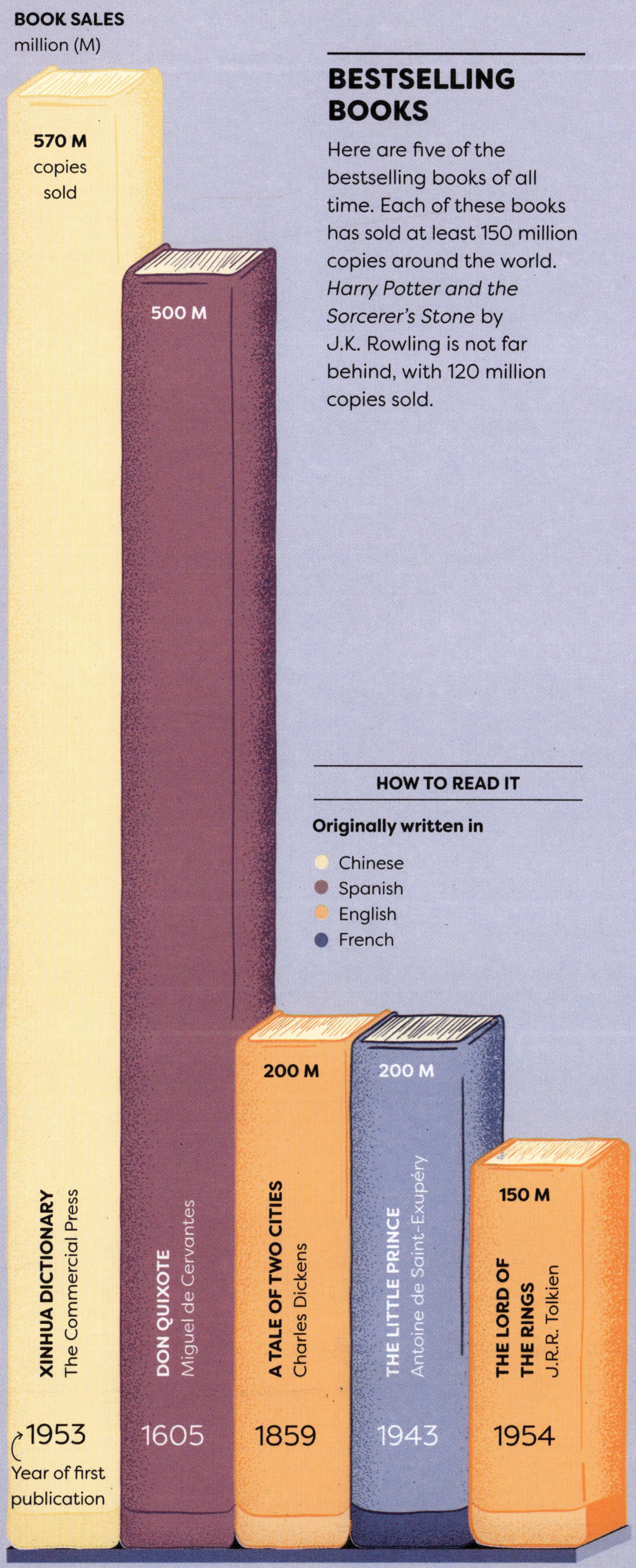

HOW TO READ IT

Originally written in

- Chinese
- Spanish
- English
- French

Music makers

Do you love music? According to the latest archeological evidence, humans have been creating music together for tens of thousands of years. But although music is a common feature of human cultures all around the world, the instruments people use to make it are different and have changed over time. Here, you can see when various popular musical instruments were first played, from prehistoric bone flutes to the modern electric synthesizer.

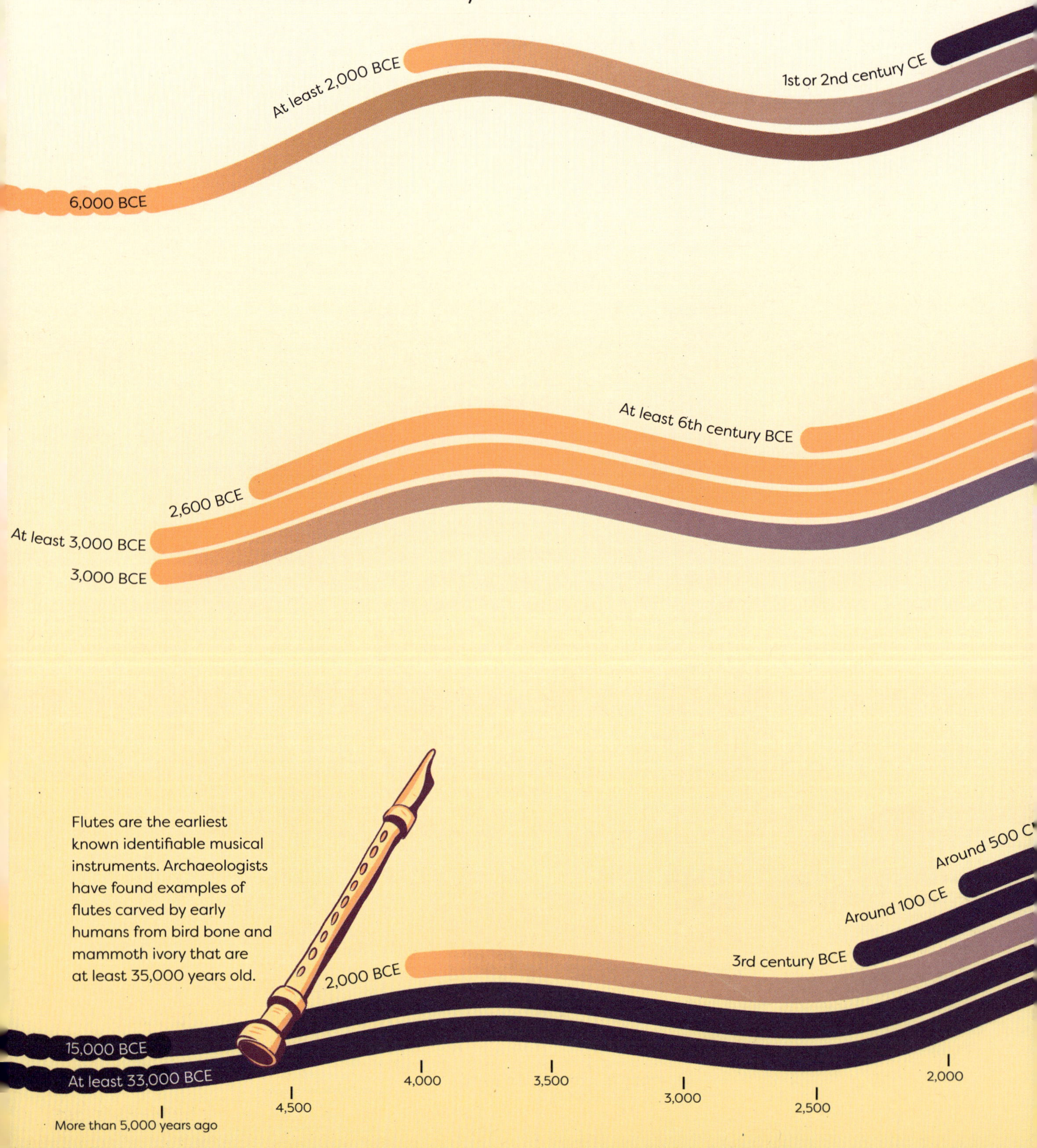

INSTRUMENT
ELECTRONIC
1955 Synthesizer
1920 Theremin
1874 Musical telegraph, keyboard
1761 Electric harpsichord, keyboard
PERCUSSION
By 14th century Triangle
Gong
Cymbals
Drum
STRINGED
1936 Electric guitar
1709 Piano
Around 1550 Violin
Around 1550 Cello
16th century Sitar
16th century Guitar, Spanish
16th century Banjo
15th century Harpsichord
Guzheng (Chinese zither)
Lyre
Lute
Harp
WIND
1844 Saxophone
1835 Tuba
1821 Harmonica
1820s Accordion
Early 18th century Clarinet
Mid-17th century Oboe
Mid-17th century French horn
17th century Bassoon
15th century Trombone
14th century Recorder
Didgeridoo
Bagpipe
Pipe organ
Trumpet, metal
Trumpet, shell
Flute
,500
1,000
500
0
FIRST PLAYED OR INVENTED
Number of years ago
HOW TO READ IT
Origin
Africa
Americas
Asia
Europe
Oceania
Asia / Europe
Asia / Africa

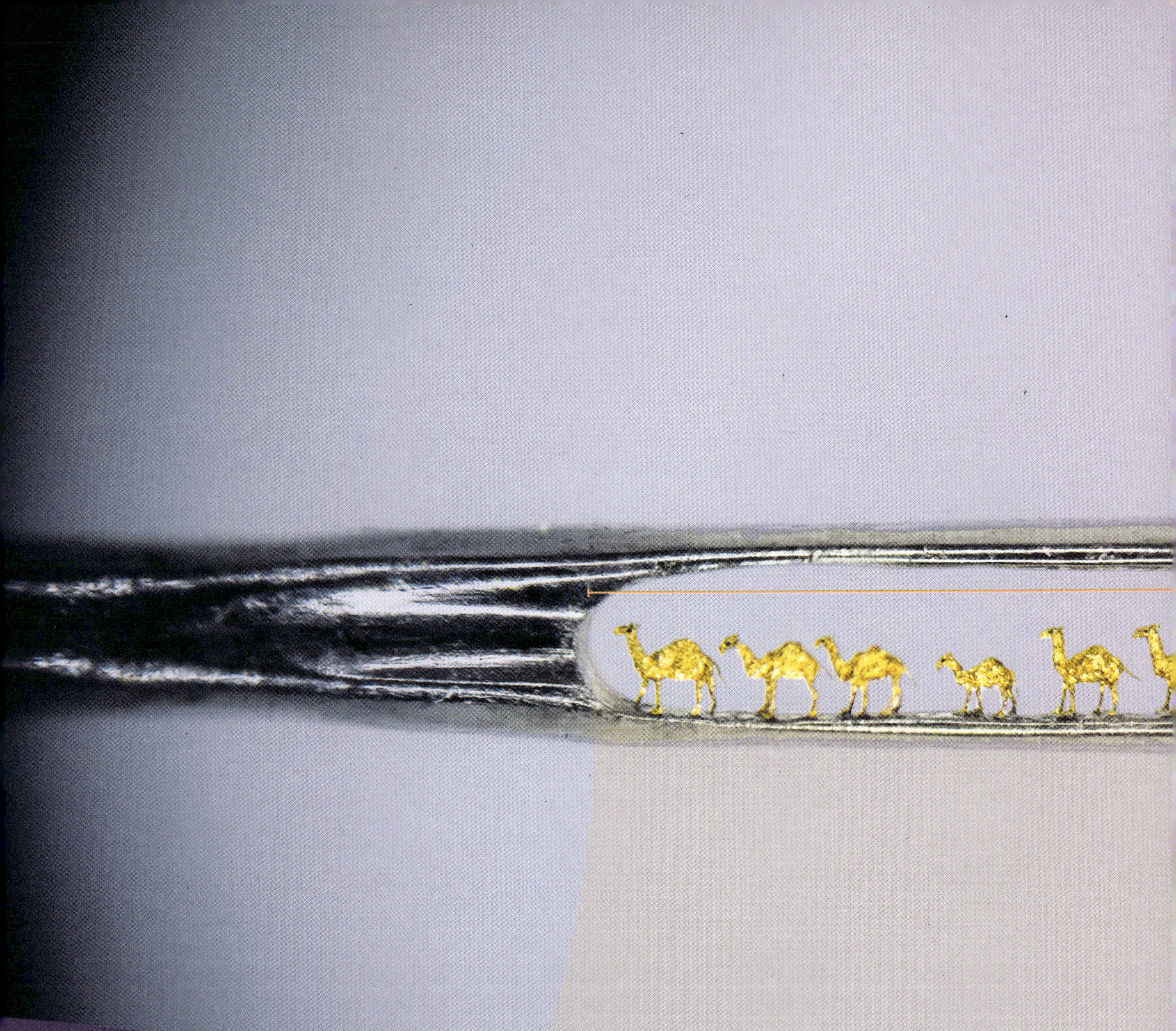

This scale diagram shows how big the needle in the photograph is in real life.

All of the 14 camels fit in here, the eye of the needle. It's only $\frac{1}{32}$ inch (0.9 mm) long and $\frac{1}{100}$ inch (0.3 mm) wide!

To see some more tiny things, go to page 148.

Mini masterpieces

This tiny sculpture, inspired by a story in the Bible, shows a herd of camels inside the eye of a needle, which is the small loop through which the thread is passed. It was created by the British sculptor Willard Wigan, who also holds the world record for the smallest sculpture made by hand. That sculpture—of a human embryo—is $\frac{1}{1,000}$ inch (0.05 mm) wide, which is roughly the size of a human blood cell.

Say goodbye!

A language is a system we use to share information. Humans have developed more than 7,000 languages altogether.

IF THE WORLD WERE 100 PEOPLE...

This infographic represents the world as 100 people and shows how many people speak different languages as their first, or native, language. The people illustrated here are all saying "goodbye."

Zài jiàn

(simplified Mandarin)

18 people
SPEAK CHINESE LANGUAGES
(including Mandarin, Cantonese, and 11 other languages)

Adiós

7 people
SPEAK SPANISH

Goodbye

5 people
SPEAK ENGLISH

This infographic shows the most commonly spoken first languages. If it also included second, third, and fourth languages, English would be the most spoken language.

Ma'a al-salāmah

5 people
SPEAK ARABIC LANGUAGES

Namaste

5 people
SPEAK HINDI

3 people
SPEAK BENGALI

3 people
SPEAK PORTUGUESE

2 people
SPEAK RUSSIAN

2 people
SPEAK JAPANESE

50 people
SPEAK OTHER LANGUAGES

Emojis are symbols used to create a type of visual "language" to convey information, such as emotions, animals, nature, food, and activities. The term emoji is a combination of two Japanese words: *e*, meaning "picture," and *moji*, meaning "written character." By 2022, the Unicode Consortium, the organization that reviews and releases emojis and other characters, had standardized more than 3,600 of them.

MEET THE EXPERT CONSULTANT

Professor Ganna Pogrebna

Behavioral data scientist

TELL US ABOUT YOUR JOB

I help people and organizations understand how they make decisions and teach them how to make them better. For example, if a city wants to become greener and more sustainable, I can help them figure out how to get people to recycle more.

HOW DID YOU BECOME A DATA SCIENTIST?

I started my career writing mathematical models to predict human behavior and then testing these models in the laboratory. But I wanted to make a difference in the real world rather than in the lab. Working with data allows scientists like me to make predictions about what might happen in the future, such as how many people might get sick with a disease or where we can expect a flood. This allows us to ensure help is available for people when it is needed.

WHAT EXCITING DISCOVERY ARE YOU LOOKING FORWARD TO SEEING IN THE FUTURE?

Computers are good at solving problems, but they don't think and solve problems in the same way that people do. Sometimes, when we use computer programs, they do something that we don't expect or understand. This is because the computer program is like a "black box": we can't see what's going on inside. I am looking forward to computer programs changing from being black boxes into something that we can explain. This will develop better understanding between people and machines.

WHAT IS YOUR FAVORITE THING ABOUT DATA SCIENCE?

My favorite thing about studying human behavior with data science is that I get to work on lots of different types of projects. For example, today I may study how people make choices in a shop and tomorrow I might help astronauts to make decisions in space.

SCAVENGER HUNT!

Can you track down the answers to this quiz in the pages of this book? (Turn to page 305 to see if you are right!)

1. In which country is the game of chess thought to have been invented?

2. The *Lucky Lady II* was the first airplane to do what?

3. In which year was the electronic synthesizer invented?

4. On average, how many babies are born around the world every second: 2, 4, or 7?

5. Michael Phelps is the most successful modern Olympian. How many gold medals did he win?

6. Namaste means "goodbye" in which language?

7. What is the world's estimated total wealth in US dollars: $464 million, $464 billion, or $464 trillion?

8. What is the name of the world's tallest building?

Sources

An infographic is only ever as accurate and trustworthy as the data used to create it. In this book, we have worked hard to use the most reliable data available at the time of publication and to present it clearly and objectively. We have also used data and facts that are as globally representative as possible. You can find a list of our main data sources for every infographic here.

Welcome!, pp.vi–vii:
'Information theory: Physiology', britannica.com; 'In the blink of an eye', news.mit.edu; 'Visual perception', sciencedirect.com; '45 years ago, *Pioneer 10* first to explore Jupiter', nasa.gov

SPACE, PP.1–47

A timeline of everything, pp.2–3:
Dates compiled mainly from the following sources: cosmiccalendar.net; 'Timeline: the evolution of life', newscientist.com; 'The cosmic timeline', scienceabc.com; 'Gaia', esa.int *[Date of the Milky Way]*

Where are we in the universe?, pp.4–5:
'The Milky Way galaxy', imagine.gsfc.nasa.gov; 'Universe', britannica.com. *[Note that the galaxies illustrated at the bottom are 'zoomed in'. In reality, at this scale, each galaxy would be only a minuscule dot!]*

Welcome to our solar system!, pp.6–7:
[Note that planets Saturn and Jupiter measure significantly wider across the middle instead of being perfect spheres, as represented in the illustrations.] 'Planet compare', solarsystem.nasa.gov; 'Planets', solarsystem.nasa.gov; 'Solar system', britannica.com; 'Mercury, planet', britannica.com; 'Venus, planet', britannica.com; 'Mars, planet', britannica.com; 'Jupiter, planet', britannica.com; 'Saturn, planet', britannica.com; 'Uranus, planet', britannica.com; 'Neptune, planet', britannica.com

Why is Earth so special?, pp.8–9:
'The planet Mercury', weather.gov; 'The planet Venus', weather.gov; 'The planet Earth', weather.gov; 'The planet Mars', weather.gov; 'The planet Jupiter', weather.gov; 'The planet Saturn', weather.gov; 'The planet Uranus', weather.gov; 'The planet Neptune', weather.gov; 'Planetary fact sheet – metric', nssdc.gsfc.nasa.gov; 'Habitable zone', britannica.com; 'Kepler occurrence rate', nasa.gov

What protects Earth from the Sun?, pp.10–11:
'Magnetosphere', britannica.com

How many moons do the planets have?, pp.12–13:
'Moons', solarsystem.nasa.gov; 'Jupiter, planet', britannica.com; 'Saturn, planet', britannica.com; *[Note that on Jupiter and Saturn, not all moons are shown in the graphics because the data is not yet available on their size and distance from the planets.]*

How far away is the Moon?, pp.14–15:
[Inspired by an illustration by Dr James O'Donoghue.] 'How far away is the Moon?', spaceplace.nasa.gov; 'Moon in motion', moon.nasa.gov; 'Moon', britannica.com

Phases of the Moon, pp.16–17:
'Moon in motion', moon.nasa.gov; 'Moon', britannica.com

Mapping the stars, pp.18–19:
'Constellation', britannica.com; 'Meet Libra the scales, a zodiacal constellation', earthsky.org

What is an eclipse?, pp.20–21:
'Our Sun', solarsystem.nasa.gov; 'The frequency of solar and lunar eclipses', britannica.com; 'How do you tell the difference between total, annular, solar, and lunar eclipses?', britannica.com; 'Eclipses', moon.nasa.gov

Fly me to the Moon!, pp.22–3:
[Note that the infographic shows a selection of future missions, but not all. For a full list of future missions, see: https://nssdc.gsfc.nasa.gov/planetary/upcoming.html.] 'Moon missions,' moon.nasa.gov; 'Missions to the Moon', planetary.org

Humans in space, pp.24–5:
[Note that this infographic shows the first time an astronaut has been in space chronologically, so does not display repeat visits.] 'Chronological order of all FAI first flights', worldspaceflight.com; 'Women astronauts and the International Space Station', nasa.gov

What is the Sun?, pp.26–7:
'Sun', britannica.com; 'How big is the Sun?', nineplanets.org; 'How much has the size of the Sun changed in the last few billion years?', image.gsfc.nasa.gov; 'White dwarf star', britannica.com; 'What is the Sun?', Brau, 2016, pages.uoregon.edu; 'Layers of the Sun', nasa.gov

The place where stars are born, pp.28–9:
'NASA's Webb reveals cosmic cliffs, glittering landscape of star birth', nasa.gov; 'Nebula', britannica.com; 'Light year', britannica.com

The fastest thing in the universe!, pp.30–31:
'Fastest aircraft, rocket-powered', guinnessworldrecords.com; 'Parker Space Probe', blogs.nasa.gov *[Note that the Parker Space Probe figure that appears on the page is a conversion of the estimated speed (430,000 mph) that the space probe will attain in 2024.]*; 'Our Sun', solarsystem.nasa.gov; 'Speed of light', britannica.com; 'Neptune, planet', britannica.com; 'Proxima Centauri, closest star to our sun', earthsky.org/astronomy-essentials; 'The galaxy next door', nasa.gov; 'Speed of sound calculator', weather.gov; 'Sound, physics', britannica.com

The largest known star in the universe, pp.32–3:
[Inspired by Philip Park's illustration of the approximate size of UY Scuti compared to the Sun, see en.wikipedia.org.] 'Our Sun', solarsystem.nasa.gov; 'UY Scuti', star-facts.com

You are made of stars!, pp.34–5:
'The chemistry of life: the human body', livescience.com; 'The origin of the solar system elements', blog.sdss.org; 'The early universe', home.cern; 'Populating the periodic table: Nucleosynthesis of the elements', Johnson, 2019, pubmed.ncbi.nlm.nih.gov

The awesome power of black holes!, pp.36–7:
'Black hole', britannica.com; 'What are black holes?', nasa.gov; *Cosmos: The Infographic Book of Space* by Stuart Lowe and Chris North (Aurum Press, 2015); 'What would happen if you got sucked into a black hole?', newscientist.com

Rocks from outer space, pp.38–9:
'Comet Hale-Bopp', jpl.nasa.gov; 'Halley's comet', britannica.com; '955 years ago: Halley's comet and the Battle of Hastings', nasa.gov; 'Asteroid impacts: 10 biggest known hits', nationalgeographic.com; 'Vredefort crater', earthobservatory.nasa.gov; 'Sediment swirls off the Yucatán', earthobservatory.nasa.gov; 'Morokweng crater', daviddarling.info; 'Meteorite impacts and craters', dmp.wa.gov.au; 'How an asteroid ended the age of the dinosaurs', nhm.ac.uk

Mega asteroids!, pp.40–41:
'Asteroids', solarsystem.nasa.gov; 'Asteroid', britannica.com; 'Ceres, dwarf planet', britannica.com

Extraordinary exoplanets!, pp.42–3:
'All discoveries', exoplanets.nasa.gov; 'Jupiter', solarsystem.nasa.gov

The end of the universe, pp.44–5:
'Dark energy', britannica.com; 'Dark matter', britannica.com; 'Big crunch', kids.britannica.com; 'A big freeze, rip or crunch: how will the universe end?', wired.co.uk; *Seven Brief Lessons on Physics* by Carlo Rovelli (Penguin, 2016)

LAND, SEA, SKY, PP.48–95

Introducing Earth, pp.50–51:
'How much water is there on Earth?', usgs.gov; 'Introduction to the oceans', physicalgeography.net; 'Earth fact sheet', nssdc.gsfc.nasa.gov/; 'International Commission on Stratigraphy', stratigraphy.org; 'The pregeologic period', britannica.com; *[Surface areas of continents and planets from britannica.com. Note that percentages for each individual continent are rounded here to the nearest whole number, meaning that in the detail of the infographic, they add up to 30% instead of 29%.]*

What's inside Earth?, pp.52–3:
'Inside the Earth', pubs.usgs.gov; 'The Earth's structure', gsi.ie; 'Development of Earth's structure and composition', britannica.com; 'Earth's interior', nationalgeographic.org; 'Evaluation of different egg quality traits and interpretation of their mode of inheritance in White Leghorns', Kumar Rath et al., 2015, ncbi.nlm.nih.gov *[Data about egg]*

Volcanic explosion!, pp.54–5:
'Volcano hazards program', volcanoes.usgs.gov; 'Volcanic Explosivity Index', nps.gov; 'Mount Tambora', britannica.com; 'Kīlauea', volcano.si.edu; 'Six types of eruptions', britannica.com

The Ring of Fire, pp.56–7:
Volcanic eruptions plotted by Addy Pope and his colleagues at ESRI, esri.com; 'Global volcanism project', Smithsonian Institution, volcano.si.edu; 'Monitoring volcanoes', nps.gov/articles; 'Ten thousand years of volcanic eruptions', mediaspace.esri.com

Reading the rocks, pp.58–9:
'Igneous rock, geology', britannica.com; 'Metamorphic rock, geology', britannica.com; 'Sedimentary rock, geology', britannica.com

How to measure a mineral, pp.60–61:
'Mineral ID hardness', pinalgeologymuseum.org; 'The Mohs scale of hardness for metals: why it is important', jewelrynotes.com; 'Mohs hardness, mineralogy', britannica.com

Where's all the water?, pp.62–3:
'How much water is there on Earth?', usgs.gov; 'Hydrosphere', britannica.com

Iceberg ahead!, pp.64–5:
'End of the iceberg life cycle', earthobservatory.nasa.gov; 'Iceberg size and shape', britannica.com; 'Icebergs', terrain.org; 'Whale tales', education.nationalgeographic.org *[Data for whale measurement];* 'Antarctica', britannica.com

Longest rivers, pp.66–7:
'Distribution of rivers in nature', britannica.com; 'Largest rivers by discharge in the world', rlist.io; 'Nile River', britannica.com *[see also data on other featured rivers on britannica.com]*; 'Parana', geol.lsu.edu; 'Waterfalls', britannica.com

Deep caves, pp.68–9:
'World's longest caves', caverbob.com; *Caves* by David Shaw Gillieson (Wiley, 2021); 'Mammoth cave', nps.gov; 'Transcaucasia', britannica.com

Stalactites and stalagmites, pp.70–71:
'Stalactite and stalagmite, mineral formation', britannica.com

The sky and beyond, pp.72–3:
'Troposphere, atmospheric region', britannica.com; 'Stratosphere, atmospheric region', britannica.com; 'Layers of the atmosphere', weather.gov; 'Earth's atmosphere: a multi-layered cake', climate.nasa.gov *[Note that sources vary on the upper range of the*

exosphere.]; 'Highest freefall parachute jump (official FAI)', guinnessworldrecords.com

Dazzling auroras, pp.74–5:
'Aurora, atmospheric phenomenon', britannica.com

Cloudy skies, pp.76–7:
'Clouds', metoffice.gov.uk; *The Cloudspotter's Guide* by Gavin Pretor-Pinney (Sceptre, 2007); 'Cloud, meteorology', britannica.com

Extreme planet, pp.78–9:
Surface temperatures are from 1981–2010, ERA5 dataset from Copernicus Climate Change Service Information [2020], arcgis.com; 'What is the highest point on Earth as measured from Earth's center?', oceanservice.noaa.gov *[Note that the height level given for Mount Chimborazo on the infographic is the measurement above sea level, as no specific data is available about the distance from the centre of Earth. Chimborazo is the highest point above sea level as it is on the highest part of Earth's bulged shape.]*; 'How deep is the ocean?', oceanservice.noaa.gov; 'World Meteorological Organization global weather and climate extremes archive', wmo.asu.edu; 'Snowfall statistics', mtbaker.us

The driest places on Earth, pp.80–81:
'Antarctica', britannica.com; 'Sahara Desert, Africa', britannica.com; 'Facts about the Sahara Desert', globaladventurechallenges.com; 'WMO verifies one temperature record for Antarctic continent and rejects another', public.wmo.int

Lightning and thunder, pp.82–3:
'WMO certifies two megaflash lightning records', public.wmo.int; 'A global LIS/OTD climatology of lightning flash extent density', Peterson et al., 2021, agupubs.onlinelibrary.wiley.com; 'Lightning facts and information', nationalgeographic.com; 'Lightning, meteorology', britannica.com; '10 striking facts about lightning', metoffice.gov.uk

Wind made visible!, pp.84–5:
'Wind, meteorology', britannica.com; Map created by Cameron Beccario, earth.nullschool.net

Tsunamis, pp.86–7:
'Notable tsunamis', britannica.com; 'JetStream Max: Tsunamis vs. Wind Waves', weather.gov; 'Dinosaur-killing asteroid triggered mile-high tsunami that spread through Earth's oceans', livescience.com; 'Tsunami event information', ngdc.noaa.gov; 'M 9.5 - 1960 Great Chilean earthquake (Valdivia Earthquake)', earthquake.usgs.gov; 'Ten years after the tsunami', earthobservatory.nasa.gov; 'Tsunami wave run-ups: Indian Ocean – 2004', sos.noaa.gov

Highest points on Earth, pp.88–9:
'Giraffes', ifaw.org; 'What was the biggest dinosaur? How scientists determine giant prehistoric record-breakers', guinnessworldrecords.com; 'Sauroposeidon', prehistoric-wildlife.com; 'The tallest tree in the world', monumentaltrees.com; 'Pyramids of Giza', britannica.com; 'Eiffel Tower information', toureiffel.paris; 'Burj Khalifa', britannica.com; 'Airplane height', pilotinstitute.com; 'What height (altitude) do private jets fly at?', privatefly.com; 'Mount Everest', britannica.com; 'The highest settlement in the world', earthobservatory.nasa.gov; 'How big are the Hawaiian volcanoes?', usgs.gov; 'Angel Falls, waterfall, Venezuela', britannica.com

Mount Everest, pp.90–91:
'How tall will Mount Everest get before it stops growing?', bbc.com; 'Mount Everest', britannica.com; 'The Himalayan database', himalayandatabase.com; 'Mount Everest to reopen for first climbers post-pandemic', cnn.com

In deep water, pp.92–3:
'Giant squid', britannica.com; 'Deepest diving whale sharks', livescience.com; 'The truth about the world's deepest oil well', oilprice.com; 'Mariana trench', britannica.com; 'Deepest fish ever recorded – documented at depths of 8,178 m in Mariana Trench', jamstec.go.jp; 'Titanic', britannica.com; 'Deepest descent in the sea by a manned vessel', guinnessworldrecords.com; 'Challenger expedition, oceanography', britannica.com

LIVING PLANET, PP.96–143

Survival and extinction, pp.98–101:
'Extinctions', ourworldindata.org; 'International chronostratigraphic chart', stratigraphy.org; 'What are mass extinctions, and what causes them?', nationalgeographic.com; 'Six extinctions in six minutes', amnh.org/shelf-life; 'What is mass extinction and are we facing a sixth one?', nhm.ac.uk; 'Learn about the dodo and know the reasons behind its extinction', britannica.com; 'Thylacines', ucl.ac.uk; *[Note that Colossal Inc. and the University of Melbourne's Thylacine Integrated Genomic Restoration Lab are attempting to resurrect the Tasmanian tiger and reintroduce it to Tasmania. See 'Thylacine', britannica.com.]*

Clues about the past, pp.102–3:
Individual dinosaurs on paleobiodb.org; 'Fossil, paleontology', britannica.com

Life on Earth now, pp.104–5:
'The biomass distribution on Earth', pnas.org

Where does oxygen come from?, pp.106–7:
'Save the plankton, breathe freely', nationalgeographic.com; 'The rise of atmospheric oxygen', Kump, 2008, nature.com; 'Timeline of photosynthesis on Earth', scientificamerican.com

Tremendous trees, pp.108–9:
'El Árbol del Tule (the Tule Tree)', atlasobscura.com; 'Baobab; Africa's tree of life,' worldofsucculents.com; 'Why is the strangler fig tree called so?', worldatlas.com; 'Bellingen fig', nationalregisterofbigtrees.com.au; 'World's

largest trees', wondermondo.com; 'Tallest tree living', guinnessworldrecords.com; 'The 27 tallest trees in the world', arboroperations.com.au; *[Note that the calculation used for holding hands in 'World's Widest Trees' section is based on 1.2-m span (1.4-m span, estimating 0.2 m lost per hand linkage), rounded up to nearest whole number because children cannot stretch more than their span but more children can join the circle.]*

Leaf spotting, pp.110–11:
'Glossary of leaf morphology', en.wikipedia.org; 'Leaf or leaflet dissection', idtools.org

Flower power!, pp.112–13:
'Learn all about bees!', mileeven.com; 'How many bees does it take to make a jar of honey?', onehoneybee.com; 'Honey trivia', honeyassociation.com; 'Pollination, ecology', britannica.com

The world's biggest flower, pp.114–15:
'Colossal blossom', harvardmagazine.com; '5 awesome parasitic plants', britannica.com

Seeds great and small, pp.116–17:
'Nuts for coco de mer: islanders rally to save world's biggest seed', theguardian.com; 'Double coconut: the largest seed in the world', kew.org; 'Dandelion', canr.msu.edu; 'Seeds', britannica.com

The Wood Wide Web, pp.118–19:
'The role of the mycorrhizal symbiosis in nutrient uptake of plants and the regulatory mechanisms underlying these transport processes', Bücking et al., 2012,intechopen.com; 'Wood wide web: Trees' social networks are mapped', bbc.co.uk; 'The secrets of the Wood Wide Web', newyorker.com; 'Humongous fungus is older than Christianity and weighs 400 tonnes', newscientist.com

Heroes of the underground, pp.120–21:
[The infographic shows actual 'wet' weight of both humans and earthworms, not dry biomass.]; 'Nature article to commemorate Charles Darwin's birthday on 12th February', vermecology.wordpress.com; 'World population growth', ourworldindata.org; 'Rapper giant earthworm', inaturalist.org; 'Common earthworm', nationalgeographic.com

Humans and our planet, pp.122–3:
[The infographic displays the 'Out of Africa' theory to show how humans migrated across the globe. But note that there is some scientific debate about when humans inhabited the Indo-Malaya area. Some evidence suggests that human ancestors lived in Indonesia about 1.7 million to 1.8 million years ago.]; 'Oldest footprints in Saudi Arabia reveal intriguing step in early human migration', nationalgeographic.com; 'Global human journey', education.nationalgeographic.org; 'The origin of humans and early human societies', khanacademy.org; *Human Journey* by Professor Alice Roberts (Egmont, 2020); 'Population, 10,000 BCE to 2021', ourworldindata.org

Where do humans live now?, pp.124–5:
Infographic created by Alasdair Rae, which depicts population in 2020; 'Data portal, population division', population.un.org *[Data for population by global area]*; 'World population', worldometers.info; '2022 World population by country', worldpopulationreview.com

Friends with animals?, pp.126–7:
'Taming the past: ancient DNA and the study of animal domestication', MacHugh et al., 2017, palaeobarn.com; 'Domestication', education.nationalgeographic.org; 'Dog, the breeds', britannica.com *[Note that sources differ widely for the date of dog domestication, see 'How accurate is the theory of dog domestication in "Alpha"?', smithsonianmag.com.]*; 'Domesticated sheep, britannica.com; 'The origin of domestication genes in goats', Zheng et al., 2020, science.org; 'First settlers domesticated pigs before crops', nytimes.com; 'Cow, mammal', britannica.com; 'Cats domesticated themselves, ancient DNA shows', nationalgeographic.com; 'Llamas and alpacas', jefferson.extension.wisc.edu; 'Origin of horse domestication', britannica.com; 'Dromedary (*Camelus dromedarius*) and Bactrian camel (*Camelus bactrianus*) crossbreeding husbandry practices in Turkey and Kazakhstan: An in-depth review', Dioli, 2020, pastoralismjournal.springeropen.com; 'Domestication of the donkey: Timing, processes, and indicators', Rossel et al., 2008, pnas.org; 'Water buffalo, mammal', britannica.com; 'The origin of ducks', Laatsch, livestock.extension.wisc.edu

The rise of the chicken, pp.128–9:
[Number of farm animals worldwide is counted from 1961–2020. Meat production worldwide shows data from 2020. Wild vs domesticated mass data is from 2018.]; 'Food and agriculture organization of the United Nations', fao.org; 'Humans and big ag livestock now account for 96 percent of mammal biomass', ecowatch.com; 'The biomass distribution on Earth', pnas.org; 'Biodiversity and wildlife', ourworldindata.org

Life in the rainforests, pp.130–31:
'Deforestation fronts', wwfint.awsassets.panda.org/downloads; 'Rainforest', education.nationalgeographic.org; 'Drivers of deforestation 2005–2013', ourworldindata.org; 'Forest pulse: the latest on the world's forests', research.wri.org; 'Meet Borneo's organic barometers', wwf.panda.org; 'Amazon wildlife', wwf.panda.org

Energy sources, pp.132–3:
'Global primary energy consumption by source, 1800–2021', ourworldindata.org; 'Net zero by 2050: a roadmap for the global energy sector', iea.blob.core.windows.net; 'Nuclear energy', kids.britannica.com; 'Nuclear energy', education.nationalgeographic.org

Changing temperatures on Earth, pp.134–5:
Data visualisation courtesy of Ed Hawking, Reading University, 'Climate stripes', reading.ac.uk; 'Show your stripes', showyourstripes.info

Shrinking ice, pp.136–7:
'The Arctic has warmed nearly four times faster than the globe since 1979', Rantanen et al., 2022, nature.com; 'Arctic sea ice minimum extent', climate.nasa.gov *[Data shows 1979–2021]*

Animals in danger, pp.138–9:
IUCN Red List, iucnredlist.org *[All population data from here]*; 'Population of Eurasian beaver (*Castor fiber*) in Europe', sciencedirect.com

Conservation in action, pp.140–41:
'Grand Cayman blue iguana', iucn.org

ANIMALS, PP.144–191

How many species do we know about?, pp.146–7:
'Animals', eol.org; 'Biodiversity', education nationalgeographic.org; 'Number of species evaluated in relation to the overall number of described species, and numbers of threatened species by major groups of organisms.', iucnredlist.org

Tiny creatures, pp.148–9:
'Smallest Insect', entomology.uni.edu; '*Ammonicera minortalis*', conchology.be; 'Smallest spider', guinnessworldrecords.com; 'The world's tiniest land snails from Laos and Vietnam (Gastropoda, Pulmonata, Hypselostomatidae)', Barna Páll-Gergely et al., 2022; 'Tardigrade, animal', britannica.com; 'The battle to identify the world's smallest vertebrate', phys.org; 'Highlight: big surprises from the world's smallest fish', Casey McGrath, *Genome Biology and Evolution*, 2018; '"Smallest reptile on Earth" discovered in Madagascar', bbc.co.uk; 'At the lower size limit in snakes: two new species of threadsnakes (*Squamata: Leptotyphlopidae: Leptotyphlops*) from the Lesser Antilles', S. Blair Hedges, *Zootaxa*, 2008; '*Mellisuga helenae*', animaldiversity.org; 'Smallest mammal', guinnessworldrecords.com

Biggest beasts of the land and sky, pp.150–53:
A Dazzle of Dragonflies, Forrest Lee Mitchell et al. (Texas A&M University Press, 2005); 'The aerodynamics of *Argentavis*, the world's largest flying bird from the Miocene of Argentina', Sankar Chatterjee et al., 2007; 'Andean Condor', María Rosa Cuesta et al., in *Endangered animals: a reference guide to conflicting issues* (Greenwood Press, 2000); 'Largest wingspan for a bird species (living)', guinnessworldrecords.com; 'Biggest ever flying bird and the beast that dwarfed it', newscientist.com; 'Flight performance of the largest volant bird', Daniel T. Ksepka, 2014, PNAS; 'Functional morphology of *Quetzalcoatlus* Lawson 1975 (Pterodactyloidea: Azhdarchoidea)', Kevin Padian et al., *Journal of Vertebrate Paleontology*, 2021; '*Macropus rufus*', animaldiversity.org; 'Tinamous and ratites to hoatzins,' in *Grzimek's Animal Life Encyclopedia*, Vol. 8: Birds I, 2003; '*Gigantopithecus*, extinct ape genus', britannica.com; '*Ceratotherium simum*', animaldiversity.org; '*Loxodonta africana*', animaldiversity.org; 'Columbian mammoth', nps.gov; '*Mammathus columbi*', prehistoric-wildlife.com; '*Hippopotamus amphibius*', animaldiversity.org; '*Giraffa camelopardalis*', animaldiversity.org; *Rhinoceros giants: the paleobiology of Indricotheres*, D.R. Prothero, 2013; 'Neck biomechanics indicate that giant Transylvanian azhdarchid pterosaurs were short-necked arch predators', Darren Naish et al., 2017; '*Triceratops*, dinosaur genus', britannica.com; 'What is the biggest snake in the world?', nhm.ac.uk; 'A computational analysis of limb and body dimensions in *Tyrannosaurus rex* with implications for locomotion, ontogeny, and growth', John R. Hutchinson et al., 2011; 'A re-evaluation of *Brachiosaurus altithorax* Riggs, 1903, (dinosauria, sauropoda) and its generic separation from *giraffatitan brancai* (Janensch, 1914)', Michael P. Taylor, *Journal of Vertebrate Paleontology*, 2009; '*Dreadnoughtus*, dinosaur', britannica.com; 'Determining the largest known land animal: a critical comparison of differing methods for restoring the volume and mass of extinct animals', Gregory Paul, *Annals of Carnegie Museum*, 2019; 'The biggest insect ever was a huge "dragonfly"', eartharchives.org; 'Argentinosaurus', a-z-animals.com; '*Hatzegopteryx*', a-z-animals.com; '*Tyrannosaurus rex*', si.edu; '*Quetzalcoatlus*', pteros.com; '*Indricotherium*, fossil mammal genus', britannica.com; 'Argentavis, the largest flying bird, was a master glider', nationalgeographic.com; 'Columbian mammoth', floridamuseum.ufl.edu

Giants of the sea, pp.154–7:
'Polar bear: facts', worldwildlife.org; 'Japanese spider crab', ocean.si.edu; 'My, what big eyes you have...', Ivan R Schwab, 2002; 'Crocodile, reptile order, Crocodylia', britannica.com; 'White shark, fish', britannica.com; 'Giant manta ray', oceana.org; 'Sizing ocean giants: patterns of intraspecific size variation in marine megafauna', Craig R. McClain et al., 2015; 'Basking shark', hwdt.org; 'Killer whale, mammal', britannica.com; 'Devourer of gods: The palaeoecology of the Cretaceous pliosaur, *Kronosaurus queenslandicus*', Colin McHenry, 2009; 'Plesiosaur, fossil marine reptile', britannica.com; 'Giant squid', nationalgeographic.com; 'Whale shark: facts', worldwildlife.org; 'In pursuit of giant pliosuarids and whale-sized ichthyosaurs', markwitton-com.blogspot.com; 'Sperm whale', oceana.org; 'Megalodon, fossil shark', britannica.com; 'Blue whale', nwf.org

What's for dinner?, pp.158–9:
'Carnivore', britannica.com; 'Omnivore', britannica.com; 'Herbivore', britannica.com

What goes in... must come out!, pp.160–61:
'Estimation of global recoverable human and animal faecal biomass', David M. Berendes et al., *Nature Sustainability*, 2018; 'The diet of individuals: a study of a randomly-chosen cross section of British adults in a Cambridgeshire village', Bingham, Sheila et al., 2007, cambridge.org; 'Hydronamics of defecation', Patricia J. Yang et al., *Soft Matter*, 2017; 'Rabbit manure price', rabbitpros.com; 'The bamboo-eating giant panda harbors a carnivore-like gut microbiota, with excessive seasonal variations', Xue, Zhengsheng et al., *American Society for Microbiology*, 2015; 'Elephant facts',

elephantsforafrica.org; 'Blue whale, world's largest animal, caught on camera having a poo', abc.net.au; 'Blue whale', nationalgeographic.com

Tongues and tails, pp.162–3:
'How long is a giraffe's tongue? What colour is it?', giraffe.conservation.org; 'Anteater, mammal', britannica.com; 'Off like a shot: scaling of ballistic tongue projection reveals extremely high performance in small chameleons', Christopher V. Anderson, *Scientific Reports*, 2016; 'Green woodpecker tongues are so long they wrap around their skulls', earthtouchnews.com; 'The bat with the incredibly long tongue', newscientist.com; 'Giraffe', en.wikipedia.org; 'Thresher sharks use tail-slaps as a hunting strategy', Simon P. Oliver et al., *PLoS*, 2013; 'Angola colobus', en.wikipedia.org; 'Ring-tailed lemur', en.wikipedia.org; 'Geoffroy's spider monkey', en.wikipedia.org; '*Euchoreutes naso*', animaldiversity.org; 'Roughtail stingray', en.wikipedia.org; '*Basiliscus basiliscus*', animaldiversity.org; 'Whydah, bird', britannica.com

Symmetry, pp.164–5:
'Symmetry, biology', britannica.com

The strongest animals on Earth, pp.166–7:
'Strongest bird of prey', guinnessworldrecords.com; 'Harpy eagle facts', pbs.org; 'Grizzly bear', nwf.org; 'Foot pressure distributions during walking in African elephants (*Loxodonta africana*)', Olga Panagiotopoulou et al., *Royal Society Open Science*, 2016; '*Ovibos moschatus*', animal diversity.org; 'Tiger fact sheet', pbs.org; '"I will continue raising the bar": Tamara Walcott lifts record weight in competition', guinnessworldrecords.com; 'How strong are gorillas?', nyungweforestnationalpark.org; 'Mountain gorilla', nationalgeographic.com; 'Large ants do not carry their fair share: maximal load-carrying performance of leaf-cutter ants (*Atta cephalotes*)', Paolo S. Segre et al., *Journal of Experimental Biology*, 2019; 'Rhinoceros Beetles', nwf.org; 'Small but powerful: the oribatid mite *Archegozetes longisetosus* (Acari, Oribatida) produces disproportionately high forces', Michael Heethoff et al., *Journal of Experimental Biology*, 2007; 'Pulling power points the way to the world's strongest insect', eurekalert.org; 'Dung beetle species introductions: when an ecosystem service provider transforms into an invasive species', Min R. Pokhrel et al., 2020; *[Note that the data on the oribatid mite and the dung beetle were gathered in specially designed strength experiments, and so are not representative of the amount they carry on a regular basis.]*

The fastest animals on Earth, pp.168–9:
'Peregrine falcon, bird', britannica.com; fs.usda.gov/Internet/FSE_DOCUMENTS/stelprdb5303500.pdf; 'Supercharged swifts take flight speed record', news.bbc.co.uk; 'The fastest animals on earth', britannica.com; 'What is the fastest fish in the ocean?', oceanservice.noaa.gov; 'The fastest fish in the world', thoughtco.com; 'Up close with a Mahi Mahi', ocean.si.edu; 'Cesar Cielo Filho', olympics.com; 'World's fastest cheetah dies – watch her run', nationalgeographic.com; 'Springbok, mammal', britannica.com; 'Ostrich, bird', britannica.com; 'How fast is the world's fastest human?', britannica.com

Jumping champions!, pp.170–71:
'Amazing facts about the flea', onekindplanet.org; 'Kangaroo', britannica.com

Nature's survivors, pp.172–3:
'Absurd creature of the week: the incredible critter that's tough enough to survive in space', wired.com; '*Gynaephora groenlandica*', en.wikipedia.org; 'Polar bear', itsourplanettoo.co.uk; 'Emperor penguin', en.wikipedia.org; '*Rana sylvatica*', sciencedirect.com; 'Fennec fox (*Vulpes zerda*) fact sheet: physical characteristics', ielc.libguides.com; '8 animals that live in extreme environments', britannica.com; 'Sahara Desert ant, insect', britannica.com; 'Snow leopard', iucnredlist.org; 'Wild Yak', iucnredlist.org; 'Discovery of the world's highest-dwelling mammal', Jay F. Storz et al., PNAS 2020; 'High altitude and hemoglobin function in the vultures *Gyps rueppelli* and *Aegypius monachus*', Roy E. Weber et al., 1988; '*Geophilus hadesi*: new species of cave-dwelling centipede discovered', sci.news; 'Subterranean worms from hell', Nadia Drake, *Nature*, 2011; 'Go deep, small worm', sciencenews.org; 'What lives at the bottom of the Mariana Trench?', iflscience.com

How big is a penguin?, pp.174–5:
'Extinct mega penguin was tallest and heaviest ever', newscientist.com; 'Emperor penguin, bird', britannica.com; 'King penguin, bird', britannica.com; 'Humboldt penguin, bird', britannica.com; 'Galapagos penguin, bird', britannica.com; 'Gentoo penguin, bird', britannica.com

Epic migrations, pp.176–7:
Infographic based on 'Migration flows' map by Kenneth Chmielewski; 'Dorado catfish: the Amazon fish with the world's longest freshwater migration', internationalrivers.org; 'Monarch butterfly', nms.ac.uk; 'Record-breaking bird migration revealed in new research', ncl.ac.uk; 'The Bar-tailed godwit undertakes one of the avian world's most extraordinary migratory journeys', datazone.birdlife.org; 'During epic migrations, great snipes fly at surprising heights by day and lower by night', sciencedaily.com; 'Grey whale', fisheries.noaa.gov; 'Leatherback turtle', fisheries.noaa.gov

Super senses!, pp.178–9:
'What is echolocation? Definition and examples in the animal and human worlds', treehugger.com; 'Magnetoreception in fish', Krzysztof Formicki et al., *Journal of Fish Biology*, 2019; 'To hunt, the platypus uses its electric sixth sense', amnh.org; 'Snake infrared detection unravelled', Janet Fang, *Nature*, 2010; 'How do other animals see the world?', nhm.ac.uk; '11 animals that have a sixth sense', treehugger.com

Transformers!, pp.180–81:
'Selection for social signalling drives the evolution of chameleon colour change', Devi Stuart-Fox, *PLoS Biology*,

2008; 'Night vision by cuttlefish enables changeable camouflage', Justine J. Allen et al., *Journal of Experimental Biology*, 2010; 'Mimic octopus makes home on Great Barrier Reef', blogs.scientificamerican.com; 'Some shape-shifting animals that can morph to fool others', theconversation.com; 'Phenotypic plasticity raises questions for taxonomically important traits: a remarkable new Andean rainfrog (*Pristimantis*) with the ability to change skin texture', Juan M. Guayasamin et al., *Zoological Journal of the Linnean Society*, 2015

Which animals kill the most humans?, pp.182–3:
'Shark attacks are in the news again, but plenty of other phenomena are far more dangerous', cbs58.com; '9 of the world's deadliest mammals', britannica.com; 'What are the world's deadliest animals?', bbc.co.uk; '*Ascaris*, nematode genus', britannica.com; 'Aberystwyth University research tackles "killer" snails', bbc.co.uk

Eggs great and small, pp.184–5:
'Smallest bird egg', guinnessworldrecords.com; 'Hummingbirds at Weltvogel Park Walsrode', Anne Hoppmann, aviculture-europe.nl; 'British birds' eggs', birdspot.co.uk; 'Carrion Crow', bto.org; 'Egg sizes and dimensions', brinsea.co.uk; 'Golden eagle', bto.org; *Biology of Birds*, D.R. Khanna et al. (Discovery Publishing, 2005); 'Trumpeter swan', en.wikipedia.org; 'Ostrich, bird', britannica.com; 'Largest bird egg ever', guinnessworldrecords.com; 'Beibeilong', en.wikipedia.org; 'Horn shark: *Heterodontus francisci*', sharksandrays.com; 'Haaniella', eol.org; 'Chapter 40: largest eggs', in *Book of Insect Records* (University of Florida, Salvatore Vicidomini, 2005); 'Early development and embryology of the platypus', R.L. Hughes et al., 1998; 'Gnaraloo sea turtle conservation – news from the field', gnaraloo.org; '*Conraua goliath* (Boulenger, 1906)', gbif.org; 'A practical staging atlas to study embryonic development of *Octopus vulgaris* under controlled laboratory conditions', Astrid Deryckere et al., *BMC Developmental Biology*, 2020; 'The effect of spatial position and age within an egg-clutch on embryonic development and key metabolic enzymes in two clownfish species, *Amphiprion ocellaris* and *Amphiprion frenatus*', A. Kunzmann et al., 2020

How long do animals sleep?, pp.186–7:
'How much do animals sleep?', faculty.washington.edu; 'How do giraffes sleep?', tuftandneedle.com; 'Do cows need beauty rest, too?', thecattlesite.com; '15 things you didn't know about goats', goatsontheroad.com; 'Why humans sleep less than their primate relatives', smithsonianmag.com; 'How do whales and dolphins sleep without drowning?', scientificamerican.com; 'How many hours does a dog sleep in a day?', petmd.com; 'Cat sleeping habits', purina.co.uk; 'You're sure to be jealous of some of these lazy animals', news.cgtn.com; 'Sleeping and nesting habits of squirrels', animalsake.com; 'Animals that sleep the least and most', discovermagazine.com; 'Species spotlight: the little brown bat', mass.gov

Staying alive, pp.188–9:
[Timeline inspired by 'How long do animals live?' by Otto Neurath.]; 'Dragonfly lifespan: how long do dragonflies live?', a-z-animals.com; 'Common shrew', wildlifetrusts.org; 'Blackbird', woodlandtrust.org.uk; 'Foxes lifespan: how long do foxes live?'; 'Species – mole', mammal.org.uk; 'Red kangaroo fact sheet', racinezoo.org; 'Green anaconda', nationalzoo.si.edu; 'Sheep in nature', goodheartanimalsanctuaries.com; 'How long do dogs live?', petmd.com; 'How long do lions live?', discoveryuk.com; 'Wild cat', animalspot.net; 'Moose', a-z-animals.com; 'Reindeer fact sheet', pbs.org; 'How long do geese live?', birdfact.com; 'Giraffe', a-z-animals.com; 'How long do sandhill cranes live?', birdfact.com; 'Harbour seal', dfo-mpo.gc.ca; 'Common carp', chesapeakebay.net; 'Rhinoceros fact sheet', pbs.org; 'Alligators lifespan: how long do alligators live?', a-z-animals.com; 'Asian elephant', nationalgeographic.com; 'Life expectancy', ourworldindata.org; '7 animals with incredibly long life spans', vetstreet.com; 'Do lobsters live forever?', livescience.com

HUMAN BODY, PP.192–239

The building blocks of the body, pp.194–5:
The Complete Human Body: The Definitive Visual Guide, 2nd edition, by Professor Alice Roberts (Dorling Kindersley, 2016); 'Human body', kids.britannica.com

How bony are you?, pp.196–7:
Gray's Anatomy: The Anatomical Basis of Clinical Practice (Elsevier, 2020); 'What are bones made of?', healthline.com; 'Six fun facts about the human skeleton', theconversation.com

The growing skull, pp.198–9:
Gray's Anatomy: The Anatomical Basis of Clinical Practice (Elsevier, 2020); 'Anatomy of the newborn skull', stanfordchildrens.org

Your biggest muscle is... behind you!, pp.200–201:
'Remarkable human muscles', livescience.com; 'Relationship between muscular and bony anatomy in native hips', pubmed.ncbi.nlm.nih.gov; 'Stapedius', sciencedirect.com; 'Extraocular muscles', britannica.com; 'Fact or fiction: the tongue is the strongest muscle in the body', scientificamerican.com; '13 fun facts about owls', audubon.org

Take a deep breath!, pp.202–3:
'Respiratory system', bbc.co.uk; 'How long can you go without air?', bbc.com; 'Sperm whale', seaworld.org; 'Longest time breath held voluntarily', guinnessworldrecords.com; 'Alveoli area', med.libretexts.org

Inhale, exhale, pp.204–5:
'Physiology, lung capacity', ncbi.nlm.nih.gov

How does blood get around the body?, pp.206–7:
'Blood flow and blood pressure regulation', bio.libretexts.org;

'Blood and the cells it contains', ncbi.nlm.nih.gov; '11 surprising facts about the circulatory system', livescience.com; 'Whole blood and what it contains', redcrossblood.org

Pump, pump, pump, pp.208–9:
'Your heart rate', bhf.org.uk; 'Cardiac output', webmd.com; 'Life expectancy at birth for both sexes combined', data.un.org

Eat, then excrete!, pp.210–11:
[Inspired by 'How long is the digestive tract? A visual synthesis', elegantexperiments.net.]; 'Human digestive system', britannica.com; 'Rectum', britannica.com; 'Appendix', britannica.com; 'Three-dimensional model of an average human stomach', R. Paul Singh, researchgate.net, 2011; 'Esophagus', britannica.com; 'Standard height of a multi-storey building', civilsir.com

How much snot do you make?, pp.212–13:
'Mucus', britannica.com; 'Mucus, snot, boogers', vox.com; *[Note that the lifetime mucus production data are based on the average human life expectancy of 72.6 years.]*

Poo and farts, pp.214–5:
'Feces', britannica.com; 'The characterization of feces and urine', Rose et al., 2015, ncbi.nlm.nih.gov; 'Bristol stool form scale', pediatricsurgery.stanford.edu; 'Characterization, recovery opportunities, and valuation of metals in municipal sludges from U.S. wastewater treatment plants nationwide', pubs.acs.org; 'Investigation of normal flatus production in healthy volunteers', Tomlin et al., 1991, pubmed.ncbi.nlm.nih.gov

The wonders of wee, pp.216–7:
'The characterization of feces and urine', Rose et al., 2015, ncbi.nlm.nih.gov; 'Duration of urination does not change with body size', ncbi.nlm.nih.gov; '"Universal urination duration" wins Ig Nobel prize', bbc.co.uk

What does skin do?, pp.218–9:
'Surface area of human skin', bionumbers.hms.harvard.edu; 'Surface area of human skin', hypertextbook.com; 'The mattress size guide', dreams.co.uk *[Data used for bed size]*; 'Human skin', britannica.com

Long lashes, pp.220–21:
'Anatomy, head and neck, eyelash', Patel et al., 2022, ncbi.nlm.nih.gov

Can you hear me?, pp.222–3:
'The audible spectrum', *Neuroscience*, 2nd edition, ncbi.nlm.nih.gov; 'Hearing with an atympanic ear: good vibration and poor sound-pressure detection in the royal python, *Python regius*', C.B. Christensen et al., 2012, journals.biologists.com; 'Structure and function of the auditory system in fishes', Kasumyan, 2005, researchgate.net; 'Avian hearing and the avoidance of wind turbines', Dooling, 2002, nrel.gov; 'Elephant senses', seaworld.org; 'Moth hearing and sound communication', Nakano et al., 2015, pubmed.ncbi.nlm.nih.gov; 'Hearing range of the domestic cat', Heffner, 1985, pubmed.ncbi.nlm.nih.gov; 'Neural coding of sound frequency by cricket auditory receptors', Imaizumi et al., 1999, jneurosci.org; 'Baseline hearing abilities and variability in wild beluga whales (*Delphinapterus leucas*)', Castellote et al., 2014, researchgate.net; 'The effect of signal duration on the underwater detection thresholds of a harbor porpoise (*Phocoena phocoena*) for single frequency-modulated tonal signals between 0.25 and 160 kHz,' R.A. Kastelein et al., *The Journal of the Acoustical Society of America*, 2010; 'Hearing sensitivity and amplitude coding in bats are differentially shaped by echolocation calls and social calls', Lattenkamp et al., 2021, royalsocietypublishing.org

The eye cells, pp.224–5:
'Structure and function of photoreceptors', britannica.com; 'Cones, retinal cell', britannica.com; 'Rods, retinal cell' britannica.com; 'Anatomical distribution of rods and cones', *Neuroscience*, 2nd Edition, Purves et al., 2001, ncbi.nlm.nih.gov; 'Feline vision: how cats see the world', livescience.com

Your body's control centre, pp.226–7:
'Brain anatomy and how the brain works', hopkinsmedicine.org; *New Scientist*, *The Brain: A User's Guide* (John Murray, 2020)

Brain networks, pp.228–9:
'Nervous system', kids.britannica.com

How brainy are humans?, pp.230–31:
New Scientist, *The Brain: A User's Guide* (John Murray, 2020); 'Brain size predicts problem-solving ability in mammalian carnivores', Benson-Amram et al., 2008–9, pnas.org

What is DNA?, pp.232–3:
'Genetics by the numbers', Toledo et al., 2012, nigms.nih.gov; 'Bonobos join chimps as closest human relatives', science.org; 'Animals that share human DNA sequences', sciencing.com; 'Do people and bananas really share 50 percent of the same DNA?', science.howstuffworks.com

How old is your body? (Younger than you think!), pp.234–5:
New Scientist, *The Brain: A User's Guide* (John Murray, 2020); 'Growth rate of human fingernails and toenails in healthy American young adults', onlinelibrary.wiley.com; '6 ways to make your hair grow faster and stronger', healthline.com *[Data is for scalp hair growth]*; 'Taste bud regeneration and the search for taste progenitor cells', Miura et al., 2010, ncbi.nlm.nih.gov; 'Cell types numbers and turnover rates database', static-content.springer.com *[Note that fat cells are adipose tissue, and lung cells are bronchial epithelial cells]*; 'Dynamics of cell generation and turnover in the human heart', Bergmann et al., 2015, researchgate.net; 'Brain basics: the life and death of a neuron', ninds.nih.gov. *[There is a debate about whether adult humans can grow new brain cells, a process called 'neurogenesis'. We are born with most of our neurons and in healthy adults they do not die as we grow older. See 'Discovering the brain', Ackerman, 2019, ncbi.nlm.nih.gov; and 'We may be unable to grow new brain cells after we enter adulthood', newscientist.com.]*

How long does it take to grow a baby?, pp.236–7:
'Week by week guide to pregnancy', nhs.uk; 'Pregnancy week by week', whattoexpect.com; 'Gestation', britannica.com

HUMAN WORLD, PP.240–287

The world as 100 people, pp.242–3:
'Population by 5-year age groups and sex', population.un.org; 'Literacy for a human centred recovery: narrowing the digital divide', en.unesco.org *[Note that this data refers to the literacy rate of people over 15.]*; 'Human handedness: A meta-analysis', Papdatou-Pastou et al., 2020; 'Percentage of global population accessing the internet from 2005 to 2022, by market maturity', statista.com; 'Urbanization', ourworldindata.org; 'Population lacking basic sanitation, 2015 and 2020', washdata.org *[Note that we have grouped washdata.org's categories: 'Safe drinking water at home' = 'Safely managed'; 'Safe drinking water outside the home' = 'Basic' and 'Limited'; 'No safe drinking water' = 'Unimproved' and 'Surface water'.]*; 'Continent populations', populationstat.com *[Note that a few thousand people do live on Antarctica, mainly scientists. See: 'Antarctica population 2023', worldpopulationreview.com.]*; 'Southern Hemisphere countries 2023', worldpopulationreview.com

Life and death, pp.244–5:
'This is how many humans have ever existed, according to researchers', weforum.org

Every second..., pp.246–7:
'Numbers of births and deaths per year, World', ourworldindata.org; 'Number of cars sold worldwide from 2010 to 2022, with a 2023 forecast', statista.com; 'Frozen pizza market worldwide from 2020-2027', statista.com *[Note that the figure for money spent on frozen pizzas has been converted from $570 into pounds sterling as per the exchange rate in 2023, and rounded up.]*; 'Fact sheet: single use plastics', earthday.org; 'Email Statistics Report, 2021–2025', radicati.com; *[Data for plastic bottles entering the ocean is based on the estimate that 11 million metric tons of plastic enter the ocean annually.]* 'How a source-to-sea approach can curb the threat of plastic pollution', unep.org; *[Data for chocolate bars consumed is based on estimated chocolate consumption per capita per year, see: 'Global pressures on chocolate industry prompt alternative formulations', ingredientsnetwork.com.]*; 'Number of flights performed by the global airline industry from 2004 to 2022', statista.com *[Note that the calculation of planes taking off every second assumes that flights are equally distributed over time.]*

How much money do people have?, pp.248–9:
'Global wealth report', credit-suisse.com; 'Mūsā I of Mali', britannica.com; 'How much?: this Duffel bag was designed to carry 1 million dollars cash', kolormagazine.com; 'Here's what a billion dollars looks like in cash (and how much it weighs)', commoncentsmom.com

Coming together, pp.250–51:
'World city populations 2023', worldpopulationreview.com; 'Kumbh Mela, Hindu festival', britannica.com

Human conflict, pp.252–3:
[Illustrations inspired by Great War 1914–1918 by Otto Neurath.]; 'Casualties of World War I', britannica.com; 'How many people died during World War II?', britannica.com; *[Note that the estimated cost of the First World War is $208 billion, which according to 'CPI Inflation Calculator', data.bls.gov, is approximately $4 trillion today. The estimated cost of the Second World War is $1 trillion, which equates to approximately $17 trillion today.]*

Eureka! A timeline of inventions, pp.254–7:
'Oldest stone tools pre-date earliest humans', bbc.co.uk; *Catching Fire: How Cooking Made Us Human* by Richard Wrangham (Basic Books, 2009); 'Evidence for early hafted hunting technology', Jayne Wilkins et al., 2012, science.org; 'Colored Pigments and complex tools suggest humans were trading 100,000 years earlier than previously believed', smithsonianmag.com; 'UF study of lice DNA shows humans first wore clothes 170,000 years ago', news.ufl.edu; 'Indications of bow and stone-tipped arrow use 64,000 years ago in KwaZulu-Natal, South Africa', Marlize Lombard et al., 2010, antiquity.ac.uk; 'Naturally perforated shells one of the earliest adornments in the Middle Paleolithic', sciencedaily.com; 'Ngwenya Mines', whc.unesco.org; 'Oldest ceramic figurine', guinessworldrecords.com; 'First evidence of farming in Mideast 23,000 years ago', sciencedaily.com *[Note that the recorded figure for agriculture was a very early attempt; agriculture did not become widespread until between 15,000 and 10,000 years ago. See: 'Origins of agriculture', britannica.com.]*; 'Bread, food', britannica.com; 'Writing', britannica.com; 'Brick', en.wikipedia.org; 'Water technology in Ancient Mesopotamia', Aldo Tamburrino, in *Ancient Water Technologies* (Springer Netherlands, 2010); 'Irrigation: An Historical Perspective', R.E. Sojka et al., 2002; 'History of ships', britannica.com; 'Wheel', britannica.com; 'Glass', britannica.com; 'History of energy-conversion technology', britannica.com; 'Papermaking', britannica.com; 'Chess, game', britannica.com; 'First mechanical clock', guinnessworldrecords.com; 'Playing cards', britannica.com; 'History of gunpowder', en.wikipedia.org; 'Gunpowder', in *Encyclopaedia of the History of Science, Technology, and Medicine in Non-Western Cultures* (ed. Selin, Springer Science, 1997); 'Compass, navigational instrument', britannica.com; 'Printing press, printing', britannica.com; 'History of optical microscopes', britannica.com; 'From turrets to toilets: a partial history of the throne room', smithsonianmag.com; 'Telescope', en.wikipedia.org; 'Steam engine, machine', britannica.com; 'History of the automobile', britannica.com; 'Smallpox vaccines', who.int; 'Voltaic pile', en.wikipedia.org; 'Railroad history', britannica.com; 'Concrete, building material', britannica.com; 'Electric power, physics', britannica.com; 'Telegraph', britannica.com; 'Incandescent lamp, lighting', britannica.com; 'History of anaesthesia', wfsahq.org; 'Refrigeration', britannica.com;

'Celluloid, synthetic plastic', britannica.com; 'Gatling gun, weapon', britannica.com; 'Bicycle, vehicle', britannica.com; 'Development of gasoline engines', britannica.com *[Note that the data for the internal combustion engine refers to the first four-stroke cycle internal combustion engine built by Nikolaus Otto in 1876. The first internal combustion engine is generally credited to Belgian inventor Étienne Lenoir in 1860.]*; 'X-ray, radiation beam', britannica.com; 'Radio's early years', britannica.com; 'Washing machine', en.wikipedia.org; 'The history of antibiotics', microbiologysociety.org; 'Television', britannica.com; 'Development of rockets, rockets', britannica.com; 'Early business machines, computer', britannica.com; 'When was the microwave invented? The accidental creation of this household appliance.', eu.usatoday.com; 'Transistor, electronics', britannica.com; 'Alan Turing and the beginning of AI, artificial intelligence', britannica.com; '5 fascinating facts about fetal ultrasounds', livescience.com; 'The first video game?', bnl.gov; 'Integrated circuit, electronics', britannica.com; '1971: first ever email', guinnessworldrecords.com; 'Meet Marty Cooper – the inventor of the mobile phone', news.bbc.co.uk; '3D printing, manufacturing', britannica.com; 'Robotic surgery', britannica.com; 'Tablet computer', britannica.com; 'A short history of the Web', home.cern; '1990s: Birth of search engines', en.wikipedia.org; 'Augmented Reality: the past, the present and the future', interaction-design.org; 'Smartphone', britannica.com; 'Hybrid electric vehicle', en.wikipedia.org; 'What Is the International Space Station?', nasa.gov; 'Graphene: the wonder material of the 21st century', europarl.europa.eu; 'Blockchain, database technology', britannica.com; 'World's first lab-grown burger is eaten in London', bbc.co.uk; 'A Timeline of Voice Assistant and Smart Speaker Technology From 1961 to Today', voicebot.ai

How smart is AI?, pp.258–9:
'Artificial intelligence', britannica.com; 'Top artificial intelligence fails in image and facial recognition', skywell.software

Engineering masterpieces, pp.260–61:
'Grand Canal, canal, China', britannica.com. *[Note that, despite its name, the Jing-Hang canal is a series of constructed waterways linking various natural waterways together and so is not a 'canal' in the strictest sense. Although the waterway system was started in the 4th century BCE and rebuilt in 607 CE, it did not take its definitive form until about 1327 CE. See also: 'The Grand Canal', whc.unesco.org.]*; 'Trans-Siberian Railroad, railway, Russia', britannica.com; 'Pan-American Highway', britannica.com *[Note that the Pan-American Highway is technically not one continuous road because of the Darién Gap.]*; 'Delaware Aqueduct, water works, New York, United States', britannica.com; 'Danyang-Kunshan Grand Bridge, bridge, China', britannica.com; 'Burj Khalifa, skyscraper, Dubai, United Arab Emirates', britannica.com; 'India unveils Statue of Unity, world's tallest statue and twice the size of Lady Liberty', nytimes.com; 'The world's largest Ferris wheel just opened in Dubai', npr.org; 'The Pyongyang Metro – DPRK Guide', youngpioneertours.com *[Note that the average depth of the Pyongyang metro is 100 m, but sources such as 'The Pyongyang metro' on north-korea-travel.com suggest that it can reach 110 m underground.]*; 'Deepest mine', guinnessworldrecords.com *[Note that, although the main shaft was first completed in 1986, the mine did not reach a depth of around 4 km until later expansions in and after 2012.]*; 'Angkor Wat, temple complex, Angkor, Cambodia', britannica.com; 'Palm Jumeirah, island, United Arab Emirates', britannica.com

Rise of the toys, pp.262–3:
[Note that the estimated growth of the LEGO minifigure population assumes that approx. 340 million minifigures will continue to be made each year. See: '10 Top LEGO Facts!', natgeokids.com and 'International LEGO Day – Our Favourite LEGO Facts', bricksmcgee.com.]; 'Population', un.org; 'World population growth, 1700-2100', ourworldindata.org

Moving at speed!, pp.264–5:
[Note that the train location is where the speed record was broken, whereas the car location is where they were built.]; 'Rainhill Trials', historic-uk.com; 'Stephenson's *Rocket*', collection.sciencemuseumgroup.org; 'London & North Eastern Railway steam locomotive "Mallard"', collection.sciencemuseumgroup.org; 'W. German train sets speed record', latimes.com; 'A CRH380BL EMU train sets a world record with a speed of 487.3 kilometers per hour on the Beijing-Shanghai high-speed railway on Dec 3, 2010', en.sasac.gov.cn; 'Fastest maglev train', guinnessworldrecords.com; 'Steam train anniversary begins', news.bbc.co.uk; 'First to sixty: *La Jamais Contente*', motortrend.com; 'What is the fastest F1 car of all time?', motorsportmagazine.com; 'Bugatti delivers final Chiron Super Sport 300+, its fastest, and weirdly, greenest car', carscoops.com; 'Proteus Bluebird CN7', nationalmotormuseum.org.uk; 'ThrustSSC', transport-museum.com; 'The first automobile', group.mercedes-benz.com

How many planes are in the sky?, pp.266–7:
'Lucky Ladies I, II and III', afhistory.af.mil; Map courtesy of Flightradar24; *[Note that the flights depicted in the map were recorded at 3pm UTC.]*

Mega space rockets, pp.268–9:
'What Was the Saturn V?', nasa.gov; 'The world's tallest rockets: how they stack up', space.com; 'Soyuz-U', astronautix.com; 'Delta IV Launch Vehicle', mobile.arc.nasa.gov; 'Atlas 5 rocket launches six military research satellites into orbit', space.com; 'Launch vehicle', mars.nasa.gov; 'Facts About SpaceX's Falcon Heavy rocket', space.com; 'Falcon Heavy', spacex.com; 'Artemis I update', blogs.nasa.gov; 'Space Launch System lift capabilities', nasa.gov; 'Space Launch System configurations', nasa.gov; 'Nasa's giant SLS rocket: A guide', bbc.co.uk; 'Space Launch System at a glance', lpi.usra.edu; '1st orbital test flight of SpaceX's Starship Mars rocket pushed to March at the earliest', space.com; 'Starship', spacex.com; 'Space X's Starship rocket: specs, size, history, and more', history-computer.com; 'Russia sets out Yenisei super-heavy launch vehicle timetable and

budget', spacewatch.global; 'Russian engineers draft super rocket', russianspaceweb.com; 'China officially plans to move ahead with super-heavy Long March 9 rocket', arstechnica.com; 'China reveals details for super-heavy-lift Long March 9 and reusable Long March 8 rockets', spacenews.com; 'China scraps expendable Long March 9 rocket plan in favor of reusable version', spacenews.com *[Note that the heights and weights of rockets that have not yet been built are estimates and are likely to be subject to change.]*; 'Statue of Liberty, monument, New York City, New York, United States', britannica.com

Space junk, pp.270–71:
'How much space junk orbits Earth?', earthhow.com

Looking into space, pp.272–3:
'Building the 100-inch Telescope', mtwilson.edu; 'The 200-inch (5.1-meter) Hale Telescope', sites.astro.caltech.edu; 'The MMT Observatory', mmto.org; 'Hubble Space Telescope', nasa.gov; 'W.M. Keck Observatory, about', keckobservatory.org; 'Hobby-Eberly Telescope', mcdonaldobservatory.org; 'Very Large Telescope', esp.org; 'About the Subaru Telescope', subarutelescope.org; 'International Gemini Observatory, about', gemini.edu; 'Magellan Telescopes (6.5m)', obs.carnegiescience.edu; 'The University of British-Columbia Liquid-Mirror Observatory', astro-canada.ca; 'SALT Telescope', salt.ac.za; 'Large Binocular Telescope Observatory', lbto.org; 'Introducing the Gran Telescopio CANARIAS', gtc.iac.es; 'James Webb Space Telescope, about', jwst.nasa.gov; 'About Rubin Observatory', lsst.org; 'Revolutionizing our knowledge of the universe', giantmagellan.org; 'Timeline', tmt.org; 'ESO moves one step closer to the first Extremely Large Telescope', eso.org

Going for gold, pp.274–5:
'All-time medal count at the Summer Olympics by country and color from 1896 to 2020', statista.com; 'Average number of medals won per capita at the Summer Olympic Games from 1986 to 2020', statista.com; 'Michael Phelps, American swimmer', britannica.com; 'Larisa Latynina, Soviet athlete', britannica.com; 'Aladar Gerevich', olympics.com; 'Shaunae Miller-Uibo', olympics.com

Sporting success, pp.276–7:
'The Paralympics have gone from strength to strength', economist.com

Read all about it, pp.278–9:
'Major techniques of printmaking', britannica.com; 'History of printing', britannica.com; 'Printing press', britannica.com; 'Earl Stanhope invents the first completely iron hand press; output increases to 250 sheets per hour', historyofinformation.com; 'Koenig's mechanical press (early 19th century)', britannica.com; 'History of printing', britannica.com; 'Michael Hart, inventor of the ebook, dies aged 64', theguardian.com; *[Note that the statistic that 86% of the global population can read and write refers only to people aged 15 and older.]*; 'Best-selling book', guinnessworldrecords.com; 'The 22 best-selling books of all time', entertainment.howstuffworks.com; '*The Little Prince*, fable by Saint-Exupéry', britannica.com

Music makers, pp.280–81:
'Flute, musical instrument', britannica.com; 'Why a musician breathed new life into a 17,000-year-old conch shell horn', text.npr.org; 'Trumpet, musical instrument', britannica.com; 'Organ, musical instrument', britannica.com; 'Bagpipe, musical instrument', britannica.com; 'Didgeridoo', en.wikipedia.org; 'Recorder, musical instrument', britannica.com; 'Trombone, musical instrument', britannica.com; 'Bassoon, musical instrument', britannica.com; 'Horn, musical instrument', britannica.com; 'Oboe, musical instrument', britannica.com; 'Clarinet, musical instrument', britannica.com; 'Accordion, musical instrument', britannica.com; 'Harmonica, musical instrument', britannica.com; 'Tuba, musical instrument', britannica.com; 'The inventor of the saxophone', nationalsaxophonemuseum.com; 'Harp, musical instrument', britannica.com; 'History of lute-family instruments', en.wikipedia.org *[Note that what is known today as the lute descended from a plucked instrument found in ancient Mesopotamia c.3100 BCE, as shown in the timeline.]*; 'A history of world music in 15 instruments', britishmuseum.org; 'Zheng, musical instrument', britannica.com; *Ethnomusicology: The Folk Banjo: A Documentary History*, Dena J. Epstein (University of Illinois Press, 1975); 'Guitar, musical instrument', britannica.com; 'Harpsichord (Renaissance)', caslabs.case.edu; 'Sitar, musical instrument', britannica.com; 'Cello', vsl.info; 'Piano, musical instrument', britannica.com; 'The birth of the electric guitar', yamaha.com; 'Drum, musical instrument', britannica.com; 'Cymbal, musical instrument', britannica.com; 'Gong, musical instrument', britannica.com; 'Triangle, musical instrument', britannica.com; 'Electronic instrument, music', britannica.com; 'Elisha Gray', en.wikipedia.org; 'The theremin: The strangest instrument ever invented?', bbc.com; 'Music synthesizer', britannica.com

Mini masterpieces, pp.282–3:
willardwiganmbe.com; Needle dimensions courtesy of Dr Willard Wigan MBE

Say goodbye!, pp.284–5:
'Summary by language size', ethnologue.com

Glossary

agriculture Growing and harvesting crops, and raising livestock.

air pressure The pressure of the atmosphere pushing down on everything it touches.

algae A large group of simple plants and plant-like organisms (such as seaweed) that usually grow in water and photosynthesise but do not produce seeds.

altitude Height above a certain level and especially above sea level.

amphibian Any of a group of cold-blooded vertebrate animals (such as frogs and toads) that have gills and live in water as larvae but breathe air as adults.

anaesthetic Something that produces loss of feeling in all or part of the body.

antibiotic A substance able to inhibit or kill microorganisms.

arthropod Any of a large group of animals (such as crabs, insects and spiders) with jointed limbs and a body made up of segments.

artificial intelligence The ability of a computer or a robot to learn and to deal with new situations.

asteroid A rocky object made from clay, rock and sometimes metal that travels around the Sun. Asteroids are smaller than planets and come in lots of different shapes and sizes.

atmosphere (physics) The layer of gases that surrounds a planet, such as Earth.

atom The smallest unit into which matter can be divided without the release of electrically charged particles. Matter is the stuff that makes up everything around us, from air and water to the Sun and the Moon. Even you are made of atoms.

axis A straight line about which a body, such as Earth, rotates or may be thought of as rotating.

blockchain A system that keeps track of transactions across different computers.

carbohydrate A substance (such as starch and sugar) that is rich in energy and is made up of carbon, hydrogen and oxygen.

carnassial teeth Typically found in carnivores, teeth that have adapted for shearing or cutting flesh.

carnivore An organism, usually an animal, that feeds on meat.

ceramics The art of making things (such as pottery or tiles) of baked clay.

circumference The line that goes around a circle.

civilian A person who is not a member of a military, police or firefighting force.

compass A device with a magnetic needle that indicates direction on Earth's surface by pointing towards the North.

concentration camp A place where people are held as prisoners for political reasons.

conflict An extended struggle.

conservation The protection of animals, plants and natural resources.

constellation A certain group of stars that has been imagined to form a recognisable pattern. Many constellations represent animals, mythological people and creatures, and scientific instruments.

continent One of the great divisions of land on the globe – Africa, Antarctica, Asia, Australia, Europe, North America or South America.

crater A circular depression in the surface of a planet, moon or other celestial body caused by a meteorite impact or by volcanic action.

crewed mission A flight operation of an aircraft or spacecraft with people on board.

dehydrate To lose water or fluids.

diameter The distance through the centre of an object or shape from one side to the other; an object's width.

diet The food and drink that a person or another organism usually takes in.

digest To break down food into simpler forms that the body can use for nourishment.

diurnal Active during the day.

DNA A large molecule that carries genetic information in the chromosomes and resembles a twisted ladder. (DNA is short for deoxyribonucleic acid.)

domesticated Living things, such as animals or plants, that humans care for and make use of, for food, for work or for companionship.

drinking water Water that is safe to drink.

dwarf planet A round object orbiting the Sun that is generally bigger than a comet or asteroid but smaller than a planet, and is not a moon. Its gravity is not big enough to clear other objects from its orbit. The most famous dwarf planet is Pluto.

eclipse The total or partial hiding of a planet, star or moon by another celestial body.

economic cost The cost in money, time and other resources to make something or that results from a change.

emoji A symbol in electronic communication used to express information, such as a human emotion, food or flag.

endangered species A species that may soon become extinct.

equator An imaginary line that runs around the middle of a planet, moon or other celestial body.

equatorial circumference The distance around the equator of a planet such as Earth.

eruption column height The height reached by the ash that rises directly above a volcano during an eruption.

excrete To separate and give off waste matter from the body usually as urine, sweat or faeces.

exoplanet A planet that travels around a star other than the Sun.

extinct No longer existing.

extinction The state of being, becoming or making extinct.

festival A time or event of celebration.

fish A large group of vertebrate animals that live in water, breathe with gills, and usually have fins and scales.

fossil The remains or traces of an ancient living thing that has been preserved in the ground.

frequency (physics) For any type of wave, such as a sound wave, frequency is the number of waves that reach or pass a point within a certain amount of time.

fresh water Water that is not salty, usually inland, in rivers and lakes.

galaxy A huge collection of stars, gas and dust. Our galaxy is known as the Milky Way.

generator A machine that produces electricity.

geologist A person specialising in the study of geology, a science that deals with the history of Earth and its life, especially as recorded in rocks.

gestation The carrying of young in the uterus during pregnancy.

glacier A huge, slow-moving river of ice. Glaciers are made from layers of snow that are squeezed over hundreds of years until they become ice.

global population The total number of people living in the world.

graphene A single layer of carbon atoms bound in a hexagonal lattice, which is 200 times stronger than steel and conducts electricity and heat very well.

gravity A force that pulls objects towards each other. Earth's gravity pulls everything on it, including people, towards its centre. The Sun's gravity pulls Earth, and the other planets, towards it.

groundwater Any water under the ground that is not chemically combined into rocks and minerals.

guzheng A Chinese zither-like stringed instrument.

habitat The place where a plant or animal grows or lives in nature.

harpsichord A keyboard instrument similar to a piano with strings that are plucked.

hemisphere One of the halves of Earth as divided by the equator or by a meridian.

herbivore An animal that feeds on plants.

hibernate To pass all or part of the winter in an inactive state in which the body temperature drops and breathing slows.

human cost The damage or loss caused to people or societies.

influenza A contagious viral disease that affects the nose, throat and lungs and can cause a fever, chills and aches.

insect One of a group of small and often winged animals that are arthropods, with six jointed legs and a body formed of a head, thorax and abdomen.

internal combustion engine An engine that creates its energy by burning fuel inside itself.

invertebrate An animal that doesn't have a backbone, such as a worm, jellyfish, insect, spider or crab.

irrigation An act or process of supplying with water or cleaning with a flow of liquid.

lava Molten rock flowing from a volcano or other crack in Earth's surface.

left-handed Using the left hand better or more easily than the right.

lifespan The length of time for which a person or animal lives.

light year The distance light travels in one year. It is used to describe things that are very, very far away. One light year is about 9.5 trillion kilometres.

lightning bolt The single flash of light caused by the passing of electricity within a cloud, between clouds, between a cloud and the air, or between a cloud and the ground.

literacy The ability to read and write.

locomotive A vehicle that moves under its own power and is used to haul railway cars.

lunar eclipse A darkening of the Moon caused when it enters the shadow of Earth.

magma Semi-solid rock when it is below Earth's surface. When it reaches the surface, it is called lava.

magnetosphere A region around a planet that is affected by its magnetic field.

malaria A serious disease with chills and fever that is spread by the bite of a mosquito.

mammal A warm-blooded animal (such as a dog, mouse, bear, whale, or human being) with a backbone that feeds its young with milk produced by the mother and has skin usually more or less covered with hair.

mass The amount of stuff, known as matter, an object is made up of.

microbe A microscopic living organism, especially a bacterium.

microchip A very small piece of material inside a computer that contains electronic circuits and can hold large quantities of information or perform mathematical and logical operations.

microscopic So small as to be visible only through a microscope.

migration Travelling a long distance, especially a regular to-and-fro movement of animals from one region to another.

military Members of the armed forces.

milk teeth The first 20 temporary teeth that humans grow. Milk teeth usually loosen and fall out between the ages of 5 and 13 to be replaced by 32 permanent adult teeth.

mineral A natural substance with a definite chemical composition that is not part of a living thing. For example, gold is a mineral.

moon A natural object that travels around a planet, dwarf planet or asteroid. Some planets, including Saturn, have many moons. Earth has only one moon.

mouth (river) The place where a river or stream enters a larger body of water.

nebula (plural: nebulae) An enormous cloud of dust and gases found in space that can appear in many shapes and colours. Stars often form in nebulae.

nectar A sweet liquid produced by plants and used by bees in making honey.

nocturnal Active at night.

non-renewable energy Energy that comes from sources that are not restored or replaced by natural processes in a short period of time. For example, oil and gas are non-renewable energy sources.

Northern Hemisphere The half of Earth that lies north of the equator.

nutrients Substances in food that help your body to work, such as vitamins and minerals.

observatory A place that has instruments for making observations (such as of the stars).

offspring The young of a person, animal or plant.

omnivore An animal that feeds on plants and other animals.

orbit The route of a body in space, such as a planet, moon, or artificial satellite, when it is circling a larger body, under the influence of gravity. For example, the Moon orbits Earth.

organism Any living thing. Examples are plants, animals and bacteria.

parasite A living thing (such as a flea, worm or fungus) that lives in or on another living thing and gets food and sometimes shelter from it and causes harm to it.

permafrost Permanently frozen ground, particularly common in Arctic and Antarctic regions.

photosynthesis The process by which plants use sunlight, water and carbon dioxide to make their own food, giving off oxygen as a waste product.

phytoplankton Microscopic plant-like organisms floating in the surface layers of the ocean. They are the main source of food for marine ecosystems.

pigment A substance that gives colour to other materials.

planet A large spherical object in space that travels around the Sun or another star. It must be big enough for its gravity to clear the area around it of other large objects. Earth is one of eight planets that travel around the Sun; the others are Mercury, Venus, Mars, Jupiter, Saturn, Uranus and Neptune.

plumbing A system of pipes and fixtures for supplying and carrying off water in a building.

poisonous Containing poison, a substance that by its chemical action can injure or kill a living thing.

polar circumference An imaginary circle around Earth that passes through both the North and South Poles.

population The total number of people living in a country, city or area.

precipitation Water that falls to Earth as hail, mist, rain, sleet or snow.

predator An animal that lives mostly by killing and eating other animals.

prehistoric Relating to or existing in the time before written history began.

prey To hunt or kill for food. Also, an animal that is hunted and killed for food by a predator.

printing press A machine that makes copies of text and images.

propulsion The act or process of moving something forwards.

proteins Large molecules in the body that do many important jobs. They are needed to build cells and regulate tissues and organs. We get proteins into our bodies by eating protein-rich foods, including meat, milk, eggs and beans.

rabies A deadly disease of the nervous system that affects animals and can be passed on to people by the bite of an infected animal.

radius A straight line extending from the centre of a circle to the outside edge or from the centre of a sphere to the surface.

regulate To control the time, amount, degree or rate of a process.

renewable energy Energy that comes from sources that will not run out or can be replaced.

reptile A cold-blooded animal (such as a snake, lizard, turtle or alligator) that breathes air and usually has skin covered with scales or bony plates.

resilin A highly elastic substance found in many insects and arthropods (including fleas).

right-handed Using the right hand better or more easily than the left.

rival Someone or something that tries to defeat or be more successful than another.

robotic surgery Surgery carried out using mechanical arms controlled by the surgeon.

rodent A small mammal (such as a squirrel, rat, mouse, or beaver) with sharp front teeth used in gnawing.

round trip A journey in two directions (there and back).

satellite An object that travels around another larger object. Satellites can be natural, such as the Moon, or human-made, such as the International Space Station.

scale The size or extent of something, especially in comparison to something else.

schistosomiasis A disease caused by parasitic worms.

senses The ways humans and other animals perceive the world around and inside them, including sight, hearing, touch, smell and taste.

sinews Bands of tough fibres connecting muscles to another part of the body (such as a bone).

singularity A point of infinite density, where the ordinary laws of physics break down. Scientific theory predicts that singularities should exist at the centres of black holes.

sitar An Indian lute with a long neck and a varying number of strings.

sleeping sickness A tropical disease that causes fever, chills and pain in the arms and legs.

solar eclipse A complete or partial hiding of the Sun, as caused by the Moon's passing between the Sun and Earth.

source (river) The beginning of a stream of water.

Southern Hemisphere The half of Earth that lies south of the equator.

species Any one kind of animal or other living thing. Members of the same species can breed with each other to produce young that can also produce young to continue the species.

star A huge ball of exploding gases that glows in space. Stars are made mostly of the gases hydrogen and helium. The Sun is the closest star to Earth, but we can see lots of other stars on a clear night.

supernova (plural: supernovae) The incredibly bright and powerful explosion that happens when a massive star comes to the end of its life.

symmetry Close agreement in size, shape and position of parts that are on opposite sides of a dividing line or centre; an arrangement involving regular and balanced proportions.

tardigrade Any of a group of microscopic invertebrates with four pairs of stout legs that live usually in water or damp moss. They are also called moss piglets or water bears.

tectonic plates Large, moving pieces that make up the outer layer of Earth, known as its crust.

terawatt A unit of power equal to one trillion watts. (Watts are the standard unit for measuring electric power.)

theremin An electronic musical instrument played by moving the hands in the electromagnetic fields surrounding two projecting antennae.

thorax The part of a body of a vertebrate that lies between the neck and the abdomen and contains the heart and lungs. In an insect, the thorax is the middle of the three major divisions of its body.

toxin A poison produced by a living thing (such as an animal or bacterium).

transformation The act or process of changing completely; a complete change.

transistor A small solid electronic device used for controlling the flow of electricity.

ultrasound Vibrations of the same physical nature as sound but with frequencies above the range of human hearing. In medicine, ultrasound can be used to examine internal body structures without having to cut into the body, such as looking at a baby while it is still in the mother's womb.

urban Of, relating to, or being a city.

USSR The Union of Soviet Socialist Republics, also known as the Soviet Union. A former country (existing between the years 1922 and 1991) in eastern Europe and northern Asia.

vacuum A space completely empty of matter.

vein One of the blood vessels that carry the blood back to the heart.

vertebrate Any animal with a backbone, such as a mammal, reptile, bird, fish or amphibian.

vitamins A group of substances that are found naturally in many foods, are necessary in small quantities for good health and normal development and functioning, and are designated by a capital letter and sometimes a number.

wealth A large amount of money or possessions.

wingspan The distance from the tip of one wing to the tip of another wing.

yellow fever A disease carried by mosquitoes in parts of Africa and South America.

zika A virus transmitted by mosquitoes.

Scavenger hunt answers

SPACE, p.47
1. 1,300,000 Earths; **2.** The planet Saturn; **3.** Aquila; **4.** Light moves faster; **5.** The year 1972; **6.** 150 times; **7.** Sagittarius A*; **8.** A meteor.

LAND, SEA, SKY, p.95
1. 71%; **2.** Page 53; **3.** Exosphere; **4.** Antarctica; **5.** Cirrus; **6.** 10 on the Mohs Scale; **7.** Downwards; **8.** Mariana snailfish.

LIVING PLANET, p.143
1. USA; **2.** 100 km; **3.** All the earthworms; **4.** Alpaca; **5.** The North Pole; **6.** Rotting meat; **7.** Going up; **8.** Page 131.

ANIMALS, p.191
1. 200 litres; **2.** 5; **3.** Carnivore; **4.** 11; **5.** Horn shark; **6.** 200 times; **7.** 10 metres; **8.** 20 hours.

HUMAN BODY, p.239
1. Enamel; **2.** The tongue; **3.** A human; **4.** Five cups; **5.** 60%; **6.** A cantaloupe melon; **7.** Gold; **8.** 3 metres.

HUMAN WORLD, p.287
1. India; **2.** Fly non-stop around the world; **3.** 1955; **4.** 4; **5.** 23; **6.** Hindi; **7.** $464 trillion; **8.** The Burj Khalifa.

Picture credits

The publisher would like to thank the following for permission to reproduce their photographs and illustrations. While every effort has been made to credit images, the publisher apologises for any errors or omissions and will be pleased to make any necessary corrections in future editions of the book.
t = top; l = left; r = right; c = centre; b = bottom

WELCOME!, pp.vi–vii
p.vi NASA; p.viib Recreated from the copy of the plaque carried by *Pioneer 10*, NASA.

SPACE, pp.1–47
pp.4–5 Adapted from illustration that appeared D'Efilippo, Valentina and Ball, James, *The Infographic History of the World* (HarperCollins, 2013); pp.10–11 NASA/SOHO; p.16br NASA/Goddard/Arizona State University; pp.18–19 Constellation maps by Mark Ruffle, background photograph ChaNaWiT/Getty Images; p.22–23 Infographic adapted from the graphic 'Missions to the Moon' by Valentina D'Efilippo, *Science Focus*, July 2019; p.23t National Space Science Data Center, NASA's Goddard Space Flight Center; pp.28–9 NASA, ESA, CSA, and STScI; p.36br NASA/ESA; pp.40–41 NASA/JPL-Caltech/UCLA/MPS/DLR/IDA; pp.44–45 Timeline adapted from illustration that appeared D'Efilippo, Valentina and Ball, James, *The Infographic History of the World* (HarperCollins, 2013); p.46 Courtesy of Fabien Sena.

LAND, SEA, SKY, pp.48–95
p.52 iStock/Nerthuz; pp.58-9t ehrlif/iStockphoto; pp.58–9c Konoplytska/iStockphoto; pp.58–9b Baloncici/Dreamstime; pp.70–71 David Kalisinski Photography/iStockphoto; pp.74–5 Kamil Nureev/EyeEm/Getty Images; p.80 Edwardje/Dreamstime; p.81 Oleg Seleznev/Dreamstime; pp.84–5 Cameron Beccario (https://earth.nullschool.net); pp.90–91 Daniel Prudek/Alamy; p.94 Courtesy of Professor Christopher Jackson.

LIVING PLANET, pp.96–143
pp.102–103 James L. Amos (Wikimedia Commons/CC0 1.0); pp.114–15 Paul Williams/Nature Picture Library; pp.124–5 Alasdair Rae (automaticknowledge.co.uk); pp.134–5 Professor Ed Hawkins MBE/University of Reading (https://showyour stripes.info); pp.140–41 reptiles4all/iStockphoto; p.142 Courtesy of Dr Christopher Fernandez.

ANIMALS, pp.144–191
pp.146–7 pixelprof/iStockphoto; pp.158–9 Janpiter Frans S/EyeEm/Getty Images; p.164 OGphoto/iStockphoto; p.165 Aquanaut4/Dreamstime; pp.170–71 Scenics & Science/Alamy; pp.174–5 David Merron/Getty Images; pp.178–9 Claud Lunau/Science Photo Library; p.189 Tui De Roy/Nature Picture Library; p.190 Courtesy of Miranda Lowe CBE.

HUMAN BODY, pp.192–239
pp.198-9 D Roberts/Science Photo Library; pp.204-205 Zephyr/Science Photo Library; pp.208-209 Zephyr/Science Photo Library; pp.220-21 Steve Gschmeissner/Science Photo Library; pp.224-5 Alfred Pasieka/Science Photo Library; pp.226-7 Large image adapted from illustration that was first published in *New Scientist, The Brain: A User's Guide* (John Murray, 2020); pp.228-9 Nancy Kedersha/Science Photo Library; pp.230-1 Adapted from illustration that was first published in *New Scientist, The Brain: A User's Guide* (John Murray, 2020); p.235 Adapted from illustration that was first published in *New Scientist, The Brain: A User's Guide* (John Murray, 2020); p.238 Courtesy of Professor Claire Smith.

HUMAN WORLD, pp.240–287
pp.244–5 Nacho Calonge/Alamy; pp.250–51 Alison Wright/Getty Images; pp.258–9 (muffin) mtreasure/iStockphoto; pp.258–9 (cupcake) Antoniu Rosu/500px/Getty Images; pp.258–9 (younger chihuahua) Galina Kovalenko/Shutterstock; pp.258–9 (older chihuahua) dahuang1231/iStockphoto; pp.262–3 seewhatmitchsee/Alamy; pp.266–7 Flightradar24; pp.270–71 NASA; p.271 NASA; pp.276–7 Adam Pretty/Getty Images; pp.282–3 Dr Willard Wigan MBE; p.286 Courtesy of Professor Ganna Pogrebna.

FIND OUT MORE!, pp.308–11
p.306t British Library; p.306c Wikipedia (Public Domain); p.306b Wikimedia/2012rc; p.307t Library of Congress, Washington, D.C.; p.307c Courtesy of marieneurath.org; p.307b Free material from gapminder.org.

Find out more!

If this book has inspired you to find out more about infographics, then you'll be delighted to discover that humans have been creating infographics for thousands of years! There are countless more out there, each with its own fascinating visual story to tell. Here are some famous examples to get you started.

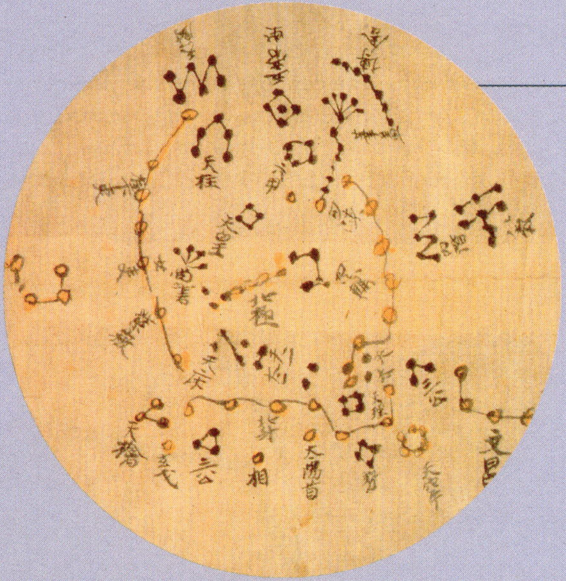

DUNHUANG STAR MAP, 700 CE

This is the earliest known atlas of the stars, created hundreds of years before the invention of the telescope. It was discovered among thousands of ancient manuscripts in a cave in Dunhuang, China. Find out more at www.bl.uk/collection-items/chinese-star-chart.

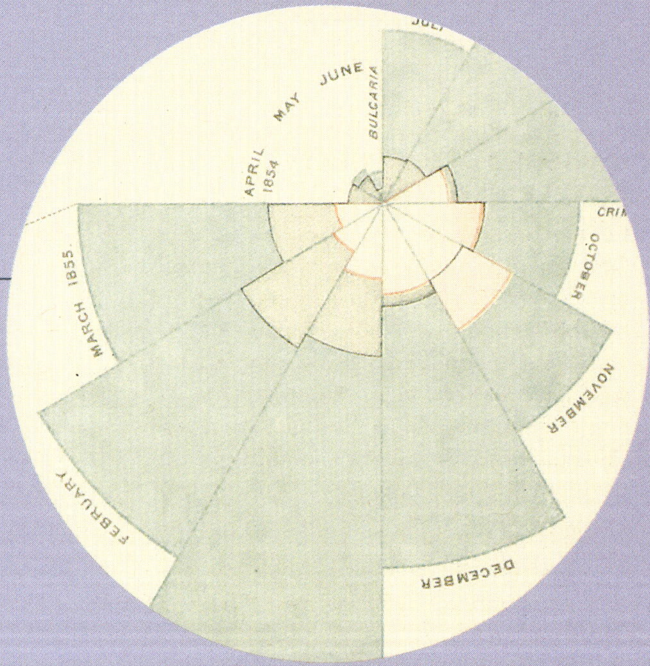

FLORENCE NIGHTINGALE'S WAR MORTALITY DIAGRAM, 1858

British nurse Florence Nightingale created an infographic called a rose diagram to persuade politicians of the importance of cleanliness and hygiene in hospitals. The improvements in sanitation that she fought for have saved millions of lives. Find out more at www.britannica.com/biography/Florence-Nightingale.

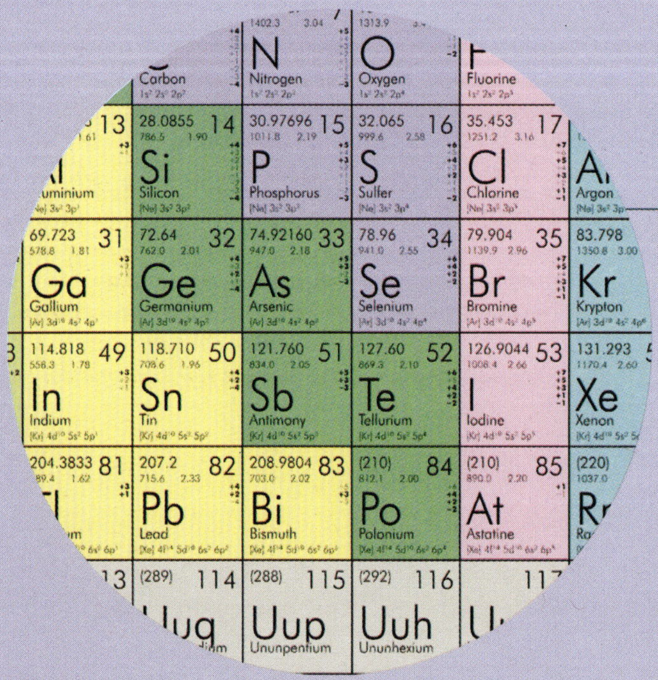

DMITRI MENDELEEV'S PERIODIC TABLE, 1869

All the matter in the universe is made from basic chemical elements, and the Russian scientist Dmitri Mendeleev created a system for arranging them called the periodic table. Mendeleev's table helps scientists to understand how elements behave – and even make predictions about the properties of elements we have yet to discover. The modern version of the periodic table is illustrated here. Find out more at www.britannica.com/biography/Dmitri-Mendeleev.

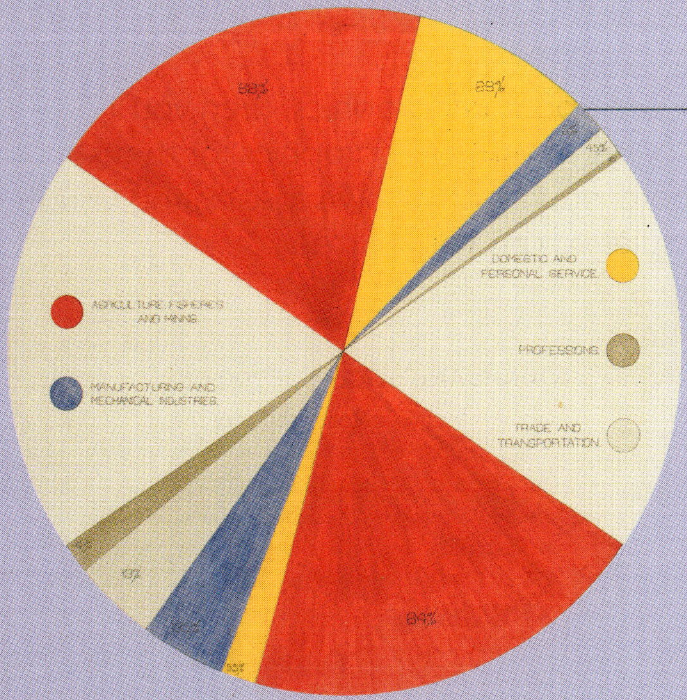

W.E.B. DU BOIS'S JOBS OF BLACK AND WHITE AMERICANS IN GEORGIA, USA, 1900

W.E.B. Du Bois was an influential African-American thinker and an early leader of the movement for the equal treatment of Black and white people in the United States. He created around 60 infographics to challenge people's perceptions of the lives of Black Americans. Find out more at www.tableau.com/blog/how-web-du-bois-used-data-visualization-confront-prejudice-early-20th-century.

MARIE AND OTTO NEURATH'S ISOTYPE INSTITUTE, 1940s

German and Austrian designers Marie and Otto Neurath founded the Isotype Institute, which aimed to educate children using pictures. The Neuraths' slogan was: 'Words divide, pictures unite.' They created beautiful books of infographics that communicate information visually, on topics ranging from how plants grow to the structure of atoms. Find out more at www.marieneurath.org.

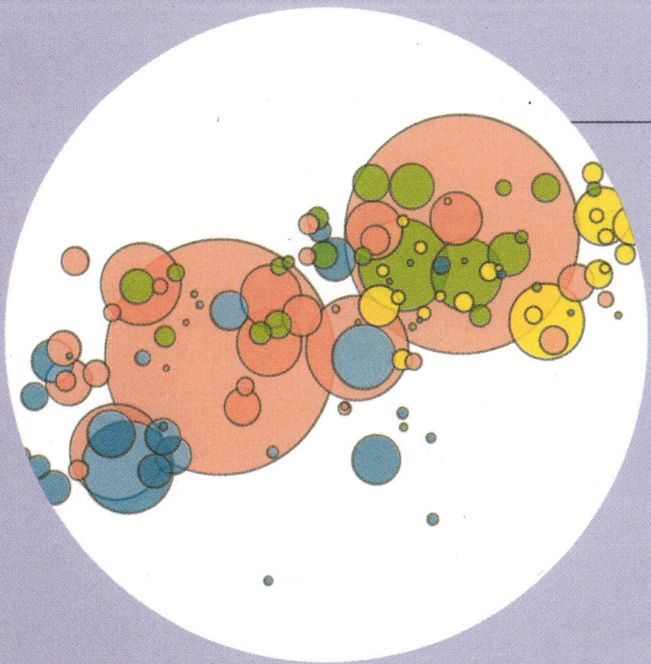

GAPMINDER, 2005

Set up by a team of Swedish scientists and statisticians, the Gapminder foundation uses data and infographics about global wealth, society and the environment to increase people's understanding of the modern world. Gapminder's mission is to challenge ignorance and popular misconceptions with 'a fact-based worldview everyone can understand'. Find out more at www.gapminder.org.

Books and websites

Here is a selection of books and websites that we found useful in our research.

BOOKS

D'Efilippo, Valentina and Ball, James, *The Infographic History of the World* (HarperCollins, 2013)

DK, *Timelines of Everything* (Dorling Kindersley, 2018)

Gifford, Clive, *The Book of Comparisons* (Quarto, 2018)

Harford, Tim, *The Truth Detective* (Wren & Rook, 2023)

Jenkins, Steve, *Animals by the Numbers* (Houghton Mifflin Harcourt Publishing, 2016)

Lowe, Stuart and North, Chris, *Cosmos: The Infographic Book of Space* (Aurum, 2015)

McCandless, David, *Knowledge is Beautiful* (Harper Design, 2014)

New Scientist, *The Brain: Everything You Need to Know* (John Murray, 2018)

Pretor-Pinney, Gavin, *The Cloudspotter's Guide* (Sceptre, 2006)

Roberts, Professor Alice, *The Complete Human Body* (Dorling Kindersley, 2016)

Rovelli, Carlo, *Seven Brief Lessons on Physics* (Penguin, 2016)

Smith, David J., and Armstrong, Shelagh, *If the World Were a Village* (Bloomsbury Education, 2017)

Taschen, *History of Information Graphics* (Taschen, 2021)

Tufte, Edward R., *The Visual Display of Quantitative Information* (Graphics Press, 2001)

WEBSITES

amnh.org (American Museum of Natural History)

atlasobscura.com

bbc.co.uk

britannica.com

earthobservatory.nasa.gov

flightradar24.com

guinnessworldrecords.com

iucnredlist.org (Red List of Threatened Species)

livescience.com

marieneurath.org

metoffice.gov.uk

nasa.gov

nationalgeographic.com

ncbi.nlm.nih.gov (National Library of Medicine)

newscientist.com

nhm.ac.uk (Natural History Museum, UK)

ourworldindata.org

pnas.org (Proceedings of the National Academy of Sciences)

si.edu (Smithsonian Institution)

statista.com

usgs.gov (US Geological Survey)

Index

A

B

C

D

E

F

G

H

I

J

K

L

M

N

O

T

U

V

W

X

Y

Z

Meet the team!

This encyclopedia was made through the collaborative efforts of a creative team. Here you can find out more about some of the key people behind the book.

THE AUTHORS

Valentina D'Efilippo is an award-winning data designer and illustrator. She is the co-creator of *The Infographic History of the World* (Firefly, 2013) which has been sold in eleven languages, she presented a TEDx talk on Data Design in 2021, and she leads workshops for students and professionals, including masterclasses with the *Guardian* about visual storytelling with data. This is her first children's book.

Andrew Pettie is a writer, editor and journalist who has contributed to *The Times*, *The Sunday Times* and the *Daily Telegraph*, where he was Head of Culture. Andrew is the author of *Listified!* (published by Britannica Books) and the editor of *Britannica Magazine*.

Conrad Quilty-Harper is a journalist at Bloomberg News in London. He previously worked at *New Scientist*, *British GQ*, the *Daily Mirror* and the *Daily Telegraph*, often using data and infographics to tell stories. He plays the trombone, likes aeroplanes, and his favourite type of graph is the Sankey diagram (see pages 34–5 for an example of one!).

THE DATA RESEARCHERS

Elizabeth Gregory is a journalist and researcher based in London. She has written for publications including London's *Evening Standard* and the *Sunday Times*.

Simon Hunt is a journalist working in data reporting and research.

Rachel Kenny is an environmental scientist and data analyst. She now works at the World Resources Institute.

Miriam Quick is a data journalist and researcher. Her first book, *I am a book. I am a portal to the universe.*, co-authored with Stefanie Posavec, won the Royal Society's Young People's Book Prize 2021 and an Information is Beautiful Award 2022.

THE EXPERT CONSULTANTS

Dr Christopher Fernandez is an ecologist at Syracuse University, USA, specialising in mycorrhizal ecology.

Professor Christopher Jackson is a geologist and professor at Imperial College London. He has done geological fieldwork in the Argentinian Andes, the Borneo rainforest and the Sinai Desert in Egypt. He also presented the Royal Institution Christmas Lectures in 2020.

Miranda Lowe CBE is a principal curator at the Natural History Museum, London. She specialises in crustacea and cnidaria, and has worked at the museum for 30 years. She also lectures on science and curation, mentors students and conducts outreach in schools. She is a STEM ambassador, volunteering for the Aspiring Professionals Programme, a scheme that connects students who lack a professional network to top people in their field.

Dr James O'Donoghue is a planetary scientist specialising in ground-based astronomy of giant planet upper atmospheres, in particular Jupiter, Saturn and exoplanets. In his spare time he makes videos that explain the scales, motions and mechanisms of the solar system and beyond, which are used in schools, universities, planetariums and museums worldwide. For this outreach work he was awarded the 2021 Europlanet Society Prize for Public Engagement.

Professor Ganna Pogrebna is the Executive Director of AI and Cyber Futures Institute at Charles Sturt University (Australia), an Honorary Professor of Behavioural Business Analytics and Data Science at the University of Sydney (Australia), and the Lead for Behavioural Data Science at the Alan Turing Institute (UK). Her work blends behavioural science, AI, computer science, data analytics, engineering and business model innovation to help cities, businesses, charities and individuals optimise their behaviour to achieve higher profits, better social outcomes and improved wellbeing. In 2020, she won the TechWomen100 prize, which recognises leading female experts in STEM in the UK.

Professor Claire Smith is head of anatomy at Brighton and Sussex Medical School. She has published over 100 peer-reviewed articles and is the lead author of *Gray's Surface Anatomy and Ultrasound for Students*. Professor Smith is an associate editor for *Anatomical Sciences Education*, the world-leading journal for anatomy education. She was the first in the UK to print 3D anatomy body parts for students scanned from a donated human cadaver.

Acknowledgements

Creating this encyclopedia would have been impossible without our brilliant and indefatigable editor Natalie Bellos, who led the project in so many vital ways. This book is as much Natalie's achievement as it is ours.

We would also like to thank:

Nancy Feresten at What on Earth Publishing and Alison Eldridge at Encyclopaedia Britannica for their editorial insights and wise judgement.

Christopher Lloyd, for championing the project from start to finish.

Judy Barratt, for her meticulous editing; Julie Brooke, for her help keeping everything on track; and Meg Osborne and Lucy Buxton, for their help managing the project, attention to detail, and ideas.

Andy Forshaw, for his work on the cover and both Andy and Daisy Symes for their meticulous work on the layouts; Mark Hickling for his expert knowledge and support with the book design; and design interns Camila Coelho, Joana Carvalho, Cinzia Bongino and Alena Boack for their fantastic help with data preparation, design and illustration work.

Data researchers Miriam Quick, Rachel Kenny, Elizabeth Gregory and Simon Hunt for their many hours spent reviewing scientific papers, collecting and collating data, and unearthing fascinating and unlikely facts to include. (Not many people are happy to spend their days scouring academic research papers to estimate the mass of a giant panda's poo.)

Dr James O'Donoghue, Professor Christopher Jackson, Dr Christopher Fernandez, Miriam Lowe CBE, Professor Ganna Pogrebna, Tim Harford, Michael Ray, Erik Gregersen and John P. Rafferty, for all their expert insights and advice.

Encyclopaedia Britannica's fact-checking supervisors Will Gosner and Michele Rita Metych; fact-checkers Mic Anderson, Fia Bigelow and R.E. Green; and Kenneth Chmielewski for his help with the maps.

Susannah Jayes for picture research; Vanessa Bird for the index; Sarah Epton, Ingrid Court-Jones and Lori Merritt for proofreading; and Lauren Fulbright for all her work on the production and printing.

The sales, marketing and publicity team: Helen Thewlis, Patty Sullivan, Olivia Galyer, Gracia Lukombo, Laura Smythe, and everyone at PGW, Bounce, Publisher Spotlight and Walker Books Australia.

Alasdair Rae, and all the contributors who generously agreed for their infographic work to be featured: Warming Stripes by Ed Hawking,

Volcanic Eruptions by Addy Pope and his colleagues at ESRI, Wind Map by Cameron Beccario, Migration Flows by Kenneth Chmielewski, and Air Traffic made with data from Flightradar24.

Richard Atkinson and Peter Dawson for their advice and support.

All the young readers who contributed invaluable suggestions and feedback along the way.

And, finally, thank you to everyone who reads the book. We hope you enjoy it and are able to amaze your friends and family with the facts that you learn.

FROM VALENTINA

First, I am indebted to James Cheshire, who thought I would be a good fit for this project and introduced me to Natalie. And to Natalie herself, who trusted his judgement and welcomed my creative vision.

My heartfelt thanks to my family and friends for their continued support and enthusiasm. Thanks especially to my mother, Maria Rita, who taught me the joy that comes from loving a craft and from creative practice. I dedicate this book to my children, Rita Blue and Ray, who have filled my life with awe and wonder.

Last, but certainly not least, thanks to my partner, Timothy, who knew from experience that creating another book would not be easy on anyone, even more so because we were embarking together on another ambitious project – expanding our family. His boundless love, creative ideas and constructive feedback have been matched only by his unlimited patience when the book took over evenings and weekends.

FROM ANDREW

I would like to thank May and Nat; my parents, Tony and Jill; and my brother, Nick – for their love, encouragement and support. Thanks especially to May, for her brilliant insights and ideas.

FROM CONRAD

Thank you to my wife Annabel for her constant love and support and for making me tea when I was working on the book. And to my parents, Fiona and Dominic, and sisters, Ciara and Juliette, for their encouragement throughout. And a big thank you to everyone who has asked how the book is going over the years.

BRITANNICA BOOKS

Britannica Books is an imprint of What on Earth Publishing, published in collaboration with Britannica, Inc.
The Black Barn, Wickhurst Farm, Leigh, Tonbridge, Kent TN11 8PS, UK
30 Ridge Road Unit B, Greenbelt, Maryland, 20770, United States

First published in the United Kingdom in 2023

Written by Andrew Pettie and Conrad Quilty-Harper
Editorial development by Conrad Quilty-Harper and Andrew Pettie
Infographics and art direction by Valentina D'Efilippo
Infographics and illustration support by Camila Coelho, Joana Carvalho, Cinzia Bongino, and Alena Boack
Cover design by Andy Forshaw
Data research by Miriam Quick, Rachel Kenny, Elizabeth Gregory and Simon Hunt
Project editing by Judy Barratt
Project managing by Julie Brooke
Picture research by Susannah Jayes
Topic consultancy by Dr James O'Donoghue, Professor Christopher Jackson, Dr Christopher Fernandez, Professor Claire Smith, Miranda Lowe CBE, Professor Ganna Pogrebna

Encyclopaedia Britannica: Alison Eldridge, Managing Editor; Will Gosner and Michele Rita Metych, Fact Checking Supervisors; Mic Anderson, Fia Bigelow and R.E. Green, Fact Checkers

What on Earth Publishing: Nancy Feresten, Publisher and Editor-in-Chief;
Natalie Bellos, Editorial Director; Meg Osborne, Editor; Lucy Buxton, Editorial Assistant;
Andy Forshaw, Art Director; Daisy Symes, Senior Designer; Lauren Fulbright, Production Director

A CIP catalogue record for this book is available from the British Library

ISBN: 978-93-5954-195-2

Published and Distributed in India by
Scholastic India Pvt. Ltd.

First edition 2023
This Reprint Edition: September, 2024

Printed in India At : VK Global Digital Private Limited